TUNNEL OF HOPE

Escape from the Novogrudok Forced Labor Camp

TUNNEL OF HOPE

Escape from the Novogrudok Forced Labor Camp

Dr. Betty Brodsky Cohen
Foreword by Prof. Yehuda Bauer

gefen גפן
publishing house בית חוצאה לאור
JERUSALEM • NEW YORK   Est. 1981

Excerpts from Jack Kagan, "Surviving the Holocaust with the Russian Partisans," in the
Memorial (Yizkor) Book of the Jewish Community of Novogrudok, Poland, ed. Rabbi Helen Cohn
(New York: JewishGen, Inc., 2013), originally published as *Pinkas Navaredok*, eds. Eliezer
Yerushalmi and David Cohen (Tel Aviv: Alexander Harkavy Navaredker Relief Committee in
the USA and Israel, 1963), reproduced by permission of JewishGen.org.
Photo of the members of the 1934–1935 Novogrudok Maccabi team, in Jack Kagan,
Novogrudok: The Story of a Shtetl (London: Vallentine Mitchell, 2006), reproduced by
permission of Vallentine Mitchell.
Photos of the Bielski partisans reproduced by permission of the Yad Vashem Photo Archive,
Jerusalem.
Novogrudok-area map, from Peter Duffy, *The Bielski Brothers* (New York: Perennial, 2003),
reproduced by permission of Peter Duffy and Jeffrey Cuyubamba.
The original escape list, recorded by escapee Yitzchak Rosenhaus in the Novogrudok forced
labor camp, reproduced by permission of Ghetto Fighters' House (Lochamei Hagetaot).
Photo of a section of the tunnel with a memorial candle, reproduced by permission of Dror
Shwartz, director of the documentary film *Tunnel of Hope* (2015).
Cover photograph of tunnel escapees Memorial Wall courtesy of Shiran Cohen. This wall,
funded by Charles and Seryl Kushner, the son and daughter-in-law of the escapee Raya
Kushner, is based on the author's research. Inaugurated in Novogrudok in July 2019, it honors
all the escapees, lists their names, and indicates their fates.

Research and Content Editor: Melanie Rosenberg
Manuscript Editor: Kezia Raffel Pride
Cover design: Dragan Bilic
Typesetting: Optume Technologies

ISBN: 978-965-7801-29-1

1 3 5 7 9 8 6 4 2

Gefen Publishing House Ltd.
6 Hatzvi Street
Jerusalem 9438614, Israel
972-2-538-0247
orders@gefenpublishing.com

Gefen Books
140 Fieldcrest Ave.
Edison NJ, 08837
516-593-1234
orders@gefenpublishing.com

www.gefenpublishing.com
Printed in Israel

Library of Congress Control Number: 2024935720

The research and writing of this book were carried out with the assistance and support of the
Conference on Jewish Material Claims Against Germany

Claims Conference ועידת התביעות
The Conference on Jewish Material Claims Against Germany

In memory of my mother, Fanya Dunetz, escapee #142

and

in honor of all the escapees for teaching me the meaning
of courage, determination, and persistence

In Memoriam

We are grateful to these generous donors for making this book possible through donations in memory of their loved ones:

Shlomit Adivi – in memory of Moshe Wasserman and his family

Tali Alt – in memory of the Yarmovski and Weiner family members of Novogrudok murdered in the Holocaust

Anonymous donor – in memory of the Novogrudok community that once was

Susan Bach and Art Abrams – in memory of the Abramowicz, Giershenowski, Grinberg, and Broinitsky families

Chaim Barkan (Berkowicz) and Mascha Dalva – in memory of their dear parents, escapee Eliyahu Berkowicz and Chana Berkowicz Gelfer; their aunt, escapee Chaya Sara Luska; Yakov Konskowolski, and all the relatives that were murdered in the Holocaust

Sybil and Joel Berk – in memory of Eta bat Alter Yaakov and escapee Myer (Meir ben Baruch) Berkowicz (Berk) and their family members martyred in the Holocaust

Bonnie Bienstock – in memory of Wendy Small

Lea Blumenfeld – in memory of Esther Dunec (Klubock)

Iris and Sharon Broyde – in memory of Rosalyn and Ben Broyde and escapee Fanya Dunetz

Zophy Chermoni – in memory of escapees Moshe and Alter Nignevitcky

Grandchildren of Savta Genya Cohen (Kagan) – in memory of escapee Dr. Yakov Kagan

Meir Cohen – in memory of the family members of escapee Fanya Dunetz

Guy Czertok – in memory of escapee Abram Czertok, his first wife Fanny Kantorovich Czertok, and their baby daughter, who were murdered in the Holocaust, as well as his second wife Marcelle Sherman Czertok

Agi and Arthur Dunec – in memory of escapee Helena (Lena-Leah) Kitayevich (Klubok), Bogdana Lidski (Klubock), and Avraham and Tsipora Klubock

Caryn and Mark Dunec – in memory of the members of the Dunetz, Klubok, Zicherman, Klein, Borger, Goldman, Folk, and Zeisel families, who perished in the Holocaust

Tsafi Erez – in memory of escapee Natan Yankelevich

A Friend – in tribute to the Novogrudok forced labor camp inmates who upon their deaths were the last living members of their families. With no one left to say Kaddish, may their names and their memories be blessed.

Bronia and Milan Gofman – in memory of escapees Yisrael and Shmuel Kolachek

Howard and Judy Gold – in memory of escapee Nachman (Natan) Feifer

Chaya Goldhaber – in memory of escapee Batia Gradis Rabinowitz

Tsipora Gorodynski; Avi, Azrikam, and Tamir Ganot (Gorodynski) – in memory of escapees Shaul and Sonya Gorodynski Oshman

Hana Gotian, Shimon and Lev Wolkowicki – in memory of escapee Perez (Peretz) Wolkowicki

Stephen Greenberg – in memory of Harry and Sonia Greenberg

Boris Ioselevich (Yoselevich) – in memory of escapee Yakov Ioselevich and Dvosha Yoselevich (Velkin)

Jack (Idel) Kagan, escapee – in memory of Dvora, Yankel, Nechama, Shoshke, Moshe, and Leizer Kagan, and Hannah Gitel Gurevitz

Paula Kalinowski – in memory of Charna and escapee Akiva Schmulewicz

Ludmila Karpukhin – in memory of escapee Shmuel Niselevich and Yenta Kaplinsky

Dorit Kay – in memory of escapee Perla Ostashinski and her husband Moshe (Moniek) Hirschprung; escapees Daniel and Chaim Zeev Ostashinski, Esther, Yitzchak, Batya, and Rivka Ostashinski

Alex Kritz – in memory of escapee Herman Kritz and Bertha Kritz

Charles and Seryl Kushner – in memory of escapee Rae and Joseph Kushner, and escapee Naum Kushner

Murray Kushner – in memory of escapees Chanan, Raya (Rayka), Leah (Leyka) and Naum Kushner, and Chaim Leibowitz

Linda and Murray Laulicht – in memory of escapee Rae and Joseph Kushner, escapee Naum (Nachim) and Hindel Kushner, Chonon Kushner, Esther Kushner, and escapee Leah (Liza) Reibel

Simon Lazowsky – in memory of escapee Sara Zamosczyk Lazowsky

Moshe Lusky – in memory of Yehuda and Dvora Lusky

Chaya, Shmaya, and Ruthie Magid; Rachel Malik – in memory of the family members of Chaya Magid and tunnel escapee Avraham Magid and his family members

Pnina Maman and Ella Abramowicz – in memory of Pesach Abramowicz

Avishay (Gertzovski) Morag – in memory of his father Aaron (Arke) Gertzovski, his grandparents, escapee Zalman and Sara Gertzovski, and their family members from Zhetl; Chaya (Dvora) Zamkov-Gertzovski, Avraham and Chana Zamkov and their family members from Novogrudok.

Shula (Shulamis) Mordechowicz, her children Zvi Mor and Lea Ben-Yelid, her grandchildren and great-grandchildren – in memory of escapee Mordechai (Motl) Morduchowicz; and the Kosower, Tunik,

Machlis, Rusak, and Rabinowicz families of Ivenets, Derevna, and Rubiezewicze

Pierre and Ziva Nochimowsky – in memory of Yehoshua and Mera Czertok and escapee Abram Czertok

Shaul Nochimowski – in memory of Yehoshua and Mera Czertok and escapee Abram Czertok

Sara and Yanek Okonski – in memory of all those murdered in the Novogrudok forced labor camp and in the tunnel escape

Adi and Gil Ostashinski – in memory of escapees Chaim Zeez, Daniel, and Paula Ostashinski, Pesach Ostashinski, and their murdered family members: Zipora, Yitzchak, Esther, and Rivka Batya Ostashinski

Sonia Palkis – in memory of escapees Roza Giershenowski Wodakow, Basia and Sara Giershenovski

Yisrael Portnoj – in memory of escapee Lionke Pornoj and all the other tunnel escapees

Hyman Ryback – in memory of his parents, escapee Chana Ivanetka of Novogrudok and Shlomo Ryback of Radun, who rebuilt their lives to inspire a generation of youth in Montreal, Canada

Effie Rosenhaus – in memory of escapees Yitzchak and Genia Rosenhaus

Esther Schulder – in memory of escapees Rae and Joseph Kushner

Steve and Linda Shell – in memory of escapees Efroim and Sima Selubski; Dora and Avraham Kalmanowitz

Mania and Mendel Shor – in memory of Mania's father, escapee Aaron Kirzner

David Silberklang – in memory of Yisrael Senderovski, his wife and two daughters; Hillel and Malka Senderowski; Yisrael and Hanna Frieda Belous; Zisl and Pesia Kalbstein, their daughter and son Mordechai; Mordechai (Mota), Nechama, and Yudl Zakroiski;

Hirsz and Esther Belous, daughter Ruth and a seven-year-old son; escapee Chaim Belous

Neal and Debby Silver – in honor of the memory of Holocaust survivors Jean and Albert Silver

Michael Skakun – in memory of Joseph Skakun and his murdered parents, Chaikel and Chaya Elovich Skakun, all from Novogrudok

Sylvia Ryback Sklar – in memory of Ephraim Ryback, the baby brother she never knew

Rita Wilenski Standig – in memory of escapees Simcha and Aaron Wilenski; Rochel, Yehuda, Eliyahu, Perl, Baila, and Yehudit Wilenski

Nili Tauber – in memory of escapees Mordechai and Leib Orzuchowski

Shiri Tsur – in memory of Tina and Hertz Benzionowski (Benson), their daughter Yolanda, Yitzchak (Itchke) Benzionowski (Benson), and members of the extensive family from Novogrudok and Lubcha who were murdered in the Holocaust

Haim, Drora, and Benny Weinstein; Tsafrit Grinberg – in memory of Binyamin, Cherna, Moti, and Sheina Weinstein of Zhetl

Seymour Wodakow – in memory of escapees Roza Giershenowski Wodakow, Basia and Sara Giershenovski

Bracha Steiner and Shimon Yarom – in memory of escapees Isaac and Zlata Yarmovski

Nechama Zakok and Yisrael Klar – in memory of Chana Golda Mayevski Klar; escapee Pesia Mayevsky Nadel, Chaya, Yisrael, Chonia and Hinda Mayevski of Zhetl; Avraham Klar of Rava Ruska, and Mordechai Nadel of Lodz

Zalmanovich family – in memory of escapee Berko (Dov) Zalmanovich

Helen Zelig – in memory of her mother, escapee Leah Kushner; her father, Joseph Reibel; and their many family members who perished in the Holocaust

Contents

Foreword

Tunnel of Hope: Escape from the Novogrudok Forced Labor Camp relates the extraordinary story of a mass escape of 240 or so Jews, inmates of a German slave labor camp in a former courthouse in the town of Novogrudok (Navardok), today in Belarus, in September 1943. With unbelievable courage and immense resourcefulness, they secretly dug a long tunnel from the camp. Originally intended to lead to a field nearby, it was lengthened when it became clear that it was an open field in which the grain had been harvested so that there was no protection at all.

Of the escapees, some were hidden by local Baptists, others were caught by the Germans, but the majority managed to reach partisan units, mainly but not exclusively the detachment (otriad) of the Bielski brothers. The book relates the personal stories of all 227 identified escapees, as well as those of another four whose participation in the escape is uncertain. It is a very valuable addition to our knowledge of the only case we know of a successful venture like this. The author, the daughter of one of the survivors, made a successful effort at telling the stories of other escapees, through her research and as they were told to her by their descendants.

In addition to the identification of the escapees and their fates, the author has proven that there were at least 133 definite survivors of the breakout, making it one of the most successful prisoner escapes of the Holocaust.

Tunnel of Hope: Escape from the Novogrudok Forced Labor Camp is a story of resistance, because organizing the escape and escaping is no less an act of resistance than fighting with arms in hand. We should be thankful to Dr. Cohen for this important addition to our knowledge.

Professor Yehuda Bauer
Jerusalem, December 27, 2020

Preface

As this book was going to press, Israel was recovering from its worst attack on civilians since the Holocaust. Its soldiers were destroying tunnels in the Gaza Strip that were specifically designed for murder and heinous acts such as those committed on what has been dubbed the Black Sabbath of October 7, 2023. In contrast, this book is about a different kind of tunnel – one that offered hope and enabled people to live.

Based on my research to date, the Novogrudok forced labor camp tunnel escape may be considered to be the most successful prisoner escape of the era through the longest hand-dug tunnel of World War II.

I initially learned of the little-known breakout from the Novogrudok forced labor camp when I made the first of three visits to Belarus and to the site where the labor camp had stood. My mother, Fanya Dunetz, had been interned in this camp during the Holocaust.

During this visit in 2007, I met Tamara Vershitskaya, then the director of the Museum of Jewish Resistance located in the former labor camp. It was then that I offered to help with the transcription of the escape list from Yiddish to English. This list, recorded in the camp by inmate Yitzchak Rosenhaus, delineated the order in which the inmates were to exit the tunnel during the planned escape.

Little did I know that this meeting with Tamara would change my life and that deciphering the largely illegible list (a more legible list, probably the original, was located many years later in the Ghetto Fighters' House in Kibbutz Lochamei Hagetaot) would become my passion for over a decade. During this time, I have interviewed survivors and their children, sifted through endless written and oral testimonies, and reviewed Holocaust databases in order to identify escapees.

Tamara first gave me a list of 113 partial and full names that had been transliterated from Yiddish to English. Through my own subsequent research, I have compiled a list that includes the names of 227 confirmed escapees, as well as four individuals whose participation in the escape is uncertain. I have deciphered the majority of the names on the original list, as well as added twenty names of known escapees whose names could not be found in the original compilation.

A word about the spelling of names: Among the documents and reference volumes referred to in this book, a great many inconsistencies exist in the English spelling of Polish and Yiddish names. To determine the spelling of each tunnel escapee, we searched for original signatures wherever possible. Otherwise, we chose to use a phonetic spelling. In footnote sources, however, names are spelled as on the original documents (i.e., Red Cross documents, Yad Vashem Pages of Testimony, and so on) when they appeared in the Latin alphabet.

While working on the list and collecting names of escapees, I began discovering the captivating, riveting life stories of many of these men and women. The seed was thus planted to write this book and tell the amazing, often tragic, but always inspiring stories of the tunnel escapees.

My book is not only about the escapees themselves, but about what and whom they left in the world. With the help of a genealogist, I have located many of the second generation from genealogical, International Red Cross, Holocaust-related, and population databases.

An unexpected outcome of my research has been a mutually enlightening relationship with other second-generation tunnel survivors whom I have met in the course of my work. Through them, I have learned how their parents chose life and contributed to their new societies. Having researched each escapee's prewar life, I was able to inform many of the children about the past their parents had been unable to share with them directly. As a result, many of the second generation have found their place among the extended families that they never knew existed. Learning of their parents' bravery, both in the tunnel escape and in the partisans, often changed their view of a parent from victim to hero.

It is impossible to write about the tunnel escape without discussing the Bielski brothers, Tuvia, Alexander ("Zus"), and Asael, who ran one of the most inclusive Jewish partisan units that ever existed, and who absorbed the majority of the survivors of the Novogrudok forced labor camp escape. Although some of the escapees joined Russian partisan units, *all* the escapees were inspired and given hope by the possibility of reaching the one detachment, the one address, where they were assured of being taken in and cared for. This book is therefore as much a tribute to the Bielski brothers as it is to the tunnel escapees. Without the Bielskis, the escape could not and would not have happened.

Many of the tunnel escapees who fell were the very last remnants of their families. It is my hope that as a result of this research, their lives and their courageous deaths will now be known and remembered.

In the words of Teddy Roosevelt:

> Credit belongs to the man who is actually in the arena, whose face is marred by dust and sweat and blood; who strives valiantly; who errs, who comes short again and again, because there is no effort without error and shortcoming; but who does actually strive to do the deeds; who knows great enthusiasms, great devotions; who spends himself in a worthy cause, who at best knows in the end the triumph of high achievement, and who at the worst, if he fails, at least fails while daring greatly, so that his place shall never be with those cold and timid souls who neither know victory nor defeat.[1]

Even as their faces were *marred by dust and sweat and blood*, all the tunnel escapees *strived valiantly*. All were devoted to life. Even those who failed in their mission *dared greatly*. For this, they should be remembered. For this, may their memory be blessed.

Jerusalem, Israel
February 2024

Acknowledgments

This book would not have taken the form it did without the talents of my friend of over thirty years, Melanie Rosenberg. Melanie served as my research and content editor, as well as my genealogist and researcher. As my initial editor, she sharpened my thoughts, seeking the right words to describe my meaning in the clearest possible way. She was a true partner in this endeavor, for which I am extremely grateful.

As my researcher, Melanie found members of the second generation all over the world whom I myself could never, ever have found. The gratitude of the second generation at having been found was matched only by my own at having found them. Having researched and discovered details about their parents' prewar lives, I was able to answer many questions children had never dared to ask their parents while they were still alive. Thank you, Melanie, for bringing a sense of completion both to the children as well as to myself. Thank you to the second generation for sharing with me their lives, as well as the lives of their parents, a process that was not always easy. Not for them, and not for me.

This book would never have been written without three people. The first is my good friend Ruth Begin, to whom I am thankful for insisting that together we visit Zhetl, our mothers' town, as well as Novogrudok, and for arranging the trip in 2007. The second is Tamara Vershitskaya, then director of the Jewish Resistance Museum in Novogrudok. During that visit, Tamara first taught me about the escape. After I decided to go far beyond her request to decipher and complete a nearly illegible copy she possessed of the original Yiddish-language escape list, Tamara encouraged me throughout my work and provided invaluable information, primarily for survivors who remained in the former Soviet Union, where civil records are quite difficult to obtain. The third is the survivor Jack Kagan, of blessed memory, who by first teaching Tamara about the Jews of Novogrudok and about the escape inspired her to become one of the foremost Holocaust educators in the former Soviet Union. I thank Jack for providing me with materials as well as spending hours with me during several visits to Jerusalem, relating invaluable information about the escapees and the escape.

My sincere gratitude to the late Chaya Magid, widow of escapee Avraham Magid and a fellow townsperson of my mother's from Zhetl. In spite of her "young age," her near-encyclopedic memory regarding her former townspeople, coupled with her willingness to share, have greatly contributed to our knowledge of the Zhetlers who participated in the breakout, the second-largest group of escapees. I am greatly sorrowed that due to her death in January 2023, she did not live to hold a copy of this book.

Thank you to my husband Meir and my children Yanai and Shiran, who have stood by me as I worked day and night for many years to bring this project to fruition. They have become part of the story, having participated in the group that traveled to Novogrudok in 2012 to find the remains of the tunnel, within the context of Dror Schwartz's movie about the search, also named *Tunnel of Hope* by my mother. During one of her two additional trips to Novogrudok during which she accompanied me, Shiran photographed the incredible image of the tunnel escapees Memorial Wall that appears on the front cover. Thank you, Shiran.

Thank you, Dror, for traveling across Israel during the COVID-19 pandemic when the Yad Vashem library was closed in order to bring me the *Novogrudok Memorial Book*, generously loaned to me by the family of the late Yakov Berman of Novogrudok.

I also wish to express my appreciation to my late uncle, the Yiddish journalist Max Mordechai Dunetz, for his invaluable help in deciphering the original Yiddish-language list of tunnel escapees.

My typist, Esther Rosenfeld, was not just a typist, but having grown up in a home for Kindertransport children, she appreciated the content, expressed a deep interest in the topic, and proved to be a source of encouragement throughout the process.

Many thanks to Shulamit Rosenthaler, director of the Tracing Department of Magen David Adom in Israel, a member organization of the International Red Cross, for her help in locating several formerly untraceable relatives of escapees. Her diligence and perseverance were indispensable in helping us complete some of the stories presented.

Michael Goldstein, former president of the International Association of Jewish Genealogical Societies (IAJGS), has also helped us crack the mystery surrounding the postwar whereabouts of several escapees.

Special thanks to Steve Rosenberg for his technical support and his belief in me.

My great appreciation to editorial consultants Michael and Susie Kadish, whose sharp insight and guidance was invaluable. Thank you, Michael, for your editorial contributions to the initial manuscript.

Thank you to Dr. David Zilberklang, senior historian at Yad Vashem, for his editorial comments and help in telling the story of his family members from Zhetl, one of whom was a tunnel escapee. Thanks as well to the dedicated and patient staff of the Yad Vashem Library, especially Joshua Bernhardt, and to all the contributors who have filed Pages of Testimony for their murdered family members. These testimonies have proven invaluable in reconstructing prewar family compositions of the tunnel escapees.

I wish to express my gratitude to journalist and author Peter Duffy for his encouragement and for recognizing the need for a book on the Novogrudok tunnel escape. My thanks to him and to Jeffrey Cuyubamba for their wonderful map of the Novogrudok area.

I am indebted to Professor Yehuda Bauer for taking the time to meet with me and to clarify the mutual influences of what may be considered the two greatest resistance events of the Holocaust: the Warsaw ghetto uprising and the Novogrudok tunnel escape.

I am extremely grateful to the Claims Conference on Jewish Material Claims Against Germany for supporting my research, and especially to Adina Shudofsky for her mentorship, ongoing support, patience, and encouragement.

Thank you to the many families of escapees who have donated to this project so that their parents and grandparents may be honored and the story of their bravery may be told. Special thanks to Murray Kushner, Charles and Seryl Kushner, Esther Schulder, Zophy Chermoni, and Bonnie Bienstock for their extraordinary generosity.

To all the second-generation tunnel escapees, thank you for opening your hearts and sharing your parents' and your own stories and perspectives. It was not always easy, but I couldn't have done this without you. You were all true partners in this project.

I thank the late Lord Rabbi Jonathan Sacks for teaching the world – and myself – about the immense power of hope as well as the importance of collective responsibility. He has been an inspiration in the completion of this work, which is really about what one can achieve in the presence of hope and the belief that we truly are our brothers' keepers. And I wish to thank my longtime mentor, the late Professor Reuven Feuerstein, who also taught me about hope, perseverance, and the power of the human spirit.

Thanks to the Gefen team: first of all, to owner and publisher Ilan Greenfield, who recognized and appreciated my vision in making the Novogrudok tunnel story known; to Senior Editor Kezia Raffel Pride for her razor-sharp eye and ability to find innovative solutions; to the talented graphic designer Dragan Bilic, and to Project Manager Binyamin Greenfield, who put everything together. It was a pleasure to work with you all.

Thank you to escapee #142, my mother Fanya Dunetz, of blessed memory, for having been an invaluable fount of information about the labor camp and the escapees, for providing the name of this book, as well as for teaching me firsthand the importance of never, ever giving up the fight for life.

Background

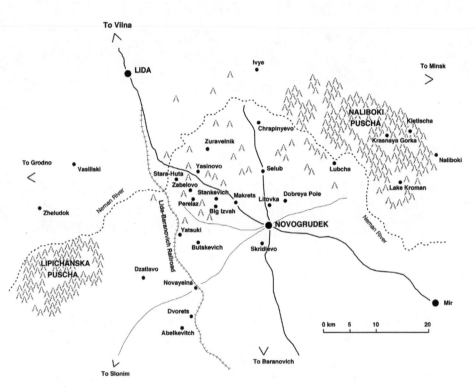

Novogrudok-area map, from Peter Duffy, *The Bielski Brothers* (New York: Perennial, 2003), reproduced by permission of Peter Duffy and Jeffrey Cuyubamba

Introduction:
The Tunnel Escape from the
Novogrudok Forced Labor Camp, 1943

Based on the author's research carried out to date, the Novogrudok tunnel escape was likely the most remarkable prisoner breakout of the Holocaust. It also appears to constitute the most successful escape through the longest hand-dug tunnel of World War II. In presenting the results of the research, this book strives to give a personal glimpse of the men and women who planned and carried out this spectacular feat.

The following is a brief description of the escape and the background against which it transpired.

For generations, the dynamic, close-knit Jewish community of Novogrudok was a source of pride to all. Despite omnipresent anti-Semitism, this city in the Russian Empire and later Poland (in today's Belarus) offered fertile ground for Jewish merchants, craftsmen, bankers, physicians, and others to ply their trades and even to prosper, while Jewish education, social services, and religious institutions flourished. Children gathered savory chestnuts from Novogrudok's trees in autumn, then crisscrossed snow-covered slopes on homemade sleds in winter. On the Sabbath day, families strolled together through the green, tree-covered hills of the countryside.

By mid-1939, the winds of war ushered in a reign of terror for the Jews of Novogrudok, the surrounding towns, and greater Europe. By September 17, the Polish rulers had abandoned the Novogrudok area as Soviet soldiers took control. The city's Jews warmly welcomed the Soviet troops, believing that the Soviets would be an improvement over their anti-Semitic Polish predecessors. Within mere months, the Soviets closed Jewish-owned shops and dissolved the main Jewish organizations.

Yet the Russians were soon to beat a retreat when Germany invaded the Soviet Union on June 22, 1941, in an opening move to conquer Europe. Their declared intention was to annihilate the entire Jewish population every step of the way.

Two days later, bombs fell over Novogrudok. The central part of town, which included Jewish neighborhoods, stores, and synagogues, was destroyed. Nearly three hundred Jewish residents were dead.[1] With the ensuing German occupation of Novogrudok on July 4, 1941, anti-Jewish laws were enacted to strip the Jews of citizenship. Men aged twelve to sixty were forced to report for slave labor. Forbidden to walk on the pavement, all Jews were forced to wear a yellow star patch on the front and back of their clothing.[2]

The bone-chilling cold of Saturday, December 5, 1941, set the backdrop for the German order for Novogrudok's some sixty-five hundred Jews to assemble in the yard of the town's courthouse. Once the families arrived clutching photos, clothing, and small possessions, the soldiers locked the gates of the yard behind them. For two days, the Jews were denied food and sleep. On December 8, between four thousand and fifty-one hundred Jews were slaughtered.

Those who remained alive were locked in the courthouse compound before being taken to the newly built, extremely overcrowded Pereseka ghetto, enclosed in barbed wire and enforced by armed guards. Here they subsisted on a daily ration of two hundred grams (seven ounces) of bread. As escapee Sonya Gorodynski described it, "Those working inside [the courthouse] workshops were skilled craftsmen, saved for their skills. Each morning, the ghetto gates would open, and tailors, shoemakers, metalworkers, carpenters, saddlers, and mechanics, along with their families, were ushered at gunpoint to their workshops to sew fur linings into boots, manufacture guns, or mend German Army uniforms."[3]

On August 7, 1942, the second mass extermination targeted the thousands of Jews now crowded into the Pereseka ghetto after having survived mass slaughters in nearby towns. Some fifty-five hundred men, women, and children were hauled to their deaths and hurled into a mass grave in the nearby village of Litovka. Only around five hundred Jews remained alive in Novogrudok's Pereseka ghetto and the courthouse, which had changed its status from a ghetto to a forced labor camp.[4]

Six months later, on February 4, 1943, Novogrudok's third mass slaughter annihilated all but two of the Pereseka ghetto's inhabitants, with the bodies of the murdered Jews thrown into a pre-dug ditch. Weeks later, the near-starving, distraught inmates in the forced labor camp made desperate plans to stage an uprising against the ghetto guards. Planning to storm the ghetto gates, the inmates acquired arms by bribing guards and stealing iron rods and knives from their workshops. Yet just before the first grenade was to be thrown, a sudden reinforcement of guards arrived at the camp to thwart any chance of the mini-rebellion. The plan had been exposed to the Germans either by the mother of Moshe Burshtein, a prisoner held in jail,[5] or by the wife of Dr. Jakubowicz to protect her husband who had been shot in the leg.[6] Had the uprising taken place, both would have been left behind and killed.

Soon afterwards, on May 7, 1943, the fourth savage Novogrudok massacre took place. In clear view of inmates in the labor camp, over 250 of their fellow workers – including husbands, wives, and children – were forced to undress before being led to prepared pits and systematically gunned down in groups of ten.[7]

Days later, the estimated 240 forced labor camp inmates who remained alive became aware of evidence that their German captors planned to murder the vast majority of them in the near future.[8] Each of these inmates had lost countless members of their families, often slaughtered before their eyes. Now the last remnants of their Jewish communities of Novogrudok and the surrounding towns, they had nothing left to lose.

Working feverishly against time, a core group of leaders led by inmate Berl Yoselevich began meeting surreptitiously to plan a breakout from the well-guarded camp. The idea to dig an escape tunnel with their bare hands and the most rudimentary self-made tools emerged as the best option to enable the inmates a chance at freedom.[9] Moreover, the plan's acceptance was sealed by the benevolent promise of partisan leader Tuvia Bielski to provide refuge to all escapees who reached the Bielski detachment in the nearby forest.[10]

Inmates who were carpenters risked their lives to smuggle wood from the carpentry workshop for use in building the tunnel. (The missing lumber did not go unseen by the German officers, yet despite cruel punishments, the inmates never exposed the top-secret project.) A rigorous digging schedule was set up for those healthy inmates able to toil by night after performing slave labor by day. From their own terribly meager portions, other inmates gave extra bread to help sustain the diggers. Men, women, and the few children in the camp took part in hauling sacks of dug-up dirt, which they later unpacked to hide the dirt under the floors and in specially built double walls. In time, the genius of one talented inmate came to the fore to create a makeshift trolley on a track to facilitate moving the heavy loads of dirt.[11]

An important role in the tunnel digging was played by children and small men who could maneuver the narrow walls. The children dug lying down, bellies against the earth. To protect their only clothing and to avoid suspicion, the children dug naked or wore robes of burlap sacks or old cloth. Describing her experience digging, escapee Sonya Gorodynski admits, "I did not smell or feel a thing. We were anxious to get out as fast as we can because we had death waiting for us. I don't even know whether I was breathing or not.... We were so full of worries that we forgot about anything else. We just wanted to get out. We wanted our lives."[12]

The stories of the Novogrudok tunnel escapees describe not only the details of the escape, but the inmates' largely untold struggle for survival and meaning. This book is a tribute to their fierce devotion to life.

An Eyewitness Account of the Escape

The following excerpts from the memoirs of escapee Jack (Idel) Kagan (#95) detail a priceless eyewitness account of the events. This is JewishGen's lightly edited English translation of the original Yiddish-language account. No changes have been made in the spelling of the names, but for clarity, escape list numbers have been inserted.

After this massacre (of May 7th, 1943)…the first plan was to wait for a dark night, throw hand grenades into the guard-room and escape.… However, after about a week, this plan was dropped and a new one devised: to dig a tunnel one hundred meters (328 feet) long to the other side of the barbed wire, into a field of growing wheat. The plan was worked out by Berl Yoselevitz. The work had to start immediately. The aim was to dig two meters per day. Digging actually started in the second week in May. A works committee was formed, and they met in the room where I lay on the top bunk.… They used to meet three–four times a week to discuss the progress.… It is difficult to know how many members served on the committee; people were called in as they were needed. The word "tunnel" changed the whole atmosphere in the camp. For people who believed in the escape, it gave a hope for salvation.

People who did not want to escape did not have to make up their minds on the spot. It was decided to start digging in the stable. It was the furthest building from the guards and least occupied. I can't be certain, but I believe that in the stable was an earthen floor. Notke Sucharski [#4] and Lionke Portnoy [#19] promised to make available the necessary tools within a week and to keep them in perfect condition.… A two-meter-deep vertical shaft was dug. Sosnovski [#11] the tailor was called in and told to collect blankets and to make 60 bags, each 40 cm x 50 cm [16 x 20 inches] in size. A joiner was called in and asked to cut a trap door from the stable to the loft of the next building. Salek Jakubowicz [#28], the policeman, was responsible for the selection of diggers and for finding extra food for them. It was established that the tunnel should be 65 cm x 70 cm [26 x 28 inches] in cross section. The soil was to be stored on either side of the loft. There was a builder in the camp. (I can't remember his name.)[13] He was later sent to Koldichevo. He was responsible for storage of the dug-out earth and to make sure that the loft would not cave in under the weight of the earth. After two weeks, it was realized that it would be impossible to maintain the rate of two meters per day. The lamp in the tunnel did not burn properly. It was difficult for people to sit inside the tunnel and to pass on the bags filled with soil.

We had no electric light in the living quarters. Rukovski [#10], the best electrician in the camp, was called in and told to look for an active electric cable and to provide electric light in the tunnel. After a few days, he reported that he found the main cable and that he could do it.

Skolnik [#210], the carpenter from Karelich, was called in and told to make as quickly as possible a platform on wheels 50 cm x 50 cm [20 x 20 inches] in size. They asked my father to stitch up two reins, each 50 m [165 feet] long. They had to be strong and to have rings at the ends. It was like magic, everything materialized under such difficult conditions. Skolnik built the platform in pieces to be able to smuggle them out from the joiners' workshop.

I think that within three weeks, electricity was provided inside the tunnel. The platform was functioning, but not good enough. Earth was spilling over, and the platform was hitting the walls.

Skolnik was called in again, this time to produce four panels, 50 cm x 50 cm x 50 cm in size, fitted to the sides of the platform. Two of the panels were hinged, for quick loading and unloading of the soil. Wider wheels and guiding rails for the wheels were made, so that the platform would move in a straight line and not hit the walls. The request was enormous. It meant making and stealing four one-meter rails a day to extend the rails....

The aim was to pull out nine to ten trollies of earth a day and move the soil in the night. In the shaft at the entrance to the tunnel, a space for two people was made. They passed on the bags of soil. From the entrance to the tunnel, sixty or seventy people sat in a row and passed to each other the bags that were emptied at the other end on both sides of the loft.... On a Sunday morning at the end of June, Lionke Portnoy installed an air pipe to let air into the tunnel. At the same time, a test was made to measure the depth and the position of the tunnel. This was not a simple exercise. He needed to push through a two-meter [6.5 foot] rod from a 65 cm [26 inch] cavity. Lionke brought with him four sticks. They had to be assembled into one. The top one was painted white so that it should be easily seen. At the same time, Joselevitz went up on the loft and took out some tiles to be able to see the direction the tunnel took. Everything was perfect....

The digging of the tunnel progressed well. The escape plan was set in motion. Rukovski, the electrician, managed to make a switchboard so that he could control the two large searchlights. To the end, the Germans could not find out the reason the searchlights were not functioning properly. The escape was planned for the second week in August. The wheat outside the camp was the best camouflage.

Then one day in August, the Germans brought a tractor into the field and cut the wheat. We were afraid that the tunnel would collapse under the weight of the tractor, but luckily it held. However, we were left with a problem. Escape was impossible into an open field....

The committee met and decided to dig further to the end of the ridge, in excess of 150 meters [492 feet] more. Nobody can imagine how much earth accumulates from such a project. First the loft was filled, then double walls were built and filled. We had to hide any incriminating evidence. Sunday was the sanitary day in the camp. We had to make sure that outside the buildings all was clean. New toilets had to be built, and that gave us an opportunity to dispose of earth from the tunnel.

At the end of August, there were further problems: rain was seeping through, and earth was falling from the roof of the tunnel. Timber had to be stolen and some bunks destroyed to make supports to prevent the tunnel from collapsing.

In the middle of September, a meeting was called and a vote taken. There were still people who said it was better to die in the camp than to run, but the majority preferred escape, so a list was drawn up. Mr. Yitzchak Rosenhouse [#30] put together a list of the inmates and gave it to the committee to decide on the order people would go out through the tunnel....

The first to go through the tunnel would be the tunnel diggers, followed by five armed men, and then followed all fit persons.

On September 19, 1943, another meeting was called, and we were notified that the tunnel would be completed in the following week. So started the longest week in my life, but I was not afraid. People were saying goodbye to each other and exchanging tips about the route and the best way to go. It was thought that if we all went our separate ways, we would stand a better chance of survival.

The day arrived on September 26, 1943, our chosen day of escape. We assembled in the rooms of the front building. There were about ten rooms in the front building. Orders were given for some people to go up to the loft. This was a test. The committee was afraid that if 250 people would go up into the loft at the same time, the ceiling might collapse.

The night was dark and stormy. It was made to order. The searchlights had been cut off and some of the nails removed from the zinc roof in the stable, to make them rattle a lot in the wind. The leaders did not let anybody into the tunnel till they had broken through to the surface, to make sure that there would be enough air for the first 120 people to go into the tunnel. Only then did they go into the tunnel. The rest went up into the loft and formed a line which moved slowly forward towards the stable. The first group that went into the tunnel sat there for about ten to fifteen minutes until the hole was enlarged. Then the line started to move forward. But we had not allowed for the effect of the light in the tunnel. When people came out at the other end, the sudden darkness after the brightness in the tunnel disoriented them and they ran towards the camp, whereupon the guards opened fire. Although the searchlights were cut off, the guards could still see movement in the dark and probably thought partisans had come to liberate the camp.

When I came out of the tunnel, I could see the whole field alive with flying bullets. I saw figures in the dark running towards the forest and was certain that in the morning, the Germans would search that area....

Dawn started to break...[14]

Novogrudok – A Tale of Contrasts

The beauty of the Novogrudok area belies the horrors that transpired there. Situated around ninety miles southwest of Minsk, the city lies close to the Brichinke stream, which flows into the Neman River.[15] Nearby Lake Svityaz, the largest lake in the area, has been glorified in ballads composed by Adam Mickiewicz, the renowned nineteenth-century Polish poet, whose Novogrudok home is now a popular museum. The poet also wrote of the smaller Lake Litovka,[16] which carries the name of the village in which the second and third mass slaughters of Jews from Novogrudok and the surrounding towns took place.

Novogrudok's mountain climate is moderate in summer and cold in winter, with clear, dry air. The water from the Brichinke was famed for its high quality in cooking and preparing tea in a samovar.[17] Much of the Novogrudok area abounds with forests, including the Lipiczanski Forest to the southwest and the Naliboki Forest to the northeast.[18]

Within the city is a mound called the Zamok, where the ruin of the citadel of the ancient Lithuanian princes lies. Before the Holocaust, on Friday nights, Jews in their Sabbath best would make their way to the Schloss Gass (Castle Street) Shul at the entrance to the Zamok;[19] they'd take strolls in the area on Saturdays as well.[20] Today, the mountain continues to offer a breathtaking view of the trees, fields, and forests in the distance beyond.

To this day, a major market square in Novogrudok's center stands at the vortex from which the main streets continue to emanate, bearing the names of some of the towns to which they lead. Stately houses from prewar days continue to surround the square where market days once took place on Mondays and Thursdays. Incredibly, half of Novogrudok's grand House of Culture, located on the square and containing a large auditorium, was once the private home where escapee Lena Kitayevich (#62) grew up.[21]

On the banks of the Panikva River and surrounded by a pine forest, a resort popular with Russian tourists now lies between Novogrudok and nearby Zhetl, from which the second-largest group of tunnel escapees hailed. Amid the scenic countryside of both towns, one to the right of the resort and one to the left, the bodies of thousands of murdered Jews lie in mass graves.

The Power of Collective Responsibility

"To be a Jew," wrote Elie Wiesel, "is to believe in that which links us to one another."[22] Indeed, Jewish Rabbinic tradition posits, "If I am not for myself, who will be for me? But when I am only for myself, what am I?"[23]

Rabbi Joseph B. Soloveitchik writes that "shared suffering finds its expression in the awareness of shared responsibility and liability."[24] He translates the phrase "*Kol Yisrael areivim zeh ba'zeh*," which denotes the notion of collective responsibility among the Jewish people, as "all Jews are guarantors for one another." The rabbi attributes to Maimonides the idea that "the common situation of all Jews without distinction – whether manifested on the objective level as shared historical circumstances or on the subjective level as shared suffering – opens up founts of mercy and lovingkindness in the heart of the individual on behalf of his brethren in trouble…"[25] In Soloveitchik's view, all Jews are brothers, as it is stated in the Book of Deuteronomy (14:1), "Ye are the children of the Lord your God." He asks: "If brother shows no compassion to brother, who will show compassion to him? And unto whom shall the poor of Israel raise their eyes? Unto the heathens, who hate and persecute them? Their eyes are therefore uplifted solely to their brethren."[26]

Rabbi Shmuel Goldin translates the same phrase as "All within Israel are responsible one for the other," declaring that this implies that "we are inextricably bound to one another, connected heart to heart."[27]

Israeli journalist Sivan Rahav-Meir explores why when Moses pleaded to God to forgive the Children of Israel for the sin of the Golden Calf, he cried, "Forgive *our* iniquity and *our* sin." Why did he use the plural *our* and thus include himself in a sin that he had not committed? Rahav-Meir cites the explanation of Rabbi Yosef Chayim of Baghdad, the eighteenth-century kabbalist and expert on Jewish law known as the Ben Ish Chai, who wrote:

In addition to being punished for sins he did commit, he is also punished for his fellows' sins because of collective responsibility. The children of Israel are one body with many limbs. When the sages composed the Viduy confessional prayer, they wrote it in the plural, "We have transgressed, we have betrayed," etc., rather than in the singular. A person says the entire prayer in the plural even if he is certain that he is not guilty of any of these transgressions, and he need not fear that he is saying untruths because he is demonstrating his collective responsibility toward all other Jews. It is thus clear why Moses, a righteous person, begged for forgiveness for "our iniquity and our sin," because he was part of them.[28]

When Pope John Paul refers to the concept of collective responsibility in his encyclical *Sollicitudo Rei Socialis* (On Social Concern) to the bishops of the Roman Catholic Church on December 30, 1987, he writes: "We are all really responsible for all."[29] He echoes Dostoyevski's declarations in *The Brothers Karamazov*: "One is responsible to all men for all and everything.... Every one of us is undoubtedly responsible for...everything on earth...each one personally for all mankind and every individual man."[30]

Writing about feelings of loyalty and belonging, journalist, author, and filmmaker Sebastian Junger posits that "the earliest and most basic definition of community would be the group of people that you would both help feed and help defend."[31] Reporting that the incidence of post-traumatic stress disorder has risen considerably among combat veterans all over the world with Israel the only exception, he attributes the fact to the country's "sense of community,"[32] or in other words, its deep sense of collective responsibility.

Stressing that "all Israelites are responsible for one another," Rabbi Jonathan Sacks describes Judaism as a "collective faith" whose "central experiences are not private but communal"[33] and notes that even the Hebrew word for responsibility (*achrayut*) comes from the word *other* (*acher*).[34] Emphasizing that Moses thought of *all* the people under his leadership, while Noah thought *only* about his family, Rabbi Sacks holds that Noah "failed the test of collective responsibility."[35] Although the rabbi stresses the collective responsibility inherent in Judaism, he does, however, allow for the possibility that "being human…involves collective responsibility," noting Maimonides's claim that regardless of one's faith, we are all responsible for one another.[36]

The idea of collective responsibility appears in the Book of Deuteronomy. On his last day on earth, Moses gathers the Israelites as they prepare to enter the Promised Land. Entering them into a covenant with God, he says to the assembled:

> You stand this day all of you before the Lord your God; your captains of your tribes, your elders, and your officers, with all the men of Yisrael, your little ones, your wives, and thy stranger that is in thy camp, from the hewer of thy wood to the drawer of thy water; that thou shouldst enter into the covenant of the Lord thy God. (Deuteronomy 29:9)

Just as the Israelite captains of the tribes, the hewers of wood, and the drawers of water entered a covenant together as one people whose members became responsible for one another, the Novogrudok forced labor camp inmates also entered a pact of collective responsibility. Like the Israelites in the desert, they were people of all walks of life. Among the inmates were doctors, lawyers, housewives, carpenters, seamstresses, and even a mushroom picker. All were united in their will to live. Without each other, without the cooperation of every single inmate, none would survive.

With the inmates jointly responsible for the construction of the tunnel, keeping the breakout plan a secret, and maintaining their daily production in their specialized workshops, they epitomized the notion of collective responsibility. Only together could they hope to reach the partisans, where the notion of collective responsibility was exemplified to the utmost, where each and every partisan was responsible for the life of his or her comrade. Only by turning to one another could they fulfill their dream of freedom. Only together did they have a chance at life.

The Bielski Detachment: The Address of Hope

Rabbi Jonathan Sacks posits that "The greatest achievement in life is to have been, for one other person, even for one moment, an agent of hope."[37] In their indefatigable passion to save Jewish lives, brothers Tuvia, Asael, and Zus Bielski became agents of hope for some twelve hundred men, women, and children who found refuge in their partisan detachment. Escapee Jack (Idel) Kagan views the existence of the Bielski detachment as having been the trigger for the breakout. "Everybody was ready to escape [from the Novogrudok forced labor camp] because they had an address to go to."[38] For the Novogrudok tunnel escapees, the Bielskis were the *sole hope* to counter their despair, granting a vision of freedom that helped save at least 133 escapees from almost certain death.

The famed Bielski partisan leaders were three of the twelve children of David and Beila Bielski, mill owners and farmers (and the sole Jewish family) living in the tiny village of Stankiewicze between Lida and Novogrudok. Born over a span of twenty-five years, the ten sons and two daughters never lived together all at once in the family's two-room hut. Tuvia (Anatoli), born in 1906,[39] was two years older than Asael and four years older than Zus.[40]

Following their escape from German-occupied Stankiewicze in early 1942, the Bielski family began wandering through the forests of Bochkovichi. By spring and summer, as they were joined by small groups of friends and relatives who escaped from the Novogrudok ghetto, the core of the makeshift partisan detachment headed by Tuvia Bielski was established. In time, the group obtained arms and began to carry out missions against anti-Semitic peasants and Nazi collaborators. When plagued by heightened dangers and difficulties in supplying the camp over the winter of 1942–1943, the unit was forced to divide into five groups in the Novogrudok area. While some tried to abandon the unarmed groups of partisans, Tuvia issued an order forbidding anyone to desert another Jew in the forest.[41]

By the summer of 1943, the Bielski partisans relocated to the thick Naliboki Forest, splintering into many small groups and once again pitting the armed against the unarmed. In September 1943, when Soviet partisan leaders attempted to reorganize the different groups operating in the area, the Bielskis found themselves attached to the Kirov Brigade. Only then were the fighting men finally separated from the unarmed, non-fighting "family group."[42] Although the family group was only officially designated as "the Bielski detachment" on April 1, 1944,[43] this had been its moniker even when formally titled the "Kalinin detachment" (for Mikhail Kalinin, former head of the Soviet Union).[44] The fighting group, called the Ordzhonikidze detachment, was named for Georgian Communist leader Sergo Konstantinovich Ordzhonikidze, who had died in 1937.[45]

Throughout the years of Tuvia's partisan leadership, danger and shortage of supplies often spawned resistance among the fighters in having to care for the *malbushim* (unarmed partisans). Only due to Tuvia's insistence was no Jew ever turned away.

Tuvia Bielski admitted everyone to his detachment without exception: the young, the old, men, women, children, the sick and the weak, those with weapons, and those unarmed. Historian and Bielski partisan Dr. Shmuel Amarant recalls Tuvia saying repeatedly, "I wish that thousands of Jews would join us – we will absorb them all."[46] One man who made his way to the detachment in May 1943 along with a group of escapees from Lida recalls being saluted by Tuvia as he greeted the newcomers in a tear-choked voice: "Comrades, this is the most beautiful day of my life because I lived to see such a big group come out of the ghetto! ...I don't promise you anything, we may be killed while we try to live. But we will do all we can to save more lives. This is our way, we don't select, we don't eliminate the old, the children, the women. Life is difficult, we are in danger all the time, but if we perish, if we die, we die like human beings."[47]

In the spring of 1943, Dr. Yakov Kagan (#3a) and Berl Yoselevich, underground resistance leaders in the Novogrudok forced labor camp, reached out to Tuvia Bielski for assistance in organizing a breakout to the forest. Regretfully, Tuvia was unable to offer aid in the escape effort, yet he managed to send a letter assuring the underground leaders, "Whoever comes will be well received."[48]

Armed with the promise of safety within the partisan detachment, the inmates first devised a camp breakout scheduled for April 15, 1943.[49] When that plan failed to materialize, the inmates clung all the stronger to the hope of being received with open arms in the nearby partisan unit, inspiring and empowering them to dare to attempt the tunnel escape.

In founding this unique, miraculous partisan detachment, Tuvia Bielski became a prophet of hope and a leader who can truly be considered a modern-day Moses. By establishing the clandestine enclave in the Naliboki Forest known as "Jerusalem,"[50] Tuvia created a sphere in which each and every individual became the guarantors of *all*. There, in the forest, collective responsibility was exercised to an ultimate, life-saving degree.

Utilizing the skills of the escapees, a range of makeshift workshops was created deep in the woods which serviced both the Bielskis and other partisan groups. Most of the workshops were situated in a large hut and separated by wood partitions, with others located throughout the camp. The shoemakers were constantly occupied repairing the tattered shoes of escapees. The tailors were in demand to patch the threadbare clothing of the partisans as well as to fill orders from other partisan units. The tanners supplied leather to the shoemakers, and the saddlers fashioned belts for the partisans and harnesses and saddles for the horses. The carpenters made barrels for the tanners, lasts for the shoemakers, and wooden soles for sandals. The barbershop, adjacent to the workshops, was staffed by three barbers and served as a meeting place for partisans. Nearby was the smithy, where blacksmiths serviced the horses of the detachment as well as those of neighboring partisan units. The sausage factory, watch repair, and metal workshops were also in high demand among the other partisans in the area, who often brought gifts of cattle and arms to be cleaned, repaired, and rebuilt in the metal workshop.[51]

In addition, the Bielski partisans worked together to maintain a medical clinic, quarantine hut, bakery, mill, and communal bathhouse consisting of a bathing room next to a Turkish bath.[52] With bathing compulsory for public health, a bathing schedule was organized. When Tuvia learned that one partisan could make soap from ashes and animal fat, a small soap factory was created in the extraordinary detachment in the forest.[53]

By the end of 1943, even a school was established for about twenty children. Although this school was bereft of books, pencils, paper, and any semblance of formal instruction, the children are reported to have been delighted to play, sing, and exercise together.[54]

In their *zemlyankas*, the underground dugouts that served as living quarters, the partisans savored the occasional evenings with time to share songs and stories around the wood-burning stove in each hut. At times, they would be joined by Tuvia as he walked from hut to hut. When a guitar, violin, and mandolin were acquired during food expeditions, a trio was formed which took a starring role in special festivities in honor of Red Army Day on February 23, 1944.[55]

Shmuel Amarant stressed that almost everyone in the Bielski camp was productive in some way, either as a fighter or in non-military tasks. In whatever capacity they served, their productivity was mutually beneficial, raised morale, and helped the partisans temporarily put aside their sense of pain and loss.[56] Their struggle to stay alive became a constant collective effort of concern for one another. The victorious result: over twelve hundred partisan survivors, including over a hundred tunnel escapees, proudly marched out of the Naliboki Forest on July 10, 1944, led by their Moses, Tuvia Bielski, together with his brothers Zus and Asael. If not for the hope and the vision they had provided, there would never have been a large contingent of forced labor camp escapees among the marchers. There would never have been a tunnel escape.

Partisan leader Tuvia Bielski
(courtesy of Yad Vashem
Photo Archive, Jerusalem,
503/7415)

Asael Bielski
(courtesy of Yad Vashem
Photo Archive, Jerusalem,
503/7373)

Zus Bielski and his wife Sonia Bielski
(courtesy of Yad Vashem Photo Archive, Jerusalem, 5674/3)

A group of Bielski partisans in the Naliboki Forest, May 1944
(courtesy of Yad Vashem Photo Archive, Jerusalem, 5674/3)

Other Notable Escapes of World War II

My research has proven that the Novogrudok forced labor camp tunnel escape was in all likelihood the most successful prisoner escape of the Holocaust, as well as the most successful tunnel escape of the era.

Every escape attempt during the Holocaust is to be lauded as an example of hope in the face of despair, as well as heroism in the face of barbarism. Each life saved was an extraordinary feat.

The most remarkable escapes of the Holocaust years include the following:

- Within just seven and a half weeks of the Novogrudok tunnel escape, one thousand prisoners staged an uprising at the Treblinka extermination camp on August 2, 1943. Of the roughly two hundred who succeeded in escaping, the Germans reportedly caught and murdered some one hundred escapees.[57]
- In Mir, Lithuania, Oswald (Shmuel) Rufeisen, a Jew from the Krakow District, obtained false papers and began working as

a police translator. On August 9, 1942, Rufeisen smuggled weapons to enable some two hundred inmates to escape from the Jewish ghetto to the forest to join the partisans,[58] although the exact number of survivors from this escape remains unknown.

- On October 14, 1943, nearly three weeks after the tunnel escape in Novogrudok, six hundred inmates in the Sobibor extermination camp made a mass escape attempt. Only some sixty survived the ensuing German manhunt.[59]

- Although known attempts to dig escape tunnels were carried out in the then-Polish towns of Pruzhany, Slonim, and Dokszyce,[60] when I began my research, it appeared the Novogrudok breakout was the sole successful escape via a tunnel. To the contrary, a 2016 archaeological expedition at Ponar, six miles from Vilna, revealed a killing site where an estimated seventy thousand people, mostly Jews, were gunned down into gigantic pits previously excavated by the Germans for fuel storage. In time, the eighty prisoners assigned to the "burning brigade," a special unit charged with pulling the bodies from the pits, arranging them in piles, and burning them, became aware that they themselves were soon to be murdered. Forty prisoners then clandestinely dug a 130-foot (40 m) escape tunnel. As in Novogrudok, this tunnel was dug by hand using the most rudimentary tools. Although it was completed almost seven months after the Novogrudok tunnel escape, there is no evidence of any contact having taken place between the Ponar inmates and the former Novogrudok prisoners. Of the forty Ponar prisoners who attempted to escape on April 15, 1944, most were discovered by the Germans and shot. Only eleven are reported to have successfully escaped to the forests.[61]

In contrast to these other notable escapes, I have identified 227 inmates as having definitely participated in the Novogrudok tunnel escape.

Dug with nothing but bare hands and the most rudimentary self-made tools, the Novogrudok tunnel was measured in 2020 by the then director of the Jewish Resistance Museum, located in the former labor camp, and found to be 650 feet (200 m) long.[62] Michael Kagan, the son of the escapee Idel Kagan (#95), had already measured the tunnel length using Google Earth during the filming of the documentary film in 2012 and found it to be 208 meters.[63] Of the 227 participants identified, at least 133, more than half, survived the breakout on September 26, 1943.[64] This includes six inmates who participated in the digging of the tunnel while not actually escaping with the others. Of the nine inmates whose fate is unknown, some may also have survived.

Not only was the Novogrudok tunnel escape perhaps the most successful breakout of the Holocaust era, it also appears to be the most successful escape through a hand-dug tunnel, the longest of World War II.

Stalag Luft III was a German prisoner-of-war camp for Allied airmen located in then Nazi Germany (today Zagan, Poland). It was the setting for the 1963 film *The Great Escape*,[65] which reveals the story of seventy-six British Commonwealth prisoners who, on March 24, 1944, escaped through a 350-foot (106-meter) hand-dug tunnel. It was referred to as "the longest tunnel" of the war in the 1990 book by the same name.[66] Of the seventy-six escapees who escaped in the breakout, seventy-three were recaptured within two weeks.

A November 19, 2019, headline on the Polish news site TVP World reads: "Longest WWII-Era Escape Tunnel Discovered in Northwestern Poland."[67] This refers to the 459-foot (140-meter) tunnel built by French officers in a German prisoner-of-war camp near Klomino, Poland,[68] through which seventeen prisoners crawled their way to freedom on March 16, 1942.[69]

While every escape can be considered a testament to man's desire for freedom, it thus seems that the Novogrudok tunnel escape was not only a *great* escape but the *greatest* breakout through a hand-dug tunnel of World War II known to date.

The Story of the Escape List

Just as the secret tunnel construction neared completion in mid-September 1943, the growing opposition of many inmates gave rise to a final vote to determine whether to proceed with the planned escape or to remain in the Novogrudok forced labor camp. Some inmates expressed fear of being trapped in the tunnel,[1] while others deemed it preferable to die in the camp rather than be killed on the run.[2] In his testimony, escapee Eliyahu Berkovitz reports that the secret ballot vote resulted in the majority (165 out of 230) opting in favor of the escape plan.[3]

To properly organize the now-imminent mass escape from the labor camp, an evacuation committee was formed with the power to enforce the exit of all prisoners.[4] At the instruction of Berl Yoselevich, referred to as "the organizer and living spirit of the tunnel escape,"[5] Yitzchak Rosenhaus (#30) drew up an initial list of all the inmates to enable the escape committee to determine the order in which each would exit the tunnel.[6] (Among the permanent members of the escape committee were Nota Sucharski (#4) and Ruvke Shabakovski (#5), with others added as needed.)[7] Berkovitz notes that due to the desire of so many to be first in line, each inmate merely received a piece of paper with the name of the person he or she would follow.[8]

On my first visit to Novogrudok in 2007, I was presented a nearly illegible copy of the original escape list written in Yiddish, from which I diligently worked for the coming years to decipher and research the fate of each escapee. Only in February 2020, when the task was nearly completed, was a document likely to be the original escape list discovered in the archives of the Ghetto Fighters' House in Kibbutz Lochamei Hagetaot.

The revised version of the original escape list that follows presents the fate and prewar residences of 206 known escapees whose names were researched and deciphered, as well as those of twenty-one additional tunnel escapees whose names do not appear on the original list.

The Escape List

The names on the escape list were originally recorded by the inmate Yitzchak Rosenhaus in the Novogrudok forced labor camp. See appendix 2 for an image of the original list. Updated compilation, revisions, and research have been done by the author.

	Name	Fate	Prewar Residence
1	Jakubowicz, Dr. Majer	Survived	Lodz
2	Jakubowicz, Sarafima	Survived	Lodz
3	Mazurkevich, Etya	Survived	Ivenets
3a	Kagan, Dr. Yakov	Murdered	Baranovich
4	Sucharski, Natan (Nota)	Survived	Novogrudok
5	Shabakovski, Reuven (Ruvke)	Murdered	Novogrudok
6	Yarmovski, Isaac	Survived	Novogrudok
7	Yarmovski, Zlata	Survived	Novogrudok
8	Selubski, Efroim	Survived	Novogrudok
9	Gurvich, Hirsh	Survived	Novogrudok
10	Rakovski, Abraham (Avram)	Survived	Novogrudok
11	Sosnovski, Noah	Murdered	Novogrudok
12	Gershanovich, Mairim	Survived	Novogrudok
13	Gershanovich, Shevach	Survived	Novogrudok
14	Yoselevich, Yisrael	Murdered	Novogrudok
15	Illegible		
16	Illegible		

	Name	Fate	Prewar Residence
17	Iwinetzki, Chana	Murdered	Novogrudok
18	Zak, Yoel	Survived	Ivenets
19	Portnoj, Pesach (Lionke)	Survived	Novogrudok
20	Portnoj, Sima	Survived	Novogrudok
21	Kirzner, Aaron (Rozke)	Survived	Baranovich
22	Abramowicz, Chaim	Survived	Karelich
23	Belous, Chaim	Murdered	Zhetl
24	Crossed out and illegible		
25	Illegible		
26	Illegible		
27	Rabinowitz, Batia	Survived	Zhetl
28	Jakubowicz, Shlomo	Murdered	Lodz
29	Michalevich, Gershon	Murdered	Novogrudok
30	Rosenhaus, Yitzchak	Survived	Baranovich
31	Rosenhaus, Genia	Survived	Baranovich
32	Ostashinski, Chaim	Survived	Novogrudok
33	Ostashinski, Perla	Survived	Novogrudok
34	Orlinski, Hirsh	Murdered	Zhetl
35	Chernichovski, Hirsh	Murdered	Unknown
36	Chernichovski, Moshe	Murdered	Unknown
37	Glicksman, Moshe	Presumed murdered	Unknown
38	Leipuner and Israelit	(crossed out; see 73a and 74a)	
39	Shepsman, Yakov (Yankel)	Survived	Radom

	Name	Fate	Prewar Residence
40	Meiersdorf, David	Presumed murdered	Unknown
41	Razvaski, Yosef	Survived	Novogrudok
42	Orzuchowski, Mordechai (Motl)	Survived	Novogrudok
43	Lipchin	Presumed murdered	Unknown
44	Engler, Shlomo (Moniek)	Presumed murdered	Unknown
45	Czertok, Abram	Survived	Novogrudok
46	Pinchuk, Leiba	Survived	Novogrudok
47	Feivelevich, Moshe	Survived	Novogrudok
48	Illegible		
49	Berkowicz, Eliyahu (Elya)	Survived in hiding	Novogrudok
50	Rozin, Zisel	Survived in hiding	Novogrudok
51	Nevachovich, Yakov (Jankef)	Murdered	Novogrudok
52	Pozniak, Yechezkel (Chatzkel)	Survived	Ivenets
53	Notkovich, Kalman	Survived	Zhetl
54	Wasserman, Dov	Murdered	Mezrich
54a	Wasserman, Frieda	Murdered	Mezrich
54b	Wasserman, Leah	Murdered	Mezrich
55	Jakubowski, Aaron	Survived	Lubien Kujawski
56	Distiler	Presumed murdered	Unknown
57	Borowski, Wolff (Velvel)	Survived	Novogrudok
58	Borowski, Aaron	Survived	Novogrudok
59	Bitenski, Ita	Presumed murdered	Nowa Mysz
60	Kritz, Herman	Survived	Novogrudok

	Name	Fate	Prewar Residence
61	Katz, Manya	Unknown	Unknown
62	Kitayevich, Helena (Lena)	Murdered	Novogrudok
63	Maslovati, Gedalia	Survived	Novogrudok
64	Zalmanovich, Berko (Berl)	Survived	Novogrudok
65	Wilenski, Aaron	Survived	Novogrudok
66	Shleimovich, Naum	Survived	Novogrudok
67	Angelchik, Yakov	Survived	Novogrudok
68	Halperin	Unknown	Unknown
69	Kulik, Aaron	Presumed murdered	Unknown
70	Kulik, Sarah	Presumed murdered	Unknown
71	Wolozhinski, Rita	Murdered	Novogrudok
72	Wolkin, L.	Presumed murdered	Unknown
72a	Kabak, Matus	Survived	Novogrudok
73	Abush, Dr.	Presumed murdered	Unknown
73a	Leipuner	Presumed murdered	Unknown
74	Zilberman, Gitel (Gita)	Murdered	Novogrudok
74a	Israelit	Presumed murdered	Unknown
75	Golanski, Shlomo	Survived	Novogrudok
76	Kushner, Chanan	Murdered	Novogrudok
77	Gorodynski, Shevel (Shaul)	Survived	Novogrudok
78	Gorodynski, Sonya	Survived	Novogrudok
79	Oshman, Aaron	Survived	Ivenets
80	Oshman, Yakov	Survived	Ivenets
81	Kolachek, Yisrael	Survived in hiding	Ivenets

	Name	Fate	Prewar Residence
82	Kolachek, Shmuel	Survived in hiding	Ivenets
83	Schmulewitz, Akiva (Kiwa)	Survived	Lubcha
84	Yankelevich, Natan (Nota)	Survived	Lubcha
85	Ofsejewicz, Betzalel (Salek)	Survived	Lubcha
86	Shapiro, Gutel	Survived	Novogrudok
87	Gorodynski, Shlomo	Survived	Karelich
88	Niselevich, Shmuel	Survived	Zhetl
89	Okonski, Shlomo	Survived	Novogrudok
90	Okonski, Efraim	Survived	Novogrudok
91	Leibowitz, Chaim Noah	Survived	Novogrudok
92	Leipuner	(crossed out; see 73a)	
93	Israelit	(crossed out; see 74a)	
94	Yanson	Presumed murdered	Unknown
95	Kagan, Idel	Survived	Novogrudok
96	Yoselevich, Yakov	Survived	Novogrudok
97	Bruk, Moshe	Survived	Novogrudok
98	Gurvich, Alter	Survived	Lubcha
99	Kaplinski, Mordechai	Presumed murdered	Unknown
100	Shelkovich, Kalman	Survived	Zhetl
101	Crossed out and illegible		
102	Zacharevich, Mordechai	Survived	Novogrudok
103	Zacharevich, Yitzchak	Murdered	Novogrudok
104	Kabak, Matus	(crossed out; see 72a)	
105	Jakubowski	(crossed out; see 55)	

	Name	Fate	Prewar Residence
106	Bekenshtein, Chaim	Murdered	Zhetl
107	Lewin, Malka	Survived	Novogrudok
108	Tzimerman, David	Murdered	Novogrudok
109	Mirski, Yosef (Yosel)	Murdered	Zhetl
110	Ginden, Sholom	Survived	Novogrudok
111	Wilenski, Simcha	Survived	Novogrudok
112	Berkovich, Leah	Presumed murdered	Unknown
113	Levkovich, Nina	Survived	Novogrudok
114	Novogrudski, Michael	Survived	Zhetl
115	Leibovich, Rachmiel	Murdered	Zhetl
116	Shklarski, David	Murdered	Zhetl
117	Gertzovski, Zalman	Murdered	Zhetl
118	Shimshelevich, Shmuel	Murdered	Zhetl
119	Lidski, Isaac	Survived	Zhetl
120	Bitenski, Aaron	Murdered	Nowa Mysz
121	Samsonowicz, Hirsz	Survived	Novogrudok
122	Meyerovich, Yevel	Survived	Karelich
123	Ryback, Shlomo	Survived	Novogrudok
124	Ryback, Chana	Survived	Novogrudok
125	Shmerkovich, Tevel	Survived	Novogrudok
126	Shmerkovich, Feige	Survived	Novogrudok
127	Provizor	Presumed murdered	Unknown
128	Goldshmid, Abram	Survived	Novogrudok
129	Skakun	Presumed murdered	Unknown

	Name	Fate	Prewar Residence
130	Nignevitcky, Moshe	Survived	Novogrudok
131	Nignevitcky, Sheina	Survived	Novogrudok
132	Nignevitcky, Alter	Survived	Novogrudok
133	Zamosczyk, Nachum	Survived	Zhetl
134	Zamosczyk, Sara	Survived	Zhetl
135	Ribatzki	Presumed murdered	Unknown
136	Yoselevski, Zacharia	Murdered	Zhetl
137	Eisenshtadt, Shepsel	Survived	Novogrudok
138	Grande, Yehezkiel (Chatskel)	Survived	Novogrudok
139	Landau, Miriam	Presumed murdered	Warsaw
140	Landau, Linka	Murdered	Warsaw
141	Novolenski, Eliyahu	Murdered	Zhetl
142	Dunetz, Fanya	Survived	Zhetl
143	Kushner, Naum (Zeidel)	Survived	Novogrudok
144	Kushner, Raya	Survived	Novogrudok
145	Kushner, Leah	Survived	Novogrudok
146	Kaganowicz, Riva	Survived	Novogrudok
147	Maloshitzki, Yitzchak	Murdered	Novogrudok
148	Maloshitzki, Mordechai	Murdered	Novogrudok
149	Giershenowski, Sara	Survived	Novogrudok
150	Giershenowski, Basia	Murdered	Novogrudok
151	Giershenowski, Roza	Survived	Novogrudok
152	Lidski, Sara	Murdered	Zhetl
153	Altman, Hirsh	Murdered	Novogrudok

	Name	Fate	Prewar Residence
154	Garbar, Chana	Murdered	Novogorudok
155	Mikulitzki	Unknown	Unknown
156	Weinrid, Yakov	Survived	Unknown
157	Chechanovski, Yosef	Presumed murdered	Unknown
158	Davidovich, Frieda	Survived	Novogrudok
158a	Davidovich, Leah	Survived	Novogrudok
159	Patzovski, Hirsh	Survived	Zhetl
160	Mayevski, Pesia	Survived	Zhetl
161	Patzovski, Yakov (Yanek)	Murdered	Zhetl
162	Lev, Chanan	Survived	Bialystok
163	Niselevich, Moshe Yakov (crossed out; participation in escape uncertain)	Murdered	Novogrudok
164	Niselevich, Berl (crossed out; participation in escape uncertain)	Murdered	Novogrudok
165	Niselevich?, Raizel (crossed out; participation in escape uncertain)	Unknown	Unknown
166	Tiles, Etel	Murdered	Novogrudok
166a	Tiles, Yocheved (Yacha)	Survived	Novogrudok
167	Feifer, Nachman	Survived	Jesow
168	Luska, Chaya Sara	Survived in hiding	Novogrudok
169	Shleimovich, Eliezer (Leizer)	Unknown	Unknown
170	Galai	Presumed murdered	Unknown
171	Stein	Unknown	Unknown

	Name	Fate	Prewar Residence
172	Skora, Faivel	Unknown	Lodz
173	Gertzovski, Berl	Murdered	Zhetl
174	Gertzovski, Yosef	Murdered	Zhetl
175	Paretzki, Shmuel	Murdered	Zhetl
176	Paretzki, Moshe	Murdered	Zhetl
177	Mazurkevich, Yitzchak	Survived	Unknown
178	Epshtein, Tanchum	Murdered	Zhetl
179	Bielitski, Betzalel (Tsala)	Murdered	Zhetl
180	Daichovski, Leib	Murdered	Zhetl
181	Milovanski, Abram	Presumed murdered	Zhetl
182	Milovanski, Moshe	Presumed murdered	Zhetl
183	Ochonovski, Yedidia	Murdered	Zhetl
184	Shlachtman, Chaim (participation in escape uncertain)	Murdered	Novogrudok
185	Lusky, Rafael	Murdered	Zhetl
186	Gorodynski, Moshe	Murdered	Karelich
187	Gorodynski	Unknown	Unknown
188	Rolnik, Moshe	Presumed murdered	Ivenets
189	Rolnik, Nechama	Presumed murdered	Ivenets
190	Goberman, Natan (Nota)	Survived	Novogrudok
191	Zusmanovich, Samuil	Survived	Novogrudok
192	Zusmanovich, Eliezer (Leizer)	Survived	Novogrudok
193	Chernevich, Avram	Survived	Novogrudok
194	Chernevich, Notek	Survived	Novogrudok

	Name	Fate	Prewar Residence
195	Yarmovski, Henia	Survived	Novogrudok
196	Rabinovich, David	Presumed murdered	Unknown
197	Kopernik, Zelda	Survived	Karelich
198	Potasznik	Unknown	Unknown
199	Wolkowicki, Peretz	Survived	Lida
200	Bruk, Henia	Presumed murdered	Unknown
201	Senderovski, Menachem	Presumed murdered	Unknown
202	Shofer, Rafael	Survived	Novogrudok
203	Pozniak, Av. or Ab.	Presumed murdered	Unknown
204	Skiba	Unknown	Unknown
205	Abramowicz, Pesach	Survived	Novogrudok
206	Svinik, Dvora	Survived	Ivenets
207	Svinik, Shalom	Survived	Ivenets
208	Dinciolski	Presumed murdered	Unknown
209	Shuster, Yosef (Yosel)	Survived	Novogrudok
210	Shkolnik, Hirsch	Survived	Karelich
211	Berman, Leib	Murdered after possibly hiding	Zhetl
212	Kokin	Unknown	Unknown
213	Vainshtein, Shmuel	Murdered	Zhetl
214	Gertzovski, Saadia	Survived	Karelich

Additional Escapees Not on Original List

Compilation and research of the following list has been undertaken by the author.

Name	Fate	Prewar Residence
Berkowicz, Meir	Survived	Novogrudok
Epshtein, Chana	Survived in hiding	Zhetl
Ginenski, Bella	Survived	Novogrudok
Ginenski, Rivka (Riva)	Survived	Novogrudok
Kantorovich, Yakov	Survived	Slutzk
Koniak, Yosef	Presumed murdered	Unknown
Kozuchovski	Murdered	Unknown
Lazowsky, Isaac	Survived	Novogrudok
Magids, Avraham	Survived	Belice
Majerowicz, Morduch (Mordechai)	Survived	Karelich
Morduchowicz, Mordechai	Survived	Karelich
Notkovich, Chaim	Murdered	Zhetl
Orzuchowski, Leib	Survived	Novogrudok
Ostashinski, Daniel	Survived	Novogrudok
Reznitzki, Shalom	Survived	Zhetl
Shuster, Yitzchak	Survived	Novogrudok
Shvarzbord, Morduch	Survived	Rakov
Ulert, Isaac	Survived	Mlawa
Yoselevich, Berl	Murdered	Novogrudok
Avraham, son-in-law of Chaim Notkovich	Murdered	Zhetl
Moshe (Moshele), grandson of Chaim Notkovich	Murdered	Zhetl

Escapee Stories

Dr. Majer (#1) and Sarafima (#2) Jakubowicz

As the escape list bears witness, Dr. Majer Jakubowicz and his wife Sarafima (Sara) were the two Novogrudok forced labor camp inmates designated to be first in line to grope their way through the make-shift escape tunnel. Yet for days and weeks preceding the breakout on September 26, 1943, the couple had stood at the core of a heated ideological controversy threatening their own life and death, as well as that of their approximately 240 fellow inmates.

Majer Jakubowicz, born in 1911, was a native of Lodz, Poland,[1] while Sara née Zilberman was born in 1920 in the Polish town of Mlawa. Prior to the war, the couple had lived in Lodz. As to how and why they later reached Novogrudok, 335 miles away, we can speculate that they fled Lodz following the September 1939 German invasion to join family or friends in the then-safer Novogrudok area under Russian control. Possibly Majer escaped from the Lodz ghetto at some point, as his name appears on a list of ghetto inhabitants during the period 1940–1944.[2]

In July 1941, the Nazis occupied Novogrudok, unleashing three systematic mass executions of thousands of Jewish men, women, and children in the overcrowded Novogrudok and Pereseka ghettos. Majer and Sara Jakubowicz, a physician and nurse, were among the last few hundred Jews to remain alive, thanks to having occupations or skills deemed essential to the Nazi war machine. These men and women assigned to hard labor in the forced labor camp became the last remnants of Novogrudok Jewry.

While smoking a cigarette in the doorway of the labor camp in April 1943, Majer was shot in the leg when the Germans suddenly opened fire.[3] This injury, by domino effect, may have forced the cancellation of a gallant, meticulously planned ghetto breakout the inmates had scheduled for April 15, 1943. Researcher Nechama Tec reports that at the very last minute, with all plans in place, a sudden unexpected reinforcement of camp guards arrived on the scene to stymie the mass breakout attempt. She cites testimony given by Eliyahu Berkowicz (#49) of a subsequent investigation by the camp's resistance leaders which determined that Sara Jakubowicz had divulged the rebellion plans to the Germans for fear her injured husband would be unable to flee with the inmates.[4] Escapee Chaim Leibowitz (#91), however, attributes the leaked plans to the mother of jailed prisoner Moshe Burshtein.[5]

According to the escapee Shaul Gorodynski (#77), Sara's continued threats to sabotage any other escape plans nearly resulted in her and her husband being assassinated at the hands of their fellow prisoners. Majer's own brother Salek, who served as the Jewish police commandant in the camp, proposed that Majer and Sara be killed, arguing that the entire inmate population should not be sacrificed for a few people, even if they were his own brother and sister-in-law. Eventually, the couple agreed to participate in the breakout on the condition they be first in line and the injured physician be carried the first 110 yards after exiting the tunnel.[6]

Majer and Sara survived the tunnel escape, but at a tragic cost: Majer's brother Salek, the man who carried him not only 110 yards but a full 220 yards, was shot to death during the heroic rescue.[7]

As to Dr. Majer's fate following the escape, Zafrir Ostashinski recalls his father Daniel, also interned in the labor camp, mentioning he carried the wounded doctor to the Bielski partisan detachment. This is corroborated by Shaul Gorodynski in his Yad Vashem testimony, in which he recounts having come across a group of Jews including Leiba Pinchuk (#46), Moshe Feivelevich (#47), and Daniel Ostashinski, who had all carried the injured doctor on their backs.[8]

Dr. Majer Jakubowicz's father Berek, a merchant, and his mother Yehudit née Hershkovitz[9] were the parents of six children, five of whom we can positively identify: Moshe, born in 1902,[10] and Salek (#28), born in 1904,[11] were both merchants and single at the time of their deaths. Moshe died in 1941 in the Lodz ghetto, and Salek, as mentioned, was shot to death in the 1943 tunnel escape. Zlata Zosia Jakubowicz Braun, born in 1919, was married with no children. Although she had been interned in the Lodz ghetto, she is reported by Majer to have died in Tarnopol in 1944.[12] The youngest child, Sara, born in 1921, died in the Lodz ghetto in 1943.[13] In 1942, Berek Jakubowicz died of starvation in the Lodz ghetto[14] along with his second wife, Sura née Krenik, whom he married following Yehudit's death in 1929.[15]

Sara Jakubowicz's mother Chava née Turover, a housewife,[16] and her father Eliyahu David Zilberman, a merchant,[17] were murdered in one of the 1942 transports from their native Mlawa to Auschwitz. With Chava and Eliyahu in the deadly transport were their children: Rivka, married with three children;[18] Avraham, born in 1909, married with one child;[19] Miriam, born in 1924;[20] Zisa[21] and Bina,[22] both born in 1927; Ziskind, born in 1930,[23] and Baruch, born in 1933.[24] The mass murder of nearly Sara's entire family was part of the horrifying statistic that only forty of Mlawa's seven thousand Jewish residents survived the Holocaust.[25]

Following their harrowing escape through the Novogrudok forced labor camp tunnel, Sara[26] and Majer Jakubowicz joined the Budenny partisans, a Soviet detachment.[27]

As for their fate following liberation from the forest in 1945, a lengthy genealogical search revealed that Majer and Sara returned to Lodz after the war, and their only child Bronislaw was born on February 10, 1946.[28]

The family eventually immigrated to Israel, where they resided on Nordau Street in Tel Aviv,[29] and Dr. Majer Jakubowicz resumed practicing medicine. Majer's name appeared in the Israeli Registry of Physicians from 1948 to 1957.[30]

By 1960, the Jakubowiczes had moved to the United States. They first lived in Kansas City, Missouri,[31] before settling permanently in

Framingham, Massachusetts.[32] Majer died on December 13, 1979,[33] nearly twenty-two years before Sara's death on August 14, 2001.[34] Both are buried in the Framingham Natick Jewish Cemetery.[35]

Their son Bronislaw currently lives in St. John's, Florida. Reached by the author in 2019, he shared photos of his parents from their youth. His mother described the tunnel escape to him in detail, he reports, although her account included no mention of the controversial details surrounding her participation as reported by other inmates.[36]

Dr. Majer Jakubowicz, undated photo (Jacob Family Tree, Ancestry.com)

Sara Jakubowicz and her son Bronislaw, undated postwar photo, Lodz, Poland (courtesy of Bronislaw Jakubowicz)

Etya Mazurkevich (#3)

Etya Mazurkevich, daughter of Samuil, was born in 1913. Prior to the war, she lived in Ivenets, a town situated between Novogrudok and Minsk.[1]

Etya was spared death by virtue of being a seamstress,[2] a skill greatly needed by the Nazi war machine to produce uniforms and accessories for their massive troop deployments. Interned in the Novogrudok forced labor camp, Etya joined other skilled workers coerced into performing grueling tasks under subhuman conditions.

It is also probable that Etya took her turn working secretly by night to dig out the earth from beneath the camp in the furious effort to build the tunnel. Ultimately, she survived the breakout and made her way through treacherous terrain to reach the Bielski partisan *otriad* (detachment)[3] hidden deep in the Naliboki Forest.

Unfortunately, our search of Holocaust-related, genealogical, and population databases has revealed no information regarding Etya Mazurkevich's prewar life and family status, nor of her whereabouts following the war.

Yakov Kagan (#3a)

One must wonder what emotions Genya Cohen of Kibbutz Beit Alpha experienced in 1955 when she completed a Yad Vashem Page of Testimony for Yakov, the fourth of her seven sons. As she wrote that Yakov had died in an "escape attempt," had she known of the tunnel escape from the Novogrudok forced labor camp, and of Yakov's role as a vital, leading force in the attempt? Was she aware that the majority of escapees her son inspired would survive one of the most successful prisoner escapes of the Holocaust, and generations of Jews would be born to their descendants?

If she didn't know in 1955, perhaps Genya learned of her son's greatness when Yakov's leadership was acclaimed in the *Novogrudok Memorial Book*, originally published in 1963.[1] Yet Genya's grandchildren attest that until her death in 1979, she never once spoke of the murders of Yakov, of her daughter-in-law Rachel, nor of her three-and-a-half-year-old granddaughter Aviva.[2]

Yakov Kagan was born in 1898 in the Belarusian forest town of Buda to Genya, a housekeeper, and Shmaryahu, a lumber merchant. Once Shmaryahu could finally afford to buy a house for his family in the "big city" of Baranovich in 1914, they were caught in the maelstrom of revolution, pogroms, and civil war, forcing their exile within Russia. After wandering to the city of Alexandria in Ukraine, the Kagans moved into a comfortable home on a street lined with chestnut trees. Nearby lived the neighborhood Provoslavian priest and his wife, who, despite her marked anti-Semitism, treated her new neighbors with respect. Only thanks to the priest's warning to hide was the family saved from a violent pogrom in which seventy-two of their neighbors were murdered. The Kagans' home was vandalized and ruined. Shortly afterwards, Yakov's younger brother Yitzchak, age sixteen and a civil guard member, was brutally murdered by Ukrainian farmers who mutilated his face beyond recognition with a hatchet before hurling his body into a pit.[3]

Genya, Shmaryahu, and four of their sons then fled Alexandria for the Ukrainian town of Kremenchug. Here they lived in two rooms in poverty and constant fear of the native population known to rob, beat, and rape the Jews. Yakov and his older, well-loved brother Aaron ("Archik") were then living together in Kharkov, where Yakov attended a Hebrew teachers' seminary. Soon after he began teaching Hebrew, Yakov was forced to cease due to new Bolshevik prohibitions. He then completed his law degree under the conviction that the Bolsheviks would not remain in power.[4]

Yakov, like Aaron, helped supplement the family's income from his earnings as a Hebrew teacher. Upon learning of their family's plan to flee Russia and return to Baranovich around 1920, both Yakov and Aaron left Kharkov to join them. There Yakov founded the local branch of the Tse'irei Zion (Young Zionists) youth movement, which championed immigration to Palestine. He found work as an accountant for a lumber merchant, while resuming his Hebrew teaching. Following Shmaryahu's sudden death from a heart attack, Yakov increased his efforts to financially assist the family.[5]

With the Bolsheviks remaining firmly in power, Yakov left his careers in law and Hebrew teaching to study medicine. In 1922, he began medical school in Berlin, where his brother Aaron had begun his university studies as well. Ultimately, the two were forced to transfer to universities in the neighboring German city of Jena. There they were allowed to complete their exams in Russian. Upon Yakov's completion of his studies and the brothers' return to Poland, the Polish authorities refused to recognize Yakov's German credentials as a physician. With characteristic persistence, he moved to Vilna, where his credentials were accepted. After two years, he returned to Poland to become a nationally renowned dermatologist.[6]

By the mid-1930s, the eldest Kagan son, Chaim, had remained in Russia, and the second son, Nachman, had moved to the United States. Genya, Aaron, and twins David and Moshe had immigrated to Palestine. Yakov opted to remain in Poland until his own pending emigration.

In 1939, Yakov visited his family in Palestine, where he began to plan his own aliyah (immigration of Jewish person to the Land of Israel). Although he found work in Tel Aviv, his intention to remain in Palestine was instantly changed by a letter from his future wife Rachel Kroshinski requesting he return to Poland so they could wed.[7]

On March 3, 1938, Yakov and Rachel were married in Baranovich, and on June 7, 1939, the couple celebrated the birth of their daughter.[8] Her Hebrew name, Aviva, signified their hopes for future immigration to Israel.

In Poland, Yakov continued his Zionist activities. As a member of the Central Committee of the Socialist-Zionist Poalei Zion organization,[9] he was sent as a delegate to the Zionist Congress in Switzerland in 1939.[10] Yakov is lauded in the *Baranovich Memorial Book* as having been a positive, honest, and reliable individual, who worked toward mutual understanding, the good of the community, and the prevention of arguments in all his dealings. As director of a community-run bank, he would find ways to help needy individuals even after refusing them a bank loan.[11]

The Nazi onslaught of June 27, 1941,[12] cruelly dashed Yakov and Rachel's hopes to immigrate to Palestine. Under German order to leave Baranovich, the couple fled for the nearby town of Zhetl.[13] There, unspeakable tragedy struck soon afterwards when both Rachel and little Aviva were murdered.

For many years, Yakov's family in Israel had believed Rachel and Aviva were murdered in the German command center in Baranovich immediately after Yakov received orders to leave Baranovich. Evidently, Yakov's nephew Shmaryahu Kagan was told by Holocaust historian Shalom Cholawsky that Rachel and Aviva had been murdered instantly when Yakov asked whether his wife and daughter could join him in exile from their home.[14]

Yet in a March 2017 meeting with Yakov's niece and nephew, the author's mother, escapee Fanya Dunetz (#142), disproved the contention that Rachel and Aviva were killed in Baranovich. Fanya, who had known Rachel Kroshinski and her younger sister Dveyre in 1935 when she studied in a Baranovich high school, was a frequent visitor to the girls' home.

Still recalling Dveyre's "large green eyes" some eighty-five years later, Fanya testified that Dveyre, Yakov, Rachel, Aviva, and the rest of the Kroshinski family were among the refugees who came to Zhetl in 1941 in search of safety. Admitting that she wondered what had brought that family to the small, seemingly insignificant town of Zhetl, she told of a bold attempt with Dveyre to flee the town together. With all exits blocked, the two were unsuccessful. This was the last time Fanya was to see her friend Dveyre,[15] whose name appears on a list of murdered individuals in Zhetl in 1941–1942.[16]

When Genya Cohen submitted testimony in 1955 noting the murders of her daughter-in-law Rachel and granddaughter Aviva in Novogrudok on August 8, 1942, she was apparently correct regarding the dates of their deaths, while incorrect as to the place. Fanya recalls that in the forced labor camp, Yakov would often come into her room to spend hours talking with Batia Rabinowitz (#27), her "plankmate" in the column of wooden slabs where the inmates slept.[17] Consequently, in 1957, Batia submitted a Page of Testimony for Rachel and Aviva stating they had been killed in Zhetl (not Novogrudok) on August 8, 1942.[18] Considering the long conversations between Batia and Yakov in the labor camp and the fact she had been a neighbor of the family in Zhetl, Batia could credibly testify to the details of their fate. Rachel and Aviva's murders in Zhetl are also noted on a Russian list of individuals from Zhetl murdered in 1941–1942.[19]

In the aftermath of the horror of having lost his wife and little daughter, Yakov was forced to grapple with the near-hopeless task of serving as a doctor in the Novogrudok forced labor camp, bereft of even basic medicine. Yet Fanya Dunetz attests to his popularity, declaring, "Everybody loved him. He was such a kind man."[20]

Yakov's role as a resistance leader was already solidified after Novogrudok's third massacre ravaged the ghetto during the first week of February 1943. At this time, five hundred Jews were escorted not to their jobs in the labor camp but to ditches outside the city, stripped of their clothing, and forced to stand naked in the cold before being shot. A death blow not only to the forced labor camp inmates, but to the Pereseka ghetto itself,[21] this slaughter spurred the inmates to action. Realizing the stark probability that they were the next to be murdered, a secret committee was formed to plan an escape. The prominent leaders of this early resistance effort were noted as having been Dr. Yakov Kagan and Berl Yoselevich.[22]

The first strategy involved a prisoner escape to be coordinated with a simultaneous Jewish partisan attack from outside the camp. In the spring of 1943, Yakov and Yoselevich successfully contacted Tuvia Bielski, requesting that his partisans attack the labor camp. Bielski responded that although his fighters were not sufficiently prepared to participate in such an operation, he would nonetheless accept any escapee who reached the detachment.[23]

Tuvia Bielski's letter drove the labor camp inmates into planning an independent breakout. With passion and pathos, Yakov is reported to have declared that "[the inmates'] lives must not be sacrificed cheaply, [they] should aim to take a head for every head killed by the Germans.... It is disgraceful to die like our misled brothers and sisters died. It is an insult to live such a shameful life. There is only one way left – a worthy death. We must attack the Germans with any means available – using knives, stones, with teeth and nails. And only then will we be united with the souls of the fallen."[24]

In response, an armed uprising by the inmates was planned for April 15, 1943, with Dr. Yakov Kagan chosen as the leader. The "infirmary" that he shared with Dr. Majer Jakubowicz (#1) was designated as the command center. At the secret moment when the uprising was to start, the inmates were armed with five rifles, six revolvers, and four hand grenades purchased for hefty sums from camp guards; the main gate had been slipped open using surreptitiously copied keys; and the inmates waited for a shot to signal the attack on a guard. Yet the mass breakout was suddenly cancelled due to a swift, unanticipated, and significant increase of security guards in the camp.[25] According to some, the sudden rush of policemen came in response to the screams of the mother of jailed resistance fighter Moishe Burshtein, who feared her son would be left behind during the breakout.[26] A second version holds that the plan had been exposed by Sara Jakubowski (#2) in an attempt to protect her husband Majer (#1), whose recent injury would have prevented his escape.[27]

The fourth Nazi massacre of the remaining Jews of Novogrudok, just three months after the third, once again drove Dr. Kagan into a leadership position.[28] Together with Berl Joselewicz, Yakov is credited by sociologist Nechama Tec[29] as having initiated the idea for a tunnel escape, and by the former Novogrudker Yehoshua Yaffe as having been the "commander" of the escape.[30] Fanya Dunetz personally named Yakov as having been a major organizer of the escape.[31]

When the escape list was compiled to determine the order in which the inmates would flee the tunnel, Yakov sought no privileges for himself, despite being a below-the-knee amputee who used a prosthetic device (due to a prewar jump from a moving train). Following the war, his family in Israel was told by survivors that Yakov had refused to take his assigned preferential position as the fourth in line, moving back to the end of the line instead.[32]

As to the details of Yakov's tragic death in the escape, Yakov's niece and nephew report that following the war, survivors informed the family that Yakov, like many others, had lost his way after emerging from the tunnel into the general bedlam on the dark, stormy night.[33] (This is confirmed by Fanya Dunetz, as well.[34]) With visibility almost nil and Yakov an amputee, the double liability became fatal.

Yehoshua Yaffe's account, however, presents a different scenario: Several days after the breakout, a clash broke out between a group of Russian leader Victor Panchenko's partisans and nine tunnel escapees, including Dr. Yakov Kagan. When the escapees refused to surrender the two weapons in their possession, they were all murdered.[35]

At his death, Yakov Kagan was the last remaining member of his immediate family. Yet his life and death continue to be commemorated by his numerous nieces and nephews, now numbering into the fifth generation. As for Yakov's siblings, all but one immigrated to Israel; twin brothers David and Moshe remained on Kibbutz Beit Alfa throughout their lives, and each had children and grandchildren. Aaron settled in Tel Aviv, where he taught Hebrew literature at the Shalva High School until retirement. He married Shifra, an English teacher and an American immigrant who had a daughter and two grandchildren. Chaim immigrated to Israel from Russia, settled in Ramat Gan, and had children and grandchildren. Nachman settled in the USA, where he married an American-born woman. They had no children of their own.

Yakov Kagan will be forever remembered as the man who inspired so many to seek life, or at the least to die a meaningful death. In their lives and through their descendants, those who survived the Novogrudok forced labor camp escape can be considered a tribute to his leadership. Those who died gave meaning to their deaths by their valiant efforts to live. Dr. Yakov Kagan's life was to offer meaning in a time and place that seemed to defy its very definition.

Dr. Yakov Kagan in his clinic, 1936
(courtesy of Yitzchak Cohen and Hagar Sezaf)

Natan (Nota) Sucharski (#4)

Born in Lida in 1897[1] to Yisrael and Sheina,[2] Natan ("Nota") Sucharski, along with Berl Yoselevich, is largely credited with having been a driving force behind the conception of a tunnel escape.[3] A tinsmith by profession, Nota Sucharski is recalled by fellow inmate Daniel Ostashinski as also having been a skilled carpenter known before the war for his expertise in crafting skis. In the escape effort, Ostashinski notes that Nota designed much of the woodwork in the tunnel, including planks, supports, rails, and carriages.[4]

In a personal interview, Jack (Idel) Kagan (#95) explained that Nota Sucharski was married to his father's sister.[5] Prior to the war, Nota had made a good living as an expert tinsmith from his basement workshop in the marketplace. A well-known public figure in Novogrudok, Nota was a devoted activist in community work and served as a member of the Jewish Community Council, the Council of the Jewish Hospital, the Home for the Aged Committee, and more.[6] Nota took a heightened role in the United Jewish Artisans Association, whose Artisans and Small Business Bank helped improve the lives of those engaged in small businesses and crafts, which was about 80 percent of the town's population. As a member of the association's subcommittee supporting poor tradesmen, he discreetly helped impoverished families obtain food for the Sabbath as well as for holidays, especially Passover.[7]

At Nota Sucharski's marriage to Chaya "Haike" Kagan, their dowry was a house adjacent to one shared by the families of two brothers and two sisters: Dov Cohen's parents Moshe Kagan and Shosh née Gurevitz, and Jack Kagan's parents, Yankel Kagan and Dvora ("Dvore") née Gurevitz. The Sucharskis and both Kagan families lived in the low-income Jewish neighborhood of Racelo Street, where they were considered wealthy and respectable.[8]

On summer evenings, the Sucharskis would entertain their many friends in their lovely garden, graced by a table and benches surrounding an old apple tree.[9] Haike Sucharsky helped Nota support the family by mending umbrellas. She is described by her nephew Dov Cohen as having been a kind, gentle woman who allowed Nota to be the disciplinarian for their three children, all of whose young lives ended tragically.[10]

The couple's youngest child, daughter Idele, born in 1931, died at the age of three from appendicitis.[11] Sixteen-year-old Srulik (Yisroel) was shot and killed on August 6, 1942, while attempting to escape from the military barracks where he had been employed. His failed attempt came just one day before the second brutal execution in which five thousand men, women, and children were massacred in Litovka and thrown into pre-dug mass graves.[12]

Jack Kagan relates that his uncle Nota's oldest child, eighteen-year-old Sheindel, escaped from the Novogrudok forced labor camp in February 1943 together with Henia, the daughter of Noah Sosnovski

(#11). The two girls then headed for the marketplace, where arrangements had been made for them to meet a non-Jew hired to lead them to Reuven Openheim, who was to have escorted them to the Bielski partisans. Yet when they reached the marketplace, the girls were betrayed by a local resident, leading to their arrest, torture, and murder in prison.[13] Three months later, Haike Sucharski was slain on May 7, 1943, in the fourth and final Novogrudok massacre.[14]

Testimony by fellow escapee Shaul Gorodynski (#77) sheds light on the fact that Nota Sucharski was a key member of the group that planned an uprising in early 1943, when around five hundred inmates were interned in the Novogrudok forced labor camp. Other leaders in the planning were Dr. Yakov Kagan (#3a), Berl Yoselevich, and Aaron Oshman (#79), as well as those with prior military experience, such as Abram Rakovski (#10), Gershon Michalevich (#29) and Isaac Yarmovski (#6).[15] Originally scheduled for April 15, 1943, the uprising was ultimately cancelled, reportedly due to increased Nazi security in the camp. The arrival of these extra guards has been attributed to Sara Jakubowicz (#2) leaking the plans for fear that her husband would be left behind because of his injured leg.[16]

Against the backdrop of the failed uprising, as well as the massacre of May 7, 1943, in which Nota's beloved wife Haike and half the camp's population was murdered within sight and earshot of the inmates, those remaining resolved to "die like heroes" rather than being "killed like chickens."[17] Thus the brave plan was born to dig a secret tunnel to freedom.

Sucharski and Berl Yoselevich were designated to head the committee to plan the tunnel escape, along with Shmuel Kolachek (#82), Chaim Leibowitz (#91),[18] Ruvke Shabakovski (#5), and others. Sucharski and Shabakovski lived in the same room as Idel Kagan (#95), who reports that clandestine meetings were held there three to four times weekly.[19]

Kagan also recalls that both Nota Sucharski and Lionke Portnoj (#19) gave a one-week commitment to make the tools needed to dig the tunnel, plus a promise to maintain them afterwards.[20] Kagan credits

Nota's expertise in ingenious tool design as having evolved from his experience in improvising makeshift tools to clear the rubble of German bombing raids in the July 4, 1941, Nazi invasion of Novogrudok. At the time, Kagan was a fellow laborer in the task, along with Efroim Selubski (#8), Dov Cohen, and Noah Sosnovski.

Nota Sucharski survived the tunnel breakout from the forced labor camp for which he had toiled day and night. Fellow escapee Abram Czertok (#45) testifies that he and Nota banded together immediately afterwards with Isaac Yarmovski, Hirsh Gurvich (#9), and father and son Mairim (#12) and

Natan (Nota) Sucharski, undated prewar photo (*Memorial Book of the Jewish Community of Novogrudok, Poland*)

Shevach (#13) Gershanovich to set out for the Bielski partisan detachment. After two days of trekking through the forest with no food or water, the six escapees were given shelter by a non-Jewish farmer. A young girl who had taken cover with them later led the group to a Jewish-founded partisan unit, the Frunze detachment of the First Baranovichskaya Brigade.[21]

Czertok testifies that the six men remained in this detachment until liberation, when all, save for Shevach Gershanovich, were drafted into the Red Army.[22] Yet Nota is listed in the National Archive of the Republic of Belarus (NARB) as having joined the Bielski detachment in September 1943,[23] implying the possibility that he transferred there after a period with the Frunze partisans.

The sole survivor of his immediate family, Nota Sucharski died at the age of forty-seven in Novogrudok in October 1944 following abdominal surgery performed by the renowned Dr. Kalman Gordin. He is buried in the Novogrudok Jewish cemetery.[24]

Reuven (Ruvke) Shabakovski (#5)

Despite unspeakably brutal torture, Reuven (Ruvke) Shabakovski tenaciously withstood Nazi demands to reveal information on resistance efforts within the Novogrudok forced labor camp. Prior to the mass execution of May 7, 1943, Ruvke and his fellow inmate Moshe Burshtein had been arrested and tortured by the Germans, critically endangering the lives of the hundreds of Jews interned in the camp. Moshe Burshtein survived long enough to smuggle out a message written on his shirt in his own blood: "I am waiting for my death. I am in great pain – I will not betray you."[1]

Ruvke miraculously escaped death to take a leading role just months later in planning the tunnel escape. He became an active member of the clandestine works committee that met three to four times weekly to plan and discuss the progress of the prospective breakout.[2] During this period, Shabakovski shared a room with Nota Sucharski (#4), another permanent committee member, and with Idel Kagan (#95), a fourteen-year-old whose unsuccessful attempt at escape in December 1942 had necessitated the furtive amputation (sans anesthesia) of all his toes.[3] In his writings, Kagan recalled that following the amputation, Ruvke was dispatched to town by the commandant for a special task and returned with a purloined half-full sack of flour and a radio. The precious radio, carefully hidden in a loft, became a vital means of informing the inmates of current events.[4]

Ruvke was born in Novogrudok in 1912 to Shprintze and Kalman.[5] Although Ruvke was said to have married,[6] we have no information regarding his wife's name, fate, or the names and fate of any children they may have had. Ruvke was perhaps a twin to Charna, whose date of birth was also listed as 1912 in a Yad Vashem Page of Testimony. Charna Furman was murdered together with her seven-year-old son Kalman in

1942, most likely in the November 7 mass execution of Novogrudok's Jews.[7] Her husband Motl was murdered at some point as well.[8] Liba Boretzki, a sister to Ruvke and Charna, was murdered in one of the 1943 Novogrudok massacres, along with her daughters Chaya, age nine, and Lia, age twelve, as well as the family matriarch Shprintze.[9] Remarkably, Liba's husband Yosef and their son Yitzchak (born in 1928) survived to become Bielski partisans.[10]

Reuven Shabakovski, undated prewar photo (*Memorial Book of the Jewish Community of Novogrudok, Poland*)

Although Ruvke Shabakovski endured his terrible torture, he did not survive the tunnel escape. His name appears among the Holocaust victims commemorated in the *Novogrudok Memorial Book*.[11]

Both Ruvke's brother-in-law Yosef and his nephew Yitchak Boretzki immigrated to Israel after World War II. Although Yitzchak, who died in 2003, is described by his daughter Leah as having been withdrawn and reticent to speak about the war years,[12] it is through his Pages of Testimony at Yad Vashem that details of Ruvke's family are preserved.

Ruvke's brother David, three years his junior, survived the war with the Bielski partisans.[13] The last of his immediate family to remain alive, David immigrated to Brooklyn and changed his surname to Zaks. His niece Leah notes that David died around 2014, leaving two sons, a daughter, and grandchildren.[14] To date, we have been unable to make contact to tell them of the legacy of courage and bravery their great-uncle Ruvke Shabakovski left for posterity.

Isaac (#6) and Zlata (#7) Yarmovski

Isaac and Zlata Yarmovski were one of the few married couples in the Novogrudok forced labor camp to survive and remain together throughout the war – in the ghetto, in the labor camp, in the tunnel escape, and in the partisans. A source of mutual support throughout the brutally difficult times, they rebuilt their lives in the immediate postwar period to make a new life for their family in Israel.

Born on New Year's Day 1911, in Smolchika, near Novogrudok,[1] Isaac was the son of Shimon, a miller, and Chana née Zizemski, a housewife. He was one of six siblings, three of whom were killed with their parents and families in Novogrudok's first mass slaughter on December 8, 1941.[2] His sister Etl Bytenski, a thirty-six-year-old housewife, was murdered together with her two sons, fifteen-year-old Lolik and thirteen-year-old Yitzchak.[3] Brother Efraim Yarmovski, a merchant married to Raizl, was thirty-four years old at his death.[4] Brother Moshe, a merchant married to Rachel, was forty years old when murdered.[5] Only one sister, Leah Rodnitzki, was spared the Novogrudok atrocities thanks to having immigrated to pre-state Israel prior to the war.[6] Isaac and his brother Shlomo, born in 1907,[7] were to become the sole family members to survive the Novogrudok slaughters. The two brothers are reported to have remained extremely close until Shlomo's death in Israel in 1964.[8]

Zlata Gordin Yarmovski was born on July 27, 1912, in Volchichi, a hamlet near Novogrudok. Like Isaac's parents, Zlata's parents Rafael and Bracha Gordin were millers. Zlata's four siblings included Chana, Berl, Sara, and Kalman, who became a renowned surgeon. At some point prior to the war, the family members relocated to Novogrudok. Save for Zlata and Kalman, the entire Gordin family was murdered along with the Yarmovski family and over five thousand others in the Novogrudok mass murder of December 8, 1941.[9]

Isaac and Zlata were hurriedly married in a religious ceremony soon after the German occupation of Novogrudok on July 3, 1941.[10] Isaac's technical skills and Zlata's proficiency as a seamstress enabled them both to survive all selections, be assigned to the forced labor camp, and remain alive. In his testimony, fellow inmate Shaul Gorodynski (#77) notes that prior to the war, Isaac had worked for Shaul's father Avraham in Novogrudok where he repaired sewing machines, typewriters, and bicycles.[11] In the labor camp, Isaac continued repairing the all-important sewing machines[12] and worked together with Shaul in the mechanical welding shop. Thanks to his having served in the Polish Army at the rank of corporal, Isaac was tapped with other military veterans to serve on the top-secret escape committee that devised and planned the breakout from the forced labor camp.[13]

Thanks to the 1968 testimony of fellow escapee Abram Czertok (#45), we know that upon fleeing through the tunnel, Isaac joined up with him, Natan Sucharski (#4), Hirsh Gurvich (#9), and father and son Mairim (#12) and Shevach (#13) Gershanovich to make their way together through the forest to the partisans. After two days along the treacherous journey, they were given shelter by a Christian farmer and later directed to the Frunze partisan detachment of the First Baranovichskaya Brigade.[14] As for Zlata, we are unaware whether Czertok inadvertently neglected to name her among the members of this group or whether Zlata and Isaac were separated and reunited at some other point after the escape. In any case, both Zlata and Isaac are reported to have ultimately served together in the Frunze partisan detachment.[15]

Despite the liberation of Belorussia in the summer of 1944 by victorious Soviet forces, hostilities continued to rage elsewhere in Europe. Isaac Yarmovski was immediately drafted into the Red Army, together with Czertok, Sucharski, Gurvich, Mairim Gershanovich, and Abram Rakovski (#10).[16] Isaac is said to have taken part in heavy fighting until reaching Berlin, where he was injured by a shrapnel wound to the knee.[17]

For reasons unknown to their children, following the war, Isaac and Zlata chose to return to Novogrudok to set down new roots. (With the notable exceptions of Abram Goldshmid [#128] and Leiba Pinchuk [#46], the overwhelming majority of tunnel escapees avoided resettling in Novogrudok.) Together with Dr. Kalman Gordin and his family, Isaac and Zlata eventually returned to the home that Zlata and Kalman's father had built, close to the *zamek* (castle fortress), once a popular destination for Novogrudok's Jews on a Sabbath stroll. There their two children Bracha and Shimon were born in 1946 and 1951, respectively. Bracha was named for Zlata's mother, and Shimon for Isaac's father.[18]

By 1959, the family was repatriated to Poland. One year later, they immigrated to Israel, reunited at last with Isaac's sister Leah Rodnitzki, who played a major role in their resettlement. Isaac and Zlata (who Hebraicized their first names to Yitzchak[19] and Zahava[20]) eventually settled in Rishon Lezion, where Isaac worked in construction and resumed his penchant for repairing bicycles. Zlata occasionally worked at home as a seamstress as she concentrated her efforts on raising the children. Today Bracha is a retired agricultural researcher for the Hebrew University,[21] and Shimon is a retired Israeli Air Force lieutenant colonel.

Although they had been told about the tunnel escape during their childhood and youth, Shimon[22] and Bracha were unaware of the details of the escape and of their parents' partisan experiences. As children, despite having resided in close proximity to the scenes of horrendous wartime atrocities in Novogrudok, they insist that they lived a "normal" life in a home unclouded by the shadow of Holocaust trauma. Thus, they never felt compelled to ask their parents questions about their past. While Bracha recalls that Zlata was somewhat reserved in manner, Isaac loved to dance and exuded his joy at being alive. She also notes that the family enjoyed good relations with their

Christian neighbors in Novogrudok, making certain that those individuals who extended help during the war were recognized by Yad Vashem as Righteous Among the Nations.[23] This rare "normative" lifestyle may well be attributed to Isaac and Zlata's mutual support, as well as to the close relationships between the surviving siblings and members of their families – Zlata and her brother Kalman and Isaac and his brother Shlomo – all of whom remained in Novogrudok until at least 1959.

Isaac passed away in Israel on October 21, 1984,[24] nineteen years before Zlata's death on November 25, 2003.[25] If they were alive as of September 2023, they would be the proud grandparents of four and the great-grandparents of nine.[26]

Isaac Yarmovski, during his Polish Army service, undated (courtesy of Shimon Yarom)

Zlata Yarmovski, undated prewar photo (courtesy of Shimon Yarom)

Efroim Selubski (#8)

Just one day before the Passover Seder night, when Jews celebrate their exodus from Egypt, the author received a return call from Efroim Selubski's son, Steve Shell. During the ensuing telephone conversation, Steve learned for the first time of his father's own personal exodus from the Novogrudok forced labor camp.[1]

Not unlike many other second-generation Holocaust survivors, Steve knew almost nothing of his father's Holocaust experiences, including his internment in a labor camp. Efroim had been determined to remain silent about the life he left behind after immigrating to America. The only giveaway of his hidden pain and sorrow were the cries he uttered when he thought his children were out of hearing distance.[2]

Born on May 15, 1903, Efroim Selubski was the son of Shlomo and Malka née Warecki. Prior to the war, he lived in Novogrudok, where he worked as a saddler and shoemaker.[3] We learn from the memoirs of fellow Novogrudok native and labor camp inmate Jack (Idel) Kagan (#95) that Efroim was employed for many years by the Kagan family and that in the forced labor camp, Efroim helped care for thirteen-year-old Idel when the boy's frostbitten toes were amputated following a failed escape attempt.[4]

Other than the fact that two sisters came to the United States prior to the war, we have no information regarding Efroim's family of origin. Although no official record exists of the murder of Efroim's first wife and baby daughter in one of the Novogrudok massacres, Steve recalls a relative inadvertently relaying the information of their existence and slayings.[5]

In his memoirs, Idel Kagan relates that following the bombing raids in the Nazi invasion of Novogrudok on July 4, 1941, Kagan and Efroim were part of a team ordered to clear the rubble from the streets.

Kagan recounts the chilling details of German gunfire ripping the air as the two took cover in the cellar of a stone building along with Natan Sucharski (#4), Noah Sosnovski (#11), and Dov Cohen. As the townspeople looked on, fifty-two Jews were executed in this coldblooded massacre in the market square, to the accompaniment of a German orchestra.[6]

We can assume that his profession as a leather worker spared Efroim's life, resulting in his internment in the Novogrudok forced labor camp from July 1941 until the escape in September 1943.[7] Here he probably worked in the labor camp's shoe workshop, where footwear was prepared for the German army, and repairs were made for the local populace.

After surviving the tunnel escape and his subsequent flight to freedom through the forest, Efroim joined the Bielski partisans. There he met his second wife Sima née Chytovich, a former bakery owner from Novogrudok.[8] After registering in Warsaw with the Central Committee for Polish Jews,[9] which supervised repatriation of Jews from the Soviet Union and attended to the needs of survivors from 1944 to 1950,[10] the young couple and their two-month-old daughter Sarah were among the first refugees to inhabit the Bindermichl Displaced Persons Camp in Linz, Austria,[11] when it opened in October 1945.[12]

On January 8, 1947, four years and four months after the tunnel escape, Efroim, Sima, and two-and-a-half-year-old Sarah boarded the SS *Marine Marlin* under the sponsorship of the Hebrew Immigrant Aid Society, bound for their new home of New York City.[13] There they were warmly received by Efroim's sister Dora, who had last seen her brother before the war.[14]

The family settled in the Williamsburg section of Brooklyn, where Steve was born in 1947, moving seventeen years later to the Flatbush area. Laboring intensely to support his family at the only job he ever held in the United States, Efroim worked eleven hours a day on the night shift at Ratner's, the landmark New York kosher dairy restaurant on the Lower East Side. From 7:00 p.m. until 6:00 a.m., Efroim was either at the counter or in the restaurant's bakery. Coincidently, the distinct possibility exists that among Efroim's customers was the author, who regularly frequented this restaurant.[15]

Efroim Selubski upon entry to the United States, 1947 (courtesy of Steve Shell)

Described by his son as "one of the nicest, kindest men one could ever know," Efroim is said to have been a gentle man who "never let his anger out" despite all his past suffering. At his death in July 1975, Efroim was the proud grandfather of two-year-old Ilya, Steve's son. He defied the intense pain of his cancer to crawl on the floor and play with the toddler he loved so dearly. Efroim's second grandson, his namesake Jeremy Efroim, was born in 1980.

Sima, also a longtime Ratner's Restaurant worker, died in 1998, twenty-three years after her husband's death. Daughter Sarah, whose name became Sally in America, devotedly cared for Sima during her mother's last thirteen years. Sally worked in computer data entry before her death in 2017. She never married.

Steve Shell (who changed his surname prior to the birth of his first child in 1973), is a retired teacher and educational administrator married to Linda, a financial and business manager. Both Ilya and Jeremy Efroim are successful in their respective fields of finance and real estate. If Efroim were alive at the time of this writing (2018), he would be the great-grandfather of four.[16]

Now that his father's story is known to Steve, he appears proud of the chapter of his father's life that he has only now discovered. He even speaks of the possibility of visiting Novogrudok to see where it all took place.

Hirsh Gurvich (#9)

Although virtually no civil records for Hirsh Gurvich have been found to date, the testimony of two Novogrudok *landsmen* (fellow country-men) – a chronicler and a comrade – have shed a priceless light on several distinct aspects of his life.

The son of Chaim, Hirsh Gurvich was born in 1911 and worked as a tailor in Novogrudok prior to the war.[1] We have no details about his family of origin or whether he was married before the Holocaust. Yet thanks to the postwar testimony of fellow Novogrudok resident Abram Czertok (#45), who was interned together with Hirsh in the Novogrudok forced labor camp, we learn that Hirsh's brother had been an inmate of the camp as well. Czertok reveals that this brother, whose name he did not mention, was injured in the camp some time prior to the escape. Fearing that the injury would hinder Hirsh's brother's swift flight through the tunnel, he and his comrades faced the chilling pros-pect that he would be caught by the Germans in the escape attempt and horribly tortured. To prevent this, he was injected with a lethal amount of morphine by one of the camp doctors, in a true mercy killing.[2]

Hirsh Gurvich survived the treacherous escape through the tunnel, where he joined fellow escapees Nota Sucharski (#4), father and son Mairim (#12) and Shevach (#13) Gershanovich, Abram Czertok, and Isaac Yarmovski (#6) to traverse the forest in search of partisans. Two long days later, bereft of food or water, the escapees found shelter with a non-Jewish farmer. Later, a young girl who had taken cover with them guided the men to the Frunze detachment of the First Baranovichskaya Brigade, where they became partisan fighters at last.[3]

An additional glimpse of Hirsh Gurvich's life is found in the *Novogrudok Memorial Book*. Here Dr. S. Openheim notes that in his youth, Hirsh had been an active member of the Freiheit Socialist-Zionist youth movement.[4] Although his Freiheit affiliation promoted the ideology of creating a Jewish nation, this Zionist was not fated to see Israel reach statehood in 1948. After liberation, Hirsh Gurvich was conscripted into the Red Army and fell in battle at the front.[5]

Avraham (Abram) Rakovski (#10)

Abram Rakovski was not only a leader of the resistance in the Novogrudok forced labor camp, but also reputed to be the electrical genius who devised a method to cut off the electricity in the camp and provide the blanket of darkness essential to usher in the escape.

Born in 1911, Abram Rakovski resided in Novogrudok.[1] Apparently from a Zionist family, he was active in the Hashomer Hatzair Zionist youth movement[2] and educated in the city's Chaim Nachman Bialik Tarbut Hebrew School, in which Hebrew was the language of instruction in all subjects except for Polish history and geography.

Abram's parents Sara Feigel and Yitzchak Yaakov Rakovski, along with his siblings Chaya, Moshe, Rivka, and Chana Sheina, were all murdered in the Holocaust. Only his sister Adela (Man) survived the war; she placed a memorial notice for her entire family in the *Novogrudok Memorial Book*.[3]

As for Abram, his skills as an electrician earned his entry to the Novogrudok forced labor camp, where he soon became a leader in the inmates' clandestine resistance endeavors against their Nazi captors. The prisoners' first major undertaking was an armed uprising.

Despite the opposition of some who felt that such an operation would be suicidal, Abram, along with Jankef Nevachovich (#51), Berl Yoselevich, and an inmate known as Mandri, was appointed to lead one of the four groups designated to attack the Germans in the uprising planned for April 15, 1943. This endeavor was ultimately called off at the last minute when a German guard became informed of the plan.[4]

As described, the horrific massacre of May 7, 1943, which ensued soon afterwards, as well as rumors of the camp's impending liquidation gave rise to the heroic tunnel escape plan. Inmate Shaul Gorodynski (#77) notes in his Yad Vashem testimony that when plans for the tunnel escape began in earnest in May 1943, all those with prior military experience were tapped to serve on the top-level escape committee. This included Abram, who had most likely been a veteran of the Polish Army.[5]

Though fellow inmate Eliyahu Berkovicz (#49) attributes the electrical wizardry of the escape to Gershon Michalevich (#29),[6] others write of the major role played by Abram Rakovski. Idel Kagan (#95) credits Rakovski as having been the best electrician in the camp, and as such, he was asked to search for a live electric cable to provide light in the tunnel. Several days later, Rakovski found the main cable. Besides installing a warning bell at the site of the top-secret tunnel digging, he also managed to fashion a switchboard that enabled him to control the two large camp searchlights.[7] Fellow escapee Shaul Gorodynski (#77) recalls that Abram began causing frequent short circuits to avoid suspicion when this would happen in real time during the escape. Thanks to Abram's electrical prowess, the Germans never discovered why the searchlights were not functioning properly.[8] The night of the escape, the searchlight cut off flawlessly.

It is quite possible that without Abram Rakovski's electrical genius, the tunnel escape would have never achieved its extraordinary success. Abram, too, was able to reap the benefit of his work to survive the escape. Making his way to the forest, he joined a Jewish-founded partisan unit, the Frunze detachment of the First Baranovichskaya Brigade,[9] where he fought valiantly against the Germans.[10]

Following liberation, Abram was drafted into the Russian Army along with fellow tunnel escapees Isaac Yarmovski (#6) and Abram Czertok (#45). Czertok's son Guy reports that the three saw action together in battling the German enemy.[11]

Although he survived all four Novogrudok massacres, the tunnel escape, and his partisan service, Abram Rakovski was not destined to remain alive. Killed in the battle for Berlin, he was highly decorated posthumously by the Soviet government.[12] His medal was received by Adela,[13] the last living member of the immediate family.

Noah Sosnovski (#11)

Noah Sosnovski was a tailor from Novogrudok who played an important role in the construction of the Novogrudok forced labor camp escape tunnel. According to Jack (Idel) Kagan (#95), Sosnovski was called upon by the escape committee to collect blankets and sew them into sixty bags, each sixteen inches by twenty inches. After nine to ten trolley loads of earth were dug out daily, these bags were used by night to move and hide the soil. Sixty or seventy people would sit in a line from the entrance to the tunnel and pass the bags along to the next person. In time, the bags were emptied on both sides of the loft in the adjacent building.[1]

In his Yad Vashem testimony, Shaul Gorodynski (#77) mentions that despite the strict curfew imposed, several inmates did manage to flee by night in the period prior to the great escape. One escapee, he notes, was one of Noah Sosnovski's two daughters.[2] As we know that twenty-year-old Michal Sosnovski was killed with her mother in the camp massacre of May 7, 1943,[3] this had to have been her sister, seventeen-year-old Henia, who escaped from the forced labor camp in February 1943 together with Sheindel Sucharski, the daughter of Nota (#4). After being betrayed by a local resident in the marketplace, both girls were reported to have been arrested, tortured, and killed in prison.[4]

Despite his struggle to remain alive as the sole living member of his immediate family, Noah Sosnovski did not survive the tunnel escape to which he had contributed so greatly.[5] His death is commemorated in the *Novogrudok Memorial Book*.[6]

Mairim (#12) and Shevach (#13) Gershanovich

Father and son Mairim and Shevach Gershanovich crawled out of the tunnel together to freedom, with Mairim leading the way. Tragically, they were now the last surviving members of their immediate family: their wife and mother, whose first name is unknown, had in all likelihood been murdered in one of Novogrudok's four mass executions. According to family friend Jack (Idel) Kagan (#95), Shevach's sister, his only sibling, had been murdered in one of the slaughters.[1]

Mairim Gershanovich, the son of Idel, was born in 1895 and resided in Novogrudok.[2] A tailor by profession, Mairim most probably taught the trade to Shevach, born in Novogrudok in 1923,[3] and in doing so enabled him to survive. Both men were conscripted by the Nazis to the Novogrudok forced labor camp, where tailors' skills were greatly needed by the German Army.

Among the first to break out of the tunnel, father and son Mairim and Shevach survived to band together with Natan Sucharski (#4), Isaac Yarmovski (#6), Hirsh Gurvich (#9), and Abram Czertok (#45) to navigate the forest. Along the difficult trek, a Christian farmer offered the men shelter in his home. After several days, a young girl who had been in hiding together with them showed the escapees the way to the Frunze partisan detachment of the First Baranovichskaya Brigade.[4] According to Jack Kagan, Shevach's escape was all the more remarkable considering that the young man had been sickly as a child.[5]

Mairim Gershanovich, who survived all four Nazi "selections" in Novogrudok, as well as the tunnel escape and partisan life in the forest, did not survive the war. Mobilized by the Red Army, he met his death on the Russian front.[6]

Shevach, now the sole member of his family to remain alive, returned to live and work in Novogrudok following the war.[7]

Yisrael (#14) and Berl Yoselevich

From a memorial notice submitted by a surviving brother of Yisrael and Berl Yoselevich, we learn that the Yoselevich family of Novogrudok included parents Rafael and Chaya Sara and at least six children. Five of the children were murdered in the Holocaust.[1] Among them, both Yisrael and Berl were destined to take part in the Novogrudok forced labor camp tunnel escape, for which Berl's contribution was renowned for its extraordinary impact.

Fellow escapee Chaim Leibowitz (#91) writes that the Yoseleviches were a family of tradesmen, noting that Rafael had been extremely active in Novogrudok Jewish communal affairs.[2] Nothing is known of Chaya Sara other than that she was killed along with Rafael in one of the Novogrudok massacres.[3] According to the testimony of relatives, three of the couple's children were murdered in 1942: Yehudit, born in 1902, single and a seamstress by profession;[4] Yente, born in 1906, single and a photographer;[5] and Mira, for whom no details were given.[6] One son, Avraham, survived to submit the names of his parents and siblings to be listed among the murdered in the *Novogrudok Memorial Book* published in 1963.[7] We know nothing more about Avraham or even where he resided.

Yisrael Yoselevich was born in Novogrudok in 1900. Yisrael was married to Ida. The couple had a daughter, Chaya, who was three years old at her death in 1942.[8] Yisrael's profession as a tailor enabled him to survive the massacres by being conscripted to the Novogrudok forced labor camp. Sadly, Yisrael did not survive the tunnel escape.[9]

Berl Yoselevich, born in 1904, has been referred to as "the organizer and living spirit of the tunnel escape."[10] According to former classmate Chaim Leibowitz, Berl had a traditional Jewish education and was a good pupil. For two years, the two learned together in the Menaker Cheder.[11]

Although active in Hashomer Hatzair, one of the most popular youth movements in Novogrudok until the 1939 outbreak of World War II, Berl mainly enjoyed athletics with the Maccabi sporting organization.[12] A photo of the 1934–1935 Novogrudok Maccabi Team appearing in Jack Kagan's book *Novogrudok: The History of a Jewish Shtetl* shows Berl along with two teammates destined to become fellow tunnel escapees, Jankef Nevachovich (#51) and Simcha Wilenski (#111).[13]

Thanks to his teenage pursuit of photography, Berl was employed as a photographer[14] prior to the war. In the forced labor camp, he was ordered to work as a locksmith.[15]

Jack Kagan (#95),[16] Chaim Leibowitz,[17] and Peter Duffy[18] all credit Berl Yoselevitz with having independently conceived the idea of digging a tunnel under the camp to break through to freedom, although both Yehoshua Yaffe[19] and Daniel Ostashinski[20] cite Berl Yoselevich together with Nota (Natan) Sucharski (#4) as having initiated the concept. Alternately, Nechama Tec attributes the plan for a tunnel escape to both Berl and Dr. Yakov Kagan (#3a).[21]

Whether or not Berl was the sole initiator of the escape, a general consensus is that he also took responsibility for all the working plans and details involved in the endeavor. Chaim Leibowitz names him as the technical manager of the tunnel construction,[22] while Nechama Tec refers to him as having not only been "in charge of the actual building," but also having "coordinated the different parts of the job."[23] Former inmates Fanya Dunetz (#142)[24] and Jack Kagan[25] also corroborate that the plans for the tunnel were engineered by Yoselevich.

Before the tunnel escape was undertaken, Berl Yoselevich had assumed a key role in an earlier attempt to free the Jewish prisoners from the yoke of German rule. Perhaps thanks to their prior military experience,[26] both Yoselevich and Abram Rakovski (#10) had been selected to lead two of four groups covertly organized to wage an armed uprising. Yoselevich and Rakovski, along with Jankef Nevachovich and an inmate referred to only as "Mandri," were to head groups slated to attack their captors from all four corners of the ghetto on April 15,

1943.[27] However, the uprising was ultimately cancelled due to sudden stepped-up security in the camp.

While planning the subsequent organized resistance and escape into the forest in the spring of 1943, Berl Yoselevich and Dr. Yakov Kagan contacted Tuvia Bielski to seek the reinforcement of a simultaneous Jewish partisan attack on the ghetto during the breakout. Bielski's letter of response: "I am ready to accept all of you.… But we are not sufficiently organized to send people to you. Whoever comes will be received well."[28] Historian Nechama Tec scrutinizes Bielski's response within the context of the *otriad's* lack of a permanent base and the partisans' relentless ongoing struggle for survival. Yet the knowledge that a safe place existed to run to following a breakout was a key factor in influencing the organizers to pursue a tunnel escape.

Upon first introducing the tunnel concept, Berl Yoselevich was roundly elected to the position of coordinator by the ten inmate committee members present.[29] From the outset, fifty individuals were recruited for work directly related to the tunnel construction;[30] however, all the inmates were obligated to dig during assigned turns. According to Daniel Ostashinski, anyone who was unable to dig due to health or work constraints was to compensate by contributing to the tunnel construction in some other possible way.[31] On the long-awaited night of September 26, 1943, Berl Yoselevich was said to have stood at the entrance to the tunnel with the other planners, holding the carefully prepared list of escapees close at hand to ensure the smooth escape. Nechama Tec[32] notes that in the aftermath, several of the escapees took pains to stress the care and concern exhibited by the organizers during the perilous breakout.[33]

The disorientation that many of the escapees faced after crawling through the brightly lit tunnel[34] into the pitch-black darkness was further compounded by the heavy German shooting and rocket fire. As the Germans suspected that their fears of a partisan-led breakout had been realized,[35] the bombardment either came in response to the commotion caused by the disoriented escapees running in all directions,[36] the unextinguished lights at the tunnel entrance,[37] or the fire that broke out there.[38] Chaya Magid, widow of escapee Avraham Magid, reports having been told by her late husband that many inmates found themselves overdressed when reaching the mouth of the narrow tunnel and quickly shed excess clothing at the entrance. When the pile of discarded clothes somehow became ignited, her husband was convinced that this fire was the primary trigger for the intensity of the German response.[39]

Berl Yoselevich's name does not appear on the escape list, although it is possible that his is one of several names that faded from the fragile paper over the decades. One such "vanished" space is found directly underneath the name of Berl's older brother Yisrael. Yet the organizers were the last to leave,[40] thus he probably was to be found among them.

The Germans immediately scoured the area searching for Jews. Many of the escapees who were caught were gruesomely tortured,[41] although Yehoshua Yaffe attests that Berl, along with Kozuchovski and six other armed escapees, were killed for their weapons by partisans of the Russian leader Victor Panchenko.[42] Leibowitz reports that following his capture, Yoselevich was killed by German soldiers in a forest less than three miles (5 km) from Novogrudok, near the village of Horodechno. He notes the date of the murder as September 27, one day after the escape.[43]

All descendants of the tunnel escapees, the author included, owe their lives to Berl Yoselevich.

Berl Yoselevich (*third from left*) with members of the Novogrudok Maccabee Team, 1934–35 (courtesy of Vallentine Mitchell Publishers)

Chana Iwinetzki (#17)

Yad Vashem Pages of Testimony reveal that there were two women from the same family named Chana Iwinetzki. Over eight decades later, the precise identity of the Chana Iwinetzki who took part in the escape from the Novogrudok forced labor camp remains a mystery.

In 1971, Abe Wind (formerly Iwinetzki) submitted Pages of Testimony to memorialize what was probably his entire family. The testimonies include both a Chana Iwinetzki (Lachowski) born in 1906, who was his sister,[1] as well as a Chana Iwinetzki, born around 1926, who was his niece.[2] Although he testified that both women were massacred in Novogrudok's first mass slaughter of December 8, 1941, Abe Wind was unaware that one of them had been conscripted to the forced labor camp and attempted to flee in the 1943 escape.

Abe's sister Chana Iwinetzki was the daughter of Zvia née Slutzki and Israel Iwinetzki. Born around 1906, Chana was married to Vilna-born Misha Lachowski,[3] and the couple lived at 25 Leninskaya Street in Novogrudok.[4] It does not appear that they had children. If this is the Chana Iwinetzki conscripted to the labor camp, she would have been around thirty-seven years old at the time of the breakout.

Abe's niece Chana Iwinetzki was the daughter of Ovsey, a movie theater owner[5] born in 1897,[6] and Rachel née Mikolayevski, born in 1899.[7] Abe notes that Chana's twin sister was named Leah,[8] which coincidentally (or not) gives them the same names as their paternal aunts. In addition to testifying to Chana and Leah's murders in December 1941, he names their two brothers Berko (Dov), age eighteen,[9] and Avraham, age twenty,[10] as having been killed at that time as well. If this Chana Iwinetzki somehow survived to be conscripted to the forced labor camp, she would have been around seventeen years old at the time of the escape.

Whether Chana Iwinetzki, the seventeenth in line to break out of the forced labor camp, was a married woman near forty or a young girl of seventeen, her name does not appear in the compilation of Jewish partisans in Belorussia from 1941 to 1944.[11] We may thus assume that she did not survive the escape to reach the safety of the partisan detachment.

As for Abe Wind, born Abram Iwinetzki, he apparently lost his entire immediate family in the Holocaust. Records show that he arrived in the United States as a refugee in 1951.[12] Two decades later, when he completed Pages of Testimony for his family in August 1971, he was living in Springfield, New Jersey.[13]

Following his death on December 16, 1979, Abe Iwinetzki Wind was buried in Livingstone, New Jersey. His tombstone bears no indication of a spouse or of any children or grandchildren who might have preserved the legacy of Chana Iwinetzki, who bravely attempted to escape to freedom.[14]

Yoel Zak (#18)

Very little is known about Yoel Zak, save for the fact that he survived the tunnel escape. The memorial book from his native town of Ivenets notes that he died in combat as a partisan,[1] although his name does not appear in the compilation of Jewish partisans in Belarus.[2]

It is quite possible that Yoel belonged to the extensive Zak family that hailed from Ivenets, located some forty miles from Novogrudok.

Pesach (Lionke) Portnoj (#19)

Pesach (Lionke) Portnoj, a metalworker, played a pivotal role in the construction of the tunnel from its inception. Born on February 5, 1910,[1] in Sumy, Ukraine, to Eliezer and Kunia[2] née Ostrowska,[3] Lionke had two sisters: Nusia, born in 1908 in Sumy,[4] and Sima (#20), born in 1916 in Novogrudok.[5] Eliezer and Kunia were killed during the Soviet occupation of Novogrudok in 1939–1941,[6] while Nusia was murdered in the Novogrudok ghetto in 1942.[7] Only Sima survived to accompany Lionke throughout the war until liberation.

Lionke's skills as a metalworker enabled him not only to be spared death and assigned to the Novogrudok forced labor camp in August 1942,[8] but to take a lead in assuring the creation of the tunnel. Fellow escapee Idel Kagan (#95) testifies that once the decision was taken to start digging the tunnel, both Lionke and Nota Sucharski (#4) pledged to surreptitiously obtain the necessary tools within one week and to maintain them in perfect condition.[9]

When the secret tunnel digging commenced underground, kerosene lamps were utilized to illuminate the area, yet the lack of air beneath the earth's surface snuffed out the lamplight. Lionke Portnoj saved the day by installing air vents that enabled oxygen to flow through the tunnel.[10] According to escapee Eliyahu Berkowicz (#49), Lionke created these pipes in the shape of cones, wide at the bottom and narrow on top where they penetrated to the outside. Lionke also performed a series of tests from aboveground to measure the depth and position of the tunnel.[11]

Records in the National Archive of the Republic of Belarus attest to the fact that Lionke Portnoj joined the Bielski partisans soon after the escape in September 1943.[12] The author's mother Fanya Dunetz (#142) recalls that after Lionke reached the *otriad*, he shared a *zemlyanka* (dugout) lodging with her and his sister Sima, as well as other tunnel escapees including Batia Rabinowitz (#27), Pesia Mayevski (#160), Hirsh Patzovski (#159), and Chaim (#32) and Perla (#33) Ostashinski. Others occupying the dugout included Lyuba Epshtein of Zhetl, Raisl Wolkin of Wsielub, Eshke (Essie) Levine and her father from Novogrudok, Frieda and Yitzchak Sklar of Lida, and a couple from Naliboki whose son later succumbed to tuberculosis.[13]

After liberation from the forest in July 1944, Lionke remained in Soviet-controlled Novogrudok and worked as a plumber for several months before being repatriated to Poland. In October 1944, Lionke made his way from Lodz to the displaced persons camp in Waldenberg, Germany, where he remained until moving to Berlin in June 1945 to be employed by UNRRA. By June 1949, Lionke was working for the Jewish Committee in the Kadima (Gabersee) Displaced Persons Camp in the Munich District,[14] from which point he immigrated to Israel in 1950, as did Sima.[15]

In Israel, Lionke worked as a house-painter while he and his wife Miriam née Koenigsburg raised Miriam's daughter from a former marriage as well as their own son Yisrael. In time, Yisrael became a carpenter, married, and had three children, Liron, Liat, and Oded. Lionke passed away in Israel in 2001. At the time of the author's interview with his widow Miriam in 2012, Miriam expressed sorrow that Lionke did not live to see his first great-grandchild, Liron's granddaughter.[16]

Miriam passed away in her sleep in March 2019 at the age of ninety-six.[17] A Holocaust survivor from a small

Pesach (Lionke) Portnoj, Munich, 1946 (courtesy of Yisrael Portnoy)

town near Cracow, she had been incarcerated in Auschwitz and met Lionke in Germany following the war. Like Lionke, she is said to have never once spoken about her life before, during, or immediately after the war.

Yisrael relates a difficult youth as the only child of two traumatized Holocaust survivors. He admits that he only learned of the tunnel escape following his father's death. As for Lionke's vital contribution to the construction of the tunnel, Yisrael learned of this for the first time from the author.[18]

If he were alive at the time of this writing in October 2023, Lionke Portnoj would be the great-grandfather of two.[19]

Sima Portnoj (#20)

In September 1943, twenty-seven-year-old Sima Portnoj crawled out of the tunnel immediately behind Lionke, her older brother and sole surviving family member, to break out of the Novogrudok forced labor camp. Their parents Eliezer and Kunia had been murdered during the 1939–1941 Soviet occupation of Novogrudok,[1] and their sister Nusia was slain in the Novogrudok ghetto in 1942.[2] Sima's last permanent address appears on a partisan list as having been Leninskaya Street in Novogrudok.[3] We can assume that as a single woman at the time, she resided there with her family.

Even though Sima survived the Holocaust to become an educator, and her husband Eliyahu, a fellow survivor, became a well-known journalist and Holocaust researcher, their son Eli (Eliezer) reports that the war period was not discussed in their home. The heroic tunnel escape and her prewar family life were barely mentioned. Eli, named for his maternal grandfather, knows only that his namesake had been an agent for Singer sewing machines in Novogrudok.[4]

Although he knew little about his mother's prewar years, Eli was aware that Sima had been active in Novogrudok's Hashomer Hatzair Zionist youth movement and had attended a teachers' seminary in Vilna.[5] In an article published in 1963, Sima wrote that in 1933 she began teaching in the kindergarten of Novogrudok's Tarbut school. Located on Pilsudski Street, her kindergarten consisted of one large room and two smaller ones, where the daily schedule was filled mainly with playtime activities, singing, and crafts. The happiness and laughter that characterized the kindergarten's holiday celebrations appear in stark contrast to the heartbreaking scene she describes of seeing her pupils for the last time. In December 1941, as the toddlers stood hungry and shivering in the cold together with their parents outside the district court for "selection" during Novogrudok's first massacre, Sima helplessly looked on as many were hauled away in a crowded, open truck for "their last journey."[6]

Kindergarten teacher Sima Portnoj was conscripted to the forced labor camp to work as a seamstress in the production of leather bags.[7] She and her brother Lionke both survived the tunnel escape to arrive at the Bielski partisan detachment before the end of September 1943, as recorded in the National Archives of the Republic of Belarus.[8]

After liberation from the forest, both Sima and Lionke were repatriated to Lodz, Poland.[9] There she worked as a teacher before traveling to Germany, where from November 1946 to February 1948, she took refuge in the Schlactensee Displaced Persons Camp in Berlin before moving to Munich.[10] It was in Germany that Sima met her future husband, Eliyahu Yones, a Holocaust survivor born in Vilna.[11] Like Sima, he had served in a forced labor camp, Kurvitse (near Lvov), as well as joining a partisan unit in the forest.[12] While later serving in the Red Army, Eliyahu was badly injured in battle.[13]

Active in the secular socialist Bund movement prior to the war, Eliyahu later became the founder and editor of the Bundist survivors' newspaper *Unzer Leben* (Our Life).[14] An ardent Zionist, he was among the organizers of the brave underground Bricha movement, which helped survivors break the British ban on immigration to Palestine.[15] As mentioned, Sima had in her youth been active in the Hashomer Hatzair Zionist youth movement, through which she had planned to join a group that settled in Kibbutz Eilon in northern Israel.[16] Although the war disrupted this dream, in September 1950, newlyweds Sima and Eliyahu emigrated from Munich to the new State of Israel.[17]

After residing in the city of Ramla, where Sima and Eliyahu's only child Eli was born in 1951, the young family moved to Jerusalem in 1953. There Sima resumed her teaching career and Eliyahu gained prominence in the field of communications. He served as the Israel Broadcasting Authority's director of Yiddish broadcasting, as director of its training center, as well as director of East European broadcasting. In addition, he was named secretary of the Jerusalem Journalists' Association. Late in life, Eliyahu obtained a doctorate in history with his dissertation focusing on the Holocaust in Lvov.[18]

Eli Yones, who holds degrees in the fields of economics and business administration, has held leading positions in the world of finance, including serving as the chief executive officer of several banks and as the accountant general of the State of Israel. The father of three children, Eli is the grandfather of three, as of this writing in 2020.[19] Sima died in 1996, fifteen years before her husband Eliyahu.[20]

Shortly after the 2009 release of the film *Defiance*, which presents the story of the Bielski brothers' partisan detachment, Eli's father revealed to him: "Your mother was there."[21] Only then did Eli begin to fully realize the bravery that characterized his mother's Holocaust experiences in the past she so desperately tried to hide.

Sima Portnoj, Germany, circa 1947 (courtesy of Eli Yones)

Aaron (Rozke) Kirzner (#21)

The trail leading to information regarding Aaron (Rozke) Kirzner was quite exciting. We present it here as an example of the research process involved in finding family members of the escapees. Knowing only that Aaron was born in 1908 to Isaac, that he lived in Baranovich before the war,[1] and that he became a Bielski partisan after surviving the tunnel breakout,[2] the author was stymied when no information was found in the Holocaust-related, genealogical, and population databases researched to learn about Aaron's postwar life.

Returning to Yad Vashem's Central Database of Shoah Victims' Names, a last effort was made to locate members of Aaron's family of origin. There a 1977 Page of Testimony was discovered for Aaron's sister, Miriam Rimer, daughter of Isaac and Dvora, who had been killed in 1943. The submitter of the Page of Testimony was Miriam's daughter and Isaac's niece, Rachel Falik of Kibbutz Nir David.[3] In contacting the secretariat of Kibbutz Nir David, we learned that although Rachel had died over twenty years earlier, her daughter Osnat Rabin continues to reside on the kibbutz. Excitedly, Osnat reacted to the author's query about her great-uncle: "Of course, Uncle Aaron from Russia! He died, but he has family here."[4]

Contacting Aaron's daughter Mania Shor in Kiryat Yam, the author introduced herself as a researcher writing a book on the escape from the Novogrudok forced labor camp. Like many other children of escapees interviewed, Mania had no knowledge of the escape and first learned details from the author. "I knew my father was in a labor camp after being in the Baranovich ghetto," she responded, "but I didn't know where. I knew he escaped, but I didn't know how."[5]

We learned from Mania that Aaron was a watchmaker both before and after the war, not a hatter as erroneously reported on a partisan list.[6] We also learned that in postwar Soviet Union, his nickname was no longer Rozke, as on the escape list, but Arche. Mania noted that Aaron's first wife Kejla[7] and their young child had been killed in the war. After liberation, Aaron somehow made his way to Kishinev, Moldavia, where he met and married Leyke, a fellow survivor. Mania, their only child together, was born in December 1946.[8]

Aaron (Rozke) Kirzner, Kishinev, Moldova, 1947 (courtesy of Mania Shor)

Mania relates that Miriam Rimer was her father's only sibling. Miriam, her husband Shmuel,[9] and their teenage daughter Osnat[10] had all met their deaths in the Baranovich ghetto, yet Aaron dreamt of coming to Israel to be reunited with her two daughters Rachel and Shulamit, a member of Kibbutz Beit Zera.

This dream was realized in 1975, when Aaron and his family immigrated to Israel, first living in Upper Nazareth before settling in Kiryat Yam the following year. Aaron is said to have loved his life in Israel, where he and Leyke lived close to Mania and her family until Aaron's death in 1980.

Mania is currently retired from her work as a nurse-midwife. Leyke lived until 2011, the year before Aaron and Leyke's first great-grandchild Lily was born to Mania's only child Aviv, a draftsman. A second great-grandchild, Eitan, was born in 2016.[11] As a result of this research, these children will someday learn of the heroic escape in which their great-grandfather participated, enabling him to survive and bring his family to Israel.

Chaim Abramowicz (#22)

Chaim Abramowicz was fated to live a life of challenge, meeting adversity with strength.

A carpenter by trade, Chaim was born in Karelich on October 3, 1910.[1] His father Abraham Yehoshua,[2] a carpenter and glazier[3] born in 1882,[4] was married to Zicha née Gerszowicz, born in 1884.[5] In handwritten notes found after his death, Chaim's younger brother Yosef recorded that both their parents, their twelve-year-old brother Moshe, and their twenty-four-year-old sister Chaya[6] were among the hundreds of Karelich Jews expelled from their homes on a thirteen-mile (21 km) forced march to Novogrudok's Pereseka ghetto in spring 1942.[7] Although we have no details of the time and place the Abramowitz family members were murdered, their deaths were commemorated in a memorial notice placed by Chaim and Yosef in the *Novogrudok Memorial Book* published in 1963.[8]

Yosef, a carpenter, escaped death by being transferred out of the ghetto with other skilled Karelich craftsmen and assigned to the courthouse workshops in the Novogrudok forced labor camp. There, Yosef reunited with Chaim, who informed him of the horrific murder of his wife and two children.[9] Their names, which were never memorialized in Pages of Testimony,[10] remain unknown.

Soon after Yosef's arrival in the forced labor camp, the two brothers made a daring attempt to escape to the partisans. Yosef first slipped out under the camp fence into a small trench, where he was met by prearrangement with a Bielski partisan. Chaim, who had intended to follow, suddenly heard footsteps approaching. Fearing for his life, he gave up this chance at freedom, although his brother Yosef safely reached the Bielski detachment.[11]

Now alone in the forced labor camp, Chaim pursued his work as a carpenter. Although his name is not mentioned specifically in any account of the tunnel construction, we know that the inmate carpenters played a major role in acquiring materials for and constructing the secret underground passage.[12]

Chaim survived the breakout to make his way to the Bielski partisan detachment, where he was reunited with Yosef.[13] In his memoirs, Commander Tuvia Bielski writes how the discovery of a cache of arms in the forest enabled the establishment of two groups of armed partisan warriors. Chaim Abramowicz was tapped to become the commander of one of the groups.[14] It was also in the forest that widower Chaim met and married Cype (Tsipora),[15] a fellow Bielski partisan,[16] with whom he would build a new family. In a 1946 World Jewish Congress list of survivors, Cype is noted as having been born in Novogrudok in 1912 to Meir and Lea.[17]

Following liberation, Chaim and Cype took refuge from 1945 to 1946 in the displaced persons camp in Graz, Austria,[18] described as having been cold and generally unpleasant, with insufficient food provisions.[19] After moving to and from DP camps in Rome, Oscia, and Cremona, the couple finally set sail from Naples on the MSS *Saturno* in August 1948 to their new home in New York.[20] One year later, they were joined by Chaim's brother Yosef, together with his wife Ester née Grinberg and their two-year-old daughter Sara Zishe, later to become Susan, who made the same ocean journey from Naples.[21]

By the time he became a naturalized citizen of the United States of America on August 9, 1954, Chaim was living in the Bronx in New York City under the name Herman Abrams,[22] and Cype had become known as Cilie.[23] Taking advantage of his carpentry skills, Chaim became an upholsterer and eventually opened his own upholstery business.[24]

Chaim and Cype's sons Melvin and Albert both moved to Florida. Melvin, who married and has several children, currently works in retail sales.[25] Albert, born in 1951, who also worked in retail sales, died on

June 20, 2018. He is survived by his wife Louise and children Cheryl Lori and Mark, both born in the 1980s.[26]

At some point before Cypa's death on January 13, 1980, she and Chaim moved from the Bronx to Florida as well.[27] Residing in Fort Lauderdale,[28] Chaim was said to have taken an active part in the local synagogue.[29] (Although we have been unable to make contact with Chaim's son Melvin, Yosef's daughter Susan Abrams Bach and his late son Art Abrams were extremely helpful in providing information for this report.)

Chaim Abramowicz of Karelich died as Herman Abrams on August 21, 1996, in Fort Lauderdale, Florida,[30] forty-eight years after fleeing the European continent that brought him much pain and loss. Till his dying day, Chaim remained close to his brother Yosef, the sole surviving member of his immediate family. Just as Yosef had followed Chaim to America, he followed him to Florida in the mid-1980s, where he lived until his death in 2003.[31]

Chaim Abramowicz (*seated, fourth from left*), New York, 1950s
(courtesy of Susan Abramowicz Bach)

Chaim Belous (#23)

On August 6, 1942, the Germans ordered the mass of men, women, and children crushed into the Jewish ghetto in Zhetl to report to the town square. Just over three months beforehand, a similar order had resulted in the heinous massacre of over a thousand Jews, with only those possessing work permits being spared.

At this second German edict to assemble, Chaim Belous, a mechanic by trade, was the only member of his immediate family to report to the town square. In a perilous attempt to escape certain death, Chaim had helped his parents, his two married sisters and their families, as well as several other unidentified people to prepare an attic hideout. For reasons unknown, Chaim opted not to join them, but to take his place in the town square.[1]

There, Chaim, a bachelor born in 1919, was conscripted to the Novogrudok forced labor camp thanks to his skill as a mechanic being essential for the Germans.[2] The twenty-five hundred Jews alongside him who were not assigned to the labor camp were marched to their deaths in the second mass murder, completely annihilating the remaining Jewish population of Zhetl.

Left in hiding in the attic were Chaim's parents, Yisroel and Chana Frieda née Dzienczelski; Chaim's sister Nechama, her husband Mordechai (Mote) Zakroiski, and their two-year-old son Yudel; and Chaim's sister Pesia, her husband Zisl Kalbstein, their three-year-old son Mordechai[3] and older daughter, either a six-year-old named Masha, as recalled by Zisl's nephew,[4] or a four-year-old named Cila, as recalled by Pesia's first cousin.[5]

Prior to the war, Zisl Kalbstein had worked as a butcher,[6] Pesia as a seamstress,[7] and Chaim's father,[8] sister Nechama,[9] and Nechama's husband Mote[10] had all been bakers in Zhetl. In all probability, they worked together with Chaim's paternal aunt Yachna in a bakery located near the Catholic church in the center of town.[11] Originally from the hamlet of Morozovich, the Belous clan had made Zhetl their home for many years before the war.[12]

These family members, who had worked closely in life, now found themselves cramped together in a dire bid to survive. To the horror of the stowaways, as German troops stormed through the area searching for Jews, the two toddlers Yudel and Mordechai began to cry. Unable to silence them and terrified at the impending danger, the decision was made to smother the little boys to death in order to save the lives of the others in the hideout.[13]

Yet despite their most noble efforts, the hideout was discovered that very day, and Pesia, her parents, and her little daughter were murdered. Somehow Nechama, her husband Mote, and Pesia's husband Zisl managed to evade death,[14] albeit for a limited time. Both Nechama[15] and Mote are reported to have escaped to join a Zhetl partisan unit in the Lipiczanska Forest,[16] where Mote the baker took charge of preparing bread for the detachment. Nechama[17] and Mote died as partisans, with his death in a German ambush coming on July 16, 1944, just one day before liberation.[18] Zisl survived to be liberated from a partisan unit and drafted into the Red Army, where he fell in battle against the Germans near Wolkowysk.[19]

Chaim Belous, one of the last of his immediate family to remain alive, was killed in the tunnel escape from the Novogrudok forced labor camp at the age of twenty-three.[20] One might wonder if, while crawling through the tunnel, he was still hoping to be reunited with the loved ones he left behind in the hiding place he had prepared.

Chaim Belous (*top row, second from right*) with the Zhetl Volunteer Fire Brigade Band, Zhetl, 1933 (*Memorial Book of the Jewish Community of Novogrudok, Poland*)

Batia Rabinowitz (#27)

Thanks to the love and the urging of her grandchildren, then seventy-five-year-old Batia Rabinowitz broke her near silence to give a testimony of her Holocaust experiences, including an eyewitness account of the tunnel construction and escape.

Batia was born in 1917, lived in Zhetl before the war, and worked as a bookkeeper in a local bank.[1] Her parents were Chaya née Perlman, a housewife born in 1883,[2] and Baruch Mordechai, a merchant born in 1873. Both Chaya and Baruch Mordechai were killed in Zhetl's first massacre on April 30, 1942.[3]

In a testimony Batia wrote in 1992 for a grandchild's school project, she recounts that after being confined to Zhetl's ghetto for over a year, she was taken to the Novogrudok forced labor camp. There, she reports, twenty-five people lived in a room with three levels of wooden planks that served as sleeping berths for the inmates.

In her testimony, Batia describes the pain of being left alone after her sister Leahle was killed[4] in the massacre of forced labor camp inmates on May 7, 1943.[5] Batia also touches on the inability of the surviving inmates to provide support to one another as they mourned their murdered loved ones.[6]

In recounting the digging of the tunnel from beneath one of the houses in which the inmates were confined, Batia details the nightly transfer of sand from inmate to inmate to an adjacent building where double walls had been built to covertly store the sand. Tools that the inmates lifted from their workplaces to use for the clandestine digging were returned in the morning.

In her account of the tunnel escape, Batia writes of the Germans' attempts to repair the electrical power failure that signaled the beginning of the escape and the extraordinary fact that despite the soldiers firing in the air, including in the direction of the tunnel door, many of the inmates survived. (Fortunately, her estimate that only sixty survived is far below the actual number.)[7]

Batia's name appears on a Minsk Archives document as having joined the Bielski partisan detachment in September 1943.[8] Her name and birthdate also appear on Gerasimova, Selemenov, and Kagan's list of 7,742 Jews who were members of the Belarusian partisan movement from 1941 to 1944. There, Batia is listed as Basya Mordukhovna Rabinovich, a member of the Kalinin Brigade.[9]

Batia reported having known prior to the tunnel escape about the Bielski partisans and how to find them. She notes that the Bielski *otriad* was the only Jewish partisan detachment that was open to women and the sick. Describing her arrival at the *otriad*, she tells of finding people living underground in pits about ten feet deep with long benches used as makeshift beds.[10]

In her testimony, Batia describes the kitchen and bakery of the *otriad* as communal, noting that the partisans came to the kitchen to receive food. Although she states that bread was sliced and distributed each morning in the kitchen,[11] Batia modestly omits mention of what Fanya Dunetz,[12] Chaya Bielski,[13] and Tuvia Bielski[14] all report: Batia Rabinowitz oversaw bread distribution, a most coveted position in the forest.

After liberation from the forest, Batia made her way to Italy via Baranovich and Warsaw. There, from the port of Bari, she left for Palestine on an illegal immigration ship to arrive on September 26, 1945, two years to the day after escaping from the tunnel. She describes how young men awaited the ship's passengers in Palestine's territorial waters to hoist any non-swimmers ashore on their shoulders.[15]

After several days on a kibbutz, Batia reached the home of her sister Rachel, who had immigrated to Tel Aviv before the war.[16] In Israel, Batia was also reunited with her brothers Shmuel, Yitzchak, and Moshe.[17] Sarah, the eldest sibling, had been killed in the first of Zhetl's massacres on April 30, 1942, while Rivka, the family's third child, had immigrated to the United States before the Holocaust.[18] Batia's daughter Chaya Goldhaber praises her grandparents' foresight in having sent most of their children abroad prior to the war, thus saving their lives.[19]

As for why Batia had remained behind, her employment in a bank in Zhetl was said to have been an important source of income for her family.[20] She continued to work in the bank when it came under Russian control.[21] When Batia arrived in Tel Aviv, she began working at the Anglo-Palestine Bank (later Bank Leumi).[22]

Two and a half years after immigrating to Israel, Batia married Nahum Gradis, a

Batia Rabinowitz, Tel Aviv, 1946 (courtesy of Chaya Goldhaber)

survivor from Riga, Latvia, who escaped from Iraq while serving in Anders's Army (the informal name of the Polish Armed Forces in the East commanded by Władysław Anders, also called the Polish Army in the USSR). Their daughter Chaya (Goldhaber), a sociologist, is married to Gad, an architect.[23]

Upon her death in Tel Aviv on November 25, 2004, Batia was also survived by three grandchildren. After years of silence, it was only with her older grandchildren that Batia became able to speak about the Holocaust. Chaya reports that as a child, she heard about her mother's wartime experiences only when she feigned sleep and listened as Batia and her childhood friends from Zhetl would peruse *Pinkas Zhetl*, the Zhetl memorial book.

If Batia were alive as of this writing in August 2023, she would have surely been proud of her three grandchildren and her eight great-grandchildren.[24]

Shlomo (Salek) Jakubowicz (#28)

From a Page of Testimony completed by Salek's brother Dr. Majer Jakubowicz (#1), we learn that Salek (Shlomo) was born in Lodz in 1904 to Berko (Beresh or Berek) Jakubowicz and Yehudit née Hershkovich. Salek was single and worked as a merchant prior to the war.[1] According to Majer's testimony, Berek Jakubowicz died of starvation in the Lodz ghetto in 1942[2] along with his second wife, Sura née Krenik, whom he married following Yehudit's death in 1929.[3] Two of Berek's six children, Moshe[4] and Sara,[5] also met their deaths in the Lodz ghetto, while their sister Zlata survived the ghetto but died in Tarnopol in 1944.[6]

Against the backdrop of the Novogrudok forced labor camp, the relationship between Salek and his brother Majer and sister-in-law Sarafima (Sara) became extremely complex from the moment Majer, a physician, was shot in the leg in April 1943.[7] His injury consequently thwarted a ghetto breakout that had been carefully planned for April 15, 1943. At the last minute, the rebellion was aborted due to the sudden, unexpected arrival of a large number of guards. It subsequently became apparent that the plans had been divulged to the Germans by Sara Jakubowicz in order to prevent her lame husband from being left behind.[8]

When Sara continued to threaten to inform the Germans of any impending plans for an escape, Salek, who served as the camp's Jewish police commandant, proposed that she and Majer be killed. He claimed that the entire remaining camp population should not be sacrificed for a few people, even if those few were his brother and sister-in-law.[9]

Fellow inmate Daniel Ostashinski notes that once plans for the tunnel escape went into action, Salek Jakubowicz was in charge of assigning the shifts of tunnel digging to each and every inmate capable of hard labor.[10] In addition, Salek was responsible for ensuring that each tunnel digger received extra food.[11]

Dr. Majer Jakubowicz and his wife ultimately agreed to take part in the clandestine tunnel escape on condition that they be first in line and that Dr. Jakubowicz be carried for the first 110 yards.[12]

Salek Jakubowicz carried Majer a full 220 yards before he was shot to death.[13] Salek died a hero, saving his brother's life.

Gershon Michalevich (#29)

Gershon Michalevich, an electrician who is lauded for his contribution to the success of the Novogrudok forced labor camp tunnel escape, was born in Novogrudok in 1905 to Shabtai, a grain merchant, and Sarah Bluma née Rabani. According to Pages of Testimony filed by a relative, the 1942 Novogrudok massacres took the lives of Shabtai, Sarah Bluma, and their children Urcze, forty, a salesman; Leyb, thirty-nine, an electrician;[1] Perla, thirty-eight, a housemaid; Galia, thirty-six, a student; and Jakob, thirty-four, an electrician.

Fellow forced labor camp inmate Shaul Gorodynski testified that in light of Gershon's prior military experience (of which we have no details), Gershon was appointed to the planning committee for the camp uprising set for April 15, 1943. After its cancellation due to increased security in the camp, Michalevich took a lead in planning the tunnel escape.[2]

The unprecedented success of the tunnel escape was due in great part to the keen electrical prowess of several of the inmates. While Jack (Idel) Kagan (#95) attributes this electrical wizardry primarily to Abram Rakovski (#10), Eliyahu Berkowicz (#49) reports that Gershon Michalevich was the electrician responsible for the remarkable electrical feats carried out in the escape. He acclaims Michalevich for providing electric light in the tunnel (by running a concealed connection through the loft), as well as for engineering an electrical cutoff enabling the escapees to control the two large camp searchlights during the escape.[3] Berkowicz credits Gershon Michalevich with signaling the escape at 8:00 p.m. on Sunday, September 26, 1943, by short-circuiting the current to the searchlight atop the courthouse roof that illuminated the entire area. After blinking on and off several times before dimming into darkness, the non-functioning searchlight served as a sign to the escapees to begin crawling through the tunnel.[4]

Tragically, the ingenious electrician did not survive the escape. Gershon Michalevich's death in Novogrudok is recorded in a 1956 Page of Testimony completed by a cousin, who noted that Gershon was murdered in 1942 along with perhaps the entire Michalevich family.[5] Ironically, this cousin was not only unaware that Gershon was alive until late 1943, but that he is likely to have played a crucial role in enabling others to live.

Yitzchak (#30) and Genia (#31) Rosenhaus

Of the many miracles that Yitzchak and Genia Rosenhaus were to experience in their lives, their flight to freedom through the Novogrudok forced labor camp tunnel was all the more remarkable since they were among the very few couples to survive the escape together.

Yitzchak Rosenhaus was born in Baranovich in 1909 to Moshe and Chana née Kantorovich.[1] Moshe[2] and Chana[3] met their deaths in the Baranovich ghetto in 1943, together with two of their four children: Genia, born in 1914,[4] and Esther, born in 1919.[5] Their son Zev had immigrated to Palestine prior to the war.[6]

Genia née Slutzki was born in Lida in 1912.[7] Prior to the war, she obtained her university degree in Warsaw and became a teacher of English, French, and Latin.[8] Genia's father Moshe was a merchant born in Zhetl, and her mother Kunia née Dvilanska a housewife. Moshe[9] and Kunia Slutski[10] were murdered in Zhetl's second Nazi massacre on April 30, 1942, along with their son Avram (Genia's only sibling), an unmarried clerk at the time of his death.[11]

After his father's death in 1996, Effie Rosenhaus found a Yiddish-language letter Yitzchak had written on May 12, 1943 (five days after the third Novogrudok massacre) to a friend or relative identified only as "Yitzchak." In this letter, which appears in its entirety in appendix 3 of this book, Yitzchak Rosenhaus relays his hope that it would be smuggled out by the only local Christian allowed entrance into the forced labor camp. Here Rosenhaus details the "tragic experiences and spiritual suffering" that he and Genia, whom he married in Baranovich on December 24, 1939, had endured from the outbreak of the war. Outlining their wanderings, he described how shortly after their marriage, they were evicted from their house in Baranovich and forced to leave the city. After reaching Grodno, they were "miraculously" saved after being buried under the ruins of a bombing raid on the first day of the German-Russian War. In June 1941, the couple took refuge in Zhetl, where they went into hiding together with Genia's parents, who had also arrived in the town.

In his letter, Yitzchak Rosenhaus mentions the isolation of Zhetl's Jews from the rest of the population after being forced into the town's ghetto on April 22, 1942. He also describes the restrictions imposed upon them prior to the second massacre on August 6, 1942, in which twenty-five hundred Jews were killed, essentially "cleansing" Zhetl of Jews. (In the prior massacre of April 30, 1942, a thousand Jews had been murdered in the Kurpishtz Forest.) Yitzchak notes the enforced wearing of yellow star patches as well as prohibitions against Jews walking on the sidewalk, engaging in business, moving freely on the roads, and even wearing a watch. He reports that the Germans had taken possession of houses, fields, horses, cows, goats, furs, textiles, leather, gold, silver, nickel, and even kitchen utensils and bed linens.[12]

Former coworker, camp inmate, fellow escapee, and partisan Fanya Dunetz (#142) recalls Yitzchak and Genia's arrival in Zhetl in June 1941 in their attempt to evade the Germans. Both she and Yitzchak worked as secretaries in Zhetl's Judenrat under the direction of Alter Dvoretzky, Judenrat chairman and commander of the ghetto's underground.[13] Fanya's memories of Genia go even further back to when teenage Genia worked during school vacations in the town's bakery owned and operated by the Vinokur family, perhaps relatives or friends of Genia's Zhetl-born father.[14]

In Yitzchak's letter, he writes of yet another miracle for Genia and himself – that of escaping death in Zhetl and being transferred in August 1942, along with just over two hundred people with essential occupations, to the Novogrudok forced labor camp (which he termed a "concentration camp").

Despite having found several opportunities to escape from the camp on their own, Yitzchak and Genia opted to wait for the spring. Yet by then, an increase of guards, the construction of a barbed-wire fence, and placement of searchlights and cannons had made escape a near-impossible feat.[15]

In mid-September 1943, with the imminent completion of the tunnel construction, a final vote was taken among the inmates as to whether to proceed with the planned organized escape or remain in the camp, as some maintained would be preferable. Eliyahu Berkowicz (#49) wrote that a secret ballot vote resulted in the majority (165 out of 230) opting in favor of the escape plan.[16] It was Yitzchak Rosenhaus who then drew up a list of all the inmates so that the escape committee could determine the order in which each one would exit the tunnel.[17]

Yitzchak's letter of May 1943 was written while he fully expected to be killed. He wrote of his great love for Genia, describing her as being his "only comfort," who continually provided courage and helped create the mutual strength that enabled them to survive together.[18]

Besides having known the Rosenhauses in Zhetl as well as in the Novogrudok forced labor camp, Fanya Dunetz also remembers them from the Bielski detachment. Her recollection of Yitzchak as having overseen the partisans' kitchen for a time [19] was corroborated by Tuvia Bielski in his memoirs,[20] as well as by Asael Bielski's widow Chaya in a list she prepared of senior positions held in the detachment.[21] According to this list, and corroborated as well by Effie Rosenhaus,

Yitzchak was both the kitchen manager as well as the detachment's pharmacist, thanks to his degree in pharmacy from Baranovich prior to the war.[22]

Being a pharmacist in the *otriad* could not have been an easy task. Although all partisans were required to hand over whatever medications they had managed to acquire, medicines were extremely scarce. Patients were often treated in unconventional ways, such as mixing fat with sulphur from bullets to serve as a disinfectant.[23]

According to both Effie Rosenhaus and Fanya Dunetz, Yitzchak and Genia eventually joined the Ordzhonikidze partisans,[24] originally consisting of 180 Bielski fighters and many of their wives. Situated at the edge of the Naliboki Forest, this fighting unit was commanded primarily by Russians and is reported to have offered a modicum of protection to the partisans of the *otriad* or family group. Members of the family group are said to have frequently been provided with information regarding road conditions by Zus Bielski, the head of reconnaissance and the only Jewish commander after Asael Bielski's early return to the Bielski *otriad*.[25]

Following liberation, Yitzchak and Genia made their way to northern Italy, where they waited several months for an illegal immigration boat to take them to British-blockaded Palestine. After finally arriving on Palestine's shores in 1945, they spent their first night in Kibbutz Yagur and moved to Tel Aviv the following day. There Yitzchak worked for a pharmaceutical import company before establishing his own concern. As a licensed pharmacist, he served in the Israeli Medical Corps during his army service, which began in the period of the War of Independence in 1948. Effie Rosenhaus reports that during his parents' early years, while his father was establishing himself in business, his mother was employed as a secretary at the Pittman Secretarial School.[26]

Yitzchak and Genia raised two sons. The elder, Moshe, was named after both his grandfathers, Moshe Rosenhaus and Moshe Slutski. Born in 1948, the year of the establishment of the State of Israel, Moshe was serving in the Israel Defense Forces when he fell in an Egyptian bombing raid near the Suez Canal one month after the Six-Day War in 1967. Moshe was nineteen years old at his death.

Effie Rosenhaus reports that his parents never recovered from the tragedy of losing their elder son. He remembers that their once "open home" became significantly less so and that the sadness in their eyes became a permanent feature. Effie also recalls the feeling of responsibility suddenly thrust upon his shoulders at age sixteen.[27]

Today, Effie Rosenhaus is a prominent businessman who resides in Tel Aviv. Yitzchak and Genia's three grandchildren are all successful in their respective fields, Ran in psychology, his twin sister Gili in business administration, and their older brother Omer as a teacher of drama and theater direction. Had they been alive, Yitzchak and Genia would have become first-time great-grandparents to Ori, Ran's daughter, in May 2022.[28]

Yitzchak Rosenhaus died in Tel Aviv in 1996 after a long illness.[29] As part of his legacy, he leaves the escape list that he recorded, which enabled so many to reach freedom. The names of all the brave individuals who participated in this remarkable escape of the Holocaust will now remain known for present and future generations.

Genia Rosenhaus died in Tel Aviv in 2001,[30] fifteen years after Yitzchak, her soulmate and partner in a life filled with both upheaval and love.

Yitzchak Rosenhaus,
Baranovich, Poland, undated
prewar photo (courtesy of
Effie Rosenhaus)

Genia Rosenhaus, undated
photo (courtesy of Effie
Rosenhaus)

Chaim Zeev Ostashinski (#32)

Chaim Zeev Ostashinski, a tailor, was born in Novogrudok on the twentieth of either September or November 1891[1] to Pesach and Kayla Fruma née Chaitovich. Kayla was known for collecting charity for the Novardok Yeshiva in the city and for opening her home to yeshiva students for Shabbat meals with her family. As one of the only women in the city who could read and write, Kayla voluntarily became "the reader" of letters friends and acquaintances brought to her.[2]

Prior to the war, Chaim is said to have made a comfortable living from his tailor shop, where he employed around fifty tailors, often contracted to make uniforms for policemen and other government workers.[3] Chaim and his wife Zipora née Abramovich, eight years his junior and a housewife,[4] had six children: Daniel, born in 1921[5]; Esther, born in 1923;[6] Perla (#33), born in 1924;[7] Yitzchak, born in 1927;[8] Batya Rivka, born in 1933;[9] and Pesach, born around 1931.[10]

Following the confinement of the family to the Novogrudok forced labor camp, Chaim's wife and three of his children were brutally murdered in Novogrudok's fourth massacre on May 7, 1943.[11] This massacre was sadistically carried out in full view of surviving family members, who witnessed the slaughter of their loved ones from the courthouse windows. Before his eyes, Chaim's beloved wife Zipora and his daughters Batya Rivka, sixteen, and Esther, twenty, were among those forced to lie face down before being shot to death in groups of ten and tossed in a pit.[12] At the same time, Yitzchak and Perla's hazardous attempt to flee the slaughter resulted in sixteen-year-old Yitzchak being fatally shot in the back as he raced after Perla. Perla somehow managed to escape the horror, jump over a fence, and reach the courthouse, where she rejoined her father and Daniel.[13]

Ultimately, Chaim succeeded in saving the lives of both of his two remaining sons. We do not know how his youngest son Pesach survived the slaughter of May 7. However, there is clear evidence that sometime after that point and from the confines of the labor camp, Chaim managed to arrange for a Christian couple, Jan and Josefa Jarmolowicz from the nearby village of Kuscin, to conceal Pesach in a hiding place under their farm's pigsty. One of the farm workers, Magdalena Cimoszko, was sworn to secrecy as she prepared food and looked after Pesach and several other Jews in hiding.[14] Here the youngster survived the war crouched cross-legged on the floor, unable to stand up for over one year. After the tunnel escape, Chaim's son Daniel eventually reached Pesach to carry him nearly nine miles to the Bielski encampment.[15] In 1990, Josefa, Jan, as well as Magdalena were recognized by Yad Vashem as Righteous Among the Nations for risking their lives to save Jews.[16]

Pesach's miraculous survival came on the heels of two separate perilous episodes in which Daniel and Chaim saved each other from the hand of Nazi killers. For a time, Daniel had held the important, powerful position of Judenrat head in the ghetto. During a "selection" by the Nazis, Chaim was sentenced to death. Protesting the order, Daniel attempted to save his father by threatening to leave his essential post, declaring, "If you take him, I go." The threat was effective: Chaim was spared death to survive and eventually save Daniel's life in turn.

At a later point in time, Chaim and Daniel once again stood alongside each other in another deadly "selection." Chaim instructed his son, now no longer serving as head of the Judenrat, to stand upright to appear more mature. Despite his improved posture, Daniel was selected for death. Chaim refused to release his son's hand, even as a Nazi officer ruthlessly pulled the young man toward him. With Chaim's insistent shouts of "He stays with me" met by the draw of a pistol, his tug-of-war with the Nazi lasted just long enough for the German to be called away by another officer, leaving no time to either kill Daniel or send him to his death.[17]

Ultimately, Chaim, Daniel, and Perla survived the tunnel escape on September 26, 1943, and reached the Bielski partisans,[18] although not simultaneously. Following liberation, it is uncertain as to whether Chaim and his daughter Perla ever lived in the confines of a displaced persons camp.[19] Although details are sparse, documentation shows that in October 1945, Chaim registered his whereabouts with the Central Jewish Committee as being in transit through Vienna at that time.[20] At a later date, Chaim and Perla joined Daniel in Italy, where he was serving as head of the local Etzel (Irgun Tzva'i Leumi) Jewish underground fighting unit. Chaim and Perla remained in Italy until their immigration to Israel in August 1949,[21] six years after most of their extended family had been lost and just over one year after the Jewish state gained independence.

Awaiting Chaim and Perla in their new homeland was Chaim's youngest son Pesach. A fellow member of the Etzel underground, Pesach had sailed to Israel from France on June 11, 1948, aboard the ill-fated *Altalena*,[22] which carried 940 Etzel fighters and a large quantity of arms and ammunition. In a deadly confrontation that ensued on June 20 between the newly formed Israel Defense Forces and the Irgun fighters on the *Altalena*, sixteen Etzel fighters and three IDF soldiers lost their lives.[23]

Pesach survived the traumatic events of the *Altalena* affair and eventually made many contributions to the State of Israel. In addition to having held a senior position in the Ministry of Finance, he was appointed a representative of the Jewish Agency in Rome. Pesach Ostashinski also strengthened Israel's ties with other nations through cultural events with the European diplomatic corps and through his work as president of the Israel-Finnish Friendship League.[24] He and his wife Linda née Mallis lived on Moshav Chavatzelet Hasharon prior to his death in 1999 at the age of sixty-eight. Although Pesach had a great love of children, he never became a father.[25]

Once Chaim arrived in Israel, he made his home in Tel Aviv, where he worked sporadically as a tailor and received assistance from his family.

He lived close to both Perla and Daniel's families in North Tel Aviv and spent almost every evening in Daniel's home until his last years. From the moment Perla became a young widow left alone to raise an eight-year-old daughter, Chaim devoted much time at her home as well in his efforts to fill the void.[26]

Chaim was a traditional Jew who enjoyed attending synagogue on Friday nights. Described by his grandson as quiet and modest, he is said to have spoken very little and never mentioned the loss of his family members during the war.[27]

Chaim Ostashinski, undated postwar photo (courtesy of Zafrir Ostashinsky)

Only fifty-eight at the time of his immigration, Chaim was reportedly a sought-after widower, yet he never remarried. When his son once gently broached the subject of remarriage, Chaim vehemently declared, "I had one wife, and I will never have another."[28]

Chaim Ostashinsky died in Tel Aviv in 1989. While alive, he was the proud grandfather of Daniel's three sons and of Perla's one daughter. One of Daniel's sons bears the name of Chaim's murdered son Yitzchak; another is named Zafrir in memory of Zipora, the wife Chaim loved so dearly.

If he were alive at the time of this writing in August 2023, Chaim would doubtless have much joy from his twelve grandchildren and about eighteen great-grandchildren, including his namesake, Perla's grandson Aviv Zeev Hirshsprung.[29]

Perla Ostashinski (#33)

Perla Ostashinski was born in Novogrudok in 1925[1] to Chaim (#32), a tailor, and Zipora née Abramovich, a housewife.[2] Perla's siblings were Daniel, born in 1921;[3] Esther, born in 1923;[4] Yitzchak, born in 1927;[5] Batya Rivka, born in 1933;[6] and Pesach, born in the early 1930s.[7] The family is remembered to have been involved with the city's renowned Novardok Yeshiva before the war, with Perla's grandmother Kayla Fruma Chaitovich responsible for collecting charity for the yeshiva and often hosting yeshiva students at the family's Shabbat table.[8]

Chaim was said to have made a good living from his tailor shop, which employed nearly fifty tailors. Fortunately, Chaim was able to pay a Christian family to hide his young son Pesach while the other members of the family were interned in the Novogrudok forced labor camp. Although Pesach was initially crippled after being confined to a cramped position for over a year in hiding,[9] he was luckier than his siblings Yitzchak, Esther, and Batya Rivka who were murdered along with approximately half the inmates of the Novogrudok forced labor camp on May 7, 1942. The massacre took place in full view of surviving family members, who watched the horror from the windows of the courthouse.[10] Yitzchak was fatally shot in the back as he ran after Perla, who miraculously jumped over a fence to reenter the safety of the courthouse.[11] Esther[12] and Batya Rivka,[13] along with their mother Zipora,[14] were among those forced to lie face down before being shot dead and thrown into a pit.

During the tunnel escape sixteen months later, Daniel became separated from his father and sister. Perla and Chaim were reunited with Daniel in the forest when they eventually reached the Bielski partisan detachment.

Pursued in the forest by Yisrael Cotler, the aide-de-camp of Asael Bielsky, Perla Ostashinski is described by Asael's widow Chaya as having been a tall, pretty, charming, and feminine woman with a winning smile. After liberation, Yisrael and Perla were to go their separate ways.[15]

During the post-liberation period, Perla, like her brother Daniel, became extremely active in the underground Etzel (Irgun) Zionist paramilitary organization. A commander in the organization, she reached Vienna, where she was responsible for hiding arms in the apartment she shared with her father. These weapons were then clandestinely shipped to Palestine to arm fighters in the battle for an independent state.[16] While in the Austrian capital, Perla met and fell in love with the young medical student and fellow Etzel member Moshe (Moniek) Hirshprung, originally from Cracow and a survivor of Mauthausen. The couple married in Vienna prior to their immigration to Israel on October 6, 1948.[17]

After living in Jerusalem as Moshe pursued his medical studies at the Hebrew University, the couple eventually moved to Tel Aviv, where Moshe established himself as an internist. Perla, who had attended Novogrudok's Hebrew-language Tarbut school and arrived in Israel fluent in Hebrew, worked as a senior secretary in the Jewish Agency and was frequently dispatched to Belgium as an immigration emissary.[18]

Fourteen years after Perla and Moshe married, their only child Dorit was born in 1961. The family maintained a religiously traditional home, and Dorit attended religious schools. Following Dorit's birth, Perla ceased to work and devoted herself solely to caring for her daughter. Tragedy struck in 1969 when Dorit was eight years old, and her beloved father died suddenly of a heart attack at the age of forty-five. The family rallied to Perla's aid: her brothers became great sources of support to the new widow, and her father Chaim took a major role in attempting to fill the void left by his son-in-law's demise. Always considered to have been the more optimistic spouse, Perla ultimately succeeded in creating a happy home for her daughter.[19]

Involved in the lives of her two grand-children as they were growing up, Perla spent long periods with the family during their stay in Boston in the late 1980s. There she volunteered to teach Russian immigrant children in the city's Hebrew Academy, where Dorit was employed as a Hebrew teacher.[20]

During Perla's last years when she suffered from ill health, Dorit lovingly cared for her, returning the care and devotion that her mother had extended for a lifetime. Perla, who never remarried, passed away in Tel Aviv in 2012.

Perla Ostashinski, undated photo (courtesy of Dorit Kay)

Dorit has served as an organizational consultant, vocational counselor, and junior high school principal. In 2019, she received her doctorate in human resource management.[21] Her daughter Tal is an accountant, and her son Aviv, who holds a managerial position in the Israel Defense Forces, has publicly spoken of his personal experiences as a third-generation survivor of the Holocaust on both sides of his family.[22]

Hirsh Orlinski (#34)

Hirsh Orlinski's name and the date and place of his birth (Zhetl, 1923) appear in a Soviet postwar document listing the murdered of Zhetl. Hirsh is noted there to have been a student at the time of his death. No further information has been located regarding his parents' names or his own marital status.

Five months before the tunnel escape from the Novogrudok forced labor camp, Hirsh Orlinski was an integral member of a team involved in planning the bold, ultimately cancelled uprising against the Germans scheduled for April 15, 1943. On September 26, 1943, Orlinski survived the tunnel breakout, reached the Bielski partisan detachment in the Naliboki Forest, and immediately joined the ranks. Three days later, Hirsh, together with former labor camp inmates Kozuchovski, a Chernichovski brother, and five other fighters, encountered a group of "Victor partisans" who demanded their weapons. When the Novogrudok escapees refused to surrender the two weapons in their possession unless by death, they were murdered in cold blood by the Russian partisans.[1]

These murders occurred despite the friendship and cooperation said to have been established between leaders Tuvia Bielski and Victor Panchenko during the summer of 1942 in response to the fierce competition among the Russian, Jewish, and Belarusian partisans in the area for obtaining food and supplies.[2]

A native of the Smolensk region to the east, Panchenko was a former lieutenant in the Red Army who served during the invasion of Finland. When his machine-gun battalion stationed along the western border of the Soviet Union was attacked by the Nazis in 1941, he retreated to Novogrudok, where he founded his partisan unit.[3]

Described as good-natured, friendly, and charming, Victor headed the strong, influential Octiaber detachment, named for the Soviet Revolution and comprised of many ex-Soviet soldiers and disenchanted Belarusian peasants, whose raids on Belarusian and German police stations procured arms and ammunition. Victor's influence was particularly apparent around the towns of Lida, Novogrudok, and Zhetl.[4] Once cooperation between Bielski and Victor's detachments was established, Victor divided the area into two sections for the purpose of food raids. While the Bielski partisans were to take provisions from farms close to Lida and Novogrudok, Panchenko's group would conduct raids in and around Zhetl.[5]

In a document filed with the National Archive of the Republic of Belorussia on September 16, 1944, signed by detachment commander Tuvia Bielski, his chief of staff Malbin, as well as the detachment commissar Shemyatovetz, contact between the Bielski and Panchenko partisans was first established in September 1942 and followed by many impressive joint operations.[6]

Despite Tuvia Bielski's appreciation of Panchenko's strategic importance in the combat against the Nazis, and despite Bielski's communiqué to newly arrived partisans stating, "Commander Victor is a good man and will help us all he can.... We must fight together with Victor's unit against the Germans,"[7] we must not forget who murdered Hirsh Orlinski and several of his fellow tunnel escapees.

Hirsh (#35) and Moshe (#36) Chernichovski

Both Chaim Leibowitz (#91) and Chaya Bielski, wife of partisan leader Asael Bielski, write of "Chernichovski" (no proper name noted), who was a leading resistance fighter in the camp and the man designated to cut the barbed-wire fences during the ill-fated uprising planned for April 15, 1943.[1] Testimonies also recount how after successfully fleeing through the tunnel, Chernichovski banded together with eight or nine comrades, including Dr. Yakov Kagan (#3a), Hirsh Orlinski (#34), Berl Yoselevich, and Kozuchovski, on their trek to the Bielski partisan detachment in the Naliboki Forest. Upon reaching the Butskovitz Forest, this group encountered a band of partisans under the command of the anti-Semitic Russian officer Victor Panchenko. At gunpoint, Panchenko's men demanded that the Jewish fighters surrender their weapons. The newly fled prisoners steadfastly refused to hand over the only two weapons they shared, declaring to the Russians that only death would make them give up their arms. Ruthlessly slain, none of these Jews lived to become partisans.[2]

Although the names Hirsh and Moshe Chernichovski appear consecutively on the escape list, we are unaware of the relationship between the two. While they may have been brothers born in Ozorkow, Poland,[3] the advanced age of these two men (between sixty and eighty years old by 1943) casts major doubt that either of the two had been a leading resistance leader.

Alternatively, the Chernichovski inmates on the escape list may have stemmed from the southeastern Polish town of Opatow. One may have been David Hersz, born in 1884,[4] or Hersz Fauwel, born in 1879.[5] The ages of these men, as well, also leads one to question whether either of them would have even been conscripted as an essential worker, let alone able to fulfill a leadership position. As for Moshe, he may have been Moshei, a child born in 1931,[6] or Mozek, born in 1917.[7]

Hirsh and Moshe Chernichovski may have been father and son, brothers, or cousins. Their precise identity and the circumstances of their lives and deaths remain an enigma to this day.

Moshe Glicksman (#37)

Yad Vashem's Central Database of Shoah Victims' Names contains listings for over sixty individuals named Moshe Glicksman, vastly complicating the search for the one man by that name who took part in the tunnel escape from the Novogrudok forced labor camp.

Of the multiple listings, only one Moshe Glicksman hailed from the Novogrudok environs, with all the others being natives or residents of different areas of Poland. While there is no proof that he is the actual tunnel escapee, we can only note that statistically speaking, the greatest number of escapees were natives of the Novogrudok region.

This Moshe Glicksman came from the very small hamlet of Sokolnica (Sokolnichi), so small that it does not even rate a dot on most maps. A student born in 1924, Moshe was the son of Leah Dina née Lerman, a housewife, and Chaim Yosef, a merchant.[1] According to a Page of Testimony completed in 1957 by a niece of Chaim Yosef, both he and Leah Dina were murdered in their village in 1940[2] along with their daughters Mirl, age eight,[3] and Zelda, age twelve.[4] Moshe was also listed as having been murdered along with his family.[5]

While Moshe of Sokolnica may have been the only member of his nuclear family to have survived the village massacre, he did not survive the war. Whether or not he was the Novogrudok tunnel escapee, we may never know. As the name Moshe Glicksman does not appear on the list of Jewish partisans in Belorussia during the years 1941–1944, we may assume that this escapee did not survive the breakout to reach the forest and the partisans.[6]

Yakov (Yankel) Shepsman (#39)

Born in Radom, Poland, in 1926,[1] Yakov (Yankel) Shepsman followed his father Mendel as well as his grandfather to become a shoemaker. In his 1996 Spielberg oral testimony,[2] Yankel proudly emphasizes that his father was no ordinary shoemaker, but one who made "special" shoes for private customers. He recalls his mother Eta née Brickman as having been quite busy caring for him and his six younger brothers and sisters, noting that both Mendel and Eta were sixteen years old at their marriage. While Eta was the daughter of a rabbi who fathered twenty-two children,[3] Mendel was described as having been more of a traditional Jew who attended synagogue on the Sabbath and holidays.

Yankel fondly recalls how his relatives would gather together to celebrate Jewish holidays, especially Passover.[4]

The eldest of his siblings, Yankel was the sole survivor of his immediate family.[5] A document from the International Committee of the
Red Cross (ICRC) Tracing Services at Magen David Adom Israel
notes that in 1942, Yankel's parents, two brothers, and two sisters were
deported to the Lodz ghetto, where they met their deaths.[6] As there
are no Pages of Testimony at Yad Vashem and no listings for members
of the immediate family among the tens of Radom-born Shepsman
victims in the Central Database of Shoah Victims' Names, we have no
further information on the circumstances of their deaths.

Yankel fondly recalls having had a "normal life" before the war,
describing having been an avid soccer player with the family's large garden as his practice field. As a youngster, he was often caught up in scuf-
fles with non-Jewish friends who dared to make anti-Semitic remarks
in his presence. In time, he observed the growing violence toward the
Jewish population, witnessing such acts as Jewish-owned wagons being
overturned in the marketplace.[7]

To a major extent, Yankel owes his life to his mother. Despite his
father's repeated dismissal of Yankel's pleas to go into hiding and his
younger brother Itche's refusal to leave their parents and flee with him
to the nearby forests, it was his mother who bravely gave Yankel her
blessing to escape. Refusing his parents' offer to take their gold jewelry
with him, Yankel joined about twenty other local young people who
fled to the woods for safety.[8]

It is not clear how Yankel traversed some 320 miles away from the
forests near Radom to Novogrudok, where he was ultimately conscripted as a shoemaker to the forced labor camp. In his testimony,
he describes the camp as having been poorly guarded, noting how
several fellow inmates succeeded in escaping in January or February
1942, only to be forced to return due to the deadly frostbite that
crippled them. Apparently a member of the camp resistance faction,
Yankel reports having been involved in obtaining arms, including six

rifles as well as several hand grenades and handguns, from outside the camp.[9]

In their testimonies, escapees Eliyahu Berkowitz (#49),[10] Chaim Leibowitz (#91),[11] and Jack (Idel) Kagan (#95)[12] have detailed the crucial role that the carpenters played in the building of the tunnel, risking their lives to sneak out wood to reinforce its wall and build trolleys to carry out the dirt. Yankel adds how the carpenters came to the rescue by reinforcing the bottom of the loft in which the heavy dug-up earth was clandestinely stored, thus preventing the ceiling from crashing onto the living quarters.

Yankel remembers keeping to the right after escaping through the tunnel and then beginning a six-day trek to the Bielski partisan detachment, subsisting on apples and carrots as he fled through villages on the way. His daughter Ze recalls her father telling her that during his journey to the partisans, he helped carry fellow escapee Idel Kagan much of the way, since Idel could barely walk due to the crude amputation of his frostbitten toes following a failed escape attempt.[13]

Upon reaching the partisan detachment, Yankel took part in nightly ambushes for food in the surrounding towns. He speaks of how even the older shoemakers, tailors, and other craftsmen were engaged in productive activity in the detachment, where all had "jobs." Sounding almost nostalgic for the "old days" in the forest, Yankel notes that despite the tragic losses they all experienced, "the atmosphere was good," with much camaraderie, singing, and bonfires in the evenings.

After liberation in September 1944, Yankel first traveled to Vilna and Lodz in a futile search for surviving relatives before taking refuge in the German Landsberg Displaced Persons Camp in the British zone. Sailing to Israel in 1946, he, like fellow tunnel escapees Efraim Okonski (#90) and Pesach Abramowicz (#205), initially joined Eliezer Sadan (formerly Senderovsky of Zhetl and Novogrudok) at Kibbutz Kinneret in the Jordan Valley. Yankel's assignments during his three-year service in the Israeli army included cleaning weapons and meeting ships carrying survivors and other immigrants. As they descended the ship, he taught the new immigrants to shoot and be war-ready even before settling in their new homes.[14]

Yankel was discharged from the Israeli army in 1950, the same year in which he married Lola Berkowitz, a survivor of the Lodz ghetto and of Auschwitz.[15] Their first child Menahem (now Martin) was born in 1951. With Yankel unable to find employment and finding life difficult in the newly born state,[16] the family returned to Europe in 1953, where they took refuge in the Föhrenwald Displaced Persons Camp, in the American zone of Germany. There, daughter Zisel (Ze) was born the following year. Until at least 1956, the Shepsman family remained in the DP camp awaiting resettlement to yet another country.[17]

Settling at last in London, Yankel was reunited there with two maternal aunts and a cousin. Fellow tunnel escapee Idel Kagan, the man he carried through the forest to the Bielski detachment, even gave Yankel his first job as a plastic welder.[18] A British acquaintance describes Yankel – now called Jack – Shepsman as having been a "soft, nice, reliable man who could be trusted to keep to his word." The early job opportunity provided by Kagan eventually led to the establishment of Yankel's own successful plastics concern, Zena Plastics. How fitting that before eventually settling in Middlesex, this amateur football player from Poland should spend his early years in London's Wembly area near the famed Wembly Football Stadium.[19]

Today, Yankel's son Martin is a retired pharmaceutical software company owner who resides in London. As of this writing in October 2020, Martin is the father of a son and a daughter and the grandfather of two. Martin admits having known very little of his father's past, partly due to his father's reticence to offer information and partly due to his own discomfort with the topic.[20]

Interviewed from her home near Oxford, Yankel's daughter Zisel, now known as Ze, relates that she was trained in business and has now retired from her position with the National Health Service, Ze, like Martin, has a son and a daughter. She currently has three grandchildren.

Unlike Martin, Ze knows many details of her father's Holocaust past, noting that while she was still in primary school, her father would gladly answer her many questions about that period of his life. She reports that Yankel was exceptionally proud of his participation in the tunnel escape and shared with her many of the details surrounding the breakout.[21]

Ze lovingly describes her father as having been a serious man who "lived for his family."[22] In his oral testimony one year before his death in 1997, Yankel expressed satisfaction that both his children and grandchildren "have a normal life," just as he once had, long ago.[23]

Yakov (Yankel) Shepsman, Kibbutz Kinneret, Israel, circa 1950 (courtesy of Ze Roberts)

David Meiersdorf (#40)

We may never know the identity of escapee David Meiersdorf.

In all likelihood, Meiersdorf did not originate from the Novogrudok area, as the *Novogrudok Memorial Book* contains no listings for any Meiersdorf family members.[1] Accordingly, Yad Vashem's Central Database of Shoah Victims' Names contains no testimonies for anyone with the Meiersdorf surname from Novogrudok or its environs.

There are, however, two records for men named David Meiersdorf from central Poland – one from Lodz, 340 miles from Novogrudok, and the other from Pultusk, 250 miles from Novogrudok. Neither record provides place, circumstance, or date of death. As a number of Novogrudok forced labor camp inmates had fled considerable distances from areas invaded by the Germans in September 1939, it is conceivable that one of these men was the David Meiersdorf who took part in the tunnel breakout.

Of the two, it is highly unlikely that Lodz native David Meiersdorf, a merchant born in 1860, would have been conscripted to the labor camp, due to his age.[2] As we know nothing of David Shamai Meiersdorf of Pultusk other than that he was murdered,[3] perhaps he was indeed the escapee from the Novogrudok forced labor camp.

Regardless, the inmate David Meiersdorf apparently did not survive the tunnel escape. Had he survived, he is likely to have joined the other escapees in the partisan detachments of the Belarusian forests. Unfortunately, his name does not appear on the list of Jewish partisans in those forests during the years 1941–1944.[4]

Yosef Razvaski (#41)

Thanks to the testimony of Dr. S. Openheim in the Yizkor book (memorial book) of the Jewish community of Novogrudok, Poland, we learn that Yosef Razvaski took part in the Novogrudok forced labor camp tunnel escape, joined the partisans, and was slain in battle in the forest.[1]

Yosef Razvaski, the son of Moshe, was born in 1895.[2] Beyond Dr. Openheim noting that Yosef was a tailor by profession[3] and the compilation of Jewish partisans in Belorussia stating that he joined the Soviet-led Kirov Brigade of partisans in the forest,[4] we have no additional personal information about Yosef. While details of Yosef's life are sparse, records of his death are unfortunately more prevalent. Dr. Openheim reports that Yosef was killed in a skirmish in the forest with the "fleeing German troops,"[5] which occurred as the Russian troops were liberating the area in 1944. Yosef's death is commemorated in the compilation of Jewish partisans in Belorussia.[6]

It is likely that the first initial of Yosef's name was written erroneously on the escape list, which instead of a *yud* (Y) lists the initial *aleph* (the Hebrew letter corresponding to A, E, or I). A search of Yad Vashem's Central Database of Shoah Victims' Names for Razvaskis with the first initial *aleph* was inconclusive. Aaron Razvaski of Zhetl, the only partisan with this surname listed in the compilation of Jewish partisans in Belorussia,[7] has been ruled out as having taken part in the tunnel escape, following our inquiry of an eyewitness and of Aaron's children.[8] In light of the published accounts of Yosef Razvaki's escape through the tunnel and his heroic service as a partisan, we may assume that he was indeed the forty-first inmate to crawl through the tunnel.

Mordechai (#42) and
Leib Orzuchowski

Mordechai (Motl) Orzuchowski was born in Karelich, where he lived until the outbreak of World War II. As a saddler, he earned his living making saddles, harnesses, and other leather goods for horse-drawn carriages, the most common means of local transportation in prewar days and still seen today in Belarus villages. Mordechai's eldest daughter, Nella, recalls that her father's handcrafted creations bore the mark of a true artisan.[1]

Mordechai's only known sibling is his younger brother and fellow tunnel escapee Leib (Lova). Although his date of birth is unknown, Nella estimates that Leib was born around 1920, approximately twenty years after her father.[2] It is not known if there were other children born to their parents, Yitzchak and Mania,[3] both of whom were slain in the war. Although Leib's profession is unknown, Nella recalls having seen a picture of her uncle playing an instrument in the band of the Karelich Fire Department.[4]

Despite Nella's desire to pursue a look into her family's past, she does not recall or has never known basic biographical information about her father's family. Like many children of survivors, she admits that her parents' past was an unspoken "taboo" subject. While noting that she never asked them questions about their families of origin, the few questions she did dare to ask were met with silence. Unaware of her father's date of birth and not recalling his year of death, Nella was also unable to provide the names of her paternal grandparents or of any siblings other than Leib. Only with the help of a geneal-ogist were we able to ascertain the names of Mordechai and Leib's parents.[5] An online family tree lists Mordechai's year of birth as 1902,[6] while the partisan list notes the date as 1897.[7] The family tree also indicates that Mordechai's wife and Nella's mother, Ida née Chodesh, was born in 1918.[8] Ida was a native of the Belarusian vil-lage of Smolevichi.[9]

The little that Nella had gleaned about the family's prewar life was what she overheard as a child when her parents discussed their past between themselves or with friends and neighbors. Born on March 23, 1941, Nella relates that at the age of three or four months, she was placed in hiding with Christian acquaintances of her father in a rural area nearly eight miles from Novogrudok. Although she does not remember her rescuers' surname, she recalls that Nicolai and Matka (a nickname for "mama"), as well as their son and daughter, treated her well and that she continued to visit them during summer vacations until her immigration to Israel at age nineteen.[10]

In the Novogrudok forced labor camp, Mordechai is said to have utilized his leatherworking skills to make boots for the Germans. Nella recalls that the uncle of one of her childhood Christian friends had been one of the camp guards. During his internment, Mordechai and this man had struck up a mutually beneficial relationship in which Mordechai would make an extra pair of boots to slip to the guard, who would then sell them "on the outside" and share the income with his prisoner.[11]

Miraculously, brothers Mordechai and Leib both survived the tunnel escape. (Although Lova's name cannot be deciphered on the escape list, Nella testifies to the fact that her uncle was a tunnel escapee, recalling conversations between the two brothers during visits in Novogrudok when they reminisced about the breakout.)[12]

Mordechai joined the Bielski partisans[13] for a period of time before changing allegiance to another Jewish partisan group, the Frunze detachment of the First Baranovichskaya Brigade,[14] which, like the Bielskis, cared for the elderly as well as women and children.[15] For his part, Leib became a member of the Ordzhonikidze detachment,[16] a fighting group with a Russian commander and 180 Bielski fighters.[17]

Following the war, Leib initially returned to live in Karelich. Mordechai was drafted into the Red Army, where he was wounded and awarded medals for his bravery.[18]

Nella recalls the day some time in 1945 that her parents arrived in a horse and buggy to retrieve her from her safe haven. Leaving the only parental figures she had known, she no longer recalls any emotions connected to the event.

After a temporary return to Karelich, Mordechai brought his newly reunited family to Novogrudok, where they lived at 74 Minskaya Street, only several houses away from the former forced labor camp. Nella describes her nearly two-mile daily walk to and from school, including in the darkness of the winter days. She also relates the fears she experienced while passing the building that had been the forced labor camp – whose history she knew – as she saw her shadow in the snow and heard the howling of the wind. Worried that the howls might be emanating from within the building, she recalls how she and her friends would search among the ruins for people trapped inside.[19]

The tumultuous experiences they all faced took a heavy toll upon the relationship between Nella and her parents. During the war, Ida, too, had been in hiding. Mordechai had survived the Novogrudok forced labor camp, the partisan detachment in the forest, and the Russian Army. Ultimately, their experiences, losses, and suffering understandably took an emotional toll on the couple, preventing them from ever being the warm parents involved in their daughter's life that Nella so longed for.[20]

Upon Mordechai's immigration to Israel in 1959 with Ida and their younger daughter Chana, born in 1947, Mordechai left his brother Leib behind in the USSR for what was to be forever. According to Nella, Leib married a Jewish woman after the war, eventually moved to Smolensk in Russia, and finally settled in the Soviet republic of Azerbaijan. She believes that he has two sons and a daughter.[21]

Preceding Nella's immigration to Israel by one year, Mordechai, Ida, and Chana set down roots in the northern border town of Kiryat Shmona. Yet the frequent air raid sirens and border skirmishes with Lebanon reminded them of World War II, prompting the family to relocate soon afterwards to Kfar Saba in central Israel. After a period as a road worker, Mordechai was employed for several years with the Agrexco Concern, Israel's largest export company for agricultural produce and cut flowers. Nella still recalls the bouquets she received from her father on the eve of every Sabbath.[22]

Perhaps due to their fresh start in a new land far removed from the suffering of the past, Nella felt a closer relationship with her parents after she arrived in Israel. During the last years of their lives, Nella cared diligently for Mordechai and Ida.[23]

Mordechai died on April 11, 1981,[24] sixteen years before Ida's death on May 9, 1997.[25] Were he alive today (June 2019), he would be the grandfather of five and the great-grandfather of fifteen.[26]

Neither Nella nor her sister Chana know whether Leib is still alive, nor are they in contact with their first cousins, the only other known remnants of the Orzuchovski family from Karelich.

Today Nella is a retired registered nurse, artist, sculptor, and mother of three sons. Chana raised four children and works in sales. To date, Nella has returned eight times to Novogrudok. Several of her visits were

devoted to helping find the remains of
the escape tunnel near her former home.
At a ceremony in Novogrudok on July 9,
2019, marking the seventy-fifth anniversary of the liberation of the area, she dedicated a monument and a grove of birch
trees on the site of the mass grave of labor
camp inmates – including a number of
Orzuchowski family members – murdered on May 7, 1943, in Novogrudok's
fourth massacre. The previous day, at the
inauguration of a memorial wall commemorating the names and fate of the
tunnel escapees, Nella proudly honored
the memory of Mordechai and Leib.

Mordechai Orzuchovski,
Israel, circa 1962
(courtesy of Nella Zaober)

Leib Orzuchowski (*second row from the top, far right*) in prewar photo
of the Novogrudok Volunteer Fire Brigade (Memorial *Book of the Jewish
Community of Novogrudok, Poland*)

Lipchin (#43)

As the individual with the surname Lipchin appears on the escape list without a proper name, we cannot determine his or her identity. The 877 records and documents in Yad Vashem's Central Database of Shoah Victims' Names with the Lipchin surname include men and women from across Poland. Although the tunnel escapee by this name could indeed have hailed from a locale far distant from Novogrudok, the 176 citations for Lipchins originating from the Novogrudok area are indicative of the prevalence of the family's branches there at the start of World War II.

Since no one named Lipchin appears in the compilation of Jewish partisans in Belorussia,[1] we can assume that the person by this name, slated to be the forty-third in line to escape from the Novogrudok forced labor camp, did not survive the tunnel breakout.

Shlomo (Moniek) Engler (#44)

With Moniek being the nickname for Shlomo or Salomon, there are three individuals with variations of the name "Shlomo Engler" in Yad Vashem's Central Database of Shoah Victims' Names. For two of them, their reported places of death are far from Novogrudok. Shleyman Angler of Kolomiya, Poland, was murdered there between 1941 and 1944,[1] and Munia or Moni of Zabia was slaughtered in that town's 1942 massacre.[2] Only the fate of Salomon Engler of Kosow (ninety miles from Novogrudok) remains uncertain.

Born in Kosow to his twenty-year-old mother Etel in 1925, Salomon Leizer Engler appears on a list of Jewish residents of the town prior to 1941.[3] While Etel's name also appears on this list,[4] we know nothing of the fate of mother and son or of other members of Salomon's family of origin.

If eighteen-year-old Salomon of Kosow is indeed the man who appears on the escape list of the Novogrudok forced labor camp, his name does not appear in the compilation of Jewish partisans in Belorussia.[5] It is thus unlikely that this inmate survived the tunnel breakout, and we must unfortunately presume that he was murdered before reaching the partisans in the forest.

Abram Czertok (#45)

Despite the turmoil and tragedies of war that darkened Abram Czertok's life, he clung throughout to the strong principles of justice, morality, and love of family that had been ingrained in his soul from childhood.

Known in Yiddish as Avrom-Eliezer,[1] Abram Czertok was born in Novogrudok in 1921[2] to Ovsey (Yehoshua),[3] a watchmaker,[4] and Myriam (Mera) née Berman,[5] a housewife. At their brutal deaths during Novogrudok's first slaughter on December 8, 1941,[6] Yehoshua was sixty-one years old and Mera just fifty-nine.

Although Abram was separated from his family during this first massacre, he was bravely able to rescue his wife, Fanya née Kantorovich, as well as their six-month-old baby. Yet tragically, the two were later murdered in a subsequent Novogrudok massacre.[7]

Because Abram's skills as a watchmaker were essential to the German Army, he was conscripted to the Novogrudok forced labor camp.[8] Miraculously, he survived the tunnel escape, after which he banded together with Nota Sucharski (#4), Isaac Yarmovski (#6), and father and son Mairim (#12) and Shevach (#13) Gershanovich. After two days of trekking through the forest with no food or drink, the five escapees were given shelter for a time by a non-Jewish farmer.[9]

Unlike the vast majority of escapees who made their way to the Bielski partisan detachment, Abram and his companions were led to the Frunze detachment of the First Baranovichskaya Brigade by a girl who had hidden along with them.[10] Abram told of having served as the sole armed fighter on horseback in the brigade, adding that he was the only one who could manage the horse.[11]

Although the July 1944 Soviet liberation of Belorussia marked the liberation of the partisans from the forest, the Second World War continued to rage across other parts of Europe. Together with Isaac Yarmovski and fellow escapee and partisan Avraham Rakovski (#10), Abram was soon drafted into the Red Army, where he was to reach the rank of lieutenant. Coming full circle from victim to liberator, Soviet Army officer Abram Czertok freed women prisoners from a German concentration camp.[12] Among the Soviet medals he was awarded for his distinguished conduct and his battle injuries was the prestigious Lenin and Stalin Medallion for exemplary military service against Nazi Germany.[13]

Following his military discharge at the war's end, Abram returned to Novogrudok determined to accomplish two major goals: to unearth the gold his father had buried underground before being murdered and to take revenge against a local collaborator with the Germans who had slain several members of his family. Meeting both goals successfully, he located parts of the hidden treasure as well as the collaborator, whom he beat ruthlessly but did not kill, despite the opportunity.[14]

While in Novogrudok, Abram learned of the possibility of traveling to Palestine to join in the fight for the birth of the Jewish nation. To become involved in the immigration effort, he set out for Berlin, together with fellow tunnel escapee Idel Kagan (#95),[15] taking refuge in the nearby Shlachtensee Displaced Persons Camp in the US Occupation Zone. Here the Hebrew language skills he acquired as a youngster in Novogrudok's Tarbut school enabled Abram to serve as a teacher to orphan children in the DP camp's Hebrew school. A photo of Abram together with the staff and orphan pupils at Shlachtensee's Hebrew school is displayed in the photo archive of the Diaspora Museum in Israel.[16]

Beyond his teaching endeavors, Abram joined other Zionists and soon took charge of procuring weapons for Jewish fighters in Palestine. He shared that he even exchanged watches for guns from Russian soldiers.[17]

At some point, Abram decided to change his immigration destination to the USA. He resourcefully turned to a Yiddish-speaking American Army officer for help in writing a letter in English to Abram's American cousin Bessie Colvin to request her sponsorship for his immigration. Bessie's husband Charles, a renowned American aeronautical engineer, not only agreed to sponsor him and to offer him a job, but informed Abram that his only sister Sonia was alive in France. Astounded, Abram immediately changed his destination to France.[18]

Somehow making the 585-mile (940 km) journey from Berlin to Reims, France, in 1946, Abram was at last reunited with his beloved sister Sonia.[19] Yet this near-miracle was tempered by Abram's arrival to his new home in France suffering from skeletal tuberculosis and knowing not a word of French. In time, he was treated for the tuberculosis and eventually became a fluent speaker of French, tinged with a Polish-Yiddish accent. Fortunately, Abram succeeded in improving his watchmaking skills in Reims to return to his profession and eventually open his own watch and jewelry shop. He started a new family through his 1950 marriage to French-born Marcelle Shermann and the birth of their son Guy two years later. Upon becoming a French national, Abram officially changed his name to André.[20]

Only through the help of a genealogist and a long search for next of kin was Abram's great-nephew Shaouli Nochimovski, Sonia's grandson, located in Israel, to which he emigrated from France. With Shaouli's help, we reached Dr. Guy Czertok, Abram's son, in Paris. A retired physician specializing in rehabilitative medicine, Dr. Czertok is married to a Jewish Moroccan-born physician specializing in homeopathic medicine. Both she and their son Sacha now share Guy's keen interest in exploring new aspects of his father's story.[21]

Guy shares that when life was difficult, his father would cynically quip that he had nothing to worry about, because he had encountered such close brushes with death during the war that he was now living an "extra life." Guy adds that although his father tried to be a happy man, his past would sometimes catch up with him, sending him from laughter to tears.

Despite the terrible difficulties involved, Guy stressed that his father's powerful responsibility to those killed in the Holocaust compelled him to give testimonies of his own experiences. In early 1968, Abram submitted a detailed oral testimony to the Ghetto Fighters' House Museum, and later submitted Yad Vashem Pages of Testimony for his parents. Yet Abram did not speak of his first wife and child, nor did he submit Pages of Testimony in their memory.

Abram did take pride in three things: participating in the tunnel escape, fighting with the partisans and the Soviet Army, and building a new life in France. After arriving in France as a penniless refugee who did not speak a word of French, he lived to see his family extend into the third generation with the 1992 birth of his grandchild Sacha. This, Abram declared, was his own personal revenge against the Nazis, which brought him tremendous satisfaction.[22]

Presently, Sacha belongs to a cooperative of geographers and political scientists. As a consultant in public policies, he works with central and local French public administrations on urban and regional planning and public governance issues. Sensitive to the issues of racism and anti-Semitism, Sacha served as a national delegate of the French Union of Jewish Students (UEJF) from 2014 to 2017, heading the fight against the French far-right party Le Front National.[23]

Dr. Czertok also reports that the Nochimovski and Czertok families have remained extremely close, and that he and Sonia's two sons Gérard

and Pierre are "almost like brothers."
Marcelle died quite young in 1976, Sonia
in 1990,[24] and Abram on June 18, 2000.[25]
Prior to his death, Abram made several
trips to Israel, where he enjoyed speaking the Hebrew of his youth and meeting
fellow Novogrudok survivors. One of his
close friends was Yehuda Slutski,[26] the
chronicler of the *Novogrudok Memorial
Book*'s account of the marketplace massacre of June 26, 1941.[27] Among others
he visited was his sister-in-law Esther
Yankelevich née Kantorovich, his first
wife's sister, who had immigrated to Israel

Abram Czertok, 1946
(courtesy of Guy Czertok)

before the war. According to Dr. Czertok, his family maintained contact with the Yankeleviches throughout most of Abram's life.[28]

Although Abram's grief remained inconsolable for the loved ones he
had lost in the war, he did find a source of comfort within his Judaism.
By the end of his life, he was a fully practicing Jew, greatly influenced
by his neighbor and friend Rabbi Haïm Korsia, the former rabbi of
Reims and current chief rabbi of France.[29] However, Guy shares that
like many Holocaust survivors, his father had particular difficulty when
reciting the verse of the Jewish grace after meals that states, "I have not
seen a righteous man forsaken, with his children begging for bread."
Instead, Abram would often add, "It is not true. I *have* seen…"[30]

Perhaps it is Rabbi Korsia's insight that best sheds light on Abram's
fierce inner strength: "It was incredible that this man, who looked
serene, was a true fighter. His behavior and his outcries against the
injustices of the world evoked the temperament of a warrior."[31]

Leiba Pinchuk (#46)

According to the list of partisans in Belorussia during the years 1942–1944, Leiba Pinchuk was born in 1896 and lived in Novogrudok. The son of Natan (Nota), he worked as a watchmaker.[1] Although on an additional partisan list, he is noted as having been single,[2] Leiba had been quoted as saying that he'd resided at 24 Korelicka Street with his wife and two children, all of whom were murdered.[3] Prior to the war, Leiba was known to have been active in the Bund, the secular Jewish socialist party in Poland.[4]

Leiba's skills as a watchmaker, valued by the German Army, enabled his conscription to the Novogrudok forced labor camp and probable escape from death in the city's massacres. The escape list shows that Leiba was assigned to crawl through the tunnel to freedom between two of his fellow watchmakers, Abram Czertok (#45) and Moshe Feivelevich (#47). Thanks to the eyewitness Yad Vashem testimony by Shaul Gorodynski (#77), we learn that on September 28, 1943, two days after the escape, Gorodynski came across a band of fellow escapees in the forest making their way toward the Bielski detachment. Included in this group were Leiba, Feivelevich, Majer (#1) and Sara (#2) Jakubowicz, and Daniel Ostashinski. Over the course of their two-week trek, they are said to have carried the wounded Dr. Jakubowicz on their backs.[5]

Following his safe arrival to the partisan detachment, Leiba assumed the position of chief watchmaker. Partisan commander Tuvia Bielski relates in his memoir that during a visit to the detachment on December 31, 1943, by Soviet general Platon (Vasily Yefimovich Chernyshev), the forest watch repair workshop made a tremendous impression on the general. There Leiba Pinchuk, head of the team of three expert watchmakers, provided Platon with an explanation of the origin and intricacies of each timepiece in the wide array at hand.[6] The watch repair workshops, as well as all the other workshops in the detachment, served the needs of both the local partisans and those of other detachments in the vicinity.[7]

It was in the Bielski detachment that Leiba met Nikolai Schensovich, author of the Russian-language book *Notes of an Actor and a Partisan* (Minsk, 1970), and related the tunnel story to him in great detail, including the fact that he had been a member of the committee responsible for organizing the construction. Leiba described the tunnel as having been twenty-six inches

Leiba Pinchuk, undated postwar photo (courtesy of Tamara Vershitskaya)

wide at its top, thirty inches wide at the base, thirty-five inches high, and 260 yards long. He noted that 240 inmates participated in the escape.[8]

The forest was also the site where Pinchuk met his second wife, Bella Krislav Mikhailovna, a librarian and member of the Soviet Octiaber detachment.[9] After liberation, the couple settled in Novogrudok, where Bella, a Communist, was employed by the town's executive committee. Leib became a watchmaker for the "Record" cooperative, one of the many voluntary associations of craftsmen that were originally organized by the Soviets in 1939–1941. The couple, who had no children, lived on Lamkovaya Street near the city's castle. An expert chess player, Leiba participated in many tournaments and enjoyed playing chess with the famed physician Dr. Kalman Gordin as well as with the Zabelinskis, other Jews who returned to Novogrudok after liberation. He also continued to maintain frequent contact with his cousin and fellow escapee Abram Goldshmid (#128).[10]

Leiba died in 1965 and is buried in the Novogrudok Cemetery.[11]

Moshe Feivelevich (#47)

According to a 1944 list of Jewish partisans in Belorussia, Moshe Feivelevich, the son of Leizer, was born in Karelich in 1895. Unmarried, Moshe was a watchmaker by profession[1] who rose to the position of vice-president of the board of directors of the Tradesmen's Union[2] in Novogrudok, where he resided prior to the war.[3]

Until its closure by the Polish government in 1938, the Tradesmen's Union served a prominent role in the Novogrudok Jewish community. Its members, all Jewish self-employed workers, gathered by evening on the premises to meet, enjoy leisure activities, and attend cultural events. The Tradesmen's Union membership spanned the gamut of local political and ideological factions and was charged with the mandate to intercede with governmental offices on behalf of Jewish workers. Of the members on the board of directors, Moshe was the sole non-Zionist in his political views.[4]

As a watchmaker, Moshe was conscripted to the Novogrudok forced labor camp. Fellow inmate Morduch Majerowicz shares the tantalizing fact that as Moshe crept out of the tunnel on the stormy night of September 26, 1943, he had the misfortune to encounter a German patrol on Shinzitza Street in Novogrudok, which opened fire on him. Miraculously, Majerowicz reports, the bullet only grazed Moshe's hat, and the escapee was spared death.[5]

As Moshe continued on his trek to the partisans, he is reported to have arrived at the Bielski detachment together with escapees Leiba Pinchuk (#46), Dr. Majer Jakubowicz (#1) and his wife Sara (#2), and Daniel Ostashinski. The trek is said to have taken nearly two weeks due to their having carried the injured Jakubowicz on their backs.[6]

Although Mordechai Majerowicz noted in 1961 that Moshe was then living in Paris,[7] fellow tunnel escapee Idel Kagan (#95) attested that Feivelevich returned to Novogrudok following the war, where he resided until his death.[8]

Eliyahu (Elya) Berkowicz (#49)

His professional skills as a tailor provided a living for Eliyahu (Elya) Berkowicz and his family prior to the war, saved his life during the Holocaust, and gave him a livelihood as well as a chance to rebuild his life after liberation. Moreover, the selflessness and love that drove him to risk his own life to save his ailing sister are lauded to this day.

Born in the north-central Polish town of Rypin in May 1907[1] to Dov, a shoemaker, and Perel-Malka née Dziecielska,[2] Elya's siblings included sisters Chaya Sara Luska (#168),[3] Beile Rozin,[4] and Gitel Szuster.[5] Gitel was killed in Novogrudok in 1942,[6] while her younger sister Beile was murdered in the mass slaughter of May 7, 1943,[7] after being confined to the Novogrudok forced labor camp with her husband Zisel Rozin (#50).

Prior to the war, Eliyahu was apprenticed as a tailor and worked for twelve years before opening his own tailor shop. At age twenty-four, he was married to Nechama Zuchovitsky and lived on Postovskaya Street in Novogrudok. In their tenth year of marriage, Nechama and two of their daughters were murdered. Perele, the middle child,[8] was her paternal grandmother's namesake.[9] Dvorele, less than a year old at her death, was born in the Pereseka (Novogrudok) ghetto, where the family was incarcerated during 1942.[10]

Following the destruction of the ghetto in February 1943, Elya's skill as a tailor enabled him to escape death by being interned in the forced labor camp. To his utter amazement, his oldest daughter, nine-year-old Bashe, somehow managed to escape the February massacre to make her way, on her own, to join him in the camp. Elya desperately tried to save this precious, sole surviving member of his family by hiding her in a closet. Horrifyingly, on May 7, 1943, he helplessly watched Bashe being led to her slaughter by a Belarusian policeman who discovered her hiding place. She was one of around thirty-two children that Elya witnessed being massacred some hundred yards away, in full view of the labor camp inmates.[11]

Ultimately, Elya was to become a spectator of the tunnel escape as well. Although he was one of the fifty inmates assigned to clandestinely dig underground by night in a prone position (for which he characterized his small size as an advantage), he did not actually participate in the breakout. Instead, he made herculean efforts to save the life of his sister Chaya Sara Luska, the last remaining member of his close family.

Due to Chaya Sara's chronic heart disease, it was clear that if she were unable to crawl through the precarious tunnel, she could impede others from escaping. Seeking a solution, Elya consulted with camp inmate Shmuel Kolachek (#82), who himself suffered from a heart condition and feared he would not survive the crawl through the tunnel. Kolachek's solution came in the guise of a precarious hiding place he prepared for himself and for his fifteen-year-old son Yisrael (#81) in a loft in the camp. In addition to ascertaining Shmuel's agreement for him and Chaya Sara to join them in hiding, Elya received permission to include his brother-in-law Zisel Rozin, the widower of his younger sister Beile. (In a personal interview with Yisrael Kolachek seventy-three years later, he did not recall Zisel Rozin being among the hideaways.[12]) After Shmuel prepared a twenty-inch-high double floor, as recalled by Elya,[13] or a twenty-inch-high double door, as recalled by Yisrael,[14] the two men stocked the loft with rudimentary provisions, water, and blankets.

In his testimony, Elya estimates that 250 inmates lined up to make their escape through the tunnel, whose dimensions he notes were twenty-six inches wide by twenty-eight inches high and 273 yards long. Simultaneously, he, Chaya Sara, Zisl, Shmuel, and Yisrael all climbed up to the loft unnoticed.[15] To discourage any German suspicions, the "entrance" was covered by a high pile of rotting garbage. From his hiding place, Elya was able to see the signal for the escape to start at 8:00 p.m. – the short-circuiting of the search light's electric current, an act he attributes to escapee Gershon Michalevich (#29). He also reports having heard intense shooting from town by 9:00 p.m., lasting for about half an hour.[16]

Thanks to Elya's secret vantage point, he was able to provide a valuable account of the reaction of the townspeople to the incredible escape. Describing the intense curiosity evoked by the breakout, he writes: "For the next three days, there were visitors to the entrance to the tunnel. Gentiles from everywhere came to look at the rarity and to see what people under threat were capable of."[17]

After eight long days, Elya and his fellow hideaways were finally able to emerge from the secret loft. With Elya and the others carrying Chaya Sara, he describes how they slipped out of the abandoned camp through a hole in the barbed wire that had been used by the local police to trade with the inmates. After eight torturous days of wandering in the forest, they reached the Bielski detachment, where Berkowicz declares that they "were not alone at last."[18]

It was in the Naliboki Forest that Elya met Chana Konskowolski,[19] the woman who was to become his second wife, and her two-and-a-half-year-old daughter Mascha, whom Chana had miraculously managed to keep alive. Eight years Elya's junior, Chana too was born in Rypin.[20] Prior to the war, Chana had lived in Lida with her husband Yakov, who according to his brother's testimony had been taken away by train to his death. Mascha, born in Lida on December 8, 1941,[21] was her paternal grandmother's namesake.[22]

Although the Soviet authorities attempted to persuade Elya and family to remain in Novogrudok following liberation with offers of better housing, he writes that even if he'd wished to stay, "there was no one to stay for." Together, he, Chaya Sara, Chana, and little Mascha were repatriated to Poland.[23]

After Elya and Chana's wedding in Lodz, the group continued their wanderings. Following a one-year stay in the Polish city of Szczecin, they spent around eight weeks in the Schlactensee Displaced Persons Camp in Berlin, then on to Hanover, and then to the Eshwege DP

Camp, where once again, Elya worked as a tailor. At the end of 1947,[24] Chaya Sara remained behind in Eshwege[25] while Elya and his new family moved on to the port of Marseilles, France. There they awaited a ship to bring them to their final destination of Palestine.[26]

It was during the one-year wait in Marseilles that Elya and Chana's one child together was born.[27] Chaim in Hebrew means life, the ultimate name to be given their son by parents who had suffered such painful, tragic losses.

After boarding and then being removed from an unseaworthy ship, six days later, the four Berkowicz family members set out at last for the Promised Land. By May 15, 1948, nearing the end of the journey, Elya rejoiced at being among the first legal immigrants to the newly declared State of Israel.[28]

Settling in Tel Aviv, Elya opened his own tailor shop on Nachlat Binyamin Street, where he designed and sewed high-end suits and women's coats. Reportedly distraught at the death of his cousin Shalom Yitzchak, born in Palestine in 1938, to whom he had grown very close, Eliyahu is said to have died of heartbreak several days later on February 6, 1967.[29]

Eliyahu Berkowicz's step-daughter Mascha Dalva gave a talk about her early childhood in the Naliboki Forest on Israeli Holocaust Day, 2023, in her senior residence in the Israeli city of Ramat Gan. Little did she know that in the audience sat a friend of Asaela Bielski Weinstein, a friend of the author and the daughter of Asael Bielski, one of the Bielski brothers. A visit with Asaela was soon arranged so that she could find out more about life with the partisans where she and her mother were given refuge after fleeing from Lida. With Asaela immediately calling me to inquire if the name Eliyahu Berkowicz meant anything, my years-long search for Mascha and Chaim Berkowicz came to an end.

In spite of the fact that Mascha was never formally adopted by Eliyahu, she carried his surname prior to her marriage and truly regarded him as her father in all ways. In fact, only in the sixth or seventh grade, while overhearing her mother speaking on the phone, did she accidentally learn that Elya was not her biological father when her mother told a friend that she had searched for a husband who would be a good father to her.

And a wonderful father he was. Mascha cannot use enough superlatives in describing Elya's parenting of her, describing him as an "angel," the "best friend" who made her wedding, bought her an apartment, and surprised her with all the furnishings. She recalls the beautiful coats and outfits that he would lovingly make for every one of her birthdays, before surprising her by leaving them on her bed. In summing up the kind of father he was to her, Mascha describes Elya as having been a "super-dad," one that "any child could only wish for."

Five and a half years old at the time of Chaim's birth, Mascha recalls her brother's circumcision ceremony as having been a truly joyous occasion for Elya, who was overjoyed to have a son. Although not knowing at the time that Elya had lost three daughters, she recalls often having seen his eyes cloud with tears when encountering groups of young children playing in the street.[30]

During the years of my search for Mascha and her brother Chaim, every single person with the name Chaim Berkowicz listed in the Israeli telephone directory was called. There was no way of knowing that Chaim had Hebraicized his surname to Barkan. Only after speaking to Mascha was I able to contact him. Reported by both his children to have never uttered a word about his experiences during the war, Elya also did not reveal the existence of the lengthy Yiddish-language written testimony he gave to Yad Vashem. The little that they knew, they knew from their mother. The existence of the Yad Vashem testimony was only made known to them in the course of their conversations with me, about seventy-five years after it was recorded.[31]

Reflecting on Elya's life, Chaim, a retired colonel in the Israeli Air Force, recalls having grown up with a sense of wonder. Even as a child, he often asked himself how his father, who suffered and witnessed so much, could possibly have been "so normal," so bereft of bitterness, so generous. Willing to extend help to anyone in need, Elya is reported to have even helped Tuvia Bielski purchase tickets to the United States for his family upon their departure from Israel.

Chaim also speaks of his father as having been a wonderful parent, equally generous to both Mascha and himself. Like Mascha, he too never suspected that Elya might not be his sister's biological parent and recalls being terribly upset when told by the son of a family friend at the age of twelve that she was really his half sibling.

Eliyahu (Elya) Berkowicz, Israel, 1960 (courtesy of Yad Vashem Archives, Jerusalem)

The extent to which Elya saved the life of Chaya Sara Luska, his only surviving family member during the war, is only now revealed to Chaim. He never knew that his father, in spite of having been a tunnel digger, never actually escaped through the tunnel with the others in order to join Chaya Sara in the hiding place provided by Shmuel Kolachek (#82). Nor did he know that, after eight days of hiding and crawling out of a hole in the fence, he literally carried her to the forest, aided by the others in their group. This generosity on Elya's part toward his younger sister is reported to have continued till her last day of life. Although Chaya Sara officially lived in Kiryat Motzkin, her last years were spent mostly in the three-room Tel Aviv apartment Elya shared with his family and the sewing machines he used for his trade.

In spite of Elya's initial reluctance to immigrate to Israel, he took great pride in the fact that, like Tsafi Erez, the step-daughter of escapee Natan Yankelevich (#84), his family was one of the very first to arrive in the new state on May 15, 1948, aboard the SS *Kedma*, the very first ship to carry the Israeli flag.

While expressing regret that he never inquired about his father's prewar life while he was alive, Chaim is emotional as he learns for the first time the names not only of his three sisters, but those of his two murdered aunts and his father's first wife.[32]

Eliyahu Berkowicz, who loved children as much as he loved life, would be proud of his five grandchildren and eleven great-grandchildren,[33] who can now learn about his legacy and his part in digging the tunnel for one of the greatest escapes of the Holocaust.

Zisel Rozin (#50)

Born in Novogrudok on May 15, 1912, Zisel Rozin was the son of Meir and Esther née Bielski.[1] His formal education consisted of four years, from the ages of seven to eleven, in Novogrudok's Yiddish Folk Shul.[2] Prior to the war, he worked as a tailor and resided with his wife Beila née Berkovitz[3] at 4 Krasnaya Street in Novogrudok.[4] We do not know if the couple had children. A postwar Red Cross record notes that Zisel served two stints in the Polish Army, beginning with a post in Baronovich from 1935 to 1937. His second term of duty, which began in March 1939, culminated in his capture by the German Army and incarceration in the prisoner of war camp at Dzialdow, Poland, from October 1939 to January 1940.[5]

We are unaware of the circumstances by which both Zisel and Beila were conscripted to the Novogrudok forced labor camp. Beila was among the estimated 250 women[6] slaughtered on May 7, 1943, just outside the camp, in full sight of the horrified inmates.[7]

Although Zisel's name appears on the tunnel breakout escape list, he was one of a group of five who did not escape through the tunnel, but lay in hiding in the camp until several days after the nearly 240 fellow inmates had fled. Yisrael Kolachek (#81) had helped construct a

well-hidden loft as a refuge for his father Shmuel (#82) and for Zisel's
sister-in-law Chaya Sara Luska, (#168) for fear that the two, both ill
with heart conditions, would not survive the treacherous tunnel escape.
Ultimately, Zisel joined them in hiding, along with his brother-in-law
Eliyahu Berkowicz (#49).

For eight full days, these five inmates took cover in the loft,
which had been equipped with water, blankets, and basic provisions.[8] When at last they were convinced that no German guards
remained in the area, the group dared to venture out and exit the
camp through a hole in the barbed wire used by the police to trade
with the inmates.[9]

As they made their treacherous journey through the Naliboki Forest
to the Bielski partisan detachment, Yisrael Kolachek cites the assistance given to the inmates by the local peasant Konstanty Kozlowski.[10]
Nicknamed "Koscik," Kozlowski learned the Yiddish language as well
as the shoemaking trade from having lived with a Jewish shoemaker
as a boy. Hating the Germans and their murderous anti-Semitism,
Koslowski opened his home to runaway Jews, providing them with
shelter, food, and guidance to reach the partisans. Often, Jews and
partisans would meet in Kozlowski's *hutor* or isolated farmhouse, from
where they were led to safety.[11] Yisrael recalls being sheltered for a
night by Kozlowski along with Zisel Rozin and the other loft stowaways. From there, Kozlowski moved them to another safe house. It
was from the second house that secure transfer to the Bielski partisans
was arranged for the escapees one week later, all thanks to Kozlowski,
who has since been recognized as Righteous Among the Nations by
Yad Vashem.[12]

Zisel Rozin remained with the Bielski partisan detachment for
ten months until liberation of the area. According to International
Red Cross records, Zisel was drafted into the Russian Army immediately after leaving the partisans. Upon discharge in January 1946,
Zisel returned to Poland. After approximately half a year in Lodz, he
moved to Germany. Here Zisel took refuge for several months in a

displaced persons camp in Berlin, before being transferred to the Ulm Displaced Persons Camp[13] in the Stuttgart District of the American zone.[14]

In a 1948 application for assistance, Zisel requested to be reunited with his sister, whom he noted was living in Buenos Aires, Argentina, and had agreed to support him.[15] However, by July 1951, records show that Zisel was living in the Pierre Hotel in Paris. In Paris, he registered with the Jewish Joint Distribution Committee for immigration to the United States.[16]

On August 14, 1953, Zisel Rozin departed from the French port of Le Havre on the SS *United States* bound for New York City.[17] The largest passenger ship ever built in the US, the SS *United States* sailed at the impressive top speed of forty-two knots per hour.[18] While other refugees suffered greatly during two-week journeys to the US on overcrowded military transport ships, Zisel swept into the New York harbor after only four days at sea. A Miami, Florida, address was listed for him on the ship's manifest,[19] making it probable that Zisel's passage on the luxury ship was sponsored by a relative living in Florida at the time.

Unfortunately, following his immigration, Zisel's tracks were lost. Variations of the surname Rozin are common, and there is a high probability that Zisel changed his first name upon reaching American shores; we have thus not been able to determine his identity in the United States. What is clear is that his destination listed on the ship's manifest, a fashionable Lincoln Road, Miami, address,[20] must certainly have been a far cry from the garbage-strewn loft he once inhabited in the Novogrudok forced labor camp. We can only hope that Zisel was able to rebuild his life.

Jankef (Yakov) Nevachovich (#51)

According to fellow escapee Fanya Dunetz (#142), Yakov Nevachovich was a barber from Novogrudok who did not survive the tunnel escape.[1] Unfortunately, we have no details regarding Yakov's parents' names or his date of birth.

In our quest to find information on fellow tunnel escapee Sara Zamosczyk (#134), it became apparent that Sara's first husband Efroim Nevachovich (murdered in 1941) was most likely one of Yakov's two brothers. From Sara's recollections recorded by her son Simon Lazowsky, we learned that Efroim's oldest brother – presumably Yakov – was unmarried, but had a "longtime girlfriend."[2]

Yakov and Efroim's younger brother, whose name we do not know, was said to have been taught by Efroim the skills to become a radio technician. As such, at the age of fourteen,[3] this youngster merited to play a very important role in the resistance efforts within the Novogrudok forced labor camp.[4] Employed as a radio technician by Wilhelm Reuter, commander of the Novogrudok forced labor camp, he was issued a work pass that enabled him to enter the forced labor camp.[5] Time and again, he risked his life to sneak electronic components to the camp attic, where he secretly assembled them to create a one-way radio. This makeshift radio enabled the resistance leaders to hear news, primarily the BBC, and to remain informed about the progress of the war.[6]

Along with inmates Mandri, Abram Rakovski (#10), and Berl Yoselevich, Yakov Nevachovich was a deputy head of the group planning the ill-fated armed uprising in the forced labor camp scheduled for April 1943. Yakov was to have led one of the four groups slated to attack the Germans from all four corners of the ghetto during the uprising.[7]

In his Yad Vashem testimony, Shaul Gorodynski (#77) relates how prior to the ultimately cancelled uprising, Yakov Nevachovich and his brother provided their sick, crippled, and aged father, also interned in the camp, with poison (probably morphine) to save him from falling into German hands.[8] Their mother had been murdered earlier by the Nazis as she futilely attempted to save the life of her only grandchild.[9]

Fanya Dunetz recalls that Yakov Nevachovich was the boyfriend of Linka Landau (#140) and that despite his number having been #51 on the escape list, he had joined Linka and her mother Miriam (#139) in crawling through the tunnel. Fanya recalls initially feeling quite fortunate to have been assigned a spot close behind them, mistakenly certain that Nevachovich, a Novogrudok native, would know the terrain and could be followed to safety.[10]

Instead of going in the direction of the partisans, however, a small group, which included Yakov Nevachovich, Linka, Rita Wolozhinski (#71), and her boyfriend, arrived at the Setzo Forest close to town. The following morning, they were discovered by the local police, who then killed the men and brutally raped and tortured the women to death.[11]

Yankef (Yakov) Nevachovich (*far left*) with members of the Novogrudok Maccabi team, 1934–1935 (courtesy of Vallentine Mitchell Publishers)

Yechezkel (Chatzkel) Pozniak (#52)

Born in either 1903[1] or 1905,[2] Yechezkel Pozniak of Ivenets was the son of Akiva (Kivel) and Mariascha née Segalowicz.[3] Prior to the war, he worked in Ivenets as a carpenter.[4]

Records indicate that Yechezkel was incarcerated in the Ivenets ghetto in July 1941 before being transferred to the Novogrudok forced labor camp the following year.[5] In 1943, Yechezkel survived the tunnel escape and the grueling trek through the forest to join the Bielski partisans.[6]

In July 1945, Yechezkel arrived with other refugees to Bologna, Italy, and soon made his home in Villa Emma in the town of Nonantola.[7] Here, prospective immigrants to Palestine were trained for agricultural work in the Nonantola Training Farm in preparation for their arrival to pre-state Israel. Reaching Israel on October 2, 1948,[8] to a country just five months old, Yechezkel eventually married the former Musia Zelikovski, also of Ivenets.[9]

Yechezkel Pozniak died on March 25, 1976, and is buried in the Holon cemetery alongside Musia, who passed away eleven years later. From the inscriptions on their tombstones, it appears that they had no children. Yechezkel's footstone bears the inscription "In memory of the Pozniak and Zelikovski families who were murdered in the Nazi Holocaust in Ivenets, Poland."[10]

Kalman Notkovich (#53)

Born in 1913, Kalman Notkovich was the son of Leizer. Prior to the war, he resided in Karelich, where he worked as a tailor.[1] We know nothing – other than his father's name – of his family of origin or his familial status at the outbreak of the war. We are also unaware of any possible relationship between Kalman Notkovich and fellow Novogrudok forced labor camp inmate Chaim Notkovich of Zhetl.

Kalman survived the tunnel escape and made his way through the forest to successfully reach and join the Bielski partisans' Kalinin Brigade.[2]

Kalman Notkovich's life during the post-liberation period remains a mystery. To date, efforts to obtain information on his whereabouts after the war via an examination of genealogical, Holocaust-related, and population databases have been unsuccessful.

Dov (#54), Frieda (#54a), and Leah (#54b) Wasserman

In a moving oral testimony submitted to Yad Vashem in 2006, Freida Wasserman's son Moshe declared that his mother, his aunt Leah, and his uncle Dov Wasserman had all been murdered in central Poland in 1942.[1] Yet Moshe went to his death in 2017 never knowing that the three had actually lived to escape five hundred miles away to Novogrudok, where they were interned in the forced labor camp and took part in the tunnel escape. In his testimony, Moshe recalls the

close-knit Wasserman clan, which lived and worked together in patri-
arch Tzvi's prosperous business. A merchant, Tzvi owned five acres of
land as well as two large produce warehouses that served farmers in the
area with whom he traded.[2]

Moshe describes how Tzvi and his wife Yutke's spacious wooden
house in Mezrich at 100 Lubelski Street,[3] home to the extended
Wasserman family, was divided into four units, each with separate
entrances. Tzvi and Yutke shared their unit with Dov (Berl), their
youngest child,[4] born in 1917,[5] as well as an orphaned cousin named
Shalom.[6]

In another unit lived Leah,[7] the oldest of the four siblings.[8] Born
in Mezrich in 1910, Leah was the mother of five daughters, who managed her meat business from a shop that was in the front section of the
family compound.[9] The other housing units were occupied by Leah's
younger brother Chuna,[10] his wife Pesia née Grinblat, and their two
children.[11] In addition to working with his father, Chuna also operated a business exporting hog hair to the United States used to manufacture brushes. Tzvi and Yutke's third child, Yeshayahu (Shaya),[12] his
wife Frieda née Goncjaz, and their three children[13] lived in the complex as well.

Frieda and Shaya's son Moshe notes that with all but three thousand of the twenty-one thousand inhabitants of prewar Mezrich being
Jewish, even the non-Jews of the town spoke Yiddish. The Wasserman
family was traditional, attended synagogue on the Sabbath, and
observed kashrut, the Jewish dietary laws.[14]

Moshe, born in 1928, details a childhood characterized by close
contact with the cousins from both sides of his large extended family, who were constantly in each other's homes. The idyllic life of the
Wasserman family came to a tragic halt in 1939 when World War II
broke out and Mezrich was invaded by the German Army. Moshe
reports that although Chuna Wasserman opted to flee with his family
over the border to Russia, Moshe's father Shaya refused to leave his
property.[15]

At the end of 1941, Moshe's mother Frieda was sent on a transport to the Treblinka extermination camp, from which no one was thought to return. Her brother-in-law Dov and sister-in-law Leah were alongside her, yet somehow escaped before being herded onto the transport.

Moshe's testimony relates the heartbreaking details of arriving around the end of 1942 to the dreaded Majdanek concentration camp where he and his father became separated from his twelve-year-old sister Edna,[16] five-year-old brother Tzvi,[17] and a maternal aunt. He could only assume that they were all burned in the camp's crematoria.

Moshe and his beloved father Shaya were later transferred together to Auschwitz, where they arrived on July 8, 1943. Moshe was sent to Birkenau and ordered to join the laborers building Crematorium 4. Shaya was forced to do heavy slave labor in the Buna subcamp of Auschwitz. After Moshe was transferred to the Bergen-Belsen concentration camp, Moshe and Shaya never saw one another again.

Upon liberation on April 15, 1945, Moshe weighed no more than sixty pounds. Following a period of rehabilitation in Sweden, where he joined a group of fellow survivors preparing to immigrate to Palestine, Moshe boarded a ship in February 1947 aiming to break the British embargo on entering Mandate Palestine. Unfortunately, the illegal immigration ship was discovered and ordered to Cyprus, where the refugees were held in a detention camp. Moshe finally reached Palestine in March 1948,[18] just two months before statehood.

As mentioned, following the war, Moshe submitted Yad Vashem Pages of Testimony attesting to the deaths of his mother Frieda and uncle Dov Wasserman, having had no idea that they had indeed reached the Novogrudok forced labor camp. Other relatives living in Israel erroneously filed testimony for the deaths of Leah Wasserman in Treblinka[19] and Dov Ber Wasserman in Mezrich.[20]

To date, we do not know how Frieda, Leah, and Dov Wasserman survived after the deaths of their spouses and children, or even how they came together during the horrific massacres and deportations imposed on the Jewish community of Mezrich. As for how, when, and why Leah,

Dov, and Frieda made the perilous journey several hundred miles to Novogrudok, it is probable that they came as refugees from central Poland following the German invasion of the area in September 1939.

Although we are unaware of the nature of the skills that Frieda and Leah claimed to have had in order to be conscripted to the labor camp, Dov was assigned to the shoemakers' workshop. In his Yad Vashem testimony, fellow escapee and former Judenrat chairman Daniel Ostashinski writes, "I would like to mention the cobbler Vasserman, who saw the tunnel as his life's mission and gave it the best part of his time, strength and initiative. Every new meter which was dug lit a spark in his eyes."[21]

Sadly, Leah, Dov, and Frieda Wasserman appear to have all been killed following the tunnel escape. None is listed in the compilation of Jewish partisans in Belorussia.[22]

After a lengthy search, the children of Moshe – the grandchildren of Frieda and the great-nieces and nephew of Dov and Leah – were located in southern Israel. In emotional telephone interviews, the namesakes of Moshe's murdered family members, Shai (named for Shaya) Vaserman, Shlomit Frieda Adivi, and Edna Aronada were all informed that their grandmother, great-aunt, and great-uncle did not die passively in 1942, but met their deaths fighting bravely for their lives crawling through a handmade tunnel in a far-off place none had ever heard of.[23]

Moshe's children attest to his firm desire to "have a happy home," thus he did not share his own harrowing Holocaust experiences with them or with his grandchildren until shortly before his death in 2017.

As of this writing in May 2020, Moshe's wife Rachel, a Holocaust survivor from Romania, lives in a Beersheva retirement home. Moshe, a development contractor by trade who planned and built foundations and roads,[24] had replicated his own childhood experiences in Mezrich by having two of his three children living alongside his home, where the nine grandchildren and eight great-grandchildren he lived to see[25] could roam freely and happily among their cousins. Had he been aware of his mother, aunt, and uncle's courageous attempt to survive, he would have surely been proud.

Aaron Jakubowski (#55)

"You have the wrong person," insisted Pinchas, son of Aaron Jakubowski, when located and contacted for information about his father. Adamant that his father had never participated in an escape, Pinchas ("Pini") was ready to cautiously trust the reliability of the data on his father's Holocaust experiences only after the author revealed the names of his paternal grandparents and offered to send copies of all the research documents discovered. "My father died when I was only twelve years old," he said emotionally. "This information is about the father I never knew."[1]

In the course of several conversations, Pini learned that his father's birthplace was not Lodz, as he'd thought, but a small village called Lubien Kujawski[2] some forty-six miles north-north-west of Lodz.[3] He also learned for the first time that his father was one of eleven siblings born to Pinchas and Ruchla née Gajc. Pini's brothers and sisters were Estera, Baruch, Tauba, Perla, Chil, Rosa, Sholom, Sucher, Leah (Lola), and Yona.[4] Other than Yona, who immigrated to Israel before the war, and Leah, who survived the Holocaust and settled in Israel,[5] Pini had never heard of his murdered aunts and uncles. Although Shlomo Okonski (#89), a Novogrudok forced labor camp escapee and member of a nearby moshav, had made persistent efforts to tell Pini how his armed father had fought Nazis in the forest, Pini had dismissed this portrayal of Aaron. It did not at all fit with the image of the sickly, physically weak man Pini recalls as his father.[6]

Born in 1897,[7] Aaron had been married before the war to Itta, who was killed in the Lodz ghetto[8] together with their three-year-old daughter.[9] While Red Cross documents indicate that Aaron was an inmate in the Wlodaw ghetto in 1939, we do not know how he became a refugee in Novogrudok by 1941 or became interned in the Novogrudok forced labor camp one year later.[10]

After surviving the breakout, Aaron joined the 106th Jewish partisan detachment under the command of Zorin,[11] who like Tuvia Bielski accepted every Jew, regardless of physical condition. There Aaron met his second wife, Sara née Goldin, born in 1920 in Minsk, who became an economic planner by profession.[12]

Having married in the forest, Aaron and Sara went to Minsk during the early post-liberation period to join several members of Sara's family who had survived the war.[13] According to Red Cross files, by 1946, the couple was being given aid in Italy[14] after a futile attempt to sail through the British blockade of immigration to Palestine.[15] That year, their first child, Shoshana, was born in a displaced persons camp in the Turin area.[16]

Although documents indicate that Aaron and Sara also requested to immigrate to Australia, Shoshana notes that Aaron insisted on immigrating to Israel, where he would no longer live among anti-Semitic non-Jews. Thus, the couple finally arrived in the newly established State of Israel in 1949,[17] perhaps sailing from the displaced persons camp in Senigallia, Italy, that Aaron listed for the American Joint Distribution Committee as his address in March of that year.[18]

Early life in Israel was hard for Aaron and Sara, a situation that unfortunately did not improve greatly with the years. After the birth of Pini in 1951, there were four mouths to feed. Supporting the family was difficult due to Aaron's severe heart condition, attributed to the war, which eventually became fatal. Despite his illness, however, Aaron made every effort, no matter how physically taxing, to feed his family. They had settled on Moshav Tzofit in central Israel, where his efforts included grueling agricultural work, arduous labor in a tire factory, poultry raising, and even working on Israel's National Water Carrier project in the early 1960s, laying the foundations to bring water from the Sea of Galilee to the center and south of the country.[19]

Pini remembers Aaron as having been an extremely loving and affectionate parent, who never spoke about the war years. Pini is certain that although his father died of complications of open-heart surgery in 1962, the true cause of death was a broken heart in the emotional sense. Besides having expressed his painful feeling of failure as a bread-winner, Aaron was keenly hurt by the insensitivity of established Israelis who often blamed Holocaust victims for having gone "like sheep to the slaughter."

Aaron Jakubowski was only fifty-two at his death. Sara remained alive an additional thirty years and supported the children through her work in hospital management.[20]

Pini continues to live on Moshav Tzofit. An agriculturist by profession, he works as an agricultural adviser in Angola, frequently returning for visits to Israel to see his wife Ruthi, his four children, and his grandchildren.[21]

Shoshana is a retired nurse and the mother of two married children, each of whom are parents of two children.[22]

For several years, Pini remained somewhat skeptical of his father's participation in the tunnel escape and continued to ponder whether we had a case of mistaken identity. Shoshana, however, was more accepting, acknowledging that she grew up in a house where "no one spoke," certainly not about the Holocaust. She did, however, express regret at never having asked questions while she had the chance.[23]

In January 2024, five and a half years after I last spoke with Pini Jakubowski, I not only received a photo of his father forwarded to me through Yanek Okonski, the son of his father's good friend Shlomo Okonski (#89), but also news that Pini has finally come to terms with his father's past as well as with his own identity. Having recently returned from a visit to his father's birthplace in Poland, he now looks forward to visiting the site of the Novogrudok forced labor camp, where he now acknowledges that his father's flight to freedom took place.[24]

If Aaron were alive in September 2023, he would be the grandfather of six as well as the great-grandfather of seven. Perhaps he would have even felt successful.[25]

Aaron Jakubowski and his first wife Itta, undated prewar photo
(courtesy of Pini Jakubowski)

Distiler (#56)

While the precise order was carefully formulated for the 240-odd men, women, and children to line up for the tunnel breakout, the chief organizers were acutely pressured by time. Thus, nearly eight decades later, the original escape list lamentably lacks basic details to enable us to determine the identity of certain inmates. Such is the case for the fifty-sixth man or woman in line, whose name appears simply as "Distiler," without a proper name or even an initial.

Yad Vashem's Central Database of Shoah Victims' Names contains sixty-eight citations for individuals from Poland with the surname Distiler. Since a significant number of inmates in the Novogrudok forced labor camp hailed from Novogrudok and the vicinity, we first examined the records for a Distiler from this region. However, not one such record was to be found in this database,[1] nor did any Distiler appear on the necrology list of the *Novogrudok Memorial Book*.[2]

A closer examination of the sixty-eight Distiler sources listed in Yad Vashem's database indicated that the great majority hailed from central Poland. Thus, it is entirely possible that the Distiler appearing on the Novogrudok forced labor camp escape list was a refugee from areas occupied by the Germans as early as 1939.

Unfortunately, as no one with the surname Distiler is included in the compilation of Jewish partisans in Belorussia,[3] the likelihood is that the man or woman who appears on the escape list did not survive the tunnel breakout.

Wolff (Velvel) Borowski (#57)

Wolff (Velvel) Borowski escaped from the Novogrudok forced labor camp together with two of his seven siblings, Aaron (#58) and Sheina Nignevitcky (#131). All three survived the tunnel escape to reach the Bielski partisan detachment.

At the age of ninety-three, some five years prior to his death in 2013, Velvel completed the following testimony for a book honoring Jewish immigrants to Melbourne, Australia.[1] A testament to his tenacity, optimism, and determination to survive, it is also a love story. Here are Velvel's eloquent words:

I was born in 1915 in Zelechov, a Polish shtetl located halfway between Warsaw and Lublin. Zelechov was a small impoverished township with a population of ten thousand people, seven thousand of them Jewish. I was one of eight brothers and sisters and although my parents, Yosel and Raisel Borowski, cared for us very much, we were poor, and life was tough. We grew up in a house we shared with my parents' cousins, Velvul and Sura Oshlack, and the two families got on very well. Ours was a traditional and very religious household, observing all the festivals and Shabbat. My father and Uncle Velvul made the uppers of shoes, but I was apprenticed to a tailor at the age of ten.

In the 1930s, my family moved to Novogrudok, a regional town in Belarus, 150 km [90 miles] west of Minsk. We had family living there and they told us to come, because there was more work and business opportunities. Furthermore, it offered a large choice of theater, movies, concerts and other social and cultural activities. Our family had a sandal factory where they made 15,000 pairs of leather sandals a year, all of which were sold over the summer.

My wife, Judy (Yussel) was born in 1917 to Moishe and Chana Berkowich in Karelich, a small town near Novogrudok. She grew up, like me, together with seven brothers and sisters and had a happy childhood. It was possible for a Jewish girl to get a good education in Karelich, and Judy, an excellent student, stayed at school up to year 8. During her teenage years she was a member of Hashomer Hatzair, a Zionist youth movement. The family fortunes changed after her father died of pneumonia in 1937, leaving her mother to bring up the family alone. Judy began working as a dressmaker, later moving to Novogrudok to work and live with an aunt.

We were married on December 17, 1940. I was twenty-five and Judy twenty-three. I considered myself a lucky man. She was very pretty, kind and clever. Six months after our wedding, on July 4, 1941, the Nazis occupied Novogrudok and anti-Jewish persecution began immediately. On July 26th, many Jewish men were rounded up by the local police and brought to the center of the marketplace. As an orchestra played, fifty-two were randomly selected and shot by the SS. My brother-in-law Shtasek Botakovich was one of them, and my sister Chana had to clean up the site where her husband had been murdered.

Soon after, the Germans established a ghetto which housed over ten thousand Jews from the surrounding areas. There was starvation, all manner of deprivation and constant random murders. There were two major "actions," or massacres, where nine thousand people were murdered – the first on December 8, 1941, in Skrydlevo, and the second on August 7, 1942, in Litovka. Many of my family members were killed there. After the massacres, the remaining Jews, many of them skilled tradesmen, were relocated from the ghetto to a work camp located at the regional courthouse buildings.

Meanwhile, in the nearby forests, a Jewish partisan group led by the Bielski brothers was providing safe haven for any Jew irrespective of health, age or gender. Any Jewish person who could reach them in the forest was taken in. They were over three hundred strong at the time and growing increasingly active week by week. Word of their existence soon spread to the ghetto and people dreamed of escaping, knowing there was somewhere to hide.

On December 22, 1942, Judy and I, together with thirteen others, decided to escape. It was in the middle of winter, and our plan was to act immediately to take advantage of the bitter cold. The ghetto gates were opened every evening to let in some trucks. Because of the icy conditions, the guards chose to stay inside the warmth of their guardhouse. Judy managed to escape with the others, but I became paralyzed with fear and was left behind.

I was in despair believing that I had ruined my only chance to get out, and even more so because I didn't know if Judy was safe. The escape, in fact, had been successful. After walking in heavy snow, sometimes waist-deep and wading through icy waters, Judy and the other escapees reached the nearby Naliboki Forest. They joined the Bielski partisans and, to her joy, Judy was reunited with two brothers and two sisters who had survived all the massacres. Judy often recalled the moment she first met the partisan leader Tuvia Bielski. He rode up to her on a white horse, dismounted and put his arm around her, saying, "Don't worry, I'll look after you."

Back in the ghetto, I was one of the three hundred Jews who remained alive after a third massacre, which occurred on May 7, 1943. Only too aware of our eventual fate, a mass escape was planned. We decided to dig a tunnel starting at our sleeping quarters. They had previously been the stables. The tunnel would go under the barbed wire fence and lead to the surrounding wheat fields, making it over 250 meters (820 yards) long and one meter (just over a yard) deep.

Digging started in May 1943. A secret trapdoor was hinged under a lower bunk, and we used timber from the walls and bunks as supports. A trolley system was employed to move out the displaced dirt as the tunnel progressed. The earth was placed in cloth bags made from our blankets, and then hidden in false walls and in the stable loft. An inmate who was an electrician set up a lighting system in the tunnel so that we could work at night. Digging tools were made in the ghetto's metal workshop and extra timber was stolen from around the camp. This was particularly dangerous, because anyone caught stealing was immediately hanged. We were famished and exhausted, but the diggers worked with feverish haste, knowing that time was against them.

The tunnel was never discovered because the work in the ghetto workshops was never neglected, so the output never dropped. In addition, the sanitary conditions within the sleeping quarters were so appalling that the guards never entered, leaving us to dig in secret.

The date set for the escape was Sunday, September 26, 1943, about five months after we started the tunnel. An order of escape had been organized, with the diggers the first to go through, followed by five armed men. A ballot was held to decide the order of the remaining escapees. I was number 174,[2] followed by my brother Aaron and sister Shayndel. The night we chose was cloudy and stormy. It was arranged that the power was to be cut to the camp's searchlight and some nails were to be removed from the tin roof so that it would rattle in the wind, distracting attention away from the breakout.

Of the 250 Jews who escaped that night, only 170 reached the forest and the Bielski partisans. Many were shot, others became disoriented and lost, while some were arrested over the next few days and subsequently killed. I made it to the forest, where I was reunited with Judy after nine months of separation. Finding each other again seemed truly a miracle. To be in the remarkable Jewish partisan group was the second miracle. It gave us back our dignity and hope. Although we were fearful of German attacks, we lived as free people in control of our own lives.

The forest base of the Bielski partisans developed into a little town, with semi-subterranean dugout rooms housing a bakery, a salami-producing factory, shoe, tailoring and engineering workshops and later, a tannery. Partisans from all over the region came to the Bielski camp to repair their guns, shoes and uniforms, and exchange flour for bread and cows for salami. I worked as a tailor, the trade I excelled in.

Many of the men had firearms and fought the Germans in guerrilla-style warfare, and also went out on missions to get food supplies from surrounding farmers and peasants.

You may ask why the Germans did not just come in and clean us out. Although we were under constant threat, there were a number of circumstances in our favor. It was our good fortune to be in the Naliboki Forest, which is one of the largest in Europe and very dense and difficult to traverse. There are also many swampy and marshy areas. This made it difficult for the armored vehicles of the German Army to get very far. Without such protection, it was very dangerous for them to venture into the forest, as many partisan groups in the region were armed and familiar with the terrain. Secondly, we were lucky with our outstanding commanders. They were brilliant strategists and knew how to mould the ever-increasing number of desperate men, women and children seeking their protection into a tightly disciplined and effective unit for survival.

The Germans did mount a major military offensive, from July to September 1943, codenamed Operation Hermann. There were always guards posted at the edge of the camp. So when they heard the Germans coming, the whole camp consisting of over eight hundred people was led deeper into the forest. There were many partisan casualties but most of the Jews escaped through swamps and rivers without any losses. Judy always recalled how she was frequently up to her chin in water, but never caught a cold.

I came to the forest after Operation Hermann. There were no other large incursions after that, because the Germans were by then losing the war in Russia. Even so, we still had to frequently move bases and start over again, hiding any evidence of habitation in the forest.

Our family group of nine people lived with the Bielski partisans until we were liberated by the Russians on June 16, 1944. Over 1,230 Jews walked out of the forest that day. Among them were Judy and me, her two brothers and two sisters and my surviving brother and two sisters. There is no doubt that we all owed our lives to the remarkable Bielskis.

After our liberation, the Russian Army conscripted all the able-bodied men to assist in the ongoing battles against the Germans. I was conscripted and again was separated from my wife. I was attached to a tank maintenance and repair unit, about 40 km [25 miles] behind the battlefront, where I worked as a tailor for the unit.

In 1946, with the war truly over, I was still in the unit, which was then stationed outside Vladivostok. Because of my Polish birth, I was demoted, and I traveled by the Trans-Siberian railway back to Poland. When I arrived in Lodz, I found my brother Aaron. He had lost his wife and two children in the ghetto, but had recently remarried another survivor, Hella.

The JDC relief organization had lists in various towns telling people where other surviving family and friends were. I traveled to Germany to a displaced persons camp, finding my sister Shayndel, and old friends from Zelechov whom I had not seen for many years. Traveling through different countries was dangerous and illegal. But with very little money, I managed to get to Austria and then smuggled myself across the Alps by night into Italy.

After eighteen months of separation, I was again reunited with my beloved Judy. I located her in a displaced persons camp outside Turin. We lived in very poor conditions in the camp for nearly three years. Work was scarce and we had very little money, but we had each other. In 1947, our beautiful daughter Annette was born. Everyone in the camp wanted to leave Europe and start a new life. Our brothers and sisters went to Israel, Rhodesia, Brazil, and the United States. Judy and I came to Australia because my cousin Gedalia Oshlack, a son of the family I originally lived with in Zelechov, had come to Melbourne before the war. My brother Aaron and his wife were already there.

We arrived in Melbourne in 1949 and immediately began to work. It was a wonderful feeling to start living a normal life again. In 1950, our son Jack was born. Many of my old childhood friends from Zelechov who had moved to Melbourne became our closest friends. We tried to replace, for each other, the families scattered all over the world or those we had lost during the Holocaust.

Australia has been a wonderful land for us. We had freedom, the possibility to prosper and to bring up a family in a free society. It has truly been a lucky country for us, a place where our dignity has been restored after living through the horrors of a horrific war.

We took great pleasure in seeing our children grow into good people and successful and proud Jewish-Australians. My beloved Judy passed away in April 2006 and I miss her dearly. We had been a devoted and loving couple for over sixty-five wonderful years. Today, I am surrounded by my children, six grandchildren and six great-grandchildren, all of whom keep me very active and involved in their activities. They make life worth living, even though I am now in my ninety-fourth year.

Who would have dared to believe, during my darkest times, that I would survive to enjoy so much happiness? I am truly the luckiest man in the world!

The perennial tailor, Velvel continued to work in this profession in Australia. His wife Judy, a seamstress in Poland, pursued this occupation as well after immigrating to Melbourne.[3]

Velvel Borowski passed away on March 11, 2013. According to his son Jack, a dentist, Velvel was alert and active until the last few months of his life, remaining optimistic until his last day. His daughter Annette is now a retired teacher.[4] Velvel is remembered by his grandson David, a physical therapist who lives in Israel, as "a good golfer, the most positive person I've ever met, someone to whom money meant nothing and who would do anything for his family."[5]

Wolff Borowski during his Russian Army service, 1944–1946 (courtesy of Jack Borowski)

If Velvel Borowski were alive as of this writing in August 2023, he would have six grandchildren and seventeen great-grandchildren – ten from Annette's three children and seven from Jack's three children.[6] He would have been most proud.

Aaron Borowski (#58)

According to Aaron's nephew, Dr. Jack M. Borowski of Victoria, Australia, Aaron was the oldest child of Yosef and Raisel Borowski. Born in Zelechov, Poland, in 1904, Aaron worked there as a shoemaker.[1] After his marriage to Chiena née Izraelit,[2] the couple settled in Novogrudok around 1930, where the remainder of the Borowski family later followed.[3]

Jack Borowski recalls his father Velvel (Wolff, #57) describing his sister-in-law Chiena as having been capable and clever. Both she and Aaron worked in the sandal business prior to the war. On August 7, 1942, Chiena and the couple's two children Masha and Favel were murdered in Litovka.[4]

Aaron Borowski, Melbourne, Australia, mid-to late 1970s (courtesy of Jack Borowski)

Thanks to his skills as a shoemaker, Aaron was spared death to be assigned to the Novogrudok forced labor camp, along with his younger brother Velvel and sister Sheina Nignevitcky (#131). Miraculously, all three survived the tunnel escape. Records in the National Archive of the Republic of Belarus chronicle their arrival at the Bielski detachment in September 1943.[5] In the compilation of 7,742 Jews who were in the Belarusian partisan movement from 1941 to 1944, "Aron Yoselevich Borowski" is listed as having been a member of the Bielski partisan detachment.[6]

In a memoir, Velvel Borowski writes of his return to Poland following the war. In 1946, he reached Lodz, where he was reunited with his brother Aaron, who had recently married a fellow Holocaust survivor named Hela (later Helen).[7] Records from the Joint Distribution Committee indicate that on September 2, 1948, forty-three-year-old Aaron immigrated to Melbourne, Australia, via a flight from Brussels.[8] The file lists his sponsor as "Oshlack," whom Velvel identifies as Gedalia Oshlack, a family friend from Zelechov who had settled in Melbourne prior to the war. Wolff and Judy later followed Aaron and Hela to settle in Melbourne as well.

Aaron lived in Melbourne until his death in 1982.[9] According to his nephew, Aaron never recovered from the loss of his family. He had no children with Helen and remained "a very sorrowful man all his life."[10]

Ita Bitenski (#59)

Ita Bitenski née Pinchuk was born in Nowa Mysz in 1898. The daughter of Moshe and Sheina,[1] she was married to Avraham, a merchant who was born in the same town in 1895.[2]

Prior to the war, the couple lived in Baranovich with their four children,[3] including Moshe, born in 1922,[4] Khil, born in 1924,[5] and Sheinda,[6] her maternal grandmother's namesake, born in 1934.

In a Yad Vashem Page of Testimony, Ita's niece notes that Avraham, Ita, and their children were all murdered in Baranovich in 1942.[7] Yet unbeknownst to her relatives, Ita remained alive and was interned in the Novogrudok forced labor camp, where she was assigned place #59 on the escape list to flee through the tunnel on September 26, 1943.

Regretfully, Ita Bitenski's name does not appear in the compilation of Jewish partisans in Belorussia. Thus Ita, the last survivor of her immediate family, apparently did not survive the tunnel escape.[8]

Herman Kritz (#60)

Herman (later Harry) Kritz was born Gregorz Kric in November 1910 in Tarnopol, Poland,[1] today in Ukraine. Herman was orphaned of his mother at the age of twelve and then left completely on his own at age seventeen when his father David and older siblings Yehuda and Malka immigrated to Palestine. Alex Kritz, Herman's son, surmises that his father's Communist, non-Zionist ideology dictated the youthful Herman's decision to remain behind alone.[2]

At some point before the war, Herman moved to Novogrudok, where he married and had a daughter. Though his wife's identity is unknown, Yad Vashem's Central Database of Shoah Victims' Names shows a Musia Kritz on a 1941 list of Novogrudok residents, the sole female with the surname Kritz.[3] For his part, Alex never recalls Herman speaking of his first wife and daughter, whose existence he only discovered in 1987, when Herman dictated an affidavit for German reparations.

In autumn of 1939, following the German and Soviet invasion of Poland, Herman was drafted into the Polish Army and ordered to the Soviet border. Within weeks, the Polish Army was defeated, enabling Herman to take advantage of the ensuing chaos to make his way back on foot to Novogrudok to his wife and infant daughter.[4]

Following the Soviet invasion of Novogrudok, the Germans wrenched control of the city in July 1941. Alex describes the terrifying dilemma that the couple, now confined to the Novogrudok ghetto, faced in their desperate attempt to save their child's life from an upcoming Nazi raid. The two had made careful plans to hide the little girl with non-Jewish friends. Speculating that his father's first wife may have been a nurse, Alex learned from him that she'd administered a sedative to the child to keep her asleep and enable her rescue by their friends after Herman and his wife were rounded up by the Nazis. Yet tragically, the sedative failed to take effect, and the child awoke crying just as the Nazis were searching the building.[5] Gathered with their neighbors on the street below, Herman and his wife watched in horror as their child was discovered by the Germans and hurled to her death from the window of their upper-story apartment. Shortly after this tragedy, the Germans forcibly separated the couple. Herman was never to see his wife again and could only assume that she had been murdered in the subsequent mass liquidation of the Novogrudok ghetto.[6]

In August 1942, Herman was assigned to the Novogrudok forced labor camp, probably by utilizing his past experience as an amateur boxer to present himself as being capable of hard labor.[7] No information has come to light regarding Herman's experiences in the Bielski partisan detachment, to which he fled following the tunnel escape. While his son recalls him having mentioned serving as a partisan, Herman did not specify the Bielski unit by name. In 2008, eleven years after his father's death, Alex recalls watching the Hollywood film *Defiance* without ever imagining that the movie depicted his father's wartime experiences.

Herman did speak of his service in the Red Army, to which he was drafted after liberation from the forest, where he attained the rank of sergeant or lieutenant. Propitiously, he was among the first Russian troops to enter and capture Berlin. Many years later, Alex still recalls his father's amusement when, as a child, he traded Herman's hard-earned military medals for some baseball cards in a game with a friend.[8]

In 1946, Herman returned to Novogrudok, where he married a woman with a past as tragic as his own. A former partisan had introduced him to Berta (later Bertha) née Portnoy, born in 1921 in the Belarusian town of Bobrusk, who was staying with relatives in Novogrudok following the war. Alex reports that as Herman's first act of courtship to woo Bertha, he brought a bag of potatoes for her and her relatives. The couple were married within several days of their first meeting.[9]

Prior to the war, Berta had been married to a first cousin. The couple had lived in Minsk, where her husband was soon drafted into the Red Army. As the German Army advanced swiftly into Russian territory, Berta, now far along in her first pregnancy, made the decision to join her mother and younger sister in their home in Bobryck. Urgently hoping that her husband would be granted a brief furlough from the front to visit her, Bertha delayed her departure to Bobryck until the last possible moment. Finally onboard the train bound for Bobryck, she neared the city simultaneously with the German Army's advance. From the approaching train, Bertha heard explosions and actually saw German paratroopers landing. In an effort to avoid the

Germans, the train conductor never stopped, but sped past Bobrusk to travel deeper east. Bertha, nearing delivery of her first baby, descended the train somewhere in Siberia. Here she boarded with a family that she described as anti-Semitic, who treated her with callousness and cruelty. In the midst of this chaotic nightmare, she lost her infant son to illness and malnourishment when he was just several months old. During this period, Bertha learned that her husband had been killed at the front.

At the end of the war, when she was finally able to reach Bobrusk, Bertha discovered from neighbors that her mother and sister had been betrayed by town residents who had once been friends. The two women were seen being marched naked through the streets along with other Jews, taken to an outlying area where they were forced to dig their graves before being shot. Alex recalls that till her dying day, Berta was plagued by guilt for having waited too long for the husband who never returned. She anguished endlessly over whether her choice prevented her from saving her mother and sister, who went to their deaths to the taunts and laughter of "friends" and neighbors.[10]

Following their marriage, Herman and Bella settled in the Soviet Union, where they began the daunting task of rebuilding their lives and families. In the postwar years, Herman worked as a manager in large distribution warehouses, initially in Novogrudok, where Bella was born in 1946, and then in Riga, where Alex was born in 1954. According to Bella, the family's move in 1957 from the Soviet Union to Szczecin, Poland, was triggered by the fear that Herman was at risk of being exiled to the Gulag during the political upheaval of the Soviet Union then underway. With their eye on eventually emigrating from the Communist zone entirely, Herman ran a small grocery in Sczcecin while they submitted applications and awaited permission to emigrate.

In December 1961, the family sailed to the United States and settled in the Bronx New York, where both Herman and Bertha had relatives.

There, at the age of fifty-one, Herman was once again confronted with the task of rebuilding his life and supporting his family. Herman found work in a small bakery stand and performed odd jobs, while Bertha worked as a janitor and a nursing home aide.

Life in the Bronx was hard. To ease the difficulties, the family moved in 1965 to Atlanta, Georgia, home of Bertha's cousin, who had married a fellow Russian partisan acquaintance of Herman. In 1967, Herman, Bertha, Bella, and Alex Kric were naturalized as American citizens, officially changing their names to Harry, Bertha, Bella, and Alex Kritz.

Herman first became the owner of a small grocery store in an African-American neighborhood before opening a luncheonette in downtown Atlanta at the height of the civil rights crisis of the late 1960s. At a time when blacks were boycotting food stores in protest of high prices and poor-quality foods, Herman and Bertha were cited by community leaders for their fair prices and first-rate food. Herman continued as the proprietor until his retirement in 1986.[11]

Herman and Bertha loved each other very much,[12] enjoying fifty-one years of marriage until eighty-seven-year-old Herman's death on January 25, 1997. Bertha was ninety-two at her death in 2013.[13] Their children clearly inherited the high standard of integrity that their parents championed. Bella holds a graduate degree in education and held an executive position in a major charity organization. She is married, retired, and living in Michigan. Alex worked as a lawyer among the poor of rural Georgia before changing careers to become a psychotherapist in the public sector, where he is currently employed. Alex has resided for many years in northern California. Herman had no grandchildren.[14]

The epitaph on Harry (Herman) Kritz's gravestone reads, "A man who loved his family and built a strong foundation for them, he enriched all the lives he touched. He was dearly loved by his wife and children."[15]

At the July 2019 ceremony held at the site of the former Novogrudok forced labor camp to inaugurate the tunnel escapees Memorial Wall, the author unexpectedly met with Alex Kritz. At the time, he was at the start of a journey to visit landmark points in his father's and his family's past. Admitting that in the past he had mistakenly viewed Herman as being depressed, distant, and preoccupied, Alex was gaining new insight into his father's personality. Today, he reports that his visit to Novogrudok and his deeper knowledge of the tunnel escape and the Bielski partisan experience have helped him to more fully acknowledge and appreciate his father's "quiet dignity and strength." As Alex declares, he is humbled by what he has come to understand as the greatness and depth of the legacy Herman bequeathed to him.[16]

Herman Kritz in Red Army uniform, undated photo (courtesy of Alex Kritz)

Manya Katz (#61)

Unfortunately, the identity and fate of Manya Katz is nearly impossible to trace due to the absence of any personal details to guide us in our search, compounded by the name being fairly common. "Manya" was frequently interchanged with the name "Maria" or "Masha," further complicating the research.

Without knowing Manya Katz's place of birth or father's name, we are at a loss to determine which, if any, of the 188 sources in Yad Vashem's Central Database of Shoah Victims' Names for Polish women named Manya, Maria, or Masha Katz could be the Novogrudok forced labor camp inmate we seek. The overwhelming majority of these women were murdered.[1]

There were, however, at least three women named Manya or Maria Katz who survived to join various partisan groups, as recorded in the compilation of Jewish partisans in Belorussia. If our escapee survived the breakout, perhaps she was Manya from Lachva, the daughter of David and a Kirov partisan; Manya, the daughter of Pavlov, born in 1921, and a member of the Russian Vezhnovets detachment; or Maria from Minsk, also a member of the Kirov Brigade, born to Gregory in 1921.[2]

At this time, however, we cannot determine the identity or the fate of Manya Katz, the sixty-first person in line to escape through the tunnel.

Helena (Lena) Kitayevich (#62)

A researcher often finds surprises in the course of work. Imagine the author's amazement to discover on the escape list a member of her extended family through marriage. Only through the author's research was Helena Kitayevich's participation in the Novogrudok forced labor camp tunnel escape made known to all second-generation members of her family.

According to Pages of Testimony submitted to Yad Vashem by her sister Fira Dunec, Helena Kitayevich née Klubok was born in 1909. A workshop owner,[1] she was the daughter of Avraham Klubok, an engineer born in Novogrudok in 1870,[2] and his first wife, whose name is unknown. Avraham Klubok was considered one of the town's "progressive intelligentsia," who supported the local Shokdey Melocho Trade School. Today it is clear that thanks to the skills they learned in the Shokdey Melocho school, many tradesmen were sent to the Novogrudok forced labor camp and thus were able to avoid death in the city's widespread massacres.

Following the birth of his second daughter Raya in 1911 in Leningrad and his wife's subsequent death,[3] Avraham Klubok married Tsipa née Selibera, a dentist born in 1875 in Slutsk, Poland,[4] who raised both Helena and Raya.[5] Tsipa is noted as having been a devoted committee member of the Novogrudok Jewish Orphanage, personally caring for the orphans and helping to restore the institution's financial viability.[6]

Helena (Lena) Kitayevich, undated prewar photo (courtesy of Arthur Dunec)

The family was residing in Novogrudok at the time of Avraham and Tsipa's daughter Bogdana's birth in 1914[7] and her sister Fira's arrival in 1916.

Helena married Gershon Kitayevich, a bookkeeper born in 1913 who was killed in Novogrudok in 1942,[8] the same year in which Bogdana and her husband Albert Lidski were murdered.[9] Prior to the war, Raya had married the renowned Novogrudok surgeon Dr. Kalman Gordin.[10] Both Dr. Gordin and Raya survived the war, yet each was certain that the other had perished. Beginning a new life, Raya (now Rita) married Max Slutsky and settled in Canada.[11] Their only child, Arthur Slutsky, is an internationally renowned pulmonologist residing in Toronto, where Raya died in 2006. Fira, who also survived the war and moved to Canada, married Chaim Dunec of Novogrudok and had two children, Lea and Arthur Dunec. Following in his grandmother's footsteps, Arthur is a dentist in Toronto, where Fira died in 2007. Chaim, Helena's brother-in-law, was a first cousin to tunnel survivor and mother of the author Fanya Dunetz (#142), who reports having been totally unaware of Helena's participation in the escape.[12] As for Dr. Gordon, he too remarried and lived out his last years in Israel after immigrating there in the 1990s.[13]

Helena and Fira's father Avraham Klubok was deported to Siberia by the Russians together with Fira in 1939.[14] He eventually died in Saratov, Russia, in 1943.[15] His wife, Helena's stepmother Tsipa, was an invalid when the Russians left Novogrudok. Arthur Dunec, Helena's nephew and the grandfather of a child named Lena, surmises that his wheelchair-bound grandmother was probably found and murdered at home.[16]

Helena did not survive the tunnel escape. Although in 1957 his mother submitted a Yad Vashem Page of Testimony attesting to Helena's death in Novogrudok in 1943,[17] Arthur Dunec does not recall her ever speaking of her sister.

Gedalia Maslovati (#63)

Gedalia Maslovati was born in Novogrudok in 1922 to Shlomo,[1] a baker,[2] and Chana, a housewife,[3] both natives of the nearby town of Lubcz. Prior to the war, the Maslovati family lived in Novogrudok.[4] Gedalia's brother Reuven, born in 1915, is listed in a relative's Yad Vashem Page of Testimony as having been a "baker's helper," probably in his father's bakery. Reuven was single,[5] as were two of his sisters – Shoshana, born about 1923,[6] and Rivka, born in 1919.[7] We have no information regarding Gedalia's occupation or his marital status at the onset of the war.

According to the Yad Vashem testimony, only Gedalia survived the Novogrudok slaughters.[8] The testimony of fellow Novogrudok forced labor camp inmate escapee Berl Zalmanovich (#64) sheds light on the fact that from the time of the tunnel escape until reaching the Bielski partisans, Berl was together with a friend named Gedalia. This Gedalia, he writes, was a brother-in-law to his murdered brother Michael. Since Gedalia Maslovati was the only known escapee with this first name, and since he was directly behind Berl during the breakout, we can assume that Gedalia Maslovati was the friend to whom Berl referred.

In his written testimony, Berl describes how he and Gedalia walked together the entire night of the escape, during which time they passed many bodies of murdered escapees. For three days, the two men lay motionless under a tree, miraculously escaping detection by German soldiers with dogs who stepped over them. Their salvation came at last when Bielski partisans discovered the two escapees while scouting the area for tunnel survivors. They arranged for Gedalia and Berl to be provided with food and shelter at the home of a local farmer before bringing them to the detachment two weeks later. Gedalia Maslovati and Berl Zalmanovich are reported to have been the first of the tunnel escapees to reach the safety of the partisans.[9]

To date, an examination of genealogical, Holocaust-related, and population databases has not provided information as to Gedalia's whereabouts after the war. It is hoped that he established a family and experienced some happiness after his many losses.

Berko (Berl) Zalmanovich (#64)

Although he bore the horror of losing his entire family in World War II, Berko (Berl) Zalmanovich is remembered by friends and family for his eternal sense of optimism and his penchant to sing.

Born in Novogrudok on March 31, 1926,[1] Berl was the youngest child of Faivel-Yosef (Shraga) and Shoshke. A shoemaker, Shraga specialized in making orthopedic shoes and maintained a small workshop in which several shoemakers were employed. Shoshke helped support their four children by baking bread for the well-to-do, selling milk she procured from local farmers, sewing made-to-order blankets, and raising ducks for fat. In Berl's memoirs, he notes that the family lived a traditional religious life and attended synagogue on Sabbath and holidays.[2]

Berl's eldest sibling Michael, an active member of the Hashomer Hatzair Zionist youth movement, was one of the few Jews in Novogrudok to have been accepted to high school and receive a scholarship as well. Sisters Hinda and Chana attended the local Polish elementary school, while Berl attended *cheder*, a religious school for young boys, until transferring to a Russian Jewish school after the Soviet invasion.[3]

In his written testimony, Berl describes the very first "action" of the Germans in Novogrudok, the 1942 marketplace massacre in which fifty-two Jewish men were brutally shot. Although he incorrectly reports the casualty figure as twenty-four, he accurately describes the harsh conditions promulgated by the Germans. The prohibition against Jews walking on paved streets was not only difficult, he wrote, but served to differentiate between non-Jews and Jews, who were largely forced to clear rubble from the German bombings[4] and to prepare what was to become the Pereseka ghetto on December 8, 1941.[5]

In his description of the ghetto period which lasted until after the second massacre on August 7, 1942, Berl corroborates the testimony of Sonya Gorodynski (#78) that the elderly and children were separated from their families and taken away by truck, supposedly for "easy work."[6] Berl notes that the lists of the handicapped and families with children were provided the Nazis by the Judenrat. Entire families were destroyed as the ages of the children to be delivered into the hands of the Nazi beasts were constantly raised, he writes.[7]

While in the Pereseka ghetto, brothers Michael, Shraga, and Berl were first assigned work on the German Army base. Here they were forced to clean the base as well as the rooms of the base residents, namely Lithuanian soldiers notorious for their brutality toward the Jews.[8] Subsequently transferred to work in the Gestapo headquarters, cleaning and tending their garden, Berl was "guarded" by thirteen-year-old youths and frequently beaten and humiliated.[9]

Michael Zalmanovich was the first to be slaughtered, apparently during the second mass killing of August 7, 1942. The remaining family members were then sent to the Novogrudok forced labor camp, "the courthouse ghetto" established almost immediately after the August massacre. At the time, Berl considered his to have been one of the "lucky" families, having remained relatively intact with "only" one murder victim.[10]

Berl describes the savage cruelty inflicted on the victims of what was probably the fourth mass murder on May 7, 1943, some of whom he reports were buried alive.[11] Although he does not specify in which massacre he lost his parents and sisters, by the September 1943 tunnel escape, Berl was the sole family member to remain alive.[12]

Berl's testimony provides a valuable eyewitness account of the breakout. The digging was so terribly difficult, he writes, that at times he wished for the tunnel to collapse on him. To our knowledge, Berl is also the only escapee known to report on the electric shocks suffered by the diggers in the damp soil. Reporting that just two hundred inmates were left in the labor camp at the time of the escape,[13] Zalmanovich grossly underestimates the success of the escape, claiming that just twenty-four inmates survived,[14] about one-fifth of the actual number of survivors.

Berl reports that from the time of the escape until reaching the partisans, he was together with a friend named Gedalia, his brother Michael's brother-in-law.[15] We may assume that this friend was Gedalia Maslovati (#63), the only known escapee with the proper name Gedalia, who was slated to crawl through the tunnel immediately before Berl. Following the breakout, Berl writes, the two walked together the entire night, witnessing the many bodies of escapees shot to death as they fled from the vicinity of the forced labor camp. Berl and Gedalia remained motionless for three days as they hid beneath a tree. Even as German soldiers walked over them with dogs sniffing out the tracks of escapees, the men miraculously remained undetected.[16]

Thankfully, the two hideaways were later discerned by Bielski partisans riding in a wagon in search of tunnel escapees. The rescuers brought Berl and Gedalia to farmers who fed and sheltered them until the partisans could return two weeks later to bring them to the detachment. Reportedly, Berl Zalmanovich and Gedalia Maslovati were the very first escapees to reach the safety of the Bielski partisan detachment. Gawking at the sight of the secret partisan "town" hidden deep in the forest,[17] Berl writes that he soon obtained a weapon, which he used during expeditions to procure food. He notes that although Soviet soldiers reached the area in the spring of 1944, the partisans were asked to remain in place lest the Germans return,[18] as indeed occurred just one day before liberation.[19]

Freed from the forest at the age of eighteen, Berl writes of being sent to a residential vocational school in Minsk, where as one of the few Jews, he was abused and taunted. Thanks to his good social skills and his talented singing abilities, however, he soon gained popularity among the students. Once Berl left for Lodz, which had become a center for survivors returning to Poland, he became involved with the Hashomer Hatzair Zionist movement. Inspired by their ideology to build and live on a kibbutz collective agricultural settlement in Palestine, Berl traveled to the port city of Gdansk in hopes of joining a "naval kibbutz." Although this goal did not materialize, it was here that he met fellow Hashomer Hatzair members who were to join him in eventually founding Kibbutz Megiddo.[20]

On June 22, 1946, the *Biria*, an illegal immigration ship organized by the Haganah, sailed from the small French port of Sete, 125 miles west of Marseilles. Carrying 1,086 Holocaust survivors and a mostly American crew, the *Biria* reached Haifa on July 2. On the alphabetical list of travelers appearing in a book by *Biria* passenger Meir Eldar, Berl Zalmanovich was listed as passenger number 1,052.[21]

After reaching Palestine, Berl spent two months in Atlit prior to traveling south with other pioneers to Kibbutz Negba for a training course to prepare them for kibbutz life. It was there that he spent the

first part of the War of Independence,
followed by stays in Moshav Hadar
and the town of Mishmar HaEmek. In
1949, Berl, now known as Dov, became
a founding father of Kibbutz Megiddo,[22]
affiliated with the Hashomer Hatzair
movement[23] and situated in Israel's ver-
dant Jezreel Valley. For Berl, this marked
a realization of the ideology that his
slain brother Michael had embraced as
a young adherent of Hashomer Hatzair
in Novogrudok.[24]

In 1953, Berl married Chana née
Zaituni, who arrived in Israel from
Lebanon as an infant. When she came
to visit a friend on Kibbutz Megiddo,
Chana was immediately spotted by Berl.

Berko (Berl) Zalmanovich,
Germany, 1946 (courtesy of
Dotan Traubman)

According to their daughter Shoshke, it was love at first sight. Berl and
Chana went on to create a family with four children, like Shraga and
Shoshke before them. Physically strong, Berl continued to work as a
driver of heavy trucks until the age of seventy-seven, when he transferred
to a job in the kibbutz jewelry factory.[25] Berl "Dov" Zalmanovich died
in 2007, three years before his beloved Chana's death. All four of their
children, Amos, Shoshke, Chagai, and Yuval, continue to reside on the
kibbutz established by their father. If Berl were alive today (December
2019), he would have nine grandchildren and six great-grandchildren.[26]

Although Berl refrained from speaking about the Holocaust, his
detailed testimony appears in the book *That Which We Remembered to
Tell*, an anthology of Holocaust memoirs by the founders of Kibbutz
Megiddo. Shoshke, her paternal grandmother's namesake, notes that
Berl's children and grandchildren are aware of his experiences in the
tunnel escape and with the partisans,[27] yet she expresses regret for
never asking her father about the war and about his family. Perhaps, she

ponders, his relatively early death at the age of eighty-two was hastened by all that he suppressed.[28]

Berl is remembered both on the kibbutz[29] and within his family[30] as someone who, despite his wartime losses, was always optimistic and created a positive atmosphere. From Europe to Israel, in good times and bad, Berl Zalmanovich never stopped singing. And he always encouraged others to sing along with him.[31]

Aaron Wilenski (#65)

Born in Novogrudok in 1920[1] to Yehuda, a tailor, and Rachel née Wolkowiski, a housewife,[2] Aaron was one of five children. Simcha (#111), the eldest, was followed by Perel, Beila, Aaron, and Yehudit. Perel, the only married sibling, is reported to have suffered a stillbirth in the Novogrudok ghetto before being interned in the labor camp, where she was murdered together with her sisters in the final massacre on May 7, 1943. All five of the Wilensky siblings were seamstresses and tailors, presumably taught by their father, who, together with their mother, was killed in one of the early slaughters in 1942.[3]

Thanks to Aaron and Simcha's sewing skills, essential to the German Army, they were among the skilled craftsman – the last remnants of Novogrudok Jewry – kept alive to be conscripted to the Novogrudok forced labor camp.

The sole survivors of their own family, Aaron and Simcha Wilenski successfully fled to freedom during the tunnel breakout. Both made their way to the Bielski partisans, where they served until the Russian conquest of Belorussia and liberation from the forest in July 1944.[4]

In time, the brothers lost track of one another, probably after Simcha was drafted into the Russian Army. Decades later, on July 23, 1999, Simcha, now Seymour Wilenski, living in Bayonne, New Jersey, filed an inquiry with the International Red Cross seeking the fate of Aaron. Reporting that his brother might be somewhere in the former Soviet Union, Simcha provided Aaron's last known address in the Novogrudok ghetto at 23 Welky Rinek.[5] According to his daughter Rita Standig, Simcha often speculated that Aaron, a talented clarinet player, might have joined a Soviet orchestra in the postwar mayhem and remained somewhere in the USSR following the war.

Sadly, Simcha died in 2010 without ever knowing the fate of his only surviving sibling.[6]

Aaron Wilenski (*extreme right*), undated prewar photo
(courtesy of Rita Wilenski Standig)

Naum Shleimovich (#66)

The son of Abram, Naum Shleimovich was born in 1907. Prior to the war, he lived in Novogrudok and worked as a bookkeeper.[1] We know nothing regarding his family status, nor any details of his family of origin beyond his father Abram's name.

Naum survived the Novogrudok forced labor camp tunnel escape and the trek through the forest to reach the safety of the partisans. Records indicate that he joined the Za Sovetskuyu Belarus partisan detachment of the Russian Kirov Brigade.[2] This brigade also included the Ordzhonikidze detachment, containing 180 Bielski fighters.[3]

To date, an examination of Holocaust-related, genealogical, and population databases has revealed no information regarding Naum Shleimovich's postwar life and whereabouts. It is possible that he remained in the USSR, where the lack of accessibility to Soviet vital records prohibits our search for documentation.

Yakov Angelchik (#67)

Yakov Angelchik, a hatter, was born in Novogrudok in 1911.[1] The son of Shalom and Tzirel (Tsila), Yakov was married to Chana. Their one child, Tsila, bore the name of her paternal grandmother.

The first massacre of Novogrudok on December 8, 1941, took a terrible toll on the Angelchik family. Yakov's sister Luba Stollar, spared death thanks to immigrating to pre-state Israel in 1933,[2] memorialized her slain family members by submitting Yad Vashem Pages of Testimony in 1956. Among those testimonies were pages for her brother Shlomo Angelchik, a tailor born in Novogrudok in 1906; his wife Leah née Gorsky; the couple's five-year-old son Shalom; Luba's brother Yakov Angelchik's wife Chana; Chana's daughter Tzila; and Yakov himself, whom Luba assumed had been killed along with his family.[3]

Yet unbeknownst to Luba, Yakov did not die in Novogrudok, not in 1941, and not even in the tunnel escape from the Novogrudok forced labor camp. Our research indicates that Yakov succeeded in surviving the breakout to become a partisan in the Frunze detachment.[4] Subsequently, we located testimony from Luba's one surviving sibling, Moshe, noting that their brother Yakov Angelchik had been conscripted into the Red Army and killed in 1945 while approaching Berlin.[5] The information included in his testimony was unfortunately not made available at the time to Luba and her family.

Descendants of Yakov's family of origin include the children and grandchildren of his siblings Luba and Moshe. Luba, who died in 2006, left two daughters. Atara Orr is a retired teacher with two children and grandchildren. Atara's sister Tsila Kleingberger, named for Yakov's mother, is a member of Kibbutz Hukuk and the mother of four, grandmother of eight, and great-grandmother of two children, as of this writing in January 2018.[6]

Yakov's brother Moshe, four years his junior, came to Palestine as a legal immigrant in 1938. A founding member of Kibbutz Eilon, he worked as an agronomist for the Ministry of Agriculture. At his death in 1995 at the age of eighty,[7] Moshe left three children (one of whom has since died), as well as several grandchildren.[8]

Only after the author spoke of her research on the tunnel escape before a Novogrudok Society memorial meeting did Atara learn of the breakout. Soon afterwards, Atara was shocked and moved when the author called to inform her that her uncle Yakov Angelchik had participated in and survived the escape. Noting that her mother rarely spoke of the brothers that she'd left behind in Novogrudok and assumed were murdered, Atara recalls her fervently listening to the popular Israeli radio show *Searching for Relatives* in an attempt to locate family members who may have survived the Holocaust.[9] A circle was closed when Atara was informed of Moshe's testimony for Yakov's death.[10]

Halperin (#68)

With no given name indicated, it is impossible to know the identity of the male or female inmate of the Novogrudok forced labor camp with the surname Halperin, the sixty-eighth person in line to escape the tunnel. Yad Vashem's Central Database of Shoah Victims' Names contains 2,837 sources for individuals named Halperin from Poland, of whom 254 are from the Novogrudok area alone.[1]

The compilation of Jewish partisans in Belorussia includes eleven individuals with the surname Galperin,[2] the Russian equivalent of the name, as well as one Alperin,[3] a Halpern variant. If this inmate survived the breakout, it is likely that he or she would have fled to the Bielski partisan detachment, as did the vast majority of escapees. As only one person with the surname Halpern was a member of this *otriad* (all the others joined Russian detachments), the possibility exists that the escapee from the Novogrudok forced labor camp was Chonia (Chanan) Alperin of Novogrudok.[4]

We know only that Chonia was born in 1881 to Moshe, and that prior to the war he lived on Grodenskaya Street in Novogrudok, where he worked as a shoemaker.[5] Other than these facts, our research has revealed no additional information to confirm or rule out Chonia Halpern's participation in the tunnel escape.

Aaron (#69) and Sarah (#70) Kulik

Although the identities of Aaron and Sarah Kulik remain unknown, we can make one basic assumption based on similar cases from the Novogrudok forced labor camp escape list: when two (or more) people with the same surname were placed consecutively in line, they were usually closely related.

Yad Vashem's Central Database of Shoah Victims' Names contains extensive entries of individuals from Poland with the surname Kulik. Only two, however, bear the proper name Aaron, and only six are named Sarah. Of these, only Aaron and Sarah Kulik both hail from the same city: Grodno.

Aaron Kulik, the son of Moshe and Miryam,[1] was born in Grodno in 1924. According to a Page of Testimony filed in his memory by his sister-in-law, Aaron was one of four children and was single.[2]

Sarah Kulik, born in 1880,[3] lived in Grodno with her husband Szmuel and three children.[4] It is possible to speculate that nineteen-year-old Aaron was perhaps a relative to sixty-six-year-old Sarah, and that the two somehow survived the massacres in which their family members were killed. As to how they made the ninety-three-mile (150 km) journey to Novogrudok or how they were conscripted to the forced labor camp, we can only conjecture. One further possibility is that they were somehow related to Sara Kulik Giershenowski (#149) of Karelich and took refuge with her. The numerous entries in Yad Vashem's central database for individuals with the surname Kulik hailing from Grodno and Novogrudok indicate that this family was widespread in both cities.

If indeed Sarah and Aaron Kulik fled from the city of Grodno, they could have escaped either from the Grodno ghetto, established in November 1941, or perhaps from the deadly transports to the Auschwitz or Treblinka death camps in early 1943.

Whether or not our hypothesis is correct, there is no doubt that the names Aaron and Sarah Kulik do not appear within Gerasimova, Selemenov, and Kagan's compilation of 4,772 Jewish partisans in Belorussia during the years 1941–1942.[5] We can thus assume that neither survived the breakout to reach the safety of a partisan detachment.

Rita Wolozhinski (#71)

Rita Wolozhinski was born in Novogrudok in 1920 to Osher, a dentist and physician,[1] and Aniuta (née Ostashinski), also a dentist.[2] Both Osher and Aniuta were killed in the courthouse massacre outside the Novogrudok forced labor camp on May 7, 1943.[3] Rita's dream to join her younger sibling Sulia who had fled to the Bielski *otriad* in late 1942[4] ended in a horrific tragedy: following the tunnel escape, Rita's mutilated body was found near Novogrudok.[5]

In her memoir, Sulia explains that her own early escape from the camp to the forest was prompted by Rita's determination to find a way to help their parents from outside the camp. When Sulia begged Rita to flee with her, Rita refused to leave her parents alone, saying, "I can't. My absence will be noticed, and they will shoot Papa and Mama. I won't shorten their lives even for a second. You go, and we will follow later."[6]

Skeptical of their own chance to escape to the partisans, Rita and Sulia's parents were wary of dying in the forest due to what they considered to be their advanced ages (forty-eight and fifty-one, respectively) and their feared difficulties in running from place to place.[7]

Sulia writes that after Michael (Matus) Kabak (#72a) escaped to the Bielski detachment, he broke the news that her parents had been slaughtered just outside the labor camp, in full view of Rita, who witnessed their murder through the window of the labor camp.[8]

As the steady flow of tunnel escapees kept reaching the *otriad*, Sulia prepared warm clothes for Rita, anxiously
awaiting their reunion at last. Yet Rita
never arrived with the other survivors.
After several weeks of gazing at all that
she had prepared for her sister and
finally realizing that Rita must have
been caught, Sulia reports having lost
her desire to live.[9] Her deep depression over Rita's fate even led to failed
attempts to self-abort the three-month
fetus she carried, prior to eventually
obtaining a torturous abortion in the
partisan camp's primitive hospital.[10]

Rita Wolozhinski, undated
prewar photo (courtesy of Jack
Kagan)

In her memoir, Sulia describes having been driven nearly insane by
accounts of her sister's murder from survivors who reached the partisans, particularly by one "deranged" boy who had been together with
Rita and her boyfriend, her friend Linka Landau (#140), Linka's boyfriend Jankef Nevachovich (#51), and others. As he hid in a tree, this
boy reportedly witnessed how Rita's drunken boyfriend insisted on the
group's sleeping in the Seltzo Forest, which was close to town, rather
than moving as distant from town as possible. When the group of Jews
was found by local policemen in the morning, the men were said to
have been shot, while the women were raped and tortured until they
too succumbed.[11]

Sulia, who moved to the United States with her husband following
the war, prospered and established a family, yet continued to suffer
the inconsolable pain of her sister's brutal death, never knowing where
Rita's remains lie buried.[12]

L. Wolkin (#72)

We cannot establish the identity of L. Wolkin, the seventy-second person in line to attempt to flee the Novogrudok forced labor camp through the tunnel. An extensive search of Holocaust databases for an L. Wolkin from Poland suggests that he or she may possibly have been Lev (Lovke) Wolkin, born in Lida in 1912, whose name appears among Lida's Holocaust victims,[1] or perhaps Lea Wolkin, listed among the murdered in the *Memorial (Yizkor) Book of the Jewish Community of Novogrudok, Poland.*[2]

Since Arie Leib was a very common combination of Jewish names often used interchangeably,[3] another prospect is that L. Wolkin was Arie Wolkin, whose name is commemorated in Novogrudok's memorial book.[4] Also noted in the *Novogrudok Memorial Book* is the murder in the Novogrudok jail of a Bielski partisan named Arie (Leibke) Wolkin, possibly in 1942, although no confirmation of this fact has been found to date. Nor does Arie (Leibke) Wolkin appear on the list of fallen partisans in Belorussia.

As no one with the surname Wolkin and a proper name beginning with the letter *L* appears in the compilation of Jewish partisans in Belorussia,[5] we can assume that L. Wolkin, the male or female inmate of the Novogrudok forced labor camp, did not survive the tunnel escape.

Matus Kabak (#72a)

Matus Kabak was a scion of Novogrudok's noted Kabak family, touted as one of the city's most influential families from the 1840s to the late 1880s.[1] One family member, Yousef Kabak, worked his way up from poverty to become the richest man in town, later renowned for his charitable pursuits.[2]

Matus, a lawyer, was born in Novogrudok to Yosef (possibly a namesake of Reb Yousef) and Chana.[3] While Matus's year of birth is recorded as 1911 on a partisan list,[4] it appears elsewhere as 1915.[5]

According to information he provided on a postwar application for assistance, Matus attained a degree in law from a university in Warsaw, where he later worked as an attorney until the German conquest of the city in 1939.[6]

Although we do not know the names of Matus's siblings whom he reported to have been murdered during the war,[7] we do know that his brother Michael, a former Novogrudok forced labor camp inmate, remained alive until the July 1944 liberation thanks to the selflessness of the author's mother, Fanya Dunetz (#142). After the fourth Novogrudok massacre on May 7, 1943, one of the local guards who had known her family before the war offered Fanya a chance to escape from the forced labor camp. For safety, he would allow her to take one fellow inmate to accompany her to the Bielski partisan detachment. However, Fanya gave up her own chance for freedom in order to save her younger brother Motl, whom she sent in her stead. For his escort, she chose Michael Kabuk. Her hope was that since Michael was a Novogrudok native, his knowledge of the surrounding terrain as well as his possession of a weapon would enable both men to safely reach the partisans. Fortunately, this hope was realized.

After successfully escaping through the tunnel nearly four months later, Matus was reunited with Michael in the Naliboki Forest. Lamentably, this reunion for the Kabak brothers was short-lived. Immediately after liberation, Michael was drafted into the Soviet Army, where he was killed in action.[8]

In the Bielski detachment, Matus Kabak was appointed to the prominent position of head of all the workshops. These impressive built-from-scratch workshops, including shoemaking, tailoring, watch repair, carpentry, leatherwork, gun repair, and baking, became the crucial lifeblood for providing services to the detachment's residents and to other partisans in the area.[9] In his memoirs, Commander Tuvia Bielski describes how Matus called all the craftsmen to attention during Soviet General Platon's historic visit to the Bielski workshops on December 31, 1943.[10]

In the January 1948 application for war reparations which Matus Kabak filed from a displaced persons camp in Rome, he reported having been incarcerated in the Toruń and Buchenwald concentration camps from December 1942 until his liberation from Buchenwald in May 1945.[11] We know these facts to be incorrect, with proof to show that during most of this period, Matus was an inmate in the Novogrudok forced labor camp,[12] a participant in the tunnel escape, and a Bielski partisan.

In order to understand the widespread phenomenon of falsehoods on applications for assistance from and immigration to the West, we must understand the chaotic postwar period in which stateless survivors were urgently seeking new homes and a better future. The Cold War that followed World War II's end had thrust the American-led Western Bloc against the Russian-led Eastern Bloc, posing a threat to former Jewish partisans hoping to immigrate to the West. They feared that their close brush with and/or membership in Russian partisan units could thwart their chances to enter America's gates. Thus, the vast majority of those applying for US and Canadian immigration simply invented alternative wartime experiences and locales to report in place of their actual service in the partisans. Such inaccuracies must be considered within the context of the complex global events of the day.

In his application for reparations, Matus Kabak noted having lived in the displaced persons camp in Graz, Austria, from July 1945 to December 1947 prior to moving to Rome. He also claimed to have filed an application for immigration to Palestine.

Matus was said to have been sighted in New York after the war,[13] yet a search of genealogical, Holocaust-related, and population databases has not uncovered the whereabouts of Matus Kabak since his 1948 application for assistance in Rome. It is quite possible that he changed his name at some point soon afterwards, making his identification some seventy years later all the more difficult.

Dr. Abush (#73)

With no proper name appearing on the escape list for "Dr. Abush," the quest to find his identity is a challenge. There are 449 sources in Yad Vashem's Central Database of Shoah Victims' Names for individuals with the surname Abush who either lived and/or died in Poland. None were from the Novogrudok area.[1]

The sole Yad Vashem Page of Testimony for a Dr. Abush was submitted in 1955 by a fellow physician then living in Haifa who had been his acquaintance. According to this testimony, Dr. Abush was born in 1900, had resided in Radomsko in central Poland prior to the war, and was married to Genia Lefkowitz. The submitter notes that his colleague had been killed in either 1939 or 1940 in Katyn, Russia, while serving as an officer in the Polish Army.[2] The Katyn Forest Massacre, which took place in 1940, was a brutal Stalin-ordered political mass murder of Polish generals, commanders, and intelligentsia.[3]

The Radomska memorial book cites the contribution of a Dr. Abush who arrived in the city just after World War I, when a mass typhus epidemic was raging. It was at his initiative that a section of the Jewish medical society to aid the poor was founded.[4] In his testimony, Novogrudok tunnel escapee Eliyahu Berkowicz (#49) writes of Dr. Abush as having been one of the physicians in the forced labor camp, along with Dr. Majer Jakubowicz (#1) and a Dr. Hirsch.[5] It is entirely possible that the hypothesis of Dr. Abush's death in Katyn is incorrect and that he lived to reach Novogrudok as a refugee, where he was conscripted to the forced labor camp. If so, we can presume that he did not survive the 1943 tunnel escape and reach the partisans, as his name does not appear in the compilation of Jewish partisans in Belorussia from 1941 to 1944.[6]

Leipuner (#73a)

The name Leipuner appears on the escape list without any proper name preceding it. Although thirty-nine listings for individuals with the surname appear in Yad Vashem's Central Database of Shoah Victims' Names, not one appears to have been from the Novogrudok area, nor did any survive.[1]

It is possible that the Leipuner who participated in the tunnel escape was a refugee from other parts of Poland that had earlier come under Nazi rule. It is possible that he or she came to Novogrudok due to a possible familial tie to the renowned restauranteer Yosef Leipuner, mentioned in the city's memorial book for his fame.[2] Perhaps the escapee was Yosef Leipuner himself or a member of his family for whom there is no documentation of status during the war.

As no one with the surname Leipuner is listed in the compilation of Jewish partisans in Belorussia,[3] we can assume that the Leipuner appearing on the Novogrudok forced labor camp escape list did not survive the breakout to reach the forest.

Gitel (Gita) Zilberman (#74)

Amazingly enough, the race against death that spurred the extraordinary tunnel escape of September 26, 1943, owes its decisive head start to inmate Gitel Zilberman, an expert seamstress. Zeidel Kushner (#143) recounts that rumors abounded boding the impending mass execution of all the remaining Novogrudok forced labor camp inmates (save for twelve specialists), yet the top-secret date was unknown. The key break-through came around September 19, when a Russian prisoner of war who spied for the Germans overheard the execution plans and hastened to contact her seamstress Mrs. Gitel Zilberman with an order to make her five dresses "well and quickly." Based on this information, the tunnel escape leaders cast the die for the breakout to be set for following week.[1]

Fanya Dunetz recalls that prior to the war, Mrs. Gitel Zilberman was a well-known dressmaker in Novogrudok who made Fanya's prom dress for her graduation from the Novogrudok Gymnasium in 1938. Fanya describes the creation as having been a beautiful long green dress with a cranberry sash made from material her mother had provided.[2]

Gitel Zilberman, perhaps the unknown and unwitting heroine of the tunnel breakout, did not survive the tunnel escape. Her name is commemorated in the *Novogrudok Memorial Book*.[3]

Israelit (#74a)

Who was the individual listed only as "Israelit" on the escape list?

In all likelihood, he or she was probably a member of one of the largest extended family networks in the Novogrudok region. There are

143 citations in Yad Vashem's Central Database for members of the Israelit family in the Novogrudok area alone. Very few survived. Only three individuals carrying the surname are listed in the compilation of Jewish partisans in Belorussia from 1941 to 1944. There are an additional five listings for individuals with similar surnames.[1]

After an extensive search of genealogical and Holocaust-related databases, we have not found a connection between any of the above-mentioned partisans and the Novogrudok forced labor camp where they may have participated in the tunnel escape. It is thus unlikely that this inmate survived the breakout.

If this is the case, we can only hope that this escapee may one day be identified and his or her memory honored.

Shlomo Golanski (#75)

Shlomo (Solomon) Golanski hailed from the small village of Zabalucz, ten miles from Novogrudok. At the outbreak of war, the hamlet consisted of a hundred Christian Belarusian farmers and one Jewish family, the Golanskis. Born on May 10, 1920, Shlomo was one of five sisters and two brothers born to Mordechai Aaron (known as "Aaron"),[1] a miller, and Gita Rasha[2] (or Gute Rachel[3]), a housewife.

Ultimately, Shlomo became the sole survivor among his parents and siblings Rachel, Sonia, Sheina, Chana, Miriam, and Mairim.[4] According to the memorials Shlomo placed for his family in the *Novogrudok Memorial Book*, Rachel was the only sibling to have married, and she, her husband, and daughter were all murdered.[5]

Shlomo Golanski is one of the few survivors of the tunnel escape to have given oral testimony. In a video interview conducted in 1997 by the Survivors of the Shoah Visual History Foundation, founded by

Steven Spielberg, Shlomo fondly recalls his childhood home and family. At the age of seven, Shlomo and one of his sisters were enrolled in Novogrudok's Tarbut school, where the language of instruction was Hebrew. Eventually, when his family could no longer afford the tuition for two of its children, his sister dropped out. Shlomo was left alone in Novogrudok, where he rented a room from a family, sleeping in a bed with one or two others. Remaining in school until his bar mitzvah, Shlomo enjoyed a seemingly happy time filled with many friends. When he returned home at age thirteen to work in the family mill, he did not often play with the village children, but spent his time primarily with his father, their Christian millhand, and the farmers who came with horses and buggies to grind their grain.

With the invasion of the Russians in World War II, the family moved to Novogrudok with their cow and horses and twenty wagons of grain and flour. Shlomo found work as a handyman and carpenter and learned Russian in night school. In the meantime, the city filled up with refugees from Polish areas already occupied by the Nazis.

Although it was thought that the Germans would never reach Novogrudok, Shlomo recalls the day the bombs fell on the city at the end of July 1941. He describes the destruction of the city center and the new regulations forcing Jews to wear yellow stars, stay off the sidewalks, and hand over all gold and jewelry. Shlomo recalls the ghetto in the Novogrudok neighborhood of Pereseka being established before Chanukah. By this time, Shlomo's parents, three sisters, and a two-year-old niece had been taken away on trucks to their deaths, transforming the joyous holiday to a time of tragedy.

After being interned in the Novogrudok forced labor camp during the winter of 1942, Shlomo was to remain there for one and a half years until the tunnel escape. He describes a lonely existence in which no one cared for him when he was sick, and he had no interest whatsoever in speaking with the other inmates. He no longer prayed, never washed, and watched the cockroaches on the ceiling from the plank he shared with another person in the three-tiered bunk.

In his testimony, Shlomo describes the fourth Novogrudok massacre of May 7, 1942, in which more than half the inmates of the Novogrudok forced labor camp, mostly women and children, were led to believe that they would be given more bread by coming out to the yard. Instead of bread, they received bullets and were hurled into a mass grave.[6]

Having been employed in the carpentry workshop of the forced labor camp, Shlomo gives us a detailed description of the role of the carpenters in the tunnel construction. Stating that the digging was made possible primarily by the use of wooden shovels made by the carpenters, he reports that very few shovels were made from metal. When the sides and top of the tunnel needed reinforcement due to rains, it was the carpenters who risked their lives by sneaking boards from their workshop and hiding them under their clothes. According to Shlomo, most of the work in the tunnel was completed by fifty or so carpenters who also constructed the small wagons with ropes that were used to haul out the dug-up earth.

After nearly two months of digging, the wood (intended for the construction of furniture to be sent back to Germany) was discovered to be missing. Nazi soldiers ordered all the carpenters to lie on the floor, where they were beaten with sticks to divulge the reason the wood had disappeared. Shlomo stresses that not one carpenter betrayed the others, not even one man sentenced to death by hanging who was later saved by a female inmate. (We assume that this carpenter was Rafael Shofer, #202.)

It is possible that Shlomo's youthful experience as a millworker saved not only his own life but that of three other escapees. Describing the rainy, dark night of the breakout, Shlomo tells of escaping through the tunnel and finding a father and two daughters who, like him, did not know the way through the forest to reach the Bielski partisan detachment. These had to have been Zeidel Kushner (#143) and his two daughters Raya (#144) and Leah (#145), the sole father and two daughters to escape through the tunnel. Shlomo took the three Kushners along with him as he sought shelter with a farmer who had come to the Golanski mill every spring to grind his grain. Happy to help, this farmer, whose name remains anonymous, boiled Shlomo's lice-ridden clothes and hid the escapees in his barn. Shlomo notes that the Kushners remained with the farmer for a week, while he remained in hiding one week longer. With the assistance of Russian partisans, he reached the Bielski *otriad*. Shlomo compared the living conditions in the *otriad* to those of the American Indians, only instead of tents, the partisans lived in underground bunkers covered by bushes. Impressed by the fact that the Bielskis accepted any Jew, he notes that there were old people as well as women and children in the detachment.

Once again, Shlomo's work in the family mill was to serve him well. Aided by another partisan who had owned a water mill prior to the war, Shlomo was able to construct a small makeshift mill from stones that was operated by hand, enabling the partisans to grind grain for bread. Four people were needed to operate the mill – he emphasized the cooperation and camaraderie among the partisans united by their common goal of survival.

Shlomo never returned to his hometown of Zabalucz. After liberation of the area by the Russians, he was drafted by the Russian Army to work as a carpenter and handyman, while pondering what his future would hold. At the close of the war, Shlomo spent time in Poland, Germany, and Austria before reaching Italy and the Pocking Displaced Persons Camp. In 1947, he arrived in Rome, where the former miller from Zabalucz found himself unseemingly employed as a carpenter in Castel Gondolfa, the scenic papal summer residence where Pope Pius II often came into view.

Throughout his subsequent wanderings in Europe, Shlomo spent time in several kibbutzim where groups of survivors were helped to cope with their losses while learning Hebrew and preparing for life in the Israeli nation-in-the-making. Despite his original plans to immigrate to Israel, Shlomo ultimately decided to avoid more war and danger to his life. As the only member of his family to survive, he felt that he'd best join two cousins who had immigrated to America prior to the Holocaust.

In December 1949, Shlomo left Europe for the US, originally settling in Brooklyn,[7] where one of his cousins arranged for a room and employment.[8] While visiting a relative in the Catskill Mountains, Shlomo met his future wife Etta née Sherman, originally from Nova Scotia, Canada.[9] The two married after only three dates,[10] settling in West Hartford, Connecticut, where they raised their only child, Alani. There, after first working as a carpenter, Shlomo was employed in a paper box factory for thirty-five years.[11]

As of this writing in August 2018, Alani is an attorney married to Gina, a fundraiser. The couple lives in Brooklyn with their two sons, Creeley, born in 2003, and Cy, born in 2006.[12]

Shlomo Golanski in West Hartford, Connecticut, 1950s (courtesy of Alani Golanski)

Alani describes his father as a "gentle, loving, stoic man who was never angry." Grateful to have a home and family, Shlomo never felt the need to travel and took pride that he was never on an airplane in his life. The story of the tunnel escape from the Novogrudok forced labor camp was "the centerpiece of my father's personal narrative," Alani attests. During his childhood, Alani notes, his dad would often bring home cardboard pieces for him to construct tunnels throughout the house.[13]

Shlomo died at the age of ninety-seven on November 27, 2017,[14] eleven years after the death of his wife Etta.[15] Alani reports that during his lifetime, his father had often requested that the story of his life, the escape, and the partisans be told.[16] Hopefully, he would be pleased with this research and publication.

When asked in the oral testimony how the Holocaust affected the way he raised his son, Shlomo Golanski answered: "No matter what, he should be proud to be a Jew." He aptly concluded: "Sometimes it's hard to be a Jew."[17]

Chanan (Chonie) Kushner (#76)

Chonie Kushner's colossal courage – and daring – in the face of danger and suffering remain inspiring to this day, numerous decades after the Novogrudok forced labor camp tunnel escape.

Given the name of his paternal grandfather, Chanan (Chonie) Kushner was born in Novogrudok on May 5, 1924,[1] to the hatter Naum (Zeidel) Kushner (#143), and his wife, Hinda née Bloch.[2] Of the couple's four children, only Raya (#144) and Leah (#145) survived the war together with their father. Their sister Esther was killed in the first Novogrudok massacre[3] on December 8, 1941, which claimed the lives of between forty-eight hundred[4] and fifty-one hundred[5] people in Skrydlevo, just outside the city.

Zeidel Kushner relates that his wife Hinda was killed in the fourth and last major massacre on May 7, 1943, during which 250 women, 45 men, and an indeterminate number of children were exterminated. Forced to completely undress, they were taken to pre-dug trenches in groups of ten, where they were shot face down in full view of the forced labor camp inmates.[6] Although she faced the "selection" alone, Hinda was said to have cared little for her own fate as long as her husband and three remaining children remained alive.[7]

From the start of the German occupation of Poland in 1941, Chonie Kushner had already plotted an escape to Russia via bicycle. Only due to his mother's tearful refusal to let him go did he remain in Novogrudok. His sister Raya attributes her mother's resistance to the escape plan to the death of a friend's son while fleeing to Russia, as well as to her total unawareness of the horrors awaiting them.[8]

Educated in *cheder* (religious school for young boys) and in Novogrudok's co-ed Tarbut school, Chonie's luck in surviving the Holocaust was put to the test on many occasions. According to his uncle Chaim Leibowitz (#91), in mid-December 1941, while Chonie was incarcerated with his parents and sisters in the Pereseka ghetto outside Novogrudok, Nazi district commissioner Traub ordered six Jews to install water pipes in his palace. Among these six were the nightshift workers H. Gershovich from Baranovich, a man named Florent, and Chonie Kushner. The frozen soil was nearly impenetrable by the axes and spades. Traub would occasionally watch the Jews work, threatening to kill them if the job was not completed on time. On New Year's Eve, he came out of his palace and asked the workers their names before slashing them with whips and ordering them to shout "I am a cursed Jew" as well as "Heil Hitler." All three Jews were then shot, dragged, and stacked on the fire they had lit for warmth. Florent's body was covered by Gershovich, and Chonie Kushner was flung to the top.[9]

Susan Bach, a niece of Chonie's fellow labor camp inmate Chaim Abramowicz (#22), shares that her maternal uncle Shimon Grinberg was also among those injured at Traub's New Year's Eve "party." As her mother described, Shimon was forced to dance on burning twigs and leaves, suffering burns that necessitated his being taken to the infirmary along with Chonie, who was so severely burned that he had to be carried.[10]

There are several differing versions, even among Chonie's family members, as to how he ultimately survived the horror at Traub's palace. Chronicler Dov Cohen writes that Chonie was able to crawl away from the fire unaided and unobserved before being smuggled back into the ghetto by the next shift of workers.[11] However, Chonie's uncle Chaim Leibowitz reports that after regaining consciousness, Chonie managed to jump over the fence before reaching another group of Jews working in the horse stable owned by a Gestapo member named Hose. Here Chonie was hidden in a corner of the stable and covered with straw before being spirited out by the Judenrat via horse and buggy to the ghetto infirmary for medical treatment. A day later, for reasons unknown, the high-ranking Nazi commander Wolfmayer appeared at the infirmary to inquire about Kushner and order the doctors to take good care of him, a ritual that he continued for the remainder of Chonie's recuperation.[12]

According to Zeidel Kushner's account, his son had been wearing a good fur which he left in the snow after being shot, in order to mislead the Germans while he ran and jumped a fence. After hiding in the nearby abandoned home of a Jewish girl, he made his way to a place where others were working. With a gunshot wound in the buttocks and burns on his hands and feet, Chonie was hidden in a cellar and then ferried back to the Pereseka ghetto via horse sleigh by a German who was paid for his labor. Zeidel relates that Chonie was placed in the ghetto hospital, where he was cared for by Dr. Yakov Kagan (#3a) and other physicians. He notes that the medical staff were instructed to ensure their patient's survival by a special German-ordered commission that visited Chonie in the hospital for a never-discovered motive.[13]

Chonie's sister Raya provides yet another version of his survival. She claims that Chonie was smuggled into the ghetto and hidden in an attic, where he recovered without doctors or medications after six months of suffering.[14]

By the time of the second mass execution of August 7, 1942, Chonie had recuperated from his wounds. His sole chance to remain alive now depended upon his conscription by the Germans to the Novogrudok forced labor camp, which required an official "essential worker" certificate.

Zeidel notes that although there were twelve hundred Jews in the forced labor camp workshops the day before the mass execution, only two hundred new certificates could be issued by Daniel Ostashinski, the German-appointed Judenrat head. Chonie, the sole family member without a certificate, failed in his repeated attempts to leave the Pereseka ghetto under the guise of his father's old document attesting to his "essential worker" status. Only Zeidel's perseverance in standing at the door to the ghetto finally led to Chonie's obtaining a certificate as a skilled worker in the forced labor camp.[15] As for the nature of his essential skills, we can only surmise that Chonie called to the fore his abilities as a hatter or furrier, likely taught to him in prewar days by his father.

By night, Chonie Kushner took a critical role as one of the fifty young men who were entrusted nightly to carry out the top-secret, intensive digging of the escape tunnel from beneath the well-guarded forced labor camp.[16] A Yad Vashem testimony by Chonie's cousin and friend Shaul Gorodynski (#77) details his toil for between three to five hours each night with his digging partner Chonie, following their day of grueling hard labor.[17]

On the stormy, pitch-black night of September 26, 1943, Chonie crawled his way through the escape tunnel just behind Gorodynski. Yet Gorodynski reports that due to near-zero visibility, the two mistakenly wandered back toward the gate of the camp rather than distancing themselves from it. Amid the pandemonium of gunfire and shouting, Chanan made a fatal misstep. Finding himself now painfully alone, Gorodynski set out toward the Bielski partisan detachment and to freedom, never to see Chonie again.[18]

Chanan (Chonie) Kushner's name is memorialized today by his sister Raya's son Charles (Chanan) Kushner, the prominent US businessman and philanthropist whose son Jared Kushner served as advisor to President Donald Trump.

Chanan Kushner (*second from right*) with Esther, Leah, Naum, and Raya Kushner, Novogrudok, 1938 (courtesy of Charles and Seryl Kushner)

Shaul (#77) and Sonya (#78) Gorodynski; Aaron (#79) and Yakov (Yankel, #80) Oshman

You will kill me today, but I have a son and a daughter and they will survive and tell what happened here.
   Avraham Gorodynski, November 4, 1943, as he was beaten
   to death in the Koldychevo concentration camp

These last words of Shaul and Sonya Gorodynski's father were revealed by a doctor who had witnessed the savage beating before he escaped Koldychevo.[1] And how prophetic were Avraham's words! For Sonya, memorializing the Holocaust and her family's experiences was to become a burning passion, while defending the State of Israel and sharing his own wartime encounters gave profound meaning to her brother Shaul's life.

Sonya, born in Novogrudok on December 17, 1923,[2] to Avraham, a businessman, and Tamara née Nochimovski, a housewife, was named for her paternal grandmother.[3] Before the war, Avraham and Tamara, their two daughters, and three sons resided with Tamara's parents Rivka and Mordechai Nochimovski. Sonya recalls having had a "beautiful life at home," in which her "very happy family" ate dinner and celebrated all holidays together. No one ever ate alone in what both she and Shaul described as their traditional, Zionist home.[4] The family lived comfortably from their father's store and workshop, where he sold and repaired motorcycles, bicycles, radios, and other appliances. The Gorodynskis were sufficiently influential to enable both Shaul and Sonya to be among the very few Jews accepted to Novogrudok's prestigious Adam Mickiewitz High School.[5]

The German aerial invasion of Novogrudok in June 1941 shattered the tranquility of Shaul and Sonya's lives forever. The first German bomb that fell on the city scored a direct hit on their home, miraculously causing no casualties.[6]

In a moving oral testimony, Sonya described the horrifying deaths of her grandparents. Separated from the rest of the family during the first Novogrudok massacre on December 8, 1941, they were thrown into trucks to be hauled away to their deaths together with screaming babies and children separated from their mothers. Told by the Germans that the older people were being "taken to work," Sonya speaks of her desperate wait and futile hope for her beloved grandparents to finish their work and return home.[7]

Detailing the dreadful conditions in the Pereseka (Novogrudok) ghetto, Sonya noted that her family was among the more than fifty families crowded into a house from December 1941 until August 1942. During this time, she worked as a nurse in the ghetto hospital, without any training and devoid of medications to administer. One of her brothers worked as a mechanic and another as a carpenter, while her parents cleaned for the Germans. For all their toil, they were each paid a "salary" of dirty water and a slice of bread made from uncleaned wheat. For the entire nine months, they wore the same clothes they had been wearing on the day they entered the ghetto. Despite being swarmed by enough body lice to have "carried them away," Sonya found comfort in the fact that at least they were together, and at least they were alive.[8]

Of their entire family, only Shaul and Sonya survived the war. Their fourteen-year-old brother Chonia (Charlie) was forced to dig his own grave before being murdered in the second Novogrudok massacre of August 7, 1942. Twenty-year-old Shlomo starved to death in January 1943. By now, Shaul and Sonya, their parents, and little sister Fanya were interned in the Novogrudok forced labor camp. Here Sonya worked as a seamstress and cleaner, and Shaul as a mechanic working alongside his father Avraham.[9] On May 7, 1943, Shaul, Sonya, Avraham, and all their fellow inmates bore terrifying witness to Novogrudok's fourth and last massacre. Helplessly, directly outside their window, they watched the murder of Tamara, Fanya, and scores of others.[10] At their deaths, Tamara was forty-three years old[11] and Fanya just eleven.[12] Only one week later, Abraham was transferred by the non-Jewish supervisor of the mechanics' workshop[13] to the Koldychevo concentration camp, where he was brutally murdered on November 4, 1943.[14]

Fellow inmate Aaron Oshman, whose life was to become intertwined with that of Sonya, was born in Leipzig, Germany,[15] on May 15, 1910. Aaron was one of three sons of Matus and Tema née Gurvicz of Ivenets,[16] who were wealthy hardware business owners.[17] When Aaron was a toddler, his family relocated from Leipzig to Ivenets, Belarus, his father's hometown, where his grandparents and relatives still lived.

As a young adult in the 1930s, Aaron became a passionate follower of Ze'ev Jabotinsky, whose Revisionist Zionist movement rallied Jews to leave Europe immediately and settle in Palestine. Following the Communist invasion of Belorussia in 1939, Aaron's Revisionist activities did not go unnoticed by the new rulers, who sought to exile him and his fellow Zionist activists to Siberia. At the last moment, Aaron fled Ivenets to Novogrudok, where friends arranged identification papers for him and his relocation to the nearby town of Lida.[18]

To his surprise, Aaron did well in the clerical job he landed in Lida. He was also able to bring his younger brother Yakov "Yankel" to help him, and to regularly send money to their parents, whose home and business were seized by the Russian government. Aaron admitted hating the Fascist regime so greatly that he prayed for the Germans to take power.

"The day the Germans invaded, Lida was destroyed in five minutes," he recalls ruefully in his 1995 oral testimony. Making their way back to the crowded, squalid ghetto in Ivenets in 1941, Aaron and Yankel arrived just after the terrifying massacre in which their parents

Matus[19] and Tema,[20] twenty-one-year-old brother Reuven,[21] and hundreds of others had been gunned down.

Broken, Aaron and Yankel continued on to Novogrudok, where they were interned by the Germans in the Novogrudok forced labor camp. There, in an empty workshop, Aaron met "a beautiful young girl," his future wife Sonya, who found him crying over the deaths of his parents and brother. Comforting him, she said, "Don't cry, young man. You still have a life. You'll go on, and you'll marry."[22] Indeed, Sonya and Aaron were to share not only the forced labor camp, but the tunnel escape, the forest – where they were married – and the remainder of their rich, full lives together.

With Aaron declaring the tunnel escape as "the biggest achievement of our lives,"[23] his contribution to the breakout may have been of greater significance than is widely known. While Berl Yoselevich is generally considered to have conceived of the idea of a tunnel escape, either single-handedly[24] or in collaboration with Nota Sucharski (#4)[25] or Dr. Yakov Kagan (#3a),[26] Shaul Gorodynski confirms[27] Aaron's claim in his own testimony that he, along with two friends, conceived the plan for the breakout.[28]

On the dark, rainy night of the escape, Shaul safely crawled out the end of the tunnel, followed by his sister Sonya, Aaron, and Yankel. Although the escapees had been instructed to reach out to the person emerging directly after them, Sonya recalls that her brother forgot to do so, and they became separated.[29] Shaul testified that the intense shooting that filled the air just before making his way out of the tunnel caused him to initially lose track of Sonya, Aaron, and Yankel.[30]

For weeks, the escapees wandered through the forest, fighting starvation and weakness. Sonya recounts how she and Aaron held hands the entire time, hiding in bushes covered with leaves by day and trekking toward the partisans by night.[31] After three weeks, at their near-breaking point, they caught sight of a light flickering in a secluded farmhouse ahead. Sonya was designated to enter and plead with the farmer to give them food and shelter. The sympathetic man offered them milk and potatoes, as well as a hiding place behind his barn in a pit, which Aaron subsequently described as a "grave." The darkness was so total that by the time the farmer sent them away five weeks later, Aaron was nearly blind and had to be carried by Sonya and Yankel to the Bielski partisan detachment.[32]

Arriving in the *otriad* at last, Sonya and Shaul were reunited after four months.[33] Like them, Aaron and his sole surviving sibling Yankel were to survive the forced labor camp, the tunnel escape, and the forest together.

Following liberation in July 1944, Shaul, Sonya, Aaron, and Yankel first made their way to Ivenets and then to Lodz in April 1945. There, after being provided with false papers by Jewish organizations documenting that they were Yugoslavian war refugees, they continued by train to Transylvania, crossing the Austrian-Hungarian border to find refuge in displaced persons camps in Graz, Austria, and the Italian cities of Bologna, Trevisor, and Ancona.[34] In Italy, Shaul and Yankel separated from Sonya and Aaron to realize their long-time dream of settling in Palestine. Although Aaron had shared the Zionist dream as well, he deferred to Sonya's opposition to settling in a war-torn country.[35]

In May 1946, Shaul and Yankel were two of 1,014 Jewish war refugees to board the illegal refugee ship *Dov Hoz* from the port of La Spezia, Italy, after swimming the previous night from Milan in a covert operation by the Jewish Brigade.[36] In what was to become known as the "La Spezia Affair"[37] (the inspiration for the book and movie *Exodus*[38]), the ship was intercepted by the British in port before ever setting sail. Only after much publicity and a seventy-four-hour hunger strike by the survivors on board was permission granted to sail to Haifa port. This ship was the last to enter Palestine prior to the British policy of deporting illegal immigration boats to Cyprus.[39]

Now in his new homeland, Shaul met and married Tsipora née Argevich of Sosnovitz, Poland, who had reached the country in 1946 as the sole survivor of her entire family. Shaul soon took up arms as a soldier in the Haganah, the main paramilitary unit of pre-state Israel. He subsequently rose to become one of the first career officers in the new Israeli army, where he served for decades. Sadly, he was able to enjoy retirement for only three years before succumbing to heart disease at age fifty-five. He did speak openly about his past, including the tunnel escape, to his sons Avi, Azrikam, and Tamir, who have all attended memorial meetings in Israel for the Novogrudok martyrs.[40] Living only to see his first two grandchildren, Shaul would as of August 2023 be the grandfather of twelve and the great-grandfather of five.[41]

As for Sonya and Aaron, the couple remained in Italy from 1945 till 1950, living in various institutions for survivors in Florence, Ladispoli, and Castel Gandolfo. Matthew, their first child and the namesake of his maternal grandfather, was born in Florence in 1945.[42]

Almost six years after liberation, on June 22, 1950, Sonya, Aaron, and five-year-old Matthew sailed for America from the port of Bremen aboard the USS *General A.W. Greely*,[43] a US Navy transport ship.[44] They first took up residence in the East New York section of Brooklyn, where, with the help of an American relative, they eventually bought a grocery. In 1965, the family moved to Elizabeth, New Jersey, before settling in the town of Hillside, where Aaron entered the construction business and rose to success.

Sonya, who had been forced to abandon her dream of a career in medicine once the Soviets occupied Novogrudok, had begun studying languages instead. Over three decades later in 1975, she returned at last to university to earn a BA in French and Spanish and an MA in French literature from Kean College.[45] Son Ted praises his mother as having been "a smart, dynamic woman who was engaged in life and spoke freely and openly about the Holocaust." Her many speaking engagements spanned the gamut from schools to military bases.[46] Extremely eloquent, Sonya considered it her duty to pass on knowledge of the past while living life to the fullest in the present.

In contrast to Sonya's openness about her Holocaust experiences, Aaron was more reticent. Describing his father as "the most wonderful, thoughtful, kind, gentle, smart, ethical, and moral individual," Ted notes that Aaron never discussed the death of his parents or offered details about the war. Ultimately, he did give a detailed oral testimony for posterity to the Spielberg Survivors of the Shoah Visual History Foundation.

Ever the ardent Zionist, Aaron named Ted, born in 1956, for Zionist founder Theodor Herzl. Ted's Hebrew name, Tamir, memorializes Shaul and Sonya's mother Tamara.[47]

Sonya and Aaron enjoyed a happy marriage in which they "shared everything" and were "equals" in every way. Sonya's assistance and advice, including regarding Aaron's business, was always appreciated. Sons Matthew and Ted became successful attorneys, basking in the love and pride that Sonya and Aaron felt for them and their own four children.[48] If Sonya and Aaron were alive today, in August 2023, they would surely extend this love and pride to their four great-grandchildren.[49]

Sonya continually expressed deep gratitude for living in the "beautiful country" of America. Her extremely productive life ended in 2013, eleven years after the death of Aaron, her life partner of seven decades.[50]

The publication of this book would have been extremely important to Sonya. In August 2007, at the very beginning of her research, the author contacted Sonya in the course of efforts to locate other escapees. Shortly afterwards, Sonya wrote her: "I'm very proud of you! ...To find time to honor the Holocaust survivors who dug the tunnel, and thanks to that, the world will not forget the Holocaust."[51]

As for Yankel, he married a fellow survivor from Poland named Esther. Yankel is recalled by Shaul's son Azrikam Ganot as having been "a quiet, smiling man" who worked as a floorer by trade and lived a "simple, happy" life. The couple lived in the seaside city of Netanya together with their one child, daughter Tammy. Azrikam notes that the Gorodynski and Oshman families in Israel enjoyed a close relationship by virtue of their common relatives and shared history.[52]

Sonya and Shaul Gorodynski,
Italy, 1945 (courtesy of Azrikam
Ganot)

Sonya Gorodynski and Aaron
Oshman, Italy, 1945
(courtesy of Azrikam Ganot)

Both Yankel and Esther died relatively young. Esther died in 1975,[53] seven years before Yankel's death on November 16, 1982,[54] at the age of sixty-seven. Both are buried in Netanya.

Since around the year 2000, daughter Tammy has resided with her Israeli husband in Rio de Janeiro, Brazil, where the couple have two children and two grandchildren and maintain a martial arts studio,[55] far distant from any reminders of wartime slaughter, the tunnel escape, and partisans in the forest.

Yakov Oshman (*right*), upon
reaching Haifa port on the
Dov Hoz ship together with
Shaul Gorodynski, May 1946
(courtesy of Azrikam Ganot)

Yisrael (#81) and Shmuel (#82) Kolachek

At the outbreak of World War II, Shmuel Kolachek, born in the Belarusian town of Ivenets in 1896,[1] and his wife Yente were the parents of four children: Chaya Dvora, Moshe, Yisrael, and Risha. Following the Nazi German occupation of Ivenets on June 28, 1941, the Kolachek family was interned with the town's Jewish community in the Ivenets ghetto by November 1941.[2] Here eleven-year-old Moshe met his death.[3]

On January 2, 1942, the Jews were sentenced to a forced forty-two-mile trek in the frigid Belorsussian winter to Novogrudok's Pereseka ghetto. In a 2016 interview conducted in his mother tongue of Yiddish,[4] Yisrael reported that during their six- to seven-month internment in the Pereseka ghetto, he was sent out daily to central Novogrudok to clean the bricks of buildings destroyed by Russian bombers. These bricks would ultimately be sent to Germany for use as building material.

Just before the third Nazi mass execution of February 4, 1943, and the liquidation of the Pereseka ghetto, the Kolacheks were transferred to the Novogrudok forced labor camp.

With much emotion, Yisrael related that he "owes his life to a brick." On May 7, 1943, the day of Novogrudok's fourth mass slaughter, German commander Reuter forced the entire camp population to stand outdoors on the premise of his distributing seven ounces of bread rather than the regular ration of three and a half ounces. At the sudden selection for the death of half the camp population – mostly women, children, and those too weak to work – Yisrael reported that only by standing on a brick to appear taller was he spared being sentenced to die with the other children. While escaping execution by machine-gun some two to three hundred yards away, he nevertheless witnessed the massacre from a workshop window. Among the victims were his mother Yente and sisters Chaya Dvora and Risha. Shmuel and Yisrael were now the sole family members to remain alive.

Thanks to his experience as the manager of a Soviet shoe factory in Ivenets prior to the war, Shmuel had been co-opted to work as a shoemaker in the forced labor camp. Citing Russian victories at the front as spurring even greater hardships for the Jews, who bore the brunt of Nazi frustration, Yisrael recalled the rampant rumors of an impending fifth mass execution of the remaining camp inmates. He attributes the resulting plan for a tunnel escape to Berl Yoselevich, who reportedly raised the idea during a meeting called by Daniel Ostashinski, the former Judenrat head in Novogrudok. In his postwar testimony, fellow camp prisoner Shaul Gorodynski (#77) notes that Shmuel Kolachek was appointed to the committee formed to plan the outbreak, together with Natan Sucharski (#4), Berl Yoselevich, Chaim Leibowitz (#91), and Rubin Shabakovski (#5).[5]

Yisrael described himself, only fifteen years old at the time, as having been a "very active tunnel digger" by night, following his toil by day preparing snowsuits and galoshes to outfit German soldiers for gas attacks on the Russian Army. Ironically, however, neither the youthful tunnel digger Yisrael nor the key escape committee member Shmuel were destined to reap the benefit of their labor by escaping via the tunnel.

Fearing that his heart condition would prevent him from surviving the perilous crawl through the tunnel, Shmuel prepared a hiding place for himself and his son. With Eliahu Berkowicz (#49) fearing for the life of his sister Chaya Sara Luska (#168), who also suffered from a heart condition, the two were invited to join the Kolacheks in hiding. Like Berkowicz,[6] Yisrael attests that his father outfitted the warehouse loft, which served as the group's safe haven, with a twenty-inch-high double floor.[7]

Berkowicz credits the repulsive pile of garbage that Shmuel had arranged to cover over the warehouse loft as being an effective deterrent to the discovery of the hiding place.[8] While Berkowicz notes that his brother-in-law Zisel Rozin (#50) was also included in the hideaway,[9] Yisrael did not remember Zisel having been present. Both Yisrael and Berkovicz corroborate that they remained in the loft eight days, subsisting on the water and small pieces of bread that had been collected in advance.

Once they finally emerged from the loft, the stowaways found the Novogrudok forced labor camp to be completely abandoned by both inmates and guards. Evidently, the Germans had not imagined that any Jews were left in hiding following the great escape. Berkowicz recalls walking out of the camp through a hole in the barbed wire which had been used by police to trade with the inmates.[10]

Yisrael recalled that as he and his fellow escapees were attempting to reach the Bielski detachment, they were met by a partisan representative who shepherded them to the renowned way-station for escaped Jews and Russian partisans[11] run by the Belarusian peasant Konstanty "Kościk" Kozlowski.[12] Here they were provided with water and shelter until the next morning, when Kozlowski sent them on to another protective shelter, simultaneously dispatching a message to the Bielskis that these escapees wished to join the partisan detachment. Yisrael recalled that the partisan representative who arrived to guide them to a meeting place in the forest was initially greeted with intense suspicion. Only when Yisroel Kotler, a former neighbor of the Kolacheks in Ivenets, arrived in uniform and warmly embraced them did the group agree to accompany him to the Bielski detachment.[13]

In his memoir, partisan commander Tuvia Bielski named Shmuel Kolachek as having headed a team of twenty-two shoemakers, many of whom hung their weapons alongside them as they plied their trade. During a December 31, 1943, visit to the detachment by Soviet general Platon (Vasily Yefimovich Chernyshev), Kolachek personally briefed the general on how these men, shoemakers as well as fighters, were never separated from their arms.[14]

During the Kolacheks' six months with the Bielski partisans, Yisrael reported that he prepared the horse that was dispatched on food-gathering expeditions and sometimes joined these forays himself. After half a year, he and his father transferred to the Russian partisan unit under the command of Dubov, a former Communist Party leader in the Ivenets area who had known Shmuel Kolachek prior to the war. During a visit by Dubov to the Bielski group, the two were reunited, and Shmuel was persuaded to join the Russian unit along with Yisrael. The degree of respect Shmuel had commanded during the prewar years, Yisrael notes, was exemplified by Dubov's return with a horse and buggy to personally transport the Kolacheks to his own unit. Although Shmuel's departure from his detachment is said to have sorrowed Tuvia Bielski, Dubov is reported to have treated well the fifteen to twenty Jews among his three to four hundred partisans. Yisrael attributes this in great measure to the two common goals shared by the Jews and Russians: "to kill Germans and to end the war."

With a secret radio providing the Dubov partisans with accounts of German losses at the front, plus a clandestine press to print notices of these events, Yisrael's task was to provide encouragement and boost morale by distributing these notices among the other partisan groups in the vicinity (i.e., the Zorin and Bielski detachments). For these efforts, he was awarded two medals by the Soviet government at the end of the war.[15]

Immediately upon liberation, Shmuel and Yisrael traveled to Novogrudok, where they stayed overnight before returning "home" to Ivenets. There they confronted the reality that over a hundred relatives had been murdered, and strangers were living in their former home, severely damaged during the war. After moving with his father into the home of murdered relatives, Yisrael was drafted into the Soviet Army at the age of nineteen and dispatched to the Soviet-Chinese border for a four-year term of duty.

Shmuel returned to managing the shoe factory in Novogrudok, where he was warmly received by his former co-workers. Following his 1946 marriage to a fellow survivor with no children, Shmuel continued working in the factory until retirement, shortly before he succumbed to cancer in 1962.

Prior to his death, Shmuel had taken responsibility in the 1950s for establishing a memorial at the site of the mass grave in Ivenets where eight hundred individuals, including six hundred children under the age of twelve, were savagely murdered on June 9, 1942. By the dissolution of the Soviet Union four decades later, this memorial was damaged, and the stone fence Shmuel had built to surround the grave was in disrepair. In the early 1990s, a new memorial was erected and the fence repaired, thanks to the efforts of tunnel escapee Mordechai Morduchowicz, who raised the needed funds in Israel.[16]

As for Yisrael Kolachek, following his army discharge, he moved to Minsk, where he worked in a shoe factory. There he met and married Nella, a bookkeeper from the Ukraine. Initially living in a thirty-nine-square-foot room in an apartment that they shared with another couple, Yisrael and Nella eventually obtained a larger apartment as a result of their productive work at the factory.

Shmuel Kolachek lived to see the birth of his only grandchild, Bronia, born in 1957. In 1973, Bronia immigrated with her parents Yisrael and Nella to Israel. Arriving in what was then the two-street town of Carmiel, Yisrael was to reside in this now-burgeoning city for over forty years. After retiring from his job as an inspector for Israel Aircraft Industries (now Israel Aerospace Industries), where he was employed for twenty-two years, Yisrael continued to work part-time for a mattress company for another five years. He died on June 21, 2018.

Prior to his death, Yisrael's family spanned four generations. Bronia married and worked as a kindergarten teacher prior to her early retirement. Yisrael proudly pointed out that his daughter was much loved by the children in her care. Her only son, Milan, is nicknamed "Mulka" in memory of Shmuel, the grandfather he never knew. Milan has two children, Itai, born in 2003, and Shirelle, born in 2006.

Despite the family he had established, and despite his outwardly successful adjustment to life in Israel, Yisrael admitted that over seventy years later, he continued to be haunted by the war years. Often screaming out in his sleep, he experienced the recurring frightening nightmare of running for his life from the Germans, eventually seeking shelter under a bed.[17]

In August 2012, nearly six years before his death, Yisrael returned to the site of the Novogrudok forced labor camp. He was accompanied on the journey by Bronia, fellow survivors Idel Kagan (#95) and Riva Kaganowicz (#146), as well as fifty descendants of escapees for the filming of the movie *Tunnel of Hope*.[18] During the filming in which the participants succeeded in their search to locate the tunnel, Yisrael was visibly moved as he identified the soles of shoes used in the shoe-making workshop as well as handmade tools that were unearthed in the excavations.

A "regular" at the Novogrudok memorial meetings in Israel until his death, Yisrael is now sorely missed.

Yisrael Kolachek, Minsk, circa 1951 (courtesy of Israel Kolachek)

Shmuel Kolachek, undated photo (courtesy of Israel Kolachek)

Akiva Schmulewitz (#83)

Akiva ("Kiwa") Schmulewitz was born in the town of Lubcha on October 15, 1899,[1] to Hirsh and Lea.[2] While there is no record of Hirsh having been killed in the Holocaust, Lea was murdered in the Lubcha ghetto in August 1942. In August 1942, Kiwa's twenty-year-old sister Elka was murdered in Novogrudok and a forty-four-year-old brother was killed in Baranovich.[3] At the time of his imprisonment in the Novogrudok ghetto in 1941, Kiwa was single and had worked as a mushroom picker.[4]

In a country like Belarus, where 93.1 percent of the landscape consists of natural vegetation and one-third of all green landscape is forest,[5] mushroom picking is so profitable today that a "mushroom tax" has been legislated into law for professional gatherers.[6] If this held true in the past century as well, it is possible that as a mushroom picker, Akiva Schmulewitz made a decent living.

Kiwa survived the tunnel escape from the Novogrudok forced labor camp and succeeded in reaching the Bielski partisan detachment.[7] In an application to the Bavarian State Compensation Office in which he detailed his war history, Kiwa did not reveal his partisan participation. Instead, he noted that he was hidden by farmers from September 1943 to July 1944.[8] This claim is certainly understandable if we take into account that his report, dated August 1964,[9] was made in the midst of the Cold War with the Soviet Union, during which many partisans feared that their partisan activities would make them suspect of collaboration with the Soviets, thus jeopardizing their American citizenship.

Following liberation, Kiwa Schmulewitz spent several years in the Föhrenwald Displaced Persons Camp in Germany.[10] One of the largest camps of its kind in the American zone, Föhrenwald held the distinction in 1957 of being the last displaced persons camp to close.[11] It was there that Kiwa married Czarna née Berkowicz on September 26, 1947,[12] and there that the couple's daughter Pola ("Pesze") was born one year later.[13] The date of the marriage, perhaps symbolically, marked Kiwa's flight to freedom from the tunnel five years earlier to the day.

After his six-year stay in Föhrenwald, from the year of its opening in 1945 to 1951,[14] Kiwa, Czarna, and two-and-a-half-year-old Pesze journeyed at last to the United States of America. Boarding the USS *General C.H. Muir*, a former US military transport ship during World War II,[15] the family sailed from Bremenhaven, Germany, on March 3, 1951, to arrive in New York City ten days later.[16]

What was a professional mushroom picker to do in the United States? Sponsored by the International Rescue Committee refugee aid organization, Kiwa and his family were initially sent to the Buckstone Farm in Washington Crossing, Pennsylvania,[17] a working dairy farm founded in 1945 by Jewish philanthropist Sol Feinstone.[18]

In a document Kiwa submitted to the International Red Cross in 1964, he states that the family was residing at the time in Trenton, New Jersey.[19] We learn from an obituary for Czarna Schmulewitz, who died in nearby Hamilton Square in 2001, that the she had moved there in 1995,[20] ten years after Kiwa,[21] who is referred to in the obituary as "the late Rabbi Kiwa Schmulewitz."[22] The couple was noted to have been survived by daughter Paula Kalinowski, born Pesze Schmulewitz, who as a high school student was known as Pauline.[23]

The tunnel escape took place around one week before the Jewish New Year of 1943. After several years of searching for Paula (Pola, Pesze, Pauline), we located her around one week before the Jewish New Year of 2020. Peshie, as she calls herself, currently lives on a small farm in Chesterfield, New Jersey. Overwhelmed with emotion, she explained that she had no relatives, knew no one connected to her parents, and knew nothing of their past. Never having heard of Lubcha, Novogrudok, the labor camp, the tunnel escape, or the Bielski partisans, Peshie described a difficult childhood characterized by a mother preoccupied with her wartime past and a father who "never spoke, not about the Holocaust, not about anything. He just existed." No one had ever filled in the gaps of her parents' past and her own early childhood, and Peshie was moved to first learn basic biographical information about her parents, her birth while in the Föhrenwald Displaced Persons Camp, and her arrival and early life in the United States.[24]

Akiva (Kiwa) Schmulewitz, Germany, 1951 (courtesy of Paula Kalinowski)

Peshie does not remember her family's initial placement on the Pennsylvania farm. She speaks of growing up in Trenton, New Jersey, where her father worked nights in a kosher bakery after being the victim of painful anti-Semitism while working in a factory. In his later years, Kiwa served as a cantor and non-ordained rabbi of the Adath Israel synagogue, where he seemed to find solace and self-respect. His death in 1985 followed multiple strokes.[25]

Peshie, now the mother of two sons and grandmother of five girls, is married to Ken Kalinowski, a retired police detective who is a Polish Catholic convert to Judaism. Peshie left home at an early age and completed her studies to become a registered nurse. Although the pain still smarted of her parents' refusal to attend her wedding or to speak to her for nearly eight years afterwards, Peshie selflessly brought Czarna to her home, where she cared for her mother until nursing home care was required prior to her death in 2001. Peshie continues to recite Yizkor, the memorial prayer for the dead, for her parents.

When first told of her father's participation in the tunnel escape, Peshie found it difficult to believe that he was capable of such a feat.[26] Despite her father's silence, she is now aware of Kiwa Schmulewitz's bravery on September 26, 1943, and beyond.

Natan (Nota) Yankelevich (#84)

Natan (Nota) Yankelevich, a carpenter and merchant, was born in Lubcha on April 2, 1898, to David and Bunia née Michalewicz.[1] David, born in 1868, was a housewares dealer[2] who took an active leadership role in the Lubcha Jewish community.[3] Natan's younger brother Yakov, born in 1904, was a rabbi who lived with his wife Miriam née Landau in the town of Kovel.[4] Sister Perla, born in 1910, worked as a housemaid.[5] Joel, born in 1913, was a glass dealer.[6] According to Pages of Testimony that Natan completed in 1956, David and Bunia were slain in one of the Novogrudok massacres of 1942.[7] Perla and Joel, both single at the time, were killed in 1942 in Dworzecz[8] (Dvoretz), and Yakov was murdered in the Majdanek concentration camp in 1945.[9]

Natan and his wife Yenta née Berezowicz, a housewife,[10] had three children: Zev, born in February 1928; Arie, born in 1930, and Sara, her paternal grandmother's namesake,[11] born in 1934. In 1942, Yente and the children were massacred in Novogrudok.[12]

The last member of his immediate family to survive, Natan drew on his skills as a carpenter to be interned in the Novogrudok forced labor camp from 1941 to 1943. As many survivors have noted, carpenters played an essential role, fraught with danger, in constructing the clandestine tunnel. Natan ultimately survived the breakout to make his way to the forest and join the Bielski partisan detachment.[13]

International Red Cross records indicate that following the war and four years (1945–1949) in the Föhrenwald Displaced Persons Camp, Natan Yankelevich immigrated to Israel. In 1958, he was living at 33 Keren Kayemet Street in Givatayim with his second wife, the former Genia (Gustava) Schocher.[14]

After locating Genia's daughter Tsipora (Tsafi) through the assistance of the International Committee of the Red Cross (ICRC) Tracing Services at Magen David Adom Israel, we learned that Genia was born in 1904 in Novogrudok, the town she fled just five days prior to the German invasion of the city. Helped by her first husband to escape to Russia by walking to Minsk with their five-and-a-half-year-old daughter, Genia wandered throughout the Soviet Union with Tsafi, taking cover in Kazakhstan and Siberia.

After leaving Soviet territory at the war's end and residing in the Schlachtensee and Bergen-Belsen Displaced Persons Camps in Germany, the now-divorced Genia and her daughter sailed from Marseille on the first immigrant ship to the new State of Israel. The two arrived on May 15, 1948, the day on which the country declared independence. Tsafi proudly shares that her mother's immigration documents indicate Genia's being the new state's thirteenth immigrant, while Tsafi is listed as the thirty-fifth.

Tsafi relates that Natan Yankelevich was renting a room in Givatayim when his landlords introduced him to her mother shortly after his arrival in Israel. Tsafi was around fourteen years old at the time. Her recollections of Natan are of a kind, wonderful man who was loving and warm to both her mother and herself. "He was more of a father to me than my own father," Tsafi declares.

Natan was a modest man who worked in a grocery while Genia worked in a factory. Tsafi relates that she had learned of the tunnel escape when attending memorial meetings of the Novogrudok Society. Yet until being contacted by the author, she had no idea that Natan was ever in Novogrudok or that he had participated in the tunnel escape. Although she was aware that he had lost a wife and three children, she does not recall his ever having mentioned his war experiences, noting that "in those days the survivors didn't talk, and the children didn't ask." Tsafi partly attributes the silence of survivors to the prevailing attitude of native Israelis, vividly recalling how the newcomers were greeted with the taunt "*sabonim*" (soaps).

Despite his silence by day, the Holocaust haunted Natan's dreams by night, especially during his last years. At that time, Tsafi recalls frequent screams in his sleep, as Natan was plagued by nightmares of Germans hiding under the bed in wait to kill him.

Natan (Nota) Yankelevich, undated photo (courtesy of Tsipora Erez)

Natan and Genia are said to have been very much in love. During his last two years of life, Genia single-handedly nursed him at home when he was very ill and disabled with Parkinson's disease. Besides treating Tsafi like a daughter, Natan loved her three children dearly and considered them as his own grandchildren. The feeling was clearly mutual: on his gravestone inscription, he is noted as a "dear grandfather."[15] If he were alive today in 2019, Natan would be the great-grandfather of ten.

Besides being survived by Genia and her family at his death, Natan was survived by a brother in New York whose name Tsafi does not recall. This sole surviving sibling had come to the United States prior to the war and maintained minimal contact with Natan. The two brothers had chosen very different lifestyles: Natan's brother became a devout Jew who headed a yeshiva, in stark contrast to Natan, who gave up his religious observance soon after immigrating to Israel.[16]

Natan died at the age of seventy on February 11, 1968.[17] Genia passed away nine years later on May 15, 1976,[18] her twenty-eighth anniversary in her new homeland.

Betzalel (Salek) Ofsejewicz (#85)

Born in Lubcha in 1924, Betzalel (Salek) Ofsejewicz was the son of Yosef[1] and Leah née Binimowicz. Yosef was born in Lubcha in 1898 to Yona and Tirza,[2] and Leah was born in Novogrudok in 1905 to Lazar and Chana.[3] Residing in Lubcha, the couple had four sons, the oldest of whom was Salek, born in 1924. Save for Salek, the entire family – Salek's parents and his brothers Chanoch, born in 1926,[4] Yonatan, born in 1928,[5] and David, born in 1935[6] – were all murdered by the Nazis.

Totally alone, eighteen-year-old Salek was able to leverage his skills as a tailor,[7] in high demand by the German Army, to escape death and be assigned to the Novogrudok forced labor camp. As he crouched through the tunnel to freedom in 1943, he followed on the heels of two of his fellow Lubcha natives, Kiva Schmulewitz (#83) and Natan Yankelevich (#84), who both survived the escape as well. Salek joined the Kalinin Brigade, where he became a Bielski partisan.[8]

From Yad Vashem Pages of Testimony filled out in 1992 for Yosef and Leah Ofsejewicz by Sol Savitt, who identified himself as their son,[9] the author mistakenly assumed Sol was a brother of Salek. Once Sol Savitt's son, pediatrician Dr. Joseph Steven Savitt, was located with the help of a genealogist, both Dr. Savitt and the author were in for surprises. Betzalel (Salek) Ofsejewicz, it turned out, had changed his name to Sol Savitt after immigrating to the United States, and Dr. Savitt was none other than his own son. "Joe," as he calls himself, is the namesake of his paternal grandfather Yosef.

Joe Savitt and the author provided one another with invaluable information. He related having grown up with no knowledge whatsoever of his father's prewar and war years. Salek, he said, was a quiet man who never spoke of his life in Europe. Only following his father's death in 1995 did Joe begin to access information about his family from the Yad Vashem Central Database of Shoah Victims' Names. At that point, he was also told by family friends that his father had escaped from some kind of wartime confinement somewhere and that he had been a Bielski partisan.

Just as the author was excited to be able to obtain knowledge about Salek's postwar life, Joe Savitt was keenly anxious to learn about the Novogrudok escape. As Salek's only biological child, he describes himself as "the last link to [his] father," whose story he wishes to know.

Assuming at first that Salek had worked on his father's farm prior to the war, Joe was aware that his father's dream of going to dental school was thwarted by history. Presuming that his father's journey to America had been sponsored by a relative residing in the United States, he surmised from postcards found after his father's death that Salek had immigrated on the refugee ship SS *Ernie Pyle*.

Joe knew for certain that his father had settled in Manhattan, where through hard work and resourcefulness, Salek had successfully established himself in business, first in dry cleaning, then in real estate.

It was through his dry-cleaning business that Salek met his wife-to-be, Klara née Keller, a Holocaust survivor from Gyor, Hungary. A divorcee with a two-year-old son named Peter David, Klara found herself smitten by the dry cleaner who ruined her clothes. The two married in 1960 and soon afterwards moved from Manhattan to Long Island, New York. Peter was adopted by Salek. When Joe was born in 1962, the surname was already Savitt.

Although Salek himself never fulfilled his dream of becoming a dentist, his son Joe is a successful physician specializing in the treatment and rehabilitation of severely handicapped children. He resides in Williston Park, Long Island, and is married to Joanne Marie Socci, a teaching assistant. His son Jonathan, from a previous marriage, was born in 1992. Salek, Joe reports, was extremely joyful at the birth of his only grandson, the namesake of one of his murdered brothers.

Salek's son Peter, who lives in Long Island, works as a printer as well as a self-trained cantor. His only daughter Melissa was born in 1980. As with Joe, Salek never related his Holocaust experiences to Peter.[10]

Correspondence and records from the Red Cross International Tracing Service confirm Salek's escape from the Novogrudok forced labor camp.[11] Although he appears in the compilation of Jewish partisans in Belorussia as Tsalya Yosifovich Ovseivich,[12] in postwar documents he is listed as Salek,[13] the name that his son notes was most commonly used. Betzalel, he adds, was the name his father used in the synagogue.[14]

Betzalel (Salek) Ofsejewicz as a Bielski partisan, Naliboki Forest, September 1943–July 1944 (courtesy of Joseph Steven Savitt)

Red Cross documents also indicate that from 1946 through June 13, 1947, Salek was in the Neu Freimann Displaced Persons Camp located in Schwabing-Freimann, a borough in the northern part of Munich.[15] The Neu Freimann camp operated from July 1946 until June 15, 1949.[16] Just two months before its closing, Salek sailed from Hamburg to New York City, where he arrived on March 21, 1949. Precisely as his son Joe had suspected, the ship was indeed the SS *Ernie Pyle*, a transport ship deployed for displaced persons.[17]

Betzalel Ofsejewicz of the small town of Lubcha, Poland, died in Syosset, New York, as Sol Savitt in 1995,[18] preceding his wife Klara in death by thirteen years.[19] Only seventy-one when he died, Salek lived to see his son become a doctor, as well as the birth of grandchildren. As a result of this research, they may now know of his fight for life and his heroic escape. What was apparently too painful for Salek to share during his lifetime may now finally be revealed.

Gutel Shapiro (#86)

Born in 1922 to Gutel and Doba née Eicher,[1] Gutel Shapiro was twenty-one years old at the time of the tunnel escape. Prior to the war, he resided at 22 Zamkova Street in Novogrudok,[2] where he worked as a disinfector.[3] We know no other details related to Gutel's family of origin, other than the clue deriving from the local Ashkenazic Jewish custom to name a baby boy for his father only when the father is deceased.

Interned in Novogrudok's Pereseka ghetto,[4] Gutel was imprisoned in the Novogrudok forced labor camp following the second slaughter and the ghetto's subsequent destruction in August 1942. We do not know which profession the disinfector Gutel invented in order to qualify as a skilled tradesman in the labor camp.

Gutel survived the tunnel escape and his trek through the forest to the Bielski partisans. Listed as Gutl Gutelevich Shapiro in the compilation of Jewish partisans in Belorussia,[5] his participation in the Bielski detachment is confirmed in the National Archive of the Republic of Belarus. Here it also recorded that Gutel reached the *otriad* in September 1943.[6] Following the war, Gutel was listed by the Central Committee of Jews in Poland as residing in Lodz, Poland, in January 1947.[7]

Following his immigration to Israel in 1948,[8] in a September 1955 application for German reparations, Gutel Shapiro reported having resided in the city of Petach Tikva from 1950.[9] Israeli Ministry of the Interior records indicate that at the time of his death in 2018, Gutel, now Hebraicized to "Tuvia," was living in the coastal city of Netanya.[10] According to cemetery records, his wife Shoshana had died four years earlier.[11] Gutel and Shoshana's only son Meir was born in 1960.[12] To date, our efforts have been unsuccessful to locate Meir and to learn additional details about his father.

Shlomo Gorodynski (#87)

When lining up for the perilous tunnel breakout, Shlomo Gorodynski stood within ten places behind his second cousins, Sonya (#78) and Shaul (#77) Gorodynski. Nearly a hundred places behind stood Shlomo's father Moshe Gorodynski (#186), the only one of them who lost his life in the escape.[1]

Born in Karelich in 1916,[2] Shlomo was destined to become the sole survivor of his immediate family. Although we have no information on his biological mother Rachel née Moshkovitz,[3] Shlomo completed a Page of Testimony for his stepmother Miriam née Krinki, who was murdered in one of the Novogrudok massacres.[4]

The horrific Nazi massacre of August 7, 1942, in Novogrudok took the lives of three of Shlomo's siblings, Yitzchak, age fourteen,[5] Avraham, age ten,[6] and Rachel, just two years old.[7] In a Page of Testimony for his fourth sibling, Shaul, born in 1932, Shlomo did not record the date of his murder.[8]

If Moshe taught Shlomo the art of tailoring, he essentially gave his son a key to survival. With tailors highly needed by the Germans to supply uniforms to its massive force of troops, both Shlomo and Moshe were spared death to be assigned to the Novogrudok forced labor camp.

Following liberation, Shlomo took refuge in Germany in the Föhrenwald Displaced Persons Camp,[9] the second largest DP camp in the American Zone.[10] Here he met and married Tzila née Belizniyuk, born January 1, 1919.[11] By fleeing to Russia,[12] Tzila became one of only thirty survivors out of some six hundred Jews who lived in the small Polish village of Rafalowka prior to the war.[13] Shlomo and Tzila's daughter Bilha was born in the Föhrenwald camp in 1947. Six months later, the young family immigrated to Israel.[14]

Bilha, whom we located thanks to the assistance of the International Committee of the Red Cross (ICRC) Tracing Services at Magen David Adom Israel,[15] does not recall the exact location of the immigrant tent camp in which her family was first housed in Israel. She does remember their early years in a deserted, formerly Arab-owned apartment in Haifa that they shared with a fellow immigrant family from Lodz.[16] In the Pages of Testimony Shlomo submitted to Yad Vashem in 1956, he listed his address as 57 Jaffa Street, Haifa.[17]

Bilha shares that her father, whom she describes as having been tall and quite handsome, was greatly hurt by the demeaning attitude toward survivors that pervaded during the country's early immigration surge. The Gorodynskis remained living in Haifa, where Shlomo was employed for decades as a customs agent.

Thanks to her mother encouraging Shlomo to speak of his early life, Bilha learned of her father's education in *cheder* (religious school for young boys), his prewar service in the Polish Army as a cavalryman, and his participation in the tunnel escape. Bilha notes that Shlomo was extremely proud of having been a partisan. Although he is listed as having been a Bielski partisan,[18] she recalls him telling her that he was attached to a Russian fighting unit, with which he went on suicide missions.

Bilha is also aware that her paternal grandfather Moshe was killed in the breakout from the Novogrudok forced labor camp, citing an incident that occurred when she was around seventeen years old. At the time, a seemingly important visitor whose name she no longer remembers came to their home for lunch. She clearly recalls her father declaring that after he emerged from the tunnel into the darkness, this man had saved his life by grabbing his hand, refusing to let go as Shlomo attempted running after his father, fatally headed in the wrong direction.

Bilha Gorodynski rose to the position of personnel director of a bank. Today, she is retired and living in Tel Aviv. Her brother Moshe, his grandfather's namesake, worked as a computer specialist for a bank. At his death in 2013, Moshe was survived by a son and daughter, Shlomo's only grandchildren. According to Bilha, Moshe knew nothing about their father's war experiences, nor do his children.[19]

Shlomo died on April 10, 1981, at the age of seventy-five. He is buried in the Holon Cemetery next to Tzila, who died ten years later at the age of seventy-two on March 21, 1991.[20]

Beyond Bilha's limited knowledge of her father's past, she knew very little of his immediate family, nor had she been in contact with her own Gorodynski relatives for many years. As a fortuitous outcome of the author's research into the fate of tunnel escapee Shlomo Gorodynski, Bilha is now the recipient of Pages of Testimony her father completed for murdered members of his family, as well as contact information for cousins she'd long since lost track of.

Shmuel Niselevich (#88)

Shmuel Niselevich's post-liberation whereabouts and fate, like those of many other known tunnel survivors, were nearly impossible to trace. Considering the difficulty in obtaining genealogical, archival, and civil records from the former USSR, one supposition for survivors whose tracks were lost is that perhaps they remained within the borders of the former Soviet Union. At best, we could hope that eventually some of their descendants would be found in the West, as occurred with escapees Yakov Yoselevich (#96) and Isaac Ulert. Such is now the case of Shmuel Niselevich as well. After years of searching for his postwar whereabouts, the mystery was solved in May 2022, just after the completion of this manuscript. Thanks to a memorial meeting for the town of Zhetl, Niselevich's birthplace, in which the author spoke of her tunnel escape research, the names of the forty identified escapees from

Zhetl were posted. A Russian-accented cry from a young man then rang out: "Shmuel Niselevich was my grandfather!"

Two weeks later, an emotional meeting took place between the author and Shmuel Niselevich's grandson Dmitry (Dima) Karpukhin and his mother Ludmila (Luda) in their Ramat Gan home. Here we learned that Dima had immigrated alone to Israel from Russia in 2002 at age fifteen via a Jewish Agency program, and Luda had recently immigrated in October 2021.[1] Fortuitously, this was the first time that Dima had attended a Zhetl memorial meeting, as well as the first time that the tunnel escape was discussed at the yearly gathering.

Until now, we had assumed that Shmuel Niselevich, the son of Abram, was born in 1909, as indicated on partisan records.[2] Luda, how-ever, insists that her father was born in 1910. According to Russian doc-uments, Shmuel's first wife Rachel was murdered in 1942 along with their three-year-old daughter Leah.[3] Luda, however, recalls having been told that her half-sister's name was Masha. She also maintains that the child was younger than documented, noting that her father was said to have hidden her in a pocket he'd specially sewn inside his jacket.[4]

Although Shmuel almost never spoke of his first family, his war experiences, or the tunnel escape, Luda reports having been gener-ously provided with information by her mother Feige née Kaplinski, Shmuel's second wife. A Zhetl native, Feige had survived the war years in Siberia and married Shmuel after both returned to their hometown following liberation. Feige described to her children and Dima the hor-rendous details surrounding the deaths of Shmuel's first family, while also telling them of the courageous tunnel escape. According to Feige, Shmuel had witnessed the murder of his only child, after returning to the attic hideaway he had arranged for her and Rachel. Betrayed by a non-Jew, the two had already been hauled outside, where Shmuel helplessly watched his daughter being grabbed by the legs and her head fatally bashed upon the hard pavement.[5]

Later, Shmuel's skills as a tailor enabled him to be conscripted to the Novogrudok forced labor camp. Ultimately, he survived the tunnel escape and the difficult trek through the forest to reach the Borba Russian partisan detachment of the Lenin Brigade.[6]

Shmuel and Faige Niselevich were two of the few Jews who returned to and remained in Zhetl after the war. Here Shmuel continued to work as a tailor, and their three daughters were born: Dora in 1946, Raya in 1949, and Luda in 1955. In 1963, the family moved to the Belarusian town of Radun, where Shmuel was employed in a logistics position. There he died of a stroke on November 21, 1968, at age fifty-eight. Despite the terrible

Shmuel Niselevich, undated postwar photo (courtesy of Dmitry and Ludmila Karpukhin)

wartime atrocities he witnessed, Luda reports that Shmuel was able to rebuild his family and recover his spirit. Always in good humor, he was an extremely generous man who loved joking, being with people, and entertaining many guests, for whom he personally cooked. His funeral was attended by large numbers of those who knew and loved him.[7]

Following Shmuel's death, Feige moved to Voronova in 1971 and later relocated to the Russian town of Bryansk, where Luda and her family lived. Feige died in Bryansk in 2005.[8]

Luda's two sisters immigrated to New York many years ago. The death of her husband in Bryansk two years ago spurred Luda to consider immigration to Israel to join Dima and her son Artium, who immigrated to Israel in 2008. Luda is currently learning Hebrew, Dima is employed in high tech, and Artium works in the building industry.[9]

Today, Shmuel Niselevich's descendants living in the United States and Israel include his three daughters, four grandchildren, four great-granddaughters, and a great-great-granddaughter. An optimistic man despite all that he had suffered during the war, he would have been most proud to see the near-miraculous continuation of his family.

Shlomo (#89) and Efraim (#90) Okonski

Shlomo and Efraim Okonski were born in the central Polish town of Proshnits (Przasnysz). Together with their parents and siblings, they were among the refugees who fled to Novogrudok – a 250-mile (405 km) journey – as the Germans occupied their Polish cities and towns.

Shlomo, born on June 30, 1926, and Efraim, born March 15, 1928, were two of the seven children[1] born to Aharon Yosef (Yosel)[2] and Dina née Novoveyski. The eldest, Chana Rivka, born in 1922, was a high school student at the outbreak of the war. Avraham was born in 1930, David in 1932, Natan in 1935, and Frida, the youngest, in 1938 or 1939. Yosel survived the war. Of the seven children, only tunnel escapees Shlomo and Efraim escaped murder.[3]

After the German invasion of Proshnits in 1939, the sight of the town's rabbi being dragged by his beard to his death sealed Yosel's decision to leave his hometown and head with his family to Novogrudok, close to the Russian border. Assuming that this proximity would offer a measure of safety and the possibility of escape, Yosel, a shoemaker, was fated to be saved by the Russians without ever having to flee. After the Soviet invasion of the area, Yosel was ordered into forced labor in a Siberian shoe factory. There he survived the war, not knowing the fate of the family he left behind.

Now alone, Dina and her seven children were confined to the Novogrudok forced labor camp. Fearful that her children would attempt to escape by night, she was said to have hidden their shoes each night before she went to sleep. Against impossible odds, Dina succeeded in keeping several children alive from the time Yosel was sent to Siberia in 1939 until her own murder on May 7, 1943.

The horrors began with the savage massacre of fifty-two Novogrudok townspeople on July 26, 1941. In the aftermath, Dina and her daughter Chana were among the women forced to clean the blood from the marketplace cobblestones. By December 8 of that year, the first mass murder struck the Jewish community. Chana was ordered to her death in one of the mobile gas vans used in Belorussia, joined by her fiancé, who refused to allow her to die without him at her side. Thirteen-year-old Avraham, the only member of the family not assigned to the shoemakers' workshop, was killed by a blow to the head following a failed attempt to flee to his brothers in their workshop during the second mass slaughter on August 7, 1943. Ten-year-old David was murdered in Novogrudok's third massacre on February 4, 1943.

Up to this point, Dina had survived all of the "selections" for death thanks to her sons Shlomo and Efraim, who fulfilled their mother's quota of shoe production in addition to their own. Yet in the massacre of May 7, 1943, which annihilated the last Jews of Novogrudok, Dina and her two youngest children Natan and Frida were slaughtered. For the previous three months, Shlomo had made a desperate attempt to hide his little sister Frida in a workshop drawer from the moment he'd learned that small children were being hurled to their deaths from the roof of the courthouse.

Although Yosel was far away during the entire Nazi invasion of Novogrudok – and even began a new family in Siberia – his having taught Shlomo and Efraim the art of shoemaking essentially saved their lives through all the deadly selections. Both brothers successfully survived the tunnel escape. When the breakout began in the dark of night, Shlomo is reported to have noticed the sleeping fifteen-year-old Riva Kaganowicz (#146) and heroically carried her from her bed to her place in line.[4]

Shlomo and Efraim made their way through the forest to the Bielski partisan detachment, moving by night and sleeping in cemeteries and in the homes of non-Jewish farmers who agreed to provide shelter during the day.[5]

Shlomo is listed as having served with the Kalinin or "family" group of partisans.[6] His son Yanek attests that his father had a weapon and fought in operations to kill Germans and local collaborators, blow up trains, as well as burn the homes of those who betrayed Jews to the enemy. With simple guns, Shlomo and other partisans defied the odds to shoot down a plane manned by German, Belarusian, and Ukrainian soldiers.

Upon liberation on July 9, 1944, the twelve hundred newly freed Bielski partisans left their forest refuge en masse to reach Novogrudok on foot. By July 16, Shlomo had made his way to Minsk together with Asael Bielski to participate in the great partisan parade to celebrate the city's liberation from the Nazis. From there, both he and Asael were drafted into the Red Army, where Shlomo fought in the crucial Battle of Berlin.[7]

Discharged from his military duties in 1952, Shlomo joined his father Yosel, stepmother Freida, and stepsister Pnina near the small Polish town of Valzich. There Shlomo managed three hotels for the Polish Army. In 1954, Shlomo wed Genya, a kindergarten teacher. As a child, she had been placed in hiding by her parents in a monastery in Borislav, Ukraine. Raised by nuns who were ultimately murdered by the Nazis for hiding Jewish children, prior to her death in 2022, Genya had no idea as to her biological parents' identity or of her original name. Genya and Shlomo's son Yanek was born in 1954, and daughter Dina was born two years later.[8]

In 1957, Shlomo and Yosel immigrated to Israel with their families. There they were reunited with Efraim, who had immigrated to Palestine in 1947 following two years in the Landsberg Displaced Persons Camp.[9] After a period of living in asbestos-lined shacks in the Motzkin immigrant camp, the new immigrants all moved to Kfar Saba. Shlomo worked for the Israeli telecommunications company Bezeq, where he was promoted to manager. Genya continued to work as a kindergarten teacher. Yosel remained alive until 1971.

For several years, Efraim lived and worked in Kibbutz Kinneret, where other tunnel escapees, including Pesach Abramowicz (#205) and Yakov Shepsman (#39), had also initially settled. As a soldier in the nascent Israel Defense Forces during the War of Independence, he was wounded in the leg and never fully recovered from his injury. Efraim married a native-born Israeli, Bruria née Mendel. The couple settled in Ramat Gan, where they raised their children Nili and Danny. An independent businessman, Efraim owned a garage in Jaffa as well as a motorbike shop. His nephew Yanek relates that Efraim suffered lifelong trauma from the blows to his head in the labor camp and from witnessing the horrific murder of his mother and two youngest siblings. Fearful of losing yet another loved one to war in Israel, he opted to immigrate with his family to the United States in 1983, where he established himself in the auto-glass business.[10]

While Efraim is reported by both his children to have outwardly appeared to have made a good postwar adjustment,[11] his son Danny, interviewed from his California home, admits having grown up with a father who suffered constant physical as well as emotional pain.[12] Danny and his sister Nili recall having been told as small children of the tunnel escape and life in the partisan units.[13] Their father frequently spoke of his Holocaust experiences and seemed to be constantly thinking of his murdered loved ones.[14]

While Shlomo's son Yanek also reports having grown up with frequent stories of his father's Holocaust experiences, he feels that his father's daring acts of revenge as a partisan afforded him some sense of victory and satisfaction. Yanek recalls that on a trip to Poland with his father in 1991, Shlomo spent time searching for a house in whose attic he had left a suitcase full of watches. Although his father was unsuccessful in his search, Yanek was told that if he ever wished to know how many Nazis Shlomo had killed, he should find the suitcase.[15]

Shlomo died on January 15, 2009. Despite the atrocities he witnessed and the loved ones he lost, he did not leave a legacy of hate. Acknowledging assistance given by non-Jews, he often told how a

Belarusian who worked in the camp had helped the inmates whenever possible, and how the Pole in charge of the carpentry shop had turned a blind eye when the forced laborers smuggled out wood to be used in the construction of the escape tunnel. Shlomo also spoke highly of another Pole who'd stood guard at the gate and would often allow both him and Efraim to leave the camp by night to forage for food, sell the soles from shoes they'd purloined from the shoemakers' workshop, and to spend the night at the home of a compassionate local woman known by her surname "Rajeska." The carpentry foreman and both guards paid for their kindness with their lives: discovered by the Germans, they were hanged together in the labor camp.[16]

While Yanek has visited the site of the Novogrudok forced labor camp three times, neither his sister nor Efraim's children have been to Belarus. Today, Yanek lives in an agricultural settlement where he serves as the area's coordinator for the Border Police. In his father's footsteps, he has been involved in many security actions. In 2008, Yanek was awarded a Presidential Medal for his bravery. His sister Dina is a retired kindergarten teacher in Kfar Saba.[17] Efraim's son Danny is in the construction business,[18] and Danny's sister is the manager of a law office.[19] Shlomo's five grandchildren and Efraim's six grandchildren were a tremendous source of pride to both brothers.[20] If they were alive in August 2023, Shlomo would have eleven great-grandchildren, and Efraim would have six grandchildren and one great-grandchild.[21]

Efraim, the last member of the original Okonski family from Novogrudok, died on July 3, 2013.[22] Two months earlier, his nephew Yanek had represented the Israel Border Police at a commemoration ceremony in Auschwitz during which he proudly bore the Border Police flag. With tears in his eyes, Yanek relates having felt that he had come full circle, returning to his native Poland as an officer in the armed forces of the State of Israel.[23]

Shlomo (*standing, third from left*) and Efraim Okonski (*standing, second from left*) in family picture, Novogrudok, 1939 (courtesy of Yanek Okonski)

Chaim Noah Leibowitz (#91)

Despite the unspeakable pain he endured, Chaim Leibowitz found the courage to record and recount his experiences of the horrors of wartime Novogrudok. For now and for generations to come, his writings constitute a priceless eyewitness account of atrocities, torment, bravery, and resilience.

Chaim Noah Leibowitz (originally named Chaim Kushner), a hatmaker by trade, was born in 1895[1] and lived in Novogrudok before the war. The son of Chonon, Chaim was one of nine children, seven girls and two boys. Prior to WWII, Chaim had taken a leading role in the town's charitable organizations, primarily the Shokdey Melocho

Trade School and the Jewish Orphanage. At the arrival of the Soviets to Novogrudok in 1938, Chaim became the director of both institutions.[2]

The reason and the timing for Chaim's name change remain a mystery to this day. While he appears on the 1943 Novogrudok forced labor camp escape list as "Chaim Leibowitz,"[3] he is subsequently listed as "Chaim Kushner" in the compilation of Jewish partisans in Belorussia. In a postwar listing of refugees by the American Joint Distribution Committee (AJDC), he appears as Chaim Leibowitz, the name that he then kept for life. Chaim's great-nephew Murray Kushner surmises that Chaim changed his name before the Holocaust in order to avoid conscription to the Russian Army.[4]

Prior to the war, Chaim was married and had two children, a son and a daughter. In her oral testimony, Chaim's niece Raya Kushner (#144) recalls the pre-dawn raid in which the Germans seized thousands of children from the ghetto in the Novogrudok neighborhood of Pereseka.[5] From her description, which correlates with other published reports,[6] this event took place during Novogrudok's second massacre of August 7, 1942. Raya describes scenes of parents on their hands and knees begging for their children to be spared as a white-gloved German, after attempting to separate a child from his mother, decided to make things "easy" by simply sending both mother and child together to their deaths.[7] It is probable that the white-gloved German was none other than Nazi ghetto commandant Wilhelm Reuter, who was known to have covered his hands with white gloves before hitting a Jew. Later, with the transformation of the Novogrudok courthouse into a forced labor camp, Reuter is reported to have completely avoided entering the camp for fear of contracting a disease.[8]

It was during this ghastly second Novogrudok massacre that fierce efforts were made to save Chaim Leibowitz's two children along with eight others by hiding them behind a storage space filled with newspapers. After being hidden for several days, they were eventually sniffed out by German shepherds. According to Raya Kushner, Chaim and his wife watched their ten-year-old son and eight-year-old daughter die in agony choking to death on a toxic white powder.[9] According to Zeidel's version, however, their daughter was only five or six years old at her death, and a German soldier took pity on her fourteen-year-old brother and spared him. Five months later on May 7, 1943, this boy was murdered in Novogrudok's fourth slaughter, hand in hand with his mother.[10]

Although Chaim wrote in excruciating detail about the fourth massacre, he never mentioned the fact that members of his own family were among the 302 people he reports were murdered. He carefully chronicles the horrific event, beginning with how the best workers were separated from the less skilled. Those considered less qualified were then surrounded by black-uniformed Belarusian police and heavily armed Latvians, forced to completely undress, taken in groups of ten to prepared trenches, and shot to death face down. Women who resisted were often beaten and dragged by their hair to the trenches. With the slaughter carried out in full view of the Novogrudok forced labor camp, Chaim raises the possibility that the proximity of the trenches to the camp (less than 450 yards) was purposely intended to force survivors to witness the hideous massacre of their loved ones.[11]

In a heart-wrenching testimony of this bloodbath, Raya Kushner describes Chaim's piercing cries and screams at the sight of his wife being taken to her death. The Germans abruptly ordered Chaim outside and instructed two Jews to beat him with sticks. Fearful of their own deaths, these Jews carried out the sadistic order.[12]

Chaim testifies that within three days of the May 7 massacre, the decision was taken to build the tunnel. Hinting at the possible influence of the Warsaw ghetto uprising upon resistance attempts within the forced labor camp, he notes that the committee members planning the escape had learned details of the Warsaw events via a radio receiver concealed in the camp. The existence of the radio was known solely to the committee members,[13] who, according to Shaul Gorodynski (#77), included Chaim, Natan Sucharski (#4), Berl Yoselevich, Shmuel Kolachek (#82), and Rubin Shabakovski (#5).[14]

In his testimony, Chaim notes the dimensions of the tunnel as 28 inches wide, 28 inches high, and 262 yards long.[15] He corroborates the account of Eliyahu Berkowicz (#49)[16] that upon the tunnel's completion, a secret-ballot vote was held for all inmates in order to obtain a majority opinion on the decision to carry out the escape. According to Leibowitz, 65 percent of the inmates voted in favor of the breakout.[17]

Chaim, his brother Zeidel, and Zeidel's two daughters Leah (#145) and Raya survived the escape and the complex trek through the forest to join the Bielski partisan detachment.[18]

There Chaim became the chief of the detachment's hat-making workshop, where he was responsible for five other workers. In his memoirs, partisan commander Tuvia Bielski mentions that the Soviet general Platon spoke with Chaim Leibowitz personally during the general's visit to the workshop on his December 31, 1943, tour of the detachment.[19] Fellow tunnel escapee and Bielski partisan Fanya Dunetz (#142) recalls that despite his personal tragedies, Chaim was an extremely sociable member of the Bielski partisan detachment in the forest, often surrounded by and engaged in conversation with others.[20]

Until his death, Chaim was to remain inseparable from Zeidel's family, which eventually grew to include Raya and Leah's spouses and their children. After remaining in Novogrudok for around one year following the war, Chaim traveled with the Kushners to Czechoslovakia. There they began their journey across the border to Austria, Hungary (where Raya was married), and finally to Italy. Here, the extended family – later including Raya's first child – all lived in one room in the northern Italy Cremona Displaced Persons Camp[21] for three and a half years, waiting urgently for a visa to any country that would accept them. Relatives who had immigrated before the war ultimately sponsored their immigration to the United States in 1949.[22]

As they began their new life in America at last, Chaim, Zeidel, Leah, Raya, her husband, and their two children (to be joined by another two born in 1951 and 1954) all lived in a one-bedroom, four-story walk-up in Brooklyn for five years, from which both Chaim and Zeidel

commuted to their jobs in a hat factory.[23] After
the move of the entire clan to Elizabeth, New
Jersey, in 1954, Chaim lived in a nearby room-
ing house, spent holidays with his brother and
family, and managed a building in the family's
real estate business.[24]

Although Chaim Noah Leibowitz left no
offspring or grandchildren, he leaves a rich
legacy of writings providing invaluable historical testimony of wartime and postwar
Novogrudok. Even before the war, the ardent
Zionist had edited many Zionist papers and
publications.[25] In his article "The Three Kol
Nidreis," Chaim poignantly describes Yom
Kippur eve in the Novogrudok ghetto in 1942,

Chaim Noah
Leibowitz, undated
photo (*Memorial Book
of the Jewish Community
of Novogrudok, Poland*)

in the forest after the tunnel escape in 1943, and in Rome one year
after liberation. Reflecting on his "aching heart and troubled soul" on
the eve of Yom Kippur seventeen years later in a New York synagogue,
Chaim writes that contrary to expectations, this agony had not healed
with the passage of time.[26] His description of the last Passover in the
Novogrudok forced labor camp is especially heart-wrenching, as he
depicts how the makeshift Seder evoked memories within the inmates
and how the women wept for their murdered children.[27]

While his writings on the subject of the tunnel escape are charac-
teristically detailed and highly informative,[28] Chaim Leibowitz's entire
collection of historical Holocaust accounts is eerily bereft of any mention of the details of his own personal losses. Although he rarely spoke
of his late wife and children,[29] he is said to have reminisced about his
prewar life in Novogrudok when directly questioned.[30]

Chaim's expressed wish to start another family[31] was partially
realized around 1965 with his remarriage to a fellow survivor named
Chanka. Although the new couple had no children together, this marriage was to last until Chaim's death on June 12, 1975.[32]

Chaim's name lives on today in that of his great-nephew Jonathan
Chaim Kushner.[33]

Yanson (#94)

The identity of inmate #94, who appears on the Novogrudok forced labor camp escape list simply as "Yanson," remains a mystery.

From all of Poland, Yad Vashem's Central Database of Shoah Victims' Names lists only one woman with this surname, Frieda Yanson, born in 1878,[1] whose name appears in a compilation of Lodz ghetto inmates from 1940 to 1944. Could this sixty-five-year-old woman have somehow escaped the Lodz ghetto, made her way to Novogrudok, and then participated in the tunnel escape? Chances are slim.

The sole male from Poland with the surname Yanson appearing in the central database, Volf (Velvel) Yanson of Novogrudok,[2] was the person whom the author was certain must be escapee #94.

After an extensive international genealogical search, contact was made in 2018 with Velvel Yanson's ninety-five-year-old widow, Leah Johnson. A former Bielski partisan, Leah is a well-known speaker on her Holocaust experiences. In an emotional telephone meeting, Leah recalled the author's mother (Fanya Dunetz, #142) from the partisans and from visits with her in New York. However, the author was shocked to learn that Velvel, who died in 1979 in Montreal, was never conscripted to the Novogrudok forced labor camp and did not take part in the tunnel escape. Relating that her husband escaped to the forest from the Novogrudok ghetto in 1942, Leah testifies that without a shadow of a doubt, no known member of her husband's family survived until 1943 (the year of the tunnel escape).[3]

Whatever the identity of the escapee Yanson, we can presume that he or she did not survive the tunnel escape to reach the partisan detachments. Beyond Velvel Yanson, no other person with this surname is listed among the Jewish partisans in Belorussia.[4]

The possibility exists that the name of escapee #94 was incorrectly recorded. We may never know his or her true identity.

Idel Kagan (#95)

It was in 1945 in Landsberg, Germany, while recuperating from surgery that sixteen-year-old Idel Kagan, now almost completely alone in the world, attests that he learned the true importance of giving. Unable to walk and suffering the ravages of a primitive wartime amputation of his toes, Idel suddenly received a forty-four-pound package from a Mrs. Adell in America. The moment that Mrs. Adell, a prewar acquaintance of Idel's parents, had heard that he was alive, she'd rushed to send the young orphan a splendid assortment of chocolate, food supplies, and cigarettes. Over fifty years later, Idel (now "Jack") Kagan wrote that Mrs. Adell's generosity taught him "the greatest lesson in life."[1]

Jack, in turn, became a giver. Honoring the dead, he single-handedly memorialized the murdered Jews of Novogrudok and surroundings at the sites of their massacres, where no markers or signs of remembrance had stood before. Giving to the living, Jack was unsurpassed in assuring the survivors that the murder of their loved ones would not go unrecognized. Thanks to his extensive writings, their children and grandchildren are aware of what their parents and grandparents endured. Through his contributions to Holocaust education, thousands of schoolchildren have learned of the atrocities of World War II and of the tunnel escape. As a result of his funding the Jewish Resistance Museum in Novogrudok, numbers of local and international visitors to Belarus come to learn firsthand about the escape. Contributing to the production of the movie *Tunnel of Hope*, Jack accompanied the group that came to Novogrudok in 2012 to search for and find the tunnel, giving of himself to enable the survivors to be recognized and the dead honored for their bravery. As a result of Jack's efforts, the world cannot deny what happened in Novogrudok, both to the victims and to the survivors who took part in the most successful prisoner escape of the

Holocaust through a hand-dug tunnel. Thanks to Jack's efforts, his writings, and his meetings with me in Jerusalem to provide firsthand information, this book is being written. I thank Mrs. Adell, and I thank Jack.

Although Jack's given name is listed as "Yudel" on the original Yiddish-language escape list, his son Michael declares that his father was never known as Yudel. He maintains that the correct name is Idel, the name Jack used to refer to himself all his life,[2] as well as in his writings.[3]

Born in 1929, Idel Kagan grew up in a house on Racelo Street in Novogrudok where two sisters were married to two brothers. Although each family had its own home, they opted instead to live together in one house, harmoniously and happily. Idel's father Yankel was a businessman whose brother Moshe ran the two families' small sandal factory and saddle-making workshop, which their father Leizer had founded.

Idel's mother Dvore was a businesswoman who operated the two shops where sandals and saddles were sold. Her sister Shoshke was the homemaker, cooking and cleaning for both families, which each included two children. Idel's sole sibling, his sister Nechama, was two years his senior. Moshe and Shoshke's two boys, Berl and Leizer, carried their grandfathers' names.[4] In addition to the four Kagan children, their paternal cousin Leizer Sanderovski of Zhetl grew up in their home after his mother's death in childbirth.[5]

The family home is said to have been a spacious wooden structure, and the children are reported to have enjoyed an idyllic life.[6] Even in later years when Idel would speak of the horrors of the Novogrudok Holocaust, he never forgot the extraordinary setting of his youth and longed for the wondrous aspects of his childhood.

From the age of five, Idel attended the Menaker *cheder,* the religious school where young boys were taught to read Hebrew and to pray. With lessons from early morning till sunset, the youngsters would return home to the light of the kerosene lamps they carefully held aloft. Afterwards, Idel attended the Tarbut school, where eight hundred pupils were taught primarily in the Hebrew language.[7]

Upon the Russian occupation of Novogrudok on September 17, 1939, life changed drastically for Idel and the Kagan family. With Hebrew and religious instruction forbidden, Idel began attending a Yiddish school where he also learned Russian and Belarusian. The family's shops and workshops were shuttered, and their home was searched for hidden leather products. When the authorities deemed the house too large for just two families, the Kagans were forced to accept tenants. The date April 7, 1941, became etched in Idel's memory: his twelfth birthday party was the very last family celebration.[8]

By June 28, the Kagans were homeless. German firebombs had wreaked massive destruction on the town's center, leveling Racelo Street. Unaware of the fate of Jews throughout occupied Poland and totally unprepared for the destruction to come, the Kagans located a vacant house and moved in with about eight other families. Idel was left with only the pair of shorts he was wearing and the shirt on his back. To preserve his only pair of shoes, he trekked barefoot for thirteen miles (10 km) to his grandmother's house in Karelich to bring provisions back to Novogrudok.[9]

Following the German invasion of July 4, 1941, Yankel and Moshe continued to work as saddlemakers for local farmers who paid them with bread, while Idel, Dvore, and Shoshke each received ten and a half ounces of bread and potatoes for cleaning out the rubble of bombed streets. Yet the horrors flashed before their eyes. As fifty-two men were slain to the accompaniment of Strauss waltzes in the marketplace massacre on July 26, 1941, twelve-year-old Idel crouched behind a burnt house on Racelo Street, thinking he must have imagined the music.[10]

Novogrudok's first mass slaughter, December 8, 1941, brought a devastation of terror and death. Idel watched in terror as Moshe, Shoshke, and their sons Leizer and Berl helplessly began walking to their deaths when ordered by the German officers to go "to the left." Miraculously, Berl's quick response to the sudden request for an auto mechanic saved his life.[11] Yankel and Dvore, who were among the fifteen hundred people ordered to Novogrudok's Pereseka ghetto, became two of the near-450 inmates assigned to the workshops in one of the courthouse buildings, Yankel as a saddler, and Dvore to stitch fur gloves. Thirteen-year-old Idel took his place among the 250-odd crew assigned for work duty in the former Russian barracks in nearby Skiridlevo, eerily close to where his uncle, aunt, and cousin had recently been forced to undress before being shot to death. Assigned to wheelbarrow stones, Idel recalls having constantly worn a padded jacket to avoid the lead-tipped whip of the Nazi whose pleasure was to strike the prisoners as he rode by on his horse.[12]

When Idel was ordered to work at the courthouse to learn saddle making, the youngster's resourcefulness, ingenuity, and business acumen – which became his trademarks – were already evident. Finding a fireman's hose in the basement, he brought pieces of the rubber to the ghetto to be sold as soles for shoes, then sold linen he found under a pile of municipal papers.[13]

Describing the anguished mood in the ghetto prior to the second massacre on August 7, 1941, Idel writes: "We all knew that an action would soon take place and escape was easy. But where do you go to when nobody will let you in?" The massacre in Litovka marked the horrific deaths of fifty-five hundred men, women and children, including Idel's cousin Srolik Sucharski. That same evening, when all those in the courthouse workshops were ordered to line up, Idel wore his father's jacket and trousers to appear older. Children who'd been smuggled inside by their parents and now found hidden in the loft and basement were hurled to their deaths from the windows. Those who survived were hauled by truck to join their parents in the graves of Litovka. Now, with five hundred prisoners remaining in the Pereseka ghetto and five hundred in the courthouse workshops, the courthouse officially became the Novogrudok forced labor camp.[14]

During the summer of 1942, the news that the Bielski brothers had formed a partisan detachment spurred many young labor camp inmates to consider escape.[15] In November, partisan Ishie Oppenheim sneaked into the labor camp to organize a successful breakout of young people, including Berl. Envious, Idel began planning his own escape to freedom. On December 22, while the camp gates were opened for trucks to bring in raw materials, he slipped out to join fourteen others waiting in the forest. Here, Ruvke Oppenheim, Ishie's brother, was to lead them to the way station of the righteous Gentile Bobrovski, where they would be met by Bielski partisans and taken to the forest.

Yet the young escapees reached the meeting place too late and were instructed to wait three days in a nearby forest until the partisans were due to return. Poor Idel had fallen along the way through the ice in the Britanka River, and his felt boots had absorbed the freezing water to the point that he could now barely walk. Fearful of freezing to death as he waited for the returning partisans, Idel's sole, desperate option was to return to the labor camp. Crawling to the road, he climbed onto the back of a passing peasant's sleigh. Let off near the camp, the youngster waited for a group of water carriers to carry him back to his room. There, as Idel was held down by four inmates, a dentist used his dental pliers to cut through the bone with no anesthesia to amputate all his frostbite-blackened toes.[16] Despite the trauma and unspeakable pain, in a memoir written many years later, the ever-grateful Idel gave thanks to his beleaguered feet: "Thank you, my feet, frozen, bloody, you kept creeping and crawling and you saved me from death."[17]

Looking back on the unsuccessful escape attempt, Idel expressed his appreciation for the older inmates who, despite the threat of collective punishment should an inmate be missing, still encouraged the younger people to escape.[18] Nor did he ever forget the kindness of the Bobrovski family, most of whom were later murdered by the Germans for aiding and harboring Jews. In a 2012 meeting with the descendants of the forced labor camp survivors, he recalled the bowl of soup given to him by Mrs. Bobrovski, which he credits with saving his life.[19] A champion of acknowledging wartime aid by Gentiles to their Jewish neighbors, Idel was instrumental in obtaining the status of Righteous Among the Nations for the Bobrovski family, and he continued to aid them until his death.[20]

It was while recuperating from his painful wounds that Idel parted from his mother and father. Recalling May 7, 1943, as a "nice and sunny day," he lay on his plank, incapable of even standing for roll call. From inside, he witnessed many local and foreign policemen beating the workers. Suddenly his mother appeared at the window to reassure him, saying, "It's nothing." Even as he saw the commotion as a truly foreboding sign, Idel instinctively realized that his mother's appearance and assurance was her farewell. Later that day, his father Yankel came to break the news that both Dvore and Nechama had been taken to their slaughter just opposite the camp.

Less than one month later, Yankel was the next loved one to be wrenched from Idel's life. Transferred at the beginning of July 1943 with ten other skilled tradesmen to the Koldichevo concentration camp, Yankel was murdered sometime in February 1944 at the escape of all ninety-six Koldichevo Jews. Recalling the last time he saw his father, Idel writes: "It was a very sad day for me, the parting was so quick, and to this day I see my poor father with the small packet in his hands putting on a brave face, saying he would see me soon, knowing very well that this was goodbye forever." In truth, Yankel had already planned to sacrifice his own life to die together with his son: Following the May 7 massacre, a resistance plan had been drawn up to hurl grenades into the guardroom and escape to the forest. Considering that Idel could no longer run, Yankel had prepared two nooses for them both. Upon hearing the first explosion, father and son were to hang themselves rather than be taken alive.[21]

Despite his profound losses, young Idel did not give up his dream for freedom. He had even made a successful "trial run" through the tunnel prior to the escape. His forced labor camp comrades, however, showed little hope for Idel to survive the escape and reach the safety of the forest. Describing the day of the escape, he writes: "Friends came to wish me a successful escape, as if I was the only one escaping. I understood what they meant; they thought that I didn't stand a chance. I could sense that they were feeling sorry for me." This fourteen-year-old handicapped youngster, however, remained undeterred.

On the night of September 26, 1943, at 8:00 p.m., Idel took his place in line behind Pesach Abramovicz (#205), who had lost the toes on one foot during his own failed escape attempt. Although Idel's actual number was #95, both he and Pesach opted to be among the last to exit the tunnel so as to lessen the chance of their slow pace blocking the exit for others. While their fellow escapees spoke of running to the forest, Idel and Pesach carefully deliberated over which route they would walk, considering that their limitations made it impossible to keep pace with the others.

As he waited to enter the tunnel, Idel writes: "I sat quietly behind Pesach, and thought about my family and what had happened to us in such a short time. How strange that my mother envied her dear sister for being dead. I was hoping that my father was still alive and that maybe we would both survive this living nightmare. My only wish was not to be taken alive by the enemy."[22]

Miraculously, the two lame teenagers at the end of the line survived the breakout. With Idel hobbling with rags wrapped around his feet, he and Pesach trekked blindly through the forest for five days until mercifully encountering partisans from the Ordzhonikidze detachment, who took them to their camp. There Idel was reunited with his cousin Berl, with whom he "laughed and cried at the same time." Idel notes that while Berl, too, had held little hope for him to reach the partisans, he himself never doubted that he would succeed.

Idel and Berl were to remain lifelong "brothers." Just as Berl transferred from the fighting unit to the "family camp" in order to stay with Idel,[23] the two were never to leave each other again, even when they eventually lived on two different continents. Following liberation, Idel took refuge in the Landsberg am Lech Displaced Persons Camp, from where he attempted to join Berl in his illegal immigration to Israel via the Hashomer Hatzair Zionist movement. After being rejected on medical grounds, Idel joined his cousin Rachel Konigsberg in London in June 1947. Rachel, who had immigrated in 1938, received her cousin warmly, yet Idel never relinquished his dream to immigrate to Palestine, now Israel.

Although Idel's residence in Israel only lasted from September 1949 till April 1950, when he returned to England,[24] he (now "Jack") and his family made yearly visits to Berl (now "Dov") until his cousin's death in 2013.[25] Jack's stays in Israel also gave him the opportunity to visit his other "brother" Leizer Senderovsky, who had fled to Uzbekistan with the retreating Russian Army and later joined Kibbutz Kinneret following the war. His son Dov remembers that Idel's visits until Leizer's death in 2005 were chock-full of stories of prewar Zhetl and Novogrudok. During one visit when Dov was around seven years old, he recalls learning about the tunnel escape.[26] Idel's son Michael, today living in Israel, recalls the days long ago when overseas telephone calls needed to be scheduled by the international operator. Every few months, Idel would schedule a phone call to Dov in which the two cousins would speak in the familiar, fluent Yiddish of their youth.[27]

In 1954, Idel married the former Barbara Steinfeld, a British-born child of Polish immigrants, and the couple had three children, Michael, Debbie, and Jeffrey. Today, Debbie, the namesake of her paternal grandmother, is primarily a homemaker, while Jeffrey, his paternal grandfather's namesake, is a businessman. Michael, named for his maternal grandfather, is a chemist by profession who lives in Israel. Among his many professional and creative activities, Michael declares that as the oldest sibling, he sees himself as "carrying the torch" and preserving the memories so dear to his father.[28] He frequently lectures and writes about the tunnel escape and served as co-producer of the film *Tunnel of Hope*, which chronicles the search for and discovery of the tunnel beneath the Novogrudok forced labor camp by three survivors (including Idel) and fifty descendants of escapees who traveled to the site.[29]

In a 2001 television interview, Idel related what he felt was the key to his survival: "*I never gave up, I never gave up.*"[30] Exhibiting the same sense of determination, tenacity, and his characteristic "refusal to take

no for an answer," Idel achieved great success in a series of business ventures in the
plastics industry.[31] Nor did he ever forget
his past. Following the dissolution of the
Soviet Union, Idel made the first of many
trips to Novogrudok in the winter of 1991.
There he met Tamara Vershitskaya, curator
of the local museum. Between 1993 and
1994, she was to play a pivotal role, along
with Idel's local Jewish friend Boris Krotin,
in helping to overcome formidable bureau-
cratic hurdles to erect memorials at all three
killing sites.[32] Tamara, awakened by Idel

Idel Kagan, Landsberg,
Germany, 1947 (courtesy
of Michael Kagan)

to Novogrudok's glorious Jewish past, not only went on to become a
foremost Holocaust educator in the former Soviet Union, but, with
Idel's help, to establish the Jewish Resistance Museum at the site of the
Novogrudok forced labor camp in 2007. She was appointed as its first
director.

   Although the war suspended his own education, Idel gave top priority to educating schoolchildren of all ages to know about the Holocaust
and his own experiences. A frequent lecturer in schools and universities,[33] he was awarded several honors for his work to promote Holocaust
education in Britain. In 2014, Idel (Jack) Kagan was appointed by then
prime minister Cameron to Britain's Holocaust Commission, charged
with building a permanent memorial for national commemoration as
well as to provide the educational resources to perpetuate the memory of the Holocaust.[34] That same year, he was awarded a Medal of
Heroism by the Belarusian government.[35] By his own admission, the
2015 standing ovation Idel received in Paris after a lecture before an
audience of academics was "the pinnacle of my life."[36] Idel did not
live to receive the British Empire Medal, given for "meritorious civil
or military service worthy of recognition by the Crown,"[37] that he was

awarded posthumously in 2017. Idel's medal was presented by the queen in a special ceremony attended by his wife and daughter.[38]

But beyond all his honors and medals, Idel's greatest feat was the creation of his new family and living to see the Kagan name perpetuated in three generations. In his lifetime, Idel lived to see nine grandchildren and nine great-grandchildren. By August 2023, the number of great-grandchildren has grown to fifteen.[39]

Jack Kagan, the esteemed and successful businessman, never stopped being Idel in his soul, constantly remembering from where he came. How fitting that he left this world on December 18, 2016 (18 Kislev according to the Hebrew calendar),[40] exactly seventy-five years to the day after Novogrudok's first mass slaughter and the murders of his uncle Moshe, aunt Shoshke, and cousin Leizer.

Yakov Yoselevich (#96)

Until July 8, 2019, little was known about Yakov Yoselevich other than his birth in 1900 as the son of Samuil, his residence in Novogrudok before the war, and his survival of both the Novogrudok forced labor camp tunnel escape and his Bielski partisan service.[1] As Yakov never filed an International Red Cross application for reparations following the war, it was surmised that he had not immigrated to the West and had most likely remained in the Soviet Union. The author's hunch proved correct when at the dedication ceremony of the Memorial Wall at the site of the former forced labor camp in Novogrudok on July 8, 2019, she was approached by a Soviet-born gentleman who pointed to Yakov's plaque on the wall and introduced himself as Yakov's son Boris (Berl).

In an ensuing interview, Boris shared his scant knowledge of his father's history and his desire to seek additional information. He first shed light on the sobering fact that Yakov was not only the sole survivor of his birth family, but also the only survivor of the family he created before the war. In reality, Yakov had made a systematic effort to bury all his wartime memories. Boris knows nothing of any siblings his father may have had, nor the names of Yakov's first wife and three children (a son and two daughters), whose existence he inadvertently discovered while browsing through a photo album before Yakov's death in 1976.

As a tailor, Yakov was interned in the Novogrudok forced labor camp, from which he escaped in the tunnel breakout to make his way to the Bielski partisan detachment. There he met his second wife, Dvosha Velkin. A native of the village of Mokrets near Novogrudok, Dvosha was one of ten children, including her own twin sister Golda. Out of all the children, only two brothers survived, one who had immigrated to the United States in 1913, and Chaim Velkin, a fellow Bielski partisan.[2]

Dvosha, who had also been confined to the forced labor camp, owed her own escape to the efforts of Ivan Kozlowski, a policeman and brother of the fervently anti-German Belarusian peasant Konstanty "Kościk" Kozlowski,[3] who was renowned for providing a way station for escaping Jews and helping them reach the Bielski partisans.[4] It was Ivan who let Dvosha through the well-guarded labor camp gate and enabled her survival by providing a jar of melted animal fat for sustenance on the difficult trek to the partisan detachment.[5]

Boris notes that Konstanty Kozlowski had known both the Bielski and the Velkin families during prewar times. His long-term acquaintance with the Bielskis was forged over the many years he lived in the village of Mokrets, which was near the Bielski home in the bordering village of Stankiewicze. As for the Velkins, the Kozlowski family worked on Dvosha's parents' farm in Mokrets (they were also the owners of a shoe store in Novogrudok). They became so close to the family that Konstanty learned Yiddish. To this day, Boris maintains contact with Konstanty's niece Irena, whose mother Zena was once Dvosha's babysitter.

Although Yakov hermetically locked away the secrets and events of the past, Dvosha was slightly more open about her life during the war. It was from her that Boris heard about the Bielski partisans, including one chilling incident in the forest in which she described finding herself surrounded by wolves.

Yakov and Dvosha married in the Bielski camp and after liberation, remained in Novogrodok, where Yakov worked as a tailor for a government agency. While sharing a home with Dvosha's surviving brother Chaim, the couple had two children of their own, Rivka (Riva), born in 1945, and Boris, born in 1960.[6] Between Rivka's birth and Boris's, Dvosha had given birth to eight other children who died as infants.[7]

Although Boris does not recall being told about his Jewishness while growing up in postwar Novogrudok, he grasped that his parents were fearful to discuss what he was forced to understand from his non-Jewish neighbors and peers. As the only Jewish pupil in the entire town, he reports having been made to feel that "it was not good to be Jewish" and recalls being taunted by his schoolmates with shouts of "Go to Israel." The only overt expression of Judaism he remembers is the (Passover) matzah that somehow made its way to the family table once a year. Despite growing up in Novogrudok, Boris had no knowledge of the tunnel escape.

Boris pointed out that his obviously traumatized father chose to remain in Novogrudok, where he had suffered so many losses and endured so much pain, in the hope of finding surviving relatives. Although his father had the option to freely leave the Soviet Union with his family until 1948, Boris notes that Rivka's severe visual disabilities and her placement in a residential school for the blind in Grodno delayed their emigration to the West for many years. By the time Yakov and Dvosha were at least ready to consider such a move, it was too late. Trapped behind the Iron Curtain, Yakov died in 1976, just prior to the opening of the gates of emigration.

Boris remained in Novogrudok until moving to Minsk to attend the National Technical University in 1977. There he became a mechanical engineer and met and married Yelena, a civil engineer. Dvosha passed away in 1989 in Novogrudok, where Rivka continues to live with her daughter.

In 1992, Boris left Belarus for America and resettled in the Boston area, where he currently works as a manufacturing engineering manager. Boris is the father of two adult sons and the grandfather of a boy and a girl.

Both his sister Rivka and Irena Kozlowski affirm that Boris, nicknamed "Berl" throughout his childhood, is the namesake of a relative, tunnel escapee Berl Yoselevich, whom he now knows was instrumental in conceiving the idea for the breakout.[8]

Unlike Yakov, who maintained a wall of silence until his death, Boris is openly proud of his father's participation in the tunnel breakout and his service with the Bielski partisans. Fortunately, Boris made the long journey from Boston to his native Novogrudok for the Memorial Wall inauguration and the reunion of the descendants of the Bielski partisans. This sparked the discovery of new details of his father's life and allowed Yakov Yoselevich's story to be included in the annals of the near-miraculous tunnel escape.

Yakov Yoselevich with his wife and children, Novogrudok, early 1960s
(courtesy of Boris Ioselevich)

Moshe Bruk (#97)

Moshe Bruk was born in Novogrudok on March 15, 1919,[1] to Shlomo, a merchant,[2] and Golda née Eiseman.[3] After Golda's early death, Shlomo was left alone to raise their two young sons, Moshe and his older brother David. When David immigrated to Palestine in the 1930s, only Shlomo and Moshe remained.[4] Ultimately, Shlomo was murdered in Novogrudok's first massacre on December 6, 1941.[5]

By virtue of his skills as a tailor, a profession deemed vital to the German Army, Moshe was conscripted to the Novogrudok forced labor camp. There Moshe worked by day; by night he joined the arduous clandestine efforts to dig the underground tunnel. Following Moshe's successful escape, he joined the Bielski partisan detachment.[6]

After liberation, Moshe was listed as residing in February 1947 in the Landsburg am Lech Displaced Persons Camp,[7] a former concentration camp[8] and the second largest such camp in the American zone. Known for its cultural life as well as its overcrowded conditions, Landsberg was visited in 1945 by David Ben-Gurion, who became instrumental in obtaining more room for the inhabitants.[9]

It was in Italy while serving as a leader for the Dror Zionist youth organization that Moshe first met Sara Eiseman, who was destined to become his wife. Sara hailed from a small town in the Bialystok region and had taken refuge during the war years with her parents and four siblings in Kazakhstan. Moshe and Sara's paths diverged when Moshe became involved in the dangerous mission of smuggling illegal immigrants into Palestine before Israel's declaration of statehood in 1948. As fate would have it, once they'd each reached Israel, Moshe and Sara were reunited when they met on a street in the town of Kiryat Yam. Their married life began on Kibbutz Yagur, where the couple was part of a *hachsharah*, a group being trained for kibbutz life. Moshe and Sara

Bruk went on to become two of the founders of Kibbutz Lochamei Hagetaot (the Ghetto Fighters' Kibbutz), together with such renowned Warsaw ghetto heroes as Zivia Lubetkin.[10]

By the time Moshe and Sara's oldest son Shlomo (named for his paternal grandfather) was born on September 2, 1953, they were among the early residents of Kiryat Yam, today a suburb of Haifa. There they lived for two and a half years in a one-room apartment before moving to nearby Kiryat Haim, where Shlomo and his brother Yehoshua (Shuki), born in 1956, were raised. Moshe commuted daily to his job at the Haifa port.[11]

Moshe Bruk, Israel, 1948 (courtesy of Shlomo Bruk)

Moshe is described by Shlomo as having been an extremely affectionate father who never appeared depressed, despite the painful losses he had suffered. With the education of his children holding prime importance, Moshe would be extremely proud today of his very accomplished progeny. Shlomo earned advanced degrees and is a well-respected expert in the field of security. Of Shlomo's three daughters, one is currently (November 2018) completing her medical studies, another holds a PhD in genetics, and the third is the assistant chief executive officer of her firm. Shuki Bruk is a professor of computer science at the California Institute of Technology. One of Shuki's two children is a physician; the second is a doctor of law.

Moshe Bruk died in 2002, and his wife Sara lived for another sixteen years until August 2018. At the time of his death, Moshe had seen the birth of five great-grandchildren.[12] If he were alive today in September 2023, he would undoubtedly be proud of the other five whom he did not live to see.[13]

Alter Gurvich (#98)

Alter Gurvich was born in the town of Lubcha in 1907.[1] The son of Girsh, he worked as a tailor before the war,[2] a skill that enabled him to be interned in the Novogrudok forced labor camp producing uniforms and gear for the Nazis. We know nothing of Alter's family of origin, his life before the war, or whether he was single or married prior to the Holocaust. Nor can we determine whether there is a relationship between Alter and his fellow escapee Hirsh Gurvich (#9) of Novogrudok.

Alter survived the tunnel escape to join Sholom Zorin's Jewish partisan group, the 106th detachment. Like the detachment under the command of Tuvia Bielski, the Zorin group accepted any Jew who reached the shelter of its *otriad*, regardless of age or health status. Although the Zorin unit was smaller (between six and seven hundred members), it operated under the directive of a Communist commander, thus enjoying the support of the Soviets.[3]

After liberation, Alter Gurvich settled in Russia, where he married Matlya née Shapiro. (It is possible that like many other former partisans, he was drafted into the Red Army subsequent to liberation and remained in Russia following the war's end.) At least until 1950, Alter and Matlya were living in Saratov, Russia, where their son Michael was born that year.[4] According to information on a family tree that includes Alter Gurvich's family, Michael was married twice. He is noted to have had two children, one from each wife.[5] As their names are unknown, we cannot trace the third generation in order to obtain more information regarding Alter.

Alter, Matlya, and Michael immigrated to Israel, although we do not know the year. All three died within a short time of one another. Son Michael passed away first in 2001 at the age of fifty-one.[6] Alter's death on July 28, 2002, was followed by Matlya's death only two weeks later,[7] possibly of heartbreak.

Michael's grave is located in the southern Israeli city of Ofakim.[8] His parents are buried in the northern coastal plain city of Or Akiva.[9]

Mordechai Kaplinski (#99)

The identity of escapee Mordechai Kaplinski is difficult to determine.

Unlike many of his fellow conscripts to the Novogrudok forced labor camp, it appears that he was not a resident of Novogrudok or its immediate surroundings prior to the war. The name Mordechai Kaplinski does not appear in any of the *Novogrudok Memorial Book* necrology lists, nor is there a Page of Testimony for anyone by this name from the Novogrudok area.

Yad Vashem's Central Database of Shoah Victims' Names lists four Mordechai Kaplinskis from Poland. By process of elimination, two may be excluded due to their age: the seventy-seven-year-old tailor from Minsk[1] as well as the one-year-old child from Lodz named Zalman Mordechai.[2] Motke Kaplinski of Vilna[3] would also be an unlikely candidate, as he would not have been a refugee to Novogrudok from areas of Poland occupied by Germany in 1939.

We may, however, consider the possibility of Motelle (Yiddish for Mordechai) Kaplinksi from Sokolka, a small town in close vicinity to Grodno, around 115 miles (185 kilometers) from Novogrudok. The sole details recorded testify that Motelle and his wife Beba had two daughters, Chaikeh and Liubke. All four appear among the Holocaust victims commemorated in the *Memorial Book of Sokolka*.[4]

As the name Mordechai Kaplinski does not appear on the list of Jewish partisans in Belorussia during the years 1941–1944,[5] we can assume that the escapee by this name did not survive the breakout.

Kalman Shelkovich (#100)

Kalman Shelkovich, a tailor, was born in 1910[1] and grew up in Zhetl. A member of the Hashomer Hatzair Zionist youth movement as well as the Seamsters Union, Kalman also performed with the Union's Drama Society.[2]

Kalman's father Shevel (Shaul), a teacher,[3] had been an active member of Zhetl's Va'ad Hayeshivot, an umbrella organization that supported local religious institutions.[4] While Shevel Shelkovich's name appears among the murdered of Zhetl,[5] we are unaware of Kalman's mother's name or fate or of any possible siblings. Nor do we know if Kalman had been married before the war.

According to the Yiddish-language testimony of fellow escapee Pesia Mayevski (#160), Kalman, along with Nachum (#133) and Sara (#134) Zamosczyk and Hirsh Patzovski (#159), were her four companions in a group that banded together upon fleeing the tunnel. With the escapees subsisting primarily on raw potatoes during their perilous trek to the Bielski detachment, Pesia describes the first night of their flight in a forest over two and a half miles from the Novogrudok forced labor camp. She recalls that Kalman was less bothered than the others by their first uncooked meal in the woods. His ability to eat twelve raw potatoes was a feat that reportedly evoked much envy on the women's part.[6]

With all members of the group succeeding in reaching the Bielski *otriad*, Kalman is listed in the compilation of Jewish partisans in Belorussia as Kalman Shevelevich Shelkovich.[7]

In January 1947, Kalman sailed from Poland for the United States via Bilboa, Spain. On the ship manifest for the SS *Magallanes*, Kalman listed his last place of residence as "Zhienciol," Polish for Zhetl. In February 1947, the boat, which had been converted to a refugee ship, docked in New York City carrying the new Americans Kalman, his wife Luba, and their one-year-old baby daughter.[8]

Settling in the township of North Bergen, New Jersey, at some point Kalman and Luba changed their surname to Salkin.[9/10] Records show that the baby immigrant is today called Renee Salkin, a retired social worker living in Little Falls, New Jersey.[11] Unfortunately, we have thus far been unable to make contact with her.

Luba[12] died in March 1984 and Kalman in November 1984.[13] For nearly four decades, they had made their lives in the United States, far from the terror of their former homes.

Mordechai (#102) and Yitzchak (#103) Zacharevich

According to information gleaned from a partisan list, Mordechai Zacharevich was born in 1902. The son of Yitzchak, he lived in Novogrudok prior to the war and worked as a tailor.[1]

Thanks to his tailoring skills being of necessity to the Nazis, Mordechai was assigned to the Novogrudok forced labor camp along with his adolescent son Yitzchak, his grandfather's namesake. Tragically, young Yitzchak was killed during the tunnel escape.[2] His death is memorialized in the *Novogrudok Memorial Book*.[3]

Mordechai himself survived the tunnel escape, reached the Bielski detachment, and became a member of the Chapayev detachment of the Shchors Brigade. He appears on a list of Jewish partisans in Belorussia as Mordukh Isaakovich Zakharovich.[4]

Although Mordechai emerged unscathed from both the tunnel escape and his partisan fighting unit in the forest, his ultimate fate was cruel. Jack Kagan (#95), a childhood friend of Yitzchak, reports that after liberation from the forest, Mordechai was drafted into the Red Army and met his death on the Russian front.[5]

Chaim Bekenshtein (#106)

Chaim Bekenshtein was born in Zaludek in 1910 and lived in Zhetl prior to the war.[1] A tailor, he was married to Chasia née Senderovski, a housewife born in Zhetl.[2] According to the list of murdered people from Zdzieciol (Zhetl) in 1941–1942, Chasia was murdered during this time,[3] along with the couple's two little daughters, Leya, born in 1937,[4] and Sara, born in 1939.[5] A Page of Testimony by a neighbor notes the date that Chasia and her two children were murdered as April 30, 1942,[6] Zhetl's first slaughter.

Chaim's skills as a tailor, essential to the German Army, enabled him to escape death to be conscripted to the Novogrudok forced labor camp. The sole member of his immediate family to remain alive at that time, Chaim did not survive the tunnel escape. His name is commemorated in *Pinkas Zhetl*.[7]

Malka Lewin (#107)

On five different documents, five different dates are listed for Malka Lewin's birth, ranging from 1914 to 1921.[1] Born in Novogrudok,[2] Malka was orphaned of her parents Mirela née Czarna[3] and Berl[4] when both were murdered in the Novogrudok massacres.[5] We do not know the names or the fate of any siblings.

Following Malka's internment in the Novogrudok forced labor camp and her successful breakout through the tunnel, she somehow made her way through the forest to the Bielski partisan detachment.[6] Like most other partisans, Malka did not reveal the fact of her partisan activities in her applications for war reparations,[7] most likely for fear that her partisan membership would not be regarded favorably in the post-World War II Cold War atmosphere that prevailed.

From documentation files of the International Committee of the Red Cross (ICRC) Tracing Services at Magen David Adom Israel, we know that in January 1947, Malka registered her whereabouts with the Jewish Central Committee in Warsaw, Poland.[8] Two years later, on March 4, 1949, Malka's last known address was in Italy,[9] perhaps indicating the locale of a displaced persons camp where she'd found refuge. In April 1950, documents indicate that she had passed through Vienna, Austria.[10]

Malka's October 1956 application for aid from the Red Cross was submitted from Berea, Johannesburg, South Africa, where she noted that she was living with the Paiken family.[11] Unfortunately, from that point on, no further documentation has been found. While Malka Lewin's name does not appear in the genealogical and population databases examined, it is possible that she married and changed her surname. Likewise, inquiries made to date of children of former Bielski partisans who grew up in Johannesburg have failed to shed light on Malka's identity.[12]

David Tzimerman (#108)

All that is known about Novogrudok forced labor camp escapee David Tzimerman is that he hailed from the Novogrudok area and that he did not survive the breakout. Although he does not appear in Yad Vashem's Central Database of Shoah Victims' Names, David Tzimerman is commemorated among the murdered in Novogrudok's memorial book, which encompasses Holocaust victims from Novogrudok and its environs.[1]

Yosef (Yosel) Mirski (#109)

Yosef (Yosel) Mirski[1] was born in Zhetl to Pinchas[2] and Beile,[3] who were murdered in their hometown in 1940 together with three of their children – Eliezer,[4] Yakov,[5] and Batia.[6] Yosel's sister Rivka was a childhood friend and elementary school classmate of the author's aunt, Shifra Dunetz. Prior to World War II, Rivka Mirski left Zhetl for France, where she became a Yiddish writer.[7]

Novogrudok forced labor camp escapee Fanya Dunetz (#142) reports having seen Yosel escape the camp in March 1943 along with her brother Mordechai (Motl) Dunetz. As Motl apparently lost track of Yosel in the freezing cold,[8] it is possible that Yosel returned to the camp, just as Idel Kagan (#95) reports having done during his own failed escape that very same winter.[9]

Yosel Mirski did not survive the tunnel breakout, evidently his second attempt to escape to the freedom of a partisan detachment in the forest. A Yad Vashem Page of Testimony filed by an acquaintance notes that Yosel was single at the time of his death,[10] as is also recorded in his memorial in Zhetl's memorial book.[11]

Sholom Ginden (#110)

Our genealogist, who located Sholom Ginden as having lived in Rochester, New York, was married in 1972 in Little Rock, Arkansas, by a young rabbi named Shaya Kilimnick. The rabbi was to maintain lifelong contact with the bride and groom, even after moving to Rochester in 1977 to lead Congregation Beth Sholom. When the three met in Jerusalem during Passover 2018, Rabbi Kilimnick was asked if perhaps he knew of the Holocaust survivor Sholom, now Sam, Ginden. Quoting inspirational author Irene Hannon to the effect that coincidence is a small miracle in which G-d chooses to remain anonymous, Rabbi Kilimnick replied that Shalom was a respected member of his congregation as well as a friend. Nor could it be pure coincidence that I was able to subsequently meet with Rabbi Kilimnick for him to shed light on Sholom's personality and life. I am grateful to the rabbi, whose untimely death in August 2020 we mourn.

Born in Novogrudok in 1923 to Shmuel Alter and Nechama née Zalmanovski,[1] Sholom Ginden worked as a tailor[2] and lived on Korelitzkaya Street in Novogrudok before the war.[3] Other than his father's name appearing on a list of Novogrudok residents in 1941,[4] we have no details of Sholom's early life or of other members of his family of origin.

Sholom's skills as a tailor, deemed essential to the German Army, brought about his conscription to the Novogrudok forced labor camp. Upon surviving the tunnel escape, Sholom made his way through the forest to reach and join the 106th partisan detachment, commanded by Shlomo Zorin.[5]

Rabbi Kilimnick provided the information that following liberation, Sam had been drafted into the Soviet Army, where he held a high rank and performed courageous feats.[6] At the war's end, Sholom took refuge in several displaced persons camps, including Babenhausen,[7,8] located in the Frankfurt District of the American zone in Germany. Previously a Soviet prisoner-of-war camp, Babenhausen was known for its particularly dismal conditions: survivors were assigned to stalls that had earlier housed German Army horses.[9]

On February 26, 1951, Sholom departed Bremen Harbor to sail for the United States aboard the American naval vessel *General R.M. Blatchford*, which had been transformed into a refugee ship.[10] Settling in Rochester, New York, he changed his name to Sam (becoming his father's namesake), married the former Bessie Molly Abramowitz in 1954,[11] and worked in real estate.[12]

Recollecting Sam and Bessie, Rabbi Kilimnick declared with a smile that "they were like Fred Astaire and Ginger Rodgers." Describing the couple as an integral part of the Rochester survivor community, the rabbi noted that even though Bessie was American born, she had met Sam in the Anielewicz Society, a social group of survivors with camp experiences. Sam and Bessie loved to go to parties, where they were soon stars on the dance floor. Despite his wartime experiences and probable losses, Sam was recalled by the rabbi as having had a "smile affixed on his face all the years that I knew him." Depicted as bearing an innocent face and a relatively short stature, Sam was still taller than Bessie. In Sam's eulogy for his wife, he lovingly said, "Bessie was a very short woman, but in my eyes, she was a giant."[13]

Sam is remembered as having been "sweet and kind" by another member of the community, attorney Betty Gould, whose mother had been Bessie's best friend.[14] Barbara Appelbaum, the first director of Rochester's Center for Holocaust Awareness and Information (CHAI), reports that although Sam had been repeatedly requested to give testimony of his Holocaust experiences, he was unable to bring himself to do so. Barbara Applebaum, too, describes Sam as "having loved to cut a rug" with Bessie, regardless of his hidden pain. Both are remembered as having been very active members of the survivor social circle that met in a local park on Sundays.[15]

Sam Ginden died on January 20, 2007, just over four years after Bessie's death in November 2002. Sholom and Bessie were survived by Abe, their only child.[16] (Abe, who never married or had children, did not respond to our requests for contact prior to his death at age sixty-two on November 26, 2019.)[17]

Sam's participation in the forced labor camp tunnel escape appears to have been unknown to all who knew and loved him after the war in his new home. Perhaps even the love of his life and dancing partner Bessie was unaware. Only because of a "coincidence" will Sam Ginden's legacy now include his bravery in taking part in one of the most successful breakouts of the Holocaust.

Simcha Wilenski (#111)

Simcha Wilenski owed his life to his father Yehuda Eliyahu, a tailor by trade, who taught his children to sew. In the face of the savage Nazi invasion of their Novogrudok hometown, Yehuda Eliyahu and his wife Rachel née Wolkowski were slaughtered in one of the city's early massacres. All of their five children were seamstresses or tailors, earning them internment in the Novogrudok forced labor camp, where the German Army exploited their skills. Yet on May 7, 1943, daughters Perel, Baila, and Yehudit were among the hundreds executed in close proximity to the forced labor camp, in full sight of the remaining prisoners. Of the entire Wilenski family, only Simcha, born in 1913, and Aaron, born in 1920,[1] were spared death.

According to Simcha's only child, Rita Standig, who was traced to her home in Bayonne, New Jersey, with the help of a genealogist, her father would often blame himself for not having devised a way to save his sisters.[2] The brutal May 7 massacre is said to have been the decisive point at which the labor camp workers, the last remaining Jews alive in the Novogrudok area, realized that they were next in line to be murdered.[3] Their fierce desire to live gave them the impetus to embark on the tunnel escape in which Simcha and Aaron both miraculously fled to freedom.

Born in the mid-1950s, Rita shares that she was already in her thirties when her father agreed to apply for reparations from Germany. Only when she helped him with the application did Simcha first tell her of the Novogrudok forced labor camp and the tunnel escape, sharing what he could not bring himself to speak of beforehand. Unlike many other survivors' children, who had little or no knowledge of the tunnel's construction, she described learning such details as the excavated dirt being hidden in an attic and the fears that the tunnel would collapse due to farming equipment driving over the field above it.[4]

Rita relates that upon fleeing the tunnel, Simcha and Aaron went separate ways in the hope that one of them would remain alive and reach the partisans.[5] Fortunately, both brothers independently reached the Bielski detachment,[6] where Simcha continued to work as a tailor.[7] Upon liberation from the forest, he was drafted into the Russian Army by an officer who valued Simcha's sewing skills. There Simcha joined an artillery unit, earning a medal for bravery in manning a cannon. Rita notes that when her father was asked to launch the Russian campaign against Schneidemühler, Germany, he did so by firing his cannon for each murdered member of his family.[8]

At the close of the war, Simcha lived in Lodz from October 1946 until 1947. He then found refuge in the Landsberg Displaced Persons Camp in Southwest Bavaria, Germany.[9] The second-largest refugee camp in the American zone, Landsberg housed five thousand Holocaust survivors in military barracks built for only two thousand soldiers. Landsberg was infamous for underfeeding, lack of adequate housing, and poor sanitary conditions. Nevertheless, it became the cultural center for survivors in the American zone, with its own choir, theater groups, and newspapers.[10]

In August 1949, Simcha Wilenski sailed from the port of Bremen, Germany, aboard the US Navy transport ship USS *General Haan*[11] bound for America's shores. Soon afterwards, Simcha changed his name to Seymour. At a dance, he met Sarah, who had immigrated to the US from Czechoslovakia in the 1920s at the age of nine. The two were married in the early 1950s.[12]

Daughter Rita's early years were spent in Jersey City before the family moved to the neighboring town of Bayonne. Simcha continued to work as a tailor and traveled daily to his jobs in Manhattan's garment center. He loved traveling on buses and took special delight in traveling to New York.[13]

In his youth, Simcha was an athlete and belonged to the Novogrudok branch of the Maccabi Sports Organization.[14] An amateur photographer before the war, Simcha continued this hobby in America. Having grown up in an observant home where his father attended the Novogrudok "Tailor's Synagogue,"[15] he never forgot how to recite his prayers by heart. Simcha was an active and respected member of his synagogue in Bayonne, often attending services twice daily. Rita describes her father as one who "stayed to himself," and despite his lack of education (limited to completion of *cheder*, a religious school for young boys), he knew how to get out of difficult situa-

Simcha Wilenski, undated pre-WWII photo (courtesy of Rita Wilenski Standig)

tions.[16] His son-in-law describes him as having been a quiet man who was always uncomfortable speaking English.[17]

In 1999, Simcha filed an inquiry with the International Red Cross as to the whereabouts of his brother Aaron, with whom he'd lost contact after the war, stating that Aaron might be somewhere in the former Soviet Union.[18] Unfortunately, Simcha died in 2010 without ever knowing the fate of his only surviving sibling.[19]

Simcha is survived by Rita, a trained social worker whose Hebrew name, Rachel Tzipora, memorializes her paternal grandmother Rachel Wilenski; his son-in-law Marc Standig, an enrolled agent with the US Treasury Department; as well as two millennial grandsons, Zachary, a paralegal, and Jordan, a university student. Jordan's Hebrew name, Doron Yehuda, immortalizes his great-grandfather Yehuda Eliyahu,[20] who by instructing his sons to sew enabled the continuation of the family.

In July 2019, Rita journeyed to Novogrudok to attend the reunion of descendants of Bielski partisans and the dedication of the Memorial Wall listing the names of the tunnel escapees. Here she took the opportunity to explore the town and the neighborhood where the Wilenski residence had once stood at 23 Wielki Rynek Street.[21] Three months afterwards, she wrote, "For me the trip to Novogrudok was truly amazing. There was clarification. I wanted to touch history: I did. Upon waking during my first morning there, I ate breakfast with individuals whose relatives also went through the tunnel. For the first time I was not alone. In the past when I discussed my father's story, no one understood or could relate to it.… I wish my father could have been with me.… Most importantly, he would not believe his name was on a wall remembering all who survived the tunnel escape. Of course he earned his place, but he would say he did not know how he survived."

Leah Berkovich (#112)

The identity of escapee Leah Berkovich remains unknown. Yad Vashem's Central Database of Shoah Victims' Names contains 185 entries for women named Leah Berkovich who resided in or were murdered in Poland during the war. This figure includes sixteen entries for Shoah victims by this name who resided in Novogrudok at their deaths.[1] With no information available to us beyond knowing that Leah Berkovich had been incarcerated in the Novogrudok forced labor camp, we may never know who this woman was or the fate of her loved ones.

Unfortunately, no one named Leah Berkovich succeeded in reaching the partisans,[2] thus we must assume that she was murdered following the breakout.

Nina Levkovich (#113)

Born in central Poland[1] in 1929,[2] Nina Levkovich was the daughter of Fadey,[3] a doctor who came to Novogrudok with his family in 1940.[4] We know nothing more of her prewar life, the names of other members of her immediate family or their fates, or whether she had first been interned in the Novogrudok forced labor camp with additional members of her family.

Only fourteen years old at the time of the escape, Nina survived the tunnel breakout and the trek to the Bielski partisans,[5] arriving at the detachment in the forest by the end of September 1943.[6]

Nina is reported to have settled in Israel after the war and to have established a family. She died in about 2009.[7] As her married name is unknown, we have not been able to locate records or find any descendants who might shed light on her postwar life.

Michael Novogrudski (#114)

Although the surname Novogrudski appears on the escape list with no given name preceding it, the testimony of Novogrudok forced labor camp escapee Pesia Mayevski (#160) reveals that it was her fellow Zhetl native Michael Novogrudski who participated in the breakout.[1]

Michael Novogrudski was born in 1911[2] (or in 1912[3]) in Zhetl, where he resided on Pionerskaya Street.[4] His parents Avraham Moshe, a shoemaker[5] born in 1876,[6] and Rivka (Riva) née Indershtein, born in 1878,[7] were both Zhetl natives.

Michael's known siblings included Nechama, a housewife born in 1904 who married Anshul Sokolovski and had two children;[8] Yevel, born in 1909;[9] Eliezer, born in 1919,[10] who married Sheina and had a three-year-old son;[11] Chaya, born in 1922,[12] who worked as a seamstress;[13] Yosef, a cabinetmaker born in 1923;[14] and Gabriel,[15] whose date of birth is unknown. All save for Yevel and Yosef are reported in Yad Vashem Pages of Testimony to have been murdered in Zhetl in 1942.

Like his father, Michael was a shoemaker by trade.[16] He was married to Rochel née Gurevich,[17] a seamstress born in 1913,[18] with whom he had at least three children: David, born in 1933;[19] Leib, born in 1936;[20] and Gitel, born in 1938.[21]

Michael's skills as a shoemaker, vital to the German Army, enabled his conscription to the Novogrudok forced labor camp. After surviving the tunnel escape, he reached the forest, where his brother Yosef was serving as a partisan in the Borba detachment of the Leninskaya Brigade.[22] Michael himself became a Bielski partisan.[23]

When no documentation was found regarding Michael Novogrudsky's fate following the war, the mystery was resolved for us by a consultation with Mrs. Chaya Magid, widow of tunnel escapee Avraham Magids. Chaya, a fellow Zhetler, informed us of Michael's death in battle while serving as a soldier in the Red Army after liberation from the forest.[24]

In 1983, Michael's brother Yevel submitted to Yad Vashem Pages of Testimony for his parents, siblings, and their families, including several for Michael and his murdered loved ones, whom he testified had been murdered in Zhetl in August 1942.[25] As each of Yevel's Pages of Testimony were written in Russian, he had apparently resided in the Soviet Union before immigrating to Pittsburg, Pennsylvania, his address at the time of testimony.

One year later, on November 2, 1984, Yevel passed away, never learning of his brother's bravery and his participation in the Novogrudok tunnel escape. The inscription on Yevel's gravestone in Pittsburgh's Chesed Shel Emeth Cemetery[26] bears only his name, bereft of any indication that he had ever remarried or had children beyond his three youngsters murdered during the war.[27]

Rachmiel Leibovich (#115)

Rachmiel Leibovich, a shoemaker by trade born in 1910,[1] was married to Sheyna, a housewife born in 1909.[2] On a list of those murdered in Zhetl in 1941–1942, Rachmiel and Sheyna's names appear together with a child named Ionas, born in 1927. Although no Pages of Testimony were submitted for this family, we can assume that Ionas was their son and that he and his mother were murdered in one of the 1942 Zhetl massacres.[3]

Rachmiel's skills as a shoemaker qualified him to be conscripted to the Novogrudok forced labor camp, where he may have made a crucial contribution. Though the idea for the tunnel escape has been largely attributed to Berl Yoselevich,[4] Zeidel Kushner (#143) credits the plan to "a shoemaker named Rachmiel."[5] Rachmiel Leibovich is the only inmate to meet this description.

Despite Rachmiel's name appearing on the list of those murdered in Zhetl during 1941–1942,[6] we can presume that he actually lost his life in the tunnel escape of 1943. His name is not included in the compilation of Belarusian Jewish partisans.[7]

David Shklarski (#116)

David Shklarski's birth in Zaludok[1] is variably listed as either 1906,[2] 1911,[3] or 1912.[4] In a Page of Testimony, his brother-in-law notes that David was a tailor by trade,[5] and that David, his wife Chaya née Zakroiski[6] and their two small children, four-year-old Israel[7] and two-year-old Chaim,[8] lived in Zaludok prior to the war.

Soviet documents list the names of David, Chaya, and their children as being among individuals from Zhetl who were murdered there in 1941–1942.[9] The family had apparently traveled the twenty-nine miles (47 km) from Zaludok to Zhetl, Chaya's birthplace, to seek safety with her family. Her brother reports that David, Chaya, and the children, along with Chaya's parents Abraham[10] and Batia Zakroiski,[11] were all slaughtered in Zhetl in 1942.

Despite David Shklarski's name appearing on both documents as having been murdered in 1942, the escape list testifies to the fact that he survived to be interned in the Novogrudok forced labor camp, where he was still alive by September 1943.

Unfortunately, the name of David Shklarski, the last surviving member of his family, does not appear in the compilation of Jewish partisans in Belorussia from 1941 to 1944. We may thus assume that he was killed following the tunnel escape.[12]

Zalman Gertzovski (#117)

Born in 1893,[1] Zalman Gertzovski, a shoemaker by trade, resided in Zhetl, where he served on the steering committee of the Tradesmen's Union, which represented the town's craftsmen and small business owners.[2] Zalman was married to Sara, a housewife born in 1896.[3] Together they raised four sons, Aaron, born in 1915, who became a carpenter;[4] Efraim, born in 1919,[5] who became a shoemaker;[6] Avraham, born in 1922;[7] and Zvulun, born in 1925. Aaron's widow Chaya Gertzovski testifies that Sara, Efraim, Avraham, and Zvulun were all murdered in the Zhetl massacres of 1942.[8]

Chaya Magid, widow of tunnel escapee Avraham Magid, reports that Zalman and Aaron were both conscripted to the Novogrudok forced labor camp following the murders of Zvulun, Ephraim, Avraham, and

Sara. Within several months, Zalman was left alone in the camp[9] after Aaron's escape to the Ordzhonikidze detachment of the Kirov Brigade,[10] made up of 180 Bielski fighters under a Russian commander and commissar.[11] Chaya attests that she met Aaron in the forest in November 1942 after her escape from the Dvoretz forced labor camp. She recalls him telling her that he'd left his father in the camp in order to first seek freedom for himself and then attempt to help Zalman join him in the forest.[12]

Although Pesia Mayevski (#160) claims that Zalman was hiding in the camp during the escape,[13] Chaya Magid declares that it was generally known among tunnel survivors in Israel that Zalman did participate in the tunnel breakout.[14] In any event, Zalman did not survive to reach the forest or to fulfill his fervent hope of being reunited with Aaron, the sole living member of his immediate family.[15]

After losing his first wife Sima née Sokolovski and their two-year-old son Mairim in Zhetl's second slaughter,[16] Aaron married Chaya Zamkov, a Novogrudok native whom he had met in the forest.[17]

Immigrating to Israel, Aaron and Chaya settled in Givatayim, where Aaron opened a carpentry shop. The couple had two children, Avishay and Sara, who was named for Aaron's mother.[18]

Avishay, now named Avishay Morag (Gertzovski), first learned of Zalman's participation in the tunnel escape upon being contacted by the author in search of information on his grandfather. Expressing a mixture of shock and pride, Avishay noted that his father had divulged nothing beyond his partisan experiences during the war.[19]

Zalman was described by Chaya Magid as having been extremely well-liked, clever, and active in support of Zhetl's charitable institutions, yeshivot, and loan societies;[20] his sense of caring for the less fortunate was apparently passed on to his children. Avishay describes Aaron as having been a very generous man, recalling early memories of accompanying his father across Israel to extend aid and monetary loans to former townspeople or relatives in need.[21]

Through Aaron, Zalman leaves four generations of descendants. Aaron's daughter Sara Menachem, a graphic artist, has three children and four grandchildren.

Avishay, an innovator and researcher in the field of agriculture, also has three children and four grandchildren. Avishay only discovered the existence of his murdered half-brother Mairim from the author. Both amazed and grateful at learning the "missing gaps" in his personal history, Avishay looks forward to sharing what he has learned with his own children.[22]

Avishay notes that at his father's death in 1988, Aaron was extremely proud of the five great-grandchildren he had lived to see.[23] Zalman, fated to see his only grandson murdered during the war, would surely be overjoyed with the generations that followed.

Zalman Gertzovski (fourth from right), Association of the Tradesmen's Union of Zhetl, Zhetl, 1930 (*Pinkas Zhetl*)

Shmuel Shimshelevich (#118)

Shmuel Shimshelevich of Zhetl was married to Keyla, a seamstress born in 1892.[1] Shmuel and Keyla were the parents of Shimon, a shoemaker,[2] Perla,[3] and Yitzchak.[4] The three children were killed together with their mother in Zhetl's second massacre on August 6, 1942.[5] At the time of their deaths, Shimon was twenty-two years old,[6] Perla was sixteen years old,[7] and Yitzchak was fourteen years old.[8]

The last of his family to survive until 1943, Shmuel participated in the tunnel escape, as confirmed by fellow escapee Pesia Mayevski (#160).[9] Unfortunately, he lost his life in the breakout. Shmuel Shimshelevich is commemorated in the *Novogrudok Memorial Book*.[10]

Isaac Lidski (#119)

Born in 1907, Isaac Lidski, a shoemaker by profession, lived in Zhetl prior to the war. Although he was married,[1] we have no information about his wife or any children the couple might have had.

Isaac may have been the sole member of his immediate family to survive the Holocaust. Both his mother Nechama, a housewife born in 1884,[2] and his father Shlomo, a male nurse born in 1879,[3] were killed in Zhetl's first massacre on April 4, 1942.[4] His married sister Batia, born either in 1915[5] or 1918,[6] was also murdered in Zhetl in 1942.[7]

Isaac's skills as a shoemaker enabled him to remain alive to be conscripted to the Novogrudok forced labor camp. Here he survived the tunnel escape to make his way to the Grodishche District near Pinsk, where he joined the Kotovski Russian partisan detachment of the Budyonny Brigade active in the area.[8]

We know nothing of Isaac's postwar life. To date, a search of genealogical, Holocaust-related, and population databases has revealed no information. Since he served in a Russian partisan unit, Isaac may have remained in the Soviet Union, where vital records are not readily available for research.

Aaron Bitenski (#120)

Although documentation is scarce for Novogrudok forced labor camp inmate Aaron Bitenski, it is known that he hailed from the small town of Nowa Mysz, around forty miles (65 km) from Novogrudok. On the eve of the Holocaust, Aaron and his family were among the 630 Jews residing in Nowa Mysz, constituting around one-third of the total population. Nearly every Jewish man, woman, and child of the town was annihilated by the Nazis in a mass murder in the late summer of 1942.[1]

One Soviet document indicates that Aaron Bitenski was murdered along with four family members between 1941 and 1944.[2] A second document notes that he was killed between 1941 and 1942 along with three family members.[3] Although his loved ones were evidently slaughtered, Aaron Bitenski somehow escaped death in Nowa Mysz to flee to Novogrudok. To date, we are unaware of the professional skills he possessed that enabled his conscription into the forced labor camp, nor do we have any details regarding his probable relationship with Ita Bitenski (#59), a fellow inmate from Nowa Mysz.

Despite the mysteries surrounding Aaron Bitenski's identity, we can make the assumption that since his name does not appear within the compilation of Jewish partisans in Belorussia from 1941 to 1944, he did not survive the tunnel escape.[4]

Hirsz Samsonowicz (#121)

Hirsz Samsonowicz was born in Novogrudok[1] on May 1, 1913,[2] to Mendel, a livestock trader,[3] and his wife Miriam[4] (Mari[5]) Samsonowicz. One of at least four children, Hirsz worked as a state purchasing agent prior to the war.[6]

In 1941, both Mendel and Miriam were killed in Horodyszcze,[7] a town twenty-one miles (34 km) from Novogrudok.[8] That same year, Hirsz's oldest sibling Chaim, born in 1900 and a livestock trader like his father, was shot to death in Horodyszcze together with his wife Malke née Kantorovich and their three children.[9] Brother David was thirty-two years old in 1942 when he was murdered in the town of Turetz with his wife Feige née Mendelevski and their two-year-old daughter Luba.[10]

Of the known siblings, the sole survivors were Hirsz and his brother Yehuda (Yudel), a carpenter born in 1912 who had lived in Baranowicz.[11] At the start of the war, Hirsz lived in Novogrudok with his wife Hodl née Shmulevich and their two youngsters Shulamit and Moshel. In 1943, Hirsz suffered the unspeakable loss of Hodl, Shulamit, and Moshel, all murdered in Novogrudok.[12]

One might question how Hirsz's occupation as a state purchasing agent granted him the skills deemed essential by the Nazis to assign him to forced labor rather than execution. The answer apparently lies in Hersz's International Red Cross file, where he listed his occupation as shoemaker, a delineation he may well have invented to remain alive.[13]

Left alone in the labor camp after the murder of his wife and children, Hirsz survived the tunnel escape to reach the Bielski partisans, where he was reunited with his brother Yehuda.[14]

The Red Cross file also notes that from 1946, Hirsz, now liberated, took refuge in the Bad Worishofen and the Landsberg Displaced

Persons Camps, which are both near Munich.[15] The Landsberg Camp, founded in 1945 after the liberation of the Landsberg Concentration Camp, was the second-largest displaced persons camp in the American Zone. Located in former military barracks, it was infamous for its overcrowding and poor housing and sanitary conditions.[16]

Hirsz married his second wife, the former Chaya Shapiro of Vilna, in November 1947 at the St. Ottilien Benedictine Monastery[17] compound near Landsberg, which housed a Jewish hospital for displaced persons as well as a yeshiva.[18] Within a year, Hirsz was once again a father. On January 7, 1950, the couple and their two-year-old daughters, Merry and Pessie, sailed on a thirteen-day journey aboard the former American navy transport ship *General C.C. Ballou* from the port of Bremen, Germany, to New York City.[19]

By the time his naturalization petition was filed in 1956, Hirsz Samsonowicz of Horodyszcze had changed his name to Harry Simpson and was living at 92 Tapscott Street in the Brownsville neighborhood of Brooklyn, New York.[20] During the first decade of postwar immigration to New York City, this neighborhood was quite popular as an initial residence for many survivors, including the author's own parents, although it subsequently became a notoriously high-crime area.

Later documents indicate that Hirsz also called himself Harry Samson (and Chaya became Ida) and that the couple eventually moved to the more upscale Brooklyn residential area of Georgetown.[21] Hirsz's decision to immigrate to the United States separated him from his only known surviving sibling Yehuda, who immigrated to Israel and settled in the northern port city of Haifa. We have not determined whether Yehuda had descendants.

To date, the current names and whereabouts of Pessie and Merry Simpson remain unknown to us. Hirsz died on April 4, 1992,[22] predeceasing Chaya, who died on January 17, 1998,[23] three days before what would have been the family's forty-eighth anniversary in their adopted homeland.

Yevel Meyerovich (#122)

Yevel (Yoel) Meyerovich was born in Karelich to Benzion, a gardener, and Musza née Slutska.[1] Documents variably list his year of birth as 1903, 1906, or 1907.[2]

Yevel's four known siblings who were murdered in the Holocaust include Judah Kode, a grocer born in 1908[3] (along with his wife Rachel née Busel);[4] David, a merchant born in 1913;[5] Nechama, a seamstress born in 1911;[6] and Sara Minna, a saleswoman born in 1915.[7] David, Nechama, and Sara Minna were single at their deaths.[8] In a postwar 1948 application for financial assistance, Yevel testified that he'd completed seven years of schooling in Karelich before following in his father's footsteps to become a gardener.[9]

Eyewitness accounts of Karelich following the German occupation of the area on June 22, 1941, detail how the invaders encouraged the local population to beat, rob, and murder their Jewish neighbors and former friends. Yevel is specifically mentioned as having been tortured, robbed, and nearly killed by the local Belarusian police.[10]

Yevel Meyerovich was conscripted to the Novogrudok forced labor camp and numbered among those who safely fled through the tunnel to the forest. He went on to join the Bielski partisan detachment in 1943 at a time when Soviet partisan leaders were anxious to establish control over the various partisan groups in the area. As a result, part of the Bielski detachment found itself unwillingly but officially attached to the Russian-led Kirov Brigade in the fall of 1943. Knowing that any challenge to the authority of Kirov commander Vasiliev would probably result in his own death, Tuvia Bielski reluctantly agreed to split his detachment in two. Although the Bielski detachment was officially called the Kalinin detachment, it continued to be called the Bielski detachment. Yevel Meyerovich belonged to a second group of 180 Bielski fighters[11] commanded mainly by Russians in the Ordzhonikidze detachment,[12] named for Bolshevik leader General Sergo Ordzhonikidze.[13]

Following the war, Yevel's 1948 applications for financial assistance and help in immigrating to the United States made no mention whatsoever of his service in the Ordzhonikidze partisan detachment.[14] As explained previously, the end of World War II coincided with the beginning of the Cold War between the American-led Western Bloc and the Russian-led Eastern Bloc, causing former partisans such as Yevel to fear that their wartime activities would raise the suspicion of collaboration with the Soviets and thus jeopardize their entry to the United States.

Besides deleting his record of partisan service in his applications, Yevel even denied the veracity of his name, testifying that he was in fact Joseph Friedman of Karelich, who for various reasons had changed his name during the war.[15] As there was an individual named Joseph Friedman from Karelich who was reported to have been murdered in 1942,[16] it is plausible that Yevel "adopted" his identity in the hope of erasing any trace of partisan membership that might prevent his entry to the US.

Regardless of his true identity and the actual places he was interned during World War II, Yevel testified in 1947 that he had lost two fingers by Nazi torture.[17] During the pre-immigration period, Yevel was in Lodz, Poland, in 1945,[18] followed by residences in such towns and cities across Italy as Padua, Casa Bianca, Aquasanta, and Anzio, where he took part in various preparatory programs for immigration to Israel. However, his desire to immigrate to the United States was clearly stated in his application of September 13, 1948, completed in Anzio.[19]

According to an article in the Karelich memorial book, Yevel succeeded in reaching the United States.[20] To date, we have been unable to trace the whereabouts of Yevel Meyerovich, aka Joseph Friedman, following his immigration.

Shlomo (#123) and
Chana (#124) Ryback

Shlomo and Chana Ryback were among the sparse number of couples who embarked on the tunnel escape together, survived together, and took refuge in the forest together. Moreover, they both played important roles in saving the lives of other escapees and partisans.

Two years older than her husband, Chana née Iwiniecki was born in Novogrudok on March 31, 1912, to Meir, a tailor, and his wife Tsipora (Tsipa) née Leibowicz. Meir, Tsipa, and their children Leibke, Motel, Chana, and Mary (Mirke) resided on Pozhtova Gaas. Trained as a *feldshur* (paramedic) prior to the war in Vilna's TOZ Nursing School,[1] Chana returned to her hometown, where she worked in the Novogrudok Jewish Hospital together with the author's aunt Shifra Dunetz, who had been a fellow nursing student in Vilna.[2]

Shlomo was born in Radun, Poland, on March 12, 1914, to Gisia and Ephraim. At the age of only four, Shlomo suffered the first of many losses when his mother died in the 1918 Spanish influenza pandemic. Raised by his father, a beekeeper, along with siblings Shimon, Yehuda, Velvel, and Yentl, Shlomo cherished the memory of receiving a kiss on the forehead from the renowned Rabbi Israel Meir Kagan (the "Chofetz Chaim"), who as a rabbinical student had occasionally joined the Ryback family for meals.

A serendipitous fall from a horse not only broke Shlomo's collarbone, but saved the youth from conscription into the Polish Cavalry. Following his subsequent graduation from a teachers' seminary in Vilna, Shlomo began an illustrious career as a Hebrew teacher in the small Belarusian town of Turetz. Then in 1938, after only one year as a teacher in Novogrudok's Tushia School, Shlomo was appointed principal of this private Jewish religious school on Kostchelna Gass (Church Street). The following year, as Novogrudok fell under Soviet control with the enactment of the Molotov-Ribbentrop Pact partitioning Poland, Shlomo was forced to adapt his curriculum to reflect Communist ideology.[3]

Against the backdrop of the great upheaval wreaked by the Soviet annexation just three months beforehand, Chana and Shlomo were married in Novogrudok on December 31, 1939. The joy of the birth of their first child Ephraim the following year turned to terrible tragedy in 1942 while the young family was interned in the Pereseka ghetto. Shlomo had been sent out of the ghetto on a forced work detail when word came that the Germans were preparing an *aktzia* to slaughter the children. With nowhere to hide the toddler Ephraim, they feared that his presence would endanger the lives of others in the ghetto and that he would be tortured and slaughtered by the Germans. In desperation, Chana and her sister Mirke "put their children to sleep forever with painless injections." Chana's agonizing decision was to torment the couple for the rest of their lives, even while rebuilding their family after the war.[4]

In the Novogrudok forced labor camp, Shlomo became a kitchen supervisor by day and a surreptitious tunnel digger by night. After surviving the tunnel escape, he and Chana set out to reach the Bielski partisan detachment. Accompanied by other escapees, Shlomo, Chana, and their band stopped at the home of a sympathetic Polish farmer named Jan Jarmolowicz, who was hiding Jews in his barn and granary. Before the war, Jarmolowicz had been a client of Chana's father, and he was now quite pleased to help the new arrivals. Not only did he feed them, but he also cleaned and bandaged the wound that Shlomo had suffered during the escape. Moreover, before sending the group off in the direction of the Bielski detachment, this kind and brave farmer taught Shlomo how to raid houses and "act like a partisan."[5]

Beyond Chana's unspeakably painful sacrifice of her own child to save others in the Pereseka ghetto, both she and Shlomo went on to save the lives of other escapees and partisans. In his writings, Chaim

Noah Leibowitz (#91) describes the harrowing moments immediately after exiting the tunnel when, under a hail of gunfire, he fell into a hole over knee-deep in water. Helpless, Chaim was dragged out of the deadly trap by Chana and Shlomo, who risked their own lives to grasp him by the arms and flee together for their lives.[6]

Upon reaching the Bielski partisans, Chana became an assistant to the physician Dr. Max Hirsch, who had lived in Ivenets prior to the war. Together in the forest with his wife Rosalia and their two young sons Binyamin and Lyudvik, Dr. Hirsch is reported to have been an expert in performing abortions. Operating on women from distant partisan units in his forest hut on "Main Street" near that of Commander Tuvia Bielski, he was assisted by several other qualified nurses, including his own wife.[7]

By the winter of 1943–1944, when the Zhukov partisan detachment moved out of the Naliboki Forest, the commander requested that Tuvia accept several of his wounded and ill, as well as several women who were considered burdensome. In exchange for Tuvia's acquiescence, the Bielski detachment was given "gifts" – food, cows, horses, kitchen tools, and, most unfortunately, lice-infected clothing.

With the lice came a severe typhus epidemic in the *otriad*, sending the many infected partisans to Dr. Hirsch for treatment. The task of transporting them to the increasingly overcrowded "hospital" huts several times daily fell to Shlomo Ryback in his horse and buggy.[8] In all likelihood, when the author's own mother contracted the dreaded disease, she was one of those transferred to the "hospital" by Shlomo.

After liberation from the forest in 1944, Shlomo could not face the trauma of working in schools bereft of Jewish children, despite the request of the Russians to help reorganize the schools after the war. Alternatively, Shlomo preferred to fight at the front with the Red Army. Only thanks to Chana's efforts was Shlomo hired instead as a bookkeeper for the Novogrudok jail, the police station, and the fire station. During this immediate post-partisan period, Chana worked in the Russian Army infirmary as well as in the jail, where at risk to her own life, she was able to assist many Jewish prisoners. While trying to help tunnel escapee Raya Kushner (#144) pass a message to her imprisoned father Zeidel (#143), Chana was taken in for questioning. Without Shlomo's intervention, she would likely have been deported to Siberia.[9]

After the couple eventually made their way to Lodz, in 1945 Shlomo was asked by the Bricha underground organization to lead a group of stateless Jewish refugees attempting to illegally enter British-ruled Palestine (then closed to immigration). After journeying from Lodz to Bratislava, the group passed through Budapest, Hungary; Leibnitz, Austria; Zagreb and Belgrade, Yugoslavia, before finally arriving in Italy, where they were to board a ship. There, in the central Italian town of Ascoli Piceno, Chana gave birth to twins on May 27, 1946.[10] Tzipora was named for the maternal grandmother she never knew, while her brother's name, Amitzur (meaning "rock of my people"), alludes to the fortitude and very survival of his parents.

With the family settling in a refugee camp located near Castel Gandolfo and the Vatican summer palace, one would be hard pressed to imagine a more surrealistic picture than that of a Novogrudok tunnel escapee and Bielski partisan working in the Vatican only two years after liberation from the forest. Such was Shlomo, who became a Vatican library employee in Castel Gandolfo during this period.[11] Perhaps Shlomo's path crossed that of fellow tunnel escapee Shlomo Golanski (#75), who worked for a time as a carpenter at the summer palace.[12]

Chana ultimately opposed the original plan to immigrate to Israel, for fear of the ongoing conflict in the region. Sponsored by cousins of Shlomo who had immigrated to Montreal,[13] on March 2, 1950, the family sailed for Canada aboard the SS *Samaria*,[14] a former Cunard Line cruise ship that had been transformed to a troopship during the war.[15]

Although Ephraim's tragic death cast a lifelong shadow over Shlomo and Chana, they succeeded in rebuilding their lives. Shlomo, the erstwhile teacher, soon reestablished himself as a master Hebrew instructor at Montreal's Herzliya High School, in addition to editing Hebrew textbooks. Chana became a respected private-duty nurse in her adopted city's Jewish General Hospital.

Both of Ephraim and Chana's children followed in their parents' footsteps by making significant contributions in the fields of education and medicine. Tsipora, who changed her name to Sylvia, became a professor of education at McGill University in Montreal. Of her two children, Alissa Gisea is the namesake of Shlomo's mother, and Jamie Ephraim carries the name of his baby uncle.[16] Sylvia's brother Amitzur, who changed his name to Hymie, went on to become a successful otolaryngologist (head and neck surgeon) at New York's prestigious Mt. Sinai Hospital. He has three children. Both Hymie and Sylvia are currently retired.[17] As of August 2023, between them, they have ten grandchildren, who would have been great-grandchildren to Shlomo and Chana.[18]

Chana died in 2005. Until Shlomo's death in 1997 at age eighty-three, he often looked back upon their partisan days, reflecting on how strong and proud they were to be in the forest, alive and free.[19]

Sylvia and Hymie have continued to commemorate their parents' past. Together with several of their own children, they traveled to Novogrudok to attend the July 2019 inauguration of the Memorial Wall for the tunnel escapees. Sylvia's dedication at the beginning of this book reads: "In memory of Ephraim, the baby brother I never knew."

Shlomo and Chana Ryback with their twins in Italy, 1946
(courtesy of Sylvia Ryback Sklar)

Tevel (#125) and Feige (#126) Shmerkovich

Tevel and Feige Shmerkovich were one of the few married couples to have survived both the Novogrudok forced labor camp and the exceptional tunnel escape. Yet tragedy was to strike seven months later, deep in the forest.

Tevel Shmerkovich, the son of Girsh[1] and Michla,[2] was born on March 3, 1911, in the town of Nesvizh,[3] sixty miles (97 km) southwest of Minsk.[4] Tevel had six or seven siblings, including a sister said to have immigrated to South Africa prior to the war.[5] His younger brother, Yakov (Yankel), born in 1905, survived the war with the Kutuzov partisans,[6] a Russian detachment named for Michael Kutuzov, the Russian military commander who drove off Napoleon's troops.[7] Girsh, Michla, and the remainder of their children were all murdered in the Holocaust.[8]

Very little is known of Feige beyond the fact that she was the daughter of Samuil (surname unknown) and born in 1894.[9] Prior to the war, she and Tevel lived in Novogrudok,[10] her hometown.[11] Apparently, the couple had no children. While we are unaware of the nature of Feige's occupation that enabled her to be conscripted to the Novogrudok forced labor camp, it is clear that Tevel's skills as a carpenter[12] were deemed of importance to the German Army. We can assume that Tevel played a critical role along with his fellow carpenters in constructing the impressive clandestine tunnel.

During the breakout, Feige crawled directly behind her husband through the tunnel, and together the two fled through the forest to the Bielski *otriad*.[13] In the spring of 1944, Feige was killed in the woods as a partisan.[14] Tevel became a widower three days before his thirty-third birthday, just three months prior to liberation.

Records of the Red Cross International Tracing Service indicate that from 1946 to 1949, Tevel took refuge in the Hohne Displaced Persons Camp, the largest displaced persons camp and the center of survivor activities in the British-occupied zone.[15] Despite the notoriously poor hygienic conditions, shortage of food and clothing, and extreme overcrowding, a thriving community life became organized in the camp.[16] It was there while working as a British policeman that Tevel met his second wife, Sima née Korman. A native of Brisk, Sima had survived the war in Uzbekistan, yet bore the tragedy of losing a child during this time. By September 1946, Yitzchak, Tevel and Sima's only child, was born in the camp.[17]

In 1949, the young family immigrated to the newly established State of Israel,[18] following the arrival of Tevel's brother Yakov two years earlier. Here Tevel rebuilt his life, under the new name of Tuvia Shmerkovich. His son Yitzchak and granddaughter Noga praise Tuvia as having been a caring father to his only son, a loving husband to Sima (who died in 1980), and a warm grandfather to his only grandchild, Noga. Interviewed in 2020 from her home in Long Beach, California, where she works as an architect, Noga, thirty-seven, fondly recalls sleeping at her grandfather's house on the Sabbath and spending Passover with him, as well as his delight at taking her to visit the neighborhood park near his home.[19]

Yet the war had left its mark. Yitzchak points out that his father had been wounded in the head and in the leg, with one injury occurring during his prewar service in the Polish Army and the second as a partisan. Although Tuvia often suffered fears and uncontrollable panic attacks, Yitzchak emphasizes that his father persevered to continue his work as a carpenter for Israel Railways near his home in Haifa, where the family settled after one year in Tel Aviv.[20]

Yitzchak and his own family have been living primarily in the United States since 1999. A former driving instructor in Israel, he currently resides in Las Vegas, where at one point he made use of the basic carpentry skills he learned from Tuvia to build kitchen cabinets.[21]

Although Yitzchak and Noga recall having vaguely heard that Tuvia had escaped through a tunnel and had been a partisan, neither had heard of Novogrudok, the forced labor camp, or the Bielski partisans. Noga was just seven years old when her beloved grandfather died on February 2, 1990.[22] Yitzchak admits having found it difficult to speak to his father about the Holocaust, something he regrets to this day.[23]

Yitchak recalls that in his entire life, he only encountered one person who was with his father during the war, a former partisan named Sonia whom he met as a little boy in Haifa. He now hopes to learn about the tunnel breakout beyond the little his father told him, and perhaps even to visit Novogrudok, the site of the great escape and his father's fight for life.[24]

Provizor (#127)

The identity of the man or woman listed only by the surname "Provizor" remains a mystery. Out of the 206 citations in Yad Vashem's Central Database of Shoah Victims' Names for Holocaust victims from Poland with the surname Provisor or Provizor, not one is from the Novogrudok area,[1] thus we may presume that this escapee had taken refuge in the region from elsewhere in Poland.

Geographical origins notwithstanding, nearly every one of the Provisors\Provizors in the Yad Vashem central database were listed as having been murdered. The fate of only seventeen is classified as unknown.[2]

As there is no one with the Provizor surname among the compilation of Jewish partisans from Belorussia in 1941–1944,[3] we may assume that this man or woman most likely did not survive the tunnel escape.

Abram Goldshmid (#128)

Born to Yosel in 1904, Abram Goldshmid was a shoemaker by trade. He is reported to have lived in Voranova,[1] but at some point prior to the war made the fifty-mile journey to Novogrudok, where he resided with his family.[2]

Yosel's shoemaking skills, greatly needed by the German Army, led to his conscription to the Novogrudok forced labor camp. Here he survived the tunnel escape to join the Ordzhonikidze partisan detachment of the Kirov Brigade.[3] The majority of this detachment was made up of 180 Bielski fighters and their wives.[4]

The biographical sketch of Abram Goldshmid below was written by Tamara Vershitskaya, former director of the Museum of History and Regional Studies and of the Jewish Resistance Museum in Novogrudok, following a meeting in 2017 with Abram's stepson David Markovich and his wife.

> Abram Goldshmid…lived with his family on Sverdlov Street in Novogrudok. In 1941, his wife and two daughters, Sonya and Rima, were killed in their own house before Abram's eyes. When the attackers shot at him, the gun misfired and Abram managed to escape. He remained in hiding for some time before entering the [Novogrudok] ghetto in Pereseka. From August 1942, he was in the forced labor camp on Karelich Street where he escaped through the tunnel.
>
> Abram's daughter-in-law notes that in the aftermath of the escape, Abram's familiarity with the area enabled him to bring another five escapees to the village of Baranovich, in the Karelich District. From there, Abram joined the Bielski partisans and was a fighter in the Ordzhonikidze detachment.

Following liberation in July 1944, he was drafted into the Soviet Army and served as a private at the front. He fought in the Berlin Operation and was granted a medal for taking part in the capture of Berlin on June 9, 1945.

Abram Goldshmid, Novogrudok, circa 1951 (courtesy of David Slavin)

After demobilization, Abram returned to Novogrudok and in 1951 married Minia Markovich, who had been widowed during the war. She and her son David (born in 1921) had been evacuated from Vitebsk to the Saratov Region, where they lived in the village of Shiling. At the war's end, they were placed on the train to Belarus, overslept the stop in Vitebsk, and got off the train only when it stopped in Baranovichi. A Belarusian woman invited them to come with her to Novogrudok and to live in her house.

Abram and his new family lived at 23 Tsvetnaya Street in Novogrudok, where Abram continued to work as a shoemaker. He and his cousin Leiba Pinchuk (#46) often used to meet and reminisce about the escape and the partisans.

Abram Goldshmid died in 1966 and is buried in the Novogrudok cemetery.[5]

Skakun (#129)

No proper name accompanies the surname "Skakun" on the escape list, rendering his or her identification difficult to determine. Yad Vashem's Central Database of Shoah Victims' Names lists thirty-five entries for Skakuns from throughout Poland, all of whom were reported to have been murdered.[1]

In the 1963 publication of *Pinkas Navaredok*, the *Novogrudok Memorial Book*, Leizer Mishe Zamkov commemorated his Skakun family members who were slain in the Holocaust: his uncle and aunt Yitzchak and Chana, and their children Malka and Rivka.[2] A memorial notice for Chaya Skakun in *Pinkas Navaredok* was filed by her son Yosef.[3] Forty-two years later, Chaya's grandson Michael submitted a Yad Vashem Page of Testimony stating that she was murdered on December 8, 1941.[4]

Michael Skakun raises the likelihood that having survived the first two Novogrudok massacres, his paternal great-uncle Itche (Yitzchak)[5] mentioned above may be the Skakun who participated in the tunnel escape. Unfortunately, we have no proof.

Prior to the war, Itche and Chaya, grocery owners, lived at 20 Koscielna Street (Yiddishe Gass) in Novogrudok with their family.[6] Michael notes that following the murders of his wife and children, Itche was so grieved that he could not be persuaded to join an "escape party" organized by his nephew Yosef after the town's second massacre in August 1942.[7]

To his knowledge, Michael attests, his father Joseph (Yosef) was ultimately the only Skakun to survive the war. In a remarkable memoir about his father, who remained alive by posing as a Christian and a member of the SS, Michael poignantly describes the torturous atmosphere in his relatives' improvised prayer house in the Novogrudok ghetto. If the Skakun of the escape list was, in fact, one of these relatives, it is likely that he or she participated in the family prayers held there. We therefore include Michael's haunting description:

> Kaddish, an intercession for the souls of the dead…was constantly recited. A chant of praise to God, the Kaddish was counterpointed by a recitation of a passage from Psalm 44.

> > Rouse Yourself; why do You sleep, O Lord?
> > Why do You hide Your face
> > Ignoring our affliction and distress?

> No family was spared in Novardok, and those who were left were paralyzed by grief. In the twilight gloom, many now said the mourning prayer for themselves, cognizant that their days were numbered.[8]

Although the days of the Skakun recorded on the escape list were apparently longer than those of his family members, his days, too, were ultimately numbered. With no known survivors carrying the family name other than Yosef Skakun, and with no Skakun listed in the compilation of 7,742 partisans,[9] we must assume that Skakun, the Novogrudok forced labor camp inmate slated to be the 129th to crawl through the tunnel, did not survive to reach the safety of the forest.

Moshe Nignevitcky (#130)

The youngest of the six children of Zipora née Bitansky and her second husband Shmuel, Moshe Nignevitcky was born in Novogrudok in 1916 and grew up on the town's Yiddishe Gasse (Jewish Street). Alter (#132), the oldest sibling and twenty years Moshe's senior, was the only child in the family who was born to Zipora and her first husband Yosef, whose family name is unknown. Before the war, Moshe's sister Miriam (Mara) and brother David immigrated to Palestine. Of the five siblings who remained in Europe, only Moshe and Alter survived. Their brother Zvi was killed after refusing to leave his girlfriend, despite having been assigned to the Novogrudok forced labor camp through Moshe's intervention. We do not know the circumstances of the deaths of sisters Yehudit and Itka.[1]

At the age of seven, Moshe was orphaned of his father on the Jewish holiday of Simchat Torah. The following Sabbath, the renowned rabbi Avraham Yeshaya Karelitz, known as the Chazon Ish (the title of his magnum opus), happened to visit Novogrudok. Taking the orphaned Moshe aside, he prophesized that after suffering a traumatic experience, Moshe would eventually reach the Land of Israel.[2]

Moshe was a pupil in the Tarbut school, a day school comprising seven grades. From first grade, the language of instruction was Hebrew,[3] which Moshe learned to speak fluently. Despite hailing from one of the poorest families, he excelled in his studies and won awards and certificates.[4]

Perhaps as a result of the Chazon Ish's prophecy, already as a youth, Moshe was thinking of his future life in what was then Palestine. Joining the Zionist Hashomer Hatzair youth movement, he learned about and underwent training for kibbutz life. It was in the movement that Moshe met his future wife, fellow counselor Sheina née Borowski

(#131). The young couple married before the German occupation and lived on Novogrudok's Pilsudski Street. Moshe and Sheina were interned together in both the Pereseka ghetto and the Novogrudok forced labor camp. Moshe's daughter Zophy Chermoni recalls being told by fellow escapee Jack (Idel) Kagan (#95) that Moshe and Sheina's little daughter was killed during the war.

Thanks to having specialized in carpentry in the Tarbut school, Moshe became a master carpenter. His talents were such that much of the furniture he made in the camp's carpentry workshop was sent to Germany for the family of Wilhelm Reuter, the camp commander. Reuter had reportedly studied furniture restoration in Paris before the war and was able to appreciate Moshe's work – to the point that besides having intervened on behalf of his brother Zvi, Moshe was also able to arrange for Alter, a shoemaker, to be allowed to serve as his assistant in the labor camp. Even when Moshe was twice punished by hanging when suspected of pilfering wood and tools, it was Reuter who had his prized worker lowered from the tree. The wood and tools, of course, were clandestinely used in the construction of the escape tunnel. Zophy reports having been told by former labor camp inmate Dov Cohen that Moshe was not only in charge of the carpentry workshop, but at a certain point managed all the labor camp workshops as well.

Moshe, Sheina, and Alter crawled through the tunnel together and miraculously survived. Like all escapees, the three now had to make the life-and-death decision of which route to take to reach the partisan detachment in the distant forest. In their case, they relied upon a dream that Alter had had prior to the escape in which a large black dog warned against heading directly toward the forest. Moshe, Sheina, and Alter, along with several friends, heeded the warning to reach the Bielski partisans via a roundabout route, which ultimately saved their lives.

Utilizing the skills in construction he had gleaned as a carpenter, in the forest Moshe became a master builder of *zemlyankas*,[5] the earth-and-wood dugouts, two-thirds within the ground and one-third above, which served as rectangular bunkers. As the upper part formed a pyramid consisting of branches or sticks, the structure was then covered with foliage or sheets of bark. These outer coverings served the dual purpose of protecting from the sub-zero temperatures and concealing the dugouts from view. The *zemlyankas* were so well hidden that when German reconnaissance planes flew overhead in search of partisans, the bunkers could not be detected.[6]

Moshe's carpentry skills were to be literally lifesaving in lining the *zemlyankas* with wood in order to keep the soil from collapsing. The frigid temperatures in the winter and forest insects rampant in the summer dictated the need to construct wooden bunks around the walls on which straw, leaves, or flour sacks would be piled.[7] In addition to his *zemlyanka*-building efforts, Moshe is also said to have taken part in such military activities as ambushes, food raids, and acts of revenge on villages that disclosed the whereabouts of Jews.[8]

Moshe's daughter Zophy reports that her father joined the Soviet Army while in the forest, prior to the partisan exit on July 10, 1944. As a member of the forces under the command of the renowned General Georgy Zhukov, Moshe returned to Novogrudok only after the war to search for loved ones.[9]

For reasons unknown, Moshe and Sheina are reported to have separated in the forest.[10] While in the Pocking-Waldstadt Displaced Persons Camp,[11] the largest such camp in the American zone and the second-largest in all of Germany after Bergen-Belsen,[12] Moshe met his future second wife, survivor Esther Grushka from Rozan, Poland. After traveling to the port of Marseille, Moshe and Esther sailed to Palestine on the *Pan York*,[13] one of the two largest illegal immigration ships.[14] Due to having contracted typhus on board ship, he was unable to join any of the pre-state paramilitary militias in action prior to the Israeli War of Independence. Once the perilous journey ended safely on Israel's shores, Moshe was reunited with his sister Mara, who cared for him in her Tel Aviv home. When he finally recovered, Moshe and Esther were married.[15]

An expert carpenter, Moshe continued to work in his profession in his new homeland. Although he was unable to serve in the IDF as a conscripted soldier, he contributed a great deal to the security of Israel in his role as a civilian charged with carpentry services on army bases.[16]

Moshe Nignevitcky, during his Soviet Army service, 1944–1945 (courtesy of Zophy Chermoni)

Remembered as a loving family man, Moshe is recalled for his kindness and modesty, as well as for his continual aspiration for perfection in every endeavor. Despite his hardships and losses, Moshe never lost his faith and remained religiously observant his entire life. During Jewish holidays, he would often speak of his wartime attempts to uphold his traditions, even in the labor camp: Chanukah was celebrated by lighting small scraps of wood Moshe managed to smuggle out of the carpentry workshop; Yom Kippur prayers were recited by memory in small groups, even in the midst of performing slave labor.[17]

Moshe proudly related the story of the tunnel escape to his family. Today, his daughter Zophy continues to transmit the legacy of the breakout to the next generation, bringing her own children to the site of the forced labor camp as well as supporting this research.

Moshe died in 2002 at the age of ninety-six, sixteen years before his beloved Esther's death. As of August 2023, he leaves behind Zophy, a retired meteorologist, Yossi, a businessman, as well as five grandchildren and eleven great-grandchildren.[18]

Sheina (Sheindel) Nignevitcky (#131)

One of eight children, four girls and four boys, Sheina Nignevitcky née Borovski was born on May 15, 1923,[1] in the town of Zelechow to Yosef and Raisel.[2] After Sheina's older brother Aaron (#58) moved from Zelechow to Novogrudok following his marriage around 1930, the remainder of the Borovski family followed him there.[3] In Novogrudok, Sheina met and married Moshe Nignevitcky (#130), a carpenter.[4] Together with her husband[5] and two of her brothers, Aaron[6] and Wolff (Velvel, #57),[7] Sheina was interned in the Novogrudok forced labor camp, where she worked as a seamstress making dresses, coats, and gloves for the wives of the Nazi officers.[8] All four escaped through the tunnel on September 26, 1943, and survived to become Bielski partisans.[9] Although Sheina's parents, brothers Faivel[10] and Eli, and sisters Sarah and Chana (Bokatowicz)[11] were all murdered in the Novogrudok massacres, the three surviving Borovskis were reunited in the forest with their sister Anna, who had married Jacob Duszkin[12] in the ghetto, survived in hiding with her husband, and joined the partisans.[13]

Reported to have separated from her husband while in the partisan detachment, Sheina then married Tzadok Flaster,[14] a butcher from Mlawa, Poland, who fled to Belorussia during the war.[15] The couple's only child, Mendel, was born in Novogrudok on February 4, 1945.[16] The family took refuge in the Föhrenwald Displaced Persons Camp prior to immigrating to Rio de Janeiro, Brazil, in 1952.[17] Here Tzadok became known as Sergei and reestablished himself as a kosher butcher.[18]

Around eighteen years after her second marriage, tragedy struck when Sheina became widowed at the age of forty-five. Once again, Sheina's resilience came to the fore as she immigrated to the United

States, sponsored by Anna, who had moved to America in 1950 and settled in Cleveland, Ohio.[19] After living for several years in Cleveland, Sheina (who later changed her name to Sonia[20]) relocated to Brooklyn, New York, where in 1972 she remarried Sucher (Sol) Papier,[21] a Polish-born[22] refugee who worked in the garment industry.[23] The couple lived in the Coney Island neighborhood.[24]

Sheina Nignevitcky, Germany, 1945 (courtesy of Sonia [Sheina] Papier)

Following Sol's death in 1996,[25] Sheina lived for another fifteen years until her death on September 14, 2011.[26] Her niece Judy Freedman recalls Sheina as a very ambitious woman who mastered English very quickly. Despite the distance from her siblings, Judy notes that Sheina maintained close contact with them until Aaron's death in Melbourne in the mid-1980s and Anna's death in Cleveland in 2002.

If Sheina were alive, she would undoubtedly be proud of her descendants. Mendel, who cared for his mother during her last years, is currently retired from his work as a supermarket department manager.[27] His two sons, Sammy and Sergei (Tzadok's namesake), are now parents themselves. As of September 2023, Sheina would be the great-grandmother of ten.[28] By any measure, this is an extraordinary feat for a woman who fled for her life through a tunnel at the age of twenty and endured so many painful losses throughout her life.

Alter Nignevitcky (#132)

Alter Nignevitcky, a shoemaker by profession, was born in Novogrudok in 1896 to Zipora née Bitansky and her husband Yosef. Following Yosef's death when Alter was a youngster, Zipora remarried Shmuel Nignevitcky, a shoemaker, who adopted Alter, gave him his surname, and most probably taught him his trade. Zipora and Shmuel had six children together.

While we know that Alter's siblings Yehudit and Itka were murdered during the war, we have no details of their deaths. His brother Zvi was killed after refusing to leave his girlfriend, despite having been assigned to the Novogrudok forced labor camp thanks to the intervention of brother Moshe (#130). The lives of his sister Mara and brother David were saved by their immigration to pre-state Israel prior to the Holocaust. As for Alter, the oldest sibling, and Moshe, the youngest, their lives became deeply intertwined during their internment in the Novogrudok forced labor camp and ever onwards, despite the twenty years that separated their births.

As a shoemaker for the Russian Army before the war, Alter met his future wife in one of his postings, despite having been engaged at the time to a local Novogrudok girl. Returning home with his new fiancée, Alter became socially ostracized in the town of his birth, necessitating his move to the nearby town of Zhetl, where he married and had two small sons. Yet the Nazi occupation forced Alter's return to Novogrudok, where ultimately his mother Zipora, his wife, and his children were all murdered in one of the city's massacres. After the slaughter, it was his brother Moshe who physically held Alter back from certain death as he tried to run to the bodies.

In the Novogrudok forced labor camp, Alter slept in a room with fellow inmates from Zhetl. The secret entrance to the tunnel was just under his bunk. During his internment in the camp, he is recalled as having served as a cantor at the clandestine services for holidays and Shabbat.

In all probability, Alter and Moshe saved each other's lives. Moshe's talents as an expert carpenter were greatly esteemed by the German camp commander Wilhelm Reuter, who had studied furniture restoration in Paris prior to the war. Thus, when Moshe personally intervened to request that Alter be allowed to serve as his assistant in the labor camp, the request was granted. Alter the shoemaker suddenly became the assistant to a master craftsman who made furniture to be shipped to Germany for the personal use of Reuter's family.

In turn, the brothers may have been saved by Alter's dream. As he fell into a fitful sleep just prior to the escape, Alter dreamt of a large black dog which warned him to walk via the villages upon exiting from the tunnel, rather than heading directly to the forest. Heeding this seemingly illogical warning, Alter and Moshe took the indirect route toward the Bielski detachment. Other escapees, including several friends and Moshe's first wife Sheina née Borowski (#131), joined them on the ultimately successful trek.

Prior to liberation, Alter is said to have left the partisans for an unknown destination, followed by his illegal immigration to Palestine from Italy. At some point after his arrival in Palestine, Alter married Sara Liba, a fellow survivor from Zhetl. Alter and Sara Liba had no children together. Living out the rest of his life in a third-floor apartment in the Sheinkin neighborhood of Tel Aviv, Alter lived near his sister Mara Lipchin and her family.

Alter Nignevicki, Zhetl, 1932 (courtesy of Zophy Chermoni)

Although his adverse heart condition prevented him from holding steady work, when his health allowed, Alter would return to his profession as a shoemaker to work in his brother-in-law Dov Lipchin's shoe factory.

From her frequent childhood visits to Alter with her father prior to Alter's death in the mid-1970s, Moshe's daughter Zophy Chermoni remembers her uncle as being depressed and constantly speaking of his murdered children. Ironically, his Tel Aviv window faced an ongoing panorama of parents together with their children on happy outings to the zoo.[1]

Nachum (#133) and Sara (#134) Zamosczyk ("Panikarter") and Isaac Lazowsky

Sara and Nachum Zamosczyk were two of seven children who at a young age became orphaned of their parents Shimon and Laya née Lauferman[1] Zamosczyk. We learned from former Zhetl resident Mrs. Chaya Magid[2] that the nickname "Panikarter" had been given by the townspeople to Nachum, Sara, and their siblings Label, Eeser, Yussel, Peshe, and Esther[3] after these children made their way on their own to Zhetl from the nearby tiny hamlet of Panikarti following their parents' death.[4] On the escape list, Nachum and Sara were both listed under the surname "Panikarter," posing a major challenge to determine their actual identity.

Although we do not know the dates of birth of her five siblings, Sara, known as "Sorkeh," was born on May 1, 1915.[5] According to Sara's son Simon Lazowsky, she came to Zhetl only around the age of fifteen, after spending several years in the Novogrudok orphanage with one of her sisters.[6]

Nachum, Sara's older brother, was born in 1909. (His name appears as "Naum" on the list of Jewish partisans in Belorussia during the years 1941–1944,[7] and on the escape list with only the first two letters of Nachum.) Like Sara, Nachum was married prior to the war. His wife Rachel née Novogrudski, born in Zhetl in 1907, is likely to have been a relative of tunnel escapee Michael Novogrudski (#114), also of Zhetl. Pages of Testimony attest to the death of Rachel, a seamstress, during the Holocaust; however, the date and circumstances of her murder are unspecified.[8] Nachum and Rachel were the parents of Henia, just four years old at the time she was killed in one of the Zhetl massacres of 1942.[9]

In 1936, after a five-year courtship, Sara married Efroim Nevachovich of Novogrudok, a radio repairman by profession. Their daughter Leahleh was born around 1938 in Novogrudok, where Sara and Efroim had settled. In 1941, with Germany opening an eastern front, Efroim was mobilized into the Red Army as a driver. In an ill-fated attempt to escape, he went AWOL and was caught by the Germans and brutally murdered in Novogrudok's first massacre of July 26, 1941.[10]

Evidently, the younger brother (whose first name is unknown) of Efroim and Yakov (Jankef) Nevachovich (#51) played a pivotal role in resistance efforts within the Novogrudok forced labor camp. Thanks to Efroim having taught his fourteen-year-old brother the skills to build and repair radios, the youngster was co-opted by labor camp commander Wilhelm Reuter to work as a radio technician.[11] We can assume that this young man is the acclaimed radio technician who managed to smuggle electronic parts into the camp and assemble them into a one-way radio. As fellow escapee Daniel Ostashinski describes in his testimony, the brother of tunnel escapee Yakov (Jankef) Nevachovich was the miraculous radio technician who enabled camp resistance leaders to clandestinely monitor BBC broadcasts and glean information on the war's progress.[12]

In his Yad Vashem testimony, Shaul Gorodynski (#77) relates how Yakov Nevachovich and his brother provided their sick, crippled, and aged father, also interned in the camp, with poison (probably morphine) in order to save him from falling into German hands.[13]

The fate of Sara and Efroim's five-year-old daughter Leahleh and the story of a grandmother's boundless love were told to Chaya Magid (widow of escapee Avraham Magid) by Novogrudok native Chaya Gertzovski, daughter-in-law of escapee Zalman Gertzovski (#117). As Chaya described, during one of the subsequent mass executions (possibly that of May 7, 1943 as well), all children were separated from their parents, assembled in the courtyard of the forced labor camp, and thrown onto trucks to be hauled to their deaths. When Sara's daughter was forcibly wrenched from her arms, her mother-in-law climbed onto the truck as well, worried that "the child will cry" unless accompanied by a family member. The Germans happily approved the grandmother's action, giving them "another Jew to kill."[14]

Her son Simon recalls that Sara described a somewhat different account of her mother-in-law's brave, anguished attempts to save little Leahleh. She told of her mother-in-law hiding in a closet with Leahleh, thus allowing Sara to appear without her child at roll call and increase her chances of remaining alive. German soldiers then raided the building, found the grandmother and little girl, and sent them to their deaths.[15] By either account, it is clear that this grandmother made heartbreakingly valiant efforts to protect her precious Leahleh.

Although we do not know the circumstances, Sara's five siblings were all murdered during this time as well.[16] Only Sara and her brother Nachum (#133), whose proficiencies were deemed essential to the German Army – Sara as a seamstress[17] and Nachum as a shoemaker[18] – were assigned to the Novogrudok forced labor camp.

In the tunnel breakthrough of September 1943, Sara crouched behind Nachum as they crawled to freedom. The two then joined a small band of escapees who headed together for the Bielski partisan detachment. One member of the group, Pesia Mayevski (#160), notes in her account that during the several-week trek through the Naliboki Forest, they subsisted on rainwater and raw potatoes until finally reaching the safety of the Bielski detachment.[19]

Both Sara and Nachum served in the Ordzhonikidze detachment of 180 Bielski fighters under Russian command until liberation in 1944.[20] Nachum was then drafted into the Red Army, where he was killed in combat with the Germans.[21]

Postwar International Red Cross records document that for five years after the war, Sara continued to live on the European continent as a stateless refugee. While residing in the Trofaiach Displaced Persons Camp in the British-occupied zone of Austria in 1945, she married Isaac Lazowsky,[22] a fellow labor camp inmate, tunnel escapee, and Bielski partisan.[23]

Isaac (Isidore) Lazowsky, the son of Falko (Feivel) and Duszka née Itzkowitz, was born in August 1911 in the city of Minsk.[24] Records indicate that both Isaac[25] and Feivel had relocated to Novogrudok (ninety miles from Minsk) prior to the war.[26] As a welder by profession,[27] Isaac was conscripted to the Novogrudok forced labor camp.

Following their marriage, Isaac and Sara took refuge in the Villach Displaced Persons Camp in Austria, the Grugliasco DP Camp outside of Turin, Italy, and the Ostia DP camp near Rome.[28] Their son Simon, the namesake of his maternal grandfather, was born in the Ostia camp in 1947.[29]

The three-strong Lazowsky family sailed to the United States from the port of Bremen, Germany, on September 11, 1949, aboard the USS *General C.C. Ballou*.[30] In 1955, Sara and Isaac, now called "Isidore," became naturalized citizens of the United States of America.[31] At the time, Sara, Isaac, and Simon were living in an apartment that they shared with another family in the East New York section of Brooklyn, New York. When they became the sole tenants in later years, they sublet the extra bedrooms to supplement Isaac's salary as a cabinetmaker and Sara's work at home as a seamstress.[32]

A genealogical search led us to discover the existence and where-abouts of Simon and his younger sister Diane, who was born in Brooklyn in 1956.[33] When the author contacted Simon and Diane, neither had ever heard of Panikarti, their mother's birthplace. Nor had they been aware of their parents' membership in the Bielski partisans, although there had been mention of "the forest." Like many other children of survivors, both Simon and Diane had heard bits and pieces about the forced labor camp and the tunnel escape, but never in a coherent fashion.

As for the tragic murder of their sister Leahleh, her picture was displayed in the house, yet questions regarding the identity of the little girl in the photo were dismissed until Diane was about twenty-five years old and Simon was nearly forty. Only at that point did Sara tell each child some of the story of her past.[34]

Diane laments that the period of Sara and Isaac's "good years" in America came to an end in 1967. Tragedy befell the family shortly after their move to the more upscale Brighton Beach neighborhood, when Isaac suffered a disastrous stroke at the age of fifty-five. For the remainder of his life, Isaac was confined to a nursing facility as a mute quadriplegic. Until his death in 1973,[35] Sara would travel on four buses daily to be at his bedside.[36] At the same time, she continued to support the family by working as a dressmaker, a profession she disliked immensely but was forced to pursue in order to support the family.[37]

At her death in 2004, Sara had outlived her second husband by thirty-one years.[38] Today, both Simon and Diane continue to live in New York. Simon, a retired certified public accountant, is widowed.[39] Diane is married and works as an insurance broker.[40] The last remnants of the families of both their parents, they remain extremely close.[41]

Ribatzki (#135)

The surname Ribatzki stands alone on the escape list without a proper name, making it nearly impossible to determine the identity of the man or woman slated to be the 135th inmate to crawl through the tunnel. Moreover, it is impossible to know whether he or she was native of the Novogrudok area or had fled there as a refugee from a different area of Poland.

There are 121 listings in Yad Vashem's Central Database of Shoah Victims' Names for individuals from throughout Poland with the surname Ribatzki or Ribatski. Only one Page of Testimony exists for a Ribatzki whose murder occurred in Novogrudok. His uncle testifies that Asher Ribatzki, a merchant from Voronova, was slain in Novogrudok, where he had lived prior to the war. The testimony also names Asher's wife Sara and their four-year-old son Berl as having been killed.[1] A fellow townsperson of Voronova (250 miles from Novogrudok), however, testified that Asher, a yeshiva student,[2] and his wife[3] were murdered in the Voronova ghetto on May 11, 1942.

If indeed Asher Ribatzki and his family took refuge in Novogrudok, it is unlikely this merchant and/or yeshiva student would have possessed a skill deemed vital enough for the Germans to have conscripted him to the Novogrudok forced labor camp. However, the possibility exists that, like others, he "invented" a profession useful to the Germans that enabled his being drafted into the forced labor camp.

Without clear proof of the identity of the person called simply "Ribatzki" on the Novogrudok forced labor camp escape list, we cannot ascertain his or her destiny. However, the fact that no Ribatzki surname appears on any list of partisans in the Novogrudok area gives ample reason to believe that this inmate perished in the tunnel escape.[4]

Zacharia Yoselevski (#136)

One of seven children,[1] Zacharia Yoselevski was born in Novogrudok in 1895.[2] The son of Avraham, a merchant, and Basha,[3] Zacharia worked as a builder.[4]

Zacharia and his wife Dina[5] née Rozovski[6] had three children: Rivka, born in 1927,[7] Tzvi, born in 1931,[8] and Belvina, born in 1934.[9] Tragically, Zacharia was left alone when Dina and all three children were murdered in Novogrudok's second mass execution on August 7, 1942.[10]

Zacharia was spared death in the massacre to be conscripted to the Novogrudok forced labor camp. Yet just over a year after the murder of his family, Zacharia lost his life during the tunnel escape. In a Yad Vashem Page of Testimony filed by his cousin, Zecharia's death is listed as having occurred in September 1943.[11]

Zacharia Yoselevski is commemorated in the *Novogrudok Memorial Book*.[12]

Shepsel Eisenshtadt (#137)

Shepsel Eisenshtadt, the son of Lejb and Ruchla née Sztamfater, was born in 1912.[1] According to one postwar registration card he completed, Shepsel's place of birth was Sobolew, Poland, around 120 miles (200 km) southwest of Novogrudok.[2] In a second registration, he listed his birthplace as Otwock, Poland,[3] a town near Warsaw that was a popular Jewish health resort.[4] In any case, he listed Otwock on both records as his prewar address.

The Germans bombarded Otwock on September 21, 1939, plunging the Jewish community into increasingly wretched straits.[5] As to how and when Shepsel fled Otwock for Russian-controlled Novogrudok, a 270-mile (435 km) journey, we are unaware. However, as a shoemaker by profession,[6] Shepsel was conscripted to the Novogrudok forced labor camp, where his skills were of value to the German Army.

Shepsel survived the tunnel escape and the trek through the forest to reach the Bielski partisan detachment.[7] Following the war, his registration records indicate that he resided in or near Warsaw from March until at least September 1946. By 1948, Shepsel was living in Lodz, Poland, from where he made an inquiry to the Hebrew Immigrant Aid Society (HIAS) in search of a Polish relative who was now a resident and citizen of the United States.[8]

From that point onwards, we have been unable to trace any further documentation regarding Shepsel's subsequent whereabouts.

Yehezkiel (Chatskel) Grande (#138)

Contemporary scholars testify that the traumatic expulsion of the Jewish community of Spain during the Spanish Inquisition led numbers of Sephardic Jews to settle in Belarus[1] and greater Eastern Europe after first sojourning in Ottoman or perhaps Italian territory.[2] Although Sephardim in Belarus are reported to have assimilated into the mainstream local Litvak culture of the Ashkenazi majority, a small number is said to have retained the Sephardic surnames their ancestors brought with them from the Iberian Peninsula.[3]

Yehezkiel (Chatskel) Grande may have come from such a family that retained the Sephardic name of their forefathers. "Grande" is the Spanish equivalent of "large," as well as the equivalent of the popular Ashkenazi name Gross. The son of Berl (or Berko, or Boris) and Rachel

(Risha) née Kumok,[4] Chatskel was born in Novogrudok in 1922. Single, he worked as a cabinetmaker in Novogrudok prior to the war.[5]

Berl, Risha, and Chatskel's younger siblings Shlomo and Sara lived in Swierzen, a hamlet outside of Stobtszy (Stolpce). The Yizkor book from the area notes that the four were murdered together.[6] A cousin who filed Yad Vashem Pages of Testimony for Risha,[7] Shlomo,[8] and Sara[9] lists their murder as having taken place in Stolpce on January 31, 1943. At the time of their deaths, Shlomo was just eleven years old,[10] and Sara was thirteen.[11]

Chatskel's carpentry skills, deemed valuable to the German Army, enabled him to escape death to be conscripted into the Novogrudok forced labor camp. Although Chatskel is not mentioned by name in the personal testimonies found to date, the contribution of the carpenters to the construction of the clandestine tunnel is known to have been extremely crucial.

Chatskel Grande survived the tunnel escape to successfully reach the Bielski partisan detachment. His name appears in the compilation of Jewish partisans in Belorussia.[12]

We have no information whatsoever regarding Chatskel's postwar life and whereabouts. To date, an examination of genealogical, Holocaust-related, and population databases has failed to uncover any information regarding his life after liberation.

Miriam (#139) and Linka (#140) Landau

Mother and daughter Miriam and Linka Landau were refugees from Warsaw[1] who made the 260-mile journey to Novogrudok to flee the Nazis. We have no information regarding Miriam's occupation that enabled her to be conscripted to the Novogrudok forced labor camp, her husband's identity, or whether she had other children. Yet what is known to this day is that Miriam's daughter Linka was famed for her striking beauty. Fanya Dunetz (#142) recalls her as being the most beautiful girl she ever saw.[2] Chaim Leibowitz (#91) wrote of Linka as "a veritable Jewish beauty," whom the Germans spared because of her good looks, describing her as "tall, slim, and gracious with a smooth, thin face…big black eyes and long lashes and black hair."

In his poignant depiction of Passover in the forced labor camp, Leibowitz relates how Linka sat with other women on a bunk, singing a sad song about a mother parting from her child. Many of the women burst into uncontrollable tears as they recalled their own children having been torn from their arms.[3]

Fanya Dunetz recalls that Linka was the girlfriend of Jankef Nevachovich (#51), whom she describes as having been a "good-looking barber from Novogrudok."[4] Nevachovich had been appointed the deputy leader of the group charged with planning the uprising scheduled for April 15, 1942,[5] as well as the head of one of the four groups slated to attack the Germans from all four corners of the ghetto at that time. Ultimately, this uprising was aborted before it could take place.[6]

Although Jankef Nevachovich was assigned to be #51 on the escape list, according to Fanya Dunetz, he dropped back nearly one hundred places to be directly behind Linka and Miriam. Now nearly next in line, Fanya reports having been certain that Nevachovich, a Novogrudok native, would lead them all to safety, thanks to his knowledge of the area. Unfortunately, this was not to be.[7]

In her memoir, Sulia Wolozhinski Rubin, who reached the Bielski partisan detachment prior to the tunnel escape, writes of the horrifying details she learned about the fate of her sister Rita (#71), Rita's boyfriend, Linka, and her Jankef. The four had survived the breakout, yet reportedly rested in the nearby Seltzo Forest rather than distancing themselves from Novogrudok. Discovered the following morning by local policemen, the men were shot and the women raped and brutally tortured.[8]

Although Miriam was not with her daughter at the time, she was evidently slain at some point after fleeing the tunnel. Her name does not appear in the list of Jewish partisans in Belorussia from 1941 to 1944, thus we can assume that she did not survive to reach the safety of the partisan detachment.[9]

Neither Miriam nor Linka Landau's name appears in Yad Vashem's Central Database of Shoah Victims' Names. No Pages of Testimony were filed for this mother and daughter by any surviving relatives or friends.

Eliyahu Novolenski (#141)

Eliyahu (Elya) Novolenski, the son of Feige, was a merchant born in Zhetl in 1900.[1] His wife Sara, a nurse, is listed as having been born the same year[2] in Slonim.[3]

As it is the Jewish custom to name children after the dead, we assume that Elya's mother Feige died before the Holocaust, since Elya and Sara's daughter, born in 1940, was given the name Feige.[4] We have no information regarding Elya's father, but we do know that Elya's brother Yehoshua (Ovsey) was a textile merchant and single at the time of his murder in Zhetl's second slaughter on August 6, 1942.[5]

In the listing of Novolenski family members who were murdered, *Pinkas Zhetl* cites that there were two children who perished.[6] On a Russian-commissioned list of murdered individuals from Zhetl 1941–1944, Elya and Sara's names are followed by their baby daughter Feige and a boy named Monik, born in 1937.[7] As Elya and Sara are the only married adults with the surname Novolenski from Zhetl who appear both in the memorial book[8] and in Yad Vashem's Central Database of Shoah Victims' Names, it is clear that Monik was their son. Further, fellow Zhetl resident Pesia Mayevski (#160) testifies that Sara and her two children, aged seven and four, were killed in Zhetl's second massacre.[9]

Although Eliyahu Novolenski was probably the last member of his family to survive the Nazi massacres in Zhetl, he was not destined to remain alive for long. Eliyahu's death in September 1943 as he participated in the Novogrudok forced labor camp tunnel escape is documented in a Page of Testimony submitted by the escapee Pesia Mayevski Nadel.[10]

Fanya Dunetz (#142)

This report is composed primarily from anecdotes and reminiscences related by Fanya and her brother Mordechai (Motl) to the author, Fanya's daughter, throughout their lives. Originally, the text was written in tribute to Motl, who died during the early writing of this chapter on July 21, 2019. Now, however, it is a tribute to Motl and Fanya, whose lives were not only intertwined, but whose deaths occurred two years apart on the fast day of the Seventeenth of Tammuz. Fittingly, the date signifies the beginning of a three-week period of mourning in which monumental calamities befell the Jewish people throughout history. Most of Motl and Fanya's family members were killed within this period.

Fanya Dunetz's life exemplified the fierce loyalty, courage, and willingness to risk their lives for one another that characterized her family. Born in the town of Zhetl in 1920 to Yoel David and Esther Basia née Belski, Fanya was the second of four children. Her sister Shifra was born in 1915, brother Motl in 1922, and youngest brother Antzel (Alik) in 1932.

In addition to Fanya's parents and siblings, the family home on Slonim Street was shared with her paternal grandparents, Shlomo Zalman Dunetz and Sarah Rochel née Levitt. Shlomo Zalman, who was born in Bialystok, was the grandson of Yehuda Dunetz, the *av beit din* (presiding judge) of the Rabbinical Court of Slonim. In recognition of this honor, the family became known as "Dunetz," an acronym of the Hebrew words *dayan tzedek* (righteous judge). One of the first members of the Chovevei Tzion organization, a pioneering proponent of Jewish settlement in Palestine in the early 1880s, Shlomo Zalman is said to have rarely been at home as he traveled from city to city collecting for Zionist causes, including the Jerusalem-based Etz Chaim Yeshiva.

After an earlier temporary stay in Palestine, on the second day of Chanukah 1929, Shlomo Zalman left once again for the Holy Land, this time to die. Living in poverty in the Machaneh Yehuda neighborhood near the Etz Chaim Yeshiva he had faithfully supported, Shlomo Zalman fulfilled his wish to depart this world in Jerusalem on December 13, 1932. His good deeds and idealism were lauded in an obituary published by the religious Zionist newspaper *Netiva*.[1] Shlomo Zalman remained an important figure in the life of Fanya, who mentioned him often until the end of her life.

Sarah Rochel Dunetz, on the other hand, had been as disinterested in her husband's Zionist activities as he was in the grocery store she ran on the left side of the house, three steps down. There, for over fifty years, she sold herring, flour, salt, sugar, cigarettes, and more. On market day, usually Tuesdays, peasants would come to shop, parking their horses and wagons in the backyard of the family home. Sarah Rochel is said to have been very energetic, stubborn and resolutely determined to have her own way. She died on September 18, 1939, the day the Russians occupied Zhetl. Local townspeople are reported to have said that she was so smart that "she knew when to die."

Yoel David and Golda Basia's general store, chock-full of dry goods, shoes, and textiles, stood to the right of his mother's grocery. The entire extended family lived in the back of the house, whose living room was perched between the two stores. Yoel David, referred to as David, was born in Zhetl in 1892. Serving in the Russian Army from at least 1907 (as attested by a photo he sent home that year), he was captured during World War I and deported to Germany. As a prisoner of war there from 1914 to 1918, he performed farm work, painted barns, and served as an interpreter.

Golda Basia, known as Basha, was born in 1890 in the nearby town of Meytchet (Molchad). Fanya recalls having spent every summer in Meytchet with her maternal grandparents.

Fanya's eldest sister Shifra was remembered as a child who played the mandolin and enjoyed handicrafts as a student in Zhetl's Yiddish-speaking Sholom Aleichem School. Around the age of eighteen, Shifra left for Vilna to study nursing in the TOZ Jewish Nursing School.

When Jewish Polish citizens from Germany were evicted across the border to Poland in 1938, Shifra volunteered to work in a refugee camp. She was soon chosen to escort a Kindertransport group of unaccompanied children, from the refugee camp to the relative safety of Britain. Despite the danger, Shifra insisted on first returning home to Zhetl to part from her family before ushering the children to British shores. There she became trapped by the incursion of the Russians and took a job as a nurse in the local hospital.

According to family lore, on July 23, 1941, Shifra learned that all men between sixteen and sixty had been ordered to report to the marketplace. Running to the scene, she found 120 of the town's most prominent men had been selected by the Germans for "work" in Novogrudok and ordered to enter the waiting trucks. Knowing well that these men were doomed to death, Shifra dared to beg the German officer in charge to release her father, whose name had been called. At this point, a Polish woman intervened to accuse Shifra of being a Communist and urge that she be "sent away" instead of her father. The officer heeded this advice and ordered Shifra onto the truck. In contrast, Chaya Magid, widow of escapee Avraham Magid, recalls that she and Shifra were working together as nurses when Shifra was accused by a Polish colleague of having Communist leanings, arrested, and forced to the marketplace.

What is indisputable is that two days later, on the first day of the intense nine-day period of mourning during the Jewish month of Av, Shifra Dunetz, along with 119 men, was massacred in the nearby hamlet of Skrydlevo. As witnessed decades later by the author, this mass grave is shockingly just yards away from prewar houses that continue to stand along the path to the killing field.

Yoel David was ultimately murdered in Zhetl's second mass slaughter on August 6, 1942, together with Esther Basia and son Antzel (Alik), only ten years old at his death. Fanya and Motl were left orphaned and alone.

By the time her family members were murdered, Fanya had graduated from the prestigious Adam Mickiewiez High School in Novogrudok and completed her first year of studies in Bialystok's teachers' seminary. Among her classmates was Dr. Boris Ragula, who was to become an interpreter to the German regiment commissar Traub, don a German uniform, and organize a Belarusian army to fight the partisans.[2] Fanya suspected that it was Ragula who later arranged for two of their common classmates to "visit" her at the entrance to the forced labor camp, bringing her a bit of food.

Fanya had also chalked up two years of experience from 1939 to 1941 as a Russian-language teacher in her former Polish elementary school, a job she had been assigned to during the Russian occupation, despite her lack of fluency in Russian. She attributed her surprising success in this job to her father's nightly Russian-language tutoring.

In essence, her knack for languages became Fanya's key to survival. Fluent in German from her high school studies, at some point after the Nazi invasion, she was made secretary to the Judenrat (Jewish council) of Zhetl, renowned for organizing resistance activities. In the mass murder that took the lives of her parents and brother, Fanya was spared death and assigned as a secretary to the Novogrudok forced labor camp by virtue of her knowledge of German. Here she sat in a booth outside the camp, primarily responsible for recording supplies that came through the gate.

Alone with the powerful camp commander Wilhelm Reuter on several occasions, Fanya once dared to ask him why he engaged in murder. His response: "An order is an order." At another point in time, Fanya was absent while coupons for double rations were distributed. Knowing that her non-receipt of tickets for extra rations spelled certain death in an approaching slaughter, she fearlessly approached Reuter to ask that he provide them. This was a commander questioned by no man, whose ferocious cruelty included hurling infants from the roof of the camp. Yet he gave Fanya the lifesaving tickets she requested.

Fanya's brother Motl's survival was due, at least in part, to his mother Basia's clear thinking, even in her last moments of life as she lay face down in Zhetl's New Cemetery before being executed. In the chaotic shouting that prevailed, Motl recalled that German soldiers were heard to call for electricians, shoemakers, and other professionals needed for the Nazi war machine. Basia immediately advised Motl in a whisper to present himself as a carpenter, a profession for which he actually had a certificate. Thus, Fanya's only surviving sibling was assigned along with her to the Novogrudok forced labor camp.

Here Fanya employed her trademark daring to obtain extra food for herself and Motl. She developed a scheme by which Motl, now working in the labor camp section that manufactured wooden shoes for the Germans, supplied her with scraps of wood from the workshop. She then secretly transferred these scraps to fellow inmate Sara Lidski (#152), a seamstress and childhood friend from Zhetl. Sara would use these purloined pieces of wood as handles for pocketbooks that she sewed from scraps of material in the dressmaking workshop. When Fanya would boldly "sell" these creations to a German officer as gifts for his relatives in Germany, she would be given a piece of bread. Half of the bread went to Sara, while the other half Fanya shared with Motl.

The strong bond between Fanya and Motl would last a lifetime. Motl would always recall how his escape from the forced labor camp was the result of Fanya's bravery, resilience, and willingness to give up her life for his. In May 1943, Fanya was approached by Josif Wargan, a local camp guard who had known of her family in Zhetl before the war.[3] He offered her the priceless opportunity to escape with one other person of her choice. Fearing that neither she nor Motl could successfully navigate the way to the Bielski partisan detachment in the forest, she requested that they be joined by a Novogrudok native who was familiar with the terrain. When the guard refused, Fanya made the supreme sacrifice of choosing an inmate who was born and raised in Novogrudok, brother of tunnel escapee Matus Kabak (#72a), to take her place and lead Motl to safety. Willing to pay with her life to save her younger brother, Fanya was keenly aware of the punishment she could expect should Motl's absence be discovered. With family members held collectively responsible for one who escaped, Fanya recalled how a mother and father were shot at roll call when their son failed to appear after fleeing the camp.

According to Fanya, on the dark, stormy night of September 26, 1943, 240 inmates took part in the breakout from the tunnel, which she estimated to have been 275 yards long and only 24 inches high.[4] Following her own successful escape, Fanya's journey toward the distant Bielski partisan detachment was guided by the loving hand extended to her in the darkness by Henia Yarmovski (#195), a Novogrudok native and the mother of Fanya's friend and classmate Sonia. The two, together with an elderly man who also escaped from the tunnel, took refuge in the home of Baptist farmers who had been prewar customers of the Yarmovski mill. The tale of the farmers' kindness, the chicken they cooked, and the pillow they gave her for the hayloft accommodations is one of the few wartime accounts Fanya would relate to her children. Thanks to the careful directions provided by their hosts' son, the three escapees safely traversed deep into the Naliboki Forest to reach the Bielski detachment.

Yet here, Fanya discovered that Motl had left the *otriad* to join the Zhetl partisans in the Lipiczanska Forest. She then became a *malbush*, a term used to describe those without arms and without prestige. As an unmarried woman, bereft of a man to protect her and bring back provisions from hunting expeditions, she had an especially difficult life in the forest. Even so, Fanya prides herself on her refusal to attach herself to a man for the sake of survival, as did many of the other single women.

Fanya recalled sharing her *zemlyanka* dugout with, among others, Batia Rabinowitz (#27), Hirsh Patzovski (#159), Pesia Mayevski (#160), and Lyuba Epshtein of Zhetl; Chaim (#32) and Perla (#33) Ostashinski, Lionke (#19) and Sima (#20) Portnoj, sixteen-year-old Eshka Levine and her father of Novogrudok; Frieda Slutsky Sklar and her husband Yitzchak of Lida; as well as a couple from Naliboki and their grown son who eventually succumbed to tuberculosis in the detachment.[5]

Assigned the role of a nurse, who treated patients without any supplies or medicine, Fanya eventually contracted typhus. She remained alone and comatose for six weeks in the *zemlyanka* that served as the "hospital" in which she worked. A photo taken soon after liberation bears witness to her kerchiefed head, as she had lost all her hair during the illness.

After liberation, Fanya returned to Zhetl. In an undoubtedly emotional meeting, she was reunited with Motl in the market square. Two years had passed since they'd last stood there with their parents and little Antzel for the August 6 selection that separated them forever. Returning to their former home, Fanya and Motl found it occupied by Poles who were "kind enough" to allow them to live in one of the rooms. After selling the home for a winter coat, Fanya left for Baranovich, determined to complete her studies to qualify as a teacher despite the fact that she was the only Jew in the school.

With Fanya and Motl both repatriated to Poland, they registered in Lodz with the Jewish Central Committee, listing their address as

88 Piotrkowska Street.[6] After a short period in Berlin's Schlachtensee Displaced Persons Camp, in April 1946,[7] Motl and Fanya were transferred to the newly created Eschwege Displaced Persons Camp in a former German Air Force base in the Frankfurt District of the American zone. This camp was characterized by the revitalization of Jewish life among its residents. By April 1947, it contained a kindergarten and elementary schools (where Fanya taught Hebrew) as well as high schools.[8] *Undzer Hofenung* (Our Hope), the first Yiddish newspaper to be published in Germany after the war, was founded in the camp by Motl. This Zionist paper was printed by Germans in transliterated Yiddish with Latin letters, as Yiddish or Hebrew linotype was no longer available.[9]

In 1947, Fanya married Tzunia (Getzel) Brodsky of Kremenets, a survivor who had lost his entire family. She then joined him in the Windsheim Displaced Persons Camp in Bavaria, where Tzunia was a Jewish camp administrator, and Fanya began working as a kindergarten teacher. Tired of war, Fanya overruled Tzunia's strong desire to immigrate to Israel and insisted on their applying for immigration to the United States. On October 2, 1949,[10] Fanya, Tzunia, and Motl sailed to New York aboard the USS *General M.B. Stewart*, at the time an army transport ship.[11] Having looked forward to being reunited with family in the New York area, Fanya would recall her humiliation at the fact that a relative, fearful of contracting lice, forced her to shower at a neighbor's house before allowing her into her own home.

The couple initially settled in the Brownsville neighborhood of Brooklyn, where Fanya first worked in a factory and Tzunia as a textile cutter. Moving to the then upscale neighborhood of Flatbush in the early 1950s, both became naturalized American citizens on March 29, 1955, at which time Fanya officially became Fanny, and Tzunia (Getzel) became George.[12] During the early years, Fanya was primarily a housewife raising her two children: the author (namesake of Fanya's mother Esther Basia), born in 1952, and Steven, born in 1957.

In 1964, Fanya, Tzunia, and their children moved to the Brighton Beach area. Although Fanya had obtained her teaching certificate in Europe, her responsibilities at work and home left no time for her to complete the requirements for an American teaching license. After Tzunia suffered a heart attack in 1971, he was unable to continue his heavy physical work in textiles. Ever resilient, Fanya enlisted Tzunia's help in turning her small home business of selling women's dresses into the mainstay of the family's livelihood.

Fanya always stressed the importance of education. Steven holds a degree in psychology. The author, born in 1952, holds a doctorate in social work with specializations in immigration and resettlement, as well as with families of children with special needs. She is also a certified grief counselor as well as a clinical diplomate of logotherapy. Living in Israel since 1986, she resides in Jerusalem with her husband Meir, a geographical historian, and her daughter Shiran, a clinical pharmacist. Her married son Yanai, a former commander in the Israel Defense Forces, is the father of Fanya's two great-granddaughters.

In 2008, after being widowed for twelve years, eighty-eight-year-old Fanya joined her daughter and grandchildren in Israel. Here she was reunited with Motl, who had moved with his family from New York to Israel in 1978. Extremely proud of the little brother she saved during the war, Fanya reveled in his achievements as an educator and Yiddish journalist. After working in Jewish education in the US, Motl's far-reaching activities in Israel included serving as director of two departments of the Ministry of Education while continuing to write for the Yiddish-language newspaper *The Forward*.

Fania Dunetz, Germany, circa 1946 (courtesy of Betty Brodsky Cohen)

In Israel, Fanya lived in a senior residence in Jerusalem. She continued to take Hebrew lessons and was much loved by the residents. Fanya was frequently visited by second- and third-generation descendants from Zhetl, the forced labor camp, and the forest, who came to hear her story as well as stories of their parents and grandparents. Until the end of her life on June 27, 2021, Fanya continued to proudly refer to herself as a partisan. How fitting that she is buried only yards away from the grave of her beloved commander, Tuvia Bielski.

Naum (Zeidel) Kushner (#143)

Born in Novogrudok in 1898 to Chanan, Zeidel reports in his Yad Vashem testimony that he was known in his hometown as "Zeidel Kushner the hatter." Married to Hinda Bloch in 1919, he and his wife had four children, three of whom participated in the tunnel escape: Raya (#144), Leah (#145), and Chanan (#76), named for his paternal grandfather. The oldest daughter, Esther, met her death in 1941 in Novogrudok's first massacre.[1]

Zeidel notes that before the war, he owned two shops in which workers made such fur clothing items as women's coats. Hinda and an employee worked in one of the shops, while Zeidel and several workers tended the second.[2] Hinda is credited with having been the spouse who possessed the business acumen. She even brought the first mannequins to Novogrudok to display the shops' fur clothing, much to the amazement of the townspeople, who had never seen such a sight.[3]

Quite successful in his business prior to the 1939 Soviet occupation of Novogrudok, Zeidel describes the imposition of heavy taxes upon independent shopkeepers during this period. After joining forces with three other colleagues to create a cooperative association of workers as "requested" by the Soviets,[4] life became even harder with the invasion of the Germans on July 4, 1941. Recalling that the Germans treated the Jews well in World War I, Zeidel appears to have been unprepared for the horrors to come. A witness to the marketplace massacre of July 26, 1941, together with his daughter Leah, Zeidel describes how fifty Jews were murdered while fifty local Jewish women were forced to wash the blood of their husbands and brothers from the cobblestones.[5] One of the women designated for this horrendous task was his own daughter Raya.[6]

Zeidel Kushner was spared death in the Novogrudok forced labor camp by virtue of the German Army's need for fur coats for soldiers on the front lines. Former inmate Yehoshua Yaffe writes how furriers dreamed that their much-needed skill would save their lives. He describes the scene of several dozen Jews in the courthouse workshops of what was to become the Novogrudok forced labor camp pulling thick threads through the eyes of large needles to connect pieces of fur to form coat pockets, collars, and sleeves later dispersed by German trucks to blizzard-prone areas of occupation. While other skilled tradesmen included shoemakers, carpenters, corsetieres, tailors, and knitters, the furriers – like Zeidel – were considered to have been "on top of the heap."[7] Zeidel's skills enabled him to survive all of Novogrudok's mass selections, including the fourth, which claimed the life of his wife Hinda, as well as those of the wife and son of his brother Chaim Leibowitz (#91), who were reportedly murdered hand in hand. Zeidel himself witnessed these executions, noting that the horrific killings took place in such close proximity to the courthouse that they could be seen by those in the forced labor camp.[8]

Prior to the breakout from the camp in September 1943, each inmate of the camp had been given his or her assigned place among the nearly 240 lining up to escape the tunnel. Leah and Raya Kushner were designated to be far ahead of their father. Zeidel's grandson Murray Kushner relates that instead, the sisters exchanged their places to stay back in order to be alongside their father and protect him.[9]

In his account of the escape through the tunnel, Zeidel tells how he, Raya, and Leah all held each other's hands. After they miraculously emerged alive, Zeidel felt faint and urged his daughters to go on ahead while he rested. Rejecting their father's offer to virtually abandon him, Raya and Leah lifted Zeidel by his arms and continued to flee. One of the girls helped him come to by smearing onion on his lips.[10]

While viewing the video testimony of escapee Shlomo Golanski (#75), the author learned how Zeidel, in his weakened state, was likely saved by Golanski himself. In his testimony, Shlomo Golanski, a carpenter, describes meeting a father and two daughters as they exited the tunnel who, like him, did not know how to navigate through the forest to reach the Bielskis. (Zeidel, Raya, and Leah were the sole father and two daughters known to have escaped the tunnel.) Shlomo had the presence of mind to take Zeidel and his daughters along with him to seek shelter at the nearby home of a farmer who in prewar days had come to grind his grain each spring at the Golanski family mill. The three Kushners remained hidden in the farmer's barn for an entire week.[11] Thirty-four years after the escape, Zeidel described a slightly different version of events as he recalled being aided by a carpenter named Shalom, whose father was the owner of a mill.

Zeidel recounts yet another lucky encounter along their trek to the Bielski detachment, this time with none other than Vasily, the commander of the Kirov Brigade of partisans. As Vasily had been employed by Zeidel's brother-in-law in prewar days, the two were acquainted. Zeidel, Raya, and Leah were then able to remain with these Russian partisans for around two weeks until the fighters departed from the area on the festival of Simchat Torah.

Although invited to join the small Russian Jewish partisan unit of Zorin, the Kushners had already decided to cast their lot with the Bielski detachment. Shortly after their arrival at the *otriad*, it was with tears and emotion that Zeidel caught sight of Tuvia Bielski and his chief of staff Lazar Malbin mounted on their horses. That one moment brought home the realization that there, even in the harsh conditions of the forest, they were relatively free from German clutches.[12] Zeidel's skills as a hatter came to the fore in the forest, where – assisted by his daughters – he made hats for the partisans in the detachment's make-shift hat factory.

After being liberated from the forest in July 1944, Zeidel, his daughters, and his one surviving brother Chaim remained in Novogrudok for about a year before traveling to Czechoslovakia, Austria, and Hungary (where Raya married) before reaching Italy. There, the extended family – later including Raya's first child – all lived in one room in the northern Italy Cremona Displaced Persons Camp for three and a half years while awaiting a visa to any country that would provide refuge. Eventually sponsored by relatives in the United States, the family arrived in 1949 in New York City, where for five years they lived in a one-bedroom four-story walkup in the Bushwick section of Brooklyn, even after Raya's family had grown to include four children.[13]

Zeidel is described as having been a kind, mild-mannered individual who was always impeccably dressed.[14] He had incurred a broken wrist in the past, probably in the 1904 Russo-Japanese War, and his protruding bone was always neatly covered by a handkerchief.[15] While Zeidel's niece Esther never recalls Zeidel speaking of his murdered wife and children,[16] his grandson Murray notes that Zeidel would respond to specific questions about his prewar life.[17] Always a furrier at heart, Zeidel is fondly remembered for having carefully checked his grandchildren's coats to make sure they fit properly.[18] When the family moved to Elizabeth, New Jersey, in 1954,

Naum (Zeidel) Kushner, Novogrudok, early 1930s (courtesy of Charles and Seryl Kushner)

Zeidel first lived with his children and worked in a factory before eventually renting his own apartment and working in the family real estate business.[19]

Zeidel, who never remarried, passed away in April 1982. An integral member of his daughters' celebrations and family events, he lived to see the birth of six grandchildren. If he were alive today, as of September 2023, this hatter from Novogrudok would have been the great-grandfather of twenty-one, the great-great-grandfather of sixty-eight, and the great-great-great grandfather of twenty. How very proud he would have been!

Raya Kushner (#144)

The daughter of hatter Naum (Zeidel) Kushner (#143) and his wife Hinda née Bloch, Raya was born in Novogrudok in 1923. Her siblings were Esther, Chanan (#76), and Leah (#145). Ultimately, Raya, Leah, and Zeidel were the sole members of the immediate family to survive the war.

As the proprietors of two fur stores, Zeidel and Hinda were able to support their family comfortably. Before the war, Raya attended a private school, the Bais Yaakov Seminary in Krakow.[1]

From the moment that the Nazis occupied Poland, Raya became an early witness to the worst of humanity. Even before the first mass slaughter in Novogrudok, she endured a horrific trauma: on July 26, 1941, eighteen-year-old Raya was among the fifty girls forced by the Germans to the town square, where from 50 to 150[2] Jewish doctors, lawyers, professors, and teachers were brutally murdered. During this attempt to thwart a purported rebellion against the Nazis by the town's educated intellectuals, the girls were compelled to wash the blood from the cobblestones as well as to load the corpses onto a wagon. All the while, an orchestra performed music for the Germans, who danced and celebrated their "success."[3]

The marketplace massacre was only a prelude to further horrors awaiting Raya and the Kushner family. The eldest sibling, Esther, a recent college graduate, was killed in Novogrudok's first massacre of December 8, 1941, dragged to her death in full view of her parents and siblings.[4] She was said to have been wearing a good fur coat and possessing some gold at the time;[5] we can only imagine how these were wrenched from her before her murder in the nearby village of Skirdlevo.

Confined to the Pereseka ghetto, which was created in Novogrudok after the first massacre, Raya and the remainder of the family miraculously survived the city's second and third slaughters. At some point, the family determined that the nearby court building workshops might offer them a greater measure of safety. Raya, Leah, and Zeidel surreptitiously left the ghetto to crawl under the wires surrounding the courthouse building and join Chanan, who had preceded them there. On May 7, 1943, Novogrudok's fourth slaughter, Raya, her father, and siblings watched in horror as her mother Hinda was led away to her murder. Besides viewing the actual slaughter of 250 ghetto inmates, Raya also reports seeing the massacred bodies being hurled into a mass grave nearly half a mile from the ghetto.[6]

With no time to recuperate from the trauma of witnessing their mother's murder, Raya and Leah continued their work washing and cleaning the courthouse offices, as well as handling private orders from local townspeople for goods produced in the workshops by inmates of the Novogrudok forced labor camp. Soon after the May 7 massacre, the girls threw themselves into the feverish efforts to construct the escape tunnel, beginning by smuggling out small bags of collected soil hidden inside their coats, then spilling the contents into attics and empty rooms.[7]

When the escape began, in an extraordinary show of devotion to their fifty-three-year-old father – who, as one of the "elderly" inmates, was assigned a spot further back in line – Raya and Leah gave up their better placements to stay with their father and protect him. Raya asserts that she and her sister were both prepared to die together with Zeidel.[8] The possibility of death was quite real, as the Germans would have killed all those inmates still crawling out to freedom had the first ones to escape been discovered beforehand.

Their mother Hinda's last words to her children had reverberated in Raya's mind: "Children, hold on. Maybe one of you will remain alive. Maybe one of you will be left. Hold on together!" And hold on they did, as Raya, Leah, and Zeidel escaped the tunnel. Describing the tunnel exit, Raya writes:

> It was pouring and thundering. Everyone got out of the tun-nel. They became confused and started to run in different directions. Maybe it was the excitement of freedom or the instinct of survival that made them run off instead of staying together. They lost one another.[9]

Perhaps remembering Hinda's last words, Zeidel and his two daughters never lost one another. Only Chanan, who had escaped the tunnel alone much earlier, did not survive the breakout. Miraculously, Raya, Leah, and Zeidel emerged alive from the tunnel. Yet Zeidel soon began to feel faint and urged his daughters to proceed without him while he stayed back to rest. Raya and Laya steadfastly refused to abandon him, lifting their father by the arms and smearing his lips with an onion to arouse his consciousness until he felt well enough to continue.[10]

Raya reports having been aided in the trek to the Bielski partisans by an "angel," an escapee who had been a farmer and knew the way to farms in the area and many of the non-Jewish farmers.[11] Zeidel also refers to being aided by a carpenter named Sholom who knew many of the Gentiles in the area who had once come to his family's mill in a small village near Novogrudok.[12] In all probability, both Raya and Zeidel are referring to the escapee Shlomo Golanski (#75). A carpenter in the forced labor camp, Golanski refers in his own testimony to a father and two daughters whom he brought with him to seek shelter with a farmer who had brought his grain to the Golanski mill each spring.[13]

After taking refuge for two weeks with the Russian Kirov Brigade of partisans headed by the commander Vasil, an acquaintance of Zeidel from prewar days in Novogrudok, Raya, Leah, and Zeidel reached the Bielski detachment several days after the Jewish holiday of Simchat Torah.[14]

Following their liberation from the forest in July 1944, Raya remained in Novogrudok for about one year together with Leah, her father, and Zeidel's brother Chaim Leibowitz (#91), who had also survived the tunnel escape. After traveling through Czechoslovakia and Austria, they reached Hungary, where Raya was wed (in a ceremony for twenty couples) in Budapest to Joseph Berkowitz of Korelich, whom she had known before the war. Joseph had survived the Holocaust by fleeing the Korelich ghetto in 1942 and digging a pit in the woods for himself, his sisters, and his brother. They lived in this pit for nearly three years, surviving on food Joseph would procure from the Poles at gunpoint on his nightly scavenges.[15]

With Joseph reportedly adopting the Kushner surname to facilitate receiving an immigration visa,[16] the entire family reached Italy, where they lived for three and a half years in one room in the Cremona Displaced Persons Camp in the north.[17] Waiting for a visa to any country that would accept them, Raya and her family – including her first child – were eventually sponsored by relatives in the United States. For five years, the entire clan all lived in a one-bedroom four-story walk-up in the Bushwick section of Brooklyn, even after the birth of Raya's children Linda, Murray, and Charles. While pregnant with Murray in 1951, Raya attended night school to learn English.[18] At some point, she Americanized her name to Rae.

Daughter Esther was born shortly after the family finally moved to a rented house in Elizabeth, New Jersey, in 1954. Joseph, who had previously worked as a carpenter, was now a builder and constructed the first home for his family four years later.[19]

With Joseph rapidly expanding his real estate business, Raya became an integral part of the company, managing the finances and advising on all aspects of management. Considered to be more optimistic and more of a risk-taker than her husband,[20] Raya is described by son Murray as having been "one of the guys" when it came to running the business. Active in many Jewish organizations, including the Hadassah Women's Organization, Raya was renowned for her dynamic personality.[21]

Her children declare that Raya's kindness was her hallmark. Eldest child Linda Laulicht recalls that her mother's kindness extended to all, "whether to a president or a janitor." Linda describes Raya as having been a wonderful *mensch* (Yiddish for a person of integrity) blessed with the ability to make certain that no one in need left their home empty-handed. She, too, cites her mother's sharp business acumen and the fact that Raya was a true helpmate to her husband in his business. [22]

Raya's youngest child Esther (the namesake of Raya's sister Esther, who was killed in Novogrudok's first slaughter) describes her mother as having been a "kind, decent human being with an amazing heart for everybody." Esther, who has known of the tunnel escape ever since she can remember, shares that unlike many survivors, her mother felt strongly that the Holocaust must be discussed. Acting on this conviction, Raya spoke passionately about her experiences both at home and in schools.[23]

Raya's natural optimism sustained her through the pain of being widowed at the age of sixty-two in 1985. Her grandchildren loved spending time with their "Bubbie" who would greet them "as if the crown jewels had just entered."[24] Letters and tributes her grandchildren wrote in honor of her seventy-fifth birthday attest to their intense admiration for Raya, especially for her ability to rebuild her life after the Holocaust. Here are some excerpts:

My awe for you grows as I think of your life during the Holocaust. How you survived the atrocities and then came back to build a family amazes me. I just can't imagine losing so many loved ones at one time and then going on.

— granddaughter Pamela Hirt

You have many unique, admirable qualities. But the ones that I admire most are your inner strength and your courage, which is immeasurable. Your courage is reflected in the fact that you were able to survive all the horrors of the Holocaust and come to a different country and make a new, wonderful life.

— granddaughter Abigail Herschmann

I...always seek [Bubbie's] inspiration when I need a frame of reference to apply to any situation in my life. Her lessons of confidence help me keep the courage of my convictions when faced with a challenge, and her eternal hope and appetite for making the most of life help me keep a sense of sanity and perspective when faced with adversity. For all that she is, I am deeply grateful.

— grandson Aryeh Kushner

In being a Holocaust survivor, you have been through the worst of times, and yet, you are always compassionate to those who suffer misfortunes.

— grandson Jared Kushner

It is your and Zeydeh's shining and inspirational examples that we will always aspire to live up to. I only hope that I am lucky enough to be able to build a family as beautiful as the one you created. Bubbie, you are the reason G-d created love.

You are the reason G-d created angels. And you are the reason G-d created family.

– granddaughter Jessica Schulder

The greatest part of Bubbie's personality is her love and warmth towards everyone. She has touched so many people, whether they are family, friends or simply acquaintances. She always finds a way to make the people around her feel good.

– grandson Jonathan Kushner[25]

Few survivors of the Holocaust have had the strength to confront their traumas at the very site where they took place. Raya's boundless courage drove her to overcome her aversion to return to the scenes of her childhood and wartime experiences. In 1989, five years before her death in March 2004, she returned to Novogrudok together with her son Charles, his wife, and their four children.[26]

Summing up her life, Raya states in her testimony: "Our life is a miracle. We survived the camps, the ghettos, the woods. It is a miracle that we lived to become normal people. Our lives are miracles, our children and grandchildren are miracles. We never dreamed that out of the ashes and rubble, we would survive to lead normal lives and see and build the next generation."[27]

If Raya were alive at the time of this writing in August 2023, in addition to her four children, she would have fifteen grandchildren, fiftythree great-grandchildren, and twenty great-great-grandchildren. One grandchild, Jared Kushner, served as a senior advisor to US president Donald Trump. She would have been proud of them all.

Raya Kushner, Budapest, 1947 (courtesy of Charles and Seryl Kushner)

Leah Kushner (#145)

Born in Novogrudok in 1926,[1] Leah was the youngest child of hatter Naum (Zeidel) Kushner and his wife Hinda née Bloch and sister to Esther, Raya (#144), and Chanan (#76). The two successful fur shops owned and operated by Naum and Hinda provided a comfortable living for the family.[2] Ultimately, Leah, her sister Raya, and their father Zeidel were the only members of their immediate family to survive the war.[3]

A pupil at the time of the outbreak of war, Leah's life began to change with the invasion of the Soviets in 1939. Under the Communist doctrine, her father was considered a capitalist as well as an exploiter of workers. In Zeidel's Holocaust testimony, he recalls Leah complaining to him: "Why is Mendel the shoemaker treated so well? Why was his daughter Malka accepted into the Komsomol [Communist Youth Organization] and I was not accepted? Why did you need to have the shops?"[4]

After the Nazi invasion, how Leah must have longed for the days under the Soviets! Zeidel's testimony relates the horrifying events of July 26, 1941, when he and Leah witnessed the Nazi roundup of seventy Jews in the Novogrudok marketplace, of whom fifty were brutally murdered before their eyes. Following the assassinations, young Jewish girls – including her sister Raya – were forced to wash the blood from the cobblestones.[5]

Leah's devotion to her family was absolute. After her eldest sister Esther was murdered in the first Novogrudok massacre, young, blond-haired Leah refused to save herself when warned by Poles of the upcoming second massacre. At that time, the Kushner family was confined to living in the Pereseka (Novogrudok) ghetto. As the mass shootings broke out, Leah was working with her mother and Raya on

Narodne Street in the vicinity of the marketplace. Against the advice of her non-Jewish coworkers to hide alone, Leah chose to remain with her parents and Raya. Together they risked their lives to steal into the courthouse, where her brother Chanan had taken cover.[6]

Another example of Leah's devotion to her family occurred on February 4, 1943, the day of the third massacre. At this time, workers considered most useful to the Nazis were given double bread rations and permitted to be taken to the courthouse workshops. When only Leah and Zeidel were given double rations, Leah risked her life to transfer her double ration to her older sister Raya. Then, finding herself surrounded by police and German soldiers outside the courthouse as she stood among those assigned single rations, Leah barely escaped with her life.[7]

Miraculously surviving the third as well as the fourth massacre – which claimed the life of her mother Hinda – Leah was interned in the forced labor camp together with her father, sister, brother, and uncle (Chaim Leibowitz, #91). Leah and Raya worked side by side cleaning the workshops and handling orders from local peasants for products made in the workshops. Both sisters took part in building the escape tunnel by surreptitiously digging soil and ferrying it out in small bags hidden inside their coats. Above ground, the soil was spilled into attics and empty rooms.[8]

Before the escape could be executed on the night of September 26, 1943, it was crucial to ascertain whether the alleged German spy and Viennese Jew known as Mendelson had a hunch that a breakout was in the making. Zeidel Kushner relates that Daniel Ostashinski, the former Judenrat head, chose Leah and Raya for the critical assignment to help determine if Mendelson's suspicions had been aroused.[9]

Both Leah and Raya are reported by their father Zeidel to have cleaned and washed in the "office," where Mendelson is reported to have lived in a separate room[10] attached to the side of the courthouse. There he is reported to have received extra privileges. According to Leah's daughter Helen, her mother also cooked for Mendelson, who is reported to have been quite satisfied with her culinary skills.[11] The day of the escape, following their work with Mendelson, the sisters were able to report the important fact that he had indeed questioned them as to whether anything unusual was happening that day. They reportedly replied that it was Sunday.[12]

Perhaps Leah's greatest act of selflessness occurred when she, together with Raya, willingly gave up their better places in the lineup for crawling through the tunnel in order to stay with Zeidel, who as a "senior" escapee at the age of fifty-three was assigned a place further back.[13] Leah and Raya also refused to abandon their father after exiting the tunnel when he became faint and urged them to proceed without him.[14]

Leah, Raya, and Zeidel were probably aided on their complex five-day trek to the Bielski partisan detachment by escapee Shlomo Golanski (#75). In his own testimony, Shlomo refers to a father and two daughters whom he brought with him to seek shelter with a farmer who had brought his grain to the Golanski family mill each spring.[15] As Zeidel and his daughters were the only such constellation taking part in the escape, we may assume that Golanski was referring to Leah and her father and sister.

Throughout the time they served as partisans, Leah and Raya continued to assist their father in the detachment's hat-making workshop.[16]

Following liberation, Leah and her family remained in Novogrudok for one year. By 1946, Leah, Raya, Zeidel, and Zeidel's only surviving brother Chaim Leibowitz began a grueling journey through Czechoslovakia, Austria, and Hungary until they reached Italy. There they all lived for three and a half years in one room in the Cremona Displaced Persons Camp awaiting permission to settle in any country that would have them.[17]

Eventually sponsored by relatives in the United States in 1949, the entire clan, now consisting of Raya's husband Joseph Kushner and their one-year-old daughter Linda in addition to Raya, Leah, Zeidel, and

Chaim, sailed to New York. Here their living quarters expanded to a one-bedroom four-story walkup in the Bushwick section of Brooklyn.[18]

On March 13, 1954, Leah married Joseph Reibel, a Holocaust survivor fourteen years older than herself. After her marriage, Leah lived near Raya and her family,[19] who had moved to Elizabeth, New Jersey, that same year.[20] With their children growing up together, the deep bond between Leah, known in the United States as Lisa, and Raya, who became known as Rae, was to last until Raya's death in 2004.[21]

Leah and her husband were ideal role models to their children in the virtue of acknowledging kindness. Joseph knew that he owed his life to a brave Christian Polish woman named Yanka Rybak, who during the Holocaust had hidden Joseph, his two sisters, and his brother in their town near Lvov, Ukraine. In 1965, after Joseph had established himself as a builder, he and Leah brought Yanka to America to live with them and their two daughters, Helen, born in 1955 and Cheryl, born in 1957. Yanka returned to the Ukraine one year later, but Leah and Joseph made certain to publicly acknowledge her bravery by having Yad Vashem recognize her as Righteous among the Nations, a title granted to Gentiles who risked their lives to save Jews during the Holocaust.[22]

Leah's daughter Cheryl, the mother of two daughters, lives in Washington, DC, with her family. Daughter Helen, who always lived near her mother in New Jersey, recalls that despite the atrocities her parents suffered during the war, she had a happy childhood with "wonderful, giving parents" for whom their children were top priority.

Leah died in 2015, fourteen years after her husband Joseph's death. Although her last years were marked by various illnesses,[23] this woman who stated that she "had no youth"[24] became an integral part of the lives of her grandchildren as they were growing up, attending all birthday celebrations, graduations, and school plays. Helen affirms that the love Leah gave them was returned in the love and respect they showed to her.[25] If Leah were alive as of this writing in August 2023, she would be the grandmother of six and the great-grandmother of fifteen.[26]

Leah is said to have been blessed with a sense of humor and a strong personality. Her strength came to the fore during the trip to Novogrudok she undertook eight years before her death. Wheelchair-bound, Leah traveled with family members in 2007 to attend the opening of the Novogrudok Jewish Resistance Museum which commemorates the tunnel escape. Here, Leah came full circle as she stood for the first time at the mass graves where her mother and sister lie buried. Daughter Helen recalls how this trip not only

Leah Kushner, Italy, 1946
(courtesy of Helen Zelig)

imbued her with a better understanding of the labor camp breakout, but enabled her to "look at her [own] children and grandchildren as beautiful tributes to the determination and courage" of all who fled for their lives through the tunnel.[27]

Riva Kaganowicz (#146)

The story of Riva Kaganowicz defies the notion that childhood trauma bodes a lifetime of depression or major illness. Interviewed in 2019 from her Florida home at the age of ninety, Riva had clearly rebuilt her life. Her resilience and vibrancy remained robust, despite the unspeakable tragedies that robbed her of her loved ones and her dreams.

Riva and her twin brother Bezalel (nicknamed Zalka) were born on November 26, 1928.[1] She recalled that she lived at 5 Racelo Street, which bordered the Novogrudok estate of the Polish national poet Adam Mickiewicz. Among her neighbors were fellow tunnel escapees Idel Kagan (#95) and Nota Sucharski (#4).[2] As this neighborhood was occupied primarily by Jewish artisans,[3] it was quite fitting that Riva's father Aaron David Kaganowicz, a deaf saddle maker born in 1895, would live there with his wife Chaya née Angelchik, a storekeeper born in Lubtch in 1895.[4] Of their three sons and daughter Riva, only Riva survived the war.

At the start of the war, the oldest child, (Yitzchak) Meir, born in 1923, escaped to Russia on his bicycle.[5] The family was plunged into tragedy in December 1941 when eighteen-year-old Shimon was brutally murdered[6] in front of their home. Soon afterwards, Riva, her brother Bezalel, and their parents were interned in the Novogrudok forced labor camp. Here, Riva dared to dream of escaping together with Bezalel to the partisans, only to be horrified by the murder of Zalka in Novogrudok's third massacre on February 2, 1943.[7] Within three months, both her mother[8] and father[9] were slaughtered in Novogrudok's final massacre in May 1943, leaving teenage Riva completely alone in the labor camp. Her one last cherished dream of being reunited after the war with her brother Meir gave her the strength to remain alive. Yet Meir fell in battle as a Red Army soldier fighting the Germans in Crimea in April 1944, just three months before Riva's liberation.[10]

While in the forced labor camp, Riva primarily worked sorting potatoes as a kitchen assistant, as well as helping the seamstresses. Recalling the intense, gnawing hunger that plagued her over this long period, she spoke with love of Alexandra, a young Christian girl who had been her family's household helper, who often risked her life to sneak eggs, cheese, and other foodstuffs into the labor camp for her. Riva never knew how Alexandra discovered her whereabouts. For Riva, Alexandra had been "more a mother to me than my own mother," since Chaya was largely occupied in helping her husband in his business.[11] Although Riva and Alexandra were reunited after liberation, the two women lost touch several years later. For the rest of her life, Riva lamented her inability to find any trace of Alexandra when she visited Novogrudok in 2012.[12]

Sixteen years old at the time of the tunnel escape from the camp, Riva vividly remembered being awakened in the middle of the night for the breakout that she had known nothing about. She was unable to recall how she reached the entrance of the tunnel,[13] but the author was able to solve the mystery: fellow escapee Shlomo Okonski (#89) described catching a glimpse of Riva sleeping soundly on her wooden slab at the very moment that he and others were racing toward the tunnel's secret opening. Shlomo swiftly lifted Riva and carried her in his arms.[14]

In the Bielski partisan detachment, Riva often went on patrols together with her former neighbor Idel Kagan and fellow Novogrudker Reuven Openheim. Riva recalled that although they carried a gun, she had no idea how to fire it. Still mourning the deaths of her loved ones and the dashed dream of escaping to the partisans with her twin brother Bezalel, Riva was to suffer yet another devastating loss. While first wandering in the forest after the tunnel escape, Riva had met up with Sara Giershenowski (#149) and her daughter Roza (#151), who instantly adopted Riva as their own. After first reaching the Zorin partisan detachment, made up mainly of Jews from the Minsk area, two days later the women opted to transfer to the Bielski detachment. Here Sara took loving care of Riva, becoming Riva's "mother in the forest." Sara's murder in a German ambush on July 9, 1944, the last day of the war, dealt such a heavy blow that seventy-five years later, Riva was still heartbroken by the brutal slaughter of her "mother."[15]

Totally alone, seventeen-year-old Riva made her way back to Novogrudok at the war's end. Helped by Alexdrandra, she was able to raise funds by retrieving and selling the leather goods that her father had buried on the grounds of their house before being interned in the ghetto.[16] First registering in 1945 in Lodz as a Jewish survivor and then with the Central Committee of Polish Jews in Warsaw,[17] Riva joined a group of other young survivors in Lodz who wished to immigrate to Israel. While living in a displaced persons camp in Gratz, Austria, Riva succeeded in locating her paternal grandparents, who had settled in New York before the war, along with all seven of her father Aaron David's siblings. Because his deafness had made him ineligible to obtain a visa to the United States, Aaron David had stayed behind in Novogrudok with all the family property, cherishing the hope to some-day be reunited with his family.[18]

Once Riva located her grandparents, she gave up her dream of immigrating to Israel and petitioned to join her family in the United States. As she awaited a visa, Riva lived in a displaced persons camp in Rome, where she joined an acting troupe traveling the DP camp circuit to provide entertainment for other survivors. As most of her fellow actors were older, more knowledgeable, and more worldly, Riva admits that her time with them made her realize "how much I didn't know." This realization sparked her intense desire to learn.[19]

While still in the DP camp, Riva resolved to avidly pursue her edu-cation, which had abruptly stopped after grade six in Novogrudok's Tarbut school. Thanks to her grandparents' monthly allotment of fifty dollars, she was empowered to fulfill this dream. Fueling her passion were her desires to make her grandparents proud by putting their money to good use, to do something that her extremely learned father would have admired, and to seek answers from great thinkers and phi-losophers as to how the Holocaust atrocities could have been allowed to occur. Unstoppable, the young woman proceeded to learn Italian, obtain a high school diploma, take courses in philosophy, and study in an art academy. During these four years in Rome, she was helped and guided by fellow tunnel survivor Chaim Leibowitz (#91), a prewar friend of one of her uncles who had also come to her aid in the parti-san detachment. Now living in Rome as well, Chaim managed the sti-pend that Riva's grandparents sent from America and helped her make arrangements to study in Italy.[20]

Sailing at last from Naples to New York in December 1949 aboard the US Navy transport ship *General A. W. Greely*,[21] Riva had a poi-gnantly emotional reunion at the port with her aging grandparents. Yet despite the reception and assistance she received from her large family in the US, Riva admitted "never being able to feel at home" with these "American" relatives. The distance she felt from her blood relations was all the more striking in comparison to the love she felt toward Roza Giershenowski, her "adopted" sister in the partisan encampment in the forest.[22]

Riva Kaganovich, Rome, 1945 (courtesy of Eve Bernstein)

In America, Riva remained ever fervent in her quest to obtain a good education as well as to seek answers to how the evil she personally witnessed could have been perpetrated by the most "cultured" of men. To this end, Riva enrolled in Hunter College of the City University of New York with a triple major in philosophy, education, and fine arts. After graduation, she became an art teacher in the New York City public school system.[23]

Together with her husband, American-born commercial artist Irving Bernstein, Riva raised two children, a boy and a girl. Widowed in 2005, Riva was to suffer yet another tragedy at her son Alan's sudden death in 2015. Her daughter Eve is a chiropractor who lives in California with her own three children, who were Riva's pride and joy. These grandchildren often visited Riva in Florida, where she lived for over thirty years.[24]

Until her death on April 30, 2023, Riva continued to seek answers to life's existential questions and to be curious about the world. In August 2012, then eighty-six-year-old Riva traveled with Eve and her daughter Ariana to Novogrudok in hope of locating remnants of the tunnel that had saved her life. She appears in the film *Tunnel of Hope*, which documents the search.[25]

Despite the tragedies she endured, Riva was justifiably proud of all she accomplished in the life she considered herself lucky to have lived.

Yitzchak (#147) and
Mordechai (#148) Maloshitzki

The story of Yitzchak and Mordechai Maloshitzki is the story of a father's fierce love for his son.

According to Pages of Testimony submitted by Herzl Bruk, who was Yitzchak Maloshitzki's nephew through marriage, Yitzchak, his wife, and two toddler-age children had all been murdered in the Nazi mass slaughters of Novogrudok that occurred months before the tunnel escape. As it happens, Herzl was only partially correct.

Bruk's testimony stated that Yitzchak, a hat shop owner born in Novogrudok in 1908, was either murdered in the town's second massacre of August 7, 1942, or in the third massacre on February 4, 1943.[1] He also testified that Yitzchak's wife Dvorah née Plozinski, a hat shop owner, was murdered during the first Novogrudok massacre on December 8, 1941,[2] along with their children Sara,[3] age two, and Mordechai, age four.[4]

We can attest that both Yitzchak and Mordechai survived the massacres, and that Yitzchak was conscripted to the forced labor camp. At great risk to both their lives, Yitzchak somehow succeeded in hiding Mordechai in the confines of the camp following the May 7, 1943, massacre of almost all the other children. As to how such a feat was possible, we can only marvel. Mordechai's participation in the tunnel escape makes him the youngest known escapee. He was six years old at the time.[5]

Tragically, even Yitzchak's boundless love for his child was not enough to save him. Neither Mordechai nor Yitzchak survived the tunnel escape to reach the forest and the partisans. Their names do not appear in the compilation of Jewish partisans in Belorussia during the years 1941–1944.[6]

Yitzchak Maloshitzki
(courtesy of Herzl Bruk)

Herzl Bruk, the former chairman of the Novogrudok Society in Israel, who passed away in 2009, submitted the Pages of Testimony for the Maloshitzki family. Despite having provided the author with a copy of the escape list only eight years after he submitted the Pages of Testimony in 1999, Herzl obviously never knew that his own uncle and little cousin had participated in the escape. Having always told his children that the entire family in Novogrudok had been murdered after his own immigration to Palestine in 1935, Herzl would have found no reason to search for relatives on the very list he had in his possession.[7]

As of 2022, Herzl's grandson Eran Barak serves as the chairman of the Novogrudok Society in Israel. Although he had previously heard the author speak of the tunnel escape at several memorial meetings, Eran, too, never realized that his own kin were among the participants and met their deaths in the breakout. Informed of this fact on April 21, 2020, which happened to coincide with Yom Hashoah (Holocaust Martyrs' and Heroes' Remembrance Day) in Israel, he was quite emotional at receiving the information on Yitzchak and little Mordechai.

Sara (#149), Basia (#150), and Roza (#151) Giershenowski

Sara Giershenowski and her daughters Basia and Roza had already known great loss and tragedy by 1942 when they were conscripted as seamstresses to the Novogrudok forced labor camp. Yet in their last attempt to endure the savagery of World War II, only one of the three was destined to survive.

Sara Giershenowski née Kulik was born in Karelich in 1895.[1] Prior to the war, she and her husband Shlomo,[2] a shoe store owner, and their three children had resided in Novogrudok at 1947 Karelich Street.[3] Shlomo, who served on the committee of the United Jewish Artisans' Association,[4] which supported needy craftsmen, was brutally murdered in Novogrudok soon after the German occupation in June 1941.[5] At the onset of the war, Sara and Shlomo's son Shimon escaped to Russia by bicycle.

Basia, the oldest of the three children, was born on November 8, 1924.[6] Prior to the war, she married Baruch Manusevich, and their daughter Sima was born in 1940.[7] In 1942, two-year-old Sima was killed along with her father.[8]

Spared murder thanks to their skills as seamstresses, Sara, Basia, and Roza remained living and working together in the forced labor camp. On September 26, 1943, Sara led her daughters in crawling through the tunnel in their perilous escape attempt. To their horror, Basia was killed before her mother and sister's eyes in the bloody aftermath of the exit. Broken, Sara and Roza somehow reached the Bielski partisan detachment following a very brief stay with the Zorin partisans.[9]

After having clung to life throughout the Novogrudok selections, the tunnel escape, and the difficult forest conditions, Sara was not fated to survive the war. On the very day of liberation, July 9, 1944, she was ruthlessly slain in the retreating German Army's last attack on the Bielski partisan detachment. According to historian Dr. Shmuel Amarant's eye-witness account, a force of a hundred German soldiers had marched through the forest by night to wage a surprise attack on the *otriad.*

Partisans asleep in their unguarded *zemlyanka* suddenly came under a barrage of rifle fire, and a hand grenade was hurled into one of the dugouts. At that time, many of the armed Bielski fighters had been away on a mission in the area. Upon hearing the shots, they raced back to the camp to eradicate the German troops, yet they arrived too late to prevent the terrible loss of partisan lives.[10] As to the exact number of Bielski partisan casualties on Liberation Day, both Amarant[11] and Tuvia Bielski[12] report the deaths of nine men and women. Nechama Tec, how-ever, writes that eleven people were murdered that day. Following the attack, they were buried in a common grave at the top of a hill, where Tuvia Bielski delivered a eulogy and shots were fired in salute.[13]

One of those buried on the hilltop was Sara Giershenowski, fatally shot while hiding from the Germans under her makeshift bed.[14] Her death was mourned not only by her daughter Roza, but also by Riva Kaganowicz (#146), the fifteen-year-old orphaned girl she'd "adopted" in the labor camp and ultimately in the forest. Until her death in April 2023, Riva continued to mourn the death of Sara, "the mother she lost in the forest," who cared for her like her own child, sharing her food, providing support, and even sewing underclothes for her.[15]

Roza, the sole survivor of the three Giershenowski women con-scripted to the forced labor camp, was born on November 8, 1924.[16] Eight decades later, she still vividly recalled her hometown of Novogrudok as "a small city full of life." A lifelong self-proclaimed lover of shoes, she also reminisced about frequent visits to her father's shoe shop to check whether any new shoes had arrived.[17]

Fellow escapee Fanya Dunetz (#142) recalled Roza from her high school days in Novogrudok, when she rented a room in the house next to Roza's. Following graduation, Fanya attended a teachers' seminary in Bialystock and returned to her hometown of Zhetl during the war, never dreaming she would ever again live within close proximity to Roza. Yet fate brought these two former neighbors together in the Novogrudok forced labor camp, Fanya as the camp secretary and Roza as a seamstress.[18]

In an interview six years before her death in 2018, Roza shared her memory of being stricken with typhus in the forest together with Fanya. The two young women, who had lost their hair from the disease, would meet for walks to the edge of the detachment, where they could discreetly expose their newly bald heads to the sunlight.[19]

After recuperating from the disease, Roza's myriad tasks in the detachment included guarding the base and maintaining the level of cleanliness in the *otriad*.[20] Despite her assertion that "when the Germans arrived, that was the end of our lives,"[21] despite the crushing loss of her mother on the last day of the war, and despite the formidable difficulties she encountered after the war, Roza continued to live her life to the fullest. Married in 1947 to Joseph Arlinsky, a soldier in the Russian Army, Roza was widowed shortly after giving birth to her daughter Sonia that same year. In 1949, Roza married Boris Wodakow, and their son Seymour was born the following year.

The family moved to a number of places in Russia before finally being permitted to emigrate in 1959. Repatriated to Poland, Roza and her family took up residence in Gliwice, less than twenty miles from Auschwitz. In November 1963, they left Poland aboard a ship to Montreal. Following a short stay there with relatives, on November 12, 1963, Roza, Boris, Sonia, and Seymour arrived in the United States, which became their permanent home.[22]

The family settled in Queens, New York, where Roza was employed at the United Nations as an interpreter and supervisor of interpreters.[23] In December 1984, Roza was widowed once again.[24] Her children Sonia, a teacher, and Seymour, an electrical engineer, are each married and have two children. If Roza were alive as of this writing in September 2019, she would be the great-grandmother of six.[25]

Basia Giershenowski, 1938 (courtesy of Rosalia [Roza] Giershenowski Wodakow)

Sara Giershenowski, mid-1930s (courtesy of Sy Wodakow)

Almost until her death on January 3, 2018, in West Hartford, Connecticut, Roza remained close to Riva Kaganowicz, the orphaned teenager and fellow tunnel escapee who became her adopted sister during the war years.[26] As for Roza and Basia's brother Shimon, who had fled to Russia at the start of the war, he and his family emigrated from Grodno, USSR, to Israel in the early 1990s.[27] He and Roza frequently visited each other until Shimon's death in 2003.[28]

Roza Giershenowski, Russia, 1949 (courtesy of Rosalia [Roza] Giershenowski Wodakow)

Reflecting on the source of her mother's strength, Roza's daughter Sonia Palkis maintains, "One can survive almost anything when one has no choice."[29] Roza Giershenowski (Wodakow), a woman who had a lion's share of "no choice," showed herself to be a pillar of tenacity in the face of unrelenting adversity.

From her earliest memories onward, Sonia recalls her mother frequently mentioning her murdered sister and mother. Today, one of Sonia's daughters is Basia's namesake, and one of her granddaughters carries the name of Basia's daughter Sima.[30] The bravery, devotion, and love that personified Sara, Basia, and Roza Giershenowski serve as a beacon for generations to come.

Sara Lidski (#152)

The daughter of Yisrael, a watchmaker,[1] and Rivka, a housewife,[2] Sara Lidski was born in Zhetl in either 1918[3] or 1920.[4] Her siblings include Chana Karolishki, born in 1900, married and a housewife;[5] Chaim, born in either 1912[6] or 1916, a teacher and single;[7] Risha, born in 1913 and married,[8] and Feigel, born in 1916 and single.[9]

While Sara's mother and siblings were all slaughtered in the Zhetl massacres of 1942, her good friend and fellow Zhetl native Fanya Dunetz (#142) clearly remembered that Sara's father was also taken to the Novogrudok forced labor camp. As his name does not appear on the escape list, Fanya raised the probability that Yisrael Lidski was murdered prior to the breakout.[10]

Fanya recalled that at the outbreak of war and the arrival of the Russians in Zhetl, Sara returned home from her dressmaking studies in Vilna's ORT school to be with her family. Spared death to be interned in the Novogrudok forced labor camp as a seamstress, Sara coupled her sewing skills with Fanya's resourcefulness to enable both young women to be slightly less hungry on several occasions. With Fanya's brother Motl Dunetz also in the labor camp and working in manufacturing wooden shoes for the Germans, a scheme was devised by which Motl would supply Fanya with scraps of wood. These scraps would then be clandestinely transferred to Sara, who would use the wood as handles for pocketbooks that she would sew. Fanya boldly "sold" these creations to one of the German officers as presents to be sent to his relatives in Germany. In turn, Fanya was supplied with a piece of bread, half of which she gave to Sara and the other half she shared with Motl.[11]

Fanya also recalled that although she proposed to Sara that they escape from the tunnel together (Sara was supposed to have been ten places behind Fanya), Sara insisted upon leaving alongside the armed fighters who were to be the final ones to escape.[12]

Probably the very last member of her family to survive, Sara was also the last of her family to be murdered in her perilous attempt to survive the tunnel escape.[13]

The names of Yisrael, Rivka, Chana, Chaim, Risha, Feigl, and Sara Lidski are all commemorated in Zhetl's memorial book.[14]

Hirsh Altman (#153)

Among the carpenters, watchmakers, tailors, saddlemakers, and shoe-makers who were inmates in the Novogrudok forced labor camp was a noted educator, artist, illustrator, and personal mentor of a future world-renowned artist.

At the start of our research to determine the identity of Hirsh Altman, the sole entry for this name was on the necrology list of the *Novogrudok Memorial Book*.[1] Then, thanks to the ongoing translation of the *Biographical Dictionary of Modern Yiddish Literature* (*Yiddish Leksikon*), we caught our first glimpse of Hirsh as a noted educator from Novogrudok.

According to the *Leksikon*, Hirsh studied in secular primary and secondary schools in Novogrudok, and from 1934 to 1939 was living in Warsaw teaching drawing and crafts in the Tsisho school network.[2] Established in Warsaw in 1921,[3] the Tsisho (an acronym for the Yiddish "Central Jewish School Organization") system promoted Jewish secular culture and education via an elementary through high school curriculum encompassing Yiddish language and literature, Jewish history and culture, the sciences, math, music, physical education, and arts and crafts.[4]

The *Shulvegn* (School Ways), a Warsaw-based Tsisho educational publication applying the latest pedagogical theories to secular Yiddish education,[5] gave a solid clue: among its contributors in 1934, 1937, and 1939 was Hirsh Altman,[6] fated to become a tunnel escapee in the dark years to come.

During his period in Warsaw, Hirsh was to make the acquaintance of two major cultural figures: Yiddish novelist, poet, journalist, painter, and almost Nobel Prize winner[7] Mendel Mann, as well as the future Israel Prize laureate in painting, Yosl Bergner. Mann, deemed by prominent scholar Sol Liptzin as being "among the finest novelists of the Holocaust generation," is said to have begun his prolific writing career with the publication of his poems in the Polish Yiddish press in 1938.[8] Yet thanks to the Steven Spielberg–supported Yiddish Book Center, we have a glimpse of extraordinary drawings that Hirsh Altman illustrated for a children's book penned by Mendel Mann in 1934.[9] The mere fact that Mann, a talented painter himself, had chosen Hirsh to illustrate his book speaks highly of Hirsh's talent, especially considering that for a later book of short stories called *Le Chêne Noir*, Mann chose as the illustrator his good friend Marc Chagall.[10]

Seventy-seven years after leaving Warsaw in 1937, the internationally renowned painter Yosl Bergner had not forgotten Hirsh Altman, the art teacher of his youth. In a 2014 oral testimony, Bergner speaks of having been taught art by Hirsh in the Yiddish school he attended, as well as in private lessons in the artist's home. In recalling his teacher, Bergner makes pointed mention of both Altman's talent and his poverty.[11] As he climbed to fame, Yosl Bergner continued to credit Hirsh Altman in many of his biographical sketches.[12] In awarding an honorary doctorate to Bergner in 2013, the University of Haifa categorically noted, "In Warsaw, Yosl studied painting with the famous Jewish painter Hirsch Altman."[13]

Reached in November 2020, Bergner's ninety-three-year-old widow, artist Audrey Bergner, still remembered her husband having spoken of his former art teacher in Warsaw,[14] although she no longer recalls the details.

By 1939 and the German invasion of Poland, Mendel Mann, Yosl Bergner, and Hirsh Altman had all fled Warsaw for distant destinations. Mendel was drafted into the Red Army after seeking shelter in Russia,[15] Yosl had left for Australia in 1937,[16] and Hirsh fled the occupied Warsaw cultural milieu to what he must have considered the "safety" of his hometown of Novogrudok.[17]

We have little knowledge of Hirsh's personal life or even his date of birth. Only thanks to Bergner's oral testimony do we know that Hirsh was married.[18] Possibly his wife was Zlata Altman, whose name also appears on the Novogrudok necrology list.[19] We are also unaware of the skill that qualified Hirsh for conscription to the forced labor camp, although perhaps it was related to one of the crafts he taught in Warsaw.

The testimony of fellow labor camp inmate Mordechai Majerowicz, however, credits Hirsh (referred to as "Grisha") with having been one of the key organizers of the ill-fated armed rebellion planned for April 15, 1943, that was ultimately forced to be cancelled.[20] It is unlikely that this artist's hands had ever held a gun before; his crucial role in planning the act of defiance again the German captors is a tribute to his skill and determination.

Hirsh apparently did not survive the tunnel escape to reach the forest and become a partisan. As his name does not appear in the compilation of Jewish partisans in Belorussia from 1941 to 1944, we can assume that he was killed in the aftermath of the escape.[21]

In the entry cited in the *Yiddish Leksikon* published in 1954, his colleagues report Hirsh's fate to have been "unknown."[22] As a result of this research, Hirsh Altman's participation in the tunnel escape may now be noted and acclaimed in future annals of prewar artists and Yiddish educators.

Chana Garbar (#154)

Chana (Chiena) Garbar of Novogrudok was the daughter of Uria and a sister to Zlata and Rivka.[1]

Of the three daughters, only Rivka Garber (later "Roz Kaplan") remained alive after the war. In 1963, she paid tribute to Chana and Zlata in a memorial notice in the *Novogrudok Memorial Book*.[2]

We have no information as to Chana's occupation which enabled her to be conscripted to the Novogrudok forced labor camp. Sadly, we do know that Chana did not survive the tunnel escape to reach the safety of the partisan detachments.[3]

Mikulitzki (#155)

Yad Vashem's Central Database of Shoah Victims' Names contains 150 entries for individuals from Poland with the surname Mikulitzki.[1] With the escape list giving no proper name for the Novogrudok escapee called Mikulitzki, we cannot definitively determine the identity of this man or woman.

To speculate, however, we could begin with the premise that since the majority of Novogrudok forced labor camp inmates hailed from the city of Novogrudok and its environs, there is a reasonable chance that "Mikulitzki" was a native of Novogrudok as well. Indeed, 73 out of the total 150 Mikulitzki entries in the central database are from the Novogrudok area. Of these, only four were not murdered.[2] Only one, Shmuel Mikulitzki, definitely survived the war as a partisan in the Bielski *otriad*.[3]

Shmuel, our possible escapee, was born to Girsh in 1903 and lived in Novogrudok prior to the war.[4] A boilermaker and part-time farmer, Shmuel resided on Schloss Gass (Castle Street), populated by many religiously observant Jews, who maintained a large synagogue located in the third house from the corner of Schloss Gass and the entrance to the castle area (Zamok).[5]

Shmuel Mikulitzki appears in the compilation of partisans in Belorussia as having been a Bielski partisan.[6] There he played an important role in the construction of the forest detachment's tannery. In his memoir, partisan commander Tuvia Bielski praised Shmuel as an expert in extracting tar from the bark of birch trees, essential for building the tannery.[7]

Attempts have been unsuccessful to find information on Shmuel Mikulitzki or his descendants to help ascertain whether he was, in fact, the Mikulitzki of the escape list. Unfortunately, we have no knowledge of Shmuel's whereabouts subsequent to liberation.

Yakov (Yankel) Weinrid (#156)

The only facts known about Yankel Weinrid are that he was born in 1910 to Kushel, was incarcerated in the Novogrudok forced labor camp, survived the tunnel escape, and fled to the forest, where he joined the Frunze partisans, a Russian detachment."[1] Nothing is known of Yakov's birthplace, his family of origin, his marital or family status, or his profession. His name does not appear in Yad Vashem's Central Database of Shoah Victims' Names.

An examination of genealogical, Holocaust-related, and population databases has revealed no information to date regarding his postwar life. It is possible that following the war, Yakov Weinrid remained in the Soviet Union, where historical vital records are not easily accessible.

Yosef Chechanovski (#157)

Yad Vashem's Central Database of Shoah Victims' Names includes listings for seven men from throughout Poland named Yosef Chechanovski.[1] The murders of all but one are confirmed. Only the fate of Yosef Chechanovski, a refugee in Slonim in 1940, remains unknown.[2]

Although we may never know the identity of the person named Yosef Chechanovski, the 157th inmate in line to crawl through the tunnel, we can assume that he was murdered in the aftermath of the escape. His name does not appear in the compilation of Jewish partisans in Belorussia during the years 1941–1944.[3]

Frieda (#158) and Leah (#158a) Davidovich

In the wake of the 2019 Russian-language media coverage of the seventy-fifth anniversary commemoration of the tunnel escape, Tamara Vershitskaya, then director of the Jewish Resistance Museum in Novogrudok, received a message from one of the journalists who covered the story. According to this reporter, a woman living in the southern Siberian city of Barnaul named Elena Filipyeva had contacted her to convey that her grandmother Frida Davidovich, along with her great-grandmother Leah Davidovich, had participated in the tunnel escape. Upon contacting Elena, Tamara was able to obtain the short memoir left by Frieda, which was kindly forwarded to the author. Most of the following is based on this memoir.

The fate of tunnel escapees who may have settled in the former Soviet Union after the war remains a mystery to us, primarily due to the inaccessibility of Russian civil and genealogical records. Fortunately, mother and daughter Leah and Frieda Davidovich are extraordinary exceptions.

We know that Leah's skills as an expert dressmaker enabled her and her daughter Frieda to be assigned to the Novogrudok forced labor camp, thus escaping death in the Novogrudok massacres. Here, Leah, age forty-three, and Frieda, age twenty, miraculously survived the climactic tunnel escape to freedom.[1]

Although the surname Davidovich is crossed out on the escape list, it is now clear Frieda and Leah were definitely among the escapees: Frieda's written memoir gives a vivid account of their participation in the escape, and Frieda and Leah are listed as members of the Bielski partisans both in the compilation of Jewish partisans in Belorussia[2] and in documents found in the National Archive of the Republic of Belarus.[3] Perhaps their names were crossed out in error on the escape list, or their placement was changed and written on now-illegible lines on the existing copies of the list.

Frieda testifies that her brother and sister were murdered along with other relatives in one of the Novogrudok slaughters of 1942–1943, although we have no further details.[4] Nor is there any information about Gersh, Frieda's father[5] and Leah's husband.

Prior to the war, the family lived at 5 Zamkova Street in Novogrudok.[6] Frieda attended a seven-grade Polish school, followed by two years at a private high school. During this time, she also polished her considerable musical abilities while studying piano and accordion.[7]

Frieda was in tenth grade when the Soviets occupied Novogrudok in September 1939. After continuing her studies and graduating from Secondary School No. 2, she completed a six-month course in Baranovich to gain certification as an educator in an orphanage.[8] Although she is recorded on a partisan list as having been a waitress prior to the war,[9] Frieda writes in her memoir of her work in the Novogrudok orphanage.[10]

Originally established as a Jewish institution in 1917,[11] the orphanage was transformed subsequent to the Soviet occupation in 1939 into a multinational facility housing both orphans and homeless children.[12] With the invasion of the Germans on June 22, 1941, the Jewish children were transferred from their residence on Kowalewsker Street to the former home of Israel Delatycki, who had been deported to Siberia. Escapee Chaim Leibowitz (#91), who had served in the past as director of the orphanage, was asked by the Judenrat to help with the move. The children's stay in the Delatycki home, however, turned out to be only temporary. Leibowitz relates that among the fifty-one hundred Jews killed in the first slaughter in December were the Jewish orphans. The girls were all murdered in a mass grave wearing white kerchiefs on their heads.[13] Although Frieda did not detail the horrific scene of the children's deportation, it is possible that she was a staff member of the orphanage at the time.

Desperately seeking to avoid her own deportation by going into hiding, Frieda was eventually discovered and confined to the ghetto. There she was together with her mother, siblings, and other relatives for the last time: all were murdered prior to Leah and Frieda's lifesaving conscription to the forced labor camp.[14]

In Frieda's memoir, she notes the contact that existed between the inmates in the camp and the partisans in the forest prior to the escape. According to her estimate, she and her mother Leah were among a total of 238 inmates who participated in the breakout.

In an attempt to adapt to the Russian occupation of Novogrudok in 1941, Frieda had joined the Komsomol organization, the All-Union Leninist Young Communist League, which existed from 1918 until the fall of the Soviet Union in 1992. In the partisan detachment in the forest, she continued her Komsomol activities as an official organizer, a member of the bureau of the Komsomol organization, and a counselor for orphaned schoolchildren. She participated in political activities and distributed leaflets among nearby inhabitants, as well as joining clandestine combat missions in the forest along with other Komsomol members.

Frieda and Leah marched out
of the forest together with her fellow Bielski partisans in July 1944.
Possibly rewarded for her allegiance
to the Komsomol organization, she
became chief of accounting for the
Novogrudok Komsomol branch,
a position she held until August
1945, when she was transferred to
the Sixth Engineer-Sapper Brigade
as a secretary-typist to the political
department.

Frieda Davidovich with her
husband and daughter Leah,
Kamchatka or Barnaul, Russia,
mid-1950s (courtesy of Elena
Filipyeva)

At the war's end, Frieda returned
to the musical pursuits of her childhood. As early as 1945, while working as a secretary with the army, she
became a soloist in the military pop orchestra. After marrying a career
army officer in 1946, Frieda changed her surname to Yezhova and
moved to Grodno, where she studied music, directed amateur drama
performances, and gave birth to Lev, born in 1946, and Svetlana, born
in 1949.

After a one-year stint in the rural Russian Far East region of
Kamchatka, where her husband was stationed, in 1955, Frieda and
her growing family moved to Barnaul, where she led a military choir
and taught choral music in various settings. It was in Barnaul that her
youngest child, Anna, was born in 1960.[15]

To date, brief contact has been made with Frieda's granddaughter
Elena Filipyeva, who lives in Barnaul. She reports that since she was
only six years old when Frieda died, she remembers very little about
her.[16] Yet we are indeed fortunate to have proof that thanks to Leah and
Frieda's miraculous survival and escape through the tunnel, this family
has continued at least into the third generation.

Hirsh Patzovski (#159)

Hirsh Patzovski was born in Zhetl in 1915. The son of Betzalel and Frieda,[1] he was a carpenter, as were both his father[2] and brother Yakov (#161).[3] Pesia Mayevski (#160) testifies that Betzalel died at age eighty-six on February 22, 1942, the day that Zhetl townspeople were forced into the ghetto.[4] Zlata, Hirsh's younger sister, was killed in Zhetl's second slaughter on August 6, 1942, at the age of twenty-five.[5] Thanks to their professional skills, brothers Yakov and Hirsh were spared death to be interned together in the Novogrudok forced labor camp.

In the aftermath of the tunnel breakout, Yakov was killed.[6] Now perhaps the last surviving member of his family, Hirsh walked for several weeks in his quest to reach the Bielski partisan detachment. On this journey, he was accompanied by Pesia Mayevski, Kalman Shelkovich (#100), and by siblings Noah (#133) and Sara (Sorke, #134) Zamoshchik. Pesia describes how they subsisted on raw potatoes found in fields as they navigated through the forest – and their great delight at receiving bread and cooked potatoes from peasants along the way.[7]

On July 9, 1944, the day of liberation, the unarmed Hirsh was killed with nine other partisans, all armed, who were in wait to ambush what was expected to be a small group of German soldiers retreating from the Battle of Stalingrad and scavenging for food. Overtaken by a larger number of soldiers than anticipated, the entire group of partisans was killed, along with Sara Giershenowski (#149), a forty-eight-year-old escapee who was found hiding under her "bed."[8] Hirsh and his ten fellow murdered partisans were buried the same day in a common hilltop grave not far from headquarters. They were briefly eulogized by Commander Tuvia Bielski, just as the first group of Red Army soldiers, their long-awaited liberators, was being received at the *otriad*.[9]

With no time to mourn Hirsh and his comrades, the partisans were ordered the very next day to plan to evacuate the detachment and march to Novogrudok as free men.

Pesia Mayevski (#160)

One of four children, Pesia Mayevski was born in Zhetl in 1922[1] to Yisrael Asher and Chaya née Dvoretzki. Yisrael Asher, a Torah scribe, was forty-seven years old when murdered in Novogrudok in July 1941.[2] Chaya, a seamstress, was forty-five when she was shot to death in Zhetl on August 6, 1942,[3] together with two of her children, daughter Hinda, age seventeen,[4] and son Chanan, a twenty-one-year-old artist.[5] Both children had been the namesakes of grandparents, Chanan for his maternal grandfather[6] and Hinda for her paternal grandmother.[7]

Scribe Yisrael Asher must have had a secondary "official" occupation as a tailor, as is indicated on a list of Zhetl Holocaust victims.[8] We can assume that either or both parents taught Pesia to sew, as her life was saved by sewing for the Germans in the Novogrudok forced labor camp, despite her having worked as a bookkeeper before the war.

In her writings, Pesia describes becoming quite ill in the labor camp prior to the escape. Dr. Yakov Kagan of Baranovich (#3a) came to her aid, obtaining medication for her as well as money to pay someone to smuggle food to supplement the meager rations supplied to the inmates.[9] According to eyewitness Yehoshua Yaffe, every worker received a daily allotment of nine ounces of bread, as well as two servings of soup made from beet or potato skins.[10] Fellow escapee Idel Kagan (#95) reports that after the fourth Novogrudok massacre of May 7, 1943, in which half the inmates in the forced labor camp were murdered, a "slow starvation diet" was introduced. Daily rations consisted of four and a half ounces ounces of bread mixed with straw, as well as one bowl of "soup."[11] Escapee Chaim Leibowitz (#91), on the other hand, suggests that from February 1943, the time of Novogrudok's third massacre, the daily ration was three and a half ounces of bread and a thin gruel, black in color and made with water and potato peels.[12] Although we are unaware of exactly when Pesia was ill, we know that she, like all other inmates, suffered from serious malnutrition. After her recovery, she scrubbed the infirmary in order to receive an extra piece of bread, almost certainly in addition to her hard labor as a seamstress for her abusers.[13] In a Yiddish memoir about the Novogrudok forced labor camp, she describes the slave laborers' hunger as being so intense that it blocked their sleep.[14] Even dreaming of better times and places was difficult for the inmates.

Attributing the plans for a tunnel escape to Dr. Kagan and to Yitzchak Dvoretzki, a tanner from Zhetl, Pesia meticulously describes the digging that took place through the Zhetlers' workshops as having been carried out in thirteen-hour shifts. She recalls the dirt carried out in carts, as well as the line of inmates who passed bags of soil from the tunnel entrance to be concealed in the loft, while passing the emptied bags back to each other to be refilled. Because oil lamps and candles could not remain lit in the airless tunnel, Pesia writes that this necessitated the installation of electricity, which would ultimately provide a signal to indicate the presence of Germans in the camp.[15]

Recalling the night of September 26, 1943, Pesia notes that the first and last groups of escapees consisted primarily of young, armed men. Describing the great difficulty encountered by the Zhetlers in navigating the unfamiliar terrain beyond the tunnel escape, she states that these non-natives of Novogrudok simply went where their eyes led them. Because visibility was extremely limited on the moonless, rainy night of the escape, many erred by running back toward the camp, where they were slain by German bullets. Most of those who ran toward Zhetl are also reported to have been murdered.[16]

Pesia describes her initial flight from the Novogrudok camp with a group of four other escapees originally from Zhetl: Kalman Shelkovich

(#100), Hirsh Patzovski (#159), and Noah (#133) and Sara (#134) Zamoshchik. Subsisting in the forest on rain water and raw potatoes along the trek to the Naliboki Forest, she writes that it took several weeks to reach the safety of the Bielski detachment.[17] There she worked in the kitchen under fellow escapee Yitzchak Rosenhaus (#30), who, she admits, would at times spot her efforts to take "home" a few extra potatoes she attempted to hide in her threadbare pockets.[18]

Pesia Mayevski, Germany, circa 1946 (courtesy of Chaya Ben-Tal)

Devastated by Hirsh's murder by the Germans just one day before liberation, Pesia marched out of the forest along with her fellow survivors, where her wanderings and vicissitudes were just beginning. Following a brief return to Zhetl, Pesia traveled to Nowoyelna, where she waited for two weeks for the train to Lodz. From Lodz, she traveled to Czechoslovakia and on to Landsberg, Germany, the city in which Hitler wrote *Mein Kampf*.[19] Here Pesia took refuge in the Landsberg Displaced Persons Camp, a former military camp characterized by inadequate food, housing, and sanitary conditions.[20]

Pesia subsequently moved on to Marseille, France, where she waited three months for a refugee ship to Palestine, only to become consigned to an internment camp in Famagusta, Cyprus, after the illegal immigration ship was sighted and halted.[21] One full year later, at the end of 1947,[22] Pesia's boat succeeded in breaking the British blockade of Jewish immigration to Palestine.[23]

Now newly married to Mordechai Nadel, a Holocaust survivor from Lodz, Pesia finally reached the Israeli shores of Atlit. Following one-month stays both there and in Kiryat Shmuel, Pesia and Mordechai settled at last in their new home in Petach Tikva,[24] where they were to raise their two children, son Yankel and daughter Chaya.[25] Today, in August 2023, Pesia would be the grandmother of two.[26]

Pesia, an accomplished Yiddish poet, would often read her Holocaust poetry at the Zhetl survivors' annual memorial ceremonies in Tel Aviv. Her presence there is sorely missed today.

The following poem by Pesia Mayevski, written in Yiddish in 1992 and translated into Hebrew by Yitzchak Ganoz, was translated to English by Mordechai Dunetz, a former inmate of the Novogrudok forced labor camp (see Fanya Dunetz, #142).

From Where Do I Get My Strength

Fifty years have passed, and we sink along with them,
And the night will cover our last footprints.
Our sorrow and pain of years of terror and sword will remain,
And silence will penetrate the melody of our song.

Our sleep is disturbed, our dead knock within the night.
There is not rest or solace. In the evening and during times of grief,
Our heartaches are filled with overflowing years.
Time does not heal and the earth does not cover.

To bear all this till now, from the blows of darkness,
Where then can we gather our strength?
From the ghetto, from the forest, and from smoke-filled camps,
There we fought and there we struggled for life and light.[27]

Yakov (Yanek) Patzovski (#161)

Yakov Patzovski was born in Zhetl in either 1910[1] or 1914.[2] Unmarried, he was the son of Frieda and Betzalel.[3]

Like his father[4] and his older brother Hirsh Patzovski (#159),[5] Yakov was a carpenter.[6] His sister Zlata was killed in Zhetl's second slaughter on August 6, 1942, at the age of twenty-five, yet her memory was kept alive by her boyfriend Arkady Mnuskin in a Page of Testimony he submitted for her thirty-six years later from his residence in California.[7]

Yakov's participation in the tunnel escape is confirmed by Pesia Mayevski (#160), who was assigned a place on the escape list between Hirsh and Yakov. Of the three, only Yakov did not survive the breakout. Pesia writes that although he was seen running in the direction of Zhetl, Yakov Patzovski never reached his destination.[8]

Chanan Lev (#162)

Chanan Lev was born in Bialystok in 1923.[1] From the patronymic of his name on a partisan list, we know that he was the son of Shlomo.[2] We have no additional information about him or his family. Lev was apparently a very popular surname in the Bialystok region, as evidenced by the over one thousand entries in Yad Vashem's Central Database of Shoah Victims' Names for Lev family members from the area.[3]

We do not know when or under which circumstances Chanan came to Novogrudok, or the nature of his skills for which he was conscripted to the Novogrudok forced labor camp. We do know that when the Germans occupied Bialystok on June 27, 1943, even before their incursion into Novogrudok on July 4, an order was issued sentencing all Jews between the ages of fourteen and sixteen to forced labor.[4] One day later, the Nazis herded two thousand Jews into Bialystok's Great Synagogue, where all those within were burnt alive.[5]

Spared annihilation, Chanan Lev managed to survive the tunnel escape and the perilous flight to the forest. Yet on June 24, 1944, nine months after the breakout, he was killed while serving as a Bielski partisan.[6]

Moshe (#163) and Berl (#164) Niselevich; Raizel (#165)

Moshe and Berl Niselevich, whose names are crossed out on the escape list, may or may not have participated in the tunnel escape. Two plausible explanations for their names having been struck out include the possibility that they were murdered between the time the list was recorded and the tunnel escape, or that they escaped on their own. Or, perhaps Moshe and Berl's escape positions were changed, as was the case with other inmates. However, the escape list designates no alternate numbers for Moshe and Berl, although they may be among those names that remain illegible on the escape list.

Moshe[1] and Berl Niselevich[2] were two brothers from Karelich. Their father Zalman, born in 1897, was a carpenter by trade,[3] and their mother Musya, born in 1900, was a housewife.[4] Moshe and Berl had at least three other siblings: Nechama, born in 1922;[5] Aaron, born in 1924;[6] and Beyla, born in 1925.[7] All are reported to have been murdered in 1942, along with their parents. Although we are unaware of the professions and birthdates of Moshe and Berl, we know that neither survived the tunnel escape. Their names appear on the list of the murdered in the memorial book of Karelich.[8]

Despite the fact that the surname of escapee #165 is illegible and crossed out, her proper name, Raizel, is clear. Since her name appears directly following those of Moshe and Berl, it is possible that Raizel was also a member of the Niselevich family and either escaped together with the brothers, was murdered with them, or had her position on the list changed together with them. This supposition is bolstered by a page of testimony filed for Raizel Niselevich of Karelich, born in 1924, the daughter of Feivel.[9] Feivel Niselevich[10] was a brother to Zalman,[11] making Raizel a first cousin to Moshe and Berl. She is listed as having been single at the time of her death.[12]

Etel (#166) and Yocheved (Yacha, #166a) Tiles

One after the other, Etel and Yocheved (Yacha) Tiles crouched through the tunnel in their attempt to escape the Novogrudok forced labor camp to freedom. To this day, we have no idea of the relationship between the two, nor any details as to Etel's identity or age. However, the fact that they were placed together on the escape list indicates the likelihood that the two were siblings, or at least relatives.

Fortunately, a daring act by Yacha Tiles was documented in the *Novogrudok Memorial Book* in the memoirs of Sulia Rubin, sister of Rita Wolozhinski (#71). Describing the tense days following the city's August 1942 massacre, Sulia details a secret plan that she and her friend "Yarke" Tiles devised to escape the city's courthouse ghetto and flee to the Bielski partisan detachment. When they were taken out in a small group to the water pump, the teenage girls seized a moment when their Belarusian police guards were preoccupied. Ripping off their yellow stars, the girls ran for their lives through the nearby fields. Several miles later, they were caught by the local police and flogged with whips. Given the choice of being punished by local anti-Semitic policemen, many of whom were her former classmates, or the German gendarmes, Sulia opted for the Germans. Soon imprisoned and facing execution, the girls were miraculously spared death by a Nazi officer and returned to their confinement in the forced labor camp.[1]

On her second escape attempt, Sulia did safely reach the Bielski partisan detachment. Yarka (Yocheved) Tiles eventually joined her upon her own successful escape through the tunnel.

Yocheved Tiles's parents were Dvora (Doba) née Dzhencholski, a housewife born in Novogrudok in 1886, and Yisrael, a saddler and leatherworker born in Uman, Ukraine.[2] According to a Yad Vashem Page of Testimony filed by Doba's nephew, the couple had resided in Novogrudok prior to the war with their four children.[3] In addition to Yocheved, born in 1924,[4] her sister Chana[5] is listed among the dead in the *Novogrudok Memorial Book*. A brother Hirsh, born in 1922, was evacuated to Uzbekistan in February 1942.[6] The identity of the fourth child remains unknown, although the possibility exists that this was Etel Tiles, who was together with Yocheved in the Novogrudok forced labor camp and the tunnel escape.

Etel Tiles's name does not appear in the compilation of Jewish partisans in Belorussia,[7] thus we can assume that she did not survive the escape. As for Yocheved Tiles, a search of genealogical, Holocaust-related and population databases has revealed no information on her whereabouts following the war.

Nachman Feifer (#167)

Our search to shed light on the fate of Novogrudok forced labor camp escapee Nachman Feifer emerged as a journey to discover a remarkable man who lived to rebuild his life with courage.

Our research indicated that Nachman Feifer, a photographer by profession, was born in 1911 in the small town of Jesow, near Lodz, Poland, to Nachman and Dina née Janosowicz.[1] In 1939, he fled Lodz for Novogrudok in Russian-controlled Belorussia. At the Nazi conquest of the area in June 1941, he was confined to the Novogrudok ghetto. Although Nachman appears on a 1943–1944 partisan list as having been single,[2] he was actually a young widower at the time. The names of Nachman,[3] his wife Sheva,[4] as well as their infant son Lipa, born sometime in 1942,[5] all appear on a list of those confined in the Karelich ghetto from May 20, 1942–June 20, 1942.[6] Although we did not find death records for Sheva and her newborn, we presume that they had been slaughtered in one of the widespread massacres at the time in Korelich or Novogrudok.

Nachman was conscripted by the Germans to the Novogrudok forced labor camp. Here, he survived the September 1943 tunnel escape and the difficult trek through the forest to become a member of the Bielski partisans.[7]

Following liberation, we are unaware of where Nachman spent the early postwar years until October 26, 1948, when he sailed first class (as "Aron N. Fajfer") from the Polish seaport of Gdynia aboard the MS (Motor Ship) *Batory* bound for New York City.[8] The *Batory* was one of the most famous ships in Polish maritime history. As a symbol of Polish emigration, it was not usual for the ship to carry Jewish Holocaust survivors.[9]

From the Montreal address listed as Nachman's destination on the ship's manifest, we learned of the relative who had sponsored his ticket: Nathan Feifer, who with his family operated a Montreal-based shoe business.[10] City directories showed that from 1949, Nachman, now "Aron Nathan Feifer," shared a residence with a family for many decades and that he was initially employed in various jobs before returning to the photography profession in the late 1950s.[11]

After searching for Nachman's next of kin for two years, we discovered an online obituary for Nathan Aron Feifer, listing his death in 1999 and naming among his survivors a sister, Theresa Gold, two nephews, and a niece.[12] We eventually learned that it was with these relatives that Nachman resided after his immigration to Canada.

With the help of a professional genealogist, we established contact with Nachman's niece Judy Gold, who resides in Montreal, and his nephew Dr. Howard Gold of Northampton, Massachusetts, a professor of government at Smith College.[13] Judy, a former member of the Human Rights Tribunal of Quebec, currently serves as Commissioner of the Office of Urban Projects for the city of Montréal. Although Nachman's sister Theresa is still alive, her poor hearing does not allow her to be interviewed.[14]

Both Judy and Howard describe their uncle as having been a "second father" to them from their births until his death on May 15, 1999. Known to them as Nathan, he is an indelible part of their memories of home and an integral part of the family. Both Judy and Howard use the same words to describe him: a "self-made intellectual," an avid reader of philosophy and history who frequently hosted intellectuals, artists, and diplomats.[15]

Despite his varied social contacts, Nachman reserved his closest friendships for other Holocaust survivors. Although he is said to have had many women friends, he never remarried. Until his death, Nachman kept a framed photo of his wife Sheva in his room. Sheva had been a photographer, and it was from her that Nachman learned the skills that ultimately enabled him to pursue a long career as a medical photographer in Montreal's Jewish General Hospital.

Albeit a self-taught man, Nachman was a great believer in excellence and education. He insisted that Howard, Judy, and their brother Mark, today a retired attorney, all take music lessons and excel in their studies. It was in this atmosphere of high aspirations that Theresa was inspired to become a cytotechnologist after many years as a housekeeper and stay-at-home mom.[16]

Judy describes her uncle as having been "the most generous person I ever, ever met." His generosity, she reports, extended not only to his family but to others as well, particularly to immigrants, Jews and non-Jews alike. Skillfully and enthusiastically, he helped find employment for the myriad individuals who turned to him for help.[17]

Vigorously involved with the present, Nachman did not dwell on the past and related very little about his wartime experiences. Beyond knowing that their uncle had escaped from a labor camp to the partisans, neither Judy nor Howard had ever heard of Novogrudok, the tunnel escape, or Nachman's having been a Bielski partisan. Although they knew that he'd lost his wife and child, they only learned the names of Sheva and baby Lipa from the author.[18]

With their father described as having been extremely busy with his shoe factory and working long hours before his death, Nachman's niece and nephew could not overestimate how much they cherished his involvement in their lives. Just as he was considered their "second father," Nachman delightedly took on the role of grandparent to Judy, Howard, and Mark's children born prior to his death on May 15, 1999.[19]

Judy and Howard are extremely grateful to have learned more about the man who was an inseparable part of their nuclear family, who gave so much to them as well as to others. We are grateful for learning about Nachman's postwar life and how the tunnel escape afforded him the opportunity to remain alive and contribute to the world. We take comfort in knowing that upon being reunited with his sister and becoming part of her family, this lone survivor of his family was not ever alone.

Nachman Feifer in 1947 document (courtesy of Howard Gold)

Chaya Sara Luska (#168)

Chaya Sara Luska was the sister of escapee Eliyahu (Elya) Berkowicz (#49),[1] to whom she owed her life. Thanks to his care and ingenuity, she overcame serious health issues to survive in hiding in the Novogrudok forced labor camp during the escape and ultimately to reach a partisan detachment.

Born in Novogrudok in either 1885, according to a partisan list,[2] or in 1900, according to International Committee of the Red Cross (ICRC) Tracing Services at Magen David Adom Israel documents,[3] Chaya Sara was the daughter of Dov (Berko), a shoemaker by trade,[4] and Perel-Malka née Dziecielska.[5] Besides her brother Eliyahu, Chaya Sara had two married sisters, Gitel Szuster and Beile Rozin. Gitel was murdered in the Novogrudok massacre of 1942[6] and Beile in the massacre of May 7, 1943.[7] Following Belle's death, her husband Zisel (#50) remained in the forced labor camp together with Chaya Sara and Elya.

A seamstress by trade, Chaya Sara resided in Novogrudok at 20 Pochtovaya Street.[8] Despite a thorough search of population and Holocaust-related databases, no details have been found relating to the identity or the fate of her husband and daughter. As 220 of the 278 entries in Yad Vashem's Central Database of Shoah Victims' Names for individuals with the surname "Lusky" from the Novogrudok area stemmed from Zhetl,[9] Chaya Sara's husband is likely to have been a member of the large Lusky clan from this small nearby town.

Although we are unaware of the fate of Chaya Sara's family during the war, since no documentation testifies to her reunion with any family member either during wartime or after liberation, it can be assumed that they did not survive. Her brother Eliyahu's Yad Vashem testimony related that while Chaya Sara was quite ill with a cough and heart condition in the labor camp, her daughter spoke to her in a dream, saying she would bring her berries that would help her recover. Chaya interpreted the dream as an encouraging sign that she would survive and reach the forest.[10]

It is only due to Eliyahu's care and foresight that Chaya Sara did survive to reach the forest. Once plans for the tunnel escape began to materialize, Eliyahu became fearful that his sister's heart condition would impede her ability to crawl through the tunnel. In his Yad Vashem testimony, he relates consulting with fellow inmate Shmuel Kolachek (#82), who also suffered from heart disease. Fortunately, Shmuel had meticulously planned and prepared a hiding place outfitted with provisions in the labor camp's warehouse loft for himself and his fourteen-year-old son Yisrael (#81). This makeshift hiding place became the refuge as well for Chaya Sara, Eliyahu, and their sister Beile's husband Zisel Rozin (#50) for a full eight days.[11]

When the five finally emerged to escape the now-abandoned labor camp site, Chaya Sara was so weak that she had to be carried through

the hole in the barbed wire used by the
police to trade with the inmates. During
their ensuing eight-day journey, Chaya
Sara somehow became separated from the
group. By the time she was found by Zisel
Rozin, she was so weak that she could
not speak and needed to be carried for
five miles through the Naliboki Forest to
the Bielski partisan detachment. Here she
and Eliyahu remained until liberation.[12]

Chaya Sara Luska, Germany,
1947 (courtesy of Yad
Vashem Archives, Jerusalem)

Together with Eliyahu and his newly
established family (details are found in
the report on Eliyahu Berkowicz [#49]),
Chaya Sara was repatriated to Poland
through Lodz. After a two-month stay in Berlin, Chaya Sara was
transferred in March 1946 to the Eschwege Displaced Persons Camp[13]
located in a former German Air Force base in the Frankfurt District
of the American-occupied zone.[14] In May 1947, Eliyahu and family
departed for Marseille to await their ship to Palestine.[15] As for Chaya
Sara, with the exception of two periods of hospitalization at the displaced persons hospital in Merzhausen, she remained in the Eschwege
DP Camp until September 1949.[16]

Documents indicate that Chaya Sara settled in Kiryat Motzkin after
arriving in Israel more than a year after the immigration of Eliyahu and
his family.[17]

Upon discovering the whereabouts of Eliyahu's children shortly
before publication, we learned that Eliyahu continued to care for her
until the day of her death. Continuing to suffer from heart disease even
after her arrival in Israel, she lived with Eliyahu and his family during
the last period of her life. She was buried in Tel Aviv's Kiryat Shaul synagogue upon her death on May 4, 1953.[18]

Chaya Sarah's grave continues to be visited by her nephew Chaim,
who still remembers his sickly aunt who suffered and lost so much.[19]

Eliezer (Leizer) Shleimovich (#169)

Of the thirty-nine sources in Yad Vashem's Central Database of Shoah Victims' Names for individuals from throughout Poland with the surname Shleimovich, there is no one with the given name Eliezer or Leizer.[1]

Unfortunately, we have no information regarding this Novogrudok forced labor camp escapee, nor do we know if he was related to Naum Shleimovich (#66) of Novogrudok, who survived to become a Bielski partisan.

Since the name Eliezer Shleimovich is not listed in the compilation of Jewish partisans in Belorussia from 1941 to 1944,[2] we can only assume that he was not among those who survived the tunnel escape.

Galai (#170)

Yad Vashem's Central Database of Shoah Victims' Names contains fifty-eight sources for individuals with the surname Galai who originated from the Novogrudok area alone. There are 146 entries for Shoah victims named Galai from throughout Poland. All were reported as having been murdered.[1]

As we do not know the proper name of the Novogrudok forced labor camp inmate Galai, and as there is no one with this surname who appears in the compilation of Jewish partisans,[2] we can only assume that he or she did not survive the tunnel escape. It is possible that this escapee is one of the murdered individuals whose name appears in Yad Vashem's central database.

Shtein (#171)

It is impossible for us to know the identity of the escapee, male or female, listed only by the surname "Shtein," with no given name indicated. Yad Vashem's Central Database of Shoah Victims' Names includes no fewer than 6,737 entries for persons with the prevalent Jewish surname Shtein (Stein) who resided in or were murdered in Poland during World War II. This number includes 254 entries for individuals from Belorussia – 132 from the Novogrudok area alone.[1]

The absence of a proper name makes it impossible for us to explore whether the escapee Shtein was a refugee from central Poland who fled to the Novogrudok area following the 1939 Nazi invasion, or whether he or she was a native Belarusian.

Only six individuals with the surname Shtein appear in the compilation of Jewish partisans in Belorussia.[2] Unfortunately, we have no way of knowing whether the 171st person in line to crawl through the tunnel and escape the Novogrudok forced labor camp is included among these six survivors.

Faivel Skora (#172)

As Faivel Skora's name appears crossed out on the escape list, it is uncertain whether he actually escaped through the tunnel. The fact that his name was struck out may mean that he somehow escaped prior to the breakout, that he was murdered in the interim between the recording of the list and the actual escape, or that his position was changed on the escape list and is one of the currently illegible names.

Faivel Skora was born on April 11, 1907, and lived in Lodz both prior to and during the war. He lived at 6 Schoner Street before the war, and records show that his wartime address in the Lodz ghetto was 36 Hamburger Street, apt. 4. Although nothing is known about his family of origin or his familial status at the time of the war, it is likely that Sara Rivka Eichler née Skora, two years younger than Faivel, was a sister, as she is listed as having resided at the same prewar and wartime addresses.[1]

Although we cannot be certain that Faivel exited the tunnel, we can surmise that he did not survive the Holocaust. His name does not appear on the list of partisans in Belorussia in the years 1941–1944.[2]

Berl (#173) and Yosef (Yosel, #174) Gertzovski

Up until the 1941 Nazi occupation of Belorussia that led to their brutal deaths, the Gertzovski family of Zhetl had reached a measure of success. Yosef (Yosel) Gertzovski, a Zhetl native born in 1888,[1] and his wife Asnat, two years his junior,[2] operated a kiosk[3] selling light refreshments, seltzer,[4] and more. Their son Berl, born in 1916,[5] ran a popular coffee shop. Their daughter Henia, born in 1914,[6] was a newly married clerk by 1941.[7]

As a youth, Berl had been a member of the Socialist-Zionist Hashomer Hatzair youth movement.[8] As an adult, he appears in a photo with members of the Zhetl branch of Agudas Yisrael, an Orthodox religious movement.[9] And although over eight decades had passed, Fanya Dunetz (#142) still remembered being a steady ice cream cone customer in Berl's coffee shop as a child. She described Berl as having been a mild-mannered bachelor whose sister Henia was a friend of her sister Shifra.[10]

Asnat, the matriarch of the family, was the first to be murdered,[11] most likely in one of the two 1942 massacres of the thousands of Jews forced into the Zhetl ghetto.

Both Berl and Yosef were conscripted into the Novogrudok forced labor camp. Fanya Dunetz recalled that there, she and Berl shared the same tier of "beds." Fanya slept on the top plank and Berl on the bottom.[12] Additionally, Zalman Gertzovski (#117), a cousin of Yosef and fellow Zhetl native, was also assigned to the labor camp.

During their brave attempt to break out of the camp, Berl led the way through the tunnel with Yosef crouched just behind him. Tragically, both father[13] and son[14] were slain.

In their deaths, Yosef and Berl were spared the horrific details of their daughter and sister Henia's murder the following year. Her husband Nachum Shochet testified that Henia was a partisan at the time she was caught and killed by the retreating Germans in 1944.[15] Her close childhood friend Sara Epstein Shoer elaborated that while serving as a partisan, Henia was burnt alive in Zhetl by the Nazis.[16] Sara's daughter Ruthi Begin notes that her mother had learned the circumstances of Henia's death from surviving partisans and often spoke of how just one day prior to liberation, Henia's agonizing death screams had pierced the air from the center of Zhetl all the way to the forest.[17]

The murder of this entire family – Asnat, Yosef, Berl, and Henia Gertzovski – is commemorated in the memorial book of Zhetl.[18]

Shmuel (#175) and Moshe (#176) Paretzki

Eight decades after father and son Moshe and Shmuel Paretzki were conscripted to the Novogrudok forced labor camp, their very identity has been a challenge to decipher.

Ironically, Shmuel and Moshe's names were evidently penned on the escape list as #175 and #176 respectively in a space later to be covered by transparent tape. In time, the ink beneath the tape completely faded from the fragile paper, making those lines illegible. Yet the name "Yisrael Paretzki" is scrawled on the side of the copy of the original escape list in a handwriting definitely unlike that of the original transcriber Yitzchak Rosenhaus (#30).

No one named Yisrael Paretzki appears in the Zhetl memorial book's necrology list,[1] nor does the name exist in the compilation of Jewish partisans from Belorussia.[2] Moreover, Zhetl survivors Fanya Dunetz (#142)[3] and Chaya Magid[4] have no recollection of an individual named Yisrael Paretzki who resided in the town.

Thus, with no Yisrael Paretzki appearing in any of the available resources, it is likely that this "overwrite" of the name was an erroneous postwar attempt to reconstruct illegible parts of the list. However, thanks to eyewitness testimony from fellow labor camp inmate Pesia Mayevski (#160) stating that Moshe and Shmuel Paretzki of Zhetl were among the escapees,[5] we can safely deduce that these are indeed the illegible names. As for their order, Shmuel (apparently incorrectly written as "Yisrael" later on the list) was likely placed behind his father Moshe in the line to escape from the tunnel.

Sadly, neither Shmuel[6] nor Moshe[7] survived the tunnel escape.

Moshe Paretzki, a tailor by trade, was born in 1882, according to a Russian list of murdered individuals from Zhetl.[8] Pesia Mayevski, however, notes that Moshe was born in 1887.[9] He was married to Gnesha,[10] a housewife born in 1889.[11] Besides Shmuel, the couple had a daughter, Raisl (Roza), a seamstress.[12]

As for Shmuel, Pesia Mayevski gives his year of birth as 1912,[13] while his cousin Aaron Razvaski lists the date as 1917.[14] Like his father and sister, Shmuel worked as a tailor. Shmuel was married to Esther Rivka née Razvaski. Their three-year-old daughter Chana (Moshe's only grandchild) was murdered together with her mother,[15] her aunt Raisl Paretzki,[16] grandmother Gnesha, and both maternal grandparents in Zhetl's second massacre on August 6, 1942.[17]

The names of Moshe, Gnesha, Shmuel, and Raisl Paretzki are all commemorated in *Pinkas Zhetl*. Shmuel's name is noted as "Mula."[18]

At their deaths, Moshe and Shmuel Paretzki were likely the last remnants of their immediate families.

Yitzchak Mazurkevich (#177)

Yitzchak Mazurkevich was one of the Novogrudok forced labor camp inmates with whom fellow escapee Chaim Leibowitz (#91) writes of having spent the first twenty-four hours after the breakout. The others in the group included a cobbler from Makrec named Chanan, as well as Shlomo (#123) and Chana Rybak (#124) of Novogrudok.[1]

Leibowitz relates an incident in which a farmer they encountered refused the escapees' plea for food. Mazurkevich, he notes, smoothly salvaged the situation by pointing a wooden gun straight at the farmer, who, promptly provided two large loaves of bread, about a kilo each (2.2 pounds).[2]

"Yitzchak Mazurkevich Aronovich," as he appears on a partisan list, lived in Novogrudok prior to the war. He was the son of Aaron, a merchant, and the paternal grandson of Zelig and Lea.[3] His sister Yehudit testified that Aaron, born in Skernovich in 1880, lived in Warsaw before the war and met his death in the Warsaw ghetto.[4]

Details are unknown for Yitzchak's marital status or profession before the war. Although he survived the tunnel escape, Yitzchak Mazurkevich did not survive the forest. He was killed as a fighter in the First Baranovichskaya Brigade on December 8, 1943;[5] his death as a partisan is corroborated in a Page of Testimony.[6]

Tanchum Epshtein (#178)

Tanchum Epshtein, a miller by trade, was born in Zhetl in 1897 to Moshe and Feiga.[1] He was married to Sara Rivka née Senderovski, a housewife from Zhetl.[2] Yitzchak, the oldest of the couple's three children, was born in 1922 and worked as a miller like his father.[3] Chaya, born in 1924, was a student.[4] Sheina, the youngest child, was twelve years old – the traditional bat mitzvah age – at the time of her murder together with her mother and siblings on August 6, 1942.[5]

Following the war, surviving relatives assumed that Tanchum had been slaughtered with the rest of his immediate family: in Yad Vashem Pages of Testimony, his sister-in-law testified that he was killed in Novogrudok in 1942,[6] and his niece recorded the date of his murder in Zhetl as the same day as that of his wife and children.[7]

Although he lived one additional year after having been conscripted to the Novogrudok forced labor camp, Tanchum, the last member of his family to remain alive, was not destined to survive the war. His death in the tunnel escape is noted by fellow escapee Pesia Mayevski (#160) in her account of the breakout.[8]

The names of Tanchum Epshtein and his family are commemorated in *Pinkas Zhetl*, the town's memorial book.

Betzalel (Tsala) Bielitski (#179)

Although two different Pages of Testimony contend that Betzalel "Tsala" Bielitski was murdered in Zhetl's second slaughter on August 6, 1942,[1] an eyewitness testimony from fellow escapee Pesia Mayevski (#160) confirms that Tsala was among those Zhetlers who took part in the tunnel escape on September 26, 1943.[2]

Tsala, a carpenter born in 1907,[3] was the son of Zelig and Chana (Cheinke), a housewife born in 1884 who was killed in Vilna during the Holocaust.[4] A Yad Vashem testimony submitted by her cousin notes that Cheinke was the mother of five children.[5] Ultimately, Tsala was the last to remain alive. The Zhetl massacres took the lives of three: Sula Berman, who met her death along with her three children;[6] Mordechai, a bachelor,[7] and Matilda (Matla) Ogolnik, who was killed with her daughters Beila, age two, and Gitel, age six.[8] Tsala's sister Chaya Shteinhaus, a nurse married to Moshe, was murdered in the pits of Ponar, Vilna, in 1943.[9]

Tsala Bielitski and his wife Sara, a seamstress born in 1911,[10] were the parents of a five-year-old boy named Zelig, who was killed in one of the Zhetl massacres,[11] probably on August 6, 1942, when his mother was murdered.[12] Considering that Jewish custom frowns upon naming after the living, this little boy having been named for his grandfather probably indicates that Tzala's father died before the war.

Tsala's carpentry skills enabled him to be spared murder in the Zhetl massacres by being conscripted to the Novogrudok forced labor camp. Here he joined his brother-in-law and fellow carpenter Leib Berman (#211), widower of Sula. Although Tsala and Leib are not mentioned by name, many written accounts have lauded the exceptional contribution that the carpenters made in building the clandestine tunnel.[13]

Apparently the very last member of both his family of origin and his own immediate family to remain alive, Tsala did not survive the tunnel escape. His death is commemorated in *Pinkas Zhetl*.[14]

Leib Daichovski (#180)

The bittersweet Hebrew song "You Wait for Me and I'll Come Back," a revival of an emotional Russian World War II song by the same name, was made popular in Israel in 1974 after the Hebrew words were translated from a poem composed by the Soviet war poet Konstantin Simonov.[1] It was this song that, for years, tore at the heartstrings of Roza Dzencholski, the sole surviving child of escapee Leib Daichovski. Although Leib had seemingly disappeared during World War II, Roza never gave up hope that her beloved father would one day return.

The family mystery was solved at last in 2008 during a memorial meeting of the Association of Zhetl Survivors in Israel when the author spoke about her recent trip to Zhetl and Novogrudok. Describing her attempts to decipher the contents of the barely legible tunnel escape list, she announced the names of several Zhetlers – including Leib Daichovski – that appear on the list. At the close of the meeting, a small, visibly shocked woman timidly approached the podium to introduce herself as Fanya, the granddaughter of Leib Daichovski. Only now had she learned for the first time that Leib had been incarcerated in the Novogrudok forced labor camp and killed in his attempt to flee through the tunnel (as proven by the absence of his name on any partisan roster[2]). And now she knew that he had died as a hero at age fifty-four, one of the oldest escapees.

Leib Daichovski was born to Raishke (Rose) in 1889 in the town of Baranovich. Although his father died at a young age, he managed to teach his son the art of his shoemaking trade. Leib and his wife Leah née Rabinovich[3] were parents to Roza, her paternal grandmother's namesake, who was born in Zhetl in 1913,[4] and Shulamit, born in Teraspol, Poland, in 1920.[5] Leah was murdered in Zhetl's second slaughter on August 6, 1942,[6] and Shulamit, a single nurse at her death, was murdered during 1942.[7]

At the outbreak of the war, daughter Roza was living in Warsaw with her husband Noach Dzhencholski and young Fanya, who was born in the Polish capital in 1937. The three were miraculously saved by fleeing to Gorkovskaya Oblast on the Siberian border just before the Nazi occupation. Repatriated to Poland after the war, they later relocated to Estonia. Three years after Noach's death in 1956, Roza and Fanya immigrated to Israel, where Fanya married. She had two daughters, Lilach and Iris.[8]

Leib Daichovski, during a stay in Argentina, 1924–1929 (courtesy of Lilach Yudelevich Ron and Iris Yudelevich Chatami)

Fanya speaks poignantly of a childhood lived in the shadow of her mother's longing for Leib while she listened wistfully to "You Wait for Me and I'll Come Back." Somehow, she recalls, the song gave voice to her mother's dream to someday be reunited with her father.[9] In 1999, just four years before her own death, Roza filed a Yad Vashem Page of Testimony for her father at last, listing his date of death as 1942 under the assumption that he had been slaughtered in one of Zhetl's two mass killings that year.[10] Yet the agonizing lack of hard evidence surrounding his death remained a constant source of pain and mystery.[11]

Although he could never have imagined this, his two great-grand-daughters and several great-great-grandchildren[12] will now be able to tell his story to future generations.

Abram (#181) and Moshe (#182) Milovanski

Abram Milovanski, a saddler, was born in 1898 and resided in Zhetl. He and his wife Guta, a housewife born in 1900,[1] raised three sons, each born three years apart. The eldest, Moshe, was born in 1928,[2] followed by Yakov[3] and Yitzchak.[4]

The names of Abram, Moshe, Yakov, and Yitzchak Milovanski appear on a Soviet list of persecuted individuals from Zhetl as having been murdered in 1941–1942, yet in actuality, both Abram and Moshe survived Zhetl's 1942 massacres to be conscripted to the Novogrudok forced labor camp.

Both father and son attempted to flee to freedom in the tunnel escape. Abram led the way, with Moshe crawling immediately behind him. Yet, as neither name appears in the compilation of partisan fighters, it appears that neither survived to reach the safety of the forest.[5] Moshe, the oldest son, was just fifteen years old at the time of his murder.

Yedidia Ochonovski (#183)

Yedidia Ochonovski, born in either 1906[1] or 1907,[2] was the son of Leah.[3] Although we cannot be certain, evidently his wife was Sara, born in 1909, whose name appears directly below his own on a Russian list of murdered individuals from Zhetl.[4] The two were parents to a son and a daughter.[5] As for his occupation, Yedidia is alternatively listed as having been a yeshiva student[6] and a carpenter.[7]

Although Yedidia was reported to have been killed in Zhetl during the years 1941–1942,[8] his name on the escape list proves that in truth he was interned in the Novogrudok forced labor camp until the breakout on September 26, 1943. Chaya Magid, a fellow Zhetler and widow of escapee Avraham Magid, surmises that Yedidia was kept alive through all the massacres thanks to his carpentry skills being of use to the Germans.[9] Ironically for the Germans, eyewitness accounts shed light on the substantial contribution the inmate carpenters made to the complex construction of the escape tunnel.[10]

The last member of his family to survive, Yedidia Ochonovski was slain during the tunnel escape. He is commemorated in *Pinkas Zhetl*.[11]

Chaim Shlachtman (#184)

Chaim Shlachtman was born in 1902[1] in Siedlitz,[2] a town near Warsaw. He moved to Novogrudok following his marriage to Sara ("Sorke") née Sladovski,[3] who had grown up on the town's Racelo Street. Chaim and Sorke were the parents of Yosef[4] and Bella,[5] both born in 1927, and Moishele, born in 1930.[6] Their neighbor Idel Kagan (#95) recalls that the Shlachtman family was one of the poorest in their neighborhood and often the recipients of the Kagan family's used clothing.[7]

While Sorke is described as having been shy and reserved, Chaim was the direct opposite in character. With her husband frequently unemployed, Sorke supported the family by running their small shop, which sold kerosene, ceramics, and wagon oil. When the Kagans opened a shoe shop, they provided Chaim with work to help boost his family's income.[8]

Chaim was said to have been estranged from his family in Siedlitz. Fifty years after the fact, Idel Kagan recalls how in a moment of severe financial desperation, Chaim sent a cable to his parents notifying them of their "dear son's" impending death. Upon their arrival two days later, he was found on the floor, feigning death under a sheet with candles near his head. In Idel's words:

> When his parents saw the "body," they began to cry and wail. Suddenly a miracle occurred: Chaim was resurrected.
>
> He arose and announced that he had not been admitted to the Kingdom of Heaven, but rather had been sent back to earth to provide for his family, save his children from starvation, and deliver a message to his parents: if they wanted to live to a ripe old age, they must help and support Chaim and his family. His mother fainted, and his father took out a sum of 100 zlotys and gave it to Sorke. They left without saying goodbye, returned to Siedlitz, and never came back.[9]

Although Chaim's daughter Bella is listed as "Sima," the entire family is reported in a Soviet-initiated report to have been murdered during the years 1941–1942.[10] The fact that Chaim Shlachtman's name appears on the Novogrudok forced labor camp escape list, however, proves that he had been conscripted to the camp and was alive in September 1943. Although she cannot recall her source with certainty, Director of the Jewish Resistance Museum in Novogrudok Tamara Vershitskaya claims having been told (in all probability by Idel Kagan) that Chaim was killed in the short period between the drafting of the list and the tunnel escape on September 26, 1943.[11] In any case, although Chaim's name does not appear among those who reached the forest to join a partisan detachment,[12] he was certainly present in the camp long enough to have lent a hand in digging the tunnel that enabled so many others to remain alive.

Rafael Lusky (#185)

The son of Pinchas, an innkeeper from Zhetl,[1] and Chana (Chenia),[2] Rafael Lusky had four siblings: Yitzchak (Itsel), Neta Moshe, David, and Arie-Leibel. After Chana's death, Pinchas was remarried in 1910 to Esther Hinda, a widow with two children. Their three children were Idel, Rachel, and Chaim. Of all of Pinchas' children, only Arie and Chaim remained alive after the Holocaust, thanks to having immigrated to Palestine in the 1930s.[3]

Rafael Lusky was born in Zhetl in 1898.[4] A carpenter by trade, he was married before the war to Liba née Beniaminovich, a seamstress.[5] The couple had two children, Avigdor,[6] born in 1924, and his sister Chana.[7]

Rafael was spared death by virtue of his skills as a carpenter, which were essential to the German Army. Assigned to the Novogrudok forced labor camp, he no doubt played a major role in constructing the clandestine tunnel along with the other inmate carpenters. However, Rafael did not survive the escape. Nor did his two fellow carpenters Yedidia Ochonovski (#183) and Chaim Shlachtman (#184), who crawled through the tunnel before him.

Rafael's incarceration in the labor camp and his participation in the 1943 tunnel escape were unknown to the relatives and friend who completed Yad Vashem Pages of Testimony in his name, listing his date of death as either unknown or 1942.[8]

A search for relatives who completed such Pages of Testimony led the author to Rafael's first cousin Yehuda Lusky, son of Rafael's paternal uncle Moshe, who died in Zhetl prior to the war. Already orphaned from both his parents, fifteen-year-old Yehuda immigrated to Palestine with his stepmother in May 1932, where he was reunited with a sister who had come in the 1920s. Over a hundred years old at the time of this writing in February 2018, Yehuda can still give an avid description of his uncle Pinchas's household, noting that Pinchas owned an inn used primarily by non-Jews who came through Zhetl to sell their wares. There he would provide his customers with food and drink, a place to hitch their horses and park the carriages in which they would usually sleep, as well as a room to rent if they wished. Yehuda claims that Pinchas's inn was so well known throughout the area that whenever they would travel outside Zhetl, his family would be identified by the Gentile population as "Pinchas Lusky's kin."[9]

Rafael's half-brother Chaim, who immigrated to pre-state Israel in the 1930s, followed the family tradition to become the owner and proprietor of a hotel in Tel Aviv. Hotel Lusky, adjacent to the Mediterranean Sea, is operating to this day.[10]

Chaim Lusky was completely unaware of his brother Rafael's participation in the tunnel escape. In a diary he wrote prior to his death in 1999,[11] Chaim recorded the deaths of Rafael, his wife, and his son (although he omitted mention of their daughter) as having taken place in Zhetl's second mass slaughter on August 6, 1942. He described Rafael, sixteen years his senior, as having been quiet and irritable, strong and muscular, and quite preoccupied as a young adult with his girlfriend Leiba Chana, whom he married in his late twenties. During the Russian Revolution, Chaim wrote, Rafael demonstrated in favor of the Bolsheviks, an incident which nearly led to his imprisonment. In Chaim's view, Rafael did not appear to like his stepmother, nor did he enjoy a close relationship with Chaim.[12]

The author was also able to make contact with Rafael's niece and nephew, children of Rafael's brother Arie, who died in Israel in 1997.[13] Dr. Moshe Lusky, an ophthalmologist,[14] as well as his sister Ziva Falek[15] expressed amazement at learning of the tunnel escape and that their uncle was a participant. Both stated that their father, who worked as a housepainter, never spoke to them or to their brother Pinchas about his past in Zhetl, nor of those he left behind who were murdered. Ziva relates that she only overheard the name of her uncle Rafael from her mother.

Yehuda, probably the only person alive who can intimately recall the original Lusky home in Zhetl, has no pictures from his childhood in which Rafael might appear. In fact, he expresses his doubts as to whether there were any photographers whatsoever in Zhetl over a century ago.[16]

Rafael Lusky (*mustached man standing to the right of the woman*) at his brother Natan Moshe's funeral, Zhetl, 1934 (courtesy of Moshe Lusky)

Moshe Gorodynski (#186) and Gorodynski (#187)

Moshe Gorodynski, born in 1887 in Karelich, was the father of escapee Shlomo Gorodynski (#87),[1] and a great-uncle to escapees Sonya (#78) and Shaul (#77) Gorodynski.[2] Directly behind Moshe, the escape list notes simply the surname "Gorodynski" for the person slated to follow Moshe in crawling through the tunnel. Although we can assume that he or she was a close relative, the lack of a proper name makes it quite complex to determine this person's identity.

Prior to the war, Moshe and his family had resided in Karelich where he worked as a tailor.[3] Apparently, all of his children, with the exception of Shlomo, were brutally murdered in Novogrudok in 1942. In Shlomo's Pages of Testimony for his father and siblings, he notes that his brothers Yitzchak, aged fourteen,[4] and Avraham, aged ten,[5] as well as his two-year-old sister Rachel were all slain in 1942.[6]

Although we have no information on Moshe's first wife, Rachel née Moshkovitz, or on the identity of her children,[7] we learn from Shlomo that his stepmother Miriam née Krinki, born in 1900,[8] was murdered along with her son Shaul, born in 1932.[9]

As a tailor, Moshe was spared death to be conscripted to the Novogrudok forced labor camp. On the carefully planned tunnel escape list, Moshe's son Shlomo, niece Sonya, and nephew Shaul were all assigned numbers nearly a hundred places ahead of Moshe. The mystery remains as to the identity of the person in line to follow Moshe, the probable relative with the Gorodynski surname with whom his fate was tied in their attempt to escape to freedom. Was it perhaps Esther Gorodynski of Mir, the daughter of Faivel, who became a partisan?[10] Or perhaps one of Moshe's children, or even his wife Miriam?

We may never know the identity of escapee #187. Unless it was indeed Esther, we may assume that this unknown Gorodynski was killed along with Moshe in the aftermath of the tunnel escape. Moshe was fifty-six years old at his death.[11] Miraculously, Shlomo, Sonya, and Shaul Gorodynski all successfully fled through the tunnel to reach the Bielski partisans and survive the war.[12]

Moshe (#188) and Nechama (#189) Rolnik

Unfortunately, we have very little information regarding Moshe Rolnik and nearly no information whatsoever for Nechama Rolnik.

Among the scant facts known about Moshe is that he was the son of Yosel,[1] resided on Komsomolskaya Street in Ivenets, was married to Rachel,[2] and belonged to the extensive Rolnik clan of Ivenets. The Ivenets memorial book names Moshe, Rachel, and "their children" among those massacred in the Shoah. Only forty-eight people with the Rolnik surname have proper names noted in the book, along with an undetermined number of family members whose first names could not be recalled.[3]

Moshe Rolnik did not survive the tunnel escape from the Novogrudok forced labor camp to which he was conscripted. In addition to his name appearing in the Ivenets memorial book, "Movsha" Rolnik appears in a compilation of the murdered, along with an itemization of property damages, prepared in December 1944 by the Soviet Extraordinary State Commission.[4] This commission was established in November 1942 to investigate damages caused by the Nazis and their collaborators in the former Soviet Union.

Though Moshe was killed, there is a possibility that at least one of his children survived the Holocaust. A notation for Mateush Moiseyevich Rolnik, born in Ivenets in 1927, appears in the compilation of Jewish partisans in Belorussia.[5] The patronymic, derived from the father's first name, would indicate that Mateush was the son of Moisey, which corresponds to Moshe in Russian.

Although Moshe crawled out of the tunnel immediately in front of Nechama Rolnik during the breakout, we are unaware of the relationship between the two. Her name does not appear in Yad Vashem's Central Database of Shoah Victims' Names, nor in the Ivenets memorial book list of the murdered, although she may be one of the many unidentified Rolnik family members noted there.[6] As her name is also not included in the compilation of Jewish partisans in Belorussia,[7] we can assume that Nechama, too, did not survive to reach the forest.

Were it not for the Novogrudok forced labor camp escape list and this research, the name of Nechama Rolnik is likely to have been erased from all memory.

Natan (Nota) Goberman (#190)

Natan (Nota) Goberman was born in 1888 to Moshe, a carpenter. By the age of eight, Nota was already working as a carpenter as well. After serving in the Polish Army from 1911 to 1918, he returned to his carpentry profession, joining a Soviet cooperative association in September 1939.[1]

The sole information we have obtained on Nota's immediate family is found in his son Mikhail's personal military records stored near Leningrad. These documents note that Nota's full name was Yakov Nota Movshovich and that he was married to Bella, a housewife sixteen years his junior. Besides Mikhail, the couple had at least two other children, Yura, born in 1931, and Eva, born in 1936.

Both Nota and his young teenage son Mikhail were conscripted to the Novogrudok forced labor camp in August 1941.[2] Nota's skills as a carpenter (and perhaps those of Mikhail as well), which were of significant value to the German Army, had enabled him to escape death by qualifying for the labor camp. Here he most certainly joined other inmate carpenters in their major role in the complex construction of the tunnel.[3]

Natan (Nota) Goberman, Novogrudok, undated prewar drawing (courtesy of Tamara Vershitskaya)

Tragically, Bella, Yura, and Eva are all reported to have been murdered on May 7, 1943,[4] the date of the fourth and last slaughter in Novogrudok.

In early 1943, sixteen-year-old Mikhail succeeded in his own brave escape to the Bielski partisan detachment,[5] where he was finally reunited with his father following the breakout.

Nota Goberman was wounded in battle with the Germans two months before being liberated from the forest. After returning to Novogrudok in July 1944, by the year's end he was once again working as a carpenter in a cooperative association, this time in Tikhvin. He is said to have continued to work until five days before his death at age sixty-three on August 30, 1951.[6]

Much of the information related above appeared in the extract of an article prepared by Russian historian and researcher Galina Smielova,[7] which had been sent many years ago to Tamara Vershitskaya, then director of the Jewish Resistance Museum in Novogrudok. To date, our attempts to contact Ms. Smielova for assistance in locating possible descendants of Nota have been unsuccessful.

Samuil (#191) and Eliezer (Leizer, #192) Zusmanovich

Born in January 1934, Eliezer (Leizer) Zusmanovich was only eight and a half years old at the time of the tunnel escape.[1] His story is intertwined with that of his father Samuil, who was determined to save the life of Leizer, his last surviving child, against staggering odds. Using wit and cunning, Samuil succeeded in hiding Leizer in the Novogrudok forced labor camp.[2] This extraordinary feat took place against the backdrop of the May 7, 1943, massacre in which nearly every young child in the camp had been slaughtered along with his or her mother. (Only one child younger than Leizer, six-year-old Mordechai Maloshitzki [#148], is known to have participated in the tunnel escape as well.)

Samuil, born in 1896, lived prior to the war in Novogrudok, where he made his living as a shoemaker.[3] Other than Leizer, every member of Samuil's immediate family – his wife Rachel, daughter Esther, and sons Hirsh Tzvi and Yisrael – was killed, most probably in the May 7 massacre.[4]

As young as he was, little Leizer played an important role in the secret construction of the tunnel. The child duly removed the dug-out dirt from the tunnel site all night, every night, racing to spill it out in the designated hiding places before daybreak when the tunnel diggers would return to their jobs in the labor camp workshops.[5]

Describing the escape itself in the 2014 documentary film *Tunnel of Hope*, then eighty-year-old Leizer recalls his still-vivid memories of the miraculous event. According to his description, each escapee awaited his turn to enter the tunnel in utter silence, yet the breakout itself felt like a fleeting experience that was over almost as soon as it began. In the darkness and the rain, the little boy set off in the wrong direction after scrambling out of the tunnel. Almost incredulously, his father found him in the pitch-black night to rescue him once again. Leizer recounts how he and Samuil then began a long trek to the safety of the Kaminka Forest and their first encounter with the Bielski partisans.[6] There, father and son remained for a time before Samuil joined the leading Russian Roshcha partisan detachment,[7] taking Leizer with him. Fellow inmate Mordechai Majerowicz, who also became a Roshcha partisan, testifies that his small band of escapees making their way to the detachment consisted of a nine-year-old boy and three other men carrying hand-made wooden "guns."[8] The child was undoubtedly young Leizer, and one of the men was surely Samuil.

Following liberation, Leizer and Samuil returned to Novogrudok before moving to the nearby town of Ivie, where Samuil searched for work.[9] Yad Vashem's Central Database of Shoah Victims' Names contains numerous listings for Holocaust victims from Ivie with the surname Zusmanovich,[10] thus it is possible that Samuil had known the town from relatives and decided to return there with Leizer.

The two later proceeded to Vilna, where Leizer attended school for the first time in his life. In time, he joined the Soviet military and served a three-year stint. Samuil, meanwhile, had resettled in Lithuania, where he died in 1958. According to his grandson and namesake Shmuel, at his death Samuil was a totally broken man, both emotionally and physically.[11]

At around the age of twenty-five, Leizer met his wife, the former Frieda Kabas, in Vilna. Frieda was born in Ponevezh, raised in Vilna, and spent the war years in Uzbekistan. Leizer and Frieda's first child Rachel was born in Israel in 1961, one year after her parents' immigration. Today, Rachel is a high school English teacher and guidance counselor and the mother of two. Shmuel, born in 1965, is an accountant and the father of three.[12] As of August 2023, Leizer is the grandfather of five and the great-grandfather of two.[13]

Leizer refused to be interviewed for this research, for fear that talking about the war and recalling his traumatic past would be too much of an emotional burden.[14] Declaring in the *Tunnel of Hope* documentary that the cries and screams of those selected for death during the May 7 massacre remain forever etched in his memory,[15] Leizer takes pains to avoid intensifying the horrifying nightmares that he suffers.[16] In his stead, Shmuel has provided much of the information for his father's story.

Shmuel relates that as he was growing up, his father did not utter one word about his Holocaust experiences. The first time Leizer provided basic biographical details of his life was only several years ago, for a school project for one of his grandchildren. Allowing himself to be interviewed for the *Tunnel of Hope* film was a true breakthrough for him, marking the first and only time that his family heard of what he had endured. Since the interviews for the documentary, Leizer has never again spoken of the war.[17]

Despite his very turbulent youth and sparse education, Leizer Zusmanovich rose to become a power station shift manager at the Israel Electric Company, Israel's largest electrical supplier. Against all odds, this eight-and-a-half-year-old tunnel escapee succeeded in life to build a family and contribute to the State of Israel.

Samuil Zusmanovich,
undated postwar photo
(courtesy of Shmuel
Zusmanovitch)

Eliezer (Leizer)
Zusmanovich in the Soviet
Navy, 1952–1953 (courtesy
of Samuel Zusmanovitch)

Abram (#193) and Notek (#194) Chernevich

Following our research, it appears that the proper names "Aaron" and "Moshe" Chernevich as written on the escape list are incorrect. Instead, we posit that the actual names of these Novogrudok forced labor camp inmates were Abram and Notek Chernevich, based on the following: the one individual from Poland named Aaron Chernevich listed in the Central Database of Shoah Victims' Names was a resident of Warsaw born in 1880. According to a Page of Testimony submitted by his niece, Aaron and his wife Sara were both murdered in Treblinka.[1]

Correspondingly, the two listings for Moshe Chernevich in the central database are also for residents of central Poland. Moshe Chernevich from Ostrow Mazowieka, fifty-five miles northwest of Warsaw, is highly unlikely to have been conscripted to the labor camp due to his advanced age of around seventy years.[2] The second Moshe Chernevich is reported by his widow to have resided in the village of Komorow, nine miles outside of Warsaw, before being murdered in the Ukraine.[3]

It is therefore safe to assume that Aaron and Moshe were erroneously listed as the 193rd and 194th escapees to crawl through the tunnel. Neither Aaron nor Moshe appears on the list of partisans in Belorussia.[4]

We suggest that the correct names are Abram and Notek Chernevich, which appear along with most of the tunnel survivors on the list of those who reached the Bielski partisans immediately after the September 1943 escape.[5] They are also listed in the compilation of Jewish partisans in Belorussia from 1941 to 1944.[6]

Abram Chernevich, son of Shmuel, was a tailor born in 1908 who is listed as having lived in Novogrudok prior to the war at 5 Mitzkevich

Street.[7] His son Notek, born in 1930,[8] was just thirteen when he survived the tunnel escape to join the Bielski partisans. As they are the only two people from Novogrudok with the surname Chernevich listed in the central database, it is likely that Abram and Notek were not native to the city and arrived as refugees from central Poland in the wake of the German occupation in 1939.

To date, a search of genealogical, Holocaust-related, and population databases has failed to reveal information on the postwar life and whereabouts of Abram or Notek Chernevich. Quite possibly, the father and son remained in the former Soviet Union, where it is difficult to obtain vital records and genealogical data.

Henia Yarmovski (#195)

Rabbi Jonathan Sacks, the late philosopher and Chief Rabbi of England, speaks of the miracle that can occur when "a hand reaches out and pulls you to safety, and the rest of your life becomes a gift..."[1] Henia Yarmovski literally gave such a gift to the author's mother, escapee Fanya Dunetz (#142), when she extended a hand to Fanya as she crawled out of the tunnel to carefully lead her to safety.

Fanya, a native of Zhetl, had attended high school in Novogrudok together with Henia's daughter Sonia. Henia, a Novogrudok native who had owned a local flour mill with her husband Avraham, was at an advantage upon escaping the labor camp thanks to her knowledge of the terrain and her acquaintance with many peasants who were former customers. Leading Fanya to the shelter of one such farmer's home in the aftermath of the escape, Henia likely saved Fanya's life.[2]

Henia Weiner, a seamstress, was born in Novogrudok on April 17, 1895, to Yakov and Fanya née Meckel.[3] Henia became the sole survivor of her immediate family when her brother Moshe Chaim, five years her senior,[4] his wife Sara,[5] and their two children Zeidil[6] and Feigel[7] were all murdered in Novogrudok's second mass slaughter of August 7, 1942.[8]

Henia's husband Avraham Yarmovski was also interned in the Novogrudok forced labor camp. As fate would have it, thanks to his intense efforts to protect Henia in the camp,[9] she survived all four massacres, while Avraham succumbed to hunger and torture in 1943.[10]

Henia made valiant attempts to save the lives of her two daughters, Fanya Abramowicz and Sonia, who were with her in the labor camp. Fanya, born in 1916, worked as a clerk. She was married[11] and living in Warsaw[12] prior to the war with her husband Shmulik, a teacher and fellow Novogrudok native.[13] Although the couple had no children, Henia's granddaughter Tali recalls hearing that her aunt Fanya was pregnant at the time of her internment in the labor camp.[14] Sonia, like her classmate and friend Fanya Dunetz, was born in 1920 and worked as a teacher before the war.[15] Although Henia had arranged with a Polish workshop foreman to hide her daughters in a labor camp closet, this foreman betrayed their hiding place to the Germans. Sonia and Fanya were then murdered in Novogrudok's final massacre of May 7, 1943.[16]

Bereft of her two daughters and unaware of the fate of her youngest child Uri, whom she had encouraged to cross the Russian border with several neighbors,[17] Henia surely had a heavy heart as she made her escape through the tunnel. Fleeing to the home of local Baptists, Henia, Fanya Dunetz, and an elderly escapee who joined them en route spent the night in the relative luxury of the family's hayloft. There they were fed an entire chicken, despite the farmers' own impoverished state. Unable to continue feeding their "guests" and fearful of arousing suspicion by asking neighbors for food, the hosts were forced to ask the escapees to leave the following morning. The family's son personally led them to the forest, where they were directed to the Bielski encampment, which Henia and Fanya reached together[18] in September 1943.[19]

Subsequent to liberation from the forest and repatriation to Poland, Henia eventually made her way in 1946 to the Poking-Waldstadt Displaced Persons Camp,[20] the second-largest DP camp in Germany after Bergen-Belsen.[21] Acutely alone in dire living conditions, Henia saw her fervent wish to be reunited with her son Uri suddenly come true. Having worked in Siberian coal mines until the end of the war, Uri learned by chance from an acquaintance that Henia had survived. He quickly left his Russian girlfriend to reach Poking for a very emotional reunion with his beloved mother.[22] In letters Henia sent in 1947 to a relative in Israel, she declared that Uri gave her a reason to continue living.[23]

With Uri joining her, Henia was provided with improved living conditions more suitable for the two-person family they propitiously became. Upon Uri's marriage in Poking to Pola Leviatan,[24] a survivor from Dokshitz in the Vitebsk region of Belorussia,[25] the two-person family became a unit of three, who continued to live together for over three decades until Henia's death.

Henia, Uri, and Pola left the Heidenheim DP Camp,[26] a predominantly Jewish displaced persons camp near Stuttgart in the American zone,[27] for the one-year-old State of Israel, arriving in May 1949.[28] The three initially resided in Tel Aviv before settling in Givatayim. Uri and Pola's only child Avital (Tali) was born in 1962 and named for Avraham, the paternal grandfather she never knew. One of Tali's treasured memories is of her grandmother's pride the day she became a soldier in the Israel Defense Forces.

Tali also reports that Uri and Pola compassionately cared for Henia throughout her last years until Henia's death in approximately 1981. Uri was seventy years old at his death in 1993, and Pola lived to the age of seventy-six, passing away in 2004.[29]

At the time of this writing in August 2023, Tali is a marketing professional, the mother of Henia's four granddaughters, and the grandmother of Henia's three great-grandchildren. One granddaughter carries Henia's name, while grandson Or is named for Uri.[30]

Henia, like Uri, is said to have never spoken of her losses, although she kept photographs of her murdered family members on the walls of her room. Whatever Tali learned of her family's past was either related by her mother or by Uri when he was interviewed by one of his granddaughters for a "Roots" school project. Both Henia and Uri portrayed themselves to the outside world as having had a normative past, Uri with his unflappable optimism and good humor, and Henia with her impeccable dress and her frequent get-togethers with friends.[31]

Henia and Uri Yarmovski, undated postwar photo (courtesy of Tali Yarmovski Alt)

Unlike many descendants of people whose fates are intertwined, the author and Henia's granddaughter Tali had the opportunity to meet. In an emotional gathering on July 1, 2012, Fanya joined them to share her memories of spending time with her friend Sonia at Henia's house in Novogrudok during their high school days. At a later meeting in Tel Aviv on April 24, 2019, there clearly was a special bond between the author and Tali, the granddaughter of the woman who saved her mother's life.

Asked if she would ever consider visiting Novogrudok, Tali expressed uncertainty. After all, she lamented, neither Henia nor Uri spoke of their experiences. Perhaps they would not want her to visit the place where they experienced so much pain and so many losses.

David Rabinovich (#196)

The identity of Novogrudok forced labor camp inmate David Rabinovich remains a mystery. Well over two hundred entries for individuals with this fairly common name are to be found in the Yad Vashem Central Database of Shoah Victims' Names. Of those, fifteen people named David Rabinovich hailed from the Novogrudok area, with an additional ninety-four entries hailing from cities and towns in Poland at large.[1] Not one, however, appears in the compilation of Jewish partisans in Belorussia . We can thus assume that Novogrudok forced labor camp inmate David Rabinovich, whoever he was, did not survive the tunnel escape.[2]

Zelda Kopernik (#197)

In explicit detail, the 1961 Yad Vashem testimony of fellow inmate Morduch Majerowicz provides a chilling description of Zelda Kopernik's survival in the Novogrudok forced labor camp.

Recalling the gruesome aftermath of Novogrudok's last mass slaughter on May 7, 1943, Majerowicz describes the pile of bodies strewn near the entrances of the labor camp living quarters. These were the corpses of men and women shot instantly upon refusing the order to march to their prepared graves.

Yet, Majerowicz explains, he found one woman who had remained alive by hiding in the camp's open latrine. As she was covered in feces, Majerowicz and "a tailor from Karelich" – possibly Moshe Gorodynski

(#186) or his son Shlomo (#77) – struggled to pull her out, remove her clothes, and clean her. Her rescuers soon discovered that Zelda had been shot, and the camp doctor who examined her pronounced the bullet wound to her lung to be fatal. Only thanks to Mordechai's devoted care – staunching her wounds with pieces of bread, cleaning her infected areas with moist pieces of cloth – did Zelda miraculously survive. He notes proudly that she later survived the tunnel escape to reach the Bielski partisans. In time, she remarried and gave birth to children.[1]

Zelda Kopernik of Karelich, born around 1912,[2] was the daughter of Moshe, whose surname is unknown. Prior to the war, she had been married to Aaron Kopernik,[3] also of Karelich,[4] and the two were parents to a son named Faivel.[5]

The three members of the young family are listed in official documents as having been confined together in the Karelich ghetto in 1942.[6] Sadly, the names of both Aron[7] and their son Faivel[8] appear on a Soviet list of those murdered in Novogrudok that same year. At the time of his slaughter, Faivel was only three[9] or four[10] years old.

We do not know Zelda's profession or the skills she possessed to make her eligible for conscription to the Novogrudok forced labor camp, nor do we know her postwar surname. To date, an examination of genealogical, Holocaust-related, and population databases has not disclosed further information. We remain grateful to Morduch Majerowicz, whose testimony reveals that Zelda built her life anew upon liberation from the forest.

Potasznik (#198)

To date, we cannot determine the identity of the man or woman penned on the escape list simply as "Potasznik," with no proper name preceding. Of the 903 listings for individuals from Poland with this surname in Yad Vashem's Central Database of Shoah Victims' Names, seventy-one are from the Novogrudok area alone.[1]

There are five individuals with the surname Potasznik in the compilation of Jewish partisans in Belorussia.[2] One, an electrical technician named Max Potasznik, was a member of the Bielski detachment to which most of the tunnel escapees fled. Max, born in 1915, hailed from Golshany in the nearby Baranovich Region.[3] Although he appeared likely to have been in the Novogrudok forced labor camp, subsequent to further research, it has been determined that although Max joined the Bielskis in September 1943, he did so not as an escapee but after transferring from the Russian Chapayev partisan detachment.[4]

A search of Holocaust and genealogical databases shows no indication of any other partisan with the surname Potasznik who was in the Novogrudok forced labor camp.

Unfortunately, we may never know the identity or the fate of the 198th inmate in line to crawl through the tunnel in search of freedom.

Peretz Wolkowicki (#199)

When traced to her home in New York with the help of a genealogist, the daughter of Peretz Wolkowicki had no idea of any family connection to Novogrudok and its forced labor camp. Relating that her late father had made it clear that the Holocaust was a taboo subject, Hana Wolkowicki Gotian had never heard of Novogrudok nor of the tunnel escape. When the author explained the reason for her call, Hana admitted that her father had offered so very few details of the family history that she'd suspected she was adopted. Beyond mentioning the Bielski partisans and having been in a ghetto from which he rescued his brother, Peretz remained largely silent about the war years. Even the details of the bullet wounds to his scalp and leg during the Holocaust remain unknown to Hana and her siblings to this day.[1]

Fortunately, Hana's father had been slightly more open about his wartime experiences with his son Shimon. From the information gleaned from Peretz, we learn that Hana is named for their paternal grandmother Hana (née Galpern),[2] and Shimon bears the name of their paternal grandfather. Born in 1921 in Lida, Peretz had two siblings, an older sister Esther and a younger brother Mordechai.[3] According to Shimon, after they were interned in the Lida ghetto during the war, Peretz initially escaped together with his parents, brother, and sister. Yet their father and Esther, who was pregnant, could not keep up the struggle to walk and thus were forced to return to the ghetto along with Peretz's mother. There, all three met their deaths. Peretz did speak of subsequently returning to the Lida ghetto several times to help others escape. During one of these forays, he broke the lock to the German weapons silo, enabling him and others to steal all the armaments stored inside.[4]

Since Mordechai Wolkowicki, like his brother Peretz, is listed in the compilation of Jewish partisans as having been a member of the Bielski detachment,[5] he too may have been confined to the Novogrudok forced labor camp and escaped to the forest prior to the tunnel escape.

Although we do not know how Peretz came to be interned in the Novogrudok forced labor camp, it is possible that after escaping the Lida ghetto, he made his way to Novogrudok or its environs, where he became trapped. Since Shimon notes that his father worked as a welder prior to the war,[6] this essential skill probably enabled his entry to the forced labor camp.

After surviving the tunnel breakout, Peretz joined up with a Russian partisan group prior to becoming a Bielski partisan. In the Bielski detachment, he acquired skills as a tanner. After cows were found and slaughtered for food, Peretz provided the skins to be sewn into leather coats.[7]

Although brothers Peretz and Mordechai had been together in the Bielski *otriad*, they somehow lost track of each other following liberation. Only when the two returned to Lida were they reunited. There they found their former home turned into a shelter for the homeless and the family's flour mill seized for possession by new owners. Mordechai died in the town of Ryazan near Moscow in the mid-1980s. His unmarried daughter continues to reside there, while a married son lives with his family in Israel.[8]

After the war, Peretz remained in Belorussia and married Sara (Sonia) Khartowski of Vilna. At first, the young couple resided in Grodno, where their son Shimon was born in 1947.[9] Afterwards, the family moved to Ryazan before relocating to Mogilev, where Peretz found work as a tanner.[10] There, Hana was born in 1951. Their youngest son, Arie Lev, was born in 1959, the year in which the Wolkowicki family returned to Poland in order to immigrate to Israel in 1960. In Israel, Peretz continued to work in the leather industry. However, the family was destined to change countries once more. In the footsteps of their children who emigrated from Israel to the United States from the late sixties until the early eighties, Sara and Peretz relocated to Queens, New York, in 1983.[11]

Describing her father as having been "a good worker and a good husband," Hana notes that Peretz suffered painfully from tinnitus, possibly due to a head injury he had incurred during the war.[12]

Although Peretz and Sara did not keep a religious home, some of their grandchildren have returned to Jewish traditions after attending Jewish day schools. Many have visited Israel.

Peretz Wolkowicki with his wife and eldest son Shimon, Grodno, 1947 (courtesy of Hana Gotian)

Hebrew continues to be the primary language among the siblings of the second generation and the language in which Hana and her husband Zvi speak to their three children.[13]

After a long, eventful life together, Peretz and Sara Wolkowicki both died in New York in 2004. Following Sara's death, Peretz was so profoundly grieved that he refused to eat.[14] He died forty days later on December 31, 2004.[15]

During their lifetime, Peretz and Sara Wolkowicki, two survivors, were blessed with nine grandchildren and five great-grandchildren. As of August 2023, eight additional great-grandchildren have joined the roster, including two who were named in memory of Sara and Peretz.[16]

Henia Bruk (#200)

The identity and fate of the escapee named Henia Bruk remains uncertain. With the letters *H* and *G* often interchangeable in the Russian language, women with the name Henia may also be recorded as Genia. From our research results, Henia of the Novogrudok forced labor camp escape list may have been either Genia Bruk of Lubcz or Genia Bruk of Baranovich.

Although the circumstances of her death are unknown, Genia Bruk's name appears on the list of murdered residents of Lubcz, as do the names of her husband Chaim and their daughters Gita and Manya.[1]

As for Genia Bruk of Baranovich, an appeal for her search was made to the European Headquarters of the United HIAS Service in July 1963 by her aunt. According to this document, Genia, also known as Henia, was the daughter of Mendel and Sima and was born around 1929. She had been reportedly seen by friends in an undisclosed displaced persons camp in Germany after the war before going to France.[2] As no positive identification of this Genia Bruk has been recorded, her reported sighting in Germany may well have been a case of mistaken identity, or she may have subsequently married or changed her name.

However, one must consider the fact that had tunnel escapee Henia Bruk survived, she would almost definitely have become a partisan in the forest. As no one with this name appears in the compilation of Jewish partisans in Belorussia during the years 1914–1944,[3] we may presume that Henia Bruk was murdered in the immediate aftermath of the tunnel escape.

Menachem Senderovski (#201)

The identity of the escapee Menachem Senderovski remains a mystery, although in all likelihood he stemmed from Zhetl, home of a very extensive Senderovski clan. Of the 338 entries for individuals from Poland with the surname Senderovski that appear in Yad Vashem's Central Database of Shoah Victims' Names, 286 are from this small town in the Novogrudok area.

One such man named Menachem Senderovski who lived in Zhetl prior to the war was born in either 1890[1] or 1900.[2] The son of Hirsh and Dvorah,[3] he and his wife Chaya had three children.[4] A *shochet* (ritual slaughterer) by trade, Menachem belonged to the Slonim Chassidic dynasty.[5] Although he is reported by a fellow townsperson to have been murdered in Zhetl's first massacre of April 30,[6] the date and circumstances of his death may be incorrect. This possibility is reinforced by the fact that Menachem's own daughter did not list his date of death in the Page of Testimony she submitted to Yad Vashem.[7]

Another individual named Menachem Senderovski was born in Zhetl in 1900. He was married to Chasia née Berezinski of Lubcz, where the couple resided before the war. Although he is reported to have been murdered in Lubcz in 1942, we have no way of confirming this information.[8]

As there is no Menachem Senderovski listed in the compilation of Jewish partisans in Belorussia during the years 1941–1944,[9] we may assume that the Novogrudok forced labor camp inmate by this name did not survive the breakout to reach the forest and become a partisan.

Rafael Shofer (#202)

Depending on the document, Rafael Shofer, the son of Ziml and Gitl,[1] was born in Novogrudok in 1884,[2] 1889,[3] or 1891.[4] According to information Rafael conveyed in 1946, once he completed his elementary school education at age twelve, he began working straightaway as a carpenter.[5]

Rafael's carpentry skills ultimately enabled him to be conscripted to the Novogrudok forced labor camp, where he played an important role in the construction of the tunnel – almost at the cost of his life. Fellow inmate Chaim Leibowitz (#91) recounts that at a certain stage of the secret construction, heavy rains caused the soil above the tunnel to begin to crumble, and cracks began to appear in the walls. Due to the dire need to somehow prevent the collapse of the entire tunnel, the decision was made to purloin boards intended to construct furniture for the Germans and use them instead to line the tunnel walls. Upon arriving to collect the furniture and discovering that the boards had disappeared, the Germans suspected that the lumber had been stolen by the Jews for heating. All the cabinetmakers from the carpentry workshops were then punished by flogging, but Shofer was singled out to be hanged.[6]

Chaim Leibowitz's claim that Shofer was sentenced to hanging due to his involvement in pilfering the wood comes in stark contrast to the reason given by fellow inmate Mordechai Mejerowicz. In his testimony, Mejerowicz describes Shofer's "crime" as having somehow bought several potatoes. As he cooked the precious potatoes over ignited sawdust, the hapless Shofer was caught red-handed by a sadistic carpentry supervisor. As punishment, the inmate was hanged by his arms after the potatoes were hurled in his face.[7]

The two witnesses agree that a near-miracle then occurred. Both Meirovich[8] and Chaim Leibowitz[9] write of the extraordinary act of bravery that saved Rafael from death: a woman inmate seamstress defiantly cut the rope from Shofer's neck to release him from his torture.[10] Although her identification jives in both accounts, the heroine's actual identity and fate remain a mystery. Leibowitz names her as Hodl Samsonovich of Wsielub. Mayerowicz appears to refer to the same woman, whom he identifies as "the wife of the shoemaker from Horodyszcze,"[11] a town near Novogrudok. Indeed, Hodl's husband Hirsz Samsonowicz (#121) of Horodyszcze testified that he was a shoemaker by trade.[12] Yet, a Page of Testimony submitted by Hirsz Samsonowicz in 1972 declares that his Hodl had been murdered in the slaughter of May 7, 1943, prior to the commencement of digging the tunnel and the hanging of Rafael Shofer.[13]

Shofer miraculously survived the near-hanging, fled the Novogrudok forced labor camp in the tunnel escape, and ultimately reached the forest to become a Bielski partisan.[14]

Following liberation, Rafael took refuge in the UNRRA-operated Turin and Cremona Displaced Persons Camps in Italy.[15] In his June 1946 request to immigrate to Palestine, Rafael declared that he was single or widowed (without specifying which option) with no dependents.[16]

In May 1948, Rafael Shofer immigrated to the newly declared State of Israel.[17] On November 23, 1948, aged fifty-two and living in Tel Aviv, he married Shoshana Schwartzman, age forty-eight.[18] Only six years later, Rafael died on August 1, 1954.[19]

Av. or Ab. Pozniak (#203)

The proper name for Novogrudok forced labor camp escapee #203 is indicated only by a Yiddish abbreviation equivalent to "Av" or "Ab" before the surname Pozniak.

There are seventeen individuals from throughout Poland with the name of Avraham or Abram Pozniak listed in the Yad Vashem Central Database of Shoah Victims' Names.[1]

Of these, the possibility exists that escapee #203 was Avraham Yitzchak Pozniak of Ivenets, a town within the Novogrudok radius from which the overwhelming majority of escapees hailed. Avraham Yitzchak appears together with his wife Golda and their daughters (names unlisted) on the list of the murdered from Ivenets, Kamien, and the surrounding area.[2]

Additionally, the possibility exists that escapee "Av." or "Ab." Pozniak was one of two men named Abram Pozniak who originated from the town of Mir, twenty-eight miles from Novogrudok. Abram Pozniak, a lawyer, was born in 1908.[3] One of five children of Leib, a merchant, and wife Rivka,[4] Abram was married to Zoya and is listed as having lived in Novogrudok prior to and during the war. According to records in Yad Vashem's central database, Abram was a member of the Komsolskiy partisan detachment.[5]

A younger Abram Pozniak from Mir was born in 1922. The son of Yakov, he, too, became a partisan fighter. Abram was killed while serving in the Za Sovetskuyu Belarus partisan detachment on June 1, 1943.[6]

To date, we are unable to verify if any of these three men was indeed the 203rd inmate to crawl through the tunnel in a quest for freedom.

Skiba (#204)

The surname Skiba appears on the Novogrudok forced labor camp escape list without a proper name, making the identification of this man or woman extremely complex. Yad Vashem's Central Database of Shoah Victims' Names lists nine individuals with the Skiba surname who resided in prewar Poland;[1] however, we have no means by which to determine if one was indeed the tunnel escapee.

One possibility, which cannot be confirmed, is a David Skiba who became a member of the Bielski detachment, the partisan brigade in which a majority of tunnel escapees served. This man was born in 1913, lived in Mir prior to the war, and worked as a saddler.[2]

Unfortunately, it has been impossible to ascertain the identity or the fate of Skiba, the 204th inmate slated to crawl through the tunnel to freedom.

Pesach Abramowicz (#205)

Pesach Abramowicz was born in Novogrudok in 1924[1] to Pesia née Ostashinski and Faivel, a shoemaker. The family resided in the town at 75 Pilsudski Street.[2] Although we know that Pesia did not survive the war,[3] we are unaware of the circumstances of her death. A Yad Vashem Page of Testimony that Pesach submitted in 1955 states that his younger sister Esther-Elka was murdered along with their father in 1942, most likely during Novogrudok's second massacre. At the time of their murder, Esther-Elka was seven years old, and Faivel was fifty-two.[4]

Pesach was interned in the Novogrudok ghetto in December 1941,[5] following the town's first massacre. His skills as a barber[6] enabled him to survive the second slaughter in August 1942 to be consigned to the Novogrudok forced labor camp.[7]

The tragic deaths of his parents and sister had kindled a fierce determination within Pesach to live. During the bitter winter, the eighteen-year-old's first brash attempt to escape the camp and flee to the partisan enclave in the forest was a painful failure. The crippling frostbite that soon overtook him forced his return to the camp, leaving Pesach with the loss of all the toes on one foot as an excruciating, lifetime reminder.

In his own failed escape attempt prior to the tunnel breakout, Pesach's friend Idel Kagan (#95) had lost the toes on both feet due to frostbite. Although the tunnel escape list shows Idel assigned to be the 95th in line and Pesach the 205th, their severe injuries forced them to choose to be among the last to leave, for fear they might stumble and hold back others. While some escapees had planned to break into a run upon exiting the tunnel to freedom, Pesach and Idel carefully walked together along the same route Idel had used during his prior escape attempt.[8]

Pesach, the less severely injured of the two, pulled Idel along, sometimes carrying him,[9] during their five-day trek to the Bielski encampment. The teens made only one stop along their escape at a house just over a mile from Novogrudok. The bread they were given there was to become their only sustenance throughout the entire journey. Along the way, they drank from puddles. Fortunately, they eventually met up with partisans from the Orzhonididze Brigade,[10] yet these men informed Pesach of his brother Shaya's death in a partisan battle against the Germans and local police. The devastating news crushed Pesach's cherished hope to be reunited with Shaya,[11] one year older and a tailor by profession,[12] who was the last surviving member of his family.[13]

After accompanying the Orzhonididze partisans to their base, Pesach and Idel both transferred to the Bielski family group. There, with Idel unable to walk, Pesach took responsibility for bringing him food.[14]

Liberated at last from the forest and repatriated to Poland, Pesach became a stateless refugee in the Landsberg Displaced Persons Camp[15] from November 1945 to February 21, 1947, the site of a former German military compound near Munich located in the American zone.[16] Shortly after leaving the DP camp, Pesach sailed for Palestine on an illegal immigration boat, which broke the British blockade to successfully reach the shores of Atlit.

Like at least two of his fellow tunnel escapees (Yakov Shepsman, #39, and Efraim Okonski, #90), Pesach made his first home upon arriving in Israel in Kibbutz Kinneret in the Jordan Valley. Pesach, however, remained on the kibbutz for a significantly longer period than the others. Perhaps these three new immigrants were drawn to Kibbutz Kinneret at the suggestion of Eliezer Sadan (formerly Senderovski), Idel's first cousin, who with his wife had settled on the kibbutz in 1947 to join her two sisters there. A Zhetl native, Eliezer had spent his early years in Novogrudok in his grandparents' home and continued to visit his many cousins there before the war; he may have reached out to offer his newly arrived *lantzmen* (countrymen) an initial home on Kibbutz Kinneret.[17]

Three months after settling on the kibbutz, Pesach married fellow refugee Ella Birenbaum, who had arrived in Palestine and moved into the kibbutz just before his own arrival. Like Pesach, Ella, a twenty-one-year-old Auschwitz survivor from a small central Polish town, was the only survivor of her immediate family.[18]

These two sole survivors succeeded in building a new family together. After the birth of three children in Kibbutz Kinneret, Pesach and Ella decided to leave for the city in 1964. After moving to Haifa, Pesach tried but failed to maintain a kiosk due to his difficulty with standing for any length of time. Subsequently, he was successfully employed at the Israel Military Industries.[19]

Pesach Abramovicz died in Israel in 1999 at the age of seventy-five. As of this writing in May 2019, Pesach's widow Ella is ninety-four years old and living in a geriatric facility in Rishon Lezion. Clear-headed and eager to share information about her life with Pesach, she describes her husband as having been a gentle man with a big heart who suffered all his life from pain in his mutilated foot.[20] Daughter Pnina describes her father as having had a "heart of gold" with a strong desire to help anyone in need. His constant good nature belied his tortured past; Pnina relates how her childhood girlfriends were envious and often expressed the wish for a father like Pesach.[21]

Pesach Abramowicz, undated postwar photo (courtesy of Pnina Maman)

Both Ella and Pnina note that Pesach hardly ever spoke of his past losses. Only later in life did he tell of the tunnel escape – and this with great pride.[22]

The sole survivor of his family, Pesach is said to have been extremely proud of the family he built and the children he raised. If he were alive today, in September 2023, he would be the grandfather of nine and the great-grandfather of eighteen, the number in Jewish tradition that symbolizes life, which Pesach so deeply fought to live to the fullest.[23]

Dvora (#206) and Shalom (#207) Svinik

Throughout their lives, mother and son Dvora and Shalom Svinik miraculously lived to sustain each other.

Dvora Perski, a nurse by profession,[1] was born in Ivenets in 1905[2] to Yosef and Keyla.[3] Her sister Rivka and two brothers Michael and Berl all shared deep Zionist aspirations and were ardent members of the Beitar Zionist youth movement. Following Rivka's immigration to Palestine in the 1930s, her brothers, both carpenters,[4] had undergone preparatory training in Baranovich[5] to follow suit. Unfortunately, the war thwarted their dreams.

Dvora married her childhood friend and fellow Beitar member Haim Avraham Svinik. The couple lived in a four-room house on Shul-Hoif Street in Ivenets with their three sons Shalom, born in 1929; Yitzchak Aizik, born in 1933; and Binyamin Kalman, born in 1939. Prior to the war, Haim Avraham had owned a butchery.[6] He died in Minsk in 1943 shortly after the murder of his two younger sons in Ivenets on June 9, 1942.[7]

Now alone, Dvora and Shalom were interned in the Novogrudok forced labor camp, where Dvora was assigned to the sewing workshop and later to the kitchen, and Shalom, aged thirteen, was sent to work in the carpentry workshop.[8] In a Yiddish-language account of their wartime experiences, she notes:

> Shalom signed up to work as a carpenter and was employed in the workshop. At the time, he was only thirteen years old. Still a child. He feared that the Germans would notice his age and send him to be murdered. Thus, each time he was

present at a roll call, he dragged two bricks with him, took a place in the last row, and stood atop the two bricks so as to look taller.[9]

Dvora and Shalom Svinik were erroneously entered on the escape list under the surname Pozniak. (There are no individuals with the names of Dvora and Shalom Pozniak listed either in Yad Vashem's Central Database of Shoah Victims' Names or in the compilation of Jewish partisans in Belorussia.[10])

Dvora's chilling account of fleeing through the tunnel describes the events in painstaking detail:

> The night on which it was decided to carry out the escape was pitch black. A strong wind blew, and rain fell incessantly. Before the escape began, we cut the electrical wires to the searchlight (which was atop the watch tower) and simultaneously pried off a number of tin plates from the roof. Every gust of wind caused the plates to make a terrible noise, which acted to cover the noise of the escape.
>
> The tunnel that had been dug was narrow, and we were forced to crawl inside it on all fours, one after another. The instructions we received were for each one to hold onto the person in front and not to let go until the exit from the tunnel and arrival in the forest.
>
> My son Shalom crawled in front of me in the tunnel and I held him tightly by the foot so that I wouldn't lose him in the darkness. Most unfortunately, when we exited the tunnel, there was no one awaiting us, and we had no idea in which direction to turn. The two of us were left alone in the darkness, and we were overtaken by tremendous fear.
>
> A short time afterwards we met two women. The mother had left the tunnel with two of her daughters, but one had

gotten lost in the darkness. [Author's note: most probably Sara (#149) and Roza (#151) Giershenowski.]

During the tunnel escape, the Germans succeeded in repairing the searchlight and flooded the area with light. They identified the escapees and opened with heavy fire upon them. These shootings resulted in the deaths of many of the escapees. In retrospect, it also became clear that the heavy darkness caused many of those fleeing to lose their way as they exited the tunnel and mistakenly set their sights on returning to the camp.…

With shooting sounds everywhere, Shalom and I found shelter on a small hill near the river. A number of policemen passed near us with flashlights in search of escapees, but they did not notice us. When the shooting stopped, we began crawling on all fours in order to distance ourselves from the tunnel. Very quickly, it became apparent to us that we had no idea in which direction the Germans were, and so as not to encounter them, we decided to wait until sunrise. We lay next to each other the entire night, shaking from the cold and from fright as we waited for a new day to dawn.

At sunrise, we noticed that we were quite close to the road. We quickly stood up and ran inside a nearby field of lupine flowers. Yet we immediately realized that it would be quite dangerous to remain there, as these flowers were short and provided no cover. We looked around and noticed that on the other side of the road, there was a small grove. Once again, we ran across the road and hid in a thicket at the edge of the grove. Suddenly, trucks emerged from the direction of the road carrying soldiers and police. They circled the grove and began coming in our direction, shooting all the while. Shalom was hit by a bullet and wounded in the foot. He lay bleeding on the ground but did not utter a sound so that the murderers would not discover us. We were certain that these were our last moments…but then the Germans passed by without noticing us. In retrospect, it seems that all their attention was focused on the other side of the grove, where a different group of Jews had hidden. At the start of the shooting, these Jews got up and began to flee. The murderers pursued them and shot all of them to death. In the lupine field, they also found four additional Jews and murdered them as well.

After the Nazis had moved away from the grove, I tore a piece of cloth from my dress and used it to bandage Shalom's wounded foot. As night fell, I hoisted Shalom onto my shoulders and began to walk, without knowing where to. My singular goal was to get as far away from Novogrudok as possible. I walked with Shalom on my shoulders all through the night until we reached a forest, where we hid for three days. We had no food and survived only on rainwater that dripped from the trees. We sat on the wet ground with absolutely nothing to cover ourselves. On the fourth day, ravaged by hunger and cold, we decided to take the risk and enter one of the villages to ask for help.

Ultimately, mother and son reached the Bielski partisan detachment, where Shalom was cared for and recuperated from his wounds. Throughout their time in the forest encampment, Dvora worked as a nurse.[11]

After becoming displaced persons in Germany following the war's end, Dvora and Shalom fulfilled the dream of Dvora's murdered brothers with their immigration to Israel in 1949. There Dvora continued to remain inseparable from her only surviving son, whose life she had saved by virtue of her determination and strong character.

Dvora became an integral part of Shalom's family after his marriage to Chaviva (Liba) née Rosenbloom. Born in Warsaw in 1937, Chaviva survived the war in Siberia and came to Israel on the immigrant ship *Exodus*. While completing her military service, she was introduced to Shalom through her commander, himself an immigrant from Ivenets.

Romance blossomed quickly, and by their third date Shalom and Chaviva became engaged.[12]

Having studied bookkeeping on arrival in Israel, Shalom opened an office with Chaviva working as his secretary. Once the children were born, she became an insurance agent. This enabled her to work from home while raising their seven children, all of whose names commemorate family members murdered in the Holocaust. Their eldest, Haim Avraham, born in 1960, is named after Shalom's father, killed in Minsk in 1943. Aharon Tsvi (Tsvica), born one year later, is named after Chaviva's father. Yosef, born in 1963, is named for Dvora's father, while Klila, born in 1965, is named for Dvora's mother, Keyla. Yitzchak Aizik, born in 1969, and Binyamin Kalman, born just before the outbreak of the 1973 Yom Kippur War, are named after Shalom's murdered siblings. Shalom's youngest child is named after Dvora's brother Michael. Today, all of the children are successful professionals. Their close connection to one another is exemplified by the fact that nearly all live within a radius of ten miles.[13]

Tsvica recalls that although Shalom refused to discuss the Holocaust, Grandmother Dvora's tales of how she and their father had survived the tunnel escape became the "childhood story" for the rapt seven grandchildren.[14] They so respected her that when the family lived in a two-and-a-half-room apartment, all the children (four at that time) lived in one room, and the parents slept in the living room. Only Dvora was given her own room.[15]

Despite his bitter youth and terrible losses, Shalom is described as having been a positive, happy man who was honored by thousands at his 1994 funeral and the shivah mourning week that followed.

At her death eighteen months later in 1995, Dvora had lived to see seven grandchildren as well as two great-grandchildren. Were she alive today in September 2023, Dvora Svinik would certainly be extremely proud of the extensive family Shalom and Chaviva created, which now includes her twenty great-grandchildren and four great-great grandchildren.[16] In the words of one of Shalom's children, he and Chaviva succeeded in miraculously recreating a family.[17]

Dvora Svinik (*top, center*) and newlyweds Haviva and Shalom Svinik, 1956
(courtesy of Tsvica Svinik)

Dinciolski (#208)

The surname Dinciolski is derived from *dziaciel*, Belarusian for "wood-pecker," a bird that is quite prevalent in the forests around Zhetl and Novogrudok.[1] Moreover, the Polish name for Zhetl is "Zdziecol."

Indeed, Yad Vashem's Central Database of Shoah Victims' Names includes some two hundred entries for men and women from Poland with the surname Dincioski, of whom more than half, fifty-two from each town, stemmed from either Zhetl or Novogrudok, where the family was evidently extensive. With the vast majority of these individuals reported to have been murdered, the Yad Vashem database contains only thirteen persons with the Dinciolski surname who survived to reach the safety of the forest to join a partisan group. Of these, nine became partisans in the Bielski detachment,[2] where research has established that the overwhelming number of surviving tunnel escapees sought shelter.

Was it possible that one of these Bielski partisans was a tunnel escapee? Unfortunately not, from what we learned from Asaela Weinstein, a Dinciolski descendant. According to Asela, all nine of these partisans belonged to the Dinciolski clan from the village of Duza Izwa. This group included two young children, as well as Taiba née Bielski, sister of Commander Tuvia Bielski, and Chaya Dinciolski, the fiancée of Asael Bielski, Tuvia and Taibe's brother.

Asaela, who is Chaya's daughter, affirms that all of her Dinciolski relatives had been in the forest long before the tunnel escape, and none participated in the breakout.[3] She also notes that her late mother spelled her maiden name in English as Dinciolski,[4] thus we have adopted this spelling variant of the name in referring to the unidentified Novogrudok forced labor camp escapee.

Regrettably, we may never know the identity of Dinciolski, the 208th inmate to crawl through the tunnel in search of freedom. In all likelihood, he or she did not survive the breakout.

Yosef (Yosel) Shuster (#209)

Although the name of escapee #209 is listed as Moshe Shuster, fellow escapee Jack Kagan (#95) testifies that the correct name of this Novogrudok forced labor camp inmate is not Moshe but Yosef, who was known as Yosel.[1]

The son of Yehoshua (Ovsey), Yosel Shuster was born in 1909 and lived in Novogrudok prior to the war. He worked as a saddle maker.[2] Nothing is known of his family of origin.

Yosel survived the tunnel escape. Making his way through the forest to the Bielski partisans, he later became a member of the Ordzhonikidze detachment,[3] where 180 Bielski fighters served under a primarily Russian leadership.[4]

According to Kagan, Shuster immigrated to the United States after liberation.[5] To date, an examination of genealogical, Holocaust-related, and population databases has revealed no information about Yosel's postwar life and whereabouts.

Hirsh Shkolnik (#210)

A carpenter from Karelich, Hirsh Shkolnik is noted on a partisan list as having been born in 1879, probably making him the oldest tunnel escapee. The son of Leizer,[1] he was the husband of Sonia née Cohen, who owned a notions store in the town.[2] As Sonia grew older, daughters Vitl and Merke (Miriam) took over the management.[3] Sonia was killed in Novogrudok's second slaughter in August 1942.[4]

Vitl immigrated before the war to Palestine,[5] where she adopted the Hebrew name Tsipora.[6] She subsequently encouraged the third sister in the family, Esther, to join her. Esther indeed arrived in pre-state Israel, where she married and became Esther Horowitz.[7] Like her mother, Merke remained behind in Karelich. Ultimately, she,[8] her husband Monus Lev,[9] and their four-year-old daughter Hadassah[10] were all murdered in Novogrudok's second massacre in 1942.

Thanks to his skills as a carpenter, Hirsh Shkolnik was interned in the Novogrudok forced labor camp in 1942. Hirsh played a pivotal role in the construction of the escape tunnel. Without his ingenuity, it would not have been possible to extract the soil during the building of the tunnel, and the escape could never have taken place. Responsible for building the trolley used to remove the earth as it was dug up from the tunnel, Hirsh initially prepared a twenty-inch square platform with wheels, while Yakov (#3a) stitched up two reins, each fifty-five yards long, with rings at the ends. Unfortunately, this trolley hit the walls, causing spillage of the earth that had been amassed.[11]

In an attempt to produce a more efficient trolley, Hirsh prepared four twenty-inch-square panels, which were fitted to the sides of the platform. With hinges placed on the front and back panels, the accumulated earth could be loaded and unloaded quickly.[12]

To build the platform, Hirsh daringly stole pieces of wood from the carpentry workshop in the camp, risking death by hanging as punishment for stealing German property. Moreover, he oversaw the building of four yard-long rails to ensure that the trolley wheels would move in a straight line without hitting the walls, also using materials smuggled out on a daily basis.[13]

As a result of Hirsh's efforts, nine to ten trolley loads of soil were hauled out daily. By night, the soil collected was moved via a trapdoor from the stable to a loft in an adjoining building. As the stable was the furthest building from the guards and the least occupied, it was there, in the area of the inmates from Zhetl, that the tunnel's entrance was dug. With space for only two people in the shaft, bags of earth were passed along from the tunnel entrance to the loft by the sixty or seventy inmates who would sit in a line passing the bags to one another until they arrived to be emptied in the loft.[14]

Beyond Hirsh risking his life to ensure the essential construction of the trolley, fellow inmate Shaul Gorodynski (#77) divulged another crucial contribution that Hirsh made to the bold endeavor. By collecting pieces of wood to serve as supports in order to prevent collapse of the walls,[15] Hirsh again endangered his life to help ensure the success of the escape.

Hirsh was one of the inmates who survived the tunnel escape to which he made such a major contribution. Reaching the forest, he joined the Bielski partisan detachment,[16] where he built stocks for rifles.[17]

Following liberation, in January 1947, Hirsh's name appears on a list of the Central Committee of Polish Jews as living at that time in Lodz, Poland.[18] A 1950 record of the American Joint Distribution Committee relief organization indicates Hirsh had resided in Paris and in the Bergen-Belsen Displaced Persons Camp.[19]

Subsequently, Hirsh immigrated to Israel to be reunited with his daughters Tsipora and Esther and their families. Here he became "Zvi" Shkolnik. Zvi Hirsh Shkolnik died on Yom Kippur eve, September 6, 1965, twenty-two years after the tunnel escape, and is buried in the Shikun Vatikim Cemetery in the coastal city of Netanya.[20]

Online family trees[21] indicate that today Zvi Shkolnik's descendants include a number of grandchildren and a great-grandchild. To date, efforts have been unsuccessful to contact descendants of this man who contributed so much to building the tunnel that enabled so many to live.

Leib Berman (#211)

Many discrepancies exist in the information available on Leib Berman. Did he actually escape the Novogrudok forced labor camp through the tunnel, or was he among those who stowed away in the camp during the breakout, as attested by escapee Pesia Mayevski (#160)?[1] Author Peter Duffy notes that ten such inmates took cover within the camp.[2] One of the hidden, Yisrael Kolachek (#81), insists that there were only six people in hiding.[3]

Even Leib's date of birth is open to question. Was it 1910 as a cousin testifies,[4] 1896 as his nephew writes,[5] 1894 as it appears on a list of the murdered from Zhetl,[6] or 1902 as escapee Batia Rabinowitz (#27), Leib's former neighbor, listed in her Page of Testimony?[7] Consistent in all of these records are the facts that Leib Berman, the son of Zalman and Leah, was a Zhetl native who was a carpenter by trade and married to Sula née Bielitski.

The couple's four children were Rachel, born in 1925;[8] Minna, born in 1928;[9] Bracha, born in 1932;[10] and Betzalel, born in 1935.[11] All, including their mother Sula, were murdered in the Zhetl massacres of 1942.[12]

We can assume that Leib's skills as a carpenter, essential to the Nazis' war effort, enabled him to be conscripted to the Novogrudok forced labor camp. Here Leib joined his brother-in-law and fellow carpenter Betzalel (Tsala) Bielitski (#179), brother of Sula Berman. Accounts of the escape extol the contribution that inmate carpenters made in the construction of the makeshift tunnel.[13]

While the relatives and neighbors who filled out the Pages of Testimony assumed that Leib had been murdered along with his family in the Zhetl slaughters of 1942,[14] only tunnel escapee Batia Rabinowitz lists his date of death as 1943,[15] the year in which the breakout took place.

The last member of his family to survive, Leib Berman is commemorated in *Pinkas Zhetl*.[16]

Kokin (#212)

The surname Kokin stands alone on the escape list with no proper name indicated. Of the 170 entries in Yad Vashem's Central Database of Shoah Victims' Names for individuals with this surname, most are either documented as having been evacuated to Russia or are reported in Pages of Testimony to have been murdered prior to the September 26, 1943, date of the tunnel escape.[1]

Of the records for those individuals named Kokin who hailed from the Novogrudok area, all but two with this surname were murdered.[2]

The two Kokins who survived were both named Lev, and both became partisans in detachments in which survivors of the tunnel escape served.

Lev Kokin of Lida, the son of Moshe, was born in 1910. Single and a bookkeeper prior to the war, he is listed on the roster of members of the Bielski detachment.[3] This partisan detachment absorbed the overwhelming majority of surviving tunnel escapees.

Lev Kokin, the son of Yevel, was born in 1928. According to the compilation of Jewish partisans in Belorussia, he was from the Belarusian town of Shklov in the Mogilev region.[4] On a Russian partisan list, he is noted to have been a pupil living in Minsk prior to the war. This young teenager ultimately became transformed into an armed partisan with the Ordzhonikidze detachment of the Kirov Brigade,[5] consisting of 180 Bielski fighters[6] serving under the Russian commander Lyashenko.[7]

One of these two partisans is likely to be the "Kokin" who escaped the Novogrudok forced labor camp through the clandestine tunnel. To date, attempts through genealogical, Holocaust-related, and population databases have been unsuccessful in providing a conclusive resolution.

Shmuel Vainshtein (#213)

Born in the town of Nowosiolki[1] in 1898,[2] Shmuel David Vainshtein, a carpenter, lived in Zhetl prior to the war with his wife Taiba née Rozanski[3] and their four children. Taiba, a seamstress, was murdered in Zhetl's first massacre on April 30, 1942.[4] Orphaned of their mother, sons Chanoch, born in 1927,[5] and Mairim[6] lived for only three more months until their slaughter in Zhetl's second massacre on August 6, 1942.[7] Mairim's age at death is estimated to have been either eight or thirteen.[8] The circumstances of the deaths of their siblings Leib, born in 1929,[9] and Sara, born in 1932,[10] are not detailed in the

Russian-language list of murdered individuals from Zhetl in which their names appear.

Shmuel's skills as a carpenter enabled his conscription to the Novogrudok forced labor camp. Beyond using these skills for the benefit of the Germans, he was likely to have put them to critical use in helping to build the fragile underground tunnel. History has recorded the prominent role that the inmate carpenters played in the tunnel construction.[11]

The last of his immediate family to remain alive, Shmuel bravely attempted to flee to freedom. However, his death in the tunnel escape is confirmed by fellow escapee Pesia Mayevski (#160).[12]

The names of Shmuel, Taiba, Chanoch, and Mairim Vainshtein are commemorated in *Pinkas Zhetl*, the town's memorial book.[13]

Saadia Gertzovski (#214)

Saadia Gertzovski, a harness maker by trade, was born in Karelich in 1895.[1] He was married to Rachel née Gorodynski, also of Karelich.[2] Yad Vashem Pages of Testimony filed by a fellow Karelich resident following the war noted that Saadia,[3] Rachel,[4] and their twenty-two-year-old daughter Leah[5] had all been murdered in 1942.

Yet Saadia's name on the escape list – the last in line to crawl through the tunnel – is clear proof that he did not meet his death in 1942, as testified. Since his name does not appear in the compilation of Jewish partisans in Belarus during the years 1941–1944,[6] it was assumed that following the breakout, Saadia never reached the forest and was probably murdered after exiting the tunnel. Further, as no children completed Pages of Testimony for him following the war, the assumption was that at his death, Saadia was perhaps the last member of his family to survive.

In truth, none of these assumptions regarding Saadia proved correct. After noticing that a memorial notice for him and his family had been placed in the Karelich memorial book by Perle Carson and Sonia Greenberg of Toronto,[7] the author enlisted the help of her cousin Dr. Arthur Dunec, nephew of escapee Helena Kitayevich (#62) and a Toronto resident, to locate the descendants. Upon Arthur's finding Sonia's son and Saadia's grandson, retired chiropractor Dr. Stephen Greenberg, the two men found that they shared a connection beyond having tunnel-escapee relatives: Arthur's father had been Stephen's bar mitzvah teacher![8]

Upon being contacted, Stephen shared the astonishing fact that Saadia was not murdered upon exiting the tunnel as presumed, but had resided in postwar Karelich until his death sometime between 1951 and 1957. Stephen related that his mother Sonia, Saadia's oldest daughter born in 1924, had escaped to Siberia with the fleeing Soviet troops prior to the Nazi invasion. Her sister Perle, three years her junior, had survived the war with the Bielski partisans.[9] Moreover, Saadia's wife Rachel had died of natural causes around 1937 before the Nazi invasion.[10]

Like many other children of survivors, Stephen grew up in a home almost totally bereft of talk about the Holocaust. He was persistent in asking questions – never answered – about his dearth of aunts, uncles, and cousins, as well as about the grandparents he never knew. Although he is considered the family historian, he maintains that everything he knows about his family's Holocaust background has been discovered "by accident." As a ten-year-old, it was "by accident" that he chanced upon a hidden photograph of a man in burial shrouds. Questioning his parents, he was told that in 1945 after the war's end, his mother, who had been living in Siberia, had returned to Karelich with her husband Chaim Greenberg and infant son David to be reunited with her father Saadia and sister Perle. Although Saadia had by now lost his wife, his daughter Leah, and his young son Shlomo, born in 1936,[11] he nevertheless rejected his daughters' pleas to join their planned journey to Germany in an attempt to immigrate to the West. Saadia claimed that he opted to remain in Karelich due to his "old age" of fifty years.

As for the burial photo, Stephen was told that it had arrived sometime after the 1951 birth of Jack, his parents' second son, accompanied by a letter from someone in Karelich informing Sonia that her father had died. Yet for some reason, his father had hidden the letter from his mother, only revealing it around the time of the 1957 birth of Stephen and his twin brother Robert.[12] Stephen was then chosen to be Saadia's namesake, and Robert carries the name of his paternal grandfather.[13]

Whether or not Saadia and his daughters had communicated in the years prior to his death (the date of which remains unknown) remains an enigma to Stephen, although communication between Communist countries and the West was severely limited at that time. Nor is he aware of Saadia's whereabouts in the interim period between his escape from the tunnel and his reunion with Sonia in Karelich two years later. There is no information regarding Saadia's postwar life, including whether or not he remarried.[14]

After seeing the movie *Defiance* portraying the Bielski partisans, Stephen had become an admirer of the Bielskis, only to discover "by accident" that Perle Carson, his only surviving maternal aunt, had been a member of this partisan detachment. The discovery came around 2010 during a visit to Perle's home in Ft. Lauderdale, when Stephen noticed the book *Defiance* lying on a table. Mentioning that he had recently seen the movie, Perle responded, "I lived it, but I don't want to talk about it." With Perle's refusal to speak to Stephen or to her own children about her wartime experiences, and with his own mother Sonia having died at the age of fifty-two in 1977, Stephen laments the inability to ever gain a glimpse at his aunt's partisan experiences.[15]

Perle is listed as Perla Syadova Gertzovskaya in the compilation of Jewish partisans in Belarus during the years 1941–1944.[16] According to information in the National Archives of the Republic of Belarus, she joined the Bielski detachment in 1942,[17] thus ruling out her participation in the tunnel escape together with her father, as Stephen had originally thought. As for Stephen's hunch that perhaps Saadia, too, might have been a Bielski partisan, Saadia's name does not appear on the list of Jewish partisans, as mentioned, or in any partisan list in the National Archives of Belarus.[18]

Following the war, Perle, Sonia, and her family took refuge in a displaced persons camp in Germany, probably for some time in the city of Freiberg, which was often mentioned in the Greenberg home. Perle initially immigrated to Chicago before moving to Detroit, Michigan, and then Ft. Lauderdale, Florida. Sonia and family arrived in Halifax, Canada, on the SS *Marine Tiger* on October 30, 1948, to settle in Toronto, where relatives of her husband Chaim had agreed to be their sponsors.[19] During their years in Canada, Chaim owned a hotel and engaged in real estate, while Sonia managed her household and cared for her four sons.[20] In the busy dealings of life and raising a family, it was not difficult to avoid talking of the past.

Saadia Gertzovski, undated photo (courtesy of Stephen Greenberg)

Although Stephen admits that his mother had once fleetingly mentioned her father's "having escaped through a tunnel," no details were ever forthcoming. Only at a 2018 meet in Israel with his second cousin Azrikam Gorodynski, son of tunnel escapee Shaul Gorodynski (#77) and the nephew of Shaul's sister Sonya Gorodynski (#78), did Stephen first learn details of the tunnel escape.[21]

Stephen's eldest brother David, born in Russia in 1944, is the only grandson whom Saadia lived to see, thanks to Sonia's visit to Karelich in 1945. As mentioned, Sonia died in 1977, and Chaim, a native of Opatow, Poland, who had fled to Russia and became the sole survivor of his family, died in 1992. David died nineteen years later.

If Saadia were alive as of September 2023, he would be the grandfather of nine and the great-grandfather of nine.[22] As a result of this research, his legacy as a tunnel escapee will be secured. His fate on Novogrudok's Memorial Wall will now be that of "survivor."

Meir Berkowicz

Meir Berkowicz, born in Novogrudok[1] on May 15, 1914,[2] ultimately became the sole member of his family to survive the Shoah. In Yad Vashem Pages of Testimony, Meir recorded that his father Baruch, a shoemaker and glazier born in the town of Lachowicz around 1886; his mother Sara Feige née Kapushchewski, a housewife; and his brother Wolff (Velvel) were all murdered in Novogrudok's first mass slaughter on December 8, 1941.[3] His brother Moishe was killed in either 1942 or 1943.[4] Both Wolff and Moishe were barbers by profession. [5]

Meir's only sister, Rochel, wife of escapee Yitzchak Shuster, was slain in Novogrudok's fourth massacre on May 7, 1943.[6] Nearly a year beforehand, during Novogrudok's second massacre on August 7, 1942, Rochel and Yitzchak had borne the anguish of watching their only child, three-year-old Shmulik,[7] being forced onto a truck with other small children to be transported to their slaughter.[8]

Meir escaped death to be assigned to the Novogrudok forced labor camp by virtue of his skills as a tailor, an occupation deemed essential by the German Army. Like his brother-in-law Yitzchak,[9] Meir miraculously survived the tunnel escape of September 26, 1943, to reach the forest and join the Bielski partisans,[10] with whom he remained until liberation in July 1944.

From that point on, Meir became a stateless refugee in Europe. During 1946, he made his way to displaced persons camps in Munich and in Furth, Germany. From June 1946, the Bergen-Belsen Displaced Persons Camp became his temporary home for nearly three years.[11] This camp, adjacent to the former concentration camp, held the distinction of being the only exclusively Jewish camp in the entire British zone.[12] Sometime during his period in Bergen-Belsen, Meir married Eta Fuchs of Transylvania, Romania,[13] an Auschwitz survivor.[14] In March 1948, the couple sailed from the British port of Southampton to Halifax, Canada, aboard the RMS *Aquitania*,[15] a former Cunard Line luxury ocean liner relegated after the war to transporting troops and bringing immigrants to the New World.[16]

Meir and Eta made their home in Fredericton,[17] the capital of Canada's New Brunswick province. There Meir was reunited with several first cousins and changed his name to Myer Berk.[18] This former tailor from Novogrudok reestablished himself in his profession with the opening of his own tailor shop in his new hometown.[19]

Meir remained a resident of Fredericton until his death in 1994.[20] Eta moved to Toronto following a 2016 fire in her home from which, once again, she was miraculously saved. Prior to her death on October 29, 2020, at the age of 102 and a half,[21] Eta lived not far from her children Sybil, a retired speech therapist, and Dr. Joel Berk, an optometrist.[22] Joel was located through the assistance of a genealogist and of Rabbi Yosef Goldman, his former Fredricton rabbi.[23]

As Joel explained, unlike her husband, Eta openly shared her Holocaust memoirs by writing the book *Chosen*, published in 1997.[24] Her son recalls being a young adult when his father first spoke of having taken part in the tunnel escape. While reading a newspaper article about Tuvia Bielski, Meir casually mentioned that he was "together with him in the forest."

Joel Berk categorically declined an invitation to attend the 2019 reunion of descendants of Bielski partisans in Novogrudok, declaring he would never return to the place where the blood of his family members was so brutally shed.[25]

Newlyweds Myer and Eta Berkowicz, Bergen-Belsen Displaced Persons Camp, 1947 (courtesy of Joel Berk)

Chana Epshtein

Chana Epshtein, a talented language teacher, was born in 1898 to Shevel (Shaul) in the Belarusian town of Rubezhevichi.[1]

Although she is said to have been one of the tunnel escapees, Chana's name cannot be deciphered on the escape list. Rather than crawling through the tunnel during the breakout, however, she is reported to have remained in hiding before fleeing the then-vacant forced labor camp several days later.[2] Since neither Yisrael Kolachek (#81)[3] nor Eliyahu Berkowicz (#49)[4] mention Chana as having been part of their group hiding out in a loft, she was likely to have been among the remainder of the ten inmates whom author Peter Duffy reports as having been hidden in various crevices.[5] Idel Kagan (#95) also notes that during the escape, ten people remained behind in hiding in two different groups.[6]

Motl (Mordechai, Max) Dunetz, brother of tunnel escapee Fanya (#142), recalls that prior to the war, Chana Epshtein was his Polish-language teacher in Zhetl's Hebrew-based Tarbut school. The institution was forced to close its doors subsequent to the arrival of the Russians in 1939.[7]

Zhetl native Chaya Magid, wife of tunnel escapee Avraham, remembers Chana as her Hebrew-language teacher in the Tarbut school.

Both Motl and Chaya note that Chana was married to Faivel, a native Zhetler and a bookkeeper.[8] Born in 1901,[9] Faivel was employed in the flour mill and lumber concern of Arie Leib Kaplinsky, a prosperous businessman.[10]

Extremely active in community affairs, Faivel was a member of the Zhetl branch of the Keren Hayesod Zionist Organization,[11] as well as a founder of the Chaim Nachman Bialik Tarbut Hebrew School.[12]

Chaya Magid and the Epshtein family all lived on Thedeus Holovski Street in Zhetl. Thanks to the salary provided by his wealthy and generous boss, Faivel was able to install indoor plumbing, a novelty in the town. Chaya recalls that when she and her friends would come to play with Chana and Faivel's son Shmuel, a highlight of the visit was always a glimpse of the modern invention, the bathroom.[13]

Of the three members of her immediate family, Chana was the sole survivor. Both Faivel and Shmuel, just four and a half years old at the time of his death, were massacred in one of the two 1942 slaughters in Zhetl.[14]

Widowed and childless, Chana survived to make her way to the Bielski partisans, where she remained until liberation.[15]

Despite her losses, only three months after walking out of the forest and returning to Zhetl, Chana found the strength to return to teaching. Chaim Weinstein, a child survivor from the town and the sole remnant of his own family, relates that after emerging from the woods at age fifteen and a half and being placed in a Soviet orphanage, he learned in a Russian-language school. Who was his French teacher? None other than Chana Epshtein![16]

Eventually moving to Israel, where she resided in the Mediterranean coastal city of Hadera,[17] Chana married Hirsh Volhofsky, a bachelor and fellow Zhetl survivor. They had no children.[18] Prior to her death in the mid-1980s, Chana was a regular attendee at memorial meetings of Zhetl survivors and their families.[19]

Riva (Rivka) and Bella Ginenski

Shmuel and Avshalom Weinstein are violin makers whose passion is to recover Holocaust-era violins and other string instruments. They lovingly restore these instruments, which are played in their orchestra Violins of Hope in concerts across the globe.[1] Shmuel is married to Asaela, the daughter of Asael Bielski, one of the Bielski partisan leaders. Avshalom is their son.

Little did Avshalom realize that his televised meeting with a ninety-five-year-old former Bielski partisan during a recent Violins of Hope exhibition in Chicago would lead us to discover two additional tunnel escapees. An April 27, 2023, interview with the former Riva Ginenski on NBC's nationally televised *Today Show* revealed that Novogrudok-born Riva, now Rita Boyarski, had participated in the tunnel escape along with her mother.

With the assistance of Tamara Vershitskaya, former director of the Jewish Resistance Museum at the site of the former Novogrudok forced labor camp, I reached a cousin of Rita's named Isaac Koll, who with his sister were the first children in the Bielski detachment.[2] Isaac, now living in Israel, introduced me to Rita's son Sasha, who arranged for me to telephone Rita. Thanks to his sister Ella's help and translation, our interview confirmed both Rita's and her mother Bella's participation in the escape. We then learned the fate of Rita's two sisters Grunia and Dasha.

Grunia's daughter Sima related that prior to the tunnel breakout, her mother had escaped the labor camp to the Bielski partisans by handing over her gold watch.[3] Although Republic of Belarus National Archives records indicate that Dasha Ginenski had joined the Bielski detachment in 1942[4] long before the tunnel escape, Dasha, today Doris Schilloff, adamantly denies having served in the Bielski detachment. Instead, she insists that she was a fighter in the Ordzhonikidze detachment, which actually contained 180 Bielski fighters. There she met her future husband, Israel Shilovitski of Zhetl. Eventually, the two joined the family group of the Leninskaya Brigade's Borba detachment in the Lipiczanska Forest, together with many other Zhetl natives.[5]

As of June 2023, all three Ginenski sisters are alive. Rita resides in Chicago; ninety-eight-year-old Grunia lives in Denver, Colorado; and their eldest sister Doris, age 101, is a sharp-witted resident of Grants Pass, Oregon, where she claims to be the town's only Holocaust survivor.[6]

Their father Shepsel Ginenski, a butcher by profession, was born in Novogrudok in 1892 to Isaac and Feigel.[7] Rita notes that at the time of his murder in 1942, he had been working for the Germans in a military facility,[8] possibly the military barracks in Skirdlevo.

Bella, Shepsel's wife and the mother of their three daughters, was the daughter of Aaron Rabinovich. Born in the Belorussian town of Gorodischche, she worked alongside her husband in their meat and grocery shop in Novogrudok, where the family lived on Zamkovaya Street.

Doris describes her mother Bella as having been "the best mother one could ever hope to have," noting how she mustered the strength to care for and keep her three teenage children alive after her husband's murder.[9]

Of the three sisters, only Rita remained with Bella throughout the war. Together in the forced labor camp, they crawled through the tunnel to successfully reach the Bielski detachment, where they remained until liberation. Rita describes the forced labor camp as having been a "terrible place" where both she and her mother were assigned to cook and clean. Despite their job preparing food, Rita cannot forget the intense hunger that overshadowed their lives in the camp.[10]

Rita effortlessly recalls September 26, 1943, as the day she and her mother escaped from the labor camp, which both she and Doris refer to as "the ghetto." She reports that the digging "with spoons and bare hands" commenced soon after the May 7 massacre that signaled they were next in line to be killed. While Bella would take her turn digging the tunnel, Rita's job was to collect the dug-up dirt in her pockets and transfer it to the attic to be hidden. Rita estimates that 250 prisoners crawled out of the escape tunnel, which she recalls the inmates coining "the Tunnel of Life." All the escapees, she emphasizes, fiercely desired to live.[11]

Described by her daughter Ella as intelligent, kind, and strong willed,[12] Rita remained determined to become a teacher despite the war and all she had experienced. After returning to live in Novogrudok following liberation, Rita studied in Baranovich and Minsk to become a teacher of Russian literature and language, at which she worked for thirty-eight years. Married to Avraham Boyarski in 1952, she lived and raised her two children in Baranovich until their immigration to the United States in 1992 at the fall of the Soviet Union. Bella had also moved to Baranovich, where she lived with Rita and her family until her death in 1987.[13] Ella, a retired English teacher, notes that Bella was the primary source of information regarding the family's wartime experiences.[14]

As of this writing in June 2023, Rita is a grandmother of four and great-grandmother of three. Today, her mother Bella would be the grandmother of five, great-grandmother of seven, and great-great grandmother of at least nine.[15] The very last tunnel survivor we have discovered to date, Rita is the oldest living tunnel survivor to be identified.

Yakov (Yasha) Kantorovich

Yakov Kantorovich's story is one of bravery, accomplishment, and ultimate tragedy.

Born on June 5, 1910, to Dvora and Chaim in the town of Slutsk in the Minsk region, Yakov worked as a clerk. His wife Fanya née Miliavski,[1] the daughter of Samuil and Rachel,[2] was a fellow Slutsk native born in 1914.[3] During the war, both Fanya and the couple's young daughter Anna, born in 1938, were evacuated eight hundred miles away to the town of Uryupink[4] in the Volgograd region of Russia.

Although Yakov's name does not appear on the escape list, his incarceration in the Novogrudok forced labor camp and his involvement in the tunnel escape are documented in an article on Novogrudok in the *Encyclopedia Judaica* which designates him as a member of the resistance group that planned the escape.[5] Moreover, the fact that he survived the tunnel escape to arrive safely to the Naliboki Forest and join the Bielski partisans is documented in the partisan annals.[6] However, a 1990 Yad Vashem Page of Testimony submitted by his wife Fanya attests that Yakov did not survive the war, but was killed in Gomel on February 4, 1944, as a Red Army soldier.[7]

Additional Pages of Testimony that Fanya completed reveal even more tragedies: both Yakov's brother and brother-in-law were also killed at the front. His brother Solomon Kantorovich, born in 1915, had worked as a teacher in the town of Lepel in the Vitebsk region. It does not appear that he was married. According to Fanya, Solomon went missing in action.[8] Fanya's own brother Mikhail Miliavski, a clerk born in 1909 in the Belarusian town of Khoyniki, was yet another military casualty of the war.[9]

While we are unaware whether Yakov and Fanya's daughter Anna survived the war or is still alive, Fanya listed her own address as "Minsk" on the Pages of Testimony she filed in 1990 for Yakov, Solomon, and Michael.[10]

During the war, as Fanya and Anna took refuge far from their home in Slutsk, it is doubtful they ever knew of the escape from the forced labor camp in which Yakov had participated. His tragic death as a Red Army soldier dashed the dream of this family to ever be reunited again.

Yosef (Yoshke) Koniak

Yosef Koniak, a shoemaker, may ultimately have been responsible for the decision taken on Saturday night, September 25, 1943, to set the daring escape for the following night, three nights before the start of the Jewish New Year.

In a vote taken about a week earlier, 65 percent of the inmates opted in favor of escaping, while 35 percent opposed the plan. Meanwhile, persistent rumors prevailed of an upcoming liquidation of the camp's present inhabitants, save for twelve select craftsmen. Although those strongly opposed to an escape were closely guarded in order to ensure that the breakout plan would not be sabotaged,[1] Yoshke Koniak helped turn the tide from the possibility of an escape to a reality.

Described by fellow escapee Nachum (Zeidel) Kushner (#143) as having been an expert shoemaker whose skilled craftsmanship had enabled him to survive all the massacres, Koniak was the one who revealed having been ordered to paint two rooms in the jail intended to serve as a workshop for some of the twelve tradesmen slated to remain in the camp after the "final slaughter." With his fellow inmates suddenly believing the execution rumors and realizing that they had nothing to lose, the decision to escape on the night of September 26 was finalized.[2]

As for the identity of Yosef Koniak, there are two men with this name who appear in Yad Vashem's Central Database of Shoah Victims' Names. Both are listed as originating from the Volyn region in today's Ukraine, which had been under Polish rule, annexed by the Soviet Union in 1939, and under Nazi control from 1941 until recaptured by the Red Army in 1944.

All that is recorded for Yosef Koniak of Beresteczko is that he was murdered in the Holocaust. He is likely to have been part of the Koniak family of Beresteczko, which included parents Shaul and Sara and their children Yisrael and Chaya-Bila, all of whom were murdered.[3]

Yosef Koniak of Rozyszcze, the son of Yoel and Henia née Matziver, was born in 1914. A second-generation carpenter, he was married to Feige née Rivetz.[4] Yosef's five siblings included Moshe, single and age twenty-five at his death;[5] Eliyahu (Elia), age thirty at his death, married to Chaya and the father of toddlers Yoel and Avraham;[6] Chaya, age sixteen at her death;[7] Avraham, age fourteen at his death;[8] and David, only eleven years old when murdered.[9] All members of this family, including Yosef and Feige's one-year-old daughter Rachel, are reported by Yosef's brother-in-law to have been murdered in 1942. The fact that Yosef was a carpenter may negate the possibility that he was the

Novogrudok forced labor camp inmate by this name, whom Nachum Kushner reported to have been a shoemaker.

In any case, if one of these two Yosef Koniaks is indeed the inmate who escaped through the tunnel, he would have been compelled to first escape his hometown in the Volyn region before or during the 1941 Nazi invasion to reach the Novogrudok area 250 miles away.

Unfortunately, Yosef Koniak's name does not appear on any partisan list,[10] thus we must assume that he did not survive the breakout to reach the freedom of the forest.

Kozuchovski

Although the name Kozuchovski cannot be deciphered on the escape list, fellow inmate Chaim Leibowitz attests that Kozuchovski (given name unknown) was slated to have thrown hand grenades at the watchtower during the breakout from the Novogrudok forced labor camp planned for April 15, 1943, which was subsequently cancelled.[1]

Leibowitz also testifies that after fleeing through the tunnel and joining the Bielski partisans, Kozuchovski was part of a fighting group consisting of at least one of the Chernichovski brothers, Hirsh Orlinski (#34), and five other partisans, who had two weapons among them. Three days after the tunnel escape, the group encountered a Russian partisan unit that demanded their guns. Refusing to surrender their weapons unless by death, the entire group of Jews was murdered by the Russian partisans.[2] This despite the fact that Russian partisan leader Victor Panchenko had established cooperation and friendly relations with Tuvia Bielski from the summer of 1942.[3]

Victor Panchenko was a former lieutenant in the Red Army who hailed from Smolensk in the East. When his machine-gun battalion was stationed along the western border of the Soviet Union, he was attacked by the Nazis in 1941 and consequently retreated to Novogrudok, where he founded the strong *otriad* "Octiaber."[4] Named for the October Revolution and consisting of former Soviet soldiers and Belarusian peasants, this *otriad* especially concentrated its presence around the towns of Lida, Novogrudok, and Zhetl, where raids on Belarusian and German police stations netted valuable arms and ammunition. Once cooperation between the Panchenko and Bielski partisan groups was established, Panchenko divided the area into two parts for the purpose of food raids. The Bielski partisans were to procure provisions from farms close to Lida and Novogrudok, while Panchenko's Octiaber *otriad* would conduct raids in and around Zhetl.[5]

A document dated September 16, 1944, filed with the National Archive of the Republic of Belarus and signed by detachment commander Tuvia Bielski, chief of staff Malbin, and detachment commissar Shemyatovetz, notes that contact between Bielski and Panchenko was first established in September 1942. Among the many subsequent joint military operations were the September 20, 1942, ambush against German gendarmes on the Novogrudok-Novoyelna highway, as well as the March 12, 1943, attack on police in the village of Drachilov.[6]

Despite the alleged cooperation, trust, and friendship between the Bielski and Victor partisan groups, we must remember who killed Kozuchowski and the friends with whom he escaped from the tunnel.

We know nothing about Kozuchowski's origins, occupation, or family life. The name Kozuchowski does not appear in Yad Vashem's Central Database of Shoah Victims' Names.

Avraham Magids (Magid)

A symbol of resiliency in the face of ever-changing adversities, Avraham Magids was born in 1909 in Sol, a town near Vilna. His mother Chana died when he was a small child, leaving six sons and two daughters alone with their father Shmaya. One younger, single sister, Chaike, as well as two brothers married with children were killed in the Vilna ghetto by the Nazis. Their father died of natural causes during the German occupation.

One of the younger children in the family, Avraham first learned in a local *cheder* (religious school for young boys) before being sent to the yeshiva of Rav Ezer in Vilna. An excellent student, he continued his studies in the prestigious Slobodka Yeshiva located in a suburb of the Lithuanian capital of Kovno.[1]

At age twenty-one, Avraham joined the Polish Army, where he served as a sergeant in the Pilsudski Brigade near Vilna. Upon discharge, he married Bracha Katlartski from the Belarusian town of Belice, where the young couple settled and Avraham worked in his wealthy father-in-law's turpentine factory. Avraham and Bracha became the parents of two sons, Yechezkiel and Elchanan.[2]

Called up for reserve duty in 1939, Avraham was captured by the Russians near Lvov and sent by train to a prisoner of war camp in Archangelsk, near Siberia. After a brave escape from the camp with two other prisoners, he traveled for two years until returning to Belice, only to find the town under German occupation and the residents relocated to Lida and Zhetl. Avraham succeeded in finding his wife and children in the Zhetl ghetto, where local residents are reported to have opened their doors to refugees who arrived from across Poland. Yet this reunion was short-lived. Only two days later, upon Avraham's return home from a search for relatives, he found that Bracha and their two small sons had been massacred in Zhetl's first slaughter on April 30, 1942.[3]

Avraham somehow mustered the strength to work in a local shoe polish factory until the second massacre on August 6, 1942.[4] In the immediate aftermath, Avraham and other survivors were starved and held prisoner in the local cinema for several days. When a "selection" (of those to be executed) was subsequently carried out by two Germans assisted by a Ukrainian and a Lithuanian, Avraham thought quickly and told his questioners that he was a welder by profession. Asked to present his non-existent professional identification card, his pretend search of his pocket was enough to forestall death.[5]

Having managed to fake a profession deemed useful to the Germans, Avraham was sent to the Novogrudok forced labor camp. His second wife Chaya relates that after liberation, Avraham would often speak of the inhumane conditions in the camp shrouded by the fact that one never knew if he would live until the next day. Killings were conducted in a most capricious and unpredictable manner – during a lineup, for example, the camp commander Wilhelm Reuter might spontaneously decide to murder every third person.[6]

After surviving the labor camp and the tunnel escape, Avraham reached the Lipiczanska Forest, where Zhetlers, under the command of Hirsh Kaplinsky,[7] had formed a unit of the Lenin Brigade after the second Zhetl massacre of August 6, 1942. Originally consisting of about 120 men and women, mostly armed, these partisans took action against Nazi collaborators who persecuted and betrayed Jews escaping from the various ghettos in the area. After two months of acting as an independent unit, the group joined the Russian-led Orlanski partisans commanded by Nikolai Vakhonim.[8] Having somehow obtained a weapon, Avraham was accepted as a fighter, but soon found his life in danger with the discovery of several eggs that had been pilfered by his comrades during a raid near Novogrudok.[9]

Escaping the Lipiczanska region, where he was a wanted man, Avraham joined the partisans in the Rubnitski Forest near Vilna, with whom he took part in raids to rescue Jews trapped in the Vilna ghetto.[10]

After a stop in Belice, Avraham made his way back to the Novogrudok area. Still a fugitive from the nearby Russian partisans, Avraham Magids assumed the alias surname "Abramovich." In the forest, he found refuge with Tuvia Bielski, who exacted a promise from the regional Soviet partisan commander, General Vasily Yefimovich Chernyshev (codenamed "Platon"),[11] to protect the new recruit.[12] Avraham was not alone in seeking safety from non-Jewish partisans in the Bielski *otriad*. In 1943 alone, at least twenty-two Jewish fighters from the Russian Orlanski group knew they could rely on shelter with the Bielskis after being threatened by menacing anti-Semitic remarks.[13]

It was in the forest that Avraham met his second wife, Chaya née Savitzki, who had been a fighting partisan since her escape from the forced labor camp in Dvoretz in 1942. After traveling through Hungary, Czechoslovakia, Austria, and Greece (a route taken by many survivors assisted by soldiers of Britain's Jewish Brigade, who clandestinely aided immigration to Palestine),[14] the couple was married in Italy. While awaiting illegal passage to Palestine for two years, Avraham and Chaya suffered yet another hardship when their six-month-old daughter Frida, her maternal grandmother's namesake, succumbed to pneumonia.[15]

Clinging to their hope to yet reach Palestine, the couple was among the last to leave the beach town of Anzio due to Avraham's position as leader of a group of refugees waiting to leave for pre-state Israel. Ultimately the two boarded and disembarked from ships three times due to flooding. At long last, they sailed to the Promised Land in the fall of 1947 on a refugee ship departing from the port of Bari.[16]

Initially settling in Zichron Yaakov, where Avraham had family, he and Chaya lived in a house where the Aaronsohn family (founders of a pro-British World War I espionage group) had resided. Avraham continued to exhibit his well-polished ability to adapt to change. Seeking a livelihood, he first worked in a grocery, then as an upholsterer and a restaurant owner. At last, Avraham (who had by then changed his surname to "Magid") became the proprietor of a neighborhood grocery store in Givatayim, where for three decades, "everyone knew us and we knew everybody." The Magid home was renowned as a social hub for all local Zhetlers. Chaya Magid recalls that "everybody knew that each Saturday night there was a gathering at Chaya and Avraham's place, complete with tea, potatoes, and herring. The only thing we would speak about was Zhetl."[17]

After a lifetime of challenges, losses, and victories, Avraham Magid died in 1991 at the age of eighty-two. By 2022, fourteen great-grandchildren have been born. His son Shmaya, born in 1949, has four children and eleven grandchildren. Daughter Rachel, born in 1953, is the mother of three as well as the grandmother of three. Despite his accomplishments and

Avraham Magids on guard duty in Anzio, Italy, 1945–1947 (courtesy of Shmaya Magid)

the vibrant family that he and Chaya created, the latter laments that Avraham could have lived many more years. "The war ruined him," she says simply and sadly.[18]

Morduch (Mordechai) Majerowicz

The eyewitness testimony that Morduch (Mordechai) Majerowicz submitted to Yad Vashem is profoundly difficult to read. Unlike other testimonies written by escapees regarding their prewar lives and experiences in the Novogrudok forced labor camp, Morduch does not spare the horrifying descriptions and details of the atrocities he witnessed. We have included excerpts from his testimony as a documentation of life and death outside the massive killing sites of the

Holocaust, which perhaps other escapees experienced but did not dare to relate.

Born in Karelich on June 15, 1893, to Kopel and Chaya Majerowicz,[1] Morduch, a tailor, relates having moved in 1918 to the small, undeveloped Belarusian town of Rozanka, where he was later married and his three sons were born.[2] In the Yad Vashem Page of Testimony that Morduch submitted in the 1950s for his wife Leah née Paretzki and sons Kopel, Avraham, and Reuven,[3] he listed himself as the "head of the family," despite the family having been annihilated. He specifies that Kopel[4] and Reuven[5] were murdered in their birthplace of Rozanka, and that Avraham[6] was slaughtered together with his mother in the town of Szczuczyn. In his written testimony submitted in 1961, Morduch details the horrific murder in Rozanski of his eighty-five-year-old father-in-law, who due to his slow gait was "helped" to walk by being tied up and dragged to his grave.[7]

Returning to Karelich following the murder of his family, Morduch notes the openly virulent anti-Semitism of the townspeople subsequent to the German invasion. Writing of robberies and assaults committed by the local youth toward their Jewish neighbors, Morduch relates a heinous act in which David Niselevich, a tailor from Karelich, was beaten before the gold teeth in his mouth were brutally extracted.

Majerowicz also describes the unspeakable torture of the community's rabbi, Yisrael Vernik, whose beard was torn from his face. The rabbi was saved from the flames of the burning synagogue and Torah scrolls only because the Germans determined that it would be too time-consuming to burn a man as large as he. Eventually, Rabbi Vernick was taken to Novogrudok, where he was tortured in jail before his murder.

Shortly after Morduch's own arrival in Novogrudok, fifty-two men were rounded up on the Sabbath day of July 26, 1941, and murdered in the main square.[8] While Idel Kagan (#95) wrote of the Strauss waltzes that were played during the massacre,[9] Morduch reports that the victims were also sadistically forced to dance as they were slaughtered.[10]

Returning to Karelich, where he had apprenticed as a tailor, Morduch describes the ghetto workshops where the German occupiers demanded that skilled craftsmen make repairs at no charge for the local population. Conditions in the Karelich ghetto were so abominable that the same non-Jewish population that had once stolen the property of the Jews was now moved to bring them a bit of bread or several potatoes.

Describing the melting snow in Karelich of March 1942, Morduch writes of how inmates from the forced labor camp were ordered to rescue German vehicles stuck in the mud. Often compelled to march or run many kilometers to the cars, the inmates were then commanded to lick the tires as well as the shoes of the German soldiers.

In May 1942, the Karelich Judenrat was ordered by the Germans to compile a list of skilled workers for transfer to the Novogrudok forced labor camp several weeks later. As a tailor, Morduch was assigned there as well. He writes that a patch of white material with a number was sewn on the back of each inmate who was conscripted to one of the labor camp workshops. Moreover, many widowed women were fictitiously registered as craftsmen's wives so as to enable them to escape the ghetto by being permitted to join their "husbands" in the labor camp. He also details the sadism of Kavalchik, the Polish foreman of the carpentry shop, who frequently meted out punishments of twenty-five lashes to the naked bodies of Jewish inmates.[11]

According to Morduch, inmates were allowed, sometimes even encouraged, to purchase goods outside the camp, and then sentenced to murder for their "permitted" purchases. Furthermore, he cites that those "only wounded" in the May 7 massacre were put to death by chlorine being spilled over their already-mutilated bodies sprawled in the pre-dug pits.

Perhaps most excruciating are Morduch's descriptions of atrocities against the children caught hidden in the Novogrudok forced labor camp, such as Moshele, a two-year-old hiding with his mother in the camp's basement. When the toddler began to cry, she committed the ultimate sacrifice by choking him to death in order to spare the lives of the other small children hidden in the basement.

Wilhelm Reuter, the German commander of the camp, issued the orders to search for the hidden children. When discovered, they were so violently hurled onto trucks that blood often streamed from their heads onto the street. Morduch writes of Dvorah Zaritzski, wife of Yitzchak Zavitski, a furrier from Karelich, who pleaded to lick her daughter's blood and to accompany her on her last journey. He also tells of the woman who was shot and killed together with her newborn baby, and of the five-year-old daughter of inmate Sarah Burshtein, who, after begging for her mother, was led instead to her own pre-dug grave. Eighteen years after leaving the Novogrudok forced labor camp, Morduch reported being endlessly haunted by recurring images of children with smashed skulls.[12]

In describing the tunnel escape, Morduch relates that the digging lasted twelve weeks. In preparation for the escape, he notes that each inmate prepared a fake weapon, perhaps a "knife" or a "gun" made of wood, to use if needed to procure food from farmers along their journey to the forest. While Morduch writes that Tuvia Bielski acquired real weapons from farmers selling arms left by the retreating Soviets, Jews in Russian partisan units are reported to have faced such virulent anti-Semitism that weapons from the non-Jewish farmers were arbitrarily used against them.

Describing his trek through the forest, Morduch apparently reached the Russian Roscha partisan detachment together with fellow escapees Shmuel (#191) and Eliezer (#192) Zusmanovich, aged eight and a half, who remained at Shmuel's side throughout the war.[13]

The sole survivor of his family and one of only two survivors of Rozanka, Morduch overcame his losses to make meaningful contributions subsequent to liberation. While still in Belorussia, he became involved in searching out and reporting collaborators with the Germans to the Russian security services, as well as helping to return hidden children to their relatives and to the Jewish people.[14]

Active in the Zionist movement after repatriation to Poland, Morduch helped prospective immigrants to Palestine prepare for their lives as refugees in Germany.[15] Residing in Germany from July 1946 to October 1947, he gave his address in at least one Red Cross document as the Sedan-Kaserne Displaced Persons Camp in Ulm in the American zone.[16]

Although Morduch's name does not appear on the escape list, in a postwar request for assistance, he testifies to having escaped from Novogrudok in September 1943, the month of the tunnel escape and, in a rare admission, reports having joined the partisans in the same month.[17] It is noteworthy that during the Cold War era,

Morduch (Mordechai) Majerowicz, undated postwar photo (*The Story of a Partisan*, 1978)

most applicants for immigration to the West withheld the fact of their partisan membership for fear of arousing suspicion of cooperation with the Soviets. In fact, in Red Cross documents of all the tunnel escapees researched for this book, Morduch is the sole person to have openly admitted to his wartime partisan membership.

After serving in Paris as an emissary for the Zionist movement, Morduch immigrated to the new State of Israel in 1949.[18] Known as Mordechai in his new homeland, he settled in the coastal city of Ashkelon, where he lived until his death in 1975 at the age of eighty-two.[19] In all probability, the 1978 posthumous publication of his testimony as the book *The Story of a Partisan*[20] was overseen by his second wife Chana, who arranged for his burial in the Ashkelon New South Cemetery. In an emotional letter written by Chana to the Ashkelon Burial Society in January 1976, she requests a nearby plot for her own future burial and notes that Mordechai was ill for the last fifteen years of his life and frequently hospitalized. We have no information about

Chana other than that she was born in 1916 and was indeed buried in the same cemetery as Mordechai in 1988.[21]

With Chana declaring that she was all alone in the world following Mordechai's death,[22] any hopes Mordechai may have had to once again consider himself as "head of the family" apparently never came to fruition.

Mordechai (Motke) Morduchowicz

Born in Horodyszecze in 1925[1] to Yitzchak, a saddler/leather worker, and Sheina Leah née Rabinovich, a housewife,[2] Mordechai Morduchowicz grew up in the town of Ivenets and was among the three of the family's five children who survived the war.[3] Younger brothers Baruch[4] and Zeev (Velvel),[5] aged twelve and six at their deaths, were murdered together with their mother during the Ivenets massacre of June 9, 1942. After surviving another two months, their father was then slain in Novogrudok's second slaughter on August 7, 1942, while imprisoned in the Pereseka ghetto.[6]

In his Yad Vashem testimony, Mordechai recounts memories of a childhood in which he studied in the local Jewish school, learned his father's trade after school, and endured taunts and beatings by local non-Jewish children who believed that Jews used the blood of Christians to make matzot (unleavened bread for Passover).

Perhaps the unsung hero of the Novogrudok forced labor camp tunnel escape, Mordechai took the brave initiative to use his job "on the outside" as a water carrier and deliveryman to purchase sorely needed materials for building the tunnel. During his daily horse and carriage outings for loaves of bread to be distributed to the camp inmates, as well as his two to four daily journeys to town to bring water for the camp, Mordechai was accompanied by a local policeman. This "water cop" would help Mordechai obtain potatoes by the town well, buy nails for him in the local hardware store, and purchase rope and other essential supplies, never imagining that they were to be used for digging a tunnel. The unsuspecting policeman was even requested to buy a gun, albeit this item was never delivered. Mordechai obtained the money for the purchases by selling some of the bread from his wagon to people who had gold, which in turn was exchanged for cash.

Throughout his ordeals, Mordechai never lost his humanity. Prior to his internment in the Novogrudok forced labor camp, he had been assigned to backbreaking hard labor in the town of Dworetz hauling heavy rocks out of a quarry to trains bound for Germany. Upon his release, Mordechai faced a grueling one-week trek on foot to reach his home. Forbidden to use the roads, he sought unmarked paths along the miles. "When there was a lone, isolated house," he said, "we simply entered. Among the *goyim* [non-Jews], there were some good people too. Most of the *goyim* were good people, and they respected Jews."

Although a saddler and leather worker, Mordechai did not work in his trade in the forced labor camp, preferring to give work to older inmates to enable them to prove useful and prolong their lives. Having gleaned knowledge in the realm of brush-making from his work as a saddler, Mordechai became a teacher in the brush-making workshop so that here, too, some of the older workers could be deemed essential.

Recalling his "happiness to save a Jewish life," Mordechai speaks of a request he received from a Jew to smuggle his brother into the labor camp from the ghetto. Risking his own life, Mordechai hid the man among the loaves in his bread delivery, enabling him to enter the camp, from which he escaped to the partisans.

At the further risk of death, Mordechai would obtain half loaves of bread and butter to give to tunnel diggers "so they would have strength to work."

When his younger brother Yankel was sentenced to twenty-five lashes for what was deemed to be poor work, Mordechai volunteered to be whipped in his stead. Only because the foremen had taken a liking to Mordechai, considered to be a good worker, were both brothers spared the beating.

At the climax of the breakout, it was Mordechai Morduchowicz who found Daniel Ostashinski, former Judenrat head, unconscious and barely alive. Mordechai immediately hoisted escapee Daniel over his back to carry him to safety.[7]

Testimonies report the existence of several clandestine radios hidden inside the forced labor camp, serving a compelling role in keeping the resistance leaders informed of the war's developments. At least two such radios were smuggled into the camp, one slipped inside a sack of flour by Ruvke Shabakovski (#5) in December 1942[8] and another pirated into the camp during the summer of 1943 by resistance leaders.[9] Yet one additional radio was secretly assembled within the camp itself by the young brother of inmate Jankef Nevachovich (#51). Mordechai Morduchowicz's son Zvi Mor recalls his father noting that he carried out one of the radios during the escape and tried to keep it in his grasp while fleeing to the Bielski partisan detachment.[10] This is confirmed in a book coauthored by Dov Kagan and tunnel escapee Idel Kagan (#95). They report that as tunnel survivors Shaul Gorodynski (#77) and Nachman Feifer (#167) were attempting to reach the partisans, they sighted a group of escapees, "among them Dr. and Mrs. Jakubowicz (#1, 2), Daniel Ostashinski, Pinchuk (#46), (Moshe) Feivelevich (#47), and another man from Ivenets named Motke, who had a radio."[11] Unfortunately, this prized possession was eventually seized from him by a group of Russian partisans.[12]

On his own precarious trek to the Bielski detachment in the Naliboki Forest, Mordechai saved himself from being attacked by an anti-Semitic farmer by flashing a toy gun made by one of the carpenters prior to the tunnel escape. Upon safely reaching the *otriad* deep in the forest several days later, Mordechai was reunited with his brother Yankel, who had escaped from the labor camp several months earlier.[13]

In his testimony, Mordechai recalls finding that there were only 270 weapons for the twelve hundred people in the partisan detachment. As a member of the posse that set out on food-hunting expeditions, he describes how ten horses with wagons would return to camp loaded with anything they could procure in the neighboring villages. During his very last outing for provisions, just one day before liberation, Mordechai came full circle: he encountered the same group of Russian partisans that had snatched the prize radio. Excitedly, they informed Mordechai and his companions of broadcasts on the (stolen) radio indicating that the Russians were nearing. The news of their impending freedom stirred such exhilaration that the men could hardly sleep a wink. The next morning, liberation dawned.[14]

Leaving the forest, Mordechai became one of the former Jewish partisans who now volunteered to serve in an "extermination battalion" set up by the Soviet security services to seek out anti-Semites and former Nazi collaborators and bring them to punishment.[15] After serving in the Belarusian town of Derevna from 1945 until the end of 1946, Mordechai left for Kaitish, Uzbekistan, where he was reunited with his surviving siblings Reizel and Yankel.[16] After returning to Derevna a year and a half later to marry Shulamit née Kasower in 1948, Mordechai brought his young bride to the town of Nieswicz, Belorussia, where the couple resided in the local Radziwill Castle, then utilized as a health spa for Belarusian Soviet notables. Mordechai was responsible for the food warehouse. It was in Nieswicz that yet another tragedy struck: the couple's first child, Yitzchak, his paternal grandfather's namesake, born in September 1949, succumbed to illness at the age of just eighteen months. Yitzchak's brother Zvi was born in 1952 in Nieswicz, where he was raised for the first five years of his life.[17]

Repatriated to Poland at the end of 1957, the Morduchowicz family grew with the birth of Leah, the namesake of her paternal grandmother, six months prior to the family's arrival in Israel on July 1, 1959. Settling in Netanya, Mordechai first held jobs demanding physical labor before beginning to work as an agent for a food concern. In yet another terrible blow, Mordechai lost most of his vision before he turned fifty, forcing him once again to rise above his circumstances. He and Shulamit, now Shula, opened a small store, which they managed together until Mordechai could no longer continue working.[18]

Resigned to his new reality of being severely visually impaired, Mordechai attended a workshop for the blind. But tragedy struck yet again. In his mid-eighties, he suffered a serious fall on the way home from work. Never fully recovering from this fall, Mordechai reportedly spent his last years in a state of increasing dementia,[19] during which he was lovingly cared for by Shula. When visited at home by the author in 2011, Mordechai was in a hospital bed and completely unresponsive to his children and to the author, even when spoken to in his native Yiddish.

Unlike many escapees' children who have been interviewed for this book, Mordechai's children Zvi, an accountant,[20] and Leah, a university office worker,[21] both affirm that the story of the tunnel escape was an integral part of their youth. Although the Holocaust was never forgotten in the Morduchowicz home, it did not overshadow the joy and optimism that prevailed. Zvi recalls that while growing up, many friends whose parents were Holocaust survivors would comment how this joyful atmosphere contrasted to the mood in their own families.[22]

Zvi and Leah stress that while their parents expressed appreciation for their lives and for the family they created, neither ever forgot the members of their families who were slain. Thanks to Mordechai's efforts to raise funds from Ivenets survivors, a memorial stands today near the site of a mass grave in Ivenets containing the remains of eight hundred Jews, of whom six hundred were children under the age of twelve, murdered on June 9, 1942. There lie Mordechai's mother and two younger brothers, as well as the two youngest of Shula's five siblings.[23] The new memorial replaces the long-broken one originally built by Shmuel Kolachek (#82) in the 1950s. A stone wall surrounds the grave, also repaired thanks to Mordechai's efforts. In the years following the fall of the Soviet Union, Mordechai and Shula are reported to have visited the site regularly during their yearly visits to Belarus.

In January 2021, ninety-four-year-old Shula expresses gratitude for the joy and respect she receives from her family, yet insists on eating stale bread, an eternal reminder of the Holocaust and those she lost.[24]

The significance of the escape for Mordechai is evidenced in a moving scene from the documentary movie *Tunnel of Hope*, in which descendants of escapees are filmed returning to the Novogrudok forced labor camp in 2012 to search for remains of the tunnel. Despite his near-comatose state, when told by Leah and her son Nir that

Mordechai Morduchowicz, Derevna, 1944–1945 (courtesy of Zvi Mor)

they had returned from Novogrudok and found the tunnel, Mordechai almost miraculously begins to speak and relate to the event.[25]

Mordechai Morduchowicz passed away on September 9, 2013. If he were alive in August 2023, their beloved "Motl" would surely enjoy his six grandchildren and thirteen great-grandchildren.[26] Remembered by Leah for his optimism, his love for humanity, and his determination to survive under arduous circumstances,[27] Mordechai is also recalled by his son Zvi for his virtuousness and his zeal to help others.[28]

The personality traits cited by Mordechai Morduchowicz's children shone powerfully in his actions in the Novogrudok forced labor camp and in their father's crucial role in the escape.

Chaim Notkovich, Son-in-Law Avraham, and Grandson Moshele

Chaim Notkovich, a resident of Zhetl,[1] was born in 1878. Married to Tova ("Toibe"), Chaim worked as a leather worker and saddler prior to the war.[2] Tova was murdered in Zhetl in 1942.[3]

Although their names are not found on the escape list, Pesia Mayevski (#160) testifies in her Yiddish-language account of the tunnel escape that Chaim was interned in the Novogrudok forced labor camp together with his son-in-law Avraham as well as Avraham's son Moshe ("Moshele").[4] Avraham, whose surname is unknown, was married to Chaim's daughter Gutka, who was murdered in Zhetl's massacre of August 6, 1942, together with a younger son, aged seven.[5]

Chaim Notkovich, his son-in-law Avraham, and grandson Moshele were all murdered in their attempt to escape through the tunnel to freedom. Moshele was twelve years old at his death.[6]

The deaths of Chaim, Toibe, Avraham, Guta, Moshele, and his brother are commemorated in Zhetl's memorial book.[7]

Daniel Ostashinski

Daniel Ostashinski was born in Novogrudok on January 1, 1921,[1] to Chaim Zeev Ostashinski, a tailor,[2] and his wife Zipora née Abramovich, a housewife. The namesake of his maternal grandfather,[3] Daniel was the scion of a family known for its involvement with the Novardok Yeshiva in the city. In particular, his paternal grandmother Kayla Fruma née Chaitovich was renowned for her efforts to collect charity for the yeshiva and for opening her home to out-of-town yeshiva students for Shabbat meals.[4]

Daniel was the oldest of six children: Esther, born in 1923;[5] Perla, born in 1925;[6] Yitzchak, born in 1927;[7] Pesach, born around 1931;[8] and Batya Rivka, born in 1933.[9] The children grew up in comfortable circumstances, as Chaim made a good living from his successful tailor shop, where he employed around fifty tailors.[10]

When the author's mother Fanya Dunetz (#142) met with Daniel's eldest son Zafrir in the course of this research, she expressed amazement at his resemblance to his father, whom she remembered from the age of thirteen as handsome, blond, an excellent student, and so serious that he hardly ever smiled.[11] After completing *cheder* and the Tarbut school in Novogrudok, Daniel, one year younger and two grades below her, became Fanya's schoolmate at the prestigious Polish high school in Novogrudok. Fanya recalled that she and Daniel often met after school when she visited her classmate Leah Abramovich and Daniel came to be with Leah's brother Nyoma.[12]

Daniel Ostashinsky emerged as a leader early in his youth. Despite the 8:00 p.m. curfew[13] and the school's prohibition against joining political organizations, by the age of sixteen Daniel was voted to head the local Betar youth organization,[14] the Revisionist Zionist youth movement founded in 1923 by Zeev Jabotinsky. This youthful association with Betar was later to come to the fore in Daniel's postwar experiences.

In school, Daniel excelled in all academic subjects. He became fluent in Russian, Polish, White Russian, Yiddish, and German, yet this aptitude for languages ultimately complicated his life: his ability to communicate with all segments of the local population, as well as with the Nazi occupiers, led to Daniel's appointment at the young age of twenty-one as head of the Judenrat in the Novogrudok ghetto.[15] Forced in this position to cooperate with the Germans by supplying lists or ghetto inmates before each "selection" and other operations, Daniel earned many enemies who wished him dead. Others argued that he redeemed himself through his resistance work within the Novogrudok forced labor camp, where he and his family (excluding Pesach, who had been hidden with a Christian family) had been transferred, particularly through his efforts in the planning of the clandestine tunnel escape.[16]

By the end of the winter of 1942, the Germans had gradually beefed up their watch at the forced labor camp in reaction to the occasional escape of inmates. Twelve policemen provided round-the-clock guard for the camp, which was surrounded by two walls separated by two yards. One of the two-yard-high walls was made of wood and the second from barbed wire. By night, the entire area was flooded by the beams of a large searchlight.[17]

In his testimony, Daniel reports that as early as September or October 1942, he was already part of the group of six or seven inmates who planned an armed breakout through the ghetto gates to escape through the forest.[18] Although this early plan never materialized, reportedly due to inmates' fears, later that winter the leaders contacted partisan commander Tuvia Bielski requesting his armed assistance in a newly planned breakout. In the memoir he wrote with his brother Zus, Tuvia Bielski unequivocally states that the letter requesting such help was sent and signed by Daniel, as well as by other inmates.[19] Tuvia replied, "I am ready to accept all of you…. But we are not organized enough to send fighters to you. Whoever comes [to our detachment] will be well received." Armed assistance was impossible, but camp leaders were provided with encouragement and hope of shelter following a breakout. Ultimately, the minutely planned escape slated for April 15, 1943, was cancelled at the last minute due to security considerations.[20] While we have no confirmation that this proposed breakout was actually Daniel's initiative, his son Zafrir notes that his father took credit for the idea.[21]

Although there was no longer a need for a formal Judenrat following the third Novogrudok massacre on February 4, 1943, which reduced the city's Jewish population to the five hundred-odd inmates remaining in the forced labor camp, Daniel Ostashinski continued to wield authority in the eyes of both the Jews[22] and the Germans.[23] Even so, he was unable to save three of his siblings, Batya Rivka, Esther, and Yitzchak, as well as his own mother, who were killed together with approximately half of the camp inmates in the slaughter of May 7, 1943. His inability to save these family members, especially his mother, is reported to have haunted Daniel till the end of his life. It was also Daniel who reportedly insisted, in a fiery debate following the May 7 massacre, that the Kaddish memorial prayer for the dead be recited by the survivors, "because that's what they would have wanted."[24]

In the aftermath of the murders, Daniel, his father Chaim (#32), and sister Perla (#33) were the only members of the family remaining in the camp. Miraculously, all of them survived the tunnel escape. Although in his memoir, Tuvia Bielski implies that the idea for building the tunnel was first initiated by the partisan leadership in response to Daniel's letter requesting his assistance,[25] this claim is refuted in Daniel's testimony.[26] Yisrael Kolachek (#81) maintains that the idea of a tunnel escape was raised by Berl Yoselevich in a meeting called by Daniel Ostashinski after the May 7 massacre.[27]

Zafrir Ostashinski recalls that his father spoke of having carried the wounded escapee Dr. Majer Yakubowicz (#1) to the Bielski partisan detachment.[28] This is corroborated by Shaul Gorodynski (#77) in his Yad Vashem testimony. There he reports having come across a group of Jews including Leiba Pinchuk (#46), Moshe Feivelevich (#47), and Daniel Ostashinksi, who had all carried the wounded doctor on their backs.[29]

Arriving alone to the partisan detachment after a two-week trek in which he was separated from his father and sister, Daniel did not receive a warm welcome. During the course of the trek, Daniel had had the ill fortune to come upon Berl Yoselevich and Chaim Kravitz, who considered him a traitor responsible for the deaths of their loved ones, despite Daniel's claims that he had known nothing of their impending slaughters. Berl and Chaim, coachmen by profession, now immediately prepared to shoot him.[30] Taking pains to first remove Daniel's boots to avoid having to pry off the boots of a dead man's swollen feet, the zealous brothers were halted by the providential appearance of Zus and Sonia Bielski. As Sonia and Daniel had been friends and schoolmates, the execution was stayed[31] pending a decision by Tuvia. Fortunately, Daniel's actual arrival to the Bielski detachment came at a time when Tuvia was preoccupied by the reorganization and split of the detachment into the (Kalinin) family group and the Ordzhonikidze group of 180 Bielski fighters under Russian command.

In his memoir, Tuvia Bielski reports having welcomed Daniel into the *otriad* with the promise of safety and a later trial.[32] However, Tuvia's account is contested by his brother Asael's wife Chaya Bielski, who claims that it was Zus, the third Bielski brother, who actually saved Daniel by insisting, "We will not have a trial. Not here, and not by us. After the war is behind us, in days when law and order will come, we will bring him to trial. Now we must help each Jew survive. We have enough enemies."[33] Yehuda Bauer writes that Daniel was actually brought to trial in the forest and judged not guilty for his actions as head of the Novogrudok Judenrat.[34]

It must be cited that while reports of Daniel's alleged crimes persisted, there was never any clear incriminating evidence against him.[35] Although it was said that in order to keep clear of his enemies, Daniel never left the camp, tended to stay alone, and never joined in food expeditions,[36] this is contradicted by Daniel's written testimony. In fact, he reports that on one such food expedition to a Belarusian village nearly eight miles from Novogrudok, he was first reunited with his father and sister after the tunnel escape. He describes the meeting as having taken place in the middle of the night while he was with some twenty-five partisans who, besides searching for food, had gone to seek revenge against Belarusian collaborators with the Germans or with the Belarusian police.[37]

Daniel remained with the Bielski partisans until liberation. After the war, he renewed his activities in the Betar movement, initially heading all Etzel (Betar) activities in Italy and then becoming the organization's European chief. His clandestine work brought him to pre-state Israel, first in 1946 and then again in 1948, before he finally immigrated in 1949.[38] In his testimony, Daniel describes having felt a "déjà vu" upon reaching Israel's shores and visiting the various places he had learned about as a youth in the Hebrew-language Novogrudok Tarbut school.[39]

Daniel Ostashinski, circa 1945 (courtesy of Zafrir Ostashinsky)

Daniel's wife Sonia née Popovsi and her mother, former residents of the northeastern Polish city of Suvalk, had been trapped on a train to the Treblinka death camp when her mother suddenly ordered her to jump off. Miraculously, Sonia survived the war and first met Daniel in Italy. The two were reunited in Israel at a gathering of friends from the Etzel in Tel Aviv's Park Hotel. Following their marriage, Sonia worked as a secretary for a high-ranking member of the Israeli police. Their son Zafrir reports that Sonia spoke of the Holocaust more often than Daniel, who almost never recalled his wartime experiences and never once spoke of his days as the Judenrat head.[40]

Daniel and Sonia had three sons, Zafrir, an attorney; Yitzchak, an insurance executive, and Gil, a tax advisor. Despite the traumatic experiences of their past, Daniel and Sonia are reported to have created a happy home. Daniel, who survived his share of danger during the Holocaust, died in Tel Aviv in 2005 after being hit by a car and lying paralyzed in a hospital for fifteen months. Following his death, Sonia was said to have lost her will to live and passed away in 2008.[41] As of August 2023, if Daniel and Sonia were alive, they would be the grandparents of twelve and the great-grandparents of eighteen.[42]

For those who wish to pass judgment on Daniel Ostashinski, I urge that they ask themselves how they would have reacted to the impossible position he was forced into assuming. Would they have passed up the opportunity to possibly save their five younger siblings as well as their beloved parents? In the words of Idel Kagan (#95), whose father was allegedly transferred upon Daniel's recommendation from the Novogrudok forced labor camp to Koldychevo concentration camp, where he was murdered, "No one can ever know how they would have acted in his shoes."

As Sonia Boldo Bielski, wife of Zus, pointed out in a 1994 oral testimony, "We must also not forget that even Daniel Ostashinski was unable to save his own mother as well as three of his siblings."[43]

Shalom Reznitzki

Shalom Reznitzki's story is one of unspeakable tragedy and unwavering faith, despite having lost everyone and everything dear to him.

Born in Zhetl in 1908,[1] Shalom Reznitzki was a blacksmith, following in the footsteps of his father Gersh.[2] His mother Rachel Feige[3] was a housewife.[4] She and Gersh were killed together with their daughter Chana Aberstein[5] and her husband Zacharia in Zhetl's first slaughter on April 30, 1942,[6] in the Kurpishtz Forest.

Just over three months later, Shalom's wife Miriam and their three children Yehudit, Avraham Yakov, and Rachel Feige were murdered.[7] Shalom survived by virtue of his essential skills as a blacksmith, for which the Nazis conscripted him to the Novogrudok forced labor camp. Surviving the breakout, Shalom escaped to the forest to join the Borba detachment of the Lenin Brigade of partisans.[8] His closest living relative, nephew Kalman Minuskin (the son of Yocheved, Shalom's only surviving sister, three years his senior), recalls that the family often spoke of Shalom having been a tunnel escapee who had joined other survivors from Zhetl in the forest after the breakout.[9]

Soon after returning to Zhetl following liberation, Shalom became reacquainted with Golda (surname unknown), a widow from Zhetl who had also lost a spouse and several children and was now the sole survivor of her family. The two wed in 1945, shortly before joining other Zhetlers traveling to Lodz for repatriation to Poland.[10]

Throughout the war, Shalom is said to have somehow held on to the anvil that he used as a blacksmith. Only after leaving Zhetl and realizing that he was unlikely to ever work again as a blacksmith in his future home in a Western country, Shalom hurled his anvil to the wind from the train en route to Lodz.

As stateless refugees after the war, Shalom and Golda made their way to Italy, where they eventually boarded an illegal immigration ship to pre-state Israel, blocked by the British Mandate authority to immigrants. After the ship was intercepted by the British Navy, Shalom and Golda were interned in a Cyprus detention camp for several months prior to Israel's independence. During this internment, Golda is reported to have lost the baby she was carrying, the hope that she and Shalom had harbored to somehow replace the families they'd both lost.[11]

Once they finally succeeded in immigrating to Israel after the establishment of the Jewish state in 1948, Shalom found work as a welder. Living in Tel Aviv, he remained close to his sister Yocheved, who had settled with her family in the nearby town of Kfar Saba.[12]

Golda apparently never emotionally recovered from her many losses and never held a job in Israel. The couple had no children together.[13] Golda Reznitsky died on November 24, 1987.[14]

After the war, Shalom is said to have found increasing solace in religion and to have even served as Zhetl's unofficial "rabbi" to survivors returning to the town immediately after liberation. His nephew recalls that Shalom was never heard to speak of his losses directly, nor did he express bitterness, but often spoke of "God's will."[15]

In Tel Aviv, Shalom was an active member of the city's Poale Zedek Synagogue until his death on April 15, 1993.[16] On his monument in the Holon Cemetery, the congregation's members paid tribute to Shalom and to his murdered parents, first wife, and children. Having no gravestones of their own, their names are carefully inscribed on his footstone. As Jewish custom prescribes naming after the dead, we can assume that Shalom's infant daughter Rachel Feige was named for her grandmother, murdered three months before her birth.

In his epitaph, Shalom is praised as "a humble, honest man who pursued justice and mercy" and whose love for Torah and its teachings prevailed over all.[17]

Yitzchak Shuster

Although Yitzchak Shuster's name cannot be deciphered on the escape list, it does appear as #17 on the initial comprehensive list of inmates drawn up by Yitzchak Rosenhaus (#30) just before the escape. Working from this document, the escape committee compiled the escape list to delineate the order in which each person would crawl through the tunnel.[1]

Born in Novogrudok in 1914 to Pinchas, Yitchak Shuster worked as a tailor and resided on Krasnaya Street prior to the war.[2] Yitzchak was married to Rachel, the sister of escapee Meir Berkowicz, who survived to testify to the deaths of both Rachel[3] and Shmulik, the couple's three-year-old son.[4] At his murder in Novogrudok's second mass massacre on August 7, 1942,[5] little Shmulik was the first of his family to be slaughtered. In a terrifying scene, the men of the ghetto were separated from the women, while children were wrenched from their mothers to be loaded onto trucks and driven to the ditches, where they were shot to death.[6]

Bereft of their only child, Yitzchak and Rachel remained together in the Novogrudok forced labor camp until May 7, 1943, Novogrudok's fourth massacre, in which around 250 women, 45 men,[7] and 32 children[8] were murdered. Among the victims was Rachel,[9] whose horrifying slaughter was perpetrated in full view (just over a hundred yards away) of her own husband, brother, and the remaining workers in the camp.[10]

Like his former brother-in-law Meir, a fellow tailor, Yitzchak survived the tunnel escape and joined the Bielski partisans.[11] To date, his fate following liberation remains unknown. Meir's son does not recall his father ever being in contact with his brother-in-law Yitzchak Shuster or even mentioning him.[12]

Morduch Shvarzbord

The author wishes to express gratitude to Tamara Vershitskaya, former director of the Resistance Museum in Novogrudok, for discovering the fact that Morduch Shvarzbord was a tunnel survivor. This she learned from his nephew, Yakov Beskin of Grodno, who also transferred to Tamara all the original documents in his possession pertaining to Morduch's life. Much of what is written below is based on what Tamara learned from these documents and from speaking with Yakov. Our thanks to Rabbi Yitzchak Kofman of Grodno for translating the author's questions to Yakov in an ensuing telephone interview.

Born in 1902 in the town of Lubcha,[1] Morduch Shvarzbord, the son of Matus,[2] was a saddler by trade. Prior to the German invasion, he and his wife and three children[3] lived in Rakov,[4] approximately eighty-three miles (133 km) from Novogrudok. There, Morduch's wife and children are presumed to have been murdered at the start of the war.[5]

It is unclear when or under what circumstances Morduch was conscripted to the Novogrudok forced labor camp. We do know that he survived the tunnel escape, fleeing the breakout together with Leiba Pinchuk (#46).[6] While Leiba joined the Bielski partisans,[7] Morduch served in the 106th detachment commanded by Shalom Zorin.[8] Zorin, a loyal Communist in contrast to the apolitical Bielski, followed Bielski's commitment to accept every Jewish man, woman, and child to his smaller and poorer unit.[9] Morduch's proficiency as a saddler allowed him to contribute his skills in the forest to repairing horse harnesses for the detachment.[10]

Drafted into the Red Army on July 20, 1944, Morduch belonged to the Nineteenth Guards Red Banner Minsk Brigade, in which he operated both a submachine gun and a light machine gun. At some point during his military service, he incurred an injury to the left elbow so serious that he was hospitalized from October 1944 to March 1945. The severity of his injury made it impossible for Morduch to then return to active combat service, thus he served as a security guard at the House of the Red Army in Gorky until the end of the war in September 1945. For his years of loyal military service, Morduch Shvarzbord was awarded the "Victory over Germany in the Great Patriotic War of 1941–1945" medal on April 24, 1946, and in 1965 the medal commemorating "Twenty Years of Victory in the Great Patriotic War, 1941–1945."[11]

Completely alone after the war, Morduch returned to Novogrudok,[12] where he began working as a saddler. Within several years, he exhibited the resiliency required of a tunnel survivor and partisan: taking advantage of a residential building boom underway after the war, Morduch changed his profession to become a glazier actively employed installing windows in new homes under construction.[13]

Although Morduch had lost his own three children in the war, there was yet to be a child in his life. In 1946, he married Perla née Benter,[14] and the two lived at 51 Grodnenskaya Street in Novogrudok.[15] Morduch and Perla never had children of their own. In 1947, Perla's seventeen-year-old sister Ida died just two weeks after giving birth to

her son Yakov. Although Ida's husband Yosef remarried one year later
and cared for Yakov, Morduch and
Perla lived close by in what became
Yakov's second home. It was there
that Morduch shared with Yakov his
participation in the tunnel escape.[16]
Following Morduch's death, his documents were entrusted to Yakov, who
also cared lovingly for his aunt Perla
("Aunt Pasha") from the time she was
widowed until her dying day.[17]

Morduch passed away in
Novogrudok in 1973 at the age of
seventy-one. He is buried in the town
where he escaped to freedom, built a
new life, and enjoyed the company of

Morduch Shvarzbord, undated
postwar photo (courtesy of
Yakov Beskin)

a young man he helped raise who continues to remember him by his
nickname "Motye." Most importantly, Morduch is remembered as a
having been a special human being, "clever, kind and warm."[18]

Isaac Ulert

It is a common saying that one thing leads to another. So it was with
the discovery of the previously unknown tunnel escapee Isaac Ulert.
Coincidentally, this occurred at the very site of the Novogrudok forced
labor camp, nearly eight decades after the escape. Among the guests at
the October 2018 seventy-fifth anniversary reunion for descendants
of the tunnel escapees were also several members of the Bielski family, including a cousin, Yuri Pinski of Chernigo, Russia. Shortly after

returning home, Yuri came across an interview by the American film-maker and screenwriter Vladimir (Vova) Lert. In the course of the interview, Lert disclosed that his grandfather Isaac Ulert had been an inmate in the Novogrudok forced labor camp, as well as a tunnel escapee.

After receiving a copy of the Russian-language interview, Tamara Vershitskaya, organizer of the reunion and director of Novogrudok's Jewish Resistance Museum, contacted Lert via social media to receive segments from a Russian-language book in which Isaac's war experiences were described. Since the author of these pages was unknown,[1] however, the author remained skeptical of this "proof" to ascertain that Isaac had been a tunnel escapee.

Fast-forward to July 9, 2019, and another reunion at the site of the former forced labor camp, this time for descendants of the Bielski partisans. At the historic dedication of the Memorial Wall containing the names of all known tunnel escapees, the author gave a presentation of her research which led to the identification of a number of escapees. At the farewell dinner the following evening, she was approached by none other than Vova Lert and his wife Vita. In the short time remaining to speak before the Lerts' departure for Kiev, the author was able to confirm that based on the details known to Vova, his grandfather Isaac was indeed a tunnel escapee.

One year and many trials later, the author finally made phone contact with Vova on July 1, 2020. By this time, he was famous. Following his selection as a 2018 Golden Globe nominee for his film *Tevye's Daughters*, Vova Lert was now the winner of first prize for the Best Feature Film at the 2019 Rhode Island International Film Festival. Vova reports that the character of Tevye is based on his grandfather Isaac Ulert, always good-humored, always loving, and rarely angry despite his many reasons to be so.[2]

Thanks to Vova's love and admiration, Isaac's life story became preserved and shared by a Soviet filmmaker named Chernapolski, who, like his colleague Isaac, had immigrated to Denver, Colorado, in the US. Prior to his death in the late 1990s, Chernapolski dedicated his efforts to writing a Russian-language book about individuals who led especially meaningful lives. Captivated by Vova's stories of his grandfather, Chernapolski included Isaac Ulert in this volume.[3]

The following text is based upon Vova's translation of his grandfather's story as published in the book. Also included are facts gleaned from our lengthy interview, conducted eighty-four years to the day after Isaac was born to Chaim, a shoemaker, and his wife Chana in the north central Polish town of Mlawa on July 1, 1918.[4]

At the brutal German invasion of Poland on September 1, 1939, Chana suffered serious injuries in the bombing of Mlawa. Isaac miraculously succeeded in fleeing east. In Baranovich, the barely twenty-year-old Isaac married Chaya, renowned for her beauty. They somehow made their way to the town of Karelich, where the couple's daughter Tsameret (Hebrew for "pinnacle") was born. In May 1942, the young family, by now joined by Isaac's parents and his grandmother Rivka, were all confined to the Pereseka ghetto in Novogrudok. There Chaim, Chana, Rivka, and little Tsameret were soon massacred,[5] most likely in Novogrudok's second devastating slaughter of August 7, 1942.

Chaya survived until May 1943, when she is reported to have been shot to death,[6] probably among the approximately 250 women murdered in Novogrudok's fourth massacre on May 7.[7] Alone and anguished, Isaac made a failed suicide attempt by throwing himself against the barbed wire of the forced labor camp to which he had been conscripted.[8]

Like his father, Isaac was a master shoemaker, a skill greatly needed by the Germans, who retained him in the labor camp up until the tunnel escape. His later descriptions of the Jewish spy in the camp, the murder of Moshe Burshtein, the digging of the tunnel, and arrival at the Bielski detachment are compelling proof that Isaac Ulert was indeed a tunnel escapee.[9]

Isaac is listed as having been a member of the Bielski detachment in the compilation of wartime partisans in Belarussia.[10] Upon liberation, he was deemed medically unfit to serve in the Red Army and sent instead to work in the Siberian coal mines of Prokopyevsk. Due to trumped-up charges of espionage during the Stalin era, he was sentenced to maximum security camps.[11] In Siberia, Isaac met his second wife Klava, a native Russian,[12] with whom he settled in Riga in 1947. With Isaac continuing to work as a shoemaker, the couple had three children,[13] daughters Bella and Ludmila, and a son Vladimir (Volodya). Tragedy struck once again as twenty-four-year-old Volodya was accidentally killed in a street celebration on the eve of Victory Day, 1975. Vova, born in 1979, is the namesake of his uncle Vladimir, whom he never knew.[14]

Following their move to the United States in 1993, Isaac and Klava settled in Denver, where both daughters and their families eventually followed.[15] Before his death, Isaac referred to his grandchildren as his "nursery school, the highest award in [his] old age."[16] If he were alive today in September 2023, he would be the proud great-grandfather of ten.[17]

Although Vova stresses that his grandfather's war experiences were taboo subjects for discussion, he admits that for Isaac, he "was everything." Only with Vova was he open to answering questions – and only Vova dared to ask. Vova also recalls a dim memory as a young boy of Isaac taking him to the site of the forced labor camp in Novogrudok. Here he showed Vova where he was during the war and told him about having escaped through a tunnel.[18]

Vova emphasizes his grandfather's optimistic essence by the question he posed to him shortly before Isaac's death on September 4, 2002: If he had to live his life over, with all its challenges and pain, would he choose to live it again? The answer was an unequivocal yes. "Life is worth any price," Isaac exclaimed. "I am happy to have remained alive after paying the price, however high."[19]

Isaac Ulert, Riga, 1981 (courtesy of Vova Lert)

Special Mention: Yitzchak Dvoretzki

Although Yitzchak Dvoretzki, a talented carpenter, did not live to participate in the tunnel escape, his profound role in the tunnel construction and operation merits his inclusion in this book as well. Without his important contributions, it is likely that the tunnel construction would have been discovered and the escape cruelly thwarted.

By the time he was interned in the Novogrudok forced labor camp, Yitzchak, born in Zhetl in 1908,[1] was totally alone in the world. The names of his wife Alte, born in 1907,[2] and sons Shaul, born in 1938,[3] and Shimon, born in 1941,[4] all appear on Soviet lists of murdered individuals from Zhetl in 1941–1942. Alte was reportedly slain on August 6, 1942, in Zhetl's second massacre,[5] probably along with her two toddlers. Yitzchak's parents Chaim Meir[6] and Chava Dvoretzki[7] and his sisters Nishke[8] and Rivka[9] had been murdered in Zhetl's first mass slaughter on April 30, 1942.

Yitzchak Dvoretzki's contributions to the tunnel escape have been lauded in numerous survivor testimonies. He is credited by Chaim Leibowitz (#91) as having been the structural supervisor of the tunnel.[10] Shaul Gorodynski (#77) cites Dvoretzki as the carpenter responsible for creating the brilliantly innovative underground wooden track that enabled a cart filled with heavy dug-up dirt to be pulled by an attached cord in either direction from the tunnel.[11] This invention was necessitated by the daily rains of July 1943, which had caused a constant seepage of water into the tunnel that badly hindered the removal of the soil.[12]

Although Eliahu Berkowicz (#49) slightly corrupts Yitzchak's name, he writes in praise of the "carpenter from Zhetl named Boretzki" who built two platforms on wheels to remove the soil, which would then be deposited under the floors and between double walls.[13]

The fact that the soil-carrying trolleys were built according to Dvoretzki's specification is corroborated by escapee Leiba Pinchuk (#46).[14] Fellow escapee Pesia Mayevski Nadel (#160) names "Yichke" Dvoretzki as having been one of the major planners of the daring tunnel escape, together with Berl Yoselevich.[15]

Leiba Pinchuk relates that Yitzchak's fervent hope to escape to freedom through the tunnel was dashed at the end of May 1943, with his transfer to the Koldychevo death camp.[16] Yet through Yitzchak's efforts, well over half of his fellow prisoners succeeded in reaching freedom.

The death of Yitzchak Dvoretzki is commemorated in Zhetl's memorial book.[17]

Analysis: Why Novogrudok?

Why did one of the most successful prisoner escapes, which also appears to be the most remarkable escape of the Holocaust through a hand-dug tunnel, the longest of WWII, take place in Novogrudok?

Perhaps the strongest determinant was the existence of the Bielski partisan detachment and its relatively close proximity to Novogrudok.

In the spring of 1943, the inmates of the Novogrudok forced labor camp were assured that they would be received with open arms by the Bielski partisans, provided they could reach the detachment in the dense Naliboki Forest,[1] forty-one miles away. Throughout their imprisonment, the inmates had been greatly encouraged by the occasional rescue of family members and friends by partisans who dared to slip into the camp. The Bielski detachment thus became the address of hope for the desperate prisoners, who were willing to risk their lives for a precious chance at freedom.

This chapter analyses three other major factors that contribute to the escape occurring specifically in Novogrudok, as well as to its success.

1. Prewar Jewish communal organizations. The majority of escapees originated from Novogrudok and Zhetl, where a multitude of organizations existed to serve the Jewish population. Novogrudok forced labor camp inmates and their families had been an integral part of many of these institutions. In their communal roles, these men and women gained experience in mutual aid, planning, and goal setting, all essential components for the execution of the tunnel escape.

2. Righteous Gentiles. Yehuda Bauer posits that without the presence of rescuers, it would be impossible to teach the Holocaust, due to the "unrelieved horror" this would evoke.[2] Among the evil and the horror that characterized the Holocaust of Novogrudok, a few good people stood out in their willingness to aid any Jew. Some risked their lives to help the inmates remain alive under the terrible conditions of the labor camp. Pursuing the option for the tunnel escape was surely influenced by the knowledge that certain non-Jews could be relied upon to help the escapees reach the partisans. Some of these righteous Gentiles were known personally through relationships established before the war, yet others were peasants who were strangers distinguished in their humanity.

3. The Warsaw Ghetto Uprising and Resistance in Novogrudok. The mutual influence of resistance in Novogrudok and the Warsaw ghetto uprising cannot be overestimated. Fabricated reports of an uprising in Novogrudok (detailed in the last section of this chapter) became influential in motivating Warsaw ghetto residents to rise up against their German oppressors. In turn, the uprising in Warsaw likely encouraged the labor camp inmates in Novogrudok to embark upon their escape through the tunnel.

Prewar Jewish Communal Organizations of Novogrudok

The broad scope of Jewish societies and associations that existed in prewar Novogrudok and Zhetl vigorously fostered mutual aid as a way of life. Surely the sense of collective responsibility cultivated by these extensive networks helped prepare the one hundred Novogrudker and forty-one Zhetler tunnel escapees for the biggest communal mission of their lives.

The Tarbut School

Novogrudok's Jewish community offered a range of options for their children's education. Among the streams were *cheder*s such as the Menaker School, where very young boys could learn with a *melamed* (a teacher of traditional religious texts); the religious private Mizrachi Hebrew school, known as the Wolfovich School after its owner Shloyme

Wolfovich);[3] as well as the town's largest and most central educational institution, the Chaim Nachman Bialik Tarbut Hebrew School.

A member of the nationwide Tarbut Hebrew school network in Poland, the Tarbut school is said to have had a major educational and Zionist influence on Novogrudok's Jewish youth. Boasting a curriculum similar to that of Jewish schools in Palestine at the time, Tarbut schools employed Hebrew as the language of instruction in all subjects, save for Polish history and geography.[4] This Hebrew-language school in Poland was described by its former principal as an "Israeli island in the Diaspora."[5]

Prior to the war, Avraham Ostashinski headed the school's Building Committee to raise funds for a new building. Ostashinski, the deputy mayor of Novogrudok, belonged to the town's large Ostashinski clan, which included tunnel escapees Chaim (#32) and his children Perla (#33) and Daniel Ostashinski, who studied in the school. Thanks to Avraham Ostashinski's efforts, funds were quickly raised for the new school building dedicated in 1933.[6] Other tunnel escapees educated in Novogrudok's Tarbut school include Moshe Nignevitcky (#130), Chanan Kushner (#76), Shlomo Golanski (#75), Riva Kaganowicz (#146), Avraham Rakovski (#10), and Abram Czertok (#45). It is likely that at least one escapee had been a pupil in the school's kindergarten, run by Sima Portnoj (#20).

The Shokdey Melocho Trade School

In Novogrudok's Shokdey Melocho Trade School, boys and girls from the age of thirteen were taught a trade for three years while apprenticed to various tradesmen. Boys learned to be tailors, bootmakers, carpenters, watchmakers, and more. Girls were taught to become seamstresses and corset-makers. The Shokdey Melocho organization undertook to feed the students during their first year of apprenticeship, while the tradesmen would pay their apprentices enough for the students to become self-sufficient.[7] Although the founders of the Shokdey Melocho Trade School likely never imagined such an outcome, the school probably came to play a lifesaving role. We can assume a number of tradesmen who had acquired their knowledge and expertise in Shokdey Melocho were spared death by being conscripted by the German Army to the Novogrudok forced labor camp. Ultimately, they were among the last Jews of the area to remain alive, participate in the tunnel escape, and grasp a chance at freedom.

Most of the Jews of Novogrudok supported the activities of the trade school by paying monthly membership fees.[8] In addition, the school was funded by many of the town's so-called "progressive intelligentsia," including engineer Avraham Klubok, father of Helena (Lena) Kitayevich (#62), as well as Chaim Noah Leibowitz (#91). Following the 1939 Soviet invasion, Leibowitz was requested to serve as director of the trade school as well as the orphanage whose activities are described below. Two months after his appointment, however, the regime converted the trade school into a state furniture factory.[9]

The Jewish Orphanage

In wake of the massive death toll of World War I, a Jewish orphanage was created in Novogrudok in 1917.[10] Accepting school-age orphans and children of poverty-stricken families, the orphanage attempted to create a family-like atmosphere. The children all studied in the Tarbut school until age thirteen, when they were automatically transferred to Shokdey Melocho. There, like their trade school classmates, they would obtain a certificate equivalent to the completion of five grades of elementary school.[11] Until closed by Nazi order in 1939, the orphanage cared for 119 children.[12]

When the school was plagued by a serious financial crisis around 1925, a new management team was elected, and a committee was formed to care for the orphans and restore the institution's financial ability to continue. Collecting contributions from Novogrudok and surrounding towns, the management and the committee also managed to obtain government support, enabling the orphanage to regain its financial viability within around six years. While her husband was active in supporting the trade school, Tziporah Klubok, mother of escapee Lena Kitayevich (#62), was one of the orphanage's devoted committee members.[13]

As mentioned, following the Soviet invasion in 1939, Chaim Noah Leibowitz (#91), then director of the trade school, was appointed director of the orphanage, soon to be transformed into a multinational facility housing both orphans and homeless children. Although dismissed by the Soviets from his position in January 1940, Chaim returned to the orphanage subsequent to the Nazi invasion. Under orders from the Judenrat, he helped transfer the Jewish children from the building on Kowalewsker Street to the former home of Israel Delatycki, who had earlier been deported to Siberia by the Soviets. Chaim's heartbreaking memoir describes the scene during the first mass massacre of December 8, 1941, as the children were all taken to their slaughter, with the girls wearing white kerchiefs on their heads.[14]

United Jewish Artisans Association and Tradesmen's Bank

The United Jewish Artisans Association, also known as the Workers' Union,[15] represented all Jewish craftsmen and small business owners. A former member of the association declares that it "occupied one of the leading places in the communal life of Novogrudok."[16] Cultural events would be held on the premises of the association, where members would congregate nightly to read newspapers and engage in social activities.[17]

Several inmates of the Novogrudok forced labor camp had been part of the tradesmen's union leadership, including Moshe Feivelevich (#47), who served as vice president of the directorate.[18] The association's five-member committee created to aid members in need included tunnel escapee Natan Sucharski (#4) as well as Shlomo Giershenowski, husband of escapee Sara Giershenowski (#149) and father of escapees Basia (#150) and Roza (#151).[19]

The Maccabi Sports Organization

In Poland during the 1930s, the membership of the Jewish Maccabi athletic organization numbered thirty thousand sportsmen and women in 250 clubs throughout the country.[20] The Novogrudok Maccabi club included at least three tunnel escapees: Yankef Nevachovich (#51), Simcha Wilenski (#111), and Berl Yoselevich.[21]

Zionist Organizations

While many Zionist organizations, including Hahalutz Hatzair, Freiheit, and Betar,[22] existed in Novogrudok in the decade preceding the Holocaust, the influence of the youth movement Hashomer Hatzair was one of the most significant.[23] A Socialist-Zionist secular movement,[24] Hashomer Hatzair was well known in Novogrudok for its educational programming and for the sale of bonds for Palestine.[25] Among its members were escapees Moshe Nignevitcky (#130)[26] and Berl Yoselevich.[27] Escapee Berl Zalmanovich (#64) is likely to have been influenced by his older brother Michael's strong prewar involvement in Hashomer Hatzair prior to his murder in 1942. Berl survived to become extremely active in the organization following the war. Upon immigrating to pre-state Israel, he joined a Hashomer Hatzair kibbutz.[28]

Like Hashomer Hatzair, the Poalei Zion youth movement involved a combination of Zionist and Socialist ideologies, although its members were primarily adults.[29] As in other Novogrudok Zionist groups, Poalei Zion members often spoke Hebrew to one another.[30] In time, its representatives took an even more central role than Hashomer Hatzair in selling bonds for Palestine.[31] At least two members, Chaim Noah Leibowitz (#91)[32] and Moshe Feivelevich (#47),[33] took part in the tunnel escape.

The Alter of Novogrudok and the Musar Movement

The Jewish communities of both Novogrudok and Zhetl were profoundly influenced by the musar movement, a prominent ethical, educational, and cultural movement that stresses individual self-improvement, the practice of good deeds, moral introspection, and self-examination. Founded in nineteenth-century Lithuania by Rabbi Yisroel Salanter,[34] the musar movement had a noted student called Rabbi Yosef Yoysel Horowitz, who later gained renown as the Alter of Novardok (Yiddish for the Elder of Novogrudok).[35] Beyond establishing a network of smaller yeshivas in many Polish towns,[36] the Alter founded the high-level Beit Yosef Yeshiva in 1896 in Novogrudok, based on the study and practice of musar. More than four hundred students attended this yeshiva, some from as far away as the Caucasus.[37] According to Novogrudok native Mordechai Ginsburg, prior to his departure from Novogrudok at the outbreak of World War I, the Alter influenced the entire town and "created a new way of life."[38]

The political upheaval in the aftermath of the Bolshevik Revolution caused the Novardok Yeshiva to be closed by the outbreak of World War II.[39] One may presume, however, that Novogrudok natives among the Novogrudok forced labor camp inmates grew up in families influenced by the precepts of the musar movement. With its stress upon the development of humility,[40] courage,[41] patience,[42] confidence,[43] diligence, and perseverance,[44] the musar movement championed character traits crucial one generation later in planning and executing the tunnel escape. Among those escapees from families involved with the Novardok Yeshiva were Chaim Zeev Ostashinski (#32) and his children Perla (#33) and Daniel Ostashinski. Chaim's wife Kayla Fruma née Chaitovich was renowned for her efforts to collect charity for the yeshiva and for opening her home to out-of-town yeshiva students for Shabbat meals.[45]

Prewar Jewish Communal Organizations of Zhetl

The small *shtetl* of Zhetl, as it was called in Yiddish by the Jewish townspeople (Dyatlavo in Russian, Zdziecol in Polish), was located twenty miles west-southwest of Novogrudok.[46] The four thousand

Jews of Zhetl constituted the overwhelming majority, some 80 percent of the town's population in 1941,[47] as compared with the larger city of Novogrudok, where Jews composed nearly half of the population of sixty-five-hundred in 1939.

Zhetl held the distinction of having the highest number of escapees from the area's massacres during the murderous summer of 1942.[48] When the Germans invaded Zhetl to commit their second and last massacre on August 6, 1942, the streets of the ghetto were empty, as most of the population had gone into hiding in underground bunkers. By the end of the slaughter, eight hundred Jews, 20 percent of the town's Jewish population, had managed to reach partisan detachments in the nearby Lipiczansky Forest. Of these, half joined the Borba partisans under the command of Hirsh Kaplinsky.[49]

Escapee Pesia Mayevski (#160) notes that following the second massacre, the Germans transported 154 Jewish survivors to Novogrudok. Those sent to the Pereseka ghetto were slaughtered there on February 4, 1943. The skilled craftsmen among the deportees, whose exact number is unknown, were conscripted to the Novogrudok forced labor camp.[50] According to my research, at least forty-one of these craftsmen from Zhetl remained alive to participate in the tunnel escape on September 26, 1943.

It is not surprising that a proportionally large number of Zhetlers succeeded in fleeing to the forest as well as participating in the tunnel escape. Despite its relatively small size, Zhetl was known throughout the area for its spiritual, cultural, and social activities.[51] As in Novogrudok, a plethora of prewar communal institutions existed in Zhetl. Time was to prove that these organizations provided fertile ground to develop the organizational skills and social cooperation necessary to plan and execute the tunnel escape. Those inmates lacking direct experience in such organizations were likely to have been influenced by relatives who had been active members.

Among the town's many organizations were the following.

Professional Associations

Like its Novogrudok counterpart, Zhetl's tradesmen's union represented Jewish craftsmen and small business owners. Among the ten individuals who had served on its steering committee was future escapee Zalman Gertzovski (#117), a shoemaker.[52]

Additionally, there were individual organizations for specific craftsmen. For example, escapee Kalman Shelkovitz (#100), a tailor, was a member of the seamsters' union, where he participated in the union's drama club.[53]

Zionist Organizations

The second half of the nineteenth century saw the proliferation of various Zionist organizations in Zhetl. In 1898, following the visit of a former Zhetler who had immigrated to Palestine, the Zhetl Zionist League was formed, with the blessing of the town's chief rabbi, Baruch Avraham Mirski.[54] At its head stood Aaron Hirsh Langbort and Shlomo Zalman Dunetz, grandfather of escapee Fanya Dunetz (#142),[55] who was the first Zhetler to become active in Chovevei Tzion, an organization that championed Jewish settlement in Palestine. Mordechai Dunetz, brother of Fanya, remembers his grandfather as an inspirational figure who was rarely at home, as he traveled from city to city to promote and collect for the Zionist cause.[56]

Although the anti-Zionist Bund organization existed in Zhetl, it was far outnumbered by Zionist organizations in town. These included the Socialist-Zionist Hashomer Hatzair youth movement, of which escapee Kalman Shelkovich (#100)[57] was a member; the Betar Zionist youth movement, and the Socialist-Zionist Poalei Zion for adults.[58]

In addition to these movements, the Chalutz organization cut across all political lines in preparing groups for immigration to Palestine and for life on the kibbutzim.[59]

The Keren Kayemet L'Yisrael (Jewish National Fund) was founded in 1901 at the Fifth Zionist Conference in Basil for the purpose of purchasing land in Palestine.[60] Among those active in the organization's Zhetl branch was Faivel Epshtein, husband of tunnel survivor Chana Epshtein.

Cultural and Sports Associations

Between the world wars, there was a rich cultural life in Zhetl, where drama circles of the various schools and professional associations would perform for the citizens of Zhetl and surrounding communities. Especially well known was the Fire Brigade Band, consisting of the primarily Jewish members of the town's volunteer fire department, created in 1902.[61] The band often performed at celebrations in the town square and even played in neighboring towns on Polish holidays.[62] Tunnel escapee Chaim Belous (#23), a volunteer fireman, played the clarinet in the band.[63]

Religious Organizations

The political movement Agudat Yisrael was founded in Poland in 1912 as an instrument to preserve the ultra-Orthodox lifestyle.[64] In historic photos published in *Pinkas Zhetl* (Zhetl's memorial book), Berl Gertzovski (#173) appears with members of the Agudat Yisrael movement.[65]

In addition to having had its own branch of the renowned Novardok Yeshiva,[66] by the end of World War I, Zhetl was home to a branch of the Va'ad Hayeshivot organization. Founded in 1924, this organization was sponsored by the Chofetz Chaim, an influential rabbi born in Zhetl who was associated with the musar movement, as well as by Zhetl's prestigious chief rabbi, Shlomo Zalman Sorotzkin, who served in the town from 1912 to 1929.[67] The Va'ad's mandate to sustain Jewish religious institutions in eastern Poland provided monetary and moral support to a network of these institutions.[68] Active in Zhetl's Va'ad Hayeshivot branch was Shaul Shelkovich, father of escapee Kalman Shelkovich (#100).[69]

The Tarbut School

At the onset of the twentieth century, early formal Jewish education was restricted to boys from wealthy families who could afford to send their sons to *cheder*s, private religious schools for young boys. Only in 1909 was a *talmud Torah* opened where primarily religious subjects were taught to boys in the lower grades who hailed from poor families.[70]

In 1921, Zhetl's Sholom Aleichem School opened its doors. Yiddish was the language of instruction in this anti-Zionist institution. In response, six years later, Zhetl saw the opening of a Hebrew-language Zionist school named for famed Hebrew author Chaim Nachman Bialik. As a member of the Tarbut network of Hebrew-language schools then opening across Poland, this school grew from its one-room beginning, thanks to both local donations and those of former Zhetlers living in the United States.[71] Among the school's founders was Faivel Epshtein, husband of escapee Chana Epshtein, who taught in the school.

Most importantly, the rich communal activities that most escapees from Novogrudok and Zhetl experienced prior to the war are likely to have helped them to remain alive. Without these activities, without the profound sense of collective responsibility and the social skills engendered by the self-help organizations in their midst, the inmates might never have been able to carry out the tunnel escape.

In Tribute: Righteous Gentiles and the Tunnel Escape

Fanya Dunetz (#142) did not talk about the Holocaust and the tunnel escape as her children were growing up. With a great sense of drama, excitement, and wonder, she expressed that at great risk to their own lives, Baptist farmers had opened their hearts and their barns to her and two other ragged stragglers en route to the Bielski partisans. Thanks to this family's careful directions, the escapees safely reached the Bielski detachment in the forest to survive the rest of the war.

Years later, Fanya related how another non-Jew had offered to save her life. Left alone in the world and in the labor camp with only her brother Motl after the murders of their parents, sister, and brother, Fanya was approached by a camp guard, Josif Wargan, who had known her family in Zhetl. Offered by Wargan the priceless opportunity to escape with one other inmate she'd choose, Fanya feared that together, neither she nor Motl could navigate the way to the Bielski partisan detachment. Giving up the opportunity to escape in order to save her younger brother's life, Fanya arranged for Motl to escape together with a Novogrudok native familiar with the terrain and the route to the Bielski partisans. Wargan, in effect, saved her brother's life after offering to save Fanya's. By saving Motl's life, he gave Fanya someone to live for, the hope of somehow being reunited with her only surviving family member.

Fanya was my mother. Motl was my only uncle. I remain every grateful to the Baptist farmer and to Josif Wargan.

I believe that every Jew who survived the Novogorudok slaughters and the tunnel escape to reach the forest was helped at some point by a non-Jew. We don't know most of their names, but we do know of their kindness, their morality, and the considerable risk posed to their own families. Some, though not all, of these heroes have been officially recognized as Righteous Among the Nations by Yad Vashem, Israel's Holocaust memorial museum, for risking their lives to help Jews during one of the most heinous periods of human history. Although the Holocaust brought out the worst in man, we must recognize that against the horrifying backdrop, there were still people who exemplified the best.

This book has presented just some of their stories.

While imprisoned in the forced labor camp and fighting for survival, Mordechai Orzuchowski (#42) was able to rest assured of at least one thing: his infant daughter Nella was safe from the hands of the Nazis. Nella, who was placed in hiding with Christian acquaintances of her father who lived in a rural area just outside Novogrudok, no longer recalls her rescuers' surname, yet she has wonderful memories of the couple who risked their lives to shelter her.[72]

After three weeks of wandering through the forest following the tunnel escape, Sonya Gorodynski (#77), her husband-to-be Aaron Oshman (#79), and her future brother-in-law Yakov (Yankel) Oshman (#80) caught sight of a light flickering in a secluded farmhouse. In response to Sonya's desperate plea for food and shelter, the farmer fed and harbored these Jews for five weeks in a pit behind his barn before sending them on their way to the Bielski partisan detachment.

Riva Kaganowicz (#146) was a young teenager when she was interned in the Novogrudok forced labor camp. The slaughter of her twin brother and her parents had left her completely alone. Yet Alexandra Romanuk, her family's former household helper from the small village of Niovda, frequently risked her life to sneak eggs, cheese, and other foodstuffs into the labor camp to ease Riva's intense hunger. Immediately after Riva's liberation from the partisans and her return to Novogrudok, Alexandra helped her unearth and sell the leather goods Rina's father had buried before being interned in the ghetto.[73]

Chaim Zeev Ostashinski (#32) lost his wife and three of his children when they were brutally murdered in Novogrudok's fourth massacre on May 7, 1943. From the confines of the forced labor camp, Chaim managed to arrange for a Christian couple, Jan and Josefa Jarmolowicz, to keep his youngest son Pesach hidden under their farm's pigsty in the nearby village of Kustino. One of the farm workers, Magdalena Cimoszko, was sworn to secrecy as she prepared food and looked after Pesach and several other Jews in hiding. In tribute to their kindness in the face of life-threatening danger, Josefa, Jan, and Magdalena were recognized by Yad Vashem as Righteous Among the Nations in 1990.[74]

Several other tunnel escapees, including Shlomo (#123) and Chana (#124) Ryback, were helped by the Jarmolowicz family as well. As Chana's father Meyer Iwiniecki had been Jan's tailor before the war, Jan was especially happy to help Shlomo and his friends, beginning with tending to Shlomo's wounded foot. Carefully tutoring Shlomo and the others in the art of how to "act like a partisan" by going on food raids armed with fake weapons made from wood, Jarmolowicz eventually pointed them in the direction of the Bielski detachment.[75]

The father of Shlomo Golanski (#75) owned a mill prior to the war, and Shlomo was acquainted with many non-Jews who came with their horse-drawn carriages to grind their grain there. Thanks to one of them, Shlomo was able to save his own life as well as those of three other escapees. Shlomo testified that following the escape, he met a father and two daughters – probably Zeidel Kushner (#143), Raya (#144), and Leah (#145) – who like himself were unaware of how to cross the forest to reach the Bielski partisans. Shlomo took them along with him as he sought shelter with a Christian farmer who had come to the Golanski mill every spring to grind his grain. Happy to help, this farmer, who remains anonymous, hid the escapees in his barn for several weeks.[76]

Raya Kushner cannot forget the Polish woman who opened her home to the four escapees and offered them bread, water, and onions. Plagued by fear that she would be killed for harboring Jews, the woman sent the escapees on their way. Soon afterwards, this brave woman, her husband, and the seven or eight Jews she had been sheltering were all massacred.[77]

Yanek, the son of Shlomo Okonski (#89), recalls that despite all the atrocities his father witnessed, Shlomo did not leave a legacy of hate. Instead, he always emphasized that among the local population were righteous Gentiles who did their utmost to be humane and to help the Jews in any way possible. He often spoke of the twelve-year-old girl who risked her own life to slip food through the fence of the forced labor camp, and of the Polish carpentry workshop foreman who turned away as his workers stole wood to be used in building the tunnel.

Shlomo also spoke of the two guards at the gate, a Pole and a Belarusian, who would allow him and Efraim to leave the camp at night to forage for food and to sell the leather and soles they stole from the shoemaker's workshop. During these "excursions," the two youths frequently spent the night at the home of a local woman known simply by her surname Rajeska, who had known Shlomo and Efraim's father Yosel, a shoemaker in Novogrudok. This brave woman vowed to do whatever she could for Yosel's children, even at the risk of endangering her own family. In Yanek's search for members of the Rajeska family following the war, he was told they had left the area and could not be found. As for the fate of the workshop foreman and the two guards, all three had been discovered and hanged in the labor camp as an example to others.[78]

Two families, the Kozlowskis and the Bobrovskis, stand out in their profound aid to tunnel escapees seeking to reach the partisans. Because their identities and whereabouts were known to the inmates inside the camp even prior to the breakout, these families' role in providing support and encouragement should be lauded. As Idel Kagan (#95) writes: "The name Kozlowski and that of the dogcatchers (Bobrovski) became known. The story was that if you were planning an escape, you should go 14 kilometers from Novogrudok to Lida to Kozlowski's farmstead. He would then direct you to the partisans and of course everybody knew where the dogcatchers lived. And they also had contacts with the partisans."[79]

Kagan remembers two meals non-Jews provided him at crucial junctures. He describes "the loaf of the most beautiful bread and milk" given to him by a farmer when he and fellow escapee Pesach Abramowicz (#205) knocked at the door to ask for food following their escape from the tunnel.[80] In recalling his previous ill-fated escape attempt in December 1942, Idel credits the hot bowl of soup provided him at the home of Fransiszek Bobrowski as having saved his life.[81]

With their isolated shack standing at the end of the suburb of Pereseka where the ghetto was located, this impoverished family earned their living by catching stray, unlicensed dogs found wandering in the area in order to skin them and sell the hides.[82] In their compassion for the Jews, the Bobrowskis were known for sneaking food into the ghetto. Serving as liaisons to the Bielski partisans, they informed escapees when and where the partisans could be found. Every Jew who managed to escape knew that upon reaching the Bobrowski home, they would be given shelter for a day or two as well as food for the journey to the detachment.[83]

Tragically, by the time of the tunnel escape, the Bobrowskis could no longer be of help to the Jews. In February 1943, after discovering that they were in contact with the partisans, the Germans set their house aflame. Both parents were murdered on the spot, while their six children were deported to Germany to either forced labor or concentration camps. After enduring untold suffering, five of the six children returned.[84] The fatality was a fourteen-year-old son who died in the Gross-Rosen concentration camp. His sister Maria returned home from Gross-Rosen with diabetes so severe her leg was later amputated.[85]

Yisrael Kolachek (#81) recounts that in their trek in search of the Bielski detachment after they crept out of the labor camp, he, his father, Eliyahu Berkowicz (#49), and Chaya Sara Luska (#168) were met by a partisan representative who shepherded them to the way station for escaped Jews and Russian partisans run by the Belarusian peasant Konstanty "Kościk" Kozlowski. Here they were provided with water and shelter until the next morning, when Kozlowski sent them on to yet another way station along their journey to the Bielski detachment.[86]

Ivan Kozlowski, undated prewar photo (courtesy of Tamara Vershitskaya)

As a young man, Kozlowski had lived and worked in the town of Mokrets, on the farm of a Jewish shoemaker named Velkin, father-in-law of escapee Yakov Yoselevich (#96).[87] Besides learning to make shoes and to farm the land, here Kozlowski also learned to speak fluent Yiddish. An admirer of the Jewish people and its culture, he welcomed any chance to oppose the hated Germans and their murderous policies.[88] Beyond offering his home as a stopover for labor camp escapees to be picked up by the

Bielski fighters and taken to the forest, he also risked his life by serving as a courier bringing messages and letters from the Bielskis to the inmates.[89]

Konstanty's brother Ivan even joined the German police with the direct intention of providing information to the partisans and helping Jews escape from the camp. He also supplied them with weapons and medicine. Ivan was extremely close to the Velkin family, and when he saw their granddaughter Dvosha in the labor camp, he personally helped her escape to the partisans.[90] As a parting gift, he presented her with a jar of melted animal fat

Konstanty Kozlowski, undated prewar photo (courtesy of Tamara Vershitskaya)

to help her survive the trek to the Bielskis. There, in the detachment, Dvosha met her future husband, tunnel escapee Yakov Yoselevich.[91]

Konstanty and Ivan's niece Irena Michailovna Kozlovskaya (their brother Michael's daughter) relates that at one point, Ivan and Konstanty hid and fed twelve Jews at once for several days in a nearby camouflaged pit in the forest. Eventually Konstanty arranged for them to be taken by the partisans to the detachment.[92]

During a 2013 visit to Novogrudok for the filming of the documentary *Tunnel of Hope*, Yisrael Kolachek corroborated the existence of a pit that Irena's uncle had prepared near his house in order to hide escapees until they were met by partisans.[93] In a meeting of the group with Irena, he spontaneously gave her some dollars he had in his possession, humbly attempting to repay a debt he feels he owed her family for almost seventy years.

The Kozlowski family paid a horrifying price for their kindness. Ivan and Konstanty's father Gregory was beaten by the Germans as they demanded he reveal the locale of the partisans. Their brother Michael, who was also apprenticed to the shoemaker Velkin, was cruelly beaten while carrying boots he had made for partisans. Ivan paid the ultimate price when he was murdered by the Germans.[94]

Both Franciszek Bobrowski and Konstanty Kozlowski were officially recognized as Righteous Among the Nations by Yad Vashem.[95] Yet we cannot forget the many anonymous righteous men and women who were guided by their fervent conviction to risk their lives to aid the tunnel escapees. In Judaism, "to save a life is to save the world."[96] We are eternally grateful to all those who saved worlds in Novogrudok's darkest days of the Holocaust.

Jan Jarmolowicz, undated prewar photo (courtesy of Tamara Vershitskaya)

Jan and Josefa Jarmolowicz and their two sons, the eldest of whom was killed by the Nazis in 1942, undated prewar photo (courtesy of Tamara Vershitskaya)

Maria Bobrowski (*second from right*), undated postwar photo (courtesy of Tamara Vershitskaya)

The Warsaw Ghetto Uprising and Resistance in Novogrudok

The slogan "Novogrudok is calling" resonated throughout the Warsaw ghetto following an article penned by Eliezer Geller, who headed the Gordonia youth movement. A branch of the Hechalutz movement, Gordonia aimed to train pioneers for immigration to Palestine and collective labor in kibbutzim. Adapting scout-like activities to the confines of the ghetto, Geller also maintained an underground press called *Slowo Mlocych* (The Voice of the Young).[97] There, in March 1942, he published the following rumor of a purported rebellion in Novogrudok against the German captors:

> Only in Novogrudok did the Jews know how to die with honor and to avenge their blood shed by the hand of their enemies. Only there, together with the innocent victims, local gendarmes were killed while carrying out their murderous work. The city of Novogrudok has turned into a symbol for the Jews languishing in the hands of the Hitlerite murderers and a symbol of heroism for our generation and generations to come.[98]

This item was soon copied by the underground newspapers of both Hashomer Hatzair and the left-wing Poalei Zion organizations.[99] The article in *Jutrznia* (The Dawn), Hashomer Hatzair's underground ghetto newspaper, appeared on March 28, 1942, bearing the title "The Heroes of Novogrudok." There the rumor of a rebellion in Novogrudok was repeated, now with a report of two hundred Jews rebelling and twenty Germans killed:

> There were in the city of Novogrudok 200 young Jews who refused to go to the murder site like beasts to the slaughter. They found the courage in themselves to arise with arms in hand against Hitler's butchers. True, they all fell in the unequal battle, but before they died they left 20 corpses…. The heroic

action of the 200 young people will be in vain if their self-sac-
rifice does not serve as a call to all Jewish youth.... In view
of these difficult days the Jewish young must prepare. It must
begin to mobilize all the vital forces in the Jewish street.... To
that we are commanded by the heroic deaths of the 200 Jews
in Novogrudok.[100]

Professor Ruben Feldchu was a member of the Zionist right and a prolific chronicler of daily life in the Warsaw ghetto.[101] One of the few
Warsaw ghetto diarists to survive the war, in all likelihood he was the
only one to write in Hebrew.[102] Although he managed to salvage more
than eight hundred pages of notes during his escape from the ghetto,
one year in hiding, and his difficult immigration to pre-state Israel, few
of his writings have been published. However, it is notable that in the
spring of 1942, Feldchu also recorded the rumor that his co-religionists
in Novogrudok staged a rebellion against their oppressors, when indeed
this had not taken place.[103]

Holocaust historian Shalom Cholawsky claims that it is "impossible to exaggerate the importance of such 'news' for the youth of the
Warsaw ghetto of March 1942.... This story, as it was published, was a
powerful legend influencing the underground and shaping the psychological mood in the Warsaw ghetto."[104]

Who promulgated the myth of rebellion in Novogrudok which
had not yet taken place? Both Cholawsky and historian Emmanuel
Ringelblum, who also chronicled events in the Warsaw ghetto, attribute the spreading of the false rumor to non-Jews. Ringelblum credits
the Polska Partia Robotnicza (PPR) or Polish Workers' Party as having
encouraged rebellion against the Germans, quoting a passage published
in the party's underground paper on September 2, 1942:

The invaders are merciless and relentless. The Jewish population should be equally unrelenting in defending its existence.... Only uncompromising resistance in every situation,

only action – and not passive waiting for the slaughter – can save possibly thousands and tens of thousands, though it may claim victims. Let the heroic resistance of Novogrudok and other towns serve as an example.[105]

Cholawsky, by contrast, contends that the invention of the false Novogrudok rebellion was perpetrated in the Warsaw ghetto by members of the Polish Armia Krajowa (AK) or Home Army, the dominant resistance movement. He points out that the Novogrudok area contained the AK's largest force and that the city was home to the Polish national poet Adam Mickiewicz, "symbolizing the site of Polish national consciousness."[106] Cholawsky finds it logical that in their efforts to arouse the Polish masses in the capital, the battle cry "Novogrudok is calling" would be effective in its inherent insinuation that "even" the Jews in their ghettos did all in their power to physically resist the German oppression.[107]

In support of his assumption that the AK had spread the false rumor of a Novogrudok rebellion, Cholawsky notes that some non-Jews who had attended the city's Adam Mickiewicz High School had now become AK members. In meetings known to have taken place during the war with their Jewish friends, these young men learned of the Jews' quest for weapons to avenge the atrocities committed against them and their families. Cholawsky surmises that this passion for armed resistance on the part of the Jews with whom they met was "almost certainly" passed on to the Warsaw ghetto by AK members in Warsaw.[108]

In the wake of plans for an armed uprising in the Novogrudok forced labor camp, preparations were made for a rebellion to take place on April 15, 1943, five months prior to the tunnel escape. Plans for the armed revolt were developed only after the third slaughter on February 4, 1943,[109] long after "Novogrudok is calling" became the rallying cry in the Warsaw ghetto.

A circle appears to have been closed when news of the Warsaw ghetto uprising penetrated the walls of the sealed forced labor camp in

Novogrudok, 260 miles away. How could this possibly have happened? The answer appears to lie with the several clandestine radios in the labor camp, which, as detailed in this book, played a crucial role in the inmates' resistance efforts. In addition to the radio assembled by the fourteen-year-old brother of inmate Jankef (Yakov) Nevachovich (#51) and the radio sneaked in by inmate Ruvke Shabakovski (#5), Yehuda Bauer reports that yet another radio was smuggled into the camp in the summer of 1943. These precious devices are likely to have informed the inmates of the Warsaw ghetto uprising, intensifying their determination to escape.[110]

While they may have been inspired by the revolt in Warsaw, little did the resistance leaders inside the forced labor camp know that the call for the uprising is likely to have started with the chant "Novogrudok is calling" eighteen months prior to the tunnel escape. With a fabricated act of resistance leading to two very real ones, it is unknown whether the Warsaw ghetto rebellion or the Novogrudok tunnel escape would have happened in 1943 if not for the false rumor regarding what never happened in Novogrudok in 1942.

We must agree with Professor Bauer's premise that a ripple effect was created by the false rumor of what had transpired in Novogrudok.[111] By encouraging young people in the Warsaw ghetto to rebel, this resistance appears to have played a crucial role in inspiring the inmates in Novogrudok to dig their bold tunnel to freedom.

Afterword:
The Interview Process and Second-Generation Tunnel Survivors

Only decades after settling in their new home countries did most survivors begin to speak of the horrors they experienced during the Holocaust, thus creating a "great collective silence," also referred to as "the conspiracy of silence,"[1] which pervaded for years between survivors and the world at large. The first survivors did not talk, partly because of their own inability to do so and partly because the world would not listen.

The early years of the postwar adjustment of Holocaust survivors can be divided into three periods. The immediate postwar period of the 1940s was characterized by searching for relatives and "embark[ing] on the journey of 'surviving survival,'"[2] which involved both physical recuperation as well as the emotional toll of trying to come to terms with their many losses. This constituted a largely impossible task due to the sheer magnitude involved. Clinical psychologist Yael Danieli quotes one seventy-four-year-old survivor, re-widowed and the sole survivor of a family of seventy-two: "Even if it takes one year to mourn each loss, and even if I live to be 107 [and mourn all members of my family], what do I do about the rest of the six million?"[3]

Elie Wiesel, too, expresses this near impossibility of survivors to integrate their overwhelming and innumerable losses when he writes: "Having started to speak, we would have found it impossible to stop. Having shed one tear, we would have drowned the human heart."[4] With "tears and crying, wailing and loss of self-control" considered to have been "the most dangerous reactions in the concentration camp,"[5] mourning during the Holocaust itself would have been suicidal. Although mourning was a luxury survivors could not afford during the Holocaust years, neither could they complete the mourning process upon liberation. According to Joan Freyberg, "This mourning was bound to be an extended, incomplete and impaired process, as it was shorn of the usual rituals and institutions available for helping to work through grief and loss."[6]

In addition to the lack of accessible rituals and institutions, the immediate postwar period did not provide the survivor with time to mourn. Besides searching for loved ones whose fates were unknown, the survivor was busy upon liberation crossing borders to eventually reach a displaced persons camp. There they became involved with rebuilding families and planning their emigration to different countries and continents.[7]

During the second postwar period of the 1950s, survivors were engaged in immigration and absorption into their new countries.[8] Once again, they had no time to stop and mourn the dead in their pressing search for work and housing, in addition to learning new languages and customs. Rather than being made to feel welcome in their new homes, those who settled in the nascent State of Israel found the image of the helpless, persecuted Jewish victim to be in shameful contrast to the emerging national myth of the strong, heroic new Israeli Jews who "would have fought back…" Israelis looked at the survivors with a mixture of suspicion ("How did they survive?"), contempt ("They went like sheep to the slaughter!"), and/or pity ("G-d help you poor things!").[9] From the author's own experience growing up in the United States, similar humiliating expressions regarding survivors were heard there as well.

In the third period of social adjustment to new home countries, the 1960s and '70s were characterized by intensified efforts toward integration into the new culture and economy. Again, still lacking the time to mourn or reminisce, "everyone made an effort to move on and leave the tragic past behind."[10]

By being forced to bypass the mourning process in environments unconducive to listening to their agony and grief, survivors were also forced to remain silent as they integrated into society. With the very "denial of being a Holocaust survivor" often considered "a psychological necessity for coping,"[11] many, at the very least, learned to be silent, to deny their experiences and to suppress their emotional wounds and painful memories for many years, sometimes forever. With stories of the Holocaust evoking terror and anxiety among veteran residents, survivors learned that silence was the price for acceptance and integration into their new societies.[12]

Reflecting on the early years after liberation, Elie Weisel recalled: "We were mad with disbelief. People refused to listen, to understand, to share. There was a division between us and them, between those who endured and those who read about it, or would refuse to read about it."[13] Ruth Leys notes that a similar observation was made by psychoanalyst and Buchenwald survivor Ernest Rappaport in speaking of the difficulties encountered by the survivor in the face of what he called "the preferred attitude of forgetting" on the part of others.[14] Says Rappaport:

> I survived a concentration camp but I regularly made the observation that people did not really want me to talk about my experiences, and whenever I started, they invariably showed their resistance by interrupting me, by asking me to tell them how I got out.[15]

Even trained mental health professionals are reported to have wished the survivor to forget so that they, too, could do so. With the treatment of the survivor often triggering strong emotion and anxiety in the therapist, treatment was likely to be characterized by too-early termination as well as by opposing tendencies to either automatically attribute any pathology to the Holocaust or to ignore its influence completely.[16] Journalist Howard Reich refers to psychiatrist Milton E. Jucovy's term "the curtain of silence" for this tendency on the part of his colleagues to evade hearing of the unbearable horrors experienced by their patients.[17]

At Elie Wiesel's death, *New York Times* journalist Joseph Berger notes the role guilt may also have played in forcing both survivors and American Jews to have been "frozen in silence" for decades, with both the survivor and his co-religionists guilt-ridden at their inability to rescue the victims. Reporting that the 1960 English translation of Wiesel's bestseller *Night* took more than a year to find an American publisher and then sold only just over a thousand copies during the first eighteen months after publication, Berman quotes Wiesel from a 1985 interview: "The Holocaust was not something people wanted to know about in those days."[18]

It is important to reiterate that this book would not have been made possible without the work of the professional genealogist who was instrumental not only in locating second-generation tunnel survivors, but also in helping to research the prewar and immediate postwar background of surviving escapees, often from International Red Cross files. Contrary to the possible expectation that these former partisans might have taken pride in and been willing to at least acknowledge their resistance activities, not a single tunnel escape survivor included testimony of partisan membership in postwar documents filed with the Red Cross. It has come to light that survivors in the United States were often fearful to acknowledge participation in partisan activities that might somehow associate them with cooperation with the Soviets. In the era of the Cold War, many feared such a presumed association might jeopardize their American citizenship, thus preferring to keep silent about even such a heroic event as the tunnel escape.[19] This silence was often extended by survivors to their own children as they were growing up.

Perhaps, as Berger posits, it was due to guilt that survivors were psychologically re-imprisoned, no longer by the Nazis but by a world that forced them into silence. For escapees in the US, perhaps this was for fear of being branded as Communists by assumed association with the Soviets. For survivors in Israel, perhaps this was due to shame. In some cases, it is possible survivors imprisoned themselves by deliberately choosing to remain silent to avoid burdening their children, whom they wished to raise in the stereotypical "normal, happy family." Or perhaps the survivors' silence was encouraged by those whose hearts and minds simply needed more time to absorb, believe, and attempt to cope with the magnitude of cruelty they witnessed and experienced. In essence, after being forced to repress his experiences for so long, at times even the survivor had difficulty believing what had happened to him. Bergmann and Jucovy quote writer Aharon Appelfeld, who arrived in Israel at the age of twelve after liberation from a concentration camp:

> After liberation the one desire was to sleep, to forget and to be reborn. At first there was a wish to talk incessantly about one's experience. This gave way to silence but learning to be silent was not easy. When the past was no longer talked about, it became unreal, a figment of one's imagination. The new Israeli identity, sun-burned, practical and strong, was grafted upon the old identity of the helpless victim. Only in nightmares was the past alive, but then even dreaming ceased.[20]

With the children of tunnel escapees born and raised in the first three decades after liberation, it is not at all surprising to perceive the dearth of knowledge most possessed regarding their parents' wartime experiences. Many, for the reasons given above, were totally unaware of how their parents survived. When I first began to phone members of the second generation to learn about the postwar lives of their parents, I was in for a shock. When I introduced myself by saying I'm writing a book about the escapees of the Novogrudok labor camp, many children of tunnel survivors reacted with such questions as "Novo what?" or "What does this have to do with me?" The son of one survivor even told me that I must have the wrong number, as his "weak and sickly" father could never have participated in such a daring escape or fought in the Bielski partisans. For years, even after I sent him his father's Red Cross file, this son continued to deny his father's connection to the escape. After all, he asked, wouldn't his father have told him about it?

Many second-generation tunnel survivors were initially embarrassed at their lack of knowledge regarding their escapee parents. Yet they found it comforting when I introduced myself as a second-generation tunnel escapee whose mother was together with their parent in the labor camp, the escape, and the forest. They became reassured to learn they were "in good company," and their lack of knowledge of wartime events was shared by many other offspring of tunnel escapees. My admission that even I did not know about the tunnel escape until my mid-thirties or who Tuvia Bielski was until far into adulthood served to further cement the bond with fellow children of tunnel escapees, many of whom also grew up with a loud silence as the background noise of their childhoods.

A number of these "children" ultimately expressed gratitude for finally obtaining answers to questions they'd never dared to ask. As I had researched their families from genealogical and Holocaust-related websites in advance of the calls, many learned for the first time the names of their grandparents as well as the names of the displaced persons camps where their parents took refuge. At least one child of an escapee learned for the first time of his father's important contribution to the tunnel construction. Another responded: "I knew my father was in a labor camp after being in the Baranovich ghetto, but I didn't know where. I knew he escaped, but I didn't know how."

Another first learned of her mother's important role in the partisans. One daughter of an escapee was provided with the most basic biographical information about her own father, admitting that her parents' past was an unspoken "taboo" subject, and the few questions she did dare to ask were met with the type of silence I've described. Yet another escapee's daughter who had never heard of Novogrudok or of the tunnel escape admitted that her father's resistance to providing information about his past and his family history had long led her to suspect that she was adopted.

This research also enabled relatives other than the second generation to be contacted so they could fill in gaps in their family history. Imagine the surprise of a 101-year-old nephew of a tunnel escapee upon finally learning how and when his uncle met his death. Or the shock of my own cousin, who had always wondered how his aunt from Novogrudok had been murdered, only to discover she had also been a tunnel escapee. One stepdaughter of an escapee who was traced from a Holocaust database, a cemetery website, and with help from the Red Cross, learned for the first time that like her, her stepfather was from Novogrudok, and that he had participated in the breakout. A niece of another escapee who first learned of the tunnel escape when I spoke at a Novogrudok memorial meeting was overcome with emotion when I later called to inform her that her uncle had been a tunnel escapee and was alive at least until liberation. A grandson learned for the first time not only of his grandfather's participation in the tunnel escape, but also of his father's first marriage and of his own half brother, murdered as an infant.

In many cases, the reactions to my research by many second-generation tunnel escapees are similar to people who have opened their adoption files. Through the background information I provided on the escapees' families of origin, many have now learned their parents' stories as well as the names of aunts, uncles, and cousins that might have been completely lost to them and to future generations.

A number of second-generation escapees have remarked to me privately and to each other at various gatherings, including the seventy-fifth anniversary of the tunnel escape in Novogrudok in October 2019 and the inauguration of the Memorial Wall in Novogrudok in July 2020, that our common background enables us to feel like family. Many of us now meet at one another's celebrations, and like family, we call to wish each other well before holidays. My own mother had been "adopted" by a fellow escapee's son who visited her monthly and became a member of my own family.

I am pleased to say that for many of the second-generation tunnel survivors interviewed, this research changed their lives. All expressed their appreciation for making their parents' stories known, not only to themselves, but to their children and to the world. Elie Wiesel referred to the obligation of the second and subsequent generations to take on the role of witnesses by telling their parents' and grandparents' stories; we have empowered many to now do so.[21] In the words of one escapee's son: "Your work…has made a difference in our lives – reigniting a dialogue about our pasts and being more open and alive to what our inheritance has been and is." At the very least, this tribute to the tunnel survivors of this great prisoner escape of the Holocaust has helped them view their parents in a new light: that of brave, courageous individuals who daringly crawled to freedom, contributed to their new societies, and most important, chose life.

Color Images

The original escape list recorded by Yitzchak Rosenhaus, September 1943
(courtesy of Lochamei Hagetaot, the Ghetto Fighters' House)

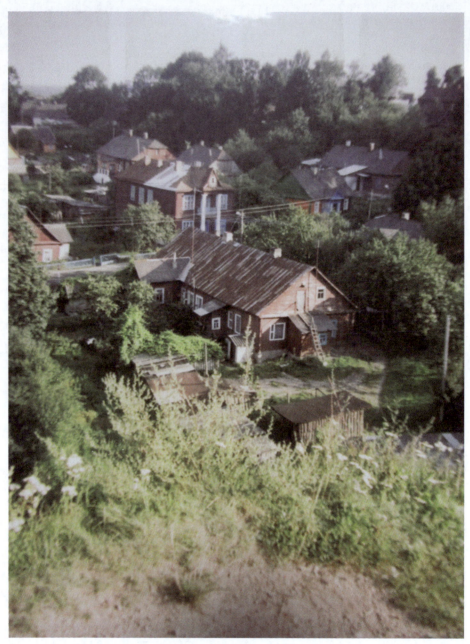

View of Novogrudok from the old Jewish cemetery
(photo by Betty Brodsky Cohen)

The Zamok (citadel), a prominent Novogrudok landmark and gathering
place for the prewar Jewish community on the Sabbath
(photo by Betty Brodsky Cohen)

The courthouse in which the Novogrudok forced labor camp workshops
were located, currently serves as a school (photo by Betty Brodsky Cohen)

Interior view of the courthouse (photo by Shiran Cohen)

Interior view of the courthouse (photo by Shiran Cohen)

Window through which inmates watched the slaughter of their families on May 7, 1943 (photo by Shiran Cohen)

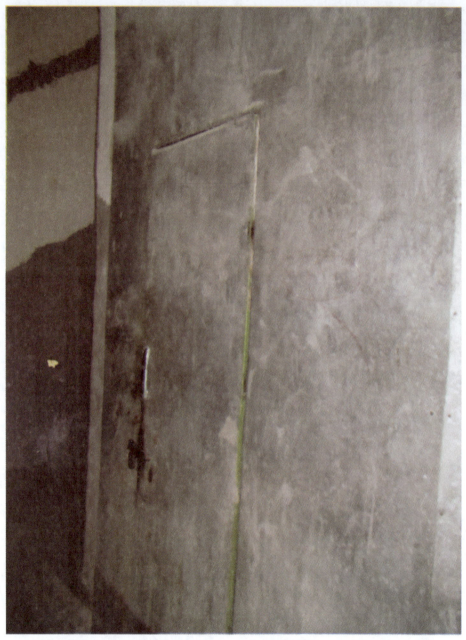

Entrance to courthouse basement where children were hidden and murdered after being discovered (photo by Betty Brodsky Cohen)

Sleeping barracks of the forced labor camp with the "Zhetler room," which housed the entrance to the tunnel, on the far right (photo by Shiran Cohen)

Three-tiered bunks in sleeping barracks with each plank holding several inmates (photo by Betty Brodsky Cohen)

Entrance to the tunnel in the "Zhetler room" under the bed of Alter
Nignevitcky (#132) and a replica of the cart built to pull out dug-up dirt
during the excavation of the tunnel (photo by Betty Brodsky Cohen)

Rudimentary hand-made tools used in digging the tunnel
(photo by Betty Brodsky Cohen)

The path of the tunnel (photo by Shiran Cohen)

Memorial Wall with tunnel escapees' names and their fates (research by
Betty Brodsky Cohen, photo by Shiran Cohen)

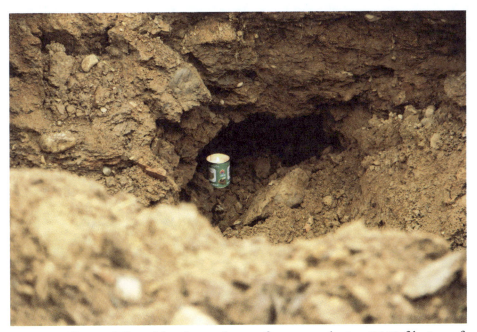

Section of tunnel found by descendants of escapees during 2012 filming of
the movie *Tunnel of Hope* (courtesy of Dror Shwartz)

Appendices

Appendices

Appendix 1
Timeline: Jewish Novogrudok, 1044–1929

1044 or 1116: Novogrudok is founded either in 1044 by Kievan prince Yaroslav the Wise, who was on a military expedition, or in 1116 by Prince Yaropolk, son of Prince Vladimir Monomach.[1]

1252: Novogrudok becomes capital of the Grand Duchy of Lithuania, Prince Mindog. Probably the era of the first settlement of Jews,[2] who become responsible for the collection of all taxes and customs duties in the Lithuanian Duchy.[3]

1563: Demand by townspeople to establish a Jewish ghetto is rejected, while poor relations with the Polish population are to continue. Jews at this time become closely connected to the Radziwill Court, which makes use of their services. Many Jews reside in a special area of town belonging to the aristocratic family.[4]

1569: Unification of Lithuania with Poland brings increased settlement of Jews to Novogrudok, which lies on the Lithuania-Moscow trade route.[5]

1648: The Great (Cold) Synagogue is erected by Karaites, who possibly arrived at the close of the fourteenth century. The synagogue later becomes the main synagogue building.[6]

1655: Russian occupation of Novogrudok.[7]

1659: Polish recapture of Novogrudok. Pogroms against the Jews.[8]

1789: Population of Novogrudok is about one-third Jewish (233 men and 204 women), as contrasted to 819 Christians.[9]

1795: End of Polish-Lithuanian Commonwealth. Novogrudok comes under Czarist rule with the partition of Poland.[10] Jews are reported to suffer from anti-Semitic acts by Russian soldiers stationed in the city.[11]

1817: Jews form the majority of Novogrudok's population of 1,571, composed of 726 Jews, 526 Christians, and 37 Tatars.[12]

1882: Beginning of wave of immigration to the United States.[13]

1888: Jews form the overwhelming majority of Novogrudok's population of 12,000. There are 8,150 Jews, 2,690 Christians, and 1,160 Muslims.[14]

1896: Beit Yosef musar yeshiva is established in Novogrudok by Rabbi Yosef Yoysl Horowitz, based on the teachings of Rabbi Israel Lipkin (Salanter) of Lithuania.[15]

1914: Jewish population decreases but is still a majority. Although still a majority of Novogrudok, the Jewish population is notably decreased due to immigration to the United States and Europe. The city's population of 8,457 consists of 5,584 Jews, 1,609 Russian Orthodox, 679 Catholics, 566 Muslims, and 19 Protestants.[16] Relatives in the USA, including Yiddish-Hebrew dictionary author Alexander Harkavy, help support Jewish life in Novogrudok.[17]

1915–1918: Occupation of Novogrudok by the Germans during World War I.[18]

February 1919: The Soviet Army enters Novogrudok.[19]

April 1919: The Polish Army enters Novogrudok.

July 1920: Departure of the Polish Army and entrance of the Red Army.[20]

October 1920: Reentrance of Polish Army. Novogrudok becomes part of newly independent Poland.[21]

1921: Court of the Justice of the Peace built,[22] whose building will serve as the workmen's ghetto under the Germans.[23]

1921–1939: Novogrudok becomes the district center of the Second Polish Republic. Many Jewish organizations flourish during this period (see section on Prewar Communal Organizations of Novogrudok in "Why

Novogrudok").[24] Anti-Semitism surges among the predominantly Polish townspeople during the Great Depression.[25]

1939: Soviet-German agreement signed on August 23, 1939. Soviet troops arrive in the city on September 17, and **Novogrudok is annexed by the Soviet Union**. The first refugees to Novogrudok from German-occupied areas bring initial reports of atrocities against Jews. Soviets are welcomed by Jews despite the dissolution of many Jewish organizations. By October 1939, all shops are nationalized and all youth movements and political parties dissolved.[26]

Appendix 2
Timeline: The Holocaust in Novogrudok, 1941–1943

June 19, 1941: Deportation to Siberia of dozens of Jewish families in advance of upcoming German attack on the Soviet Union.[1]

June 22, 1941: German attack on Soviet Union.[2]

June 24, 1941: First bombing of Novogrudok.[3]

June 26, 1941: Two hundred Jewish men are assembled in the marketplace, where they are publicly tortured.[4] Fifty-two are shot to death to the accompaniment of an orchestra playing Strauss waltzes. Jewish women are ordered to wash the blood from the cobblestones.[5]

July 4, 1941: German occupation of Novogrudok[6] At least twenty-seven Jews are murdered.[7] Promulgation of anti-Jewish laws: All Jews are required to wear yellow stars on the front and back of clothing and are forbidden to walk on the pavement. Jews aged twelve to sixty are required to report for work duty. Jews are no longer citizens, thus no longer entitled to police protection.[8] First Judenrat (Jewish council forcibly created by the Germans in Nazi-occupied European Jewish communities[9]) is established in Novogrudok, probably headed by Nachum Zeldowicz.[10] Bound to carry out German-imposed orders and regulations, Jewish council members face terrible moral conflicts over compliance with such German demands as compiling deportation lists.[11]

August 26, 1941: Additional fifty Jewish men are murdered in the market square. Both massacres are most likely committed by members of the Einsatzgruppe B,[12] the mobile killing unit operating in Belorussia and the Smolensk District, east of Moscow. The 655-man unit was assigned to execute those considered to be opponents of the Reich – i.e., Communists and Jews.[13]

September 1, 1941: Civil administration replaces former German military administration. Novogrudok becomes part of the eleven-district White Russian General Commissariat headed by Wilhelm Kube. District Commissioner Wilhelm Traub becomes the area governor.

December 7, 1941: A hundred young Jewish men are taken to disassemble the wooden fence surrounding the marketplace at the end of Karelitzer Street and ordered to carry the boards to the Novogrudok suburb of Pereseka, site of a future ghetto. Poked with sticks, rifle butts, and iron rods by the surrounding mounted Wehrmacht soldiers, Lithuanian soldiers, and Belarusian policemen, the Jews carrying the heavy, wet segments are forced to trudge through heavy snow for two kilometers. Those unable to manage the load are shot to death and their bodies carried by their brethren on wooden planks to be buried in a field in the village of Britzenko.[14]

December 8, 1941: Novogrudok's first mass slaughter led by the SIPO (German Security Police Force) from Baranovich.[15] Part of the SS, this force is assisted by the 260–280 Wehrmacht soldiers who serve under local military commander Johann Artmann;[16] by a force of auxiliary police from Lithuania, Latvia, Estonia, and by local Polish and Belarusian town police. Wilhelm Traub commands the operation.[17] After the majority of Novogrudok's Jews have been forcibly concentrated in the four buildings of the town's courthouse area from the evening of December 5, [18] women, children, and men without a skilled trade are separated from the others.[19] Taken to the forest in the nearby village of Skirdlevo, the victims are beaten and ordered to lie face down in groups of fifty. After being forced to hand over all valuables and undress in the subfreezing weather, they are driven to prepared pits and shot by the Einsatzgruppe.[20] It is estimated between four thousand and fifty-one hundred Jews are slaughtered that day. The remaining thirteen to fifteen hundred are taken to the newly built Pereseka ghetto, where they subsist on a daily ration of two hundred grams of bread.[21] Extremely small, the twenty-eight-house ghetto[22] is an open entity in which people go out to work. About 450 skilled men and women serve in the workshops of one of the courthouse buildings, while approximately 250 men work in the Russian barracks in Skirdlevo, in close proximity to the fresh mass grave of their family members.[23]

May-June, 1942: Massacres of Jews in small towns and villages near Novogrudok. Population of the Pereseka ghetto increases to six to seven thousand following the deportation of three thousand to forty-five hundred survivors of the slaughters in Zhetl, Karelich, Lubcz, Dalatycze, Ivenets, Derevna, Wsielub, Naliboki, and Ravishevits. Pereseka is described as having been a deplorable place with rampant hunger, intolerable overcrowding,[24] and people idly awaiting their deaths.

August 7, 1942: Novogrudok's second mass slaughter initiated by Wilhelm Traub. Murderers include members of the German Security Police Force from Baranovich, auxiliaries from Estonia and possibly Lithuania and Latvia, as well as the local militia.[25] As many as fifty-five hundred men, women, and children are taken two kilometers to their slaughter in the village of Litovka. That same evening, most of the children hidden in the loft and some of those hidden in the basement of the courthouse are discovered and hurled from the windows. Those remaining alive are hauled by truck to Litovka, where they are shot to death in Litovka's mass grave.[26] Their parents are then locked in a stable with the other inmates for three days without food or water.[27] Approximately five hundred Jews remain in both Pereseka and the courthouse, whose status changes from that of a ghetto to a forced labor camp.[28]

February 4, 1943: Novogrudok's third massacre, in which all but two of the approximately five hundred inhabitants of the Pereseka ghetto are slaughtered in Great Brecianka, a hamlet less than two kilometers away. The slaughter takes place in the dark of the early morning hours when the Jews are led by armed policemen to a pre-dug ditch. Most of the few who manage to escape are turned over to the Germans by local farmers. The two who remain alive manage to reach the forest to join the partisans.[29] Daily food rations in the courthouse are reduced to a hundred grams of bread mixed with straw and a thin soup of water and potato peels.[30]

February 15–April 15, 1943: Armed courthouse uprising by the forced labor camp inmates is planned for April 15, headed by Dr. Yakov Kagan (#3a). Fighters are divided into groups of five combatants plus a group leader. With arms purchased from the policemen guarding the ghetto, hand grenades are to be thrown at the guardhouse, telephone wires and wire fences are to be cut. Freed Jews are to be led to the forest to join the partisans. Plan is foiled after being exposed at the last minute, either by the mother of Moshe Burshtein, a prisoner held in jail,[31] or by the wife of Dr. Jakubowicz, to protect her husband, who had been shot in the leg.[32] Both would have been left behind and killed had the uprising taken place.

May 7, 1943: Fourth and last Novogrudok massacre. While the most highly skilled craftsmen are in the workshops, 298 of the less-skilled inmates are surrounded by black-uniformed policemen and armed Latvians in the courthouse yard at five a.m. Led out of the gate, they are forced to completely undress and lie face down. In groups of ten, they are led to prepared pits[33] in Hardzilowka,[34] just four hundred meters away, where they are shot. Many go to their deaths shouting, singing, and waving their arms to those able to view the slaughter from the window of the courthouse.[35] Many escapees later testify that the May 7 massacre is the trigger to plan a breakout from the labor camp.[36]

September 26, 1943: The rainy, stormy night of the tunnel escape. According to survivor testimonies, the number of inmates who actually participate in the tunnel escape is described as having been approximately 240,[37] or 250.[38] While estimates of the dimensions of the tunnel differ, all escapee testimonies convey the spirit of the resourcefulness, courage, and drama that culminated in the daring tunnel escape.

Appendix 3
A Letter from the Forced Labor Camp by Yitzchak Rosenhaus

After the death of tunnel escape survivor Yitzchak Rosenhaus (#30) in 1996, his son Effie found this Yiddish-language letter among Yitzchak's possessions. Penned by Yitzchak while he was a prisoner in the Novogrudok forced labor camp, the letter had been smuggled out of the camp by a non-Jew who promised to mail it. Against insurmountable odds, both Yitzchak Rosenhaus and the letter survived the war. Following his father's death, Effie gave a copy of the letter to the author's mother, Fanya Dunetz (#142), during a visit to her home.

This letter's significance cannot be underestimated: it is the sole known existing document written in real time by an inmate imprisoned in the labor camp. In this message to an unknown individual (probably a relative) also named Yitzchak, Rosenhaus provides a harrowing account of the struggle he and his wife Genia encountered from the onset of the German occupation. His stark description of the sheer desperation felt by the Novogrudok forced labor camp inmates in the wake of the May 7, 1943, massacre gives an extraordinary glimpse at the backdrop to the impetus to build the tunnel and the decision to escape to the forest.

Through this letter, Yitzchak Rosenhaus (who also undertook to salvage a copy of the original escape list he'd recorded prior to the tunnel escape) has provided generations to come with priceless testimony. Following is a translation of the Yiddish-language letter:

Novogrudok, in the concentration camp, May 12, 1943

Dear Yitzchak,

When you read these lines, I will certainly no longer be among the living. But, as it is my desire to leave behind a trace of my tragic experiences and spiritual anguish, I have decided to entrust this letter to a Christian (the only one who has authorization to enter our camp) in the hope that perhaps he will send it to you.

As of today, we have experienced forty-four months of war. I greatly regret that I wasn't killed during the first bombing on Baranovich on September 15, 1939, which took a hundred victims. During the twenty-two months of Soviet rule, we experienced a great deal. On May 20, 1940, our Sonia died due to a heart condition (following influenza). They evicted us from our house, seized the stores, and I, together with my young wife Genia (Genia Slutski of Lida), whom I married on December 12, 1939, were forced to leave Baranovich. Since I was formerly well-to-do, it was forbidden for me to remain there. We traveled to Grodno, while Mother and Esterke traveled to Slonim. Our Genia, who married a "kosher" worker, stayed in Baranovich to work as a salaried worker.

In Grodno, times were different for us. We didn't lack for unpleasantness, yet during the last half of the year, I was already managing and had started a calm life beside my beloved wife Genia, who from the first day gave me courage to overcome all the difficulties of my new proletarian life.

While in Grodno, we were in close contact with Haim Isser, who worked as a dentist in the neighboring town of Skidel.

On June 22, 1941, the first day of the German-Russian War, Grodno was very heavily bombed, and our apartment was destroyed. Genia and I were literally buried under the ruins, and only by a miracle were we saved from certain death.

On that same day, we left behind everything that we owned, packed a small bag with a change of underwear, and started out, ready to flee from the enemy. But he caught up with us. We were forced to remain in the small town of Zhetl. There we managed to get settled together with my wife's parents, who arrived there.

From the first day that our area was captured by the Germans, a sea of troubles and regulations began for us Jews. They accustomed us to this in such a sophisticated way that we imagined our former troubles were nothing compared to the new ones occurring on a daily basis. First, they ordered us to wear a yellow patch – that is, a Star of David – as a mark of shame. Then they forbade us to walk on the sidewalk – only in the gutters. They took our homes and fields; they took our horses, cows, and goats. They forbade moving freely on the roads. They took furs, textiles, skins, gold, silver, nickel, kitchen utensils, bed linens – really everything that we had. (Jews were forbidden to wear a watch.) Jews were sent into forced labor.

On February 22, 1942, they expelled us to a ghetto. That is, they arranged a neighborhood of the city – streets in which we were separated from the entire population…. During the tenth week of the ghetto's formation on April 7, 1930, the first slaughter began, in which 750 victims were murdered. After the first pogrom, they promised us that something of this nature would not happen again. The twenty-five hundred Jews who remained believed the treacherous words of the villains and continued to maintain a regular life. After three months, a new round of acts of destruction commenced anew.

One clear day, on Thursday, August 6, 1942, the town of Zhetl once again fell victim to the murderers. All the Jews were slaughtered. Zhetl remained cleansed of Jews. Skilled workers were transferred to the concentration camp in Novogrudok. During this time, we lost Genia's parents. Mother and Esterke were murdered in Baranovich on September 26, 1942. We heard from Genia that she and her husband are in a labor camp in Molodechno.

At first, we had several opportunities to escape from the labor camp to the forest, but we didn't take advantage of them. We put this off until the spring, but unfortunately, we were too late. Unexpectedly, they placed us under heavy guard, within a triple gate of wood and barbed wire, surrounded by searchlights and a row of cannons – thus, it's impossible to escape from here. From 780, our number was now "reduced" to 530 men and women. Each one a skilled worker. On Friday morning, May 7, they assaulted us once again. We paid with three hundred victims. How I saved Genia from the bullets, I myself don't know.

It's difficult to grasp our physical and spiritual suffering. The rich imagination of a writer can't even describe a speck of what we are experiencing. There are also informers from within who think they can benefit themselves on our account, and they poison our last moments.

I am summing up my short life. I hold myself accountable, for I could still do a great deal more, but I must go before my time, to the black grave, only because I am a Jew.

My only comfort is my dear Genia, who is always by my side. We draw strength from one another. You cannot even imagine what suffering the Germans are capable of wreaking. You cannot understand how people walk around in desperation, hoping to die.

Remember, dear brothers, seek revenge against the German nation for the rivers of blood shed by innocent people, men, women, and children. See to it that on the day of the great liberation, this nation of Amalekites will turn to dust....

Take revenge for those who were buried alive, the tortured, and the burnt – thousands and millions. The revenge of the Americans and the English must be total. The nation of Amalekites is forbidden resurrection. They must pay for the sea of blood that was spilled. There is no mercy in judgment! Remember that our blood will find no rest until there is complete revenge.

Read this letter to all your acquaintances. Explain and do the utmost so that we may quietly sleep our eternal sleep.

Know that as long as the Germans walk freely, the world will continue to be threatened. Invent the most severe punishments and torture for those murderers who fall into your hands.

For the government of Germany, the government of malice, there must be eternal sanctions.

Regards,

Isaak and Genia

Appendix 4
Distribution of Escapees by Prewar Residence

Town	Number of Escapees
Novogrudok	98
Zhetl	41
Ivenets	11
Karelich	9
Baranovich	4
Lubcha	4
Lodz	4
Mezrich	3
Nowa Mysz	2
Warsaw	2
Bialystok	1
Belice	1
Jesow	1
Lida	1
Lubien Kujawski	1
Mlawa	1
Ozorko	1
Radom	1
Rakov	1
Slutzk	1
Unknown	39

Appendix 5
Tunnel Survivors and Their Partisan Detachments

Tunnel Survivor	Partisan Detachment
Abramowicz, Pesach (#205)	Kalinin (Bielski)
Abramowicz, Chaim (#22)	Kalinin
Angelchik, Yakov (#67)	Frunze
Berkowicz, Eliyahu (Elya, #49)	Kalinin
Berkowicz, Myer	Kalinin
Borowski, Aaron (#58)	Kalinin
Borowski, Wolff (Velvel, #57)	Kalinin
Bruk, Moshe (#97)	Kalinin
Czertok, Abram (#45)	Frunze
Chernevich, Abram (#193)	Kalinin
Chernevich, Notek (#194)	Kalinin
Davidowicz, Frieda (#158)	Kalinin
Davidowicz, Leah (#158a)	Kalinin
Dunetz, Fanya (#142)	Kalinin
Eisenshtadt, Shepsel (#137)	Kalinin
Epshtein, Chana	Kalinin
Faifer, Nachman (#167)	Kalinin
Feivelevich, Moshe (#47)	Kalinin
Ginenski, Beila	Kalinin
Ginenski, Grunya	Kalinin
Ginenski, Rivka (Riva)	Kalinin
Gershanovich, Mairim (#12)	Frunze
Gershanovich, Shevach (#13)	Frunze

Gertzovski, Saadia (#214)	Possibly in hiding
Giershenowski, Roza (#151)	Kalinin
Giershenowski, Sara (#149)	Kalinin
Ginden, Sholom (#110)	106th detachment (Kirov)
Ginenski, Bella	Kalinin
Ginenski, Riva (Rivka)	Kalinin
Goberman, Natan (Nota, #190)	Kalinin
Golanski, Shlomo (#75)	Kalinin
Goldshmid, Abram (#128)	Ordzhonikidze
Gorodynski, Sonya (#78)	Kalinin
Gorodynski, Shevel (Shaul, #77)	Kalinin
Gorodynski, Shlomo (#87)	Kalinin
Grande, Yehezkiel (Chatskel, #138)	Kalinin
Gurvich, Alter (#98)	106th detachment
Gurvich, Hirsh (#9)	Frunze
Jakubowski, Aaron (#55)	106th detachment
Kabak, Matus (#72a)	Kalinin
Kagan, Yudel (#95)	Kalinin
Kaganowicz, Riva (#146)	Kalinin
Kantorovich, Yakov	Kalinin
Kirzner, Aaron (Rozke, #21)	Kalinin
Kolachek, Shmuel (#82)	Kalinin, Dubov
Kolachek, Yisrael (#81)	Kalinin, Dubov
Kopernik, Zelda (#197)	Kalinin
Kritz, Herman (#60)	Kalinin
Kushner, Leah (#145)	Kalinin
Kushner, Naum (Zeidel, #143)	Kalinin
Kushner, Raya (#144)	Kalinin
Lazowsky, Isaac	Kalinin
Leibowitz, Chaim Noah (#91)	Kalinin
Lev, Chanan (#162)	Kalinin
Levkovich, Nina (#113)	Kalinin
Lewin, Malka (#107)	Kalinin

Lidski, Isaac (#119)	Kotovski
Luska, Chaya Sara (#168)	Kalinin
Magids, Avraham	Borba, Kalinin
Majerowicz, Morduch	Roscha
Maslovati, Gedalia (#63)	Kalinin
Mayevski, Pesia (#160)	Kalinin
Mazurkevich, Etya (#3)	Kalinin
Mazurkevich, Yitzchak (#177)	Unknown detachment of the Baranovichskaya Brigade
Meyerovich, Yevel (#122)	Kalinin
Morduchowicz, Mordechai (Motke)	Kalinin
Nignevitcky, Alter (#132)	Kalinin
Nignevitcky, Moshe (#130)	Kalinin
Nigneviticky, Sheina (#131)	Kalinin
Niselevich, Shmuel (#88)	Borba
Notkovich, Kalman (#53)	Kalinin
Novogrudski, Michael (#114)	Kalinin
Ofsejewicz, Betzalel (#85)	Kalinin
Okonski, Efraim (#90)	Kalinin
Okonski, Shlomo (#89)	Kalinin
Orzuchowski, Leib	Ordzhonikidze
Orzuchowski, Mordechai (Motl, #42)	Ordzhonikidze, Frunze
Oshman, Aaron (#79)	Kalinin
Oshman, Yakov (#80)	Kalinin
Ostashinski, Daniel	Kalinin
Ostashinski, Chaim (#32)	Kalinin
Ostashinski, Perla (#33)	Kalinin
Patzovski, Hirsh (#159)	Kalinin
Pinchuk, Leiba (#46)	Kalinin
Portnoj, Pesach (Lionke, #19)	Kalinin
Portnoj, Sima (#20)	Kalinin
Pozniak, Yechezkel (Chatzkel, #52)	Kalinin
Rabinowitz, Batia (#27)	Kalinin

Rakovski, Avraham (Avram, #10)	Frunze
Razvaski, Yosef (#41)	106th detachment
Reznitzki, Shalom	Borba
Rosenhaus, Genia (#31)	Kalinin
Rosenhaus, Yitzchak (#30)	Kalinin
Rozin, Zisel (#50)	Kalinin
Ryback, Chana (#124)	Kalinin
Ryback, Shlomo (#123)	Kalinin
Samsonowicz, Hirsz (#121)	Kalinin
Schmulewitz, Akiva (Kiwa, #83)	Kalinin
Selubski, Efroim (#8)	Kalinin
Shapiro, Gutel (#86)	Kalinin
Shelkovich, Kalman (#100)	Kalinin
Shepsman, Yakov (Yankel, #39)	Kalinin
Shkolnik, Hirsch (#210)	Kalinin
Shleimovich, Naum (#66)	Za Sovetskuyu Belarus
Shmerkovich, Feiga (#126)	Kalinin
Shmerkovich, Tevel (#125)	Kalinin
Shofer, Rafael (#202)	Kalinin
Shuster, Yitzchak	Kalinin
Shuster, Yosef (Yosel, #209)	Kalinin
Shvarzbord, Morduch	106th detachment
Sucharski, Natan (Nota, #4)	Kalinin
Svinik, Dvora (#206)	Kalinin
Svinik, Shalom (#207)	Kalinin
Tiles, Yocheved (Yacha, #166a)	Kalinin
Ulert, Isaac	Kalinin
Weinrid, Yakov (#156)	Frunze
Wilenski, Aaron (#65)	Kalinin
Wilenski, Simcha (#111)	Kalinin
Wolkowicki, Peretz (#199)	Kalinin
Yakubowicz, Dr. Majer (#1)	Budenny
Yakubowicz, Sarafima (#2)	Budenny

Yankelevich, Natan (Nota, #84)   Kalinin
Yarmovski, Henia (#195)   Kalinin
Yarmovski, Isaac (#6)   Frunze
Yarmovski, Zlata (#7)   Frunze
Yoselevich, Yakov (#96)   Kalinin
Zacharevich, Mordechai (#102)   Kalinin
Zak, Yoel (#18)   Unknown
Zalmanovich, Berko (Berl, #64)   Kalinin
Zamosczyk, Nachum (#133)   Ordzhonikidze
Zamosczyk, Sara (#134)   Ordzhonikidze
Zusmanovich, Eliezer (Leizer, #192)   Kalinin, Roscha
Zusmanovich, Samuel (#191)   Kalinin, Roscha

Appendix 6
Distribution of Partisan Detachments among Tunnel Escapees

(Includes the multiple detachments of four tunnel survivors)

Unit	Number of Escapees
Kalinin (Bielski – includes 5 Bielski fighters in Ordzhonikidze detachment)	108
Frunze	10
106th detachment	5
Borba	3
Budenny	2
Dubov	2
Roscha	3
Kotovski	1
Za Sovetskuyu Belarus	1
Unknown	2

Endnotes

Preface

1. Theodore Roosevelt, "Citizenship in a Republic," speech given at the Sorbonne, Paris, April 23, 1910.

Introduction: The Tunnel Escape from the Novogrudok Forced Labor Camp, 1943

1. Gila Lyons, "Great Escape," *Tablet*, April 9, 2010, https://www.tabletmag.com/sections/belief/articles/great-escape.
2. Jack Kagan and Dov Cohen, *Surviving the Holocaust with the Russian Jewish Partisans* (London: Vallentine, Mitchell and Son, 1998), 138.
3. Lyons, "Great Escape."
4. Kagan and Cohen, *Surviving the Holocaust*, 160–61.
5. Chaim Leibovitz, "The Great Destruction: How 300 Jews Saved Themselves," in *Novogrudok Memorial Book*, 500–501.
6. Nechama Tec, *Defiance: The Bielski Partisans* (New York and Oxford: Oxford University Press, 1993), 187.
7. Leibovitz, "The Great Destruction," 502.
8. Nachum Kushner, Yad Vashem testimony [in Yiddish], no. 03/3929.
9. Idel Kagan, "Surviving the Holocaust with the Russian Jewish Partisans," in *Novogrudok Memorial Book*, 567–73.
10. Tec, *Defiance*, 187.
11. Shaul Gorodynski, Yad Vashem testimony, no. 3095/230.
12. Lyons, "Great Escape."
13. Kagan is obviously referring to the inmate Yitzchak Dvoretzki. See the chapter "Special Mention: Yitzchak Dvoretzki."
14. Kagan, "Surviving the Holocaust," 569–74. Reproduced by permission of JewishGen.
15. Yaakov Goldberg, "The History of the Jews of Novogudok," in *Novogrudok Memorial Book*, 19.

16 Ina Kraer, personal interview, June 17, 2021.

17 Goldberg, "The History of the Jews of Novogudok," 19.

18 Yehuda Bauer, "Nowogródek: The Story of a Shtetl," *Yad Vashem Studies* 35, no. 2 (2007): 37.

19 Eliezer Berkovich, "Schlos Gass: A Distinct Township," in *Novogrudok Memorial Book*, 242–43.

20 Miriam Ninkovski, "Four Graves of Our Fathers," in *Novogrudok Memorial Book*, 637–38.

21 Tamara Vershitskaya, personal interview, October 10, 2018.

22 Elie Wiesel, *In Modern Times – A Song for Hope*, Elie Wiesel Living Archive at 92Y.

23 Ethics of the Fathers 1:14.

24 Joseph B. Soloveitchik, *Fate and Destiny: From the Holocaust to the State of Israel* (Hoboken, NJ: Ktav Publishing House, 2000), 259.

25 Soloveitchik, *Fate and Destiny*, 53.

26 Soloveitchik, 53.

27 Shmuel Goldin, *Unlocking the Torah Text: An In-Depth Journey into the Weekly Parsha*, vol. 1, *Bereishit* (Jerusalem: Gefen Publishing House, 2007), 280.

28 Sivan Rahav Meir, *#Parasha: Weekly Insights from a Leading Israeli Journalist* (Jerusalem: Toby Press, 2017), 127–28.

29 John Paul II, *Sollicitudo Rei Socialis*, encyclical, December 30, 1987, Libreria Editrice Vaticana, https://www.vatican.va/content/john-paul-ii/en/encyclicals/documents/hf_jp-ii_enc_30121987_sollicitudo-rei-socialis.html.

30 Alexis Doval, "The Idea of Responsibility in the Brothers Karamazov," lecture, March 4, 2014, https://www.integralprogram.org/images/stories/documents/lectures/responsibilityelecture.pdf.

31 Sebastian Junger, *Tribe: On Homecoming and Belonging* (London: Fourth Estate, 2016), 109–10.

32 Junger, *Tribe*, 96.

33 Jonathan Sacks, *To Heal a Fractured World: The Ethics of Responsibility* (New York: Schocken Books, 2005), 86.

34 Sacks, *To Heal a Fractured World*, 220.

35 Sacks, 142.

36 Jonathan Sacks, *Lessons in Leadership: A Weekly Reading of the Jewish Bible* (Jerusalem: Maggid Books, 2015), 11.

37 Sacks, *To Heal a Fractured World*, 270.

38 Jack Kagan, in the documentary film *The Book of Curses*, directed by Iouri Goroulev (Israel/Belarus: Kagan Productions, 2020).

39 Inna Gerasimova, Viacheslav Selemenev, and Jack Kagan, *We Stood Shoulder to Shoulder: Jewish Partisans in Byelorussia, 1941–1944* (Suffolk: Arima Publishing, 2010), 203.

40 Tec, *Defiance*, 7–8.

41 Shmuel Amarant, "The Partisans of Tuvia Bielski," in Gerasimova et al., *We Stood Shoulder to Shoulder*, 149–50.

42 Amarant, "The Partisans of Tuvia Bielski," 50.

43 Bauer, "Nowogródek," 58.

44 Jack Kagan, "The Bielski Detachment," in Gerasimova et al., *We Stood Shoulder to Shoulder*, 142.

45 Yehuda Bauer, *The Death of the Shtetl* (New Haven: Yale University Press, 2009), 36.

46 Amarant, "The Partisans of Tuvia Bielski," 149.

47 Tec, *Defiance*, 3.

48 Tec, 187.

49 Tec, 187.

50 Allan Levine, *Fugitives of the Forest: The Heroic Story of Jewish Resistance and Survival during the Second World War* (Guilford, CT: Lyons Press, 2009), 276.

51 Amarant, "The Partisans of Tuvia Bielski," 155–59.

52 Amarant, 155–59.

53 Tec, *Defiance*, 171–72.

54 Tec, 166.

55 Tec, 193.

56 Tec, 157.

57 United States Holocaust Memorial Museum, "Jewish Uprisings in Camps," *Holocaust Encylopedia*, https://encyclopedia.ushmm.org/content/en/article/jewish-uprisings-in-camps.

58 "The Story of the Jewish Community in Mir: We Remember Oswald," Yad Vashem, https://www.yadvashem.org/exhibitions/mir/their-legacies-remain/rufeisen.html.

59 Yuri Suhl, ed., *They Fought Back: The Story of the Jewish Resistance in Nazi Europe* (New York: Schocken, 1967), 44–45.

60 Shalom Cholawsky, *The Jews of Bielorussia during World War II* (Amsterdam: Harwood Academic Publishers, 1988), 172.

61 Richard Freund, in the documentary film *The Holocaust Escape Tunnel*, directed by Kirk Wolfinger (Boston: WGBH and *Nova*, 2017).

62 Tamara Vershitskaya, personal interview, December 11, 2020.

63 Michael Kagan, personal interview, October 1, 2023.

64 Tamara Vershitskaya, personal communication, August 31, 2023.

65 Documentary film *The Great Escape*, directed by John Sturges (Beverly Hills: United Artists, 1963).

66 Alan Burgess, *The Longest Tunnel: The True Story of World War II's Great Escape* (New York: Grove Press, 1990).

67 "Longest WWII-Era Escape Tunnel Discovered in Northwestern Poland," TVP World, November 14, 2019, https://tvpworld.com/45331630/longest -wwiiera-escape-tunnel-discovered-in-northwestern-poland.

68 Anne Chatham, "The Greater Escape: Longest WWII Escape Tunnel Found along with Dozens of Trinkets," The First News, October 8, 2019, https://www .thefirstnews.com/article/the-greater-escape-longest-wwii-escape-tunnel- found-along-with-dozens-of-trinkets-7992.

69 "Longest WWII-Era Escape Tunnel Discovered."

The Story of the Escape List

1 Berkovitz, "A Sea of Troubles," 420.

2 Kagan, "Surviving the Holocaust," 573.

3 Berkovitz, "A Sea of Troubles," 420.

4 Leibovitz, "The Great Destruction," 505.

5 Shaul Gorodynski, Yad Vashem testimony, no. 3095/230.

6 Kagan, "Surviving the Holocaust," 573.

7 Kagan, 570.

8 Berkovitz, "A Sea of Troubles," 420.

Dr. Majer (#1) and Sarafima (#2) Jakubowicz

1 Meer Yakubovich," List of Partisans from the Budenny Detachment of the Pervomayskaya Brigade, Central Database of Shoah Victims' Names, Yad Vashem.

2 Majer Jakubowicz, Lodz Names – List of the Ghetto Inhabitants, Yad Vashem and the Organization of Former Residents of Lodz in Israel, Jerusalem 1994, Central Database of Shoah Victims' Names, Yad Vashem.

3 Fanya Dunetz Brodsky, personal interview, June 23, 2017.

4 Tec, *Defiance*, 187; Eliyahu Berkowicz, Yad Vashem testimony, no. 03/2774.

5 Leibovitz, "The Great Destruction," 500.

6 Shaul Gorodynski, Yad Vashem testimony, no. 3095/230.

7 Leibovitz, "The Great Destruction," 507.

8 Zafrir Ostashinski, personal interview, December 1, 2018.

9 Berek Jakubowicz, Page of Testimony submitted by Meir Yakubovich, undated, Central Database of Shoah Victims' Names, Yad Vashem.

10　Mosze Jakubowicz, Page of Testimony submitted by Meir Yakubovich, undated, Central Database of Shoah Victims' Names, Yad Vashem.

11　Salek Jakubowicz, Page of Testimony submitted by Meir Yakubovich, undated, Central Database of Shoah Victims' Names, Yad Vashem.

12　Zosia Zlata Braun, Page of Testimony submitted by Meir Yakubovich, undated, Central Database of Shoah Victims' Names, Yad Vashem.

13　Sala Sara Jakubowicz, Page of Testimony submitted by Meir Yakubovich, undated, Central Database of Shoah Victims' Names, Yad Vashem.

14　Berek Jakubowicz, Page of Testimony.

15　"Todd Cohen Family Tree," Ancestry.com., https://www.ancestry.com/family-tree/person/tree/9434902/person/800548606/facts, accessed January 20, 2019.

16　Chawa Turower Zilberman, Page of Testimony submitted by Sara Yakobowicz, undated, Central Database of Shoah Victims' Names, Yad Vashem.

17　Elias David Zilberman, Page of Testimony submitted by Sara Yakobowicz, undated, Central Database of Shoah Victims' Names, Yad Vashem.

18　Rywka Blum, Page of Testimony submitted by Sara Yakobowicz, undated, Central Database of Shoah Victims' Names, Yad Vashem.

19　Abram Zilberman, Page of Testimony submitted by Sara Yakobowicz, undated, Central Database of Shoah Victims' Names, Yad Vashem.

20　Miriam Zilberman, Page of Testimony submitted by Sara Yakobowicz, undated, Central Database of Shoah Victims' Names, Yad Vashem.

21　Zisa Zilberman, Page of Testimony submitted by Sara Yakobowicz, undated, Central Database of Shoah Victims' Names, Yad Vashem.

22　Binka Zilberman, Page of Testimony submitted by Sara Yakobowicz, undated, Central Database of Shoah Victims' Names, Yad Vashem.

23　Ziskind Zilberman, Page of Testimony submitted by Sara Yakobowicz, undated, Central Database of Shoah Victims' Names, Yad Vashem.

24　Baruch Zilberman, Page of Testimony submitted by Sara Yakobowicz, undated, Central Database of Shoah Victims' Names, Yad Vashem.

25　"Jewish Families of Mława, Poland," Geni.com, https://www.geni.com/projects/Jewish-families-of-Mława-Poland/11426, accessed January 3, 2019.

26　"Sarafima Yakubovich," in List of Partisans from the Budenny Detachment of the Pervomayskaya Brigade, Central Database of Shoah Victims' Names, Yad Vashem.

27　"Meer Yakubovich," in List of Partisans from the Budenny Detachment of the Pervomayskaya Brigade, Central Database of Shoah Victims' Names, Yad Vashem.

28　"Bronislaw Jakubowicz," in New York State Passenger and Crew Lists, 1917–1967, Ancestry.com, https://www.ancestry.com/discoveryui-content/view/4527187:1277, accessed January 14, 2022.

29 Meir Yakubovich, Pages of Testimony submitted, Central Database of Shoah Victims' Names, Yad Vashem.

30 "List of Registered Doctors in Israel 1948–1957," Sept. 15, 1957, Israel Genealogy Research Association (IGRA).

31 "Majer Jakubowicz," in New York State Passenger and Crew Lists, 1917–1967, Ancestry.com, https://www.ancestry.com/discoveryui-content/view/4527185:1277, accessed January 14, 2022.

32 "Majer Jakubowicz," in *US Social Security Death Index, 1935–2014,* Ancestry.com, https://www.ancestry.com/discoveryui-content/view/30329582:3693, accessed January 14, 2022.

33 "Majer Jakubowicz," in *US Social Security Death Index, 1935–2014.*

34 "Sara Jakubowicz," in Massachusetts Death Index, Ancestry.com, https://www.ancestry.com/discoveryui-content/view/1699915:7457, accessed January 14, 2022.

35 "Majer Jakubowicz," Memorials, Find a Grave, https://www.findagrave.com/memorial/150915106, accessed January 14, 2022; Sara Jakubowicz, Memorials, Find a Grave, https://www.findagrave.com/memorial/150915107, accessed January 14, 2022.

36 Bronislaw Jakubowicz, personal interview, February 11, 2019.

Etya Mazurkevich (#3)

1 List of Partisans from the Kalinin Detachment, Central Database of Shoah Victims' Names, Yad Vashem.

2 List of Partisans from the Kalinin Detachment.

3 List of Partisans from the Kalinin Detachment.

Yakov Kagan (#3a)

1 *Novogrudok Memorial Book,* 499–507.

2 Yitzchak Cohen and Hagar Sezaf, personal interview, January 1, 2017.

3 Details contained in a "Family Roots" project written by Omri Cohen, a great-nephew of Yakov Kagan, 1990.

4 Omri Cohen, "Family Roots" project.

5 Omri Cohen, "Family Roots" project.

6 Omri Cohen, "Family Roots" project.

7 Hagar Sezaf, personal interview, October 26, 2020.

8 Genya Kagan, dates written on back of photo, undated.

9 Leibovitz, "The Great Destruction," 499.

10 Omri Cohen, "Family Roots" project.

11 *Baranovich Memorial Book* [in Hebrew and Yiddish] (Tel Aviv: Irgun Yotsey Baranowitz, 1953), 430.

12 "Baranovichi," Yad Vashem Shoah Resource Center, https://www.yadvashem.org /odot_pdf/Microsoft%20Word%20-%205964.pdf.

13 *Baranovich Memorial Book.*

14 Hagar Sezaf, personal interview, October 26, 2020.

15 Fanya Dunetz Brodsky, personal interview, March 28, 2017.

16 List of Murdered Individuals from Zhetl, Central Database of Shoah Victims' Names, Yad Vashem.

17 Fanya Dunetz Brodsky, personal interview, November 2, 2020.

18 Rachel Kagan, Page of Testimony, submitted by Batia Gardes, March 3, 1957, Central Database of Shoah Victims' Names, Yad Vashem.

19 List of Murdered Individuals from Zhetl.

20 Fanya Dunetz Brodsky, personal interview, March 28, 2017.

21 Yehoshua Yaffe, *In the Novogrudok Ghetto and the Partisan Movement* [in Hebrew] (Tel Aviv: Navaredker Committee in Israel, 1988), 164–67.

22 Tec, *Defiance*, 187.

23 Tec, 187.

24 Leibovitz, "The Great Destruction," 499.

25 Leibovitz, 499–500.

26 Tec, *Defiance*, 187.

27 Tec, 187.

28 Leibovitz, "The Great Destruction," 505.

29 Tec, *Defiance*, 188.

30 Yaffe, *In the Novogrudok Ghetto*, 166.

31 Fanya Dunetz Brodsky, personal interview, March 28, 2017.

32 Hagar Sezaf, personal interview, October 26, 2020.

33 Yitzchak Cohen and Hagar Sezaf, personal interview, March 28, 2017.

34 Fanya Dunetz Brodsky, personal interview, March 28, 2017.

35 Yaffe, *In the Novogrudok Ghetto*, 166–67.

Natan (Nota) Sucharski (#4)

1 Gerasimova et al., *We Stood Shoulder to Shoulder*, 289.

2 Natan Sucharski, Page of Testimony submitted by Dov Cohen, December 26, 1993, Central Database of Shoah Victims' Names, Yad Vashem

3 Yaffe, *In the Novogrudok Ghetto*, 162; Daniel Ostashinski, Yad Vashem testimony, no. 6841.

4 Ostashinski, Yad Vashem testimony.

5 Jack Kagan, personal interviews, May 5, 2008; July 12, 2012.

6   Shmuel Openheim, "Personalities," in *Novogrudok Memorial Book*, 220.

7   "Samuel Nikolayevski," in *Novogrudok Memorial Book*, 247–49.

8   Kagan and Cohen, *Surviving the Holocaust*, 21, 24–25.

9   Kagan and Cohen, 28–29.

10 Kagan and Cohen, 29.

11 Kagan and Cohen, 15.

12 Kagan, personal interviews, May 5, 2008, July 12, 2012; Kagan, "Surviving the Holocaust," 566.

13 Kagan, personal interviews, May 5, 2008, July 12, 2012.

14 Kagan, personal interview, July 12, 2012.

15 Shaul Gorodynski, Yad Vashem testimony, no. 3095/230.

16 Tec, *Defiance*, 187.

17 Shaul Gorodynski, Yad Vashem testimony.

18 Gorodynski, Yad Vashem testimony.

19 Kagan, "Surviving the Holocaust," 570.

20 Kagan, 570.

21 Shalom Cholawsky, *Meri v'Lochmah Partizanit* [Resistance and Partisan Struggle] (Tel Aviv: Yad Vashem and the Moreshet Publishing House, 2001), 457.

22 Avraham-Leizer Czertok, testimony [in French], January 24, 1968, Ghetto Fighters' House Museum, Kibbutz Lochamei Hagetaot.

23 Tamara Vershitskaya, personal interview, January 2012.

24 Kagan, personal interview, May 5, 2008.

Reuven (Ruvke) Shabakovski (#5)

1   Leibovitz, "The Great Destruction," 501.

2   Kagan, "Surviving the Holocaust," 570.

3   Shaul Gorodynski, Yad Vashem testimony, no. 3095/230.

4   Kagan and Cohen, *Surviving the Holocaust*, 170.

5   Reuven Shabakovski, Page of Testimony submitted by Yitzchak Boretzki, December 12, 1998, Central Database of Shoah Victims' Names, Yad Vashem.

6   Leah Boretzki, personal interview, August 31, 2020.

7   Reuven Shabakovski, Page of Testimony.

8   *Novogrudok Memorial Book*, 714.

9   Liba Boretzki, Chaya Boretzki, Lia Boretzki; Shprintze Shabakovski, Pages of Testimony submitted by Yitzchak Boretzki, December 12, 1998, Central Database of Shoah Victims' Names, Yad Vashem.

10 Gerasimova et al., *We Stood Shoulder to Shoulder*, 303.

11 *Novogrudok Memorial Book*, 714.

12   Leah Boretski, personal interview, Nes Tziona, Israel, October 16, 2017.
13   Gerasimova et al., *We Stood Shoulder to Shoulder*, 303.
14   Leah Boretski, personal interview, August 31, 2020.

Isaac (#6) and Zlata (#7) Yarmovski

1   Bracha Shteiner, personal interview, August 18, 2019.
2   Shteiner, personal interview.
3   Etl Bytenski, Page of Testimony submitted by Lea Rodnitzki, Central Database of Shoah Victims' Names, Yad Vashem, August 1, 1956.
4   Efraim Jarmowsky, Page of Testimony submitted by Lea Dagoni, Central Database of Shoah Victims' Names, Yad Vashem, January 1, 1999.
5   Moshe Jarmowsky, Page of Testimony submitted by Lea Dagoni, Central Database of Shoah Victims' Names, Yad Vashem, January 1, 1999.
6   Bracha Shteiner, personal interview, August 18, 2019.
7   Shlyoma Yarmovski, List of Jewish Partisans in the Kalinin Detachment of the Leninskaya Brigade, Central Database of Shoah Victims' Names, Yad Vashem.
8   Bracha Shteiner, personal interview, August 18, 2019.
9   Shteiner, personal interview.
10   Shteiner, personal interview.
11   Shaul Gorodynski, Yad Vashem testimony, no. 3095/230.
12   Yitzchak Yarmovski, List of Fighters.
13   Shaul Gorodynski, Yad Vashem testimony.
14   Avraham-Leizer Czertok, testimony [in French], January 24, 1968, Ghetto Fighters' House Museum, Kibbutz Lochamei Hagetaot.
15   Shimon Yaron, personal interview, January 27, 2021.
16   Avraham-Leizer Czertok, testimony.
17   Yitzchak Yarmovski, List of Fighters.
18   Bracha Shteiner, personal interview, August 18, 2019.
19   Isaac (Yitzchak) Yarmovski gravestone, Old Cemetery Rishon Lezion, BillionGraves, https://billiongraves.com/grave/%D7%90%D7%99%D7%99 %D7%96%D7%99%D7%A7-%D7%99%D7%A6%D7%97%D7%A7- %D7%99%D7%A8%D7%9E%D7%95%D7%91%D7%A1%D7%A7 %D7%99/14201248.
20   Zlata (Zahava) Yarmovski, gravestone, Old Cemetery Rishon Lezion, BillionGraves, https://billiongraves.com/grave/%D7%96%D7%9C%D7%98%D7%94- %D7%96%D7%94%D7%91%D7%94-%D7%99%D7%A8%D7%9E%D7 %95%D7%91%D7%A1%D7%A7%D7%99/14201249.
21   Shteiner, personal interview.
22   Shimon Yaron, personal interview, August 13, 2019.

23 Shteiner, personal interview.
24 Isaac (Yitzchak) Yarmovski, gravestone.
25 Zlata (Zahava) Yarmovski, gravestone.
26 Shimon Yaron, personal interview, August 23, 2023.

Efroim Selubski (#8)

1 Steve Shell, personal interview, March 30, 2018.
2 Steve Shell, personal interview, July 17, 2018.
3 Efroim Selubski, inquiry card, TD #634303, International Tracing Service, Yad Vashem.
4 Kagan and Cohen, *Surviving the Holocaust*, 174.
5 Shell, July 17, 2018.
6 Kagan and Cohen, *Surviving the Holocaust*, 42.
7 Efroim Selubski, inquiry card.
8 Steve Shell, personal interview, March 30, 2018.
9 Efroim Szelupski, registration card for Central Committee for Polish Jews, International Tracing Service, Yad Vashem.
10 Natalia Aleksiun, "Central Committee of Jews in Poland," YIVO Encyclopedia of Jews in Eastern Europe, http://www.yivoencyclopedia.org/article.aspx /Central_Committee_of_Jews_in_Poland.
11 Efroim Selubski, inquiry card.
12 "October 1945–1950, Ramsauerstrasse/Uhlandstrasse," In Situ, Linz 2009 Kulturhaupstadt Europas, http://www.insitu-linz09.at/en/locations/39 -locations-ramsauerstrasseuhlandstrasse.html, accessed on July 16, 2018.
13 Ship manifest, SS *Marine Marlin,* January 8, 1947.
14 Steve Shell, personal interview, July 17, 2018.
15 Steve Shell, personal interview, March 30, 2018.
16 Shell, personal interview, March 30, 2018.

Hirsh Gurvich (#9)

1 "Girsh Gurevich," List of Partisans from Frunze Detachment Active in the Baranowicze District, Central Database of Shoah Victims' Names, Yad Vashem.
2 Avraham-Leizer Czertok, testimony [in French], January 24, 1968, Ghetto Fighters' House Museum, Kibbutz Lochamei Hagetaot.
3 Czertok, testimony.
4 Dr. S. Openheim, "Novogrudok Partisans Who Fell in Action," in *Novogrudok Memorial Book*, 645.
5 Openheim, "Novogrudok Partisans Who Fell in Action."

Avraham (Abram) Rakovski (#10)

1 "Abram Rakovski," List of Partisans from Baranovichskaya Brigade No. 1, Central Database of Shoah Victims' Names, Yad Vashem.

2 Openheim, "Novogrudok Partisans Who Fell in Action," 645.

3 Memorial notice for the Rakovski family submitted by Adela Rakovski Man, in *Pinkas Navaredok* [in Yiddish], ed. Dr. Eliezer Yerushalmi, David Cohen, Dr. Aharon Mirsky, et al. (Tel Aviv: Alexander Harkavy Navaredker Relief Committee in USA and Navaredker Committee in Israel, 1963), 419.

4 Shaul Gorodynski, Yad Vashem testimony, no. 3095/230.

5 Gorodynski, Yad Vashem testimony.

6 Eliyahu Berkovich, "A Sea of Troubles," *Novogrudok Memorial Book*, 421.

7 Kagan, "Surviving the Holocaust," 571.

8 Shaul Gorodynski, Yad Vashem testimony.

9 Cholawsky, *Meri v'Lochmah Partizanit*, 457.

10 Gerasimova et al., *We Stood Shoulder to Shoulder*, 277.

11 Guy Czertok, personal correspondence, August 25, 2020.

12 Gerasimova et al., *We Stood Shoulder to Shoulder*.

13 Kagan, *Novogrudok*, 257.

Noah Sosnovski (#11)

1 Kagan, "Surviving the Holocaust," 570.

2 Shaul Gorodynski, Yad Vashem testimony, no. 3095/230.

3 Jack Kagan, personal interview, May 5, 2008.

4 Jack Kagan, personal interviews, May 5, 2008; July 12, 2012.

5 Kagan, personal interview, May 5, 2008.

6 *Novogrudok Memorial Book*, 714.

Mairim (#12) and Shevach (#13) Gershanovich

1 Jack Kagan, personal interview, December 7, 2012.

2 "Mayrim Gershanovich," List of Partisans Active in the Baranowicze District, Central Database of Shoah Victims' Names, Yad Vashem.

3 " Shevakh Gershanovich," List of Partisans from Baranovichskaya Brigade No. 1, Active in the Baranowicze District, 1942.

4 Avraham-Leizer Czertok, testimony [in French], January 24, 1968, Ghetto Fighters' House Museum, Kibbutz Lochamei Hagetaot.

5 Jack Kagan, personal interview, July 12, 2012.

6 Kagan, personal interview.

7 Kagan, personal interview.

Yisrael (#14) and Berl Yoselevich

1 Yerushalmi, et al., *Pinkas Navaredok*, 414.

2 Chaim Leibovitz, "The Heroic Death of Berl Yoselevitz," in *Novogrudok Memorial Book*, 515.

3 "Khaia Sara Ioselevich," List of Murdered Jews from Yizkor Books, submitted by Avraham Ioselevich, no date indicated, Central Database of Shoah Victims' Names, Yad Vashem.

4 Yudit Joselewicz, Page of Testimony submitted by Natan Yankelevich, September 12, 1956, Central Database of Shoah Victims' Names, Yad Vashem.

5 Yente Joselewicz, Page of Testimony submitted by Natan Yankelevich, September 12, 1956, Central Database of Shoah Victims' Names, Yad Vashem.

6 "Mira Ioselevich," List of Murdered Jews from Yizkor Books, submitted by Avraham Ioselevich, no date indicated, Central Database of Shoah Victims' Names, Yad Vashem.

7 "Mira Ioselevich," List of Murdered Jews from Yizkor Books.

8 Israel Yoselewicz, Page of Testimony submitted by Natan Yankelevich, September 12, 1956, Central Database of Shoah Victims' Names, Yad Vashem.

9 Israel Yoselewicz, Page of Testimony; "Israel Ioselevich," List of Murdered Jews from Yizkor Books, submitted by Avraham Ioselevich, no date indicated, Central Database of Shoah Victims' Names, Yad Vashem.

10 Shaul Gorodynski, Yad Vashem testimony, no. 3095/230.

11 Leibowitz, "The Heroic Death of Berl Yoselevitz," 515.

12 Leibowitz, 515.

13 Kagan, *Novogrudok*, 114.

14 Kagan, 114.

15 Peter Duffy, *The Bielski Brothers: The True Story of Three Men Who Defied the Nazis, Built a Village in the Forest, and Saved 1,200 Jews* (New York: Perennial, 2003), 198.

16 Kagan, *Surviving the Holocaust*, 569.

17 Leibowitz, "The Heroic Death of Berl Yoselevitz," 515.

18 Duffy, *The Bielski Brothers*, 198.

19 Yaffe, *In the Novogrudok Ghetto*, 166–67.

20 Daniel Ostashinski, Yad Vashem testimony, no. 03/6841.

21 Tec, *Defiance*, 188.

22 Leibowitz, "The Heroic Death of Berl Yoselevitz," 515.

23 Tec, *Defiance*, 188.

24 Fanya Dunetz Brodsky, personal interview, November 14, 2016.

25 Kagan, *Surviving the Holocaust*, 569.

26 Gorodynski, Yad Vashem testimony.

27 Leibovitz, "The Great Destruction," 500.

28 Leibovitz, 187.
29 Leibowitz, "The Heroic Death of Berl Yoselevitz," 515.
30 Tec, *Defiance*, 188.
31 Ostashinski, Yad Vashem testimony, no. 03/6841.
32 Leibowitz, "The Heroic Death of Berl Yoselevitz," 515.
33 Tec, *Defiance*, 191.
34 Duffy, *The Bielski Brothers*, 202.
35 Kagan, *Surviving the Holocaust*, 572.
36 Kagan, 573.
37 Leibowitz, "The Great Destruction," 506.
38 Tec, *Defiance*, 191; Chaya Magid, personal interview, October 19, 2016.
39 Magid, personal interview.
40 Tec, *Defiance*, 191; Leibowitz, "The Heroic Death of Berl Yoselevitz," 515–16.
41 Leibowitz, "The Great Destruction," 507.
42 Yaffe, *In the Novogrudok Ghetto*, 166–67.
43 Leibowitz, "The Heroic Death of Berl Yoselevitz," 516.

Chana Iwinetzki (#17)

1   Chana Iwinetzki Lachovsky, Page of Testimony submitted by Abe Wind (formerly Abraham Iwinetzki), August 16, 1971, Central Database of Shoah Victims' Names, Yad Vashem.
2   Owsei Yeshajahu Iwinetzki, Page of Testimony submitted by Abe Wind (formerly Abraham Iwinetzki), August 16, 1971, Central Database of Shoah Victims' Names, Yad Vashem.
3   Chana Iwinetzki Lachovsky, Page of Testimony.
4   Khana Lyakhovskaya, Documentation regarding damage to property and human life of evacuees to Zhdanovsky neighborhood, Izhevsk, the Soviet Extraordinary State Commission, 09-11/1944, Central Database of Shoah Victims' Names, Yad Vashem.
5   Jeshajahu Iwiniecki, Page of Testimony submitted by Tzila Shertzer, February 13, 1957, Central Database of Shoah Victims' Names, Yad Vashem.
6   Owsei Yeshajahu Iwinetzki, Page of Testimony.
7   Rachel Iwinetzki, Page of Testimony submitted by Abe Wind (formerly Abraham Iwinetzki), August 16, 1971, Central Database of Shoah Victims' Names, Yad Vashem.
8   Leja Iwinetzki, Page of Testimony submitted by Abe Wind (formerly Abraham Iwinetzki), August 16, 1971, Central Database of Shoah Victims' Names, Yad Vashem.

9   Dov Iwiniecki, Page of Testimony submitted by Tzila Shertzer, February 13, 1957, Central Database of Shoah Victims' Names, Yad Vashem.

10   Avraham Iwinetzki, Page of Testimony submitted by Abe Wind (formerly Abraham Iwinetzki), August 16, 1971, Central Database of Shoah Victims' Names, Yad Vashem.

11   Gerasimova et al., *We Stood Shoulder to Shoulder*, 236, 323.

12   Abraham Iwinetzki, New York, U.S., Arriving Passenger and Crew Lists (including Castle Garden and Ellis Island), 1820-1957, Ancestry.com, https://www.ancestry.com/discoveryui-content/view/3026754647:7488.

13   Chana Iwinetzki Lachovsky, Page of Testimony.

14   Abraham Wind, gravestone, B'nai Abraham Memorial Park, Union County, NJ, Find a Grave, https://www.findagrave.com/memorial/207321966/abraham-wind.

Yoel Zak (#18)

1   *The Book of Ivenets, Kamien and Vicinity* [in Yiddish] (Tel Aviv: Ivenets Societies in Israel and the Diaspora, 1979), 429.

2   Gerasimova et al., *We Stood Shoulder to Shoulder*, 233, 321.

Pesach (Lionke) Portnoj (#19)

1   Peisach Portnoj, Inhaftierungsbescheinigung (Certificate of Detention), August 26, 1954, International Tracing Service, Yad Vashem.

2   Nusia Portnoj, Page of Testimony submitted by Sima Ionas, 1986, Central Database of Shoah Victims' Names, Yad Vashem.

3   Sima Jones Portnoi, Certificate of Residence #432189, International Tracing Service, Yad Vashem.

4   Portnoi, Certificate of Residence.

5   Portnoi, Certificate of Residence.

6   Yisrael Portnoy, personal interview, January 15, 2019.

7   Nusia Portnoj, Page of Testimony.

8   Peisach Portnoj, Inhaftierungsbescheinigung (Certificate of Detention).

9   Kagan, "Surviving the Holocaust," *Novogrudok Memorial Book*, 570.

10   Kagan, 571.

11   Eliyahu Berkovich, "A Sea of Troubles," *Novogrudok Memorial Book*, 419.

12   Tamara Vershitskaya, personal correspondence, January 2012.

13   Fanya Dunetz Brodsky, personal interview, November 14, 2011.

14   Correspondence from Mrs. E. B. Anderson, Welfare Officer, International Relief Organization, Munich, July 6, 1949, International Tracing Service, Yad Vashem.

15 Erklaerung (Declaration) by Peisach Portnoj, August 11, 1949, International Tracing Service, Yad Vashem.
16 Miriam Portnoj, personal interview, July 15, 2012.
17 Yisrael Portnoy, personal interview, September 29, 2020.
18 Yisrael Portnoy, personal interview, January 15, 2019.
19 Yisrael Portnoy, personal interview, September 29, 2020.

Sima Portnoj (#20)

1 Yisrael Portnoy, personal interview, January 15, 2019.
2 Nusia Portnoj, Page of Testimony submitted by Sima Yones, Central Database of Shoah Victims' Names, Yad Vashem.
3 Sima Portnoy, List of Partisans from Belorussia, Central Database of Shoah Victims' Names, Yad Vashem.
4 Eli Yones, personal interview, September 20, 2020.
5 Yones, personal interview, September 29, 2020.
6 Sima Yones-Portnoy, "Kindergarten," in *Novogrudok Memorial Book*, 162–63.
7 Yones, personal interview, September 29, 2020.
8 Tamara Vershitskaya, personal correspondence, April 29, 2019.
9 Sima Jones *geborene* Portnoi, Certificate of Residence #432189, International Red Cross, September 12, 1916, International Tracing Service, Yad Vashem.
10 Portnoi, Certificate of Residence.
11 Yones, personal interview, September 29, 2020.
12 Leyzer Ran, "Elye (Eliyahu) Yones," Yiddish Leksikon, November 28, 2016, as posted by Joshua Fogel, http://yleksikon.blogspot.com/2016/11/elye-eliyahu-yones.html.
13 Eli Yones, personal interview, October 4, 2020.
14 Yones, personal interview, September 29, 2020.
15 Ran, "Elye (Eliyahu) Yones."
16 Yones, personal interview, September 29, 2020.
17 Sima Jones *geborene* Portnoi, Certificate of Residence.
18 Yones, personal interview, October 4, 2020.
19 Yones, personal interview.
20 Yones, personal interview, September 29, 2020.
21 Yones, personal interview.

Aaron (Rozke) Kirzner (#21)

1 Aron Kirzhner, List of Partisans from the Kalinin Detachment under the Command of Bielski, 1944, Central Database of Shoah Victims' Names, Yad Vashem.

2 Gerasimova et al., *We Stood Shoulder to Shoulder*, 244.

3 Miriam Rimer, Page of Testimony submitted by Rachel Falik, September 6, 1977, Central Database of Shoah Victims' Names, Yad Vashem.

4 Osnat Rabin, personal interview, May 7, 2018.

5 Manya Shor, personal interview, May 8, 2018.

6 Aron Kirzhner, List of Partisans from the Kalinin Detachment.

7 Kejla Kirzner, Page of Testimony submitted by Rachel Falik, September 6, 1977, Central Database of Shoah Victims' Names, Yad Vashem.

8 Manya Shor, personal interview.

9 Shmuel Rimer, Page of Testimony submitted by Rachel Falik, September 6, 1977, Central Database of Shoah Victims' Names, Yad Vashem.

10 Osnat Rimer, Page of Testimony submitted by Rachel Falik, September 6, 1977, Central Database of Shoah Victims' Names, Yad Vashem.

11 Osnat Rimer, Page of Testimony.

Chaim Abramowicz (#22)

1 Herman Abrams, Application for Reparations, January 18, 1956, New York, International Tracing Service, Yad Vashem.

2 Susan Abrams Bach, personal interviews, August 30–31, 2020.

3 Herman and Cilie Abrams, gravestone, Star of David Memorial Gardens, North Lauderdale, Broward County, Florida, USA, Find a Grave, https://www.findagrave.com/memorial/43825301/herman-abrams#view-photo=23005228.

4 Yosef Abramovich, personal records, circa 1965.

5 Abramovich, personal records.

6 Abramovich, personal records.

7 Hassia Turtel-Obezhanski, "History of the Jews of Korelitz," in *Pinkas Navaredok*, 19.

8 Memorial notice for the Abromowicz family submitted by Chaim and Yosef Abromovich, *Pinkas Navaredok*, ed. Yerushalmi et al., 406; Susan Bach, personal interviews, August 30–31, 2020.

9 Bach, personal interviews.

10 Central Database of Shoah Victims' Names, Yad Vashem.

11 Susan Abrams Bach, personal interview, September 4, 2020.

12 Tec, *Defiance*, 189.

13 Gerasimova et al., *We Stood Shoulder to Shoulder*, 504–5.

14 Tuvia Bielski and Zusia Bielski, *Yehudei Yaar* [Forest Jews] (Tel Aviv: Am Oved, 1946), 209–10.

15 Bach, personal interviews.

16 Gerasimova et al., *We Stood Shoulder to Shoulder*, 98.

17 Cype Abramowicz, Jewish Holocaust Survivor List from the files of World Jewish Congress, 1918–1982, Jewish refugees in Italy, list no. 2, 1946, Ancestry. com, https://www.ancestry.com/discoveryui-content/view/61968:1385.

18 Herman Abrams, Application for Reparations.

19 Metod M. Milac, "Graz Displaced Persons Camp," in *Resistance, Imprisonment & Forced Labor: A Slovene Student in World War II* (New York: Peter Lang, 2002), cited at http://www.dpcamps.org/graz.html.

20 Herman Abrams, Application for Reparations.

21 Josef Abromowicz, New York Passenger Lists, 1820–1957, *Marine Jumper*, Ancestry.com, https://www.ancestry.com/imageviewer/collections/7488/images /NYT715_7762-0587?pId=3024932011.

22 Herman Abrams, New York, Index to Petitions for Naturalization filed in New York City, 1792–1989, Ancestry.com, https://www.ancestry.com /discoveryui-content/view/2382316:7733.

23 Cilie Abrams, US Social Security Death Index, 1935–2014, Ancestry.com, accessed on January 21, 2022, https://www.ancestry.com/discoveryui-content /view/90018:3693.

24 Bach, personal interviews.

25 Art Abrams, personal correspondence, December 18, 2018.

26 Albert Abrams, Obituary, Star of David Memorial Gardens Cemetery & Funeral Chapel, Dignitymemorial.com, https://www.dignitymemorial.com/obituaries /north-lauderdale-fl/albert-abrams-7892013, accessed on September 9, 2020.

27 Cilie Abrams, US Social Security Death Index (SSDI).

28 Herman Abrams, US Social Security Death Index, 1935–2014," Ancestry.com, https://www.ancestry.com/discoveryui-content/view/92169:3693.

29 Bach, personal interviews.

30 Herman Abrams, "US Social Security Death Index (SSDI)," Myheritage. com, https://www.myheritage.com/research/record-10002-13082643/herman -abrams-in-us-social-security-death-index-ssdi.

31 Joe Abrams, gravestone, Ohev Shalom Cemetery, Orlando, FL, Find a Grave, https://www.findagrave.com/memorial/25213370/joe-abrams.

Chaim Belous (#23)

1 David Silberklang, personal communication, May 3, 2020.

2 Haim Bielous, Page of Testimony submitted by Rywka Senderowsky Silberklang, March 5, 2000, Central Database of Shoah Victims' Names, Yad Vashem.

3 Mordechai Ela Kalbshtein, Page of Testimony submitted by Kalman Mnuskin, May 3, 1999, Central Database of Shoah Victims' Names, Yad Vashem.

4 Masha (erroneously recorded as "Moshe") Kalbshtein, Page of Testimony submitted by Kalman Mnuskin, May 3, 1999, Central Database of Shoah Victims' Names, Yad Vashem.

5 Cila Kalbstein, Page of Testimony submitted by Rywka Senderowsky Silberklang, March 5, 2000, Central Database of Shoah Victims' Names, Yad Vashem.

6 Zysl Kalbshtein, Pages of Testimony submitted by Kalman Mnuskin, August 26, 1990, April 29, 1996, Central Database of Shoah Victims' Names, Yad Vashem.

7 Pesya Kalbshteyn, List of Murdered Individuals from Zhetl, Central Database of Shoah Victims' Names, Yad Vashem.

8 Izrail Belous, List of Murdered Individuals from Zhetl, Central Database of Shoah Victims' Names, Yad Vashem.

9 Nakhama Zakroyskaya, List of Murdered Individuals from Zhetl, Central Database of Shoah Victims' Names, Yad Vashem.

10 Mote Zakroiski, Page of Testimony submitted by Rywka Silberklang, March 5, 2000, Central Database of Shoah Victims' Names, Yad Vashem.

11 David Silberklang, personal communication, May 3, 2020.

12 David Silberklang, personal communication, May 4, 2020.

13 Yudel Vital Zakroiski, Page of Testimony submitted by Rywka Silberklang, March 5, 2000, Central Database of Shoah Victims' Names, Yad Vashem, Jerusalem; First Name Unknown Kalbstein, Page of Testimony submitted by Rywka Silberklang, March 5, 2000, Central Database of Shoah Victims' Names, Yad Vashem.

14 David Silberklang, Personal Communication, May 3, 2020.

15 Mote Zakroiski, Page of Testimony.

16 Chana Mayevski Klar, "Forest Years," in *Pinkas Zhetl*, ed. B. Kaplinski, 400.

17 Nehama Zakroiski, Page of Testimony submitted by Rywka Silberklang, March 5, 2000, Central Database of Shoah Victims' Names, Yad Vashem.

18 Klar, "Forest Years."

19 Zysl Kalbshtein, Pages of Testimony.

20 Haim Bielous, Page of Testimony.

Batia Rabinowitz (#27)

1 Chaya Goldhaber, personal interview, October 2007.

2 Chaja Rabinowitz, Page of Testimony submitted by Batia Gradis, February 7, 1978, Central Database of Shoah Victims' Names, Yad Vashem.

3 Mordechaj Rabinowitz, Page of Testimony submitted by Batia Gradis, February 7, 1978, Central Database of Shoah Victims' Names, Yad Vashem.

4 Batia Rabinowitz, transcribed written testimony, 1992.

5   Leah Rabinowitz, Page of Testimony submitted by Batia Gradis, April 22, 1999, Central Database of Shoah Victims' Names, Yad Vashem.

6   Rabinowitz, transcribed written testimony.

7   Rabinowitz, testimony.

8   Tamara Vershitskaya, personal communication, January 2012.

9   Gerasimova et al., *We Stood Shoulder to Shoulder*, 275.

10 Rabinowitz, transcribed written testimony.

11 Rabinowitz, testimony.

12 Fanya Dunetz Brodsky, personal interview, November 14, 2011.

13 Tec, *Defiance*, 268.

14 Bielski and Bielski, *Yehudei Yaar*, 206.

15 Rabinowitz, transcribed written testimony.

16 Rabinowitz, testimony.

17 Goldhaber, personal interview.

18 Rabinowitz, transcribed written testimony.

19 Goldhaber, personal interview.

20 Goldhaber, interview.

21 Rabinowitz, transcribed written testimony.

22 Chaya Goldhaber, personal communication, January 1, 2020.

23 Goldhaber, personal communication.

24 Chaya Goldhaber, personal correspondence, August 21, 2023.

Shlomo (Salek) Jakubowicz (#28)

1   Salek Jakubowicz, Page of Testimony submitted by Meir Yakubovich, undated, Central Database of Shoah Victims' Names, Yad Vashem.

2   Berek Jakubowicz, Page of Testimony submitted by Meir Yakubovich, undated, Central Database of Shoah Victims' Names, Yad Vashem.

3   Todd Cohen Family Tree, Ancestry.com, https://www.ancestry.com/family tree /person/tree/9434902/person/800548606/facts, accessed January 20, 2019.

4   Mosze Jakubowicz, Page of Testimony submitted by Meir Yakubovich, undated, Central Database of Shoah Victims' Names, Yad Vashem.

5   Sala Sara Jakubowicz, Page of Testimony submitted by Meir Yakubovich, undated, Central Database of Shoah Victims' Names, Yad Vashem.

6   Zosia Zlata Braun, Page of Testimony submitted by Meir Yakubovich, undated, Central Database of Shoah Victims' Names, Yad Vashem.

7   Shaul Gorodynski, Yad Vashem testimony, no. 3095/230.

8   Tec, *Defiance*, 187.

9   Leibovitz, "The Great Destruction," 505–6.

10 Daniel Ostashinski, Yad Vashem testimony, no. 03/6041.

11 Kagan, "Surviving the Holocaust," 570.
12 Leibovitz, "The Great Destruction," 506–7.
13 Leibovitz, 507.

Gershon Michalevich (#29)

1 Gershon, Shabtai, Sarah Bluma, Urcze, Leyb, Perla, Galia, and Jakob Michalewicz, Pages of Testimony submitted by Natan Iankelevitz, September 12, 1956, Central Database of Shoah Victims' Names, Yad Vashem.
2 Shaul Gorodynski, Yad Vashem testimony, no. 3095/230.
3 Berkovich, "A Sea of Troubles,", 421.
4 Kagan, "Surviving the Holocaust," 570–71.
5 Gerszon Michalewicz, Page of Testimony.

Yitzchak (#30) and Genia (#31) Rosenhaus

1 Effie Rosenhaus, personal interview, April 15, 2013.
2 Rosenhaus, personal interview.
3 Chana Rosenhaus, Page of Testimony submitted by Yitzchak Rosenhaus, April 17, 1956, Central Database of Shoah Victims' Names, Yad Vashem.
4 Genya Rosenhaus, Page of Testimony submitted by Yitzchak Rosenhaus, April 17, 1956, Central Database of Shoah Victims' Names, Yad Vashem.
5 Estera Rosenhaus, Page of Testimony submitted by Yitzchak Rosenhaus, April 17, 1956, Central Database of Shoah Victims' Names, Yad Vashem.
6 Effie Rosenhaus, personal interview, December 17, 2019.
7 Effie Rosenhaus, personal interview, April 15, 2013.
8 Rosenhaus, personal interview.
9 Mojzesz Slutsky, Page of Testimony submitted by Genia Rosenhaus, October 20, 1956, Central Database of Shoah Victims' Names, Yad Vashem.
10 Kunia Slutsky, Page of Testimony submitted by Genia Rosenhaus, October 20, 1956, Central Database of Shoah Victims' Names, Yad Vashem.
11 Abraham Slutzki, Page of Testimony submitted by Genia Rosenhaus, October 20, 1956, Central Database of Shoah Victims' Names, Yad Vashem.
12 Yitzchak Rosenhaus, personal communication, May 7, 1943.
13 Fanya Dunetz Brodsky, personal interview, April 15, 1913.
14 Fanya Dunetz Brodsky, personal interview, September 11, 2013.
15 Rosenhaus, personal communication.
16 Berkovich, "A Sea of Troubles," 420.
17 Kagan, "Surviving the Holocaust," 573.
18 Rosenhaus, personal communication.
19 Fanya Dunetz Brodsky, personal interview, April 15, 2013.

20 Bielski and Bielski, *Yehudei Yaar*, 206.

21 Tec, *Defiance*, 267.

22 Effie Rosenhaus, personal interview, September 11, 2013.

23 Tec, *Defiance,* 172–74.

24 Effie Rosenhaus and Fanya Dunetz Brodsky, joint personal interview, September 11, 2013.

25 Tec, *Defiance,* 127, 153.

26 Rosenhaus, personal interview, September 11, 2013.

27 Effie Rosenhaus, personal interview, September 11, 2013.

28 Effie Rosenhaus, personal interview, May 8, 2022.

29 Effie Rosenhaus, personal interview, September 11, 2013.

30 Rosenhaus, personal interview.

Chaim Zeev Ostashinski (#32)

1   Compilation of Family Members & Witnesses (Zusammenstellung der Familienangehorigen und Zeugen), Ostaszynski, Chaim, International Tracing Service, Yad Vashem, Jerusalem; Correspondence to District Office for Reparation (Bezirksamt für Wiedergutmachung), Az 84871, Ostaszynski, Chaim, October 20, 1967, International Tracing Service, Yad Vashem.

2   Zafrir Ostashinski, personal interview, December 3, 2018; Dorit Kay, personal interview, December 6, 2018.

3   Zafrir Ostashinski, personal interview, December 1, 2018.

4   Cypka Ostrzynski, Page of Testimony submitted by Daniel Ostashinski, December 9, 1956, Central Database of Shoah Victims' Names, Yad Vashem.

5   Daniel Ostashinski, List of Partisans from Belorussia, Central Database of Shoah Victims' Names, Yad Vashem.

6   Ester Ostrzynski, Page of Testimony submitted by Daniel Ostashinski, December 9, 1956, Central Database of Shoah Victims' Names, Yad Vashem.

7   Perlya Ostashinskaya, List of Partisans from Belorussia, Central Database of Shoah Victims' Names, Yad Vashem.

8   Yitzchak Ostrzynski, Page of Testimony submitted by Daniel Ostashinski, December 9, 1956, Central Database of Shoah Victims' Names, Yad Vashem.

9   Batia Rivka Ostasinski, Page of Testimony submitted by Dorit Kai, June 22, 2005, Central Database of Shoah Victims' Names, Yad Vashem.

10 Ostashinski, personal interview, December 1, 2018.

11 Cypka Ostrzynski, Page of Testimony submitted by Daniel Ostashinski; Batia Rivka Ostachinski, Page of Testimony submitted by Pnina Hershprung Ostashinski, June 24, 2005, Central Database of Shoah Victims' Names, Yad Vashem.

12 Nachum Kushner, Yad Vashem testimony [in Yiddish], no. 03/3929.

13 Ostashinski, personal interview, December 1, 2018.

14 Jarmołowicz, Jan & Józefa, The Righteous Among the Nations Database, Yad Vashem, http://db.yadvashem.org/righteous/family.html?language=en&itemId=4034646.

15 Ostashinski, personal interview, December 3, 2018.

16 Jarmolowicz, Jan & Józefa, The Righteous Among the Nations Database.

17 Ostashinski, personal interview, December 1, 2018.

18 Gerasimova et al., *We Stood Shoulder to Shoulder*, 270.

19 Dorit Kay, personal interview, October 15, 2020.

20 Chaim Ostaszynski, Correspondence to District Office for Reparations.

21 Correspondence to Atty. Dr. Julius Simon, Arolsen, 25.1.56, International Tracing Service, Yad Vashem.

22 Dorit Kay, personal interview, December 8, 2018.

23 "The Altalena Affair," The Irgun Site, Etzel.org.il, http://www.etzel.org.il/english/ac20.htm.

24 Kay, personal interview, December 8, 2018.

25 Kay, personal interview, October 20, 2020.

26 Kay, personal interview, December 8, 2018.

27 Ostashinski, personal interview, December 3, 2018.

28 Ostashinski, personal interview.

29 Dorit Kay, personal interview, August 22, 2023.

Perla Ostashinski (#33)

1   Dorit Kay, personal interview, December 3, 2018.

2   Cypka Ostrzynski, Page of Testimony submitted by Daniel Ostashinski, December 9, 1956, Central Database of Shoah Victims' Names, Yad Vashem.

3   Daniel Ostashinski, List of Partisans from Belorussia, 1943–1944, Central Database of Shoah Victims' Names, Yad Vashem.

4   Ester Ostrzynski, Page of Testimony submitted by Daniel Ostashinski, December 9, 1956, Central Database of Shoah Victims' Names, Yad Vashem.

5   Yitzchak Ostrzynski, Page of Testimony submitted by Daniel Ostashinski, December 9, 1956, Central Database of Shoah Victims' Names, Yad Vashem.

6   Batia Rivka Ostasinski, Page of Testimony submitted by Dorit Kai, June 22, 2005, Central Database of Shoah Victims' Names, Yad Vashem.

7   Zafrir Ostashinski, personal interview, December 1, 2018.

8   Ostashinski, personal interview, December 3, 2018.

9   Ostashinski, personal interview.

10 Nachum Kushner, Yad Vashem testimony [in Yiddish], no. 03/3929.

11　Kay, personal interview, December 3, 2018.

12　Ester Ostrzynski, Page of Testimony.

13　Batia Rivka Ostachinski, Page of Testimony submitted by Pnina Hershprung Ostashinski, June 24, 2005, Central Database of Shoah Victims' Names, Yad Vashem.

14　Cypka Ostrzynski, Page of Testimony.

15　Chaya Bielski, *Haruach Hachaya* [A Woman Fighter with the Bielski Partisans] (Jerusalem: Yad Vashem 2012), 242.

16　Kay, personal interview, December 10, 2018.

17　Kay, personal interview, December 3, 2018.

18　Kay, personal interview.

19　Kay, personal interview.

20　Kay, personal interview.

21　Dorit Kay, personal interview, October 7, 2020.

22　Kay, personal interview, December 3, 2018.

Hirsh Orlinski (#34)

1　Leibovitz, "The Great Destruction," 507.

2　Tec, *Defiance*, 74–75.

3　Duffy, *The Bielski Brothers*, 97–98.

4　Tec, *Defiance*, 74.

5　Tec, 75; Levine, *Fugitives of the Forest*, 244.

6　Gerasimova et al., *We Stood Shoulder to Shoulder*, 40–46.

7　Duffy, *The Bielski Brothers*, 110.

Hirsh (#35) and Moshe (#36) Chernichovski

1　Leibovitz, "The Great Destruction," 500; Bielski, *Haruach Hachaya*, 229.

2　Leibovitz, "The Great Destruction," 507; Yaffe, *In the Novogrudok Ghetto*, 167.

3　Hirsh Tsernihovski, Page of Testimony submitted by Chaya Rubinovitz, April 4, 1999, Central Database of Shoah Victims' Names, Yad Vashem, Jerusalem; Moshe Chernichovski, Page of Testimony submitted by Chaya Rubinovitz, June 3, 1999, Central Database of Shoah Victims' Names, Yad Vashem.

4　David Hersz Czernikowska, List of Murdered Jews from Yizkor Books, Central Database of Shoah Victims' Names.

5　Hersz Fajwel Czernikowski, List of Murdered Jews from Yizkor Books, Central Database of Shoah Victims' Names, Yad Vashem.

6　Mojzesz Becalel Czernikowski, List of Murdered Jews from Yizkor Books, Central Database of Shoah Victims' Names, Yad Vashem.

7 Moszek Czernikowska, List of Murdered Jews from Yizkor Books, Central Database of Shoah Victims' Names, Yad Vashem.

Moshe Glicksman (#37)

1 Moshe Glicksman, Page of Testimony submitted by Minna Rozenberg, May 15, 1957, Central Database of Shoah Victims' Names, Yad Vashem.
2 Chajm Gliksman, Page of Testimony submitted by Minna Rozenberg, May 15, 1957, Central Database of Shoah Victims' Names, Yad Vashem.
3 Mirl Glicksman, Page of Testimony submitted by Minna Rozenberg, undated, Central Database of Shoah Victims' Names, Yad Vashem.
4 Zelda Glicksman, Page of Testimony submitted by Minna Rozenberg, May 15, 1957, Central Database of Shoah Victims' Names, Yad Vashem.
5 Moshe Glicksman, Page of Testimony.
6 Gerasimova et al., *We Stood Shoulder to Shoulder*, 219, 320.

Yakov (Yankel) Shepsman (#39)

1 Jakob Szepsman, Addenda to Residence Certificate of June 1, 1956, January 10, 1972, Arolsen, International Tracing Service, Yad Vashem.
2 Yakov Shepsman, oral testimony, USC Shoah Foundation Institute, October 14, 1996.
3 Ze Roberts, personal interview, October 20, 2020.
4 Jack Shepsman, oral testimony.
5 Roberts, personal interview.
6 Jakob Szepsman, Addenda to Residence Certificate.
7 Jack Shepsman, oral testimony.
8 Shepsman, oral testimony.
9 Shepsman, oral testimony.
10 Berkovich, "A Sea of Troubles," 420.
11 Leibovich, "The Great Destruction," 504–5.
12 Kagan, "Surviving the Holocaust," 570.
13 Ze Roberts, personal interview, October 20, 2020.
14 Jack Shepsman, oral testimony.
15 Shepsman, oral testimony.
16 Martin Shepsman, personal interview, September 30, 2020.
17 Jakob Szepsman, Addenda to Residence Certificate.
18 Jack Shepsman, oral testimony.
19 Victor Weisz, personal interview, April 7, 2019.
20 Martin Shepsman, September 30, 2020.
21 Ze Roberts, personal interview, October 20, 2020.

22 Roberts, personal interview.
23 Jack Shepsman, oral testimony.

David Meiersdorf (#40)

1 *Novogrudok Memorial Book*, 706.
2 Emanuel Glogovski, Page of Testimony, Central Database of Shoah Victims' Names, Yad Vashem.
3 *Pultusk Memorial Book*, translation of *Pultusk, Sefer Zikaron*, ed. Yitzhak Ivri (Tel Aviv: Pultusk Society, 1971), 636, https://www.jewishgen.org/Yizkor /pultusk/pul634.html#M.
4 Gerasimova et al., *We Stood Shoulder to Shoulder*, 262, 325.

Yosef Razvaski (#41)

1 Openheim, "Novogrudok Partisans Who Fell in Action," 645.
2 Gerasimova et al., *We Stood Shoulder to Shoulder*, 328.
3 Openheim, "Novogrudok Partisans Who Fell in Action," 645.
4 Gerasimova et al., *We Stood Shoulder to Shoulder*, 328.
5 Openheim, "Novogrudok Partisans Who Fell in Action," 645.
6 Gerasimova et al., *We Stood Shoulder to Shoulder*, 328.
7 Gerasimova, 328.
8 Chaya Magid, personal interview, April 27, 2020; Shoshi Erster and Zahava Magal, personal interviews, April 28, 2020.

Mordechai (#42) and Leib Orzuchowski

1 Nella Tauber, personal interview, June 13, 2019.
2 Gerasimova et al., *We Stood Shoulder to Shoulder*, 269.
3 Mordechai Ozuchovsky, gravestone, Kfar Saba Nordau Old Cemetery, BillionGraves, April 15, 2016, https://billiongraves.com/grave /18806770/מרדכי-אוזחובסקי.
4 Tauber, personal interview.
5 Mordechai Ozuchovsky, gravestone.
6 Nikol Falik family tree, Myheritage.com, December 29, 2008, https://www .myheritage.com/site-39778411/falik-nikol, accessed on June 19, 2019.
7 Morduch Ozchovski, List of Partisans from Baranovichskaya Brigade No. 1, Active in the Baranowicze District, 1942–1944, Central Database of Shoah Victims' Names, Yad Vashem.
8 Nikol Falik family tree.
9 Tauber, personal interview.
10 Tauber, personal interview.

11 Tauber, personal interview.

12 Tauber, personal interview.

13 Tauber, personal interview.

14 Morduch Ozchovski, List of Partisans from Baranovichskaya Brigade No. 1.

15 Jewish Partisans in Belarus, JewishGen, https://www.jewishgen.org/databases
    /Holocaust/0218_Belarus_partisans.html.

16 Gerasimova et al., *We Stood Shoulder to Shoulder*, 269.

17 Tec, *Defiance*, 126–27.

18 Tauber, personal interview.

19 Tauber, personal interview.

20 Tauber, personal interview.

21 Tauber, personal interview.

22 Tauber, personal interview.

23 Tauber, personal interview.

24 Mordechai Ozuchovsky, gravestone.

25 Ida Chorush Ozuchovski, gravestone, Kfar Saba Nordau Old
    Cemetery, BillionGraves, July 11, 2016, https://billiongraves.com/grave
    /19864463/אידה-חורוש-אוזחובסקי.

26 Tauber, personal interview.

Lipchin (#43)

1   Gerasimova et al., *We Stood Shoulder to Shoulder*, 257, 325.

Shlomo (Moniek) Engler (#44)

1   Shleyman Angler, List of Murdered Jews in Kolomyya, Central Database of
    Shoah Victims' Names, Yad Vashem.

2   Muni Engler, Page of Testimony submitted by Genya Shalmuk, February 20,
    1957, Central Database of Shoah Victims' Names, Yad Vashem.

3   Salamon Laisor Engler, List of Jews Residing in Kosow before 1941, Central
    Database of Shoah Victims' Names, Yad Vashem.

4   Etel Engler, List of Jews Residing in Kosow before 1941, Central Database of
    Shoah Victims' Names, Yad Vashem.

5   Gerasimova et al., *We Stood Shoulder to Shoulder*, 200, 313, 318, 352.

Abram Czertok (#45)

1   Guy Czertok, personal interview, August 4, 2020.

2   Abraham Dit Andre Czertok, Death Certificate, in France Death Index,
    1970–2020, Myheritage.com, https://www.myheritage.com/research/record
    -10823-13752284-/abraham-dit-andre-czertok-in-france-deathindex.

3　Owsiey Czertok, Page of Testimony submitted by André Czertok, August 1, 1978, Central Database of Shoah Victims' Names, Yad Vashem, Jerusalem; Joshua Oche Czertok, Page of Testimony submitted by Pierre Nachimovski, September 8, 1996, Central Database of Shoah Victims' Names, Yad Vashem.

4　Guy Czertok, personal interview, July 26, 2020.

5　Mera Czertok, Page of Testimony submitted by André Czertok, August 1, 1978, Central Database of Shoah Victims' Names, Yad Vashem.

6　Joshua Oche Czertok, Page of Testimony; Myriam Czertok, Page of Testimony submitted by Pierre Nachimovski, September 8, 1996, Central Database of Shoah Victims' Names, Yad Vashem.

7　Avraham-Leizer Czertok, testimony [in French], January 24, 1968, Ghetto Fighters' House Museum, Kibbutz Lochamei Hagetaot.

8　Guy Czertok, personal correspondence, August 25, 2020.

9　Avraham-Leizer Czertok, testimony.

10　Czertok, testimony.

11　Guy Czertok, personal interview, July 26, 2020.

12　Guy Czertok, personal correspondence.

13　Czertok, personal interview, July 26, 2020.

14　Czertok, personal interview.

15　Czertok, personal interview.

16　Czertok, personal interview.

17　Guy Czertok, personal correspondence, October 8, 2020.

18　Czertok, personal interview, July 26, 2020.

19　Czertok, personal interview.

20　Guy Czertok, personal interview, September 15, 2020.

21　Guy Czertok, personal interview, August 26, 2020.

22　Czertok, personal interview.

23　Guy Czertok, personal correspondence, August 11, 2020.

24　Czertok, personal interview, August 4, 2020.

25　Abraham Dit Andre Czertok, death certificate.

26　Czertok, personal interview, July 26, 2020.

27　Yehuda Slutzki, "The 52 Martyrs," in *Novogrudok Memorial Book*, 453–55.

28　Czertok, personal interview, July 26, 2020.

29　Czertok, personal interview.

30　Guy Czertok, personal correspondence, October 8, 2020.

31　Rabbi Haïm Korsia, personal interview by Guy Czertok, October 7, 2020.

Leiba Pinchuk (#46)

1　Leyba Pinchuk, List of Partisans from Belorussia, Central Database of Shoah Victims' Names, Yad Vashem.

2   Leyba Pinchuk, Personal Cards of Jewish Partisans from Belorussia, prepared 1944, Central Database of Shoah Victims' Names, Yad Vashem.

3   Nikolai Schensnovich, *Zapiski Aktiora i Partizana* [Notes of an Actor and a Partisan] (Minsk, 1976), 93–97.

4   Bielski, *Haruach Hachaya*, 239.

5   Shaul Gorodynski, Yad Vashem testimony, no. 3095/230, 27.

6   Bielski and Bielski, *Yehudei Yaar*, 216.

7   Tec, *Defiance*, 147, 268.

8   Schensnovich, *Zapiski Aktiora i Partizana*, 93–97.

9   Gerasimova et al., *We Stood Shoulder to Shoulder*, 250; List of Partisans.

10   Tamara Vershitskaya, personal communication, February 8, 2017.

11   Vershitskaya, personal communication.

Moshe Feivelevich (#47)

1   Movsha Fayvelevich, Personal Cards for Partisans from Belorussia 1944, Central Database of Shoah Victims' Names, Yad Vashem.

2   Openheim, "Politico-Communal Life in Novogrudok," 176.

3   Openheim, 175–76.

4   Openheim, 176.

5   Mordechai Majerowicz, Yad Vashem testimony, no. 0.3/2106.

6   Shaul Gorodynski, Yad Vashem testimony, no. 3095/230.

7   Majerowicz, Yad Vashem testimony.

8   Jack Kagan, personal interview, December 23, 2012.

Eliyahu (Elya) Berkowicz (#49)

1   Eliyahu Eliasz Berkowicz, Certificate of Residence #118232, International Tracing Service, June 3, 1954, Yad Vashem.

2   Eliyahu Berkowicz, Yad Vashem testimony [in Yiddish], no. 03/2774.

3   Berkovitz, "A Sea of Troubles," 421.

4   Berkovitz, 421.

5   Gitel Szuster, Page of Testimony submitted by Isaac Szuster, May 17, 1955, Central Database of Shoah Victims' Names, Yad Vashem.

6   Gitel Szuster, Page of Testimony.

7   Berkovitz, "A Sea of Troubles," 421.

8   Berkowicz, Yad Vashem testimony.

9   Yakov Konskowolski, Page of Testimony submitted by Yosef Ben Chaim, July 2, 1955, Central Database of Shoah Victims' Names, Yad Vashem.

10 Berkowicz, Yad Vashem testimony.
11 Berkowicz, testimony.
12 Yisrael Kolachek, personal interview [in Yiddish], December 6, 2016.
13 Berkovitz, "A Sea of Troubles," 421.
14 Yisrael Kolachek, personal interview.
15 Berkowicz, Yad Vashem testimony.
16 Berkovitz, "A Sea of Troubles," 421.
17 Berkovitz, 421.
18 Berkovitz, 422.
19 Berkowicz, Yad Vashem testimony.
20 Eliyahu Eliasz Berkowicz, Certificate of Residence #118232.
21 Berkowicz, Certificate of Residence.
22 Konskowolski, Page of Testimony.
23 Berkowicz, Yad Vashem testimony.
24 Berkowicz, testimony.
25 Chaya Berkowicz Luska, Certificate of Residence #113139, International Tracing Service, January 20, 1954, Yad Vashem.
26 Berkowicz, Yad Vashem testimony.
27 Berkowicz, testimony.
28 Berkowicz, testimony.
29 Avinoam and Margalit Berkovitz, personal interviews, March 1, 2020; June 2, 2020.
30 Mascha Dalva, personal interview, June 6, 2023.
31 Dalva, personal interview; Chaim Barkan, personal interview, June 7, 2023.
32 Barkan, personal interview.
33 Mascha Dalva, personal interview, June 6, 2023; Barkan, personal interview.

Zisel Rozin (#50)

1 Ziesl Rozin, Certificate of Residence, August 31, 1946, International Red Cross Committee, International Tracing Service, Yad Vashem.
2 Zisel Rozin, Application for Assistance, Preparatory Commission of the International Refugee Organization, (PCIRO), April 12, 1948, Arolsen Archives, https://collections.arolsen-archives.org/en/document/79668171.
3 Rozin, Application for Assistance.
4 Zisel Rozin, List of Partisans from Belorussia, Central Database of Shoah Victims' Names, Yad Vashem.
5 Ziesl Rozin, Certificate of Residence.
6 Nachum Kushner, Yad Vashem testimony [in Yiddish], no. 03/3929.
7 Berkovich, "A Sea of Troubles," 421.

8 Berkovich, 421.
9 Berkovich, 421.
10 Yisrael Kolachek, personal interview, December 6, 2016.
11 Eliyahu Berkowicz, Yad Vashem testimony [in Yiddish], no. 03/2774.
12 Kolachek, personal interview.
13 Rozin, Certificate of Residence.
14 "Ulm," ORT and the Displaced Person Camps, http://dpcamps.ort.org/camps
   /germany/us-zone/us-zone-i/ulm/.
15 Rozin, Application for Assistance.
16 Ziesl Rozin, Certificate of Residence.
17 Zisel Rozin, New York, US, Arriving Passenger and Crew Lists (including Castle
   Garden and Ellis Island), 1820–1957, Ancestry.com, https://www.ancestry.com
   /discoveryui-content/view/3030858336:7488.
18 SS *United States*, US Department of Transportation Maritime Administration,
   https://www.maritime.dot.gov/multimedia/ss-united-states, accessed December
   30, 2021.
19 New York, US, Arriving Passenger and Crew Lists.
20 "Lincoln Road (Miami Beach) – 2018," Trip Advisor, Miami Beach, https://
   www.tripadvisor.com/Attraction_Review-g34439-d109886-Reviews-Lincoln
   _Road-Miami_Beach_Florida.html, accessed on June 27, 2018.

Jankef (Yakov) Nevachovich (#51)

1 Fanya Dunetz Brodsky, personal interview, November 2011.
2 Simon Lazowsky, Notes on his Mother's Recollections, 1933–1941, personal
   correspondence, March 6, 2019.
3 Lazowsky, Notes .
4 Daniel Ostashinski, Yad Vashem testimony, no. 03/6041.
5 Lazowsky, Notes.
6 Ostashinski, Yad Vashem testimony.
7 Leibovitz, "The Great Destruction," 500.
8 Shaul Gorodynski, Yad Vashem testimony, no. 3095/230.
9 Lazowsky, Notes.
10 Dunetz Brodsky, interview.
11 Sulia Rubin, *Against the Tide* (Jerusalem: Posner and Sons, 1980), 149.

Yechezkel (Chatzkel) Pozniak (#52)

1 Chaskiel Pozniak, United Restitution Organization record 6.III.56, International
   Tracing Service, Yad Vashem.

2   Khatzkel Poznyak, List of Partisans from Belorussia, Central Database of Shoah Victims' Names, Yad Vashem. https://documents.yadvashem.org/index.html ?language=en&&TreeItemId=7184987.

3   Chaskiel Pozniak, United Restitution Organization.

4   Khatzkel Poznyak, List of Partisans.

5   Chaskiel Pozniak, United Restitution Organization.

6   Gerasimova et al., *We Stood Shoulder to Shoulder*, 273.

7   Chascskiel Pozniak, OOC PO record 6.III.56, International Tracing Service, Yad Vashem.

8   Pozniak, OOC PO record 6.III.56.

9   Yechezkel Pozniak, gravestone, Ha-Komemiyut St, Bat Yam, Israel, BillionGraves, May 30, 2015, https://billiongraves.com/grave/14304583/יחזקאל-פוזניאק/.

10   Yechezkel Pozniak, gravestone.

Kalman Notkovich (#53)

1   Kalman Notkovich, List of Partisans from Belorussia, Central Database of Shoah Victims' Names, Yad Vashem.

2   Gerasimova et al., *We Stood Shoulder to Shoulder*, 269.

Dov (#54), Frieda (#54a), and Leah (#54b) Wasserman

1   Moshe Wasserman, Yad Vashem oral testimony, 2006.

2   Wasserman, oral testimony.

3   Zvi Wasserman, Page of Testimony submitted by Moshe Wasserman, Central Database of Shoah Victims' Names, Yad Vashem, December 25, 2002.

4   Wasserman, oral testimony.

5   Dov Ber Waserman, Page of Testimony submitted by Tzippa Sarna, April 4, 1957, Central Database of Shoah Victims' Names, Yad Vashem.

6   Wasserman, oral testimony.

7   Leah Waserman, Page of Testimony submitted by Tzippa Sarna, April 4, 1957, Central Database of Shoah Victims' Names, Yad Vashem.

8   Wasserman, oral testimony.

9   Wasserman, oral testimony.

10   Wasserman, oral testimony.

11   Pesce Waserman, Page of Testimony submitted by Tzippa Sarna, April 4, 1957, Central Database of Shoah Victims' Names, Yad Vashem.

12   Wasserman, oral testimony.

13   Frieda Wasserman, Page of Testimony submitted by Moshe Wasserman, December 25, 2002, Central Database of Shoah Victims' Names, Yad Vashem.

14   Wasserman, Page of Testimony.

15 Wasserman, Page of Testimony.

16 Edna Vaserman, Page of Testimony submitted by Moshe Wasserman, July 10, 1987, Central Database of Shoah Victims' Names, Yad Vashem.

17 Zvi Wasserman, Page of Testimony.

18 Moshe Wasserman, Yad Vashem testimony.

19 Lea Ritza Wasserman, Page of Testimony submitted by Genendl Aleksandrovich, July 21, 1956, Central Database of Shoah Victims' Names, Yad Vashem.

20 Dov Ber Waserman, Page of Testimony.

21 Daniel Ostashinski, Yad Vashem testimony, no. 03/6841.

22 Gerasimova et al., *We Stood Shoulder to Shoulder*, 211, 319.

23 Shai Vaserman, personal interview, April 30, 2020.

24 Shlomit Frieda Adivi, personal interview, April 30, 2020.

25 Edna Aronada, personal interview, April 30, 2020.

Aaron Jakubowski (#55)

1 Pini Jakubowski, personal interview, July 1, 2018.

2 Aron Jakubowski family tree, Geni.com, https://www.geni.com/family-tree/index/6000000030646911866, accessed on January 23, 2022

3 JewishGen Town Finder, https://www.jewishgen.org/Communities/community.php?usbgn=-514283.

4 Aron Jakubowski family tree.

5 Jakubowski, personal interview.

6 Jakubowski, personal interview.

7 Aron Jakubowski, International Red Cross Committee, Arolsen, Germany, correspondence of November 13, 1958, International Tracing Service, Yad Vashem.

8 Itta Jakubowska, Lodz Names – List of the Ghetto Inhabitants 1940–1944, Central Database of Shoah Victims' Names, Yad Vashem.

9 Mordechai Even-Chen, Zikaron u'Tekumah [in Hebrew], Testimonial Stories of Holocaust Survivors)Achital Publishers, 2014), 298, https://en.calameo.com/read/0032377241030863b6b90, accessed on January 8, 2022.

10 Aron Jakubowski, "Fragebogen" document, May 1, 1957, Tel Aviv. International Tracing Service, Yad Vashem.

11 Gerasimova et al., *We Stood Shoulder to Shoulder*, 315.

12 Sara Goldina, List of Jewish Partisans Active in the Baranowicze Region, Central Database of Shoah Victims' Names, Yad Vashem.

13 Shoshana Cohen, personal interview, July 2, 2018.

14 Aron Jakubowski, International Red Cross Committee.

15 Shoshana Cohen, personal interview.

16 "Turin Area," ORT and the DP Camps, http://dpcamps.ort.org/camps/italy /turin-area.

17 "Turin Area."

18 Jakubowski, International Red Cross Committee.

19 Pini Jakubovski, personal interview.

20 Jakubovski, personal interview.

21 Jakubovski, personal interview.

22 Shoshana Cohen, personal interview.

23 Cohen, personal interview.

24 Yanek Okonski, personal interview, January 14, 2024.

25 Shoshana Cohen, personal interview, August 31, 2023.

Distiler (#56)

1 Central Database of Shoah Victims' Names, Yad Vashem.

2 *Novogrudok Memorial Book*, 693.

3 Gerasimova et al., *We Stood Shoulder to Shoulder*, 229, 320.

Wolff (Velvel) Borowski (#57)

1 Wolff (Velvel) Borowski, in *Memory, Guide My Hand: An Anthology of Life Stories by Members of the Melbourne Jewish Community from the Former Soviet Union, vol. 5*, ed. Julie Meadows and Elaine Davidoff (Caulfield South, VIC: Makor Jewish Community Library, 2008), 9–16.

2 This is at odds with his placement on the list. Numbers were changed at the last minute during the line-up for the escape, and his testimony was written many years afterwards when his memory may not have been accurate.

3 Jack Borowski, personal correspondence, August 15, 2018.

4 Jack Borowski, personal correspondence, August 12, 2018.

5 David Borowski, personal interview, August 1, 2018.

6 Jack Borowski, personal communication, August 24, 2023.

Aaron Borowski (#58)

1 Jack M. Borovski, personal communication, July 2008.

2 Cheina Borovski, Page of Testimony submitted by Itzchak Ben-Yaakov (Morduchovitz), June 28, 1999, Central Database of Shoah Victims' Names, Yad Vashem.

3 Jack M. Borovski, personal communication.

4 Borovski, personal communication.

5 Tamara Vershitskaya, personal communication.

6 Gerasimova et al., *We Stood Shoulder to Shoulder*, 208.

7   Borowski, in *Memory, Guide My Hand*, 9–16.

8   Aron Borowski, Jewish Refugees Arriving in Australia via Melbourne 1946–
     1954," JDC Archives, https://names.jdc.org/search-detail.php?id=193537.

9   Aaron Borowski, Australia, Victoria Death Index, 1836–1985, Myheritage.
     com,   https://www.myheritage.com/research/record-10547-2371871/aaron
     -borowski-in-australia-victoria-death-index.

10   Jack M. Borovski, personal communication.

Ita Bitenski (#59)

1   Ita Bitensky, Page of Testimony submitted by Khana Sevinik, undated, Central
     Database of Shoah Victims' Names, Yad Vashem.

2   Avraham Bitensky, Page of Testimony submitted by Khana Sevinik, undated,
     Central Database of Shoah Victims' Names, Yad Vashem.

3   Ita Bitensky, Page of Testimony submitted by Khana Sevinik.

4   Moshe Bitensky, Page of Testimony submitted by Khana Sevinik, undated,
     Central Database of Shoah Victims' Names, Yad Vashem.

5   Khil Bitensky, Page of Testimony submitted by Khana Sevinik, undated, Central
     Database of Shoah Victims' Names, Yad Vashem.

6   Ita Bitensky, Page of Testimony submitted by Khana Sevinik.

7   Ita Bitensky, Page of Testimony.

8   Gerasimova et al., *We Stood Shoulder to Shoulder*, 206, 318.

Herman Kritz (#60)

1   Gregorz Kric, Petition for Naturalization #8177, US Department of Justice,
     District Court Atlanta, GA, November 6, 1967.

2   Alex Kritz, personal interview, July 10, 2019.

3   Musya Krytz, List of Residents from Novogrudok 1941, Central Database of
     Shoah Victims' Names, Yad Vashem.

4   Alex Kritz, personal communication, January 5, 2019.

5   Alex Kritz, personal interview.

6   Kritz, personal interview.

7   Kritz, personal communication.

8   Kritz, personal communication.

9   Kritz, personal interview.

10   Kritz, personal interview.

11   Kritz, personal communication.

12   Kritz, personal communication.

13 Bertha and Harry Kritz, gravestone, Crest Lawn Cemetery, Atlanta, GA, Find a Grave, March 23, 2018, https://www.findagrave.com/memorial/111345728 #view-photo=167606367.

14 Kritz, personal communication.

15 Bertha and Harry Kritz, gravestone.

16 Kritz, personal interview.

Manya Katz (#61)

1 Central Database of Shoah Victims' Names, Yad Vashem.

2 Gerasimova et al., *We Stood Shoulder to Shoulder*, 242.

Helena (Lena) Kitayevich (#62)

1 Helena Kitajevic, Page of Testimony submitted by Fira Dunec, June 24, 1957, Central Database of Shoah Victims' Names, Yad Vashem.

2 Avraham Klubok, Page of Testimony submitted by Fira Dunec, June 24, 1957, Central Database of Shoah Victims' Names, Yad Vashem.

3 Arthur Dunec, personal interview, July 29, 2017.

4 Cipa Klubok, Page of Testimony submitted by Fira Dunec, June 24, 1957, Central Database of Shoah Victims' Names, Yad Vashem.

5 Arthur Dunec, personal interview.

6 "The Novogrudok Orphanage," in *Novogrudok Memorial Book*, 183.

7 Bogdana Litska, Page of Testimony submitted by Fira Dunec, June 24, 1957, Central Database of Shoah Victims' Names, Yad Vashem.

8 Gershon Kitajewicz, Page of Testimony submitted by Rachel Pentel, April 4, 1956, Central Database of Shoah Victims' Names, Yad Vashem.

9 Albert Lidski, Page of Testimony submitted by Fira Dunec, June 24, 1957, Central Database of Shoah Victims' Names, Yad Vashem.

10 Arthur Dunec, personal interview.

11 Raja (Rita) Slutsky née Klubock, MyHeritage family trees, Myheritage.com, January 21, 2022, https://www.myheritage.com/research/record-1-53830031-19-2824 /raja-rita-slutsky-born-klubock-in-myheritage-family-trees.

12 Fanya Dunetz Brodsky, personal interview, July 29, 2017.

13 Shimon Yaron, personal interview, August 23, 2023.

14 Arthur Dunec, personal interview.

15 Avraham Klubok, Page of Testimony.

16 Arthur Dunec, personal interview.

17 Helena Kitajevic, Page of Testimony.

Gedalia Maslovati (#63)

1   Gdalya Maslovaty, List of Partisans from Belorussia, Central Database of Shoah Victims' Names, Yad Vashem.
2   Shlomo Maslowaty, Pages of Testimony submitted by Zelda Grinberg, October 18, 1956, Central Database of Shoah Victims' Names, Yad Vashem.
3   Chana Maslowaty, Page of Testimony submitted by Zelda Grinberg, October 18, 1956, Central Database of Shoah Victims' Names, Yad Vashem.
4   Shlema Maslovati, Lists of Murdered Jews from Novogrudok, Central Database of Shoah Victims' Names, Yad Vashem.
5   Reuven Maslowaty, Page of Testimony submitted by Zelda Grinberg, October 18, 1956, Central Database of Shoah Victims' Names, Yad Vashem.
6   Shoshana Maslowaty, Page of Testimony submitted by Zelda Grinberg, October 18, 1956, Central Database of Shoah Victims' Names, Yad Vashem.
7   Rivka Maslowaty, Page of Testimony submitted by Zelda Grinberg, October 18, 1956, Central Database of Shoah Victims' Names, Yad Vashem.
8   Gedalia Maslowaty, Page of Testimony submitted by Zelda Grinberg; Lists of murdered individuals from Novogrudok.
9   Zalmanovich, written testimony, 235.

Berko (Berl) Zalmanovich (#64)

1   Dov Zelmanovicz, inquiry card, TD #368482, International Tracing Service, Yad Vashem.
2   Zalmanovich, written testimony, 230.
3   Zalmanovich, written testimony, 230.
4   Zalmanovich, written testimony., 231.
5   Zalmanovich, written testimony, 233.
6   Sonya Gorodynski Oshman, oral history, video transcript, 1993, Holocaust Center at Kean College of New Jersey.
7   Zalmanovich, written testimony, 231.
8   Zalmanovich, written testimony, 232.
9   Zalmanovich, written testimony, 233.
10 Zalmanovich, written testimony, 232.
11 Zalmanovich, written testimony, 234.
12 Shoshke Traubmann, personal interview, November 4, 2019.
13 Zalmanovich, written testimony, 234.
14 Zalmanovich, written testimony, 236.
15 Zalmanovich, written testimony, 235.
16 Zalmanovich, written testimony, 235.

17 Zalmanovich, written testimony, 235.
18 Zalmanovich, written testimony, 236.
19 Zalmanovich, written testimony, 236.
20 Zalmanovich, written testimony, 237.
21 Peter Landé, "The Voyage of the Olim (Immigrants) of the '*Biria*,' June 22, 1946–July 2, 1946" JewishGen, April 2009, https://www.jewishgen.org/databases/holocaust/0183_biria.html.
22 Zalmanovich, written testimony, 237.
23 David Israel, "Hashomer Hatzair Kibbutz Inaugurates First Synagogue in 70 Years," *Jewish Press*, October 18, 2019, https://www.jewishpress.com/news/israel/religious-secular-in-israel-israel/hashomer-hatzair-kibbutz-inaugurates-first-synagogue-in-70-years/2019/10/28/.
24 Zalmanovich, written testimony, 231.
25 Shoshke Traubmann, personal interview.
26 Dotan Traubmann, personal interview, December 1, 2019.
27 Shoshke Traubmann and Dotan Traubmann, personal interviews.
28 Shoshke Traubmann, personal interview.
29 Zalmanovich, written testimony, 237.
30 Shoshke Traubmann and Dotan Traubmann, personal interviews.
31 Zalmanovich, written testimony, 237.

Aaron Wilenski (#65)

1 Aron Vilenskiy, List of Partisans from Belorussia, Central Database of Shoah Victims' Names, Yad Vashem.
2 Rita Standig, personal interview, February 26, 2018.
3 Standig, personal interview.
4 Gerasimova et al., *We Stood Shoulder to Shoulder*, 212.
5 Aaron Wilensky, inquiry by Seymour Wilenski, July 23, 1999, International Tracing Service Archives, Yad Vashem.
6 Standig, personal interview.

Naum Shleimovich (#66)

1 Naum Shleymovich, List of Partisans from the Za sovetskuyu Belarus Detachment Active in the Lida District, 1942–1944, Central Database of Shoah Victims' Names, Yad Vashem.
2 Gerasimova et al., *We Stood Shoulder to Shoulder*, 307.
3 Tec, *Defiance*, 126–27.

Yakov Angelchik (#67)

1 Yaakov Angelchik, Testimony for List of Persecuted Persons submitted by Moshe Angelchik, undated, Central Database of Shoah Victims' Names, Yad Vashem.
2 Atara Stollar Orr, personal interview, March 12, 2017.
3 Szlomo, Lea, Shalom, Hana, Tzila, and Jacob Angielczyk, Pages of Testimony submitted by Luba Stolyar Orr, January 1, 1956, Central Database of Shoah Victims' Names, Yad Vashem.
4 Gerasimova et al., *We Stood Shoulder to Shoulder*, 200.
5 Yaakov Angelchik, Testimony for List of Persecuted Persons.
6 Atara Stollar, personal interviews, March 12, 2017; January 30, 2018.
7 Amnon Erez (Angelchik), "The Journey from the Galil to the Templars" [in Jewish], Maagar Siporei Moreshet, April 26, 2017, https://www.ravdori.co.il /stories/המסע-מהגליל-אל-הטמפלרים.
8 Atara Stollar, personal interviews.
9 Stollar, personal interview, January 30, 2018.
10 Stollar, personal interview, April 21, 2020.

Halperin (#68)

1 Central Database of Shoah Victims' Names, Yad Vashem.
2 Gerasimova et al., *We Stood Shoulder to Shoulder*, 215.
3 Gerasimova et al., 199.
4 Gerasimova et al., 54–55.
5 Chonia Alperin, List of Partisans from Belorussia, Central Database of Shoah Victims' Names, Yad Vashem.

Aaron (#69) and Sarah (#70) Kulik

1 Miryam Kulik, Page of Testimony submitted by Zahava Kulik, February 13, 1957, Central Database of Shoah Victims' Names, Yad Vashem.
2 Aron Kulyk, Page of Testimony submitted by Zahava Kulik, February 13, 1957, Central Database of Shoah Victims' Names, Yad Vashem.
3 Sora Kulik, List of Homeowners and Tenants from Grodno Who Paid Taxes, 1939, Central Database of Shoah Victims' Names, Yad Vashem.
4 Szmuel Kulik, Page of Testimony submitted by Mordechai Kulik, December 12, 1957, Central Database of Shoah Victims' Names, Yad Vashem.
5 Gerasimova et al., *We Stood Shoulder to Shoulder*, 251.

Rita Wolozhinski (#71)

1 Osher Wolozhinski, Page of Testimony submitted by Sulia Rubin, January 5, 1998, Central Database of Shoah Victims' Names, Yad Vashem.

2   Anuita Wolozhinski, Page of Testimony submitted by Sulia Rubin, January 5, 1998, Central Database of Shoah Victims' Names, Yad Vashem.

3   Osher Wolozhinski, Anuita Wolozhinski, Pages of Testimony.

4   Tec, *Defiance*, 54–55.

5   Lilka Kravitz, personal interview, March 2008.

6   Rubin, *Against the Tide*, 102.

7   Rubin, 109.

8   Rubin, 128–29.

9   Rubin., 146.

10 Levine, *Fugitives of the Forest*, 257–58.

11 Rubin, *Against the Tide*, 149.

12 Rubin, 145–49.

L. Wolkin (#72)

1   Lev Volkin, List of Murdered Jews from Lida, Central Database of Shoah Victims' Names, Yad Vashem.

2   *Novogrudok Memorial Book*, 718.

3   "Etymology/Connection between Ari, Aryeh, Yehudah, Leib, and Leibel," Mi Yodeya, June 30, 2015., https://judaism.stackexchange.com/questions/9065/etymology-connection-between-ari-aryeh-yehudah-leib-and-leibel, accessed July 31, 2018.

4   *Novogrudok Memorial Book*, 718.

5   Gerasimova et al., *We Stood Shoulder to Shoulder*, 213, 319.

Matus Kabak (#72a)

1   E. V. Yerushalmi, "Leaders and Ordinary Members of the Community" [in Yiddish], in *Pinkas Navaredok*, 65.

2   Yerushalmi, "Leaders and Ordinary Members of the Community," 65.

3   Matus Kabak, Application for Assistance to the Preparatory Committee of the International Refugee Organization (PCIRO), Rome, Italy, January 21, 1948. International Tracing Service, Yad Vashem.

4   Gerasimova et al., *We Stood Shoulder to Shoulder*, 238.

5   Matus Kabak, Jewish Refugees in Italy listing, Office for Statistics and Information at the Organization of Jewish Refugees in Italy 1946. International Tracing Service, Yad Vashem.

6   Kabak, Application for Assistance.

7   Kabak, Application for Assistance.

8   Fanya Dunetz Brodsky, personal interview, August 21, 2018.

9   Tec, *Defiance*, 146–47.

10   Bielski and Bielski, *Yehudei Yaar*, 206, 213.
11   Kabak, Application for Assistance.
12   Kabak, Application for Assistance.
13   Dunetz Brodsky, personal interview.

Dr. Abush (#73)

1   Central Database of Shoah Victims' Names, Yad Vashem.
2   Abusz (first name unknown), Page of Testimony submitted by illegible name, June 27, 1955, Central Database of Shoah Victims' Names, Yad Vashem.
3   Benjamin B. Fisher, "The Katyn Controversy: Stalin's Killing Fields," *Studies in Intelligence* (Winter 1999–2000).
4   M. H-D, "Institutions of Social Assistance," in *Memorial (Yizkor) Book of the Community of Radomsk and Vicinity*, ed. Gloria Freund, trans. Jerrold Landau, translation of *Sefer Yizkor le-Kehilat Radomsk ve-ha-seviva*, ed. L. Losh (Tel Aviv: Former Residents of Radomsk, 1967), 238–39, https://www.jewishgen.org /Yizkor/radomsko/rad237.html.
5   Eliyahu Berkowicz, Yad Vashem testimony, no. 03/2774.
6   Gerasimova et al., *We Stood Shoulder to Shoulder*, 198, 318.

Leipuner (#73a)

1   Central Database of Shoah Victims' Names, Yad Vashem.
2   Fruma Kamieniecki, "A Friday in Novogrudok," in *Novogrudok Memorial Book*, 345.
3   Gerasimova et al., *We Stood Shoulder to Shoulder*, 255, 324.

Gitel (Gita) Zilberman (#74)

1   Nachum Kushner, Yad Vashem testimony [in Yiddish], no. 03/3929.
2   Kamieniecki, "A Friday in Novogrudok," 345.
3   *Novogrudok Memorial Book*, 719.

Israelit (#74a)

1   Gerasimova et al., *We Stood Shoulder to Shoulder*, 236.

Shlomo Golanski (#75)

1   Mordechai Aaron Golanski, memorial notice submitted by Shlomo Golanski, in *Pinkas Navaredok*, 405.
2   Solomon Golanski, oral testimony, USC Shoah Foundation Institute, February 9, 1997.

3 Gute Rakhel Golanski, memorial notice submitted by Shlomo Golanski, in *Pinkas Navaredok*, 405.

4 Rachel Surname Unknown, Sonie Golanski, Sheine Golanski, Chana Golanski, Miriam Golanski, and Mairim Golanski, memorial notice submitted by Shlomo Golanski, in *Pinkas Navaredok*, 405.

5 Surname Unknown, First Name Unknown, memorial notice submitted by Shlomo Golanski, *Pinkas Navaredok*, eds. E. Yerushalmi, David Cohen, Aaron Mirsky et al. (Yiddish; Tel Aviv: Alexander Harkavy Navaredker Relief Committee in USA and Navaredker Committee in Israel, 1963), 405.

6 Yehoshua Yaffe, "The Tradesmen's Ghetto," in *Novogrudok Memorial Book*, 559; Kagan, "Surviving the Holocaust," in *Novogrudok Memorial Book*, 567.

7 *Solomon Golanski, US Public Records Index, 1950–1993, vol. 2, Ancestry.com*, https://www.ancestry.com/discoveryui-content/view/250779444:1732.

8 Solomon Golanski, oral testimony.

9 Etta Golanski, "Connecticut Death Index, 1949–2012," Ancestry.com, https://www.ancestry.com/discoveryui-content/view/1590282:4124.

10 Alani Golanski, personal interview, August 2, 2018.

11 Solomon Golanski, oral testimony.

12 Alani Golanski, personal interview.

13 Alani Golanski, personal interview.

14 Solomon Golanski, gravestone, Wolkowysker Society Cemetery, Hartford, CT, Find a Grave, https://www.findagrave.com/memorial/185734209.

15 *Etta Golanski, US Social Security Death Index, 1935–2014, Ancestry.com*, https://www.ancestry.com/discoveryui-content/view/78351200:3693.

16 Alani Golanski, personal interview.

17 Solomon Golanski, oral testimony.

Chanan (Chonie) Kushner (#76)

1 Chanan Kushner, Page of Testimony submitted by Naum Kushner, June 25, 1979, Central Database of Shoah Victims' Names, Yad Vashem.

2 Nachum Kushner, Yad Vashem testimony [in Yiddish], no. 03/3929.

3 Kushner, Yad Vashem testimony.

4 Kushner, Yad Vashem testimony.

5 Bauer, "Nowogródek," 14.

6 Kushner, Yad Vashem testimony.

7 Kushner, Yad Vashem testimony.

8 Rae Kushner, "The Agony of Death: The Miracle of Survival," oral history, 1996, videotape transcript, Holocaust Center at Kean College of New Jersey, Union, NJ.

9   Leibovitz, "The Great Destruction," 510.
10 Susan Bach, personal interviews, August 30–31, 2020.
11 Dov Cohen, in Kagan and Cohen, *Surviving the Holocaust*, 51.
12 Leibovitz, "The Great Destruction," 511.
13 Kushner, Yad Vashem testimony.
14 Kushner, "The Agony of Death."
15 Kushner, Yad Vashem testimony.
16 Leibovitz, "The Great Destruction," 511.
17 Shaul Gorodynski, Yad Vashem testimony, no. 3095/230.
18 Gorodynski, Yad Vashem testimony.

Shaul (#77) and Sonya (#78) Gorodynski; Aaron (#79) and Yakov (Yankel, #80) Oshman

1   Lyons, "Great Escape."
2   Sonja Oshman, Certificate of Residence #414896, March 21, 1960, International Tracing Service, Yad Vashem.
3   Abraham Gorodynski, Page of Testimony submitted by Sonya Oshman, August 20, 1991, Central Database of Shoah Victims' Names, Yad Vashem.
4   Shaul Gorodynski, Yad Vashem testimony, no. 3095/230; Sonya Gorodynski Oshman, oral history, 1993, videotape transcript, Holocaust Center at Kean College of New Jersey.
5   Sonya Gorodynski Oshman, oral history.
6   Gorodynski Oshman, oral history.
7   Gorodynski Oshman, oral history.
8   Gorodynski Oshman, oral history.
9   Gorodynski Oshman, oral history.
10 Gorodynski, Yad Vashem testimony.
11 Tamara Gorodynski, Page of Testimony submitted by Shaul (mistakenly recorded as Shmuel) Gorodynski, February 28, 1957, Central Database of Holocaust Survivors' Testimonies, Yad Vashem.
12 Fanya Gorodynski, Page of Testimony submitted by Shaul (mistakenly recorded as Shmuel) Gorodynski, February 28, 1957, Central Database of Holocaust Survivors' Testimonies, Yad Vashem.
13 Gorodynski Oshman, oral history.
14 Abram Gorodynski, Page of Testimony submitted by Shaul Gorodynski, February 28, 1957, Central Database of Holocaust Survivors' Testimonies, Yad Vashem.
15 Aaron Oshman, oral testimony, USC Shoah Foundation Institute, September 10, 1995.

16 Aron Oshman, Application to the International Red Cross, February 10, 1959, International Tracing Service, Yad Vashem.

17 Lyons, "Great Escape."

18 Aaron Oshman, oral testimony.

19 Matus Oshman, Page of Testimony submitted by Aaron Oshman, August 22, 1991, Central Database of Shoah Victims' Names, Yad Vashem.

20 Tema Oshman, Page of Testimony submitted by Aaron Oshman, August 22, 1991, Central Database of Shoah Victims' Names, Yad Vashem.

21 Rubin Oshman, Page of Testimony submitted by Aaron Oshman, August 22, 1991, Central Database of Shoah Victims' Names, Yad Vashem.

22 Oshman, oral testimony.

23 Oshman, oral testimony.

24 Kagan, "Surviving the Holocaust," 569; Leibowitz, "The Heroic Death of Berl Yoselevitz," 515; Duffy, *The Bielski Brothers*, 198.

25 Yaffe, *In the Novogrudok Ghetto*, 166–67.

26 Daniel Ostashinski, Yad Vashem testimony, no. 03/6841.

27 Gorodynski, Yad Vashem testimony.

28 Oshman, oral testimony.

29 Gorodynski Oshman, oral testimony.

30 Gorodynski, Yad Vashem testimony.

31 Gorodynski Oshman, oral testimony.

32 Oshman, oral testimony.

33 Oshman, oral testimony.

34 Gorodynski, Yad Vashem testimony.

35 Ted Oshman, personal interview, October 6, 2019.

36 Gorodynski, Yad Vashem testimony.

37 Tzvi Ben Tzur, "The La Spezia Affair – 1946," Aliya Bet Stories, Palyam.org, http://palyam.org/English/Hahapala/Teur_haflagot/hy_LSA.pdf.

38 Ilana Epstein, "Let My People Go!" *The Jerusalem Post*, April 17, 2008, https://www.jpost.com/Local-Israel/In-Jerusalem/Let-my-people-go.

39 Gorodynski, Yad Vashem testimony.

40 Azrikam Ganot, personal interview, November 4, 2019.

41 Azrikam Ganot, personal communication, August 24, 2023.

42 Ted Oshman, personal interview.

43 Aron Oshman, Application to the International Red Cross.

44 "USS/USNS *General A.W. Greely* (AP-141, Later T-AP-141), 1945–1968," Naval History and Heritage Command, February 12, 2007, https://www.ibiblio.org/hyperwar/OnlineLibrary/photos/sh-usn/usnsh-g/ap141.htm.

45 Ted Oshman, personal interview.

46 Oshman, personal interview.

47 Oshman, personal interview.
48 Oshman, personal interview.
49 Ted Oshman, personal communication, August 21, 2023.
50 Oshman, personal interview.
51 Gorodynski Oshman, personal communication, August 28, 2007.
52 Azrikam Ganot, personal interview, November 17, 2019.
53 Ester Oshman, JewishGen Online World Burial Registry – Israel Burial Record, Ancestry.com, https://www.ancestry.com/discoveryui-content/view/78351200:3693.
54 Yaakov Oshman, JewishGen Online World Burial Registry – Israel Burial Record, Ancestry.com, https://www.ancestry.com/discoveryui-content/view/78351200:1411.
55 Azrikam Ganot, personal communication, August 2, 2023.

Yisrael (#81) and Shmuel (#82) Kolachek

1 Gerasimova et al., *We Stood Shoulder to Shoulder*, 246.
2 Shmuel Spector, *Encyclopedia of Jewish Life before and during the Holocaust*, vol. 1 (New York and Jerusalem: New York University Press and Yad Vashem, 2001), 533.
3 Yisrael Kolachek, personal interview [in Yiddish], December 6, 2016.
4 Kolachek, personal interview.
5 Shaul Gorodynski, Yad Vashem testimony, no. 3095/230.
6 Berkovitz, "A Sea of Troubles," 421.
7 Kolachek, personal interview.
8 Berkovitz, "A Sea of Troubles," 421.
9 Berkovitz, "A Sea of Troubles," 421.
10 Berkovitz, "A Sea of Troubles," 422.
11 Kolachek, personal interview.
12 Tec, *Defiance*, 42–43.
13 Kolachek, personal interview.
14 Bielski and Bielski, *Yehudei Yaar*, 213–14.
15 Kolachek, personal interview.
16 Zvi Mor, personal interview, January 14, 2021.
17 Mor, personal interview.
18 Shwartz, *Tunnel of Hope*.

Akiva Schmulewitz (#83)

1 Kiwa Szmulewicz, Comité International de la Croix-Rouge, URO München, uns.Zch.L46214, April 2, 1964, International Tracing Service, Yad Vashem.

2   Kiwa Szmulewicz, Inquiry to Bavarian State Compensation Office, Az: EG 100812-7-ti, August 28, 1964, International Tracing Service, Yad Vashem.

3   Szmulewicz, Inquiry.

4   Kiva Shmuylovich, List of Partisans from Belorussia, Central Database of Shoah Victims' Names, Yad Vashem.

5   "Natural History and Wildlife," Belarus.by, http://www.belarus.by/en/about -belarus/natural-history, accessed May 6, 2017.

6   Hannah Pisarchuk, "National Traditions: Picking Wild Up Mushrooms and Berries," HiFiveBelarus!, November 10, 2017, http://hifivebelarus.com/blog -vlog/national-traditions-picking-up-mushrooms-and-berries/, accessed on January 26, 2022.

7   Gerasimova et al., *We Stood Shoulder to Shoulder*, 308.

8   Kiwa Szmulewicz, Inquiry to Bavarian State Compensation Office.

9   Szmulewicz, Inquiry.

10   Kiwa Szmulewicz, Certificate of Residence form #127543, February 17, 1955, International Tracing Service, Yad Vashem, Jerusalem; List of Partisans, Central Database of Shoah Victims' Names, Yad Vashem.

11   United States Holocaust Memorial Museum, "Foehrenwald DP Camp," Holocaust Encyclopedia, https://encyclopedia.ushmm.org/content/en/article /foehrenwald-displaced-persons-camp, accessed on December 26, 2018.

12   Kiwa Szmulewicz, Inquiry to Bavarian State Compensation Office.

13   Szmulewicz, Inquiry.

14   Kiwa Szmulewicz, Certificate of Residence.

15   "General C.H. Muir," Naval History and Heritage Command, July 10, 2015, https://www.history.navy.mil/research/histories/ship-histories/danfs/g/general -c-h-muir-ap-142.html, accessed December 12, 2018.

16   Kiwa Szmulewicz, New York, US, Arriving Passenger and Crew Lists (including Castle Garden and Ellis Island), 1820–1957, Ancestry.com, https://www .ancestry.com/discoveryui-content/view/3026761954:7488.

17   Szmulewicz, New York, US, Arriving Passenger and Crew Lists.

18   "Fields Preserved," *David Library of the American Revolution News* 15, no. 1 (Winter/Spring 2014): 2, http://www.dlar.org/pdf/dlar2014-jan-news-web.pdf.

19   Kiwa Szmulewicz, Comité International.

20   Czarna Schmulewitz, obituary, *The Times*, Trenton, New Jersey, Saturday, January 13, 2001.

21   Kiwa Schmulewitz, 1985 (January through March) Trenton Obituary Index, Trenton Historical Society, http://www.trentonhistory.org/Obit/Index1985-Jan -Mar.html.

22   Czarna Schmulewitz, obituary.

23 Pauline Schmulewitz, Trenton Central High School Yearbook 1966, Trenton, NJ, p. 149, https://www.myheritage.com/research/record-10568-131681178/trenton-central-high-school?s=226200151#fullscreen.

24 Peshie Schmulewitz Malinowski, personal interview, September 10, 2020.

25 Schmulewitz Malinowski, personal interview.

26 Schmulewitz Malinowski, personal interview.

Natan (Nota) Yankelevich (#84)

1 Natan Jankielewicz, Background Questionnaire Note, International Red Cross International Tracing Service, May 5, 1968, Yad Vashem.

2 David Jankelewicz, Page of Testimony submitted by Natan Iankelevitz, September 11, 1956, Central Database of Shoah Victims' Names, Yad Vashem.

3 David Yankelevich, 1941 List of the Religious Leaders from Lyubcha, Central Database of Shoah Victims' Names, Yad Vashem.

4 Yakow Jankelewicz, Page of Testimony submitted by Natan Iankelevitz, September 11, 1956, Central Database of Shoah Victims' Names, Yad Vashem.

5 Perla Jankelewicz, Page of Testimony submitted by Natan Iankelevitz, September 11, 1956, Central Database of Shoah Victims' Names, Yad Vashem.

6 Joel Jankelewicz, Page of Testimony submitted by Natan Iankelevitz, September 11, 1956, Central Database of Shoah Victims' Names, Yad Vashem.

7 David Jankelewicz, Page of Testimony.

8 Perla Jankelewicz, Page of Testimony; Joel Jankelewicz, Page of Testimony.

9 Yakow Jankelewicz, Page of Testimony.

10 Jente Jankelevicz, Page of Testimony submitted by Pnina Elkenbaum, undated, Central Database of Shoah Victims' Names, Yad Vashem.

11 David Jankelewicz, Page of Testimony.

12 Jente Leje Jankelewicz, Page of Testimony submitted by Natan Iankelevitz, September 11, 1956, Central Database of Shoah Victims' Names, Yad Vashem.

13 Gerasimova et al., *We Stood Shoulder to Shoulder*, 315.

14 Natan Jankielewicz, Note, International Red Cross International Tracing Service document.

15 Natan Yankelevich, gravestone, Holon Cemetery in Bat Yam, Tel Aviv, BillionGraves, March 10, 2015, https://billiongraves.com/grave/נתן-ינקלביץ/13026993.

16 Tsipora Erez, personal interviews, July 8–9, 2018.

17 Natan Yankelevich, gravestone.

18 Genia Yankelevich, gravestone, Holon Cemetery in Bat Yam, Tel Aviv, BillionGraves, March 10, 2015, https://billiongraves.com/grave/גניה-ינקלביץ/13026994.

Betzalel (Salek) Ofsejewicz (#85)

1   Tzalya Ovseevich, List of Partisans from the Kalinin Detachment under the Command of Bielski, Active in Belorussia, 1944, Central Database of Shoah Victims' Names, Yad Vashem.

2   Yosef Ofsejewicz, Page of Testimony submitted by Sol Savitt, August 26, 1992, Central Database of Shoah Victims' Names, Yad Vashem.

3   Lea Ofsejewicz, Page of Testimony submitted by Sol Savitt, undated, Central Database of Shoah Victims' Names, Yad Vashem.

4   Hanach Ofsejewicz, Page of Testimony submitted by Sol Savitt, February 9, 1992, Central Database of Shoah Victims' Names, Yad Vashem.

5   Jonathan Ofsejewicz, Page of Testimony submitted by Sol Savitt, February 9, 1992, Central Database of Shoah Victims' Names, Yad Vashem.

6   David Ofsejewicz, Page of Testimony submitted by Sol Savitt, February 9, 1992, Central Database of Shoah Victims' Names, Yad Vashem.

7   Sol Savitt/Salek Ofsejewicz, Bavarian Land Compensation Office record, February 18, 1960, International Tracing Service, Yad Vashem.

8   Tzalya Ovseevich, List of Partisans from the Kalinin Detachment under the Command of Bielski.

9   Joseph Steven Savitt, personal interview, May 27, 2018.

10 Savitt, personal interview.

11 Sol Salek Savitt, TD #771645, information card dated October 11, 1960, International Tracing Service, Yad Vashem.

12 Gerasimova et al., *We Stood Shoulder to Shoulder*, 269.

13 Joseph Steven Savitt, personal interview, May 27, 2018.

14 Savitt, personal interview.

15 Sol Savitt/Salek Ofsejewicz, Certificate of Residence, Comité International de la Croix-Rouge record, Fe. 18, 1950. International Tracing Service, Yad Vashem.

16 Savitt/ Ofsejewicz, Certificate of Residence.

17 Savitt/ Ofsejewicz, Bavarian Land Compensation Office record.

18 Sol Savitt, US Social Security Death Index (SSDI), Myheritage.com, https://www.myheritage.com/research/record-10002-7215043/sol-savitt-in-us-social-security-death-index-ssdi. Original data: Social Security Administration, Social Security Death Index, Master File.

19 Klara Savitt, "US Social Security Death Index (SSDI)," Myheritage.com, https://www.myheritage.com/research/record-10002-9350975/klara-savitt-in-us-social-security-death-index-ssdi. Original data: Social Security Administration, Social Security Death Index, Master File.

Gutel Shapiro (#86)

1. Gutel Chapiro, Request for Restitution, 1955, International Tracing Service, Yad Vashem, Jerusalem; Gutel Chapiro, List of Partisans, Central Database of Shoah Victims' Names, Yad Vashem.
2. Chapiro, Request for Restitution.
3. Gutel Shapiro, List of Partisans from Belorussia, Central Database of Shoah Victims' Names, Yad Vashem.
4. Gutel Chapiro, Request for Restitution.
5. Gerasimova et al., *We Stood Shoulder to Shoulder*, 304.
6. Tamara Vershitskaya, personal communication, January 2012.
7. Gutel Szapiro, Alphabetical Directory of Polish Jews, Central Committee of Jews in Poland, Warsaw, January 1947, International Tracing Service, Yad Vashem.
8. Shikun Vatikim Cemetery archives, Netanya, Israel.
9. Gutel Chapiro, Request for Restitution, 1955, International Tracing Service, Yad Vashem, Jerusalem; Gutel Chapiro, List of Partisans, Central Database of Shoah Victims' Names, Yad Vashem.
10. Israel Ministry of the Interior, *Itur Ma'an*, Tuvia Shapiro, July 21, 2021.
11. Shikum Vatikim Cemetery archives.
12. Israel Ministry of the Interior, *Itur Ma'an*, Meir Shapiro, July 28, 2021.

Shlomo Gorodynski (#87)

1. Mowsza Gorodinski. Page of Testimony submitted by Shlomo Gorodynski, July 11, 1956, Central Database of Shoah Victims' Names, Yad Vashem.
2. Schloma Gorodinski, Application for Reparations, TD#521962, July 16, 1956, International Tracing Service, Yad Vashem.
3. Shlomo Gorodinski, Land Compensation Office document, February 6, 1957, International Tracing Service, Yad Vashem.
4. Mirjam Gorodinski, Page of Testimony submitted by Shlomo Gorodynski, October 11, 1956, Central Database of Shoah Victims' Names, Yad Vashem.
5. Yitzchak Gorodinski, Page of Testimony submitted by Shlomo Gorodynski, October 11, 1956, Central Database of Shoah Victims' Names, Yad Vashem.
6. Avraham Gorodinski, Page of Testimony submitted by Shlomo Gorodynski, October 11, 1956, Central Database of Shoah Victims' Names, Yad Vashem.
7. Rakhel Gorodinski, Page of Testimony submitted by Shlomo Gorodynski, October 11, 1956, Central Database of Shoah Victims' Names, Yad Vashem.
8. Shaul Gorodinski, Page of Testimony submitted by Shlomo Gorodynski, October 11, 1956, Central Database of Shoah Victims' Names, Yad Vashem.
9. Schloma Gorodinski, Application for Reparations.

10 Henry Cohen, "The Anguish of the Holocaust Survivors – Camp Foehrenwald," Remember.org, April 13, 1996, https://remember.org/witness/cohen.

11 Tzila Gorodinsky, Tel Aviv Hevra Kadisha, http://www.kadisha.biz/ShowItem .aspx?levelId=59689&template=18&ID=301305.

12 Bilha Gorodinski, personal interview, December 27, 2019.

13 "Rafałówka: Historical Background during the Holocaust," Yad Vashem, https:// www.yadvashem.org/righteous/stories/rafalowka-historical-background.html.

14 Bilha Gorodinski, personal interview.

15 Shulamit Rosenthaler, Tracing Services at Magen David Adom Israel, December 27, 2019.

16 Bilha Gorodinski, personal interview.

17 Mirjam Gorodinski, Page of Testimony.

18 Gerasimova et al., *We Stood Shoulder to Shoulder*, 223.

19 Bilha Gorodinski, personal interview.

20 Shlomo Gorodinski, gravestone, Holon Cemetery in Bat Yam, Tel Aviv, BillionGraves, March 5, 2015, https://billiongraves.com/grave /12954226/שלמה-גורודינסקי.

Shmuel Niselevich (#88)

1 Dmitry and Ludmila Karpukhin, personal interviews, May 29, 2022.

2 Samuil Niselevich, List of Partisans from the Leninskaya Brigade, Active in the Baranowicz District, Central Database of Shoah Victims' Names, Yad Vashem.

3 Rakhelya and Leya Niselevich, List of Murdered People from Zdzieciol, Central Database of Shoah Victims' Names, Yad Vashem.

4 Ludmila Karpukhin, personal interview, May 29, 2022.

5 Karpukhin, personal interview.

6 Gerasimova et al., *We Stood Shoulder to Shoulder*, 268.

7 Ludmila Karpukhin, personal interview.

8 Karpukhin, personal interview.

9 Dmitry Karpukhin, personal interview.

Shlomo (#89) and Efraim (#90) Okonski

1 Yanek Okonski, personal interview, August 5, 2019.

2 Efraim Okonsky, gravestone, El Camino Memorial Park, San Diego, CA, Find a Grave, March 14, 2015, https://www.findagrave.com/memorial/143736860 /efraim-okonsky.

3 Yanek Okonski, personal interview.

4 Okonski, personal interview.

5 Yanek Okonski, personal interview, September 24, 2020.

6   Gerasimova et al., *We Stood Shoulder to Shoulder*, 269.
7   Yanek Okonski, personal interview, August 5, 2019.
8   Okonski, personal interview.
9   Okonski Efraim, registration card TD #571340, International Tracing Service, Yad Vashem.
10 Yanek Okonski, personal interview, August 5, 2019.
11 Nili Shechter, personal interview, August 11, 2019; Danny Okonski, personal interview, August 15, 2019.
12 Danny Okonski, personal interview.
13 Shechter, personal interview; Danny Okonski, personal interview.
14 Danny Okonski, personal interview.
15 Yanek Okonski, personal interview, August 5, 2019.
16 Yanek Okonski, personal interview.
17 Yanek Okonski, personal interview.
18 Danny Okonski, personal interview.
19 Shechter, personal interview.
20 Yanek Okonski, personal interview, August 5, 2019.
21 Yanek Okonski, personal interview, August 23, 2023.
22 Efraim Okonsky, gravestone.
23 Yanek Okonski, personal interview, August 5, 2019.

Chaim Noah Leibowitz (#91)

1   Khaim Kushner, List of Partisans from Belorussia, Central Database of Shoah Victims' Names, Yad Vashem.
2   Leibovich, "Shokdey Melocho," 194.
3   Chaim Leibowicz, ADJC Paris List 5, p. 61, Book I, International Tracing Service, Yad Vashem.
4   Murray Kushner, personal communication, May 17, 2018.
5   Rae Kushner, "The Agony of Death: The Miracle of Survival," oral history, 1996, videotape transcript, Holocaust Center at Kean College of New Jersey, Union, NJ.
6   Frume Gulkovitz-Berger, "The Ghetto in Peresike," in *Novogrudok Memorial Book*, 523.
7   Kushner, "The Agony of Death."
8   Naomi Baumslag, *Murderous Medicine: Nazi Doctors, Human Experimentation, and Typhus* (Westport, CT and London: Praeger, 2005), 117.
9   Kushner, "The Agony of Death."
10 Nachum Kushner, Yad Vashem testimony [in Yiddish], no. 03/3929.
11 Leibovitz, "The Great Destruction," 502.

12   Kushner, "The Agony of Death."

13   Leibovitz, "The Great Destruction," 503.

14   Shaul Gorodynski, Yad Vashem testimony, no. 3095/230.

15   Leibovitz, "The Great Destruction," 504.

16   Eliyahu Berkowicz, Yad Vashem testimony [in Yiddish], no. 03/2774.

17   Leibovitz, "The Great Destruction," 505–6.

18   Gerasimova et al., *We Stood Shoulder to Shoulder*, 252.

19   Bielski and Bielski, *Yehudei Yaar*, 213.

20   Fanya Dunetz Brodsky, personal interview, June 14, 2018.

21   Kushner, "The Agony of Death."

22   Epstein, *The Miracle of Life*, 91.

23   Epstein, 92.

24   Murray Kushner, personal interview, August 12, 2018.

25   Murray Kushner, personal communication, September 30, 2018.

26   Chaim Leibovitz, "Three Kol Niddreis" [in Yiddish], in *Pinkas Navaredok*, 201, trans. O. Delatycki, https://www.jewishgen.org/yizkor/Novogrudok/nov195.html #Page201.

27   Chaim Leibovitz, "The Last Passover" [in Yiddish], in *Pinkas Navaredok*, 293, trans. O. Delatycki, https://www.jewishgen.org/yizkor/Novogrudok/nov287.html #Page293.

28   Leibovitz, "The Great Destruction," 287; Chaim Leibovitz, "Escape through the Tunnel," in *Novogrudok Memorial Book*, 512–14.

29   Esther Schulder, personal interview, September 13, 2018.

30   Murray Kushner, personal interview, August 12, 2018.

31   Leibovitz, "Three Kol Nidreis," 201.

32   Chaim Lebowitz, New Jersey Death Index, 1920–1929, 1949–2017, Myheritage. com, https://www.myheritage.com/research/record-10747-1480963-/chaim -lebowitz-in-new-jersey-death-index.

33   Murray Kushner, personal interview, September 30, 2018.

Yanson (#94)

1   Frieda Janson, Lodz Names – List of the Ghetto Inhabitants 1940–1944, Central Database of Shoah Victims' Names, Yad Vashem.

2   Wolf Yanson, List of Partisans from the Pobeda Detachment of the Lenin Brigade, Central Database of Shoah Victims' Names, Yad Vashem.

3   Leah Johnson, personal interview, June 27, 2018.

4   Gerasimova et al., *We Stood Shoulder to Shoulder*, 315, 333.

Idel Kagan (#95)

1   Kagan and Cohen, *Surviving the Holocaust*, 236.
2   Michael Kagan, personal interview, May 21, 2021.
3   Kagan and Cohen, *Surviving the Holocaust*, 119.
4   Kagan and Cohen, 132.
5   Kagan and Cohen, 16.
6   Kagan, personal interview, May 21, 2021.
7   Kagan, personal interview.
8   Kagan and Cohen, *Surviving the Holocaust*, 136–37.
9   Kagan and Cohen, 138.
10 Kagan and Cohen, 139–40.
11 Kagan and Cohen, 141.
12 Kagan and Cohen, 150–51.
13 Kagan and Cohen, 162.
14 Kagan and Cohen, 160–61.
15 Kagan and Cohen, 162.
16 Kagan and Cohen, 166–70.
17 Idel Kagan, "How I Survived," in *Novogrudok Memorial Book*, 517.
18 Martin Pailthrope, director, *Extreme Survival* (Bristol: BBC/Travel Channel, 2001).
19 Shwartz, *Tunnel of Hope*.
20 Michael Kagan, personal interview, July 20, 2020.
21 Kagan and Cohen, *Surviving the Holocaust*, 172.
22 Kagan and Cohen, 176–82.
23 Kagan and Cohen, 183–85.
24 Kagan and Cohen, 237–39.
25 Kagan, personal interview, July 20, 2020.
26 Dov Sadan, personal interview, August 24, 2020.
27 Kagan, personal interview, July 20, 2020.
28 Kagan, personal interview.
29 Shwartz, *Tunnel of Hope*.
30 Pailthrope, *Extreme Survival*.
31 Kagan, personal interview, July 20, 2020.
32 Kagan and Cohen, *Surviving the Holocaust*, 246–54.
33 Kagan, personal interview, July 20, 2020.
34 "Prime Minister Launches Holocaust Commission," Gov.UK, January 27, 2014, https ://www.gov.uk/government/news/prime-minister-launches-holocaust -commission, accessed September 20, 2020.
35 Robert Hersowitz, "The Passing of a Courageous Survivor," *Jerusalem Post*, January 19, 2017, https://www.jpost.com/opinion/a-personal-tribute-478926.

36 Kagan, personal interview, July 20, 2020.
37 "British Empire Medal (BEM)," Forces War Records, https://www.forces-war-records.co.uk/medals/british-empire-medal.
38 Kagan, personal interview, July 20, 2020.
39 Debbie Kagan, personal communication, August 22, 2013.
40 Kagan, personal interview, July 20, 2020.

Yakov Yoselevich (#96)

1 Gerasimova et al., *We Stood Shoulder to Shoulder*, 237.
2 Boris Yoselevich, personal communication, December 7, 2019.
3 Boris Yoselevich, personal interview, October 9, 2018.
4 Tec, *Defiance*, 43.
5 Boris Yoselevich, personal communication.
6 Boris Yoselevich, personal interview.
7 Boris Yoselevich, personal communication.
8 Yoselevich, personal communication.

Moshe Bruk (#97)

1 Mosze Bruk, Certificate of Residence, Allied High Commission for Germany, September 19, 1952, International Tracing Service, Yad Vashem.
2 Shlomo Bruk, Page of Testimony submitted by Moshe Bruk, February 22, 1957, Database of Shoah Victims' Names, Yad Vashem.
3 Shlomo Bruk, personal interview, November 18, 2018.
4 Bruk, personal interview.
5 Shlomo Bruk, Page of Testimony.
6 Shlomo Bruk, personal interview, November 3, 2018.
7 Mosze Bruk, Certificate of Residence.
8 United States Holocaust Memorial Museum, "Landsberg Displaced Persons Camp," Holocaust Encyclopedia, https://encyclopedia.ushmm.org/content/en/article/landsberg-displaced-persons-camp.
9 "February 1948, Jews in the Landsberg Displaced Persons' Camp, Germany," www.Yadvashem.org, https://www.yadvashem.org/holocaust/this-month/february/1948.html.
10 Bruk, personal interview, November 3, 2018.
11 Bruk, personal interview.
12 Bruk, personal interview.
13 Shlomo Bruck, personal interview, September 6, 2023.

Alter Gurvich (#98)

1   Alter Gurvich, List of Jewish Partisans under the Command of Zorin, Central Database of Shoah Victims' Names, Yad Vashem.
2   Gurvich, List of Jewish Partisans.
3   Tec, *Defiance*, 194.
4   Michael Gurevich, Geni family tree, Geni.com, https://www.geni.com/people /Michael-Gurevich/6000000008546280328, accessed on January 31, 2022.
5   Gurevich, Geni family tree.
6   Gurevich, Geni family tree.
7   Alter and Matlya Gurvich, gravestones, Or Akiva Cemetery, Hadera, Israel, BillionGraves, https://billiongraves.com/grave/20333428/אלטר-גורביץ.
8   Michael Gurevich, "Geni Family Tree."
9   Alter and Matlya Gurvich, gravestones.

Mordechai Kaplinski (#99)

1   Mordukh Kaplinski, Page of Testimony submitted by Ela Tyapushkin, January 21, 1993, Central Database of Shoah Victims' Names, Yad Vashem.
2   Zalman Kaplinski, Page of Testimony submitted by Yekhiel Kaplinski, August 30, 1956, Central Database of Shoah Victims' Names, Yad Vashem.
3   Motka Kaplinski, Page of Testimony submitted by Ljuba Gordin, February 15, 1972, Page of Testimony, Central Database of Shoah Victims' Names, Yad Vashem.
4   "Martyrs Compiled According to Memory," in *Memorial Book of Sokolka*, trans. Ellen Sadove Renck, Ada Holtzman, and Moshe Verbi (Jerusalem: Encyclopedia of the Jewish Diaspora, 1968), 751, https://www.jewishgen.org/Yizkor/sokolka /Sok751.html#K.
5   Gerasimova et al., *We Stood Shoulder to Shoulder*, 241, 322.

Kalman Shelkovich (#100)

1   Kalman Shelkovich, List of Partisans from Belorussia, Central Database of Shoah Victims' Names, Yad Vashem.
2   Steinberg-Sarig, "Hebrew Education in Novogrudok," 142.
3   Shavel Shelkovich, List of Murdered Individuals from Zhetl, Central Database of Shoah Victims' Names, Yad Vashem.
4   Gol-Beigin, "The Communal Life in Zhetl," 171.
5   Shavel Shelkovich, List of Murdered Individuals from Zhetl.
6   Pesia Mayevski (Nadel), "Hunger" [in Yiddish], in *Pinkas Zhetl*, ed. B. Kaplinski, 320–24.
7   Gerasimova et al., *We Stood Shoulder to Shoulder*, 305.

8 Kalman Szulhovicz, Ellis Island and Other New York Passenger Lists, 1820–1957, Myheritage.com, https://www.myheritage.com/research/record -10512-27022259/kalman-szulhovicz-in-ellis-island-other-new-york-passen-ger-lists.

9 Kalman Salkin, US Social Security Death Index (SSDI), Myheritage.com, https://www.myheritage.com/research/record-10002-15818072/kalman -salkin-in-us-social-security-death-index-ssdi.

10 Luba Salkin, US Public Records Index, 1950–1993, vol. 2, Myheritage.com, https://www.ancestry.com/discoveryui-content/view/233608580:1732.

11 Renee Salkin, LinkedIn, https://www.linkedin.com/in/renee-salkin-4a61a1145, accessed on January 31, 2022.

12 Luba Salkin, US Social Security Death Index (SSDI), Myheritage.com, https://www.myheritage.com/research/record-10002-15856470/luba -salkin-in-us-social-security-death-index-ssdi.

13 Kalman Salkin, U.S. Social Security Death Index.

Mordechai (#102) and Yitzchak (#103) Zacharevich

1 Mordukh Zakharevich, List of Partisans from the Shchors Detachment, Central Database of Shoah Victims' Names, Yad Vashem.

2 Jack Kagan, personal interview, May 5, 2013.

3 Yitzkhak Zacharevits, in *Novogrudok Memorial Book*, 718.

4 Gerasimova et al., *We Stood Shoulder to Shoulder,* 234.

5 Jack Kagan, personal interview, May 28, 2013.

Chaim Bekenshtein (#106)

1 Chaim Bekenstain, Page of Testimony submitted by Shlomo Razvazhski, April 28, 1957, Central Database of Shoah Victims' Names, Yad Vashem.

2 Chasche Bekenstain, Page of Testimony submitted by Shlomo Razvazhski, April 28, 1957, Central Database of Shoah Victims' Names, Yad Vashem.

3 Khasya Bekenshteyn, List of Murdered Individuals from Zhetl, Central Database of Shoah Victims' Names, Yad Vashem.

4 Leya Bekenshteyn, List of Murdered Individuals from Zhetl, Central Database of Shoah Victims' Names, Yad Vashem.

5 Sara Bekenshteyn, List of Murdered Individuals from Zhetl, Central Database of Shoah Victims' Names, Yad Vashem.

6 Chasche Bekenstain, Page of Testimony.

7 Kaplinski, *Pinkas Zhetl*, 21.

Malka Lewin (#107)

1 Malka Levin, List of Partisans from the Kalinin Detachment under the Command of Bielski, Central Database of Shoah Victims' Names, Yad Vashem; Lewin, Malke, AJDC File F-18-253 card, 25.4.1950, International Tracing Service, Yad Vashem; Malka Lewin, AJDC Paris listing, File F18-57, 4.3.49, International Tracing Service, Yad Vashem; Malka Lewin, Bavarian State Compensation Office application, January 11, 1956, International Tracing Service, Yad Vashem; Malka Lewin, Alphabetisches Verzeichnis Polnischer Juden, Jewish Central Committee, Poland, Warsaw 1947, International Tracing Service, Yad Vashem.

2 Malka Lewin, Bavarian State Compensation.

3 Lewin, Bavarian State Compensation.

4 Malka Levin, List of Partisans.

5 *Novogrudok Memorial Book*, 703.

6 Malka Levin, List of Partisans.

7 Malka Lewin, Bavarian State Compensation.

8 Malka Lewin, Alphabetisches Verzeichnis.

9 Malka Lewin, AJDC Paris listing.

10 Malke Lewin, AJDC File F-18-253.

11 Malka Lewin, Bavarian State Compensation.

12 Eileen Fridman, personal interview, November 6, 2018; Solly Kaplinski, personal interview, November 12, 2018.

David Tzimerman (#108)

1 Yerushalmi et al., *Pinkas Navaredok*, 387.

Yosef (Yosel) Mirski (#109)

1 Yosef Mirski, Page of Testimony submitted by Moshe Iting, May 30, 1957, Central Database of Shoah Victims' Names, Yad Vashem.

2 Pinchas Mirski, Page of Testimony submitted by Moshe Iting, May 30, 1957, Central Database of Shoah Victims' Names, Yad Vashem.

3 Beile Mirski, Page of Testimony submitted by Moshe Iting, May 30, 1957, Central Database of Shoah Victims' Names, Yad Vashem.

4 Eliezer Mirski, Page of Testimony submitted by Moshe Iting, May 30, 1957, Central Database of Shoah Victims' Names, Yad Vashem.

5 Yakov Mirski, Page of Testimony submitted by Moshe Iting.

6 Batia Mirski, Page of Testimony submitted by Moshe Iting, May 30, 1957, Central Database of Shoah Victims' Names, Yad Vashem.

7 Fanya Dunetz Brodsky, personal interview, November 30, 2017.

8   Brodsky, personal interview.

9   Kagan, "How I Survived," 519.

10 Yosef Mirski, Page of Testimony submitted by Moshe Iting.

11 Kaplinkski, *Pinkas Zhetl*, 24.

Sholom Ginden (#110)

1   Sam Ginden, US Social Security Death Index, 1935–2014, Myheritage.com, https://www.ancestry.com/discoveryui-content/view/79020293:3693.

2   Sholim Ginden, List of Jewish Partisans Active in the Baranowicze Region, Central Database of Shoah Victims' Names, Yad Vashem.

3   Shmuel Ginden, List of Residents from Novogrudok 1941, Central Database of Shoah Victims' Names, Yad Vashem.

4   Ginden, List of Residents.

5   Sholim Ginden, List of Jewish Partisans.

6   Rabbi Shaya Kilimnick, personal interview, April 5, 2018.

7   Scholim Ginden, A.E.F.D.P. registration record [in German], October 2, 1946, Arolsen Archives, https://collections.arolsen-archives.org/en/document/67163502.

8   Scholim Ginden, A.J.D.C. Emigration Service Munich Record, February 6, 1951, Joint Distribution Committee Archives, http://search.archives.jdc.org/multimedia%2FDocuments%2FVMB_cardindex%2F31157_176214%2F31157_176214-00998.jpg.

9   United States Holocaust Memorial Museum, "Babenhausen Displaced Persons Camp," Holocaust Encyclopedia, https://encyclopedia.ushmm.org/content/en/article/babenhausen-displaced-persons-camp.

10 Bremen-Grohn, "Transport by USS General Blatchford, February 15, 1951" [in German], Arolsen Archives, https://collections.arolsen-archives.org/en/document/81675279.

11 Sam Ginden, New York State, Marriage Index, 1881–1967, Myheritage.com, https://www.ancestry.com/discoveryui-content/view/1413271:61632.

12 Sam Ginden, obituary, *Rochester Democrat and Chronicle*, January 22, 2007, p. 14.

13 Kilimnick, personal interview.

14 Betty Gould, personal interview, September 6, 2020.

15 Barbara Appelbaum, personal interview, September 7, 2020.

16 Sam Ginden, obituary.

17 Abe Ginden, obituary, *Democrat and Chronicle*, November 26, 2019, https://obits.democratandchronicle.com/obituaries/democratandchronicle/obituary.aspx?n=abe-gindin&pid=194565234&fhid=7324.

Simcha Wilenski (#111)

1   Rita Standig, personal interview, March 6, 2018.
2   Rita Standig, personal communication, December 27, 2019.
3   Leibovitz, "The Great Destruction," 287, https://www.jewishgen.org/yizkor/Novogrudok/nov287.html; Kagan, "Surviving the Holocaust," 569.
4   Rita Standig, personal communication.
5   Rita Standig, personal interview.
6   Gerasimova et al., *We Stood Shoulder to Shoulder*, 212.
7   Rita Standig, personal interview.
8   Rita Standig, personal communication.
9   Symcha Wilenski, Certificate of Residence, International Tracing Service, Yad Vashem.
10   "Landsberg," ORT and the DP Camps, https://dpcamps.ort.org/camps/germany/us-zone/us-zone-v/landsberg.
11   Symcha Wilenski, Certificate of Residence.
12   Rita Standig, personal interview.
13   Standig, personal interview.
14   Jack Kagan, "Novogrudok's Maccabi Swim Team 1934–1935," in *Novogrudok: The History of a Shtetl* (London: Vallentine, Mitchell, 2006), 114.
15   Shimeon Yosifun, "The Tailors' Synagogue," in *Pinkas Navaredok*, 72, https://www.jewishgen.org/yizkor/Novogrudok/nov072.html.
16   Rita Standig, personal interview.
17   Marc Standig, March 5, 2018.
18   Aaron Wilenski, inquiry record filed by Seymour Wilenski, July 23, 1999, International Tracing Service Archives, Yad Vashem.
19   Rita Standig, personal interview.
20   Standig, personal interview.
21   Rita Standig, personal communication, November 5, 2019.

Leah Berkovich (#112)

1   Central Database of Shoah Victims' Names, Yad Vashem.
2   Gerasimova et al., *We Stood Shoulder to Shoulder*, 205, 318.

Nina Levkovich (#113)

1   Jack Kagan, personal interview, July 11, 2012.
2   Gerasimova et al., *We Stood Shoulder to Shoulder*, 255.
3   Gerasimova, 255.
4   Kagan, personal interview.
5   Gerasimova et al., *We Stood Shoulder to Shoulder*.

6   Tamara Vershitskaya, personal communication, January 2012.

7   Kagan, personal interview.

Michael Novogrudski (#114)

1   Mayevski (Nadel), "In the Novardok Labor Camp," 360.

2   Mikhoel Novogrudski, Page of Testimony submitted by Yevel Novogrudski, December 2, 1983, Central Database of Shoah Victims' Names, Yad Vashem.

3   Gerasimova et al., *We Stood Shoulder to Shoulder*, 268.

4   Mikhoel Novogrudski, Page of Testimony.

5   Abraham Novogrudski, List of Murdered People from Zhetl, Central Database of Shoah Victims' Names, Yad Vashem.

6   Abraham Novogrudski, Page of Testimony submitted by Yevel Novogrudski, December 2, 1983, Central Database of Shoah Victims' Names, Yad Vashem.

7   Riva Novogrudski, Page of Testimony submitted by Yevel Novogrudski, December 2, 1983, Central Database of Shoah Victims' Names, Yad Vashem.

8   Necha Sokolowski, Page of Testimony submitted by Pesia (Mayevski) Nadel, April 24, 1957, Central Database of Shoah Victims' Names, Yad Vashem.

9   Yevel Novogrudski, US Social Security Death Index, 1935–2014, Ancestry. com, https://www.ancestry.com/discoveryui-content/view/45812802:3693.

10   Eliezer Nowogrodski, Page of Testimony submitted by Pesia (Mayevski) Nadel, April 24, 1957, Central Database of Shoah Victims' Names, Yad Vashem.

11   Scheine Nowogrodski, Page of Testimony submitted by Pesia (Mayevski) Nadel, April 24, 1957, Central Database of Shoah Victims' Names, Yad Vashem.

12   Khaia Novogrudski, Page of Testimony submitted by Yevel Novogrudski, December 2, 1983, Central Database of Shoah Victims' Names, Yad Vashem.

13   Chaja Nowogrodski, Page of Testimony submitted by Pesia (Mayevski) Nadel, April 24, 1957, Central Database of Shoah Victims' Names, Yad Vashem.

14   Iosif Novogrudski, List of Partisans from Belorussia, Central Database of Shoah Victims' Names, Yad Vashem.

15   Gawriel Nowogrodski, Page of Testimony submitted by Pesia (Mayevski) Nadel, April 24, 1957, Central Database of Shoah Victims' Names, Yad Vashem.

16   Mikhel Novogrudski, List of Partisans from Belorussia, Central Database of Shoah Victims' Names, Yad Vashem.

17   Rokhul Novogrudski, Page of Testimony submitted by Yevel Novogrudski, May 1, 1984, Central Database of Shoah Victims' Names, Yad Vashem.

18   Rakhelya Novogrudskaya, List of Murdered People from Zdzieciol (Zhetl), Central Database of Shoah Victims' Names, Yad Vashem.

19   David Novogrudski, Page of Testimony submitted by Yevel Novogrudski, May 1, 1984, Central Database of Shoah Victims' Names, Yad Vashem.

20 Leibe Novogrudski, Page of Testimony submitted by Yevel Novogrudski, May 1, 1984, Central Database of Shoah Victims' Names, Yad Vashem.

21 Gitul Novogrudskaya, Page of Testimony submitted by Yevel Novogrudski, May 1, 1984, Central Database of Shoah Victims' Names, Yad Vashem.

22 Gitul Novogrudskaya, Page of Testimony.

23 Gerasimova et al., *We Stood Shoulder to Shoulder*, 268.

24 Chaya Magid, personal interview, January 3, 2021.

25 Mikhoel Novogrudski, Page of Testimony.

26 Yevel Novogrudski, gravestone, Chesed Shel Emeth Cemetery, Pittsburgh, PA, Find a Grave, https://www.findagrave.com/memorial/206642425 /yevel-novogrudsky.

27 Reuven Novogrotzki, Chaim Novogrudski, Shayna Novogrudski, Pages of Testimony submitted by Yevel Novogrudski, December 2, 1983, Central Database of Shoah Victims' Names, Yad Vashem.

Rachmiel Leibovich (#115)

1 Rakhmiel Leybovich, List of Murdered Individuals from Zhetl, Central Database of Shoah Victims' Names, Yad Vashem.

2 Sheyna Leybovich, List of Murdered Individuals from Zhetll, Central Database of Shoah Victims' Names, Yad Vashem.

3 Ionas Leybovich, List of Murdered Individuals from Zhetl, Central Database of Shoah Victims' Names, Yad Vashem.

4 Kagan, *Surviving the Holocaust*, 569; Yad Vashem testimony; Leibovitz, "The Heroic Death of Berl Yoselevitz," 515; Duffy, *The Bielski Brothers*, 198; Yisrael Kolachek, personal interview, December 6, 2016.

5 Nachum Kushner, Yad Vashem testimony [in Yiddish], no. 03/3929.

6 Rakhmiel Leybovich, List of Murdered Individuals from Zdzieciol.

7 Gerasimova et al., *We Stood Shoulder to Shoulder*, 253, 325.

David Shklarski (#116)

1 David Shklarski, Page of Testimony submitted by David Zakroiski, May 5, 1991, Central Database of Shoah Victims' Names, Yad Vashem.

2 David Shklarski, Page of Testimony.

3 Davyd Shklyarski, List of Murdered Individuals from Zdzieciol, Central Database of Shoah Victims' Names, Yad Vashem.

4 Davyd Shklyarski, List of Persecuted Persons, Central Database of Shoah Victims' Names, Yad Vashem.

5 David Shklarski, Page of Testimony.

6   Khaia Shklarski, Page of Testimony submitted by David Zakroiski, undated, Central Database of Shoah Victims' Names, Yad Vashem.

7   Izrail Shklyarski, List of Murdered Individuals from Zhetl, Central Database of Shoah Victims' Names, Yad Vashem.

8   Khaim Skliarski, List of Murdered Individuals from Zhetl, Central Database of Shoah Victims' Names, Yad Vashem.

9   Davyd Shklyarski, List of Persecuted Persons; Khaia Shklyarskaya, List of Murdered Individuals from Zhetl, Central Database of Shoah Victims' Names, Yad Vashem; Izrail Shklyarski, List of Murdered Individuals from Zhetl; Khaim Skliarski, List of Murdered Individuals from Zhetl.

10 Abraham Zakroiski, Page of Testimony submitted by David Zakroiski, May 5, 1991, Central Database of Shoah Victims' Names, Yad Vashem.

11 Batia Zakroiski, Page of Testimony submitted by David Zakroiski, May 5, 1991, Central Database of Shoah Victims' Names, Yad Vashem.

12 Gerasimova et al., *We Stood Shoulder to Shoulder*, 307, 329.

Zalman Gertzovski (#117)

1   Zalman Gertzovski, Page of Testimony submitted by Khaia Gertzovski, undated, Central Database of Shoah Victims' Names, Yad Vashem.

2   Leizerovich, "Zhetl and the Zhetler Craftsman," 133.

3   Sara Gertzovski, Page of Testimony submitted by Khaia Gertzovski, undated, Central Database of Shoah Victims' Names, Yad Vashem.

4   Avishay Morag, personal interview, December 7, 2017.

5   Efraim Gertzovski, Page of Testimony submitted by Khaia Gertzovski, undated, Central Database of Shoah Victims' Names, Yad Vashem.

6   Efraim Gertzovski, List of Murdered Individuals from Zdzieciol, Central Database of Shoah Victims' Names, Yad Vashem.

7   Avraham Gertzovski, Page of Testimony submitted by Khaia Gertzovski, undated, Central Database of Shoah Victims' Names, Yad Vashem.

8   Zevulun Gercowski, Page of Testimony submitted by Khaia Gertzovski, undated, Central Database of Shoah Victims' Names, Yad Vashem.

9   Chaya Magid, personal interview, December 6, 2017.

10 Gerasimova et al., *We Stood Shoulder to Shoulder*, 217.

11 Tec, *Defiance*, 126–27.

12 Magid, personal interview.

13 Mayevski (Nadel), "In the Novardok Labor Camp," 361.

14 Magid, personal interview.

15 Morag, personal interview.

16 Sima Gertzovskaya, Mayrim Gertzovski, List of Murdered Individuals from Zdzieciol, Central Database of Shoah Victims' Names, Yad Vashem.

17 Magid, personal interview.

18 Morag, personal interview.

19 Morag, personal interview.

20 Magid, personal interview.

21 Morag, personal interview.

22 Morag, personal interview.

23 Morag, personal interview.

Shmuel Shimshelevich (#118)

1 Keylya Shimshelevic, List of Murdered People from Zdzieciol, Central Database of Shoah Victims' Names, Yad Vashem.

2 Szymon Szymszelewicz, Page of Testimony submitted by Pesia (Mayevski) Nadel, May 29, 1955, Central Database of Shoah Victims' Names, Yad Vashem.

3 Perla Szymszelewicz, Page of Testimony submitted by Pesia (Mayevski) Nadel, May 29, 1955, Central Database of Shoah Victims' Names, Yad Vashem.

4 Yitzchak Szymszelewicz, Page of Testimony submitted by Pesia (Mayevski) Nadel, May 29, 1955, Central Database of Shoah Victims' Names, Yad Vashem.

5 Kiejle Szymszelewicz, Page of Testimony submitted by Pesia (Mayevski) Nadel, May 29, 1955, Central Database of Shoah Victims' Names, Yad Vashem, Jerusalem; Szymon Szymszelewicz, Page of Testimony.

6 Shimon Shimshelevich, List of Murdered Individuals from Zhetl, Central Database of Shoah Victims' Names, Yad Vashem.

7 Perlya Shimshelevich, List of Murdered Individuals from Zhetl, Central Database of Shoah Victims' Names, Yad Vashem.

8 Isaak Shimshelevich, List of Murdered Individuals from Zhetl, Central Database of Shoah Victims' Names, Yad Vashem.

9 Mayevski (Nadel), "In the Novardok Labor Camp," 361.

10 *Novogrudok Memorial Book*, 715.

Isaac Lidski (#119)

1 Ayzik Litzki, List of Partisans from the Kotovskiy Detachment, Central Database of Shoah Victims' Names, Yad Vashem.

2 Nechama Lidski, Page of Testimony submitted by Pesia (Mayevski) Nadel, April 30, 1957, Central Database of Shoah Victims' Names, Yad Vashem.

3 Schloime Lidski, Page of Testimony submitted by Pesia (Mayevski) Nadel, April 30, 1957, Central Database of Shoah Victims' Names, Yad Vashem.

4 Schloime Lidski, Page of Testimony; Nechama Lidski, Page of Testimony.

5   Batia Lidski, Page of Testimony submitted by Pesia (Mayevski) Nadel, April 30, 1957, Central Database of Shoah Victims' Names, Yad Vashem.

6   Basya Lidskaya, List of Murdered Individuals from Zdzieciol, Central Database of Shoah Victims' Names, Yad Vashem.

7   Batia Lidski, Page of Testimony.

8   Gerasimova et al., *We Stood Shoulder to Shoulder*, 258.

Aaron Bitenski (#120)

1   "Nowa Mysz," in *The Yad Vashem Encyclopedia of the Ghettos during the Holocaust*, eds. G. Miron and S. Shulhani (Jerusalem: Yad Vashem, 2009).

2   Aron Bytensky, List of Jews from Nowa Mysz Who Perished 1941–1944, Prepared by the Soviet Extraordinary State Commission, Central Database of Shoah Victims' Names, Yad Vashem.

3   Aaron Bytenski, List of Murdered Jews from Nowa Mysz, Central Database of Shoah Victims' Names, Yad Vashem.

4   Gerasimova et al., *We Stood Shoulder to Shoulder*, 206, 318.

Hirsz Samsonowicz (#121)

1   Hirsch Samsonowicz, Incarceration Certificate, September 10, 1959, International Committee of the Red Cross, International Tracing Service, Yad Vashem.

2   Harry Simpson, US Social Security Death Index (SSDI), Myheritage.com, https://www.myheritage.com/research/record-10002-54977910/harry-simpson-in-us-social-security-death-index-ssdi

3   Mendel Samsonowicz, Page of Testimony submitted by Yehuda Samsonowicz, December 19, 1956, Central Database of Shoah Victims' Names, Yad Vashem.

4   Miryam Samsonowicz, Page of Testimony submitted by Yehuda Samsonowicz, December 19, 1956, Central Database of Shoah Victims' Names, Yad Vashem.

5   Mendel Samsonowicz, Page of Testimony submitted by Hershel Harry Samsonovich, March 22, 1972, Central Database of Shoah Victims' Names, Yad Vashem.

6   Girsh Samsonovich, List of Partisans from Belorussia, Central Database of Shoah Victims' Names, Yad Vashem.

7   Mendel Samsonowicz, Page of Testimony submitted by Yehuda Samsonowicz; Miryam Samsonowicz, Page of Testimony submitted by Yehuda Samsonowicz.

8   Haradzishcha, Belarus, JewishGen Communities Database, https://www.jewishgen.org/Communities/community.php?usbgn=-1943291, accessed March 18, 2019.

9   Khaim Samsonovich, Page of Testimony submitted by Hershel Harry Samsonovich, March 22, 1972, Central Database of Shoah Victims' Names, Yad Vashem.

10   Dawid Samsonovich, Page of Testimony submitted by Ieshaiahu Mendelevski, April 8, 1957, Central Database of Shoah Victims' Names, Yad Vashem.

11   Yudel Samsonowicz, American Expeditionary Force (AEF), DP registration, January 3, 1948, Arolsen Archives, https://collections.arolsen-archives.org/en/document/81675279.

12   Hodl Samsonovich, Page of Testimony submitted by Hershel Harry Samsonovich, March 19, 1972, Central Database of Shoah Victims' Names, Yad Vashem; Memorial notice for the Samsonowicz family submitted by Harry Simpson, in *Pinkas Navaredok*, ed. Yerushalmi et al., 419.

13   Hirsch Samsonowicz, International Committee of the Red Cross, Munich document, September 6, 1959, International Tracing Service, Yad Vashem.

14   Gerasimova et al., *We Stood Shoulder to Shoulder*, 284.

15   Bavarian Compensation Office document, Simpson (Samson) Harry, April 20, 1965, International Tracing Service, Yad Vashem.

16   "Landsberg," ORT and the Displaced Persons Camps, http://dpcamps.ort.org/camps/germany/us-zone/us-zone-v/landsberg/.

17   "Hirsch Samsonowicz," International Committee of the Red Cross.

18   Memorial Project 2018, "DP Hospital Sankt Ottilien 1945–1948," http://dphospital-ottilien.org/project/.

19   Chaja Samsonowicz, New York, US, Arriving Passenger and Crew Lists (including Castle Garden and Ellis Island), 1820–1957, Ancestry.com, https://www.ancestry.com/discoveryui-content/view/3026577619:7488.

20   Harry Simpson, US Naturalization Records Indexes, 1794–1995,"Ancestry.com, https://www.ancestry.com/discoveryui-content/view/52155:1192.

21   Harry Simpson, US Public Records Index, Myheritage.com,. https://www.myheritage.com/research/record-10220-63535602/harry-simpson-in-us-public-records-index.

22   Harry Simpson, US Social Security Death Index (SSDI).

23   Ida Samson, "S Social Security Death Index (SSDI), Ancestry.com, https://www.ancestry.com/discoveryui-content/view/54397323:3693.

Yevel Meyerovich (#122)

1   Jewel Meyerovich, Application for Assistance from the Preparatory Committee of the International Refugee Organization (PCIRO), International Tracing Service, Yad Vashem.

2 Jewel Majorowicz, Jewish Survivors Registered in Lodz, July 1945, Jewish Immigrant Aid Society of Canada registration card, International Tracing Service, Yad Vashem; Friedman O. Meyerowicz, Josef O. Jeil O. Jewel, Italien ITS Nr. F-816 folder, International Tracing Service, Yad Vashem; Yevsey Meerovich, List of Partisans Active in the Baranowicze District, Central Database of Shoah Victims' Names, Yad Vashem.

3 Juda Kode Mejerowicz, Page of Testimony submitted by Alte Pomerchik, May 20, 1956, Central Database of Shoah Victims' Names, Yad Vashem.

4 Juda Kode Mejerowicz, Page of Testimony submitted by Alte Pomerchik, May 20, 1956, Central Database of Shoah Victims' Names, Yad Vashem.

5 David Mejerowicz, Page of Testimony submitted by Yakov Abramowitz, undated, Central Database of Shoah Victims' Names, Yad Vashem.

6 Nachama Mejerowicz, Page of Testimony submitted by Yakov Abramowitz, undated, Central Database of Shoah Victims' Names, Yad Vashem.

7 Sara Mina Mejerowicz, Page of Testimony submitted by Alte Pomerchik, May 20, 1956, Central Database of Shoah Victims' Names, Yad Vashem.

8 Nachama Mejerowicz, Page of Testimony submitted by Alte Pomerchik, undated, Central Database of Shoah Victims' Names, Yad Vashem.

9 Jewel Meyerovich, Application for Assistance from the Preparatory Committee of the International Refugee Organization (PCIRO) August 5, 1948, International Tracing Service, Yad Vashem.

10 Hassia Turtel-Oberzhanski, "The Second World War and the Destruction of the Community," in *Korelitz: Hayeha v'churbanah shel kehilah Yehudit* [Karelich: The Life and Destruction of a Jewish Community], ed. Michael Walzer-Fass (Tel Aviv: Karelich Societies of Israel and the United States, 1982), trans. JewishGen., p. 19, https://www.jewishgen.org/yizkor/Korelicze/Korelicze.html.

11 Gerasimova et al., *We Stood Shoulder to Shoulder*, 262.

12 Tec, *Defiance*, 126–27.

13 Amarant, "The Partisans of Tuvia Bielski," 150.

14 Amarant, 150.

15 Yosef Friedman, 13.IX.48, International Tracing Service, Yad Vashem.

16 Lea Kornfeld and China Kaspi, Pages of Testimony, Central Database of Shoah Victims' Names, Yad Vashem.

17 Yosef Friedman, 13.IX.48, Friedman, Josef, Questionnaire, Case R/5172, August 5, 1948, International Tracing Service, Yad Vashem.

18 Jewel Majorowicz, "Jewish Survivors Registered in Lodz, July 1945."

19 Yosef Friedman, 13.IX.48.

20 Hassia Turtel-Oberzhanski, "The Second World War and the Destruction of the Community."

Shlomo (#123) and Chana (#124) Ryback

1   Sylvia Sklar, personal communication, June 20, 2019.
2   Sylvia Sklar, personal interview, November 15, 2012.
3   Sklar, personal communication.
4   Sklar, personal communication.
5   Sklar, personal communication.
6   Leibovitz, "The Great Destruction," 512.
7   Amarant, "The Partisans of Tuvia Bielski," 159.
8   Amarant, 159.
9   Sklar, personal communication.
10 Sklar, personal communication.
11 Hyman Ryback, personal interview, June 20, 2019.
12 Solomon Golanski, oral testimony, USC Shoah Foundation Institute, February 8, 1997.
13 Sklar, personal communication.
14 Chana Ryback, card for File F-6-194 CU, "IRO Intern.Mov.Office Bremen-Grohn," International Tracing Service, Yad Vashem.
15 "R.M.S. Samaria (II)," GreatShips.net, https://greatships.net/samaria2, accessed June 23, 2019.
16 Sklar, personal interview.
17 Ryback, personal interview.
18 Sylvia Sklar, personal communication, August 28, 2023.
19 Sklar, personal interview.

Tevel (#125) and Feige (#126) Shmerkovich

1   Tevel Shmerkovich, List of Jewish Partisans in the Kalinin Detachment of the Leninskaya Brigade, Central Database of Shoah Victims' Names, Yad Vashem.
2   Tewel Szmerkowicz, Certificate of Residence 29.VII.54, International Tracing Service, Yad Vashem.
3   Yitzchak Smerkovich, personal correspondence, November 9, 2020.
4   Nesvizh, Belarus, Jewish Gen Communities Database, https://www.jewishgen.org/Communities/jgcd.php.
5   Yitzchak Smerkovich, personal interview, October 28, 2020.
6   Yankel Shmerkovich, List of Partisans from Belorussia, Central Database of Shoah Victims' Names, Yad Vashem.
7   "Mikhail Kutuzov," *Encyclopaedia Britannica,* April 21, 2018, https://www.britannica.com/biography/Mikhail-Illarionovich-Prince-Kutuzov, accessed on June 19, 2018.
8   Yitzchak Smerkovich, personal interview.

9   Smerkovich, personal interview.

10 Feyga Shmerkovich, List of Partisans from Belorussia, Central Database of Shoah Victims' Names, Yad Vashem.

11 Feyga Shmerkovich, Page of Testimony submitted by Albert Mayzel, September 12, 1994, Central Database of Shoah Victims' Names, Yad Vashem.

12 Tevel Shmerkovich, List of Jewish Partisans.

13 Tamara Vershitiskaya, personal communication, January 2012; Gerasimova et al., *We Stood Shoulder to Shoulder*, 308, 322.

14 Feiga Shmerkovich, Page of Testimony; Central Database of Shoah Victims' Names, Yad Vashem, Jerusalem; Gerasimova et al., *We Stood Shoulder to Shoulder*, 332.

15 United States Holocaust Memorial Museum, "Bergen-Belsen Displaced Persons Camp," Holocaust Encyclopedia, https://encyclopedia.ushmm.org/content/en/article/babenhausen-displaced-persons-camp.

16 "Bergen-Belsen (Hohne)," ORT and the Displaced Person Camps, World ORT, https://dpcamps.ort.org/camps/germany/british-zone/belsen, accessed October 28, 2020.

17 Yitzchak Smerkovich, personal interview.

18 Tewel Szmerkowicz, Inquiry Form, Hanover, International Tracing Service, Yad Vashem.

19 Noga Smerkowitz Fisala, personal interview, October 27, 2020.

20 Smerkovich, personal interview.

21 Smerkovich, personal interview.

22 Smerkovich, personal correspondence.

23 Smerkovich, personal interview.

24 Smerkovich, personal interview.

Provizor (#127)

1 Central Database of Shoah Victims' Names, Yad Vashem.

2 Central Database.

3 Gerasimova et al., *We Stood Shoulder to Shoulder*, 275, 327.

Abram Goldshmid (#128)

1 Abram Golshmid, List of Partisans from Belorussia, Central Database of Shoah Victims' Names, Yad Vashem.

2 David Slavin, personal interview with Tamara Vershitskaya, February 2017.

3 Gerasimova et al., *We Stood Shoulder to Shoulder*, 222.

4 Tec, *Defiance*, 186–87.

5 Tamara Vershitskaya, personal communication, February 19, 2017.

Skakun (#129)

1   Central Database of Shoah Victims' Names, Yad Vashem.

2   Yitzchak, Chana, Malka, and Rivka Skakun, memorial notice submitted by Yosef Skakun, in *Pinkas Navaredok*, ed. Yerushalmi et al., 400.

3   Khaia Skakun, memorial notice submitted by Yosef Skakun, *Pinkas Navaredok*, 400.

4   Chaya Skakun, Page of Testimony submitted by Michael Skakun, March 16, 2005, Central Database of Shoah Victims' Names, Yad Vashem.

5   Michael Skakun, personal interview, July 15, 2017.

6   Chaya Skakun, Page of Testimony.

7   Michael Skakun, personal correspondence, February 22, 2021.

8   Michael Skakun, *On Burning Ground* (New York: St. Martin's Press, 1999), 39.

9   Gerasimova et al., *We Stood Shoulder to Shoulder*, 286.

Moshe Nignevitcky (#130)

1   Zophy Chermoni, personal interview, October 10, 2017.

2   Chermoni, personal interview.

3   Steinberg-Sarig, "Hebrew Education in Novogrudok," 147.

4   Chermoni, personal interview.

5   Chermoni, personal interview.

6   Amarant, "The Partisans of Tuvia Bielski," 152.

7   Tec, *Defiance*, 86–87.

8   Chermoni, personal interview, October 10, 2017.

9   Zophy Chermoni, personal interview, September 2, 2021.

10   Jack Kagan, personal interview, May 5, 2008.

11   Mosche Nigniewicki, Certificate of Residence #103876, Allied High Committee for Germany, International Tracing Service, November 26, 1952, Yad Vashem.

12   "Germany: Pocking," JDC Archives, https://archives.jdc.org/project/germany-pocking/, accessed June 10, 2019.

13   Chermoni, personal interview, October 10, 2017.

14   "Immigration to Israel: 'Pan Crescent' & 'Pan York' Illegal Immigration Ships," *Jewish Virtual Library*, https://www.jewishvirtuallibrary.org/quot-pan-crescent-quot-and-quot-pan-york-quot-illegal-immigration-ships, accessed June 10, 2019.

15   Zophy Chermoni, personal interview, June 10, 2019.

16   Chermoni, personal interview, October 10, 2017.

17   Chermoni, personal interview, June 10, 2019.

18   Zophy Chermoni, personal interview, August 22, 2023.

Sheina (Sheindel) Nignevitcky (#131)

1   Chejna Flaster, Brazil, Rio de Janeiro, Immigration Cards, 1900–1965, Myheritage.com, https://www.myheritage.com/research/record-30284-54629/chejna-flaster-in-brazil-rio-de-janeiro-immigration-cards.

2   Borowski, in *Memory, Guide My Hand*, 9–16.

3   Jack Borowski, personal interview, July 2008.

4   Jack Kagan, personal interview, May 5, 2008.

5   Gerasimova et al., *We Stood Shoulder to Shoulder*, 267.

6   Gerasimova et al., *We Stood Shoulder to Shoulder*, 208.

7   Borowski, in *Memory, Guide My Hand*, 9–16.

8   Judy Freedman, personal interview, May 17, 2019.

9   Gerasimova et al., *We Stood Shoulder to Shoulder*, 208, 267; Borowski, in *Memory, Guide My Hand*.

10 Andrzej Cieśla, ed. *Memorial (Yizkor) Book of the Community of Zelechow*, vol. 2, translation of *Yisker-Bukh fun der Zhelekhover Yidisher Kehile*, ed. W. Yassni (Chicago: Former Residents of Zelechow in Chicago, 1953), translated by Michael Dunayevsky and Andrzej Cieśla, https://www.jewishgen.org/yizkor/zelechow/zelechow.html.

11 Sonia (Shayndel) Papier, MyHeritage family trees, Gelfand Web Site, managed by Eden Gelfand, Myheritage.com, https://www.myheritage.com/research/record-1-428673261-1-500031/sonia-shayndel-papier-in-myheritage-family-trees, accessed February 13, 2022.

12 Jacob Duszkin, US Naturalization Records Indexes, 1794–1995, Ancestry.com, https://www.ancestry.com/discoveryui-content/view/1315444:1192.

13 Freedman, personal interview.

14 Kagan, personal interview, May 5, 2008.

15 Tzadok Flyaster, List of Partisans from Belorussia, Central Database of Shoah Victims' Names, Yad Vashem.

16 Mendel Flaster, Brazil, Rio de Janeiro, Immigration Cards, 1900–1965. Myheritage.com, https://www.myheritage.com/research/record-30284-1027386/mendel-flaster-in-brazil-rio-de-janeiro-immigration-cards.

17 Chejna Flaster, Brazil, Rio de Janeiro, Immigration Cards.

18 Freedman, personal interview.

19 Anna Duszkin, Ohio, County Naturalization Records, 1800–1977, Myheritage.com, https://www.myheritage.com/research/record-30290-156800/anna-duszkin-in-ohio-county-naturalization-records.

20 Sonia Papier, US Public Records Index, Myheritage.com, https://www.myheritage.com/research/record-10220-626026817/sonia-papier-in-us-public-records-index.

21 Sucher Papier and Chejna Flaster, New York City Marriage License Index 1908–1972, Myheritage.com, https://www.myheritage.com/research

/record-10459-4620939/sucher-papier-and-chejna-flaster-in-new-york-city-marriage-license-index.

22 Suchier Papier, US Social Security Applications and Claims Index, 1936–2007, Ancestry.com, https://www.ancestry.com/discoveryui-content/view/28503828:60901.

23 Freedman, personal interview.

24 Freedman, personal interview.

25 Sucher Papier, US Social Security Death Index (SSDI), Myheritage.com, https://www.myheritage.com/research/record-10002-13206852/sucher-papier-in-us-social-security-death-index-ssdi.

26 Sonia (Shayndel) Papier, MyHeritage family tree.

27 Papier, MyHeritage family tree.

28 Judy Freedman, personal communication, September 4, 2023.

Alter Nignevitcky (#132)

1 Zophy Chermoni, personal interviews, July 8, 2018; June 3, 2019.

Nachum (#133) and Sara (#134) Zamosczyk ("Panikarter") and Isaac Lazowsky

1 Sara Lazowsky, Certificate of Residence #169562, May 2, 1960, International Tracing Service, Yad Vashem.

2 Chaya Magid, personal interview, January 4, 2018.

3 Simon Lazowsky, personal communication, March 5, 2019.

4 Magid, personal interview.

5 Sara Lazowsky, Application for War Reparations, September 4, 1956, New York, NY, International Tracing Service, Yad Vashem.

6 Simon Lazowsky, personal interview, February 25, 2019.

7 Gerasimova et al., *We Stood Shoulder to Shoulder*, 233.

8 Rakhel Zamoshchik, Page of Testimony submitted by Yehuda Lusky, April 22, 1999, Central Database of Shoah Victims' Names, Yad Vashem, Jerusalem; Rachel Zamoszchik, Page of Testimony submitted by Shlomo Razvazhski, April 28, 1957, Central Database of Shoah Victims' Names, Yad Vashem.

9 Nachum Zamosczyk, Page of Testimony submitted by Yehuda Lusky, May 13, 1956, Central Database of Shoah Victims' Names, Yad Vashem.

10 Simon Lazowsky, Notes on his Mother's Recollections 1933–1941, personal correspondence, March 6, 2019.

11 Lazowsky, Notes.

12 Daniel Ostashinski, Yad Vashem testimony, no. 03/6041.

13 Shaul Gorodynski, Yad Vashem testimony, no. 3095/230.

14   Magid, personal interview.

15   Lazowsky, Notes.

16   Lazowsky, personal interview.

17   Sara Lazowsky, Application for War Reparations; Simon Lazowsky, personal interview.

18   Magid, personal interview.

19   Mayevski (Nadel), "Hunger."

20   Gerasimova et al., *We Stood Shoulder to Shoulder*.

21   Gerasimova et al., *We Stood Shoulder to Shoulder*; Simon Lazowsky, personal interview, February 25, 2019.

22   Sara Lazowsky, Application for War Reparations.

23   Gerasimova et al., *We Stood Shoulder to Shoulder*, 252.

24   Isidore (Isak) Lazowsky, Certificate of Residence #169561, May 2, 1960, International Tracing Service, Yad Vashem.

25   Isaak Lazovski, List of Partisans from Belorussia, Central Database of Shoah Victims' Names, Yad Vashem.

26   Fayvel Lazovski, List of Residents from Novogrudok, 1941, Central Database of Shoah Victims' Names, Yad Vashem.

27   Isidore (Isak) Lazowsky, Certificate of Residence.

28   Lazowsky, Certificate of Residence.

29   Simon Lazowski, International Tracing Service, Yad Vashem.

30   Sara Lazowsky, Certificate of Residence.

31   Sara Lazowsky, US Naturalization Records, Myheritage.com, https://www.myheritage.com/research/record-10024-800662/sara-lazowsky-in-us-naturalization-records.

32   Lazowsky, personal interview.

33   Diane Lazowsky Creaven, personal interview, February 25, 2019.

34   Lazowski and Lazowsky Creaven, personal interviews.

35   Isidore Lazowsky, US Social Security Death Index (SSDI), Myheritage.com, https://www.myheritage.com/research/record-10002-9463220/isidore-lazowsky-in-us-social-security-death-index-ssdi.

36   Diane Lazowsky Creaven, personal interview.

37   Lazowsky, personal interview.

38   Sara Lazowsky, US Social Security Applications and Claims Index, 1936–2007, Ancestry.com, https://www.ancestry.com/discoveryui-content/view/37218491:60901.

39   Lazowsky, personal interview.

40   Lazowsky Creaven, personal interview.

41   Simon Lazowski and Diane Lazowsky Creaven, personal interviews.

Ribatzki (#135)

1   Aser Ribacki, Page of Testimony submitted by Arie Movshovitz, undated, Central Database of Shoah Victims' Names, Yad Vashem.
2   Asher Ribatzky, Page of Testimony submitted by Zeev Kaplan, October 29, 2000, Central Database of Shoah Victims' Names, Yad Vashem.
3   Sara Ribatzky, Page of Testimony submitted by Zeev Kaplan, October 29, 2000, Central Database of Shoah Victims' Names, Yad Vashem.
4   Gerasimova et al., *We Stood Shoulder to Shoulder*, 278, 331.

Zacharia Yoselevski (#136)

1   Avraham Leib Josilewski, Page of Testimony submitted by Kalman Josilewski, December 6, 1955, Central Database of Shoah Victims' Names, Yad Vashem.
2   Zchariasz Joselewski, Page of Testimony submitted by Shmuel Openheim, May 15, 1955, Central Database of Shoah Victims' Names, Yad Vashem.
3   Avraham Leib Josilewski, Page of Testimony.
4   Zchariasz Joselewski, Page of Testimony.
5   Dina Joselewski, Page of Testimony submitted by Shmuel Openheim, May 15, 1955, Central Database of Shoah Victims' Names, Yad Vashem.
6   Zchariasz Joselewski, Page of Testimony.
7   Rivka Joselewski, Page of Testimony submitted by Shmuel Openheim, May 15, 1955, Central Database of Shoah Victims' Names, Yad Vashem.
8   Tzvi Joselewski, Page of Testimony submitted by Shmuel Openheim, May 15, 1955, Central Database of Shoah Victims' Names, Yad Vashem.
9   Tzvi Joselewski, Page of Testimony submitted by Shmuel Openheim, May 15, 1955, Central Database of Shoah Victims' Names, Yad Vashem.
10 Dina Joselewski, Rivka Joselewski, Tzvi Joselewski, Tzvi Joselewski, Pages of Testimony.
11 Zchariasz Joselewski, Page of Testimony.
12 Yerushalmi et al., eds., *Pinkas Navaredok*, 382.

Shepsel Eisenshtadt (#137)

1   Szepsel Ajzensztadt, registration card for Jewish Holocaust Survivors, Card #4, Warsaw, March 6, 1946, Holocaust Survivors and Victims Database, United States Memorial Holocaust Museum, https://www.ushmm.org/online/hsv/person _view.php?personid=8207906·
2   Ajzensztadt, registration card.
3   Szepsel Ajzensztadt, Registration card for Jewish Holocaust Survivors, Card #19505, Warsaw, September 13, 1946, Holocaust Survivors and Victims

Database, United States Memorial Holocaust Museum, https://www.ushmm.org
/online/hsv/person_view.php?PersonId=8207910.

4   "Otwock: History," Polin Virtual Shtetl, Museum of the History of Polish
Jews, https://sztetl.org.pl/en/towns/o/590-otwock/99-history/137815-history
-of-community, accessed February 20, 2021.

5   "Otwock: History," Polin Virtual Shtetl.

6   Szepsel Ajzensztadt, registration card for Jewish Holocaust Survivors, Card
#19505.

7   Shenshel Leibovich Aisenshtadt, in Gerasimova et al., *We Stood Shoulder to
Shoulder*, 199.

8   Szepsel Ajzensztat, F18-501, "Documents without Attributed Call Number,
Reference Code 03010105 oS, Number of documents 1014," Arolsen Archives,
https://collections.arolsenarchives.org/en/archive/80303912.

Yehezkiel (Chatskel) Grande (#138)

1   Kevin Alan Brook, "Sephardic Jews in Belarus," *Zichron Note* (Newsletter of the
San Francisco Bay Area Jewish Genealogical Society) 38, no. 1/2 (February/May
2018): 5–6, http://www.khazaria.com/sephardim-belarus.html.

2   Avraham, "Sephardim."

3   Brook, "Sephardic Jews in Belarus."

4   Rishe Granda, Page of Testimony submitted by Shira Adler Freund, undated,
Central Database of Shoah Victims' Names, Yad Vashem.

5   Khatzkel Grande, Personal Cards of Jewish Partisans of Belorussia, Central
Database of Shoah Victims' Names, Yad Vashem.

6   Janis Friedenberg Datz and Melisssa Rubin McCurdie, eds., *Memorial Volume
of Steibtz-Swerznie and the Neighboring Villages Rubezhevitz, Derevna, Nalibok
(Stowbtsy, Belarus)*, translation of *Sefer Zikaron; Steibts-Sverzhnye Ve-Ha-Ayarot
Ha-Semukhot Rubezevits, Derevno, Nalibok*, ed. Nachum Hinitz (Tel Aviv:
Former Residents of Steibtz in Israel, 1964), https://www.jewishgen.org/yizkor
/stowbtsy/sto495.html.

7   Rishe Granda, Page of Testimony.

8   Shlomo Grande, Page of Testimony submitted by Shira Adler Freund, undated,
Central Database of Shoah Victims' Names, Yad Vashem.

9   Sara (Sirke) Grande, Page of Testimony submitted by Shira Adler Freund,
undated, Central Database of Shoah Victims' Names, Yad Vashem.

10   Shlomo Grande, Page of Testimony.

11   Sara (Sirke) Grande, Page of Testimony.

12   Gerasimova et al., *We Stood Shoulder to Shoulder*, 224.

Miriam (#139) and Linka (#140) Landau

1 Fanya Dunetz Brodsky, personal interview, November 14, 2011.
2 Dunetz Brodsky, personal interview .
3 Leibovitz, "The Last Passover," 509.
4 Dunetz Brodsky, personal interview.
5 Daniel Ostashinski, Yad Vashem testimony, no. 23/6841.
6 Leibovitz, "The Last Passover."
7 Dunetz Brodsky, personal interview.
8 Rubin, *Against the Tide*, 149.
9 Gerasimova et al., *We Stood Shoulder to Shoulder*, 252, 324.

Eliyahu Novolenski (#141)

1 Eliyahu Nowolenski, Page of Testimony submitted by Pesia (Mayevski) Nadel, April 24, 1057, Central Database of Shoah Victims' Names, Yad Vashem.
2 Sara Novolenskaya, List of Murdered Individuals from Zhetl, Central Database of Shoah Victims' Names, Yad Vashem.
3 Sara Nowolenski, Page of Testimony submitted by Pesia (Mayevski) Nadel, April 24, 1057, Central Database of Shoah Victims' Names, Yad Vashem.
4 Feyga Novolenskaya, List of Murdered Individuals from Zhetl, Central Database of Shoah Victims' Names, Yad Vashem.
5 Jehoschua Nowolenski, Page of Testimony submitted by Pesia (Mayevski) Nadel, April 24, 1057, Central Database of Shoah Victims' Names, Yad Vashem.
6 Kaplinski, *Pinkas Zhetl*, 25.
7 Monik Novolenski, List of Murdered Individuals from Zhetl, Central Database of Shoah Victims' Names, Yad Vashem.
8 Kaplinski, *Pinkas Zhetl*.
9 Sara Nowolenski, Page of Testimony submitted by Pesia (Mayevski) Nadel, April 24, 1057, Central Database of Shoah Victims' Names, Yad Vashem.
10 Eliyahu Nowolenski, Page of Testimony.

Fanya Dunetz (#142)

1 "Obituary – Reb Shlomo Zalman Dunitz, z"l," *Netiva Newspaper*, March 28, 1932.
2 Jack Kagan, "Holocaust Denial" in Gerasimova et al., *We Stood Shoulder to Shoulder*, 191.
3 Lena Abramchik, personal communication, June 26, 2020.
4 Fanya Dunetz Brodsky, personal interview, June 25, 2020.
5 Fanya Dunetz Brodsky, personal interview, May 4, 2008.

6   Fanya Duniec, Registration record #F18-1o8, Central Jewish Committee in Poland, Warsaw, March 23, 1949, International Tracing Service, Yad Vashem.

7   Fanya Duniec, Registration record #T1027/Apr.46, UNRRA Team 501 Berlin-Zehlendorf, International Tracing Service, Yad Vashem.

8   United States Holocaust Memorial Museum, "Eschwege Displaced Persons Camp," Holocaust Encyclopedia, https://encyclopedia.ushmm.org/content/en/article/eschwege-displaced-persons-camp.

9   Mordechai Dunetz, "How We Made a Newspaper in a DP Camp," Wexler Oral History Project.

10   Fanny Brodsky, Certificate of Residence #146691, Comité International de la Croix-Rouge, February 10, 1956, International Tracing Service, Yad Vashem.

11   NavSource Online: Service Ship Photo Archive, "USNS *General M. B. Stewart* (T-AP-140)," Navsource.com, http://www.navsource.org/archives/09/22/22140.htm.

12   Fannie Brodsky, US Naturalization Record #7427126, Myheritage.com, https://www.myheritage.com/research/record-10024-578346/brodsky-fannie-in-us-naturalization-records.

Naum (Zeidel) Kushner (#143)

1   Nachum Kushner, Yad Vashem testimony [in Yiddish], no. 03/3929.

2   Kushner, Yad Vashem testimony.

3   Esther Schulder, personal interview, September 13, 2018.

4   Kushner, Yad Vashem testimony.

5   Kushner, Yad Vashem testimony.

6   Rae Kushner, "The Agony of Death: The Miracle of Survival," oral history, 1996, videotape transcript, Holocaust Center at Kean College of New Jersey, Union, NJ.

7   Yaffe, "The Tradesmen's Ghetto," in *Novogrudok Memorial Book*, 551.

8   Nachum Kushner, Yad Vashem testimony.

9   Murray Kushner, personal communication, September 29, 2018.

10   Murray Kushner, personal communication.

11   Solomon Golanski, oral testimony, Survivors of the Shoah Visual History Foundation, 1997.

12   Nachum Kushner, Yad Vashem testimony.

13   Kushner, "The Agony of Death."

14   Shellie Davis and Laurie Hasten, personal interview, June 17, 2018.

15   Davis and Hasten, personal interview.

16   Schulder, personal interview.

17   Murray Kushner, personal communication, September 30, 2018.

18 Davis and Hasten, personal interview.
19 Murray Kushner, personal interview, August 12, 2018.

Raya Kushner (#144)

1   Rae Kushner, "The Agony of Death: The Miracle of Survival," oral history, 1996, videotape transcript, Holocaust Center at Kean College of New Jersey, Union, NJ.
2   Nachum Kushner, Yad Vashem testimony [in Yiddish], no. 03/3929.
3   Kushner, "The Agony of Death."
4   Kushner, "The Agony of Death."
5   Nachum Kushner, Yad Vashem testimony.
6   Kushner, "The Agony of Death."
7   Nachum Kushner, Yad Vashem testimony.
8   Kushner, "The Agony of Death."
9   Kushner, "The Agony of Death."
10 Nachum Kushner, Yad Vashem testimony.
11 Kushner, "The Agony of Death."
12 Nachum Kushner, Yad Vashem testimony.
13 Solomon Golanski, oral testimony, 1997, Survivors of the Shoah Visual History Foundation, Los Angeles.
14 Nachum Kushner, Yad Vashem testimony.
15 Kushner, "The Agony of Death."
16 Murray Kushner, personal interview, August 12, 2018.
17 Epstein, *The Miracle of Life*, 92–93.
18 Epstein, 92–93.
19 Epstein, 95–97.
20 Epstein, 97–98.
21 Murray Kushner, personal interview.
22 Linda Laulicht, personal interview, October 31, 2018.
23 Esther Schulder, personal interview, October 29, 2018.
24 Laurie Hasten, personal interview, June 17, 2018.
25 Epstein, *The Miracle of Life*, 117, 127, 131, 137, 139.
26 Kushner, "The Agony of Death."
27 Kushner, "The Agony of Death."

Leah Kushner (#145)

1   Leya Kushner, List of Partisans from Belorussia, Central Database of Shoah Victims' Names, Yad Vashem.
2   Nachum Kushner, Yad Vashem testimony [in Yiddish], no. 03/3929.

3   Rae Kushner, "The Agony of Death: The Miracle of Survival," oral history, 1996, videotape transcript, Holocaust Center at Kean College of New Jersey, Union, NJ.

4   Nachum Kushner, Yad Vashem testimony.

5   Kushner, Yad Vashem testimony.

6   Kushner, Yad Vashem testimony.

7   Kushner, Yad Vashem testimony.

8   Kushner, Yad Vashem testimony.

9   Kushner, Yad Vashem testimony.

10   Kushner, Yad Vashem testimony.

11   Helen Zelig, personal communication, May 3, 2023.

12   Nachum Kushner, Yad Vashem testimony.

13   Kushner, "The Agony of Death."

14   Nachum Kushner, Yad Vashem testimony.

15   Solomon Golanski, Survivors of the Shoah Visual History Foundation, 1977.

16   Mitch Braff, director, *A Partisan Returns: A Legacy of Two Sisters* (Jewish Partisan Educational Foundation, 2008).

17   Kushner, "The Agony of Death."

18   Epstein, *The Miracle of Life*, 92–93.

19   Helen Zelig, personal interview, November 1, 2018.

20   Epstein, *The Miracle of Life*, 95.

21   Zelig, personal interview.

22   Zelig, personal interview.

23   Zelig, personal interview.

24   Reibel, *A Partisan Returns*.

25   Zelig, personal interview.

26   Helen Zelig, personal communication, August 23, 2023.

27   Zelig, personal interview.

Riva Kaganowicz (#146)

1   Zalka Kaganowicz, Page of Testimony submitted by Riva Kaganowicz-Bernstein, June 13, 2008, Central Database of Shoah Victims' Names, Yad Vashem.

2   Riva Kaganowicz-Bernstein, personal interview, September 4, 2019.

3   Dov Cohen, in Kagan and Cohen, *Surviving the Holocaust*, 24.

4   Chaja Kaganowicz, Page of Testimony submitted by Riva Kaganowicz-Bernstein, June 13, 2008, Central Database of Shoah Victims' Names, Yad Vashem.

5   Kaganowicz-Bernstein, personal interview, September 4, 2019.

6   Shymon Kaganowicz, Page of Testimony submitted by Riva Kaganowicz-Bernstein, June 13, 2008, Central Database of Shoah Victims' Names, Yad Vashem.

7   Zalka Kaganowicz, Page of Testimony.

8   Chaja Kaganowicz, Page of Testimony.

9   Aron David Kaganowicz Cohen, Page of Testimony submitted by Riva Kaganowicz-Bernstein, June 13, 2008, Central Database of Shoah Victims' Names, Yad Vashem.

10   Kaganowicz-Bernstein, personal interview, September 4, 2019.

11   Kaganowicz-Bernstein, personal interview, September 9, 2019.

12   Kaganowicz-Bernstein, personal interview, July 26, 2020.

13   Kaganowicz-Bernstein, personal interview, September 4, 2019.

14   Yanek Okonski, personal interview, August 6, 2019.

15   Kaganowicz-Bernstein, personal interview, September 4, 2019.

16   Kaganowicz-Bernstein, personal interview, September 9, 2019.

17   Riwa Kaganowicz, Record #14097 in the Alphabetical Registry of Polish Jews in Lodz, Warsaw, August 1945; Correspondence of United Restitution Organization re Bernstein Reva, March 11, 1955, International Tracing Service, Yad Vashem.

18   Kaganowicz-Bernstein, personal interview, September 4, 2019.

19   Kaganowicz-Bernstein, personal interview.

20   Kaganowicz-Bernstein, personal interview, September 9, 2019.

21   Riva Kaganowicz, Africa, Asia and Europe, Passenger Lists of Displaced Persons, 1946–1971, Ancestry.com, https://www.ancestry.com/discoveryui-content/view/28503828:60901.

22   Kaganowicz-Bernstein, personal interview, September 4, 2019.

23   Kaganowicz-Bernstein, personal interview.

24   Kaganowicz-Bernstein, personal interview.

25   Shwartz, *Tunnel of Hope*.

Yitzchak (#147) and Mordechai (#148) Maloshitzki

1   Yitzchak Maloszitzki, Page of Testimony submitted by Herzel Bruk, April 27, 1999, Central Database of Shoah Victims' Names, Yad Vashem.

2   Dvorah Maloszitzki, Page of Testimony submitted by Herzel Bruk, April 27, 1999, Central Database of Shoah Victims' Names, Yad Vashem.

3   Sarale Maloszitzki, Page of Testimony submitted by Herzel Bruk, April 27, 1999, Central Database of Shoah Victims' Names, Yad Vashem.

4   Mordechai Maloszitzki, Page of Testimony submitted by Herzel Bruk, April 27, 1999, Central Database of Shoah Victims' Names, Yad Vashem.

5   Mordechai Maloszitzki, Page of Testimony.

6   Gerasimova et al., *We Stood Shoulder to Shoulder*, 261, 325.

7   Eran Barak, personal interview, April 21, 2019.

Sara (#149), Basia (#150), and Roza (#151) Giershenowski

1   Gerasimova et al., *We Stood Shoulder to Shoulder*, 320.

2   Roza Giershenowski Wodakow, personal interview, January 3, 2012.

3   Rozalia Gershenowski Wodakow, Questionnaire for Yom Hashoah Memorial, April 2009.

4   Samuel Nikolayevski, "United Jewish Artisans Association," in *Novogrudok Memorial Book*, 247.

5   Schlomo Gerschanowski, Page of Testimony submitted by Noach Granovski (Giershenovski), February 20, 1957, Central Database of Shoah Victims' Names, Yad Vashem.

6   Rosalia Wodakow, inquiry card, Inquiry #2005061366747, January 6, 2005, International Tracing Service database, Yad Vashem.

7   Simele Sima Manusevich, Page of Testimony submitted by Shimon Germanovski, May 17, 1995, Central Database of Shoah Victims' Names, Yad Vashem.

8   Sonia Palkis, personal interview, September 8, 2019.

9   Riva Kaganowicz-Bernstein, personal interview, September 8, 2019.

10 Amarant, "The Partisans of Tuvia Bielski," 163–64.

11 Amarant, 163–64.

12 Bielski and Bielski, *Yehudei Yaar*, 230.

13 Tec, *Defiance*, 266.

14 Fanya Dunetz Brodsky, personal interview, January 2, 2012.

15 Kaganowicz-Bernstein, personal interview.

16 Wodakow, inquiry card.

17 Shwartz, *Tunnel of Hope*.

18 Roza Giershenowski Wodakow, personal interview.

19 Giershenowski Wodakow, personal interview.

20 Tec, *Defiance*, 266.

21 Schwartz, *Tunnel of Hope*.

22 Giershenowski Wodakow, questionnaire.

23 Tec, *Defiance*, 266.

24 Boris Wodakow, US Social Security Death Index, 1935–2014," Ancestry.com, https://www.ancestry.com/discoveryui-content/view/68447881:3693.

25 Seymour Wodakow, personal interview, September 17, 2019.

26 Kaganowicz-Bernstein, personal interview.

27 Palkis, personal interview, September 8, 2019.

28 Shimon Gershinovsky, gravestone, Ness Tsiyona Cemetery, Rehovot, Israel, BillionGraves, November 12, 2017, https://billiongraves.com/grave /21378409/שמעון-גרשנובסקי.

29 Palkis, personal interview, September 8, 2019.

30 Palkis, personal interview.

Sara Lidski (#152)

1   Israel Lidski, Page of Testimony submitted by Batia Gradis, April 2, 1957, Central Database of Shoah Victims' Names, Yad Vashem.

2   Yisrael Litzki, Page of Testimony submitted by Henia Rozenblum, June 25, 1956, Central Database of Shoah Victims' Names, Yad Vashem.

3   Sara Lidskaya, List of Murdered Individuals from Zhetl, Central Database of Shoah Victims' Names, Yad Vashem.

4   Sara Lidski, Page of Testimony submitted by Batia Gradis, April 2, 1957, Central Database of Shoah Victims' Names, Yad Vashem.

5   Chana Karoliszki, Page of Testimony submitted by Pesia (Mayevski) Nadel, April 30, 1957, Central Database of Shoah Victims' Names, Yad Vashem.

6   Khaim Lidski, List of Murdered Individuals from Zhetl, Central Database of Shoah Victims' Names, Yad Vashem.

7   Chaim Lidski, Page of Testimony submitted by Batia Gradis, April 28, 1957, Central Database of Shoah Victims' Names, Yad Vashem.

8   Rischa Lidski, Page of Testimony submitted by Batia Gradis, April 28, 1957, Central Database of Shoah Victims' Names, Yad Vashem.

9   Feigel Lidski, Page of Testimony submitted by Batia Gradis, April 28, 1957, Central Database of Shoah Victims' Names, Yad Vashem.

10 Fanya Dunetz Brodsky, personal interview, February 10, 2018.

11 Dunetz Brodsky, personal interview.

12 Dunetz Brodsky, personal interview.

13 Dunetz Brodsky, personal interview.

14 Kaplinski, *Pinkas Zhetl*, 23.

Hirsh Altman (#153)

1   *Novogrudok Memorial Book*, 377.

2   "Hirsh Altman," *Lerer Yisker-Bukh* [Remembrance Volume for Teachers] (New York, 1954), p. 15, posted by Joshua Fogel, Yiddish Leksikon, June 18, 2014, http://yleksikon.blogspot.com/2014/06/hirsh-altman.html.

3   Ezra Mendelsohn, *The Jews of East Central Europe between the World Wars* (Bloomington: Indiana University Press, 1983), 63.

4   Joshua D. Zimmerman, "Tsysho," YIVO Encyclopedia of Jews in Eastern Europe, https://yivoencyclopedia.org/article.aspx/Tsysho.

5   Zimmerman, "Tsysho."

6   "Hirsh Altman," *Lerer Yisker-Bukh*.

7   Zvi Mann, "Mendl Mann and the Almost Nobel Prize: Zvi Mann" [in Yiddish], Wexler Oral History Project, June 18, 2014, The Yiddish Book Center, Tel Aviv, https://www.yiddishbookcenter.org/collections/oral-histories/excerpts/woh-ex-0004917/mendl-mann-and-almost-nobel-prize.

8   Zvi Mann and David Mazower, "Signed Marc Chagall Aquarelle," *The Mendele Review: Yiddish Literature and Language*, December 21, 2008, http://yiddish.haifa.ac.il/tmr/tmr12/tmr12021.htm#i2.

9   Mendel Mann, *Noenṭ Fun Ṿayṭns Far Undzere Ḳinder* [Close from Afar for Our Children; in Yiddish], illustrated by Hirsh Altman (Warsaw: Kinder-Fraynd, 1935), digitalized by the National Yiddish Book Center, Amherst, Massachusetts, January 2009, https://www.yiddishbookcenter.org/collections/yiddish-books/spb-nybc201376/mann-mendel-altman-hirsh-noent-fun-vaytns-far-undzere-kinder.

10   Mann and Mazower, "Signed Marc Chagall Aquarelle."

11   Yosl Bergner, oral testimony, National Yiddish Book Center, Amherst, Massachusetts, June 18, 2014, https://www.yiddishbookcenter.org/collections/oral-histories/interviews/woh-fi-0000565/yosl-bergner-2014.

12   "Yosl Bergner," Dan Gallery, https://www.dangallery.co.il/artists/yosl-bergner/, accessed November 26, 2020; "Yosl Bergner," Information Center for Israeli Art, The Israel Museum, Jerusalem, https://museum.imj.org.il/artcenter/newsite/en/?artist=Bergner,%20Yosl, accessed November 26, 2020.

13   "Yosl Bergner Honorary Doctorate Ceremony," University of Haifa, June 2, 2013, https://bogcms.haifa.ac.il/images/stories/bog2013/bergner-eng.pdf, accessed November 26, 2020.

14   Audrey Bergner, personal interview, November 24, 2020.

15   Mortkhe Yofe, "Mendel Mann," Yiddish Leksikon, posted by Joshua Fogel, July 16, 2017, http://yleksikon.blogspot.com/2017/07/mendl-man-mendel-mann.html.

16   Yosl Bergner, Information Center for Israeli Art, Israel Museum.

17   "Hirsh Altman," *Lerer Yisker-Bukh* (Remembrance Volume for Teachers).

18   Bergner, oral testimony.

19   *Novogrudok Memorial Book*, 377.

20   Mordechai Majerowicz, Yad Vashem testimony, no. 03/2106.

21   Gerasimova et al., *We Stood Shoulder to Shoulder*, 200, 318.

22   "Hirsh Altman," *Lerer Yisker-Bukh* (Remembrance Volume for Teachers).

Chana Garbar (#154)

1 Memorial notice for Chana and Zlata Garbar, submitted by Rivka Roz Garbar Kaplan, in *Pinkas Navaredok*, ed Yerushalmi et al., 412.
2 Memorial notice for Chana and Zlata Garbar .
3 Gerasimova et al., *We Stood Shoulder to Shoulder*, 215, 320.

Mikulitzki (#155)

1 Central Database of Shoah Victims' Names, Yad Vashem.
2 Central Database of Shoah Victims' Namess.
3 Gerasimova et al., *We Stood Shoulder to Shoulder*, 264.
4 Gerasimova et al., 264.
5 Berkovich, "Schlos Gass," 243.
6 Gerasimova, et al., *We Stood Shoulder to Shoulder*, 264.
7 Bielski and Bielski, *Yehudei Yaar*, 215.

Yakov (Yankel) Weinrid (#156)

1 Gerasimova et al., *We Stood Shoulder to Shoulder*, 211.

Yosef Chechanovski (#157)

1 Central Database of Shoah Victims' Names, Yad Vashem.
2 Iosef Tzekanovich, List of Refugees Living in Slonim, 1940, Central Database of Shoah Victims' Names, Yad Vashem.
3 Gerasimova et al., *We Stood Shoulder to Shoulder*, 300, 329.

Frieda (#158) and Leah (#158a) Davidovich

1 Frieda Davidovich, unpublished memoir.
2 Gerasimova et al., *We Stood Shoulder to Shoulder*, 227.
3 Tamara Vershitskaya, personal communication, April 29, 2019.
4 Davidovich, unpublished memoir.
5 Frida Davidovich, List of Partisans from Belorussia, Central Database of Shoah Victims' Names, Yad Vashem.
6 Frida Davidovich, List of Partisans from Belorussia .
7 Davidovich, unpublished memoir.
8 Davidovich, unpublished memoir.
9 Davidovich, List of Partisans.
10 Davidovich, unpublished memoir.
11 "The Novogrudok Orphanage," *Novogrudok Memorial Book*, 182.
12 Leibovich, "Shokdey Melocho," 196.

13 Leibovich, 197.
14 Davidovich, unpublished memoir.
15 Davidovich, unpublished memoir.
16 Elena Filipyeva, personal communication, February 20, 2020.

Hirsh Patzovski (#159)

1   Hirsh Pacowski, Page of Testimony submitted by Pesia (Mayevski) Nadel, May 29, 1955, Central Database of Shoah Victims' Names, Yad Vashem.
2   Becalal Pacowski, Page of Testimony submitted by Pesia (Mayevski) Nadel, May 29, 1955, Central Database of Shoah Victims' Names, Yad Vashem.
3   Jacob Pacowski, Page of Testimony submitted by Pesia (Mayevski) Nadel, April 24, 1957, Central Database of Shoah Victims' Names, Yad Vashem.
4   Becalal Pacowski, Page of Testimony.
5   Zlate Pacowski, Page of Testimony submitted by Arkady Mnuskin, December 17, 1978, Central Database of Shoah Victims' Names, Yad Vashem.
6   Jacob Pacowski, Page of Testimony.
7   Mayevski (Nadel), "Hunger," 324.
8   Fanya Dunetz Brodsky, personal interview, January 14, 2018.
9   Tec, *Defiance*, 197–98.

Pesia Mayevski (#160)

1   Nechama Tzadok, personal interview, February 2, 2021.
2   Israel Ascher Maijewski, Page of Testimony submitted by Pesia (Mayevski) Nadel, April 24, 1957, Central Database of Shoah Victims' Names, Yad Vashem.
3   Chaja Maijewski, Page of Testimony submitted by Pesia (Mayevski) Nadel, April 24, 1957, Central Database of Shoah Victims' Names, Yad Vashem.
4   Hinda Maijewski, Page of Testimony submitted by Pesia (Mayevski) Nadel, April 24, 1957, Central Database of Shoah Victims' Names, Yad Vashem.
5   Chanan Maijewski, Page of Testimony submitted by Pesia (Mayevski) Nadel, April 24, 1957, Central Database of Shoah Victims' Names, Yad Vashem.
6   Chaja Maijewski, Page of Testimony.
7   Israel Ascher Maijewski, Page of Testimony.
8   Izrail Mayevski, List of Murdered Individuals from Zhetl, Central Database of Shoah Victims' Names, Yad Vashem.
9   Lipsky, *Ayaratenu Zhetl*, 135.
10 Yaffe, *In the Novogrudok Ghetto*, 166–67.
11 Kagan, *Surviving the Holocaust*, 569.
12 Leibovitz, "The Great Destruction," 498.
13 Lipsky, *Ayaratenu Zhetl*, 71.

14 Mayevski (Nadel), "Hunger," 322.

15 Mayevsky (Nadel), "In the Novardok Labor Camp," 360.

16 Mayevsky (Nadel), "In the Novardok Labor Camp," 361.

17 Mayevsky (Nadel), "In the Novardok Labor Camp," 361.

18 Mayevsky (Nadel), "In the Novardok Labor Camp," 361.

19 "Landsberg," ORT and the DP Camps, https://dpcamps.ort.org/camps /germany/us-zone/us-zone-v/landsberg.

20 Pesia Mayevski (Nadel), "From Zhetl to Petach Tikva" [in Yiddish], in *Pinkas Zhetl*, ed. B. Kaplinski, 455.

21 Haim Weinstein, personal interview, October 15, 2020.

22 Mayevski (Nadel), "From Zhetl to Petach Tikva," 454–55.

23 Mayevski, 454–55.

24 Mayevski, 454–55.

25 Nechama Tzadok, personal interview, November 12, 2011.

26 Nechama Tzadok, personal interview, August 23, 2023.

27 Pesia Mayevski (Nadel), "From Where Do I Get My Strength?" in *Ayaratenu Zhetl*, edited by Lipsky et al., 135.

Yakov (Yanek) Patzovski (#161)

1 Jacob Pacowski, Page of Testimony submitted by Pesia (Mayevski) Nadel, April 24, 1957, Central Database of Shoah Victims' Names, Yad Vashem.

2 Jacob Pacowski, Page of Testimony submitted by Lyuba Greitzer, March 26, 1957, Central Database of Shoah Victims' Names, Yad Vashem.

3 Jacob Pacowski, Page of Testimony submitted by Pesia (Mayevski) Nadel.

4 Becalal Pacowski, Page of Testimony submitted by Pesia (Mayevski) Nadel, May 29, 1955, Central Database of Shoah Victims' Names, Yad Vashem.

5 Hirsh Pacowski, Page of Testimony submitted by Pesia (Mayevski) Nadel, May 29, 1955, Central Database of Shoah Victims' Names, Yad Vashem.

6 Jacob Pacowski, Page of Testimony submitted by Lyuba Greitzer.

7 Zlate Pacowski, Page of Testimony submitted by Arkady Mnuskin, December 17, 1978, Central Database of Shoah Victims' Names, Yad Vashem.

8 Mayevsky (Nadel), "Hunger," 324.

Chanan Lev (#162)

1 Gerasimova et al., *We Stood Shoulder to Shoulder*, 324.

2 Gerasimova et al., 324.

3 Central Database of Shoah Victims' Names, Yad Vashem.

4   Isaac Czesler, "The Judenrat's Minutes and Orders," in *The Bialystoker Memorial Book* [Yiddish and English], ed. I. Shmulewitz (New York: Bialystoker Center, 1982), 67.

5   Czesler, "The Judenrat's Minutes and Orders," 67.

6   Gerasimova et al., *We Stood Shoulder to Shoulder*, 324.

Moshe (#163) and Berl (#164) Niselevich; Raizel (#165)

1   Moshe Niselewicz, Page of Testimony submitted by Lea Kornfeld, June 17, 1999, Central Database of Shoah Victims' Names, Yad Vashem.

2   Beril Niselewicz, Page of Testimony submitted by Lea Kornfeld, June 17, 1999, Central Database of Shoah Victims' Names, Yad Vashem.

3   Zalman Niselewicz, Page of Testimony submitted by Yeshayahu Mendelevski, April 8, 1957, Central Database of Shoah Victims' Names, Yad Vashem.

4   Muszka Niselewicz, Page of Testimony submitted by Yeshayahu Mendelevski, April 8, 1957, Central Database of Shoah Victims' Names, Yad Vashem.

5   Necha Niselewicz, Page of Testimony submitted by Chaim Kalmanovski, November 11, 1955, Central Database of Shoah Victims' Names, Yad Vashem.

6   Aron Niselevitz, Page of Testimony submitted by Yeshayahu Mendelevski, April 8, 1957, Central Database of Shoah Victims' Names, Yad Vashem.

7   Bela Niselewicz, Page of Testimony submitted by Chaim Kalmanovski, November 11, 1955, Central Database of Shoah Victims' Names, Yad Vashem.

8   Ann Belinsky, ed., *Korelitz: The Life and Destruction of a Jewish Community (Karelichy, Belarus)*, translation of *Korelitz: Hayeha v'churbanah shel kehilah Yehudit*, ed. Michael Walzer-Fass (Tel Aviv: Karelich Societies of Israel and the United States, 1973), 298, translated by JewishGen, https://www.jewishgen.org/yizkor/Korelicze/Korelicze.html.

9   Reisel Niselevitz, Page of Testimony submitted by Yeshayahu Mendelevski, April 8, 1957, Central Database of Shoah Victims' Names, Yad Vashem.

10   Faiwil Niselewicz, Page of Testimony submitted by Lea Kornfeld, June 17, 1999, Central Database of Shoah Victims' Names, Yad Vashem.

11   Zalman Niselewicz, Page of Testimony submitted by Lea Kornfeld, June 17, 1999, Central Database of Shoah Victims' Names, Yad Vashem.

12   Reisel Niselevitz, Page of Testimony.

Etel (#166) and Yocheved (Yacha, #166a) Tiles

1   Sula Rubin-Wolozynski, "Under the German Whip," in *Pinkas Navaredok*, ed. Yerushalmi et al., 272, https://www.jewishgen.org/yizkor/Novogrudok/nov258.html#Page272.

2   Israel Tiles, Page of Testimony submitted by Yitzchak Danieli, January 29, 1956, Central Database of Shoah Victims' Names, Yad Vashem.

3   Israel Tiles, Page of Testimony.

4   Yakha Tiles, List of Partisans from Belorussia, Central Database of Shoah Victims' Names, Yad Vashem.

5   Yerushalami et al., eds. *Pinkas Navaredok*, 82.

6   Irsh Tiles, Jewish Residents of the Soviet Union Evacuated to Tashkent 02/1942, Central Database of Shoah Victims' Names, Yad Vashem.

7   Gerasimova et al., *We Stood Shoulder to Shoulder*, 290, 329.

Nachman Feifer (#167)

1   Aron Nachman Fajfer, Government Reparation and Property Administration registration form, Wiesbaden, Germany, February 15, 1952, International Tracing Service, Yad Vashem.

2   Nakhman Fayfer, List of Partisans from Belorussia, Central Database of Shoah Victims' Names, Yad Vashem.

3   Nakhman Fayfer, List of Jews in the Karelich Ghetto 1942, Central Database of Shoah Victims' Names, Yad Vashem.

4   Sheva Fayfer, List of Jews in the Karelich Ghetto 1942, Central Database of Shoah Victims' Names, Yad Vashem.

5   Lipa Fayfer, List of Jews in the Karelich Ghetto 1942, Central Database of Shoah Victims' Names, Yad Vashem.

6   *Novogrudok Memorial Book*, 744.

7   Nakhman Faifer, erroneously listed as Nakhman Nakhmanovich Raifer, in Gerasimova et al., *We Stood Shoulder to Shoulder*, 276.

8   Aron N Fajfer, Ellis Island and Other New York Passenger Lists, 1820–1957, Myheritage.com, https://www.myheritage.com/research/record-10512-102562249/aron-n-fajfer-in-ellis-island-other-new-york-passenger-lists.

9   "Gdynia: MS Batory," In Your Pocket, https://www.inyourpocket.com/gdynia/MS-Batory_73690f, accessed February 13, 2022.

10 Lovell's Montreal Directory 1950, Bibliothèque et Archives nationales du Québec Collections, 1001.

11 Lovell's Montreal Directory, 1957, 1963, 1968, 1974.

12 Nathan Aron Feifer, obituary, *The Gazette* (Montreal), May 16, 1999, https://federationgenealogie.qc.ca/bases-de-donnees/avis-de-deces/fiche?avisID=593185.

13 Howard Gold, personal interview, December 2, 2020.

14 Judy Gold, personal interview, December 19, 2020.

15 Gold and Gold, personal interviews.

16 Judy Gold, personal interview.

17 Judy Gold, personal interview.

18 Gold and Gold, personal interviews.

19 Gold and Gold, personal interviews.

Chaya Sara Luska (#168)

1   Berkovitz, "A Sea of Troubles," 421.

2   Khaya Luskaya, List of Partisans from Belorussia, Central Database of Shoah Victims' Names, Yad Vashem.

3   Chaya Berkowicz Luska, Certificate of Residence #113139, International Tracing Service, January 20, 1954. Yad Vashem.

4   Eliyahu Berkowicz, Yad Vashem testimony [in Yiddish], no. 03/2774.

5   Chaja Luska, Certificate of Residence.

6   Gitel Szuster, Page of Testimony submitted by Isaac Szuster, May 17, 1955, Central Database of Shoah Victims' Names, Yad Vashem.

7   Berkovitz, "A Sea of Troubles."

8   Khaya Luskaya, List of Partisans from Belorussia.

9   Central Database of Shoah Victims' Names, Yad Vashem.

10 Berkowicz, Yad Vashem testimony.

11 Berkowicz, Yad Vashem testimony.

12 Berkovitz, "A Sea of Troubles," 421.

13 Chaja Luska, Certificate of Residence #113139.

14 United States Holocaust Memorial Museum, "Eschwege Displaced Persons Camp," Holocaust Encyclopedia, https://encyclopedia.ushmm.org/content/en/article/eschwege-displaced-persons-camp.

15 Berkowicz, Yad Vashem testimony.

16 Chaja Luska, Certificate of Residence #113139.

17 Chaya Luska, Review of Application for Compensation #21228, September 25, 1954, International Tracing Service, Yad Vashem.

18 Chaim Barkan, personal interview, June 7, 2023.

19 Barkan, personal interview.

Eliezer (Leizer) Shleimovich (#169)

1   Central Database of Shoah Victims' Names, Yad Vashem.

2   Gerasimova et al., *We Stood Shoulder to Shoulder*, 307, 332.

Galai (#170)

1   Central Database of Shoah Victims' Names, Yad Vashem.

2   Gerasimova et al., *We Stood Shoulder to Shoulder*, 214, 319.

Shtein (#171)
1 Central Database of Shoah Victims' Names, Yad Vashem.
2 Gerasimova et al., *We Stood Shoulder to Shoulder*, 309, 310.

Faivel Skora (#172)
1 List of Lodz Ghetto Inmates, Central Database of Shoah Victims' Names, Yad Vashem.
2 Gerasimova et al., *We Stood Shoulder to Shoulder*, 286, 329.

Berl (#173) and Yosef (Yosel, #174) Gertzovski
1 Iosif Gertzovsk, List of Murdered Individuals from Zhetl, Central Database of Shoah Victims' Names, Yad Vashem.
2 Asna Gertzovskaya, List of Murdered Individuals from Zhetl, Central Database of Shoah Victims' Names, Yad Vashem.
3 Assna Gercowski, Page of Testimony submitted by Luba Greitzer, March 26, 1957, Central Database of Shoah Victims' Names, Yad Vashem.
4 Fanya Dunetz Brodsky, personal interview, January 2, 2017.
5 Berl Dov Gercowski, Page of Testimony submitted by Nakhum Shokhet, June 25, 1956, Central Database of Shoah Victims' Names, Yad Vashem.
6 Henia Szochet, Page of Testimony submitted by Nakhum Shokhet, January 1, 1956, Central Database of Shoah Victims' Names, Yad Vashem.
7 Dunetz Brodsky, personal interview.
8 Openheim, "Politico-Communal Life in Novogrudok," 177.
9 Karpel, "Agudat Yisrael," 166.
10 Dunetz Brodsky, personal interview.
11 Asna Gercowski, Page of Testimony submitted by Nakhum Shokhet, October 26, 1956, Central Database of Shoah Victims' Names, Yad Vashem.
12 Dunetz Brodsky, personal interview.
13 Iosif Gertzovsk, List of Murdered Individuals from Zhetl; Yosef Gercowski, Page of Testimony submitted by Nakhum Shokhet, June 25, 1956, Central Database of Shoah Victims' Names, Yad Vashem.
14 Berl Dov Gercowski, Page of Testimony submitted by Nakhum Shokhet; Berko Gertzovski, List of Murdered Individuals from Zhetl, Central Database of Shoah Victims' Names, Yad Vashem.
15 Henia Szochet, Page of Testimony submitted by Nakhum Shokhet.
16 Henia Szochet, Page of Testimony submitted by Sara (Epstein) Shoer, April 18, 1999, Central Database of Shoah Victims' Names, Yad Vashem.
17 Ruthi Begin, personal interview, December 27, 2017.
18 Kaplinski, *Pinkas Zhetl*, 21.

Shmuel (#175) and Moshe (#176) Paretzki

1. Kaplinski, *Pinkas Zhetl*, 26.
2. Gerasimova et al., *We Stood Shoulder to Shoulder*, 271, 300.
3. Fanya Dunetz Brodsky, personal interview, January 27, 2018.
4. Chaya Magid, personal interview, January 27, 2018.
5. Mayevski (Nadel), "In the Novardok Labor Camp," 361.
6. Schmuel Porecki, Page of Testimony submitted by Pesia (Mayevski) Nadel, April 24, 1957, Central Database of Shoah Victims' Names, Yad Vashem.
7. Moische Porecki, Page of Testimony submitted by Pesia (Mayevski) Nadel, April 24, 1957, Central Database of Shoah Victims' Names, Yad Vashem.
8. Movsha Paretzki, List of Murdered Individuals from Zhetl, Central Database of Shoah Victims' Names, Yad Vashem.
9. Moische Porecki, Page of Testimony submitted by Pesia (Mayevski) Nadel.
10. Gnesha Paretzkaya, List of Murdered Individuals from Zhetl, Central Database of Shoah Victims' Names, Yad Vashem.
11. Gneshe Poretzki, Page of Testimony submitted by Pesia (Mayevski) Nadel, April 24, 1957, Central Database of Shoah Victims' Names, Yad Vashem.
12. Reisel Poretzki, Page of Testimony submitted by Pesia (Mayevski) Nadel, April 24, 1957, Central Database of Shoah Victims' Names, Yad Vashem.
13. Schmuel Porecki, Page of Testimony submitted by Pesia (Mayevski) Nadel.
14. Szmuel Parecki, Page of Testimony submitted by Aaron Razvaski, March 18, 1957, Central Database of Shoah Victims' Names, Yad Vashem.
15. Riwa Ester Parecki, Page of Testimony submitted by Aaron Razvaski, March 18, 1957, Central Database of Shoah Victims' Names, Yad Vashem.
16. Reisel Porecki, Page of Testimony submitted by Aaron Razvaski, March 18, 1957, Central Database of Shoah Victims' Names, Yad Vashem.
17. Gneshe Poretzki, Page of Testimony submitted by Pesia (Mayevski) Nadel.
18. Kaplinski, *Pinkas Zhetl*, 26.

Yitzchak Mazurkevich (#177)

1. Leibovitz, "The Great Destruction," 296.
2. Leibovitz, 296. The account states that the loaves were "22 pounds each," which presumably is a typo for 2.2 pounds.
3. Gerasimova et al., *We Stood Shoulder to Shoulder*, 325.
4. Aron Mazurkiewicz, Page of Testimony submitted by Yehudit Monter, January 3, 1957, Central Database of Shoah Victims' Names, Yad Vashem.
5. Gerasimova et al., *We Stood Shoulder to Shoulder*, 325.
6. Isaak Mazurkevich, Page of Testimony submitted by Albert Mayzel, December 20, 1954, Central Database of Shoah Victims' Names, Yad Vashem.

Tanchum Epshtein (#178)

1. Tana Epsztejn, Page of Testimony submitted by Khana Epshtein, June 6, 1955, Central Database of Shoah Victims' Names, Yad Vashem.
2. Tanchum Epstain, Page of Testimony submitted by Lyuba Greitzer, March 26, 1957, Central Database of Shoah Victims' Names, Yad Vashem.
3. Isaak Epshteyn, List of Murdered Individuals from Zhetl, Central Database of Shoah Victims' Names, Yad Vashem.
4. Khaya Epshteyn, List of Murdered Individuals from Zhetl, Central Database of Shoah Victims' Names, Yad Vashem.
5. Sheynya Epshteyn, List of Murdered Individuals from Zhetl, Central Database of Shoah Victims' Names, Yad Vashem.
6. Tana Epsztejn, Page of Testimony submitted by Khana Epshtein.
7. Tanchum Epstain, Page of Testimony submitted by Lyuba Greitzer.
8. Mayevsky (Nadel), "In the Novardok Labor Camp," 361.

Betzalel (Tsala) Bielitski (#179)

1. Bezalel Bielicki, Page of Testimony submitted by Shlomo Razvazhski, April 28, 1957; Cala Bielicki, Page of Testimony submitted by Chana Epshtein, June 30, 1955, Central Database of Shoah Victims' Names, Yad Vashem.
2. Mayevski (Nadel), "In the Novardok Labor Camp," 360.
3. Tzalya Belitzki, List of Murdered Individuals from Zhetl, Central Database of Shoah Victims' Names, Yad Vashem.
4. Chinke Bielicki, Page of Testimony submitted by Shlomo Razvazhski, April 28, 1957, Central Database of Shoah Victims' Names, Yad Vashem.
5. Hyena Belitzky, Page of Testimony submitted by Alte Kuznietzki, April 8, 1957, Central Database of Shoah Victims' Names, Yad Vashem.
6. Solya Berman, Page of Testimony submitted by Sara Rabinovich, October 23, 1955, Central Database of Shoah Victims' Names, Yad Vashem.
7. Mordechai Belitzky, Page of Testimony submitted by Alte Kuznietzki, April 8, 1957, Central Database of Shoah Victims' Names, Yad Vashem.
8. Matla Ogolnik, Page of Testimony submitted by Chana Epshtein, June 30, 1955, Central Database of Shoah Victims' Names, Yad Vashem.
9. Chaja Sztejnhaus, Page of Testimony submitted by Chana Epshtein, June 30, 1955, Central Database of Shoah Victims' Names, Yad Vashem.
10. Sara Belitzkaya, List of Murdered Individuals from Zhetl, Central Database of Shoah Victims' Names, Yad Vashem.
11. Zelik Belitzki, List of Murdered Individuals from Zhetl, Central Database of Shoah Victims' Names, Yad Vashem.
12. Sara Bielicki, Page of Testimony submitted by Shlomo Razvazhski, April 28, 1957, Central Database of Shoah Victims' Names, Yad Vashem.

13 Tec, *Defiance*,189; Leibovitz, "The Great Destruction," 504–5.

14 Kaplinski, *Pinkas Zhetl*, 20.

Leib Daichovski (#180)

1 Zeev Galili, "At Chaki-li v'Echzor: Makor-Hashir v'Hamanginah" [You Wait for Me and I'll Come Back: The Origin of the Song and the Melody], Higayon b'Shigayon [The Logic in Madness], August 28, 2010, http://www.zeevgalili .com/2010/08/10341, accessed October 17, 2019.

2 Gerasimova et al., *We Stood Shoulder to Shoulder*, 227, 321.

3 Fanya Yudelevich, Lilach Yudelevich Ron, Iris Yudelevich Chatami, personal interviews, May 20, 2013.

4 Yudelevich, Yudelevich Ron, Yudelevich Chatami, personal interviews .

5 Shulamit Deikhovski, Page of Testimony submitted by Roza Dzhencholski Iudelevich, April 22, 1999, Central Database of Shoah Victims' Names, Yad Vashem.

6 Lea Deikhovski, Page of Testimony submitted by Roza Dzhencholski Iudelevich, April 22, 1999, Central Database of Shoah Victims' Names, Yad Vashem.

7 Shulamit Deikhovski, Page of Testimony submitted by Roza Dzhencholski Iudelevich.

8 Fanya Yudelevich, personal interview.

9 Yudelevich, personal interview .

10 Leib Deikhovski, Page of Testimony submitted by Roza Dzhencholski, April 22, 1999, Central Database of Shoah Victims' Names, Yad Vashem.

11 Yudelevich Ron and Yudelevich Chatami, personal interviews.

12 Yudelevich Ron and Yudelevich Chatami, personal interviews .

Abram (#181) and Moshe (#182) Milovanski

1 Abram Milovanski, List of Murdered Individuals from Zhetl, Central Database of Shoah Victims' Names, Yad Vashem.

2 Movsha Milovanski, List of Murdered Individuals from Zhetl, Central Database of Shoah Victims' Names, Yad Vashem.

3 Yakov Milovanski, List of Murdered Individuals from Zhetl, Central Database of Shoah Victims' Names, Yad Vashem.

4 Isaak Milovanski, List of Murdered Individuals from Zhetl, Central Database of Shoah Victims' Names, Yad Vashem.

5 Gerasimova et al., *We Stood Shoulder to Shoulder*, 264, 326.

Yedidia Ochonovski (#183)

1   Jedidia Ochonowski, Page of Testimony submitted by Batya Gradis, March 30, 1957, Central Database of Shoah Victims' Names, Yad Vashem.

2   Yedida Okhonovski, List of Murdered Individuals from Zhetl, Central Database of Shoah Victims' Names, Yad Vashem.

3   Lea Ochonowski, Page of Testimony submitted by Batya Gradis, March 30, 1957, Central Database of Shoah Victims' Names, Yad Vashem.

4   Sara Okhonovskaya, List of Murdered Individuals from Zhetl Central Database of Shoah Victims' Names, Yad Vashem.

5   Kaplinski, *Pinkas Zhetl*, 20.

6   Jedidia Ochonowski, Page of Testimony submitted by Batya Gradis.

7   Yedidia Okhonovski, List of Murdered Individuals from Zhetl.

8   Okhonovski, List of Murdered Individuals from Zhetl.

9   Chaya Magid, personal interview, January 10, 2018.

10 Tec, *Defiance*, 189; Leibovitz, "The Great Destruction," 504–5.

11 Kaplinski, *Pinkas Zhetl*, 20.

Chaim Shlachtman (#184)

1   Khaim Shlyakhtman, List of Murdered Jews from Novogrodek, Central Database of Shoah Victims' Names, Yad Vashem.

2   Jack Kagan and Dov Cohen, *Surviving the Holocaust with the Russian Jewish Partisans* (London: Vallentine, Mitchell and Son, Ltd., 1998), 26.

3   Sara Shlyakhtman, memorial notice submitted by Leib Shmuel Sladovski, in *Pinkas Navaredok*, ed. Yerushalmi et al., 409.

4   Iosif Shlyakhtman, List of Murdered Jews from Novogrodek, Central Database of Shoah Victims' Names, Yad Vashem.

5   Bella (listed as Sima) Shlyakhtman, List of Murdered Jews from Novogrodek, Central Database of Shoah Victims' Names, Yad Vashem.

6   Moysey Shlyakhtman, List of Murdered Jews from Novogrodek, Central Database of Shoah Victims' Names, Yad Vashem.

7   Kagan and Cohen, *Surviving the Holocaust*, 26.

8   Kagan and Cohen, 26.

9   Kagan and Cohen, 26–27.

10 Sara Shlyakhtman, memorial notice; Khaim Shlyakhtman, Iosif Shlyakhtman, Moysey Shlyakhtman, and Bella (Sima) Shlyakhtman, List of Murdered Jews from Novogrodek.

11 Tamara Vershitskaya, personal communication, January 2012.

12 Gerasimova et al., *We Stood Shoulder to Shoulder*, 307, 332.

Rafael Lusky (#185)

1. Pinchas Lusky, Page of Testimony submitted by Yehuda Lusky, April 22, 1994, Central Database of Shoah Victims' Names, Yad Vashem.

2. Chana Lusky, Page of Testimony submitted by Yehuda Lusky, April 22, 1994, Central Database of Shoah Victims' Names, Yad Vashem.

3. Chaim Lusky, personal diary, submitted by Rachel Blatman.

4. Lusky, personal diary.

5. Liba Lusky, Page of Testimony submitted by Yehuda Lusky, April 24, 1994, Central Database of Shoah Victims' Names, Yad Vashem.

6. Avigdor Lusky, Page of Testimony submitted by Alte Kuznietzki, April 8, 1957, Central Database of Shoah Victims' Names, Yad Vashem.

7. Kaplinski, *Pinkas Zhetl*, 23.

8. Rafael Lusky, Page of Testimony submitted by Gabriel Sivan, April 4, 1999; Rafael Lusky, Page of Testimony submitted by Moshe Iting, May 30, 1957, Central Database of Shoah Victims' Names, Yad Vashem.

9. Yehuda Lusky, personal interview, February 8, 2018.

10. Lusky, personal interview.

11. Chaim Lusky, gravestone, Kiryat Shaul Cemetery, Tel Aviv, Israel, BillionGraves, https://billiongraves.com/grave/17628490/לוסקי-חיים.

12. Chaim Lusky, personal diary.

13. Arie Lusky, gravestone, Netanya Shikun Vatikim Cemetery, Netanya, Israel, BillionGraves, November 11, 2017, https://billiongraves.com/grave/20125716/לוסקי-אריה.

14. Dr. Moshe Lusky, personal interview, February 11, 2018.

15. Ziva Falek, personal interviews, February 11 and 12, 2018.

16. Yehuda Lusky, personal interview.

Moshe Gorodynski (#186) and Gorodynski (#187)

1. Mowsza Gorodinski, Page of Testimony submitted by Shlomo Gorodynski, July 11, 1956, Central Database of Shoah Victims' Names, Yad Vashem.

2. Mowsza Gorodinski, Page of Testimony; Abram Gorodynski, Page of Testimony submitted by Shaul Gorodynski, February 28, 1954, Central Database of Shoah Victims' Names, Yad Vashem; Abraham Gorodynski, Page of Testimony submitted by Sonya Oshman, August 20, 1991, Central Database of Shoah Victims' Names, Yad Vashem.

3. Mowsza Gorodinski, Page of Testimony submitted by Shlomo Gorodynski.

4. Yitzchak Gorodinski, Page of Testimony submitted by Shlomo Gorodynski, July 11, 1956, Central Database of Shoah Victims' Names, Yad Vashem.

5   Avraham Gorodinski, Page of Testimony submitted by Shlomo Gorodynski, July 11, 1956, Central Database of Shoah Victims' Names, Yad Vashem.

6   Rakhel Gorodinski, Page of Testimony submitted by Shlomo Gorodynski, July 11, 1956, Central Database of Shoah Victims' Names, Yad Vashem.

7   Shlomo Gorodinski, Land Compensation Office document, February 6, 1957, International Tracing Service, Yad Vashem.

8   Mirjam Gorodinski, Page of Testimony submitted by Shlomo Gorodynski, July 11, 1956, Central Database of Shoah Victims' Names, Yad Vashem.

9   Shaul Gorodinski, Page of Testimony submitted by Shlomo Gorodynski, July 11, 1956, Central Database of Shoah Victims' Names, Yad Vashem.

10 Gerasimova et al., *We Stood Shoulder to Shoulder*, 223.

11 Mowsza Gorodinski, Page of Testimony submitted by Shlomo Gorodynski.

12 Gerasimova et al., *We Stood Shoulder to Shoulder*, 223.

Moshe (#188) and Nechama (#189) Rolnik

1   Movsha Rolnik, List of Murdered Individuals from Ivenets, Soviet Extraordinary State Commission, Central Database of Shoah Victims' Names, Yad Vashem.

2   Ellen J. Eisner, Judy Prigal, and Joseph Rubinstein, eds. *The Memorial Book of Iwieniec, Kamien, and the Surrounding Region*, translation of *Sefer Iwieniec, Kamien v'Hasevivah: Sefer Zikaron* (Tel Aviv: Iwieniec Societies in Israel and the Diaspora, 1973), 436, https://www.jewishgen.org/yizkor/ivenets/ivenets.html.

3   Eisner et al, *The Memorial Book of Iwieniec, Kamien, and the Surrounding Region*, 437.

4   Movsha Rolnik, List of Murdered Individuals from Ivenets.

5   Gerasimova et al., *We Stood Shoulder to Shoulder*, 280.

6   *The Memorial Book of Iwieniec, Kamien, and the Surrounding Region*, 437.

7   Gerasimova et al., *We Stood Shoulder to Shoulder*, 280, 328.

Natan (Nota) Goberman (#190)

1   Galina Smielova, undated extract from personal file of M. N. Goberman, Archive of the Military Registration and Enlistment Office, Tikhvin, Russia, as received from Tamara Vershitskaya, personal communication, July 28, 2021.

2   Smielova, undated extract.

3   Tec, *Defiance*, 189; Leibovitz, "The Great Destruction," 504–5.

4   Smielova, undated extract.

5   Moysey Goberman, List of Partisans from Belorussia, Central Database of Shoah Victims' Names, Yad Vashem.

6   Tamara Vershitskaya, personal communication, July 28, 2021.

7   Vershitskaya, personal communication.

Samuil (#191) and Eliezer (Leizer, #192) Zusmanovich

1   Shmuel Zusmanovitch, personal interview, January 17, 2019.
2   Zusmanovitch, personal interview .
3   Gerasimova et al., *We Stood Shoulder to Shoulder*, 236.
4   Shmuel Zusmanovitch, personal interview.
5   Eliezer Zusmanovitch, in the documentary film *Tunnel of Hope*, directed by Dror H. Shwartz (Jerusalem: Go2Films, 2015).
6   Zusmanovitch, in *Tunnel of Hope*.
7   Gerasimova et al., *We Stood Shoulder to Shoulder*, 236.
8   Mordechai Majerowicz, Yad Vashem testimony, no. 0.3/2106.
9   Shmuel Zusmanovitch, personal interview.
10   Central Database of Shoah Victims' Names, Yad Vashem.
11   Shmuel Zusmanovitch, personal interview.
12   Shmuel Zusmanovitch, personal interview.
13   Shmuel Zusmanovich, personal communication, August 22, 2023.
14   Eliezer Zusmanovich, personal interview, September 1, 2018.
15   Zusmanovitch, in *Tunnel of Hope*.
16   Eliezer Zusmanovich, personal interview, September 1, 2018.
17   Eliezer Zusmanovich, personal interview.

Abram (#193) and Notek (#194) Chernevich

1   Aron Czarniewicz, Page of Testimony submitted by Genya Markovich, August 25, 1986, Central Database of Shoah Victims' Names, Yad Vashem.
2   Moshe Ceranowicz, Page of Testimony submitted by Judie Goldstein Ostroff, January 11, 2001, Central Database of Shoah Victims' Names, Yad Vashem.
3   Moche Cernowic, Page of Testimony submitted by Khava Chernovich, November 28, 1956, Central Database of Shoah Victims' Names, Yad Vashem.
4   Gerasimova et al., *We Stood Shoulder to Shoulder*, 303, 331.
5   Tamara Vershitskaya, personal communication, April 29, 2019.
6   Gerasimova et al., *We Stood Shoulder to Shoulder*, 302.
7   Abram Chereowich, List of Partisans from Belorussia, Central Database of Shoah Victims' Names, Yad Vashem.
8   Notek Chereowich, List of Partisans from Belorussia, Central Database of Shoah Victims' Names, Yad Vashem.

Henia Yarmovski (#195)

1   Jonathan Sacks, *Morality: Restoring the Common Good in Divided Times* (New York: Basic Books, 2020), 48.
2   Fanya Dunetz Brodsky, personal interview, July 1, 2012.

3   Genia Jarmowska, Certificate of Residence #105901, Allied High Commission for Germany, International Tracing Service, Yad Vashem.

4   Moshe Chaim Veiner, Page of Testimony submitted by Henia Yarmovski, May 23, 1955, Central Database of Shoah Victims' Names, Yad Vashem.

5   Sara Veiner, Page of Testimony submitted by Henia Yarmovski, May 23, 1955, Central Database of Shoah Victims' Names, Yad Vashem.

6   Zeidil Veiner, Page of Testimony submitted by Henia Yarmovski, May 23, 1955, Central Database of Shoah Victims' Names, Yad Vashem.

7   Feigel Veiner, Page of Testimony submitted by Henia Yarmovski, May 23, 1955, Central Database of Shoah Victims' Names, Yad Vashem.

8   Moshe Chaim Veiner, Sara Veiner, Zeidil Veiner, Feigel Veiner, Pages of Testimony.

9   Tali Yarmovski Alt, personal interview, April 24, 2019.

10   Avraham Jarmowski, Page of Testimony submitted by Henia Yarmovski, May 23, 1955, Central Database of Shoah Victims' Names, Yad Vashem.

11   Fanya Abramowitz, Page of Testimony submitted by Henia Yarmovski, May 23, 1955, Central Database of Shoah Victims' Names, Yad Vashem.

12   Yarmovski Alt, personal interview, April 24, 2019.

13   Mulik Abramowitz, Page of Testimony submitted by Henia Yarmovski, May 23, 1955, Central Database of Shoah Victims' Names, Yad Vashem.

14   Tali Yarmovski Alt, personal interview, April 24, 2019.

15   Sonia Jarmowska, Page of Testimony submitted by Henia Yarmovski, May 23, 1955, Central Database of Shoah Victims' Names, Yad Vashem.

16   Dunetz Brodsky, personal interview, July 1, 2012.

17   Yarmovski Alt, personal interview, April 24, 2019.

18   Dunetz Brodsky, personal interview, July 1, 2012.

19   Tamara Vershitskaya, personal communication, January 2012.

20   Genia Jarmowska, Certificate of Residence.

21   "Germany: Pocking," JDC Joint Distribution Committee Archives, https://archives.jdc.org/project/germany-pocking/, accessed April 28, 2019.

22   Yarmovski Alt, personal interview, April 24, 2019.

23   Henia Yarmovski, letters from Poking, 1947.

24   Pola and Uri Yarmovski, gravestones, Yarkon Cemetery Tel Aviv, Neshama.net, http://www.neshama.net/memorials/66131/?id=152648&media=picture&type=Profile.

25   Yarmovski Alt, personal interview, April 24, 2019.

26   Genia Jarmowska, Certificate of Residence.

27   United States Holocaust Memorial Museum, "Heidenheim Displaced Persons Camp," Holocaust Encyclopedia, https://encyclopedia.ushmm.org/content/en/article/heidenheim-displaced-persons-camp.

28   Yarmovski Alt, personal interview, April 24, 2019.

29 Pola and Uri Yarmovski, gravestones.
30 Yarmovski Alt, personal interview, August 23, 2023.
31 Yarmovski Alt, personal interviews.

David Rabinovich (#196)
1 Central Database of Shoah Victims' Names, Yad Vashem.
2 Gerasimova et al., *We Stood Shoulder to Shoulder*, 275, 327.

Zelda Kopernik (#197)
1 Mordechai Majerowicz, Yad Vashem testimony, no. 0.3/2106.
2 Zelda Kopernik, List of Jews in the Korelichi Ghetto 1942, Central Database of Shoah Victims' Names, Yad Vashem, Jerusalem; Gerasimova et al., *We Stood Shoulder to Shoulder*, 247.
3 Zelda Kopernik, List of Jews in the Korelichi Ghetto.
4 Orcia Kupernik, Page of Testimony submitted by Lea Kornfeld, September 24, 1999, Central Database of Shoah Victims' Names, Yad Vashem.
5 Fayvel Kopernik, List of Jews in the Karelich Ghetto, Central Database of Shoah Victims' Names, Yad Vashem.
6 Aron Kopernik, Zelda Kopernik, Fayvel Kopernik, List of Jews in the Karelich Ghetto 1942, Central Database of Shoah Victims' Names, Yad Vashem.
7 Aron Kopernik, List of Murdered Individuals from Novogrudok, Central Database of Shoah Victims' Names, Yad Vashem.
8 Fayvel Kopernik, List of Murdered Individuals from Novogrudok, Central Database of Shoah Victims' Names, Yad Vashem.
9 Fayvel Kopernik, List of Murdered Individuals from Novogrudok.
10 Fayvel Kopernik, List of Jews in the Karelichi Ghetto.

Potasznik (#198)
1 Central Database of Shoah Victims' Names, Yad Vashem.
2 Gerasimova et al., *We Stood Shoulder to Shoulder*, 274.
3 Maks Potashnik, List of Partisans from Belorussia, Central Database of Shoah Victims' Names, Yad Vashem.
4 Tamara Vershitskaya, personal interview, March 29, 2023.

Peretz Wolkowicki (#199)
1 Hana Gotian, personal interview, March 11, 2018.
2 Perec Wolkowycki, Application for Reparations, May 28, 1965, International Tracing Service Archives, Yad Vashem.

3   Gotian, personal interview.
4   Shimon Wolkowicki, personal interview, October 24, 2019.
5   Gerasimova et al., *We Stood Shoulder to Shoulder*, 213.
6   Shimon Wolkowicki, personal interview.
7   Wolkowicki, personal interview.
8   Wolkowicki, personal interview.
9   Gotian, personal interview.
10   Shimon Wolkowicki, personal interview.
11   Gotian, personal interview.
12   Gotian, personal interview.
13   Gotian, personal interview.
14   Gotian, personal interview.
15   Peretz Wolkowicki, gravestone, Mount Hebron Cemetery, Flushing, NY, Find a Grave, September 9, 2011, https://www.findagrave.com/memorial/76279190; Sara Wolkowicki, gravestone, Mount Hebron Cemetery, Flushing, NY, Find a Grave, September 9, 2011, https://www.findagrave.com/memorial/76279191.
16   Hana Gotian, personal interview, August 27, 2023.

Henia Bruk (#200)

1   "Martyrs of Lubtch," "Martyrs of Delatich," translation of *Lubtsh ve-Delatitsh: Sefer Zikaron*, ed. K. Hilel, Israel, 1971, p. 444, https://www.jewishgen.org/yizkor/Lyubcha/lyu444.html/.
2   United HIAS Service, Geneva, Switzerland, Letter to International Tracing Service re Henia Bruk, 1963, International Tracing Service, Yad Vashem.
3   Gerasimova et al., *We Stood Shoulder to Shoulder*, 209, 319.

Menachem Senderovski (#201)

1   Menakhim Senderovski, List of Murdered Individuals from Zhetl, Central Database of Shoah Victims' Names, Yad Vashem.
2   Menacham Senderowski, Page of Testimony submitted by Lyuba Greitzer, March 3, 1957, Central Database of Shoah Victims' Names, Yad Vashem.
3   Menachem Senderovsky, Page of Testimony submitted by Celia Sandor, October 8, 2007, Central Database of Shoah Victims' Names, Yad Vashem.
4   Menacham Senderowski, Page of Testimony submitted by Lyuba Greitzer.
5   *Sefer Zikaron Kadosh of Slonim Hassidim* [in Hebrew] (Jerusalem, 1967); Central Database of Shoah Victims' Names, Yad Vashem.
6   Menacham Senderowski, Page of Testimony submitted by Lyuba Greitzer.
7   Menachem Senderovsky, Page of Testimony submitted by Celia Sandor.

8 Menachem Sendrowski, Page of Testimony submitted by Khanan Boldo, March 24, 1957, Central Database of Shoah Victims' Names, Yad Vashem.

9 Gerasimova et al., *We Stood Shoulder to Shoulder*, 285, 328.

Rafael Shofer (#202)

1 Rafael Sofer, Certificate of Marriage, November 23, 1948, Tel Aviv, Marriages & Divorces 1921–1948, Palestine British Mandate collection, Israel Genealogy Research Association database, http://genealogy.org.il/AID/index.php?recordID=SUdSQS0xNzkxNy1NYXJyaWFnZXMtMTA1N==.

2 Rafael Szofer, UNRRA Italian Mission Information Form, June 21, 1946, International Tracing Service Archives, Yad Vashem.

3 Rafael Szafar, Application for a Certificate of Naturalization, Mandatory Government of Palestine, October 23, 1947.

4 Rafal Shofer, List of Partisans from Belorussia, Central Database of Shoah Victims' Names, Yad Vashem.

5 Rafael Szofer, UNRRA Italian Mission Information Form.

6 Leibovitz, "The Great Destruction," 504–5.

7 Mordechai Meyerowicz, Yad Vashem testimony, no. 0.3/2106.

8 Meyerowicz, Yad Vashem testimony.

9 Leibovitz, "The Great Destruction," 504–5.

10 Meyerowicz, Yad Vashem testimony.

11 Meyerowicz, Yad Vashem testimony.

12 Hirsch Samsonowicz, International Committee of the Red Cross, Munich document, September 6, 1959, International Tracing Service, Yad Vashem.

13 Hodl Samsonovich, Page of Testimony submitted by Harry Samson, March 19, 1972, Central Database of Shoah Victims' Names, Yad Vashem.

14 Gerasimova et al., *We Stood Shoulder to Shoulder*, 309.

15 Rafael Szofer, DP Camp file I3083113, Arolsen Archives, https://collections.arolsen-archives.org/en/document/80506112.

16 Rafael Szofer, UNRRA Italian Mission Information Form.

17 Rafael Sofer, *Itur Ma'an*, Israel Ministry of Interior records.

18 Rafael Sofer, Certificate of Marriage.

19 Rafael Sofer, Israel Ministry of Interior records.

Av. or Ab. Pozniak (#203)

1 Central Database of Shoah Victims' Names, Yad Vashem.

2 "Avraham Yitzkhak Pozniak," in *The Book of Ivenets, Kamien and Vicinity*, 433.

3 Abram Poznyak, List of Partisans from the Komsomolskiy Detachment, Central Database of Shoah Victims' Names, Yad Vashem.

4   Rivka Posniak, Page of Testimony submitted by Rachel Sheinbaum, January 13, 1956, Central Database of Shoah Victims' Names, Yad Vashem.

5   Abram Poznyak, List of Partisans.

6   Gerasimova et al., *We Stood Shoulder to Shoulder*, 327.

Skiba (#204)

1   Central Database of Shoah Victims' Names, Yad Vashem.

2   David Skiba, List of Partisans from Belorussia, Central Database of Shoah Victims' Names, Yad Vashem.

Pesach Abramowicz (#205)

1   Gerasimova et al., *We Stood Shoulder to Shoulder*, 198.

2   Prejsach [*sic*] Abramowicz, Deadline, Detention & Emigration Certificate, February 24, 1955. International Red Cross Committee, International Tracing Service, Yad Vashem.

3   *Novogrudok Memorial Book*, 687.

4   Feivel Abramovich, Page of Testimony submitted by Pesach Abramovich, September 24, 1955, Central Database of Shoah Victims' Names, Yad Vashem.

5   Prejsach [*sic*] Abramowicz, Deadline, Detention & Emigration Certificate.

6   Ella Abramowicz, personal interview, May 24, 2019.

7   Abramowicz, personal interview.

8   Kagan and Cohen, *Surviving the Holocaust*, 176.

9   Ella Abramowicz, personal interview.

10 Kagan and Cohen, *Surviving the Holocaust*, 182.

11 Kagan and Cohen, 183.

12 Yehoshua (Shia) Abramovich, Page of Testimony submitted by Pesach Abramovich, September 24, 1955, Central Database of Shoah Victims' Names, Yad Vashem.

13 Pnina Maman, personal interview, July 9, 2020.

14 Idel Kagan, "How I Survived," in *Novogrudok Memorial Book*, 521.

15 Pprejeach [*sic*] Abramowicz, Certificate of Residence, International Tracing Service, July 29, 1955, Yad Vashem.

16 United States Holocaust Memorial Museum, "Landsberg Displaced Persons Camp," Holocaust Encyclopedia, https://encyclopedia.ushmm.org/content/en/article/landsberg-displaced-persons-camp.

17 Dov Sadan, personal interview, August 1, 2019.

18 Abramowicz, personal interview.

19 Maman, personal interview, May 22, 2019.

20 Abramowicz, personal interview.

21 Maman, personal interview, May 22, 2019.

22 Maman and Ella Abramowicz, personal interviews.

23 Maman, personal interview, October 16, 2023.

Dvora (#206) and Shalom (#207) Svinik

1 Tsvica Svinik, personal interview, March 12, 2018.

2 Dvoyra Svinik, List of Partisans from Belorussia, Central Database of Shoah Victims' Names, Yad Vashem.

3 Svinik, personal interview.

4 Dov Ber Perski, Page of Testimony submitted by Dvora Svinik, undated Central Database of Shoah Victims' Names, Yad Vashem, Jerusalem; Michael Perski, Page of Testimony submitted by Dvora Svinik, undated, Central Database of Shoah Victims' Names, Yad Vashem.

5 Svinik, personal interview.

6 Dvora Svinik, "A Tale of a Family," in *The Book of Ivenets, Kamien and Vicinity*, 203–6.

7 Haim Avraham Svinik, including Yitzchak Aizik and Benyamin Kalman Svinik, Page of Testimony submitted by Chana Svinik, undated, Central Database of Shoah Victims' Names, Yad Vashem.

8 Dvora Svinik, "Destruction of a Jewish Community," in *The Book of Ivenets, Kamien and Vicinity*, 368–70.

9 Svinik, "Destruction of a Jewish Community," 368–70.

10 Gerasimova et al., *We Stood Shoulder to Shoulder*, 274, 327.

11 Svinik, personal interview.

12 Svinik, personal interview.

13 Svinik, personal interview.

14 Svinik, personal interview.

15 Svinik, personal interview.

16 Tsvica Svinik, personal interview, September 5, 2023.

17 Svinik, personal interview.

Dinciolski (#208)

1 Tamara Vershitskaya, personal interview, December 11, 2020.

2 Central Database of Shoah Victims' Names, Yad Vashem.

3 Asalea Weinstein, personal interview, December 8, 2020.

4 Weinstein, personal interview.

Yosef (Yosel) Shuster (#209)

1 Jack Kagan, personal communication, August 8, 2012.
2 Iosif Shuster, List of Partisans from the Ordzhonikidze Detachment of the Kirov Brigade, Central Database of Shoah Victims' Names, Yad Vashem.
3 Gerasimova et al., *We Stood Shoulder to Shoulder*, 311.
4 Tec, *Defiance*, 126–27.
5 Kagan, personal communication.

Hirsh Shkolnik (#210)

1 Girsh Shkolnik, List of Partisans from Belorussia, Central Database of Shoah Victims' Names, Yad Vashem.
2 Sonia Szkolnik, Page of Testimony submitted by Tsipora Arieli, September 10, 1956, Central Database of Shoah Victims' Names, Yad Vashem.
3 "Hershl Shkolnik the Carpenter," in *Korelitz: The Life and Destruction of a Jewish Community*, ed. Belinsky, 260, English translation at https://www.jewishgen .org/yizkor/Korelicze/kor245.html#Page260.
4 Szkolnik, Page of Testimony submitted by Tsipora Arieli.
5 "Hershl Shkolnik the Carpenter," 260.
6 Szkolnik, Page of Testimony submitted by Tsipora Arieli.
7 "Hershl Shkolnik the Carpenter," 260.
8 Merka Lev, Page of Testimony submitted by Tsipora Arieli, September 10, 1956, Central Database of Shoah Victims' Names, Yad Vashem.
9 Monus Lev, Page of Testimony submitted by Tsipora Arieli, September 10, 1956, Central Database of Shoah Victims' Names, Yad Vashem.
10 Hadasa Lev, Page of Testimony submitted by Tsipora Arieli, September 10, 1956, Central Database of Shoah Victims' Names, Yad Vashem.
11 Kagan, "Surviving the Holocaust," 570.
12 Kagan, 570–71.
13 Kagan, 571.
14 Kagan, 571.
15 Kagan, 571.
16 Gerasimova et al., *We Stood Shoulder to Shoulder*, 307.
17 "Hershl Shkolnik the Carpenter," 260.
18 Hersz Szkolnik, Alphabetisches Verzeichnis polnischer Juden, Az: F-18-1o8, International Tracing Service, Yad Vashem.
19 Hirsch Schkolnik, AJDC record File F-18-253, 19.5.1950, International Tracing Service, Yad Vashem.
20 Zvi Shkolnik, gravestone, Netanya Shikun Vatikim Cemetery, Netanya, Israel, BillionGraves, https://billiongraves.com/grave/20525085/צבי-שקולניק.

21 Gili Arieli, Gili family tree, managed by Gili Arieli, Myheritage.com, https://www.myheritage.com/site-184584952/gili-2012.

Leib Berman (#211)

1 Mayevski (Nadel), "In the Novardok Labor Camp," 360.
2 Duffy, *The Bielski Brothers*, 198; Kagan and Cohen, *Surviving the Holocaust*, 176.
3 Yisrael Kolachek, personal interview, December 6, 2016.
4 Leib Berman, Page of Testimony submitted by Alte Kuznietzki, April 8, 1957, Central Database of Shoah Victims' Names, Yad Vashem.
5 Leib Arie Berman, Page of Testimony submitted by Ephraim Shepshelevich, December 13, 1955, Central Database of Shoah Victims' Names, Yad Vashem.
6 Leyba Berman, List of Murdered Individuals from Zhetl, Central Database of Shoah Victims' Names, Yad Vashem.
7 Leib Berman, Page of Testimony submitted by Batia (Rabinowitz) Gardes, April 28, 1957, Central Database of Shoah Victims' Names, Yad Vashem.
8 Rakhelya Berman, List of Murdered Individuals from Zhetl, Central Database of Shoah Victims' Names, Yad Vashem.
9 Minya Berman, List of Murdered Individuals from Zhetl, Central Database of Shoah Victims' Names, Yad Vashem.
10 Brokha Berman, List of Murdered Individuals from Zhetl, Central Database of Shoah Victims' Names, Yad Vashem.
11 Betzalel Berman, Page of Testimony submitted by Ephraim Shepshelevich, December 13, 1955, Central Database of Shoah Victims' Names, Yad Vashem.
12 Sule Bermann, Page of Testimony submitted by Batia (Rabinowitz) Gardes, April 28, 1957, Central Database of Shoah Victims' Names, Yad Vashem, Jerusalem; Sula Berman, Page of Testimony submitted by Ephraim Shepshelevich, December 13, 1955, Central Database of Shoah Victims' Names, Yad Vashem, Jerusalem; Solya Berman, Page of Testimony submitted by Sara Rabinovitz, October 23, 1955, Central Database of Shoah Victims' Names, Yad Vashem.
13 Tec, *Defiance*, 189; Leibovitz, "The Great Destruction," 504–5.
14 Leib Arie Berman, Page of Testimony submitted by Ephraim Shepshelevich.
15 Leib Berman, Page of Testimony submitted by Batia (Rabinowitz) Gardes.
16 Kaplinski, *Pinkas Zhetl*, 20.

Kokin (#212)

1 Central Database of Shoah Victims' Names, Yad Vashem.
2 Central Database of Shoah Victims' Names.

3   Lev Kokin, List of Partisans from the Kalinin Detachment under the Command of Bielski, Central Database of Shoah Victims' Names, Yad Vashem.

4   Gerasimova et al., *We Stood Shoulder to Shoulder*, 246.

5   Lev Kokin, List of Partisans from the Ordzhonikidze Detachment of the Kirov Brigade, Central Database of Shoah Victims' Names, Yad Vashem.

6   Tec, *Defiance*, 126–27.

7   Cholawsky, *Meri v'Lochmah Partizanit*, 412.

Shmuel Vainshtein (#213)

1   Szmuel David Wainsztein, Page of Testimony submitted by Pesia (Mayevski) Nadel, May 29, 1955, Central Database of Shoah Victims' Names, Yad Vashem.

2   Samuyel Vaynshteyn, List of Murdered Individuals from Zhetl, Central Database of Shoah Victims' Names, Yad Vashem.

3   Teiba Weinstein, Page of Testimony submitted by Pesia (Mayevski) Nadel, April 30, 1957, Central Database of Shoah Victims' Names, Yad Vashem.

4   Teiba Weinstein, Page of Testimony.

5   Henoch Weinstein, Page of Testimony submitted by Pesia (Mayevski) Nadel, April 30, 1957, Central Database of Shoah Victims' Names, Yad Vashem.

6   Mairim Weinstein, Page of Testimony submitted by Pesia (Mayevski) Nadel, April 30, 1957, Central Database of Shoah Victims' Names, Yad Vashem.

7   Mairim Weinstein, Page of Testimony; Henoch Weinstein, Page of Testimony submitted by Pesia (Mayevski) Nadel.

8   Szmuel David Weinstein, Teiba Weinstein, Henoch Weinstein, and Mairim Weinstein, Pages of Testimony.

9   Leyba Vaynshteyn, List of Murdered Individuals from Zhetl, Central Database of Shoah Victims' Names, Yad Vashem.

10   Sara Vaynshteyn, List of Murdered Individuals from Zhetl, Central Database of Shoah Victims' Names, Yad Vashem.

11   Tec, *Defiance*, 189; Leibovitz, "The Great Destruction," 504–5.

12   Szmuel David Wainsztein, Page of Testimony submitted by Pesia (Mayevski) Nadel.

13   Kaplinski, *Pinkas Zhetl*, 22.

Saadia Gertzovski (#214)

1   Sadiya Gertzovski, List of Jews in the Karelich Ghetto, 1942, Central Database of Shoah Victims' Names, Yad Vashem.

2   Stephen Greenberg, personal interview, September 29, 2020.

3   Sadja Graczowski Gertzovski, Page of Testimony submitted by Lea Kornfeld, May 13, 1999, Central Database of Shoah Victims' Names, Yad Vashem.

4   Rachel Graczowski Gertzovski, Page of Testimony submitted by Lea Kornfeld, May 13, 1999, Central Database of Shoah Victims' Names, Yad Vashem.

5   Lea Graczowski Gertzovski, Page of Testimony submitted by Lea Kornfeld, May 13, 1999, Central Database of Shoah Victims' Names, Yad Vashem.

6   Gerasimova et al., *We Stood Shoulder to Shoulder*, 217, 320.

7   Memorial notice for Saadia Gertzovski, submitted by Sonia Greenberg and Perle Carson, *Korelitz: The Life and Destruction of a Jewish Community*, ed. Belinsky, translation, JewishGen., 331.

8   Stephen Greenberg, personal interview, September 22, 2020.

9   Greenberg, personal interview.

10 Greenberg, personal interview, September 29, 2020.

11 Shlema Gertzovski, List of Jews in the Korelich Ghetto, 1942, Central Database of Shoah Victims' Names, Yad Vashem.

12 Greenberg, personal interview, September 22, 2020.

13 Greenberg, personal communication, September 29, 2020.

14 Greenberg, personal interview, September 22, 2020.

15 Greenberg, personal interview.

16 Gerasimova et al., *We Stood Shoulder to Shoulder*, 217.

17 Tamara Vershitskaya, personal communication, September 23, 2020.

18 Vershitskaya, personal communication.

19 Greenberg, personal interview, September 29, 2020.

20 Greenberg, personal interview.

21 Greenberg, personal interview.

22 Stephen Greenberg, personal interview, August 31, 2023.

Meir Berkowicz

1   Meer Berkovich, Personal Cards of Jewish Partisans from The Kalinin Detachment under the Command of Bielski, Central Database of Shoah Victims' Names, Yad Vashem.

2   Majer/Myer Berkowicz, TD #718056, inquiry card, International Tracing Service, Yad Vashem.

3   Baruch Berkowicz, Sara Feige Berkowicz, and Wolff Berkowicz, Pages of Testimony submitted by Myer Berk, October 5, 1985, Central Database of Shoah Victims' Names, Yad Vashem.

4   Moishe Berkowicz, Page of Testimony submitted by Joel Berk, January 15, 1997, Central Database of Shoah Victims' Names, Yad Vashem.

5   Wolff Berkowicz; Moishe Berkowicz, Pages of Testimony.

6   Rachel Berkowicz, Page of Testimony submitted by Myer Berk, undated, Central Database of Shoah Victims' Names, Yad Vashem.

7   Shmulik Berkowicz, Page of Testimony submitted by Myer Berk, October 5, 1985, Central Database of Shoah Victims' Names, Yad Vashem.

8   Yehoshua Yaffe, "Chapters from the Holocaust: The Second Slaughter," in *Novogrudok Memorial Book*, 538.

9   Gerasimova et al., *We Stood Shoulder to Shoulder*, 311.

10   Gerasimova et al., 205.

11   Majer/Myer Berkowicz, inquiry card, International Tracing Service.

12   United States Holocaust Memorial Museum, "Bergen-Belsen Displaced Persons Camp," Holocaust Encyclopedia, https://encyclopedia.ushmm.org/content/en/article/bergen-belsen-displaced-persons-camp.

13   Joel Berk, personal interview, April 7, 2019.

14   Eta Fuchs Berk, Gilbert Allardyce, *Chosen: A Holocaust Memoir; The Eta Fuchs Berk Story* (Fredericton, Canada: Goose Land Editions, 1998).

15   Majer/Myer Berkowicz, inquiry card, International Tracing Service.

16   Daniel Othfos, "Aquitania," The Great Ocean Liners, May 2, 2018. http://thegreatoceanliners.com/articles/aquitania/.

17   Majer/Myer Berkowicz, inquiry card, International Tracing Service.

18   Berk, personal interview.

19   Berk, personal interview.

20   Myer Berk, gravestone, Sgoolai Israel Cemetery, Fredericton, Canada, Find a Grave, https://www.findagrave.com/memorial/171270066/myer-berk.

21   Berk, personal correspondence, August 11 and 15, 2021.

22   Berk, personal interview.

23   Rabbi and Mrs. Josef Goldman, personal interviews, April 4, 2019.

24   Eta Fuchs Berk, *Chosen: A Holocaust Memoir*.

25   Berk, personal interview.

Chana Epshtein

1   Gerasimova et al., *We Stood Shoulder to Shoulder*, 313.

2   Mayevski (Nadel), "In the Novardok Labor Camp," 361.

3   Yisrael Kolachek, personal interview [in Yiddish], December 6, 2016.

4   Berkovich, "A Sea of Troubles," 421.

5   Duffy, *The Bielski Brothers*, 203.

6   Kagan and Cohen, *Surviving the Holocaust*, 181.

7   Mordechai Dunetz, personal interview, February 25, 2014.

8   Chaya Magid, personal interview, January 4, 2018.

9   Fajwel Shraga Epstein, Page of Testimony submitted by Chana Epshtein, June 29, 1955, Yad Vashem.

10   Magid, personal interview.

11 Sara Gol-Beigin, "The Last Keren-Kayemet Bazaar" [in Yiddish], in *Pinkas Zhetl*, ed. B. Kaplinski (Tel Aviv: Zhetl Association in Israel, 1957), 170.

12 Dvora Goradeiski Shkolnik, "The Tarbut School" [in Yiddish], in *Pinkas Zhetl*, ed. B. Kaplinski, 215.

13 Magid, personal interview.

14 Fajwel Shraga Epstein, Page of Testimony; Shmuel Epstein, Page of Testimony submitted by Chana Epshtein, June 29, 1955, Yad Vashem.

15 Magid, personal interview.

16 Chaim Weinstein, personal interview, August 1, 2017.

17 Weinstein, personal interview.

18 Magid, personal interview.

19 Weinstein, personal interview.

Riva (Rivka) and Bella Ginenski

1 James A. Grymes, *Violins of Hope: Violins of the Holocaust; Instruments of Hope and Liberation in Mankind's Darkest Hour* (New York: Harper Perennial, 2014).

2 Isaac Koll, personal communication, June 23, 2023.

3 Sima Ginenski, personal interview, June 14, 2023.

4 Personal card of Dasha Ginenski (Russian), National Archives of the Republic of Belarus.

5 Doris Ginenski Shilloff, personal interview, June 24, 2023.

6 Ginenski Shilloff, personal interview.

7 Shepsel Ginenski, Page of Testimony submitted by Doris Ginensky Schiloff, May 16, 2005, Central Database of Shoah Victims' Names, Yad Vashem.

8 Rita Ginenski Boyarski, personal interview, June 15, 2023.

9 Ginenski Shilloff, personal interview.

10 Ginenski Boyarski, personal interview.

11 Ginenski Boyarski, personal interview.

12 Ella Odesski, personal interview, June 14, 2023.

13 Ginenski Boyarski, personal interview.

14 Odesski, personal interview.

15 Odesski, personal interview.

Yakov (Yasha) Kantorovich

1 Yakov Kantorovich, Page of Testimony submitted by Fanya Miliavski, March 12, 1990, Central Database of Shoah Victims' Names, Yad Vashem.

2 Solomon Kantorovich, Page of Testimony submitted by Fanya Miliavski, March 12, 1990, Central Database of Shoah Victims' Names, Yad Vashem.

3   Fanya Milyavskaya, List of Residents Who Were Evacuated to Uryupinsk, prepared in 1942, Central Database of Shoah Victims' Names, Yad Vashem.

4   Anna Kontarovich, List of Residents Who Were Evacuated to Uryupinsk, prepared in 1942, Central Database of Shoah Victims' Names, Yad Vashem.

5   Aharon Weiss, "Novogrudok," in *Encyclopedia Judaica*, ed. C. Roth (Jerusalem: Keter Publishing House, 1978).

6   Gerasimova et al., *We Stood Shoulder to Shoulder*, 240.

7   Yakov Kantorovich, Page of Testimony submitted by Fanya Miliavski.

8   Solomon Kantorovich, Page of Testimony submitted by Fanya Miliavski.

9   Michael Miliavski, Page of Testimony submitted by Fanya Miliavski, March 12, 1990, Central Database of Shoah Victims' Names, Yad Vashem.

10   Yakov Kantorovich, Solomon Kantorovich, and Michael Miliavski, Pages of Testimony submitted by Fanya Miliavski, March 12, 1990.

Yosef (Yoshke) Koniak

1   Nachum Kushner, Yad Vashem testimony [in Yiddish], no. 03/3929.

2   Kushner, Yad Vashem testimony.

3   Yosef Koniak, List of Murdered Individuals from Beresteczko, *There Was a Town: Yizkor Book to the Communities of Beresteczko, Boremel and Vicinity* [in Hebrew, Yiddish] (Haifa, 1961), Central Database of Shoah Victims' Names, Yad Vashem.

4   Yosef Koniach, Page of Testimony submitted by Yehoshua Dikhter, May 18, 1957, Central Database of Shoah Victims' Names, Yad Vashem.

5   Moisze Koniach, Page of Testimony submitted by Yehoshua Dikhter, May 18, 1957, Central Database of Shoah Victims' Names, Yad Vashem.

6   Elia Koniach, Page of Testimony submitted by Yehoshua Dikhter, May 18, 1957, Central Database of Shoah Victims' Names, Yad Vashem.

7   Khaia Koniach, Page of Testimony submitted by Yehoshua Dikhter, May 18, 1957, Central Database of Shoah Victims' Names, Yad Vashem.

8   Avraham Koniach, Page of Testimony submitted by Yehoshua Dikhter, May 18, 1957, Central Database of Shoah Victims' Names, Yad Vashem.

9   David Koniach, Page of Testimony submitted by Yehoshua Dikhter, May 18, 1957, Central Database of Shoah Victims' Names, Yad Vashem.

10   Gerasimova et al., *We Stood Shoulder to Shoulder*, 246, 323.

Kozuchovski

1   Leibovitz, "The Great Destruction," 500.

2   Leibovitz.

3   Gerasimova et al., *We Stood Shoulder to Shoulder*, 40; Tec, *Defiance*, 74.

4 Duffy, *The Bielski Brothers*, 97.
5 Levine, *Fugitives of the Forest*, 244; Tec, *Defiance*, 75.
6 Inna Gerasimova, "Jewish Partisan Detachments," in Gerasimova et al., *We Stood Shoulder to Shoulder*, 40–41.

Avraham Magids (Magid)

1 Chaya Magid, personal interview, January 31, 2018.
2 Shmaya Magid, personal interview, December 2013.
3 Chaya Magid, personal interview.
4 Shmaya Magid, personal interview.
5 Chaya Magid, personal interview.
6 Chaya Magid, personal interview.
7 Chaya Magid, personal interview.
8 Yitzhak Arad, *The Holocaust in the Soviet Union* (Lincoln: University of Nebraska Press, with Yad Vashem, 2009), 508.
9 Chaya Magid, personal interview.
10 Chaya Magid, personal interview .
11 United States Holocaust Memorial Museum, "The Bielski Partisans," Holocaust Encyclopedia, https://encyclopedia.ushmm.org/content/en/article/the-bielski-partisans.
12 Shmaya Magid, personal interview.
13 Tec, *Defiance*, 207.
14 Bonnie Gurewitsch, "American Jewish Chaplains in the Aftermath of the Holocaust," lecture, February 6, 2018, The Orthodox Union Center, Jerusalem.
15 Shmaya Magid, personal interview, May 12, 2020.
16 Chaya Magid, personal interview.
17 Chaya Magid, personal interview.
18 Chaya Magid, personal interview.

Morduch (Mordechai) Majerowicz

1 Morduch Majerowicz, Allied Expeditionary Forces (AEF) DP Registration Record, April 19, 1949, Arolsen Archives, https://collections.arolsen-archives.org/en/document/68238531.
2 Mordechai Majerowicz, Yad Vashem testimony [in Hebrew], no. 0.3/2106.
3 Leah Majerowicz, Page of Testimony submitted by Mordechai Majerowicz, undated, Central Database of Shoah Victims' Names, Yad Vashem.
4 Kopel Majerowicz, Page of Testimony submitted by Mordechai Majerowicz, undated, Central Database of Shoah Victims' Names, Yad Vashem.

5   Reuven Majerowicz, Page of Testimony submitted by Mordechai Majerowicz, undated, Central Database of Shoah Victims' Names, Yad Vashem.

6   Avraham Majerowicz, Page of Testimony submitted by Mordechai Majerowicz, undated, Central Database of Shoah Victims' Names, Yad Vashem.

7   Majerowicz, Yad Vashem testimony.

8   Majerowicz, Yad Vashem testimony.

9   Kagan and Cohen, *Surviving the Holocaust,* 140.

10 Majerowicz, Yad Vashem testimony.

11 Majerowicz, Yad Vashem testimony.

12 Majerowicz, Yad Vashem testimony.

13 Gerasimova et al., *We Stood Shoulder to Shoulder,* 236.

14 Majerowicz, Yad Vashem testimony.

15 Majerowicz, Yad Vashem testimony.

16 Morduch Majerowicz, Request for Assistance, No. 1, International Tracing Service TD#304671/7Bl., October 21, 1947, Yad Vashem.

17 Majerowicz, Request for Assistance.

18 Majerowicz, Yad Vashem testimony.

19 Mordechai Majerowicz, gravestone, Ashkelon New South Cemetery, Ashqelon, Israel, BillionGraves, https://billiongraves.com/grave/22119549/מרדכי-מאירוביץ.

20 Mordechai Majerowicz, *The Story of a Partisan* [in Hebrew] (Tel Aviv: Aleph, 1978).

21 Eli Yifrach, director, Ashkelon Burial Society, personal interview, May 30, 2021.

22 Yifrach, personal interview.

Mordechai (Motke) Morduchowicz

1   Mordechai Morduchowicz, Yad Vashem testimony, no. 03/6300.

2   Sheina Lea Mordukhovitz, Page of Testimony submitted by Mordechai Mordukhovitz, May 1, 1999, Central Database of Shoah Victims' Names, Yad Vashem.

3   Morduchowicz, Yad Vashem testimony.

4   Baruch Mordukhovitz, Page of Testimony submitted by Mordechai Mordukhovitz, May 1, 1999, Central Database of Shoah Victims' Names, Yad Vashem.

5   Zeev Velvel Mordukhovitz, Page of Testimony submitted by Mordechai Mordukhovitz, May 1, 1999, Central Database of Shoah Victims' Names, Yad Vashem.

6   Yitzchak Mordukhovitz, Page of Testimony submitted by Mordechai Mordukhovitz, May 1, 1999, Central Database of Shoah Victims' Names, Yad Vashem, Jerusalem; Sheina Lea Mordukhovitz, Page of Testimony.

7   Morduchwicz, Yad Vashem testimony.

8   Kagan, "Surviving the Holocaust," 570.

9   Bauer, "Nowogródek," 62.

10 Zvi Mor, personal interview, May 7, 2019.

11 Dov Cohen, in Kagan and Cohen, *Surviving the Holocaust*, 83.

12 Morduchowicz, Yad Vashem testimony; Mor, personal interview, May 7, 2019.

13 Zvi Mor, personal interview, January 14, 2021.

14 Morduchowicz, Yad Vashem testimony.

15 Moshe Kahanovich, *The Fighting of the Jewish Partisans in Eastern Europe* [in Yiddish] (Tel Aviv: Ayanot, 1954), 381.

16 Morduchowicz, Yad Vashem testimony.

17 Mor, personal interview, January 14, 2021.

18 Leah Ben Yelid, personal interview, May 2, 2019.

19 Mor, personal interview, May 7, 2019.

20 Mor, personal interview.

21 Ben Yelid, personal interview.

22 Mor, personal interview, January 7, 2021.

23 Mor, personal interview.

24 Shula Mordechowicz, personal interview, January 6, 2021.

25 Shwartz, *Tunnel of Hope*.

26 Zvi Mor, personal interview, August 27, 2023.

27 Ben Yelid, personal interview.

28 Mor, personal interview, May 2, 2019.

Chaim Notkovich, Son-in-law Avraham, and Grandson Moshele

1   Mayevski (Nadel), "In the Novardok Labor Camp," 360.

2   Chaim Notkowicz, Page of Testimony submitted by Pesia Nadel, undated, Central Database of Shoah Victims' Names, Yad Vashem.

3   Chaim Notkowicz, Page of Testimony.

4   Mayevski, "In the Novardok Labor Camp."

5   Gutke Notkowicz, Page of Testimony submitted by Pesia Nadel, undated, Central Database of Shoah Victims' Names, Yad Vashem.

6   Moshe Notkowicz, Page of Testimony submitted by Pesia Nadel, undated, Central Database of Shoah Victims' Names, Yad Vashem.

7   Kaplinski, *Pinkas Zhetl*, 24.

Daniel Ostashinski

1   Daniel Ostaszynski, Application for War Reparations, Dr. Jur Brabeck, May 4, 1957, International Tracing Service, Yad Vashem.

2   Zafrir Ostashinski, personal interview, December 1, 2018.

3   Cypka Ostrzynski, Page of Testimony submitted by Daniel Ostashinski, December 9, 1956, Central Database of Shoah Victims' Names, Yad Vashem.

4   Zafrir Ostashinski, personal interview, December 1, 2018.

5   Ester Ostrzynski, Page of Testimony submitted by Daniel Ostashinski, December 9, 1956, Central Database of Shoah Victims' Names, Yad Vashem.

6   Dorit Kay, personal interview, December 6, 2018.

7   Yitzkhak Ostashinski, Page of Testimony submitted by Daniel Ostashinski, December 9, 1956, Central Database of Shoah Victims' Names, Yad Vashem.

8   Zafrir Ostashinski, personal interview, December 1, 2018.

9   Batia Rivka Ostashinski, Page of Testimony submitted by Dorit Kei, June 22, 2005, Central Database of Shoah Victims' Names, Yad Vashem.

10   Batia Rivka Ostashinski, Page of Testimony.

11   Fanya Dunetz Brodsky, personal interview, October 10, 2017.

12   Fanya Dunetz Brodsky, personal interview, January 1, 2019.

13   Dunetz Brodsky, personal interview.

14   Daniel Ostashinski, Yad Vashem testimony.

15   Zafrir Ostashinski, personal interview, December 3, 2018.

16   Tec, *Defiance*, 177.

17   Tec, 187.

18   Daniel Ostashinski, Yad Vashem testimony.

19   Bielski and Bielski, *Yehudei Yaar*, 200.

20   Tec, *Defiance*, 187.

21   Tec, 187.

22   Dunetz, personal interview, October 10, 2017.

23   Idel Kagan, "How I Survived," in *Novogrudok Memorial Book*, 520.

24   Zafrir Ostashinski, personal interview, December 3, 2018.

25   Bielski and Bielski, *Yehudei Yaar*, 200.

26   Daniel Ostashinski, Yad Vashem testimony.

27   Yisrael Kolachek, December 6, 2013.

28   Zafrir Ostashinski, personal interview, December 3, 2018.

29   Shaul Gorodynski, Yad Vashem testimony, no. 3095/230.

30   Bielski and Bielski, *Yehudei Yaar*, 199–200.

31   Tec, *Defiance*, 177.

32   Bielski and Bielski, *Yehudei Yaar*, 202.

33   Bielski, *Haruach Hachaya*, 234.

34   Bauer, *The Death of the Shtetl*, 57.

35   Tec, *Defiance*, 177.

36   Tec, 177.

37   Daniel Ostashinski, Yad Vashem testimony.

38 Zafrir Ostashinski, personal interview, December 3, 2018.

39 Daniel Ostashinski, Yad Vashem testimony.

40 Zafrir Ostashinski, personal interview, December 3, 2018.

41 Zafrir Ostashinski, personal interview.

42 Gil Ostashinski, personal interview, September 10, 2023.

43 Sonia Boldo Bielski, oral testimony RG-50.030.0025, United States Holocaust Museum, July 11, 1994, https://collections.ushmm.org/search/catalog /irn504532.

Shalom Reznitzki

1 List of Partisans, Central Database of Shoah Victims' Names, Yad Vashem.

2 Hirshel Reznitzki, Page of Testimony submitted by Kalman Minuskin, May 3, 1999, Central Database of Shoah Victims' Names, Yad Vashem Jerusalem; Hirsch Reznicki, Page of Testimony submitted by Ioselevski, April 23, 1957, Central Database of Shoah Victims' Names, Yad Vashem.

3 Rakhel Feiga Reznitzki, Page of Testimony submitted by Kalman Minuskin, May 3, 1999, Central Database of Shoah Victims' Names, Yad Vashem.

4 Rachel Reznicki, Page of Testimony submitted by Ioselevski, April 23, 1957, Central Database of Shoah Victims' Names, Yad Vashem.

5 Chana Aberstein, Page of Testimony submitted by Shlomo Razvazhski, April 28, 1957, Central Database of Shoah Victims' Names, Yad Vashem.

6 Zecharia Aberstein, Page of Testimony submitted by Shlomo Razvazhski, April 28, 1957, Central Database of Shoah Victims' Names, Yad Vashem.

7 Shalom Roznitsky, gravestone, Holon Cemetery, Bat Yam, Israel, BillionGraves, https://billiongraves.com/grave/13244961/שלום-רוזניצקי.

8 Gerasimova et al., *We Stood Shoulder to Shoulder*, 278.

9 Kalman Minuskin, personal interview, March 26, 2019.

10 Minuskin, personal interview.

11 Minuskin, personal interview.

12 Kalman Minuskin, personal correspondence, March 28, 2019.

13 Minuskin, personal interview.

14 "Golda Roznitzki, Daughter of Yitzchak," Gravez, https://gravez.me/en /deceased/C4A671E1-2BC7-49B8-9870-FAABE927E5E1, accessed on January 5, 2021.

15 Kalman Minuskin, personal interview.

16 Shalom Roznitsky, gravestone.

17 Shalom Roznitsky, gravestone.

Yitzchak Shuster

1 Jack Kagan, "Surviving the Holocaust with the Russian Jewish Partisans," in *Novogrudok Memorial Book*, 573.

2 Isaak Shuster, List of Partisans from Belorussia, Central Database of Shoah Victims' Names, Yad Vashem.

3 Rachel Berkowicz, Page of Testimony submitted by Myer Berk, undated, Central Database of Shoah Victims' Names, Yad Vashem.

4 Shmulik Shuster, Page of Testimony submitted by Myer Berk, undated, Central Database of Shoah Victims' Names, Yad Vashem.

5 Shmulik Shuster, Page of Testimony.

6 Yaffe, "Chapters from the Holocaust," 538.

7 Nachum Kushner, Yad Vashem testimony [in Yiddish], no. 03/3929.

8 Eliyahu Berkowicz, Yad Vashem testimony [in Yiddish], no. 03/2774.

9 Rachel Berkowicz, Page of Testimony submitted by Myer Berk.

10 Nachum Kushner, Yad Vashem testimony; Leibovitz, "The Great Destruction," 502.

11 Gerasimova et al., *We Stood Shoulder to Shoulder*, 311.

12 Joel Berk, personal communication, June 23, 2020.

Morduch Shvarzbord

1 Tamara Vershitskaya, personal communication, March 7, 2020.

2 Gerasimova et al., *We Stood Shoulder to Shoulder*, 303.

3 Yakov Beskin, personal interview, July 13, 2020.

4 Gerasimova et al., 305.

5 Vershitskaya, personal communication.

6 Vershitskaya, personal communication.

7 Gerasimova et al., 273.

8 Gerasimova et al., 305.

9 Tec, *Defiance*, 194.

10 Beskin, personal interview.

11 Vershitskaya, personal communication.

12 Vershitskaya, personal communication.

13 Vershitskaya, personal communication.

14 Beskin, personal interview.

15 Vershitskaya, personal communication.

16 Beskin, personal interview.

17 Beskin, personal interview.

18 Beskin, personal interview.

Isaac Ulert

1   Tamara Vershitskaya, personal communication, October 15, 2018.
2   Vladimir Lert, personal interview, July 1, 2020.
3   Lert, personal interview.
4   Vladimir Lert, personal communication, July 17, 2019.
5   Lert, personal communication.
6   Lert, personal communication.
7   Nachum Kushner, Yad Vashem testimony [in Yiddish], no. 03/3929.
8   Lert, personal communication.
9   Lert, personal communication.
10 Gerasimova et al., *We Stood Shoulder to Shoulder*, 292.
11 Lert, personal communication.
12 Lert, personal interview.
13 Lert, personal communication.
14 Lert, personal interview.
15 Lert, personal interview.
16 Lert, personal communication.
17 Vladimir Lert, personal communication, August 31, 2023.
18 Lert, personal interview.
19 Lert, personal interview.

Special Mention: Yitzchak Dvoretzki

1   Isaac Dvoretzki, List of Murdered Individuals from Zhetl, Central Database of Shoah Victims' Names, Yad Vashem.
2   Alte Dvoretzki, List of Murdered Individuals from Zhetl, Central Database of Shoah Victims' Names, Yad Vashem.
3   Saul Dvoretzki, List of Murdered Individuals from Zhetl, Central Database of Shoah Victims' Names, Yad Vashem.
4   Shimon Dvoretzki, List of Murdered Individuals from Zhetl, Central Database of Shoah Victims' Names, Yad Vashem.
5   Alte Dworecki, Page of Testimony submitted by Pesia Nadel, April 30, 1957, Central Database of Shoah Victims' Names, Yad Vashem.
6   Chaim Meir Dworecki, Page of Testimony submitted by Betzalel Lubetkin, August 17 (year not indicated), Central Database of Shoah Victims' Names, Yad Vashem.
7   Chaim Meir Dworecki, Page of Testimony.
8   Nishke Dworecki, Page of Testimony submitted by Shlomo Razvazski, April 28, 1957, Database of Shoah Victims' Names, Yad Vashem.

9   Rivka Dworecki, Page of Testimony submitted by Shlomo Razvazski, April 28, 1957, Database of Shoah Victims' Names, Yad Vashem.

10   Leibovitz, "The Great Destruction," 504.

11   Shaul Gorodynski, Yad Vashem testimony, #3095/230.

12   Berkovitz, "A Sea of Troubles," 420.

13   Berkovitz, 420.

14   Schensnovich, *Zapiski Aktiora i Partizana*, 93–97.

15   Mayevski (Nadel), "In the Novardok Labor Camp," 360.

16   Tamara Vershitskaya, personal communication.

17   Kaplinski, *Pinkas Zhetl*, 22.

Analysis: Why Novogrudok?

1   Tec, *Defiance*, 187.

2   Bauer, *The Death of the Shtetl*, 67.

3   Moshe Steinberg-Sarig, "Hebrew Education in Novogrudok," in *Novogrudok Memorial Book*, 142.

4   Steinberg-Sarig, 147.

5   Steinberg-Sarig, 152.

6   Steinberg-Sarig, 159–60.

7   Chaim Leibovich, "Shokdey Melocho," in *Novogrudok Memorial Book*, 194.

8   Shmuel Openheim, "Politico-Communal Life in Novogrudok," in *Novogrudok Memorial Book*, 170.

9   Leibovich, "Shokdey Melocho," 196–97.

10   Openheim, "Politico-Communal Life in Novogrudok," 182.

11   Leibovich, "Shokdey Melocho," 195.

12   "The Novogrudok Orphanage," *Novogrudok Memorial Book*, 185.

13   "The Novogrudok Orphanage," *Novogrudok Memorial Book*, 183.

14   Leibovich, "Shokdey Melocho," 197.

15   Openheim, "Politico-Communal Life," 175.

16   Samuel Nikolayevski, "United Jewish Artisans Association," in *Novogrudok Memorial Book*, 247.

17   Openheim, "Politico-Communal Life," 175.

18   Openheim, 176.

19   Nikolayevski, "United Jewish Artisans Association," 248.

20   Jack Jacobs, "Sport: An Overview," The YIVO Encyclopedia of Jews in Eastern Europe, https://yivoencyclopedia.org/article.aspx/sport/an_overview.

21   Jack Kagan, *Novogrudok: The History of a Shtetl* (London: Vallentine Mitchell, 2006), 114.

22   Bauer, *The Death of the Shtetl*, 26–27.

23 Openheim, "Politico-Communal Life," 177.

24 "HaShomer HaTzair around the World," Havatzelet, October 30, 2013, https://en.havatzelet.org.il/cgi-webaxy/item?44, accessed April 11, 2021.

25 Openheim, "Politico-Communal Life," 177.

26 Zophy Chermoni, personal interview, October 10, 2017.

27 Openheim, "Politico-Communal Life," 177.

28 Dov Zalmanovich, written testimony [Hebrew], in *Asher Zacharnu Lisaper* [That which we remembered to tell], ed. Arie Haran (Tel Aviv: Sifriat Poalim, 1988), 230.

29 Samuel Kassow, "Po'ale Tsiyon," The YIVO Encyclopedia of Jews in Eastern Europe, https://yivoencyclopedia.org/article.aspx/poale_tsiyon.

30 Bauer, "Nowogrodek," 40.

31 Openheim, "Politico-Communal Life," 180.

32 Openheim, 180.

33 Openheim, 176.

34 Mordechai Ginsburg, "The Mussar Movement," in *Novogrudok Memorial Book*, 47–49.

35 Bauer, *The Death of the Shtetl*, 18.

36 Bauer, 67.

37 Ginsburg, "The Mussar Movement," 56.

38 Ginsburg, 54.

39 Shlomo Weintraub, *The Alter of Novardok* (Rahway, NJ: Mesorah Publications, 2020), 196–97.

40 Weintraub, 11.

41 Weintraub, 11.

42 Ginsburg, "The Mussar Movement," 52.

43 Weintraub, *The Alter of Novardok*, 52.

44 Weintraub, 99.

45 Zafrir Ostashinski, personal interview, December 1, 2018.

46 "Navahrudak, Belarus," Jewish Gen Locality Page, accessed December 25, 2020, https://kehilalinks.jewishgen.org/navahrudak/Home.html.

47 Bauer, *The Death of the Shtetl*, 138.

48 Haya Lipsky, Rivkah Lipsky-Kaufman, and Yitshak Ganoz, eds., *Ayaratenu Zhetl: Shishim shanah le-hurban kehilat Zhetl, 1942–2002* [Our town Zhetl: Sixty years since the destruction of the community of Zhetl] (Tel Aviv: Zhetl Association in Israel, 2002), 76.

49 Cholawsky, *The Jews of Bielorussia*, 141.

50 Pesia Mayevski (Nadel), "In the Navardok Labor Camp" [in Yiddish], in *Pinkas Zhetl*, ed. B. Kaplinski (Tel Aviv: Zhetl Association in Israel, 1957), 359.

51 Benzion H. Ayalon, "Maytchet" [in Yiddish], in *Molchadz (Maytchet): In Memory of the Jewish Community* (Tel Aviv: Molchadz Relief Society, 1973), 40.

52 Moshe Mendel Leizerovich, "Zhetl and the Zhetler Craftsmen" [in Yiddish], in *Pinkas Zhetl*, ed. B. Kaplinski, 133.

53 Dov Erezshechovski, "The Zhetler Worker after the First World War" [in Yiddish], in *Pinkas Zhetl*, ed. B. Kaplinski, 154.

54 "Political Parties in Zhetl" [in Yiddish], in *Pinkas Zhetl*, ed. B. Kaplinski (Yiddish; Tel Aviv: Zhetl Association in Israel, 1957), 142.

55 "Political Parties in Zhetl," in *Pinkas Zhetl*, ed. B. Kaplinski.

56 Mordechai Dunetz, "Shlomo Zalman Dunetz" [in Yiddish], in *Pinkas Zhetl*, ed. B. Kaplinski, 241–44.

57 Yakov Indershtein, "Hashomer Hatzair" [in Yiddish], in *Pinkas Zhetl*, ed. B. Kaplinski, 163.

58 Bauer, "Nowogródek," 40.

59 Yosef Berman, "The Chalutz" [in Yiddish], in *Pinkas Zhetl*, ed. B. Kaplinski, 155; Mordechai Dunetz, personal interview, May 15, 2000.

60 Jacob Tsur, "The Jewish National Fund (Keren Kayemeth LeIsrael)," in *Encyclopedia Judaica*, ed. C. Roth (Jerusalem: Keter Publishing House, 1978).

61 Lipsky, *Ayaratenu Zhetl*, 21.

62 Lipsky, 32.

63 Philip Zabich, "Our Orchestra" [in Yiddish], in *Pinkas Zhetl*, ed. B. Kaplinski, 180.

64 "Agudat Yisrael," The Israel Democracy Institute, https://en.idi.org.il /israeli-elections-and-parties/parties/agudat-israel/.

65 Yisrael Karpel, "Agudat Yisrael" [in Yiddish], in *Pinkas Zhetl*, ed. B. Kaplinski, 166.

66 Zimel Zimelevich, "The Navardok Community in Zhetl" [in Hebrew], in *Pinkas Zhetl*, ed. B. Kaplinski, 82.

67 Rabbi Elchanan Sorotzkin, "The Life Journey of Rabbi Zalman Sorotzkin" [in Yiddish], in *Pinkas Zhetl*, ed. B. Kaplinski, 234.

68 "Vaad Hayeshivot," YIVO Institute for Jewish Research, https://vilnacollections .yivo.org/?ca=((item.php!id__rg-25.

69 Sara Gol-Beigin, "The Communal Life in Zhetl" [in Yiddish], in *Pinkas Zhetl*, ed. B. Kaplinski, 171.

70 Lipsky, *Ayaratenu Zhetl*, 28.

71 Lipsky, 28.

72 Nella Orzuchovski, personal interview, June 19, 2019.

73 Sonya Gorodynski Oshman, oral history, 1993, videotape transcript, Holocaust Center at Kean College of New Jersey, Union, NJ.

74 "Jan & Józefa Jarmołowicz," The Righteous Among the Nations Database, Yad Vashem, https://righteous.yadvashem.org/?search=jarmolowicz&searchType=righteous_only&language=en&itemId=4034646&ind=0.

75 Sylvia Sklar, personal communication, June 20, 2019.

76 Solomon Golanski, USC Shoah Foundation Institute testimony 25649, Connecticut, February 9, 1997.

77 Ellen Robinson Epstein, ed. *The Miracle of Life: The Story of Rae and Joseph Kushner* (Arlington, VA: Virginia Lithograph, 1998), 66–67.

78 Yanek Okanski, personal interview, September 24, 2020.

79 Kagan and Cohen, *Surviving the Holocaust*, 166.

80 Kagan and Cohen, 182.

81 Dror H. Shwartz, director, *Tunnel of Hope* (Jerusalem: Go2Films, 2015).

82 Bauer, "Nowogródek," 60.

83 Kagan and Cohen, *Surviving the Holocaust*, 58.

84 Shwartz, *Tunnel of Hope*.

85 Bauer, "Nowogródek," 30.

86 Yisrael Kolachek, personal interview, December 6, 2016.

87 Boris Ioselevich, personal interview, October 9, 2019.

88 Tec, *Defiance*, 43.

89 Kagan and Cohen, *Surviving the Holocaust*, 181–82.

90 Helena Gantsevich, "The Righteous Make the World Go Round," *Novgazeta*, September 7, 2018, https://novgazeta.by/news/novogrudok-news/the-righteous-make-the-world-go-round/.

91 Ioselevich, personal interview.

92 Gantsevich, "The Righteous."

93 Yisrael Kolachek, as related by Lea Ben-Yelid in her diary of her trip to Novogrudok for filming the movie *Tunnel of Hope*, August 8, 2012.

94 Yisrael Kolachek, as related by Lea Ben-Yelid.

95 Bauer, "Nowogródek," 60.

96 Jerusalem Talmud, *Sanhedrin* 4:1 (22a).

97 Bauer, "Nowogródek," 59.

98 Cholawsky, *The Jews of Bielorussia*, 180.

99 Bauer, "Nowogródek," 59.

100 Cholawsky, *The Jews of Bielorussia*, 179–80.

101 Laurence Weinbaum, "Shaking the Dust Off: The Story of the Warsaw Ghetto's Forgotten Chronicler, Ruben Feldchu (Ben-Shem)," in *Jewish Political Studies Review* (Jerusalem: Jerusalem Center for Public Affairs, 2010), 7.

102 Weinbaum, "Shaking the Dust Off," 8.

103 Weinbaum, 20.

104 Cholawsky, *The Jews of Bielorussia*, 180.

105 Emmanuel Ringelblum, *Polish-Jewish Relations during the Second World War* (Jerusalem: Yad Vashem, 1974), 158.

106 Cholawsky, *The Jews of Bielorussia*, 181.

107 Cholawsky, 181.

108 Cholawsky, 181.

109 Leibovitz, "The Great Destruction," 498–500.

110 Kagan and Cohen, *Surviving the Holocaust*, 170.

111 Yehuda Bauer, personal interview, May 2017; Bauer, "Nowogródek," 59.

Afterword: The Interview Process and Second-Generation Tunnel Survivors

1 Eric Simenauer, "The Return of the Persecutor," in *Generations of the Holocaust*, ed. M. S. Bergmann and M. E. Jucovy (New York: Basic Books, Inc., 1982), 175; Martin S. Bergmann, "Recurrent Problems in the Treatment of Survivors and Their Children," in *Generations of the Holocaust*, ed. M. S. Bergmann and M. E. Jucovy, 249; Natan P. F. Kellermann, *Holocaust Trauma: Psychological Effects and Treatment* (Bloomington, IN: IUniverse, 2009), 23.

2 Kellermann, *Holocaust Trauma*, 22.

3 Yael Danieli, "On the Achievement of Integration in Aging Survivors of the Nazi Holocaust," *Journal of Geriatric Psychiatry* 14, no. 2 (1981): 197.

4 Elie Wiesel, "The Holocaust: Three Views," in *ADL Bulletin*, November 1977.

5 Joost A. M. Meerloo, MD, "Delayed Mourning in Victims of Extermination Camps," *Journal of the Hillside Hospital* 12 (April 1963): 96.

6 Joan Freyberg, "Difficulties in Separation-Individuation as Experienced by Offspring of Nazi Holocaust Survivors," *American Journal of Orthopsychiatry* 50, no. 1 (1980): 88.

7 Betty Brodsky Cohen, "Holocaust Survivors and the Crisis of Aging," *Families in Society: The Journal of Contemporary Social Services* 72, no. 4 (April 1991): 228.

8 Kellermann, *Holocaust Trauma*, 22.

9 Kellermann, 112.

10 Kellermann, 23.

11 Haim Dasberg, "Forward," in *Holocaust Trauma*, IV.

12 Judith S. and Milton Kestenberg, "The Experience of Survivor-Parents," in Bergman and Jucovy, *Generations of the Holocaust*, 59.

13 Elie Wiesel, "The Holocaust: Three Views," *ADL Bulletin,* November 1977.

14 Ruth Leys, *From Guilt to Shame: Auschwitz and After* (Princeton, NJ: Princeton University Press, 2007), 66.

[15] Ernest A. Rappaport, "Beyond Traumatic Neurosis: A Psychoanalytic Study of Late Reactions to the Concentration Camp Trauma," *International Journal of Psychoanalysis* 49 (1968): 720.

[16] Bergmann, "Recurrent Problems in the Treatment of Survivors and Their Children," 249.

[17] Howard Reich, *The Art of Inventing Hope: Intimate Conversations with Elie Wiesel* (Chicago: Chicago Review Press, 2019), 75.

[18] Joseph Berger, "Elie Wiesel, Auschwitz Survivor and Nobel Peace Prize Winner, Dies at 87," *New York Times*, July 2, 2016.

[19] Fanny Brodsky, personal interview, September 15, 2019.

[20] Bergmann and Jucovy, "Prelude," in *Generations of the Holocaust*, 5-6.

[21] Reich, *The Art of Inventing Hope*, 95.

Appendix 1: Timeline: Jewish Novogrudok: 1044–1939

[1] Yaakov Goldberg, "The History of the Jews of Novogrudok," *Novogrudok Memorial Book*, 7.

[2] Bauer, "Nowogródek," 37.

[3] Goldberg, "The History of the Jews of Novogudok," 8.

[4] Bauer, "Nowogródek."

[5] Bauer, "Nowogródek."

[6] Tamara Vershitskaya, "Novogrudok: Some Historical Facts," in Kagan, *Novogrudok: The History of a Shtetl*, 33.

[7] Bauer, "Nowogródek."

[8] Bauer, "Nowogródek."

[9] Vershitskaya, "Novogrudok: Some Historical Facts," 33.

[10] Bauer, *The Death of the Shtetl*, 38.

[11] Goldberg, "The History of the Jews of Novogrudok," 21.

[12] Vershitskaya, "Novogrudok: Some Historical Facts," 33.

[13] Bauer, "Nowogródek," 38.

[14] Vershitskaya, "Novogrudok: Some Historical Facts," 33.

[15] Weintraub, *The Alter of Novardok*, 67.

[16] Vershitskaya, "Novogrudok: Some Historical Facts," 33.

[17] Bauer, "Nowogródek," 39.

[18] Vershitskaya, "Novogrudok: Some Historical Facts," 33.

[19] Vershitskaya, 33.

[20] Vershitskaya, 33.

[21] Vershitskaya, 33.

[22] Vershitskaya, 33.

[23] Bauer, "Nowogródek," 38.

24   Bauer, "Nowogródek," 38.
25   Bauer, "Nowogródek," 10.
26   Bauer, "Nowogródek," 41.

Appendix 2: Timeline: The Holocaust in Novogrudok, 1941–1943

1   Bauer, "Nowogródek," 45.
2   Bauer, "Nowogródek," 44.
3   Bauer, "Nowogródek," 44.
4   Bauer, "Nowogródek," 45.
5   Kagan and Cohen, *Surviving the Holocaust*, 138.
6   Kagan and Cohen, 198.
7   Bauer, "Nowogródek," 44.
8   Kagan and Cohen, *Surviving the Holocaust*, 138–39.
9   Yad Vashem, "Judenrat," Yad Vashem Information Center, https://www
     .yadvashem.org/odot_pdf/Microsoft%20Word%20-%206389.pdf.
10   Bauer, "Nowogródek," 45.
11   United States Holocaust Memorial Museum, "Jewish Councils (Judenraete),"
     Holocaust Encyclopedia, https://encyclopedia.ushmm.org/content/en/article
     /jewish-councils-judenraete.
12   "Jewish Councils (Judenraete)," Holocaust Encyclopedia.
13   Yad Vashem, "Einsatzgruppen," Yad Vashem Information Center, https://www
     .yadvashem.org/untoldstories/documents/GenBack/Einsatzgruppen.pdf.
14   Kagan and Cohen, *Surviving the Holocaust*, 46.
15   Bauer, "Nowogródek," 48.
16   Bauer, "Nowogródek," 47.
17   Bauer, "Nowogródek," 48.
18   Kagan and Cohen, *Surviving the Holocaust*, 140.
19   Bauer, "Nowogródek," 48–49.
20   Kagan and Cohen, *Surviving the Holocaust*, 141.
21   Bauer, "Nowogródek," 49.
22   Kagan and Cohen, *Surviving the Holocaust*, 140–41.
23   Kagan and Cohen, 150.
24   Bauer, "Nowogródek," 50.
25   Bauer, "Nowogródek," 51.
26   Kagan and Cohen, *Surviving the Holocaust*, 160.
27   Bauer, "Nowogródek," 52.
28   Kagan and Cohen, *Surviving the Holocaust*, 161.
29   Yaffe, "The Final Wandering," in *Novogrudok Memorial Book*, 550–51.
30   Leibovitz, "The Great Destruction," 498.

31 Leibovitz, 500–501.

32 Tec, *Defiance*, 187.

33 Leibovitz, "The Great Destruction," 502.

34 Kagan and Cohen, *Surviving the Holocaust*, 75.

35 Kagan and Cohen.

36 Leibovitz, "The Great Destruction," 502; Kagan and Cohen, *Surviving the Holocaust*, 569; Borowski, in *Memory, Guide My Hand*, 9–16; Nachum Kushner, Yad Vashem testimony [in Yiddish], no. 03/3929.

37 Fania Dunetz Brodsky, personal interview, June 25, 2020.

38 Idel Kagan, "Surviving the Holocaust with the Russian Jewish Partisans," in *Novogrudok Memorial Book*, 573.

Bibliography

Books and Articles

Aleksiun, Natalia. "Central Committee of Jews in Poland." YIVO Encyclopedia of Jews in Eastern Europe. http://www.yivoencyclopedia .org/article.aspx/Central_Committee_of_Jews_in_Poland.

Amarant, Shmuel. "The Partisans of Tuvia Bielski." In *We Stood Shoulder to Shoulder*, edited by Gerasimova, et al., 149–50.

Arad, Yitzhak. *The Holocaust in the Soviet Union*. Lincoln: University of Nebraska Press, with Yad Vashem, 2009.

Avraham, Alexander. "Sephardim." YIVO Encyclopedia of Jews in Eastern Europe. http://www.yivoencyclopedia.org/article.aspx/Sephardim.

Ayalon, Benzion H. "Maytchet" [in Yiddish]. In *Molchadz (Maytchet): In Memory of the Jewish Community*. Tel Aviv: Molchadz Relief Society, 1973.

Baranovich Memorial Book [in Hebrew and Yiddish]. Tel Aviv: Irgun Yotsey Baranowitz, 1953.

Bauer, Yehuda. *The Death of the Shtetl*. New Haven: Yale University Press, 2009.

———. "Nowogródek: The Story of a Shtetl." *Yad Vashem Studies* 35, no. 2 (2007).

Baumslag, Naomi. *Murderous Medicine: Nazi Doctors, Human Experimentation, and Typhus*. Westport, CT and London: Praeger, 2005.

Belinsky, Ann, ed. *Korelitz: The Life and Destruction of a Jewish Community (Karelichy, Belarus)*. Translation of *Korelitz: Hayeha v'churbanah shel kehilah Yehudit*, edited by Michael Walzer-Fass. Tel Aviv: Karelich Societies of Israel and the United States, 1973. Translated by JewishGen, https://www.jewishgen.org/yizkor/Korelicze/Korelicze.html.

Ben Tzur, Tzvi. "The La Spezia Affair – 1946." Aliya Bet Stories. Palyam.org. http://palyam.org/English/Hahapala/Teur_haflagot/hy_LSA.pdf.

Berger, Joseph. "Elie Wiesel, Auschwitz Survivor and Nobel Peace Prize Winner, Dies at 87." *New York Times*, July 2, 2016.

Bergmann, Martin S. "Recurrent Problems in the Treatment of Survivors and Their Children." In *Generations of the Holocaust*, edited by M. S. Bergmann and M. E. Jucovy, 249.

Bergmann, Martin S., and M. E. Jucovy, eds. *Generations of the Holocaust*. New York: Basic Books, 1982.

Berk, Eta Fuchs, and Gilbert Allardyce. *Chosen: A Holocaust Memoir; The Eta Fuchs Berk Story*. Fredericton, Canada: Goose Land Editions, 1998.

Berkovich, Eliezer. "Schlos Gass: A Distinct Township." In *Novogrudok Memorial Book*, 242–43.

Berkovich, Eliyahu. "A Sea of Troubles." In *Novogrudok Memorial Book*, 421.

Berman, Yosef. "The Chalutz" [in Yiddish]. In *Pinkas Zhetl*, edited by B. Kaplinski, 155.

Bielski, Chaya. *Haruach Hachaya* [A Woman Fighter with the Bielski Partisans]. Jerusalem: Yad Vashem, 2012.

Bielski, Tuvia, and Zusia Bielski. *Yehudei Yaar* [Forest Jews]. Tel Aviv: Am Oved, 1946.

The Book of Ivenets, Kamien and Vicinity [in Yiddish]. Tel Aviv: Ivenets Societies in Israel and the Diaspora, 1979.

Borowski, Wolff (Velvel). In *Memory, Guide My Hand: An Anthology of Life Stories by Members of the Melbourne Jewish Community from the Former Soviet Union*, vol. 5, edited by Julie Meadows and Elaine Davidoff, 9–16. Caulfield South, VIC: Makor Jewish Community Library, 2008.

Burgess, Alan. *The Longest Tunnel: The True Story of World War II's Great Escape*. New York: Grove Press, 1990.

Chatham, Anne. "The Greater Escape: Longest WWII Escape Tunnel Found along with Dozens of Trinkets." The First News, October 8, 2019. https://www.thefirstnews.com/article/the-greater-escape-longest-wwii -escape-tunnel-found-along-with-dozens-of-trinkets-7992.

Cieśla, Andrzej, ed. *Memorial [Yizkor] Book of the Community of Zelechow.* Vol. 2. Translation of *Yisker-Bukh fun der Zhelekhover Yidisher Kehile,* edited by W. Yassni. Chicago: Former Residents of Zelechow in Chicago, 1953. Translated by Michael Dunayevsky and Andrzej Cieśla. https://www.jewishgen.org/yizkor/zelechow/zelechow.html.

Cholawsky, Shalom. *The Jews of Bielorussia during World War II.* Amsterdam: Harwood Academic Publishers, 1988.

———. *Meri v'Lochmah Partizanit* [Resistance and Partisan Struggle]. Tel Aviv: Yad Vashem and the Moreshet Publishing House, 2001.

Cohen, Betty Brodsky. "Holocaust Survivors and the Crisis of Aging." *Families in Society: The Journal of Contemporary Social Services* 72, no. 4 (April 1991): 226–32.

Cohn, Rabbi Helen, ed. *Memorial (Yizkor) Book of the Jewish Community of Novogrudok, Poland* (henceforward *Novogrudok Memorial Book*). New York: JewishGen, Inc., 2013. Translation of *Pinkas Navaredok,* eds. Eliezer Yerushalmi and David Cohen. Tel Aviv: Alexander Harkavy Navaredker Relief Committee in the USA and Israel, 1963.

Czesler, Isaac. "The Judenrat's Minutes and Orders." In *The Bialystoker Memorial Book* [Yiddish and English], edited by I. Shmulewitz, 67. New York: Bialystoker Center, 1982.

Danieli, Yael. "On the Achievement of Integration in Aging Survivors of the Nazi Holocaust." *Journal of Geriatric Psychiatry* 14, no. 2 (1981): 191–210.

Datz, Janis Friedenberg, and Melisssa Rubin McCurdie, eds. *Memorial Volume of Steibtz-Swerznie and the Neighboring Villages Rubezhevitz, Derevna, Nalibok (Stowbtsy, Belarus).* Translation of *Sefer Zikaron; Steibts-Sverzhnye Ve-Ha-Ayarot Ha-Semukhot Rubezevits, Derevno, Nalibok,* edited by Nachum Hinitz. Tel Aviv: Former Residents of Steibtz in Israel, 1964, https://www.jewishgen.org/yizkor/stowbtsy/Stowbtsy.html#TOC316.

Doval, Alexis. "The Idea of Responsibility in the Brothers Karamazov." Lecture. March 4, 2014. https://www.integralprogram.org/images/stories/documents/lectures/responsibilityelecture.pdf.

Duffy, Peter. *The Bielski Brothers: The True Story of Three Men Who Defied the Nazis, Built a Village in the Forest, and Saved 1,200 Jews*. New York: Perennial, 2003.

Dunetz, Mordechai. "Shlomo Zalman Dunetz" [in Yiddish]. In *Pinkas Zhetl*, edited by B. Kaplinski, 241–44.

Eisner, Ellen J., Judy Prigal, and Joseph Rubinstein, eds. *The Memorial Book of Iwieniec, Kamien, and the Surrounding Region*. Translation of *Sefer Iwieniec, Kamien v'Hasevivah: Sefer Zikaron*. Tel Aviv: Iwieniec Societies in Israel and the Diaspora, 1973. https://www.jewishgen.org/yizkor/ivenets/ivenets.html.

Epstein, Ellen Robinson, ed. *The Miracle of Life: The Story of Rae and Joseph Kushner*. Arlington, VA: Virginia Lithograph, 1998.

Epstein, Ilana. "Let My People Go!" *The Jerusalem Post*, April 17, 2008. https://www.jpost.com/Local-Israel/In-Jerusalem/Let-my-people-go.

Erez (Angelchik), Amnon. "The Journey from the Galil to the Templars" [in Hebrew]. Maagar Siporei Moreshet, April 26, 2017, https://www.ravdori.co.il/stories/המסע-מהגליל-אל-הטמפלרים.

Erezshechovski, Dov. "The Zhetler Worker after the First World War" [in Yiddish]. In *Pinkas Zhetl*, edited by B. Kaplinski, 154.

Fisher, Benjamin B. "The Katyn Controversy: Stalin's Killing Fields." *Studies in Intelligence* (Winter 1999–2000).

Fogel, Joshua. "Elye (Eliyahu) Yones." Yiddish Leksikon (Blog), November 28, 2016. http://yleksikon.blogspot.com/2016/11/elye-eliyahu-yones.html.

Freund, Gloria, ed. *Memorial (Yizkor) Book of the Community of Radomsk and Vicinity*, trans. Jerrold Landau. Translation of *Sefer Yizkor le-Kehilat Radomsk ve-ha-seviva*, edited by L. Losh. Tel Aviv: Former Residents of Radomsk, 1967.

Freyberg, Joan. "Difficulties in Separation-Individuation as Experienced by Offspring of Nazi Holocaust Survivors." *American Journal of Orthopsychiatry* 50, no. 1 (1980): 87–95.

Galili, Zeev. "At Chaki-li v'Echzor: Makor-Hashir v'Hamanginah" [You Wait for Me and I'll Come Back: The Origin of the Song and the Melody].

Higayon b'Shigayon [The Logic in Madness], August 28, 2010. http://www.zeevgalili.com/2010/08/10341.

Gantsevich, Helena. "The Righteous Make the World Go Round." *Novgazeta*, September 7, 2018. https://novgazeta.by/news/novogrudok-news/the-righteous-make-the-world-go-round/.

Gerasimova, Inna. "Jewish Partisan Detachments." In *We Stood Shoulder to Shoulder*, edited by Gerasimova et al., 40–41.

Gerasimova, Inna, Viacheslav Selemenev, and Jack Kagan. *We Stood Shoulder to Shoulder: Jewish Partisans in Byelorussia, 1941–1944*. Suffolk: Arima Publishing, 2010.

Ginsburg, Mordechai. "The Mussar Movement." In *Novogrudok Memorial Book*, 47–49.

Gol-Beigin, Sara. "The Communal Life in Zhetl" [in Yiddish]. In *Pinkas Zhetl*, edited by B. Kaplinski, 171.

———. "The Last Keren-Kayemet Bazaar" [in Yiddish]. In *Pinkas Zhetl*, edited by B. Kaplinski, 170.

Goldberg, Yaakov. "The History of the Jews of Novogudok." In *Novogrudok Memorial Book*, 19.

Goldin, Shmuel. *Unlocking the Torah Text: An In-Depth Journey into the Weekly Parsha*. Vol. 1, *Bereishit*. Jerusalem: Gefen Publishing House, 2007.

Goroulev, Iouri, director. *The Book of Curses*. Israel/Belarus: Kagan Productions, 2020.

Grymes, James A. *Violins of Hope: Violins of the Holocaust; Instruments of Hope and Liberation in Mankind's Darkest Hour*. New York: Harper Perennial, 2014.

Gulkovitz-Berger, Frume. "The Ghetto in Peresike." In *Novogrudok Memorial Book*, 523.

Hersowitz, Robert. "The Passing of a Courageous Survivor." *Jerusalem Post*, January 19, 2017. https://www.jpost.com/opinion/a-personal-tribute-478926.

Indershtein, Yakov. "Hashomer Hatzair" [in Yiddish]. In *Pinkas Zhetl*, edited by B. Kaplinski, 163.

Israel, David. "Hashomer Hatzair Kibbutz Inaugurates First Synagogue in 70 Years." *Jewish Press*, October 18, 2019. https://www.jewishpress.com/news /israel/religious-secular-in-israel-israel/hashomer-hatzair-kibbutz-inaugurates-first-synagogue-in-70-years/2019/10/28/.

Jacobs, Jack. "Sport: An Overview." The YIVO Encyclopedia of Jews in Eastern Europe. https://yivoencyclopedia.org/article.aspx/sport/an_overview.

John Paul II. *Sollicitudo Rei Socialis*. Encyclical. December 30, 1987. Libreria Editrice Vaticana. https://www.vatican.va/content/john-paul-ii /en/encyclicals/documents/hf_jp-ii_enc_30121987_sollicitudo-rei -socialis.html.

Junger, Sebastian. *Tribe: On Homecoming and Belonging*. London: Fourth Estate, 2016.

Kagan, Idel. "How I Survived." In *Novogrudok Memorial Book*, 519.

———. "Surviving the Holocaust with the Russian Jewish Partisans." In *Novogrudok Memorial Book*, 567–73.

Kagan, Jack. "The Bielski Detachment." In *We Stood Shoulder to Shoulder*, edited by Gerasimova, et al., 142.

———. "Holocaust Denial." In *We Stood Shoulder to Shoulder*, edited by Gerasimova et al., 191.

———. *Novogrudok: The History of a Shtetl*. London: Vallentine Mitchell, 2006.

———. "Novogrudok's Maccabi Swim Team 1934–1935." In *Novogrudok: The History of a Shtetl*.

Kagan, Jack, and Dov Cohen. *Surviving the Holocaust with the Russian Jewish Partisans*. London: Vallentine, Mitchell and Son, 1998.

Kahanovich, Moshe. *The Fighting of the Jewish Partisans in Eastern Europe* [in Yiddish]. Tel Aviv: Ayanot, 1954.

Kamieniecki, Fruma. "A Friday in Novogrudok." In *Novogrudok Memorial Book*, 345.

Kaplinski, Baruch, ed. *Pinkas Zhetl*. Tel Aviv: Zhetl Association in Israel, 1957.

Karpel, Yisrael. "Agudat Yisrael" [in Yiddish]. In *Pinkas Zhetl*, edited by B. Kaplinski, 166.

Kassow, Samuel. "Po'ale Tsiyon." The YIVO Encyclopedia of Jews in Eastern Europe. https://yivoencyclopedia.org/article.aspx/poale_tsiyon.

Kellermann, Natan P. F. *Holocaust Trauma: Psychological Effects and Treatment*, 23. Bloomington, IN: IUniverse, 2009.

Klar, Chana Mayevski. "Forest Years." In *Pinkas Zhetl*, edited by Baruch Kaplinski, 400.

Leibovich, Chaim. "Shokdey Melocho." In *Novogrudok Memorial Book*, 194.

Leibovitz, Chaim. "Escape through the Tunnel." In *Novogrudok Memorial Book*, 512–14.

———. "The Great Destruction: How 300 Jews Saved Themselves." In *Novogrudok Memorial Book*, 500–501.

———. "The Heroic Death of Berl Yoselevitz." In *Novogrudok Memorial Book*, 515.

———. "The Last Passover" [in Yiddish]. In *Pinkas Navaredok*, 293. Translated by O. Delatycki, https://www.jewishgen.org/yizkor/Novogrudok/nov287 .html#Page293.

———. "Three Kol Niddreis" [in Yiddish]. In *Pinkas Navaredok*, 201. Translated by O. Delatycki. https://www.jewishgen.org/yizkor/Novogrudok/nov195 .html#Page201.

Leizerovich, Moshe Mendel. "Zhetl and the Zhetler Craftsmen" [in Yiddish]. In *Pinkas Zhetl*, edited by B. Kaplinski, 133.

Levine, Allan. *Fugitives of the Forest: The Heroic Story of Jewish Resistance and Survival during the Second World War*. Guilford, CT: Lyons Press, 2009.

Leys, Ruth. *From Guilt to Shame: Auschwitz and After*. Princeton, NJ: Princeton University Press, 2007.

Lipsky, Haya, Rivkah Lipsky-Kaufman, and Yitshak Ganoz, eds. *Ayaratenu Zhetl: Shishim shanah le-hurban kehilat Zhetl, 1942–2002* [Our town Zhetl: Sixty years since the destruction of the community of Zhetl]. Tel Aviv: Zhetl Association in Israel, 2002.

"Longest WWII-Era Escape Tunnel Discovered in Northwestern Poland." TVP World, November 14, 2019. https://tvpworld.com/45331630/longest-wwiiera-escape-tunnel-discovered-in-northwestern-poland.

Lyons, Gila. "Great Escape." *Tablet*, April 9, 2010. https://www.tabletmag.com/sections/belief/articles/great-escape.

Majerowicz, Mordechai. *The Story of a Partisan* [in Hebrew]. Tel Aviv: Aleph, 1978.

Mann, Mendel. *Noenṭ Fun Vayṭns Far Undzere Ḳinder* [Close from Afar for Our Children; in Yiddish]. Illustrated by Hirsh Altman. Warsaw: Kinder-Fraynd, 1935. Digitalized by the National Yiddish Book Center, Amherst, Massachusetts, January 2009. https://www.yiddishbookcenter.org/collections/yiddish-books/spb-nybc201376/mann-mendel-altman-hirsh-noent-fun-vaytns-far-undzere-kinder.

Mann, Zvi. "Mendl Mann and the Almost Nobel Prize: Zvi Mann" [in Yiddish]. Wexler Oral History Project, June 18, 2014, The Yiddish Book Center, Tel Aviv. https://www.yiddishbookcenter.org/collections/oral-histories/excerpts/woh-ex-0004917/mendl-mann-and-almost-nobel-prize.

Mayevski (Nadel), Pesia. "From Where Do I Get My Strength?" In *Ayaratenu Zhetl*, edited by Lipsky et al., 135.

———. "From Zhetl to Petach Tikva" [in Yiddish]. In *Pinkas Zhetl*, edited by B. Kaplinski, 455.

———. "Hunger" [in Yiddish]. In *Pinkas Zhetl*, edited by B. Kaplinski, 320–24.

———. "In the Navardok Labor Camp" [in Yiddish]. In *Pinkas Zhetl*, edited by B. Kaplinski, 359.

Meerloo, Joost A. M., MD. "Delayed Mourning in Victims of Extermination Camps." *Journal of the Hillside Hospital* 12 (April 1963): 96–98.

Mendelsohn, Ezra. *The Jews of East Central Europe between the World Wars*. Bloomington: Indiana University Press, 1983.

Milac, Metod M. "Graz Displaced Persons Camp." In *Resistance, Imprisonment & Forced Labor: A Slovene Student in World War II*. New York: Peter Lang, 2002.

Nikolayevski, Samuel. "United Jewish Artisans Association." In *Novogrudok Memorial Book*, 247.

Ninkovski, Miriam. "Four Graves of Our Fathers." In *Novogrudok Memorial Book*, 637–38.

Novogrudok Memorial Book. See Cohn, Rabbi Helen, ed.

Openheim, Dr. Shmuel. "Novogrudok Partisans Who Fell in Action." In *Novogrudok Memorial Book*, 645.

———. "Personalities." In *Novogrudok Memorial Book*, 220.

———. "Politico-Communal Life in Novogrudok." In *Novogrudok Memorial Book*, 170.

Pinkas Navaredok. See Yerushalmi, Dr. Eliezer, et al., eds.

Pultusk Memorial Book. Translation of *Pultusk, Sefer Zikaron*, edited by Yitzhak Ivri. Tel Aviv: Pultusk Society, 1971. https://www.jewishgen.org/Yizkor /pultusk/pul634.html#M.

Rahav Meir, Sivan. *#Parasha: Weekly Insights from a Leading Israeli Journalist.* Jerusalem: Toby Press, 2017.

Rappaport, Ernest A. "Beyond Traumatic Neurosis: A Psychoanalytic Study of Late Reactions to the Concentration Camp Trauma." *International Journal of Psychoanalysis* 49 (1968): 719–31.

Reich, Howard. *The Art of Inventing Hope: Intimate Conversations with Elie Wiesel.* Chicago: Chicago Review Press, 2019.

Renck, Ellen Sadove, Ada Holtzman, and Moshe Verbi, trans. *Memorial Book of Sokolka.* Jerusalem: Encyclopedia of the Jewish Diaspora, 1968.

Ringelblum, Emmanuel. *Polish-Jewish Relations during the Second World War.* Jerusalem: Yad Vashem, 1974.

Rubin, Sulia. *Against the Tide.* Jerusalem: Posner and Sons, 1980.

Rubin-Wolozynski, Sula. "Under the German Whip." In *Pinkas Navaredok*, edited by Yerushalmi et al., 272, https://www.jewishgen.org/yizkor /Novogrudok/nov258.html#Page272.

Sacks, Jonathan. *Lessons in Leadership: A Weekly Reading of the Jewish Bible.* Jerusalem: Maggid Books, 2015.

———. *Morality: Restoring the Common Good in Divided Times.* New York: Basic Books, 2020.

———. *To Heal a Fractured World: The Ethics of Responsibility.* New York: Schocken Books, 2005.

Schensnovich, Nikolai. *Zapiski Aktiora i Partizana* [Notes of an Actor and a Partisan]. Minsk, 1976.

Simenauer, Eric. "The Return of the Persecutor." In *Generations of the Holocaust,* edited by M. S. Bergmann and M. E. Jucovy, 175. New York: Basic Books, 1982.

Skakun, Michael. *On Burning Ground.* New York: St. Martin's Press, 1999.

Soloveitchik, Joseph B. *Fate and Destiny: From the Holocaust to the State of Israel.* Hoboken, NJ: Ktav Publishing House, 2000.

Sorotzkin, Rabbi Elchanan. "The Life Journey of Rabbi Zalman Sorotzkin" [in Yiddish]. In *Pinkas Zhetl,* edited by B. Kaplinski, 234.

Spector, Shmuel. *Encyclopedia of Jewish Life before and during the Holocaust.* Vol. 1. New York and Jerusalem: New York University Press and Yad Vashem, 2001.

Steinberg-Sarig, Moshe. "Hebrew Education in Novogrudok." In *Novogrudok Memorial Book,* 142.

Suhl, Yuri, ed. *They Fought Back: The Story of the Jewish Resistance in Nazi Europe.* New York: Schocken, 1967.

Svinik, Dvora. "Destruction of a Jewish Community," in *The Book of Ivenets, Kamien and Vicinity,* 368–70.

———. "A Tale of a Family." In *The Book of Ivenets, Kamien and Vicinity,* 203–6.

Tec, Nechama. *Defiance: The Bielski Partisans.* Oxford: Oxford University Press, 1993.

Tsur, Jacob. "The Jewish National Fund (Keren Kayemeth LeIsrael)." In *Encyclopedia Judaica,* edited by Cecil Roth. Jerusalem: Keter Publishing House, 1978.

Turtel-Obezhanski, Hassia. "History of the Jews of Korelitz." In *Pinkas Navaredok*, 19.

———. "The Second World War and the Destruction of the Community." In *Korelitz: Hayeha v'churbanah shel kehilah Yehudit* [Karelich: The Life and Destruction of a Jewish Community], edited by Michael Walzer-Fass, 19. Tel Aviv: Karelich Societies of Israel and the United States, 1982. Translated by JewishGen. https://www.jewishgen.org/yizkor/Korelicze /Korelicze.html.

United States Holocaust Memorial Museum. "Babenhausen Displaced Persons Camp." Holocaust Encyclopedia. https://encyclopedia.ushmm. org/content/en/article/babenhausen-displaced-persons-camp.

———. "Bergen-Belsen Displaced Persons Camp." Holocaust Encyclopedia. https://encyclopedia.ushmm.org/content/en/article/ babenhausen-displaced-persons-camp.

———. "The Bielski Partisans," Holocaust Encyclopedia, https:// encyclopedia.ushmm.org/content/en/article/the-bielski-partisans.

———. "Eschwege Displaced Persons Camp." Holocaust Encyclopedia. https://encyclopedia.ushmm.org/content/en/article/ eschwege-displaced-persons-camp.

———. "Foehrenwald DP Camp." Holocaust Encyclopedia. https:// encyclopedia.ushmm.org/content/en/article/foehrenwald-displaced -persons-camp.

———. "Heidenheim Displaced Persons Camp." Holocaust Encyclopedia. https://encyclopedia.ushmm.org/content/en/article/heidenheim -displaced-persons-camp.

———. "Jewish Uprisings in Camps." Holocaust Encyclopedia. https:// encyclopedia.ushmm.org/content/en/article/jewish-uprisings-in-camps.

———. "Jewish Councils (Judenraete)," Holocaust Encyclopedia, https:// encyclopedia.ushmm.org/content/en/article/jewish-councils-judenraete.

———. "Landsberg Displaced Persons Camp," Holocaust Encyclopedia, https://encyclopedia.ushmm.org/content/en/article/landsberg -displaced-persons-camp.

"Vaad Hayeshivot." YIVO Institute for Jewish Research. https://vilnacollections.yivo.org/?ca=((item.php!id__rg-25.

Weinbaum, Laurence. "Shaking the Dust Off: The Story of the Warsaw Ghetto's Forgotten Chronicler, Ruben Feldchu (Ben-Shem)." In *Jewish Political Studies Review*. Jerusalem: Jerusalem Center for Public Affairs, 2010.

Weintraub, Shlomo. *The Alter of Novardok*. Rahway, NJ: Mesorah Publications, 2020.

Weiss, Aharon. "Novogrudok." In *Encyclopedia Judaica*, edited by Cecil Roth. Jerusalem: Keter Publishing House, 1978.

Wiesel, Elie. "The Holocaust: Three Views." In *ADL Bulletin*, November 1977.

Yaffe, Yehoshua. "Chapters from the Holocaust: The Second Slaughter." In *Novogrudok Memorial Book*, 538.

———. "The Final Wandering." In *Novogrudok Memorial Book*, 550–51.

———. *In the Novogrudok Ghetto and the Partisan Movement* [in Hebrew]. Tel Aviv: Navaredker Committee in Israel, 1988.

———. "The Tradesmen's Ghetto." In *Novogrudok Memorial Book*, 559.

Yerushalmi, Dr. Eliezer, David Cohen, and Dr. Aharon Mirsky, et al., eds. *Pinkas Navaredok* [in Yiddish]. Tel Aviv: Alexander Harkavy Navaredker Relief Committee in USA and Navaredker Committee in Israel, 1963.

Yerushalmi, E. V. "Leaders and Ordinary Members of the Community" [in Yiddish]. In *Pinkas Navaredok*, 65.

Yosifun, Shimeon. "The Tailors' Synagogue,. In *Pinkas Navaredok*, 72. https://www.jewishgen.org/yizkor/Novogrudok/nov072.html.

Zabich, Philip. "Our Orchestra" [in Yiddish]. In *Pinkas Zhetl*, edited by B. Kaplinski, 180.

Zalmanovich, Dov. Written testimony [Hebrew]. In *Asher Zacharnu Lisaper* [That which we remembered to tell], edited by Arie Haran, 230. Tel Aviv: Sifriat Poalim, 1988.

Zimelevich, Zimel. "The Navardok Community in Zhetl" [in Hebrew]. In *Pinkas Zhetl*, edited by B. Kaplinski, 82.

Zimmerman, Joshua D. "Tsysho." YIVO Encyclopedia of Jews in Eastern Europe. https://yivoencyclopedia.org/article.aspx/Tsysho.

Documentary Films

Braff, Mitch, director. *A Partisan Returns: A Legacy of Two Sisters*. Jewish Partisan Educational Foundation, 2008.

Goroulev, Iouri, director. *The Book of Curses*. Israel/Belarus: Kagan Productions, 2020.

Pailthrope, Martin. *Extreme Survival*. Bristol: BBC/Travel Channel, 2001.

Shwartz, Dror H., director. *Tunnel of Hope*. Jerusalem, Israel: Go2Films, 2015.

Sturges, John, director. *The Great Escape*. Beverly Hills: United Artists, 1963.

Wolfinger, Kirk, director. *The Holocaust Escape Tunnel*. Boston: WGBH and *Nova*, 2017.